Victoria Crosses on the Western Front

Battles of the Hindenburg Line – St Quentin, Beaurevoir, Cambrai 1918 and the Pursuit to the Selle

September–October 1918

Victoria Crosses on the Western Front

Battles of the Hindenburg Line – St Quentin, Beaurevoir, Cambrai 1918 and the Pursuit to the Selle

September–October 1918

Paul Oldfield

Pen & Sword
MILITARY

First published in Great Britain in 2024 by
Pen & Sword Military
An imprint of Pen & Sword Books Limited
Yorkshire – Philadelphia

ISBN 978 1 52673 575 1

A CIP catalogue record for this book is
available from the British Library

Typeset by Mac Style
Printed in the UK by CPI Group (UK) Ltd, Croydon, CR0 4YY.

Pen & Sword Books Limited incorporates the imprints of After the Battle,
Atlas, Archaeology, Aviation, Discovery, Family History, Fiction, History,
Maritime, Military, Military Classics, Politics, Select, Transport, True
Crime, Air World, Frontline Publishing, Leo Cooper, Remember When,
Seaforth Publishing, The Praetorian Press, Wharncliffe Local History,
Wharncliffe Transport, Wharncliffe True Crime and White Owl.

For a complete list of Pen & Sword titles please contact

PEN & SWORD BOOKS LIMITED
47 Church Street, Barnsley, South Yorkshire, S70 2AS, England
E-mail: enquiries@pen-and-sword.co.uk
Website: www.pen-and-sword.co.uk
or
PEN AND SWORD BOOKS
1950 Lawrence Rd, Havertown, PA 19083, USA
E-mail: uspen-and-sword@casematepublishers.com
Website: www.penandswordbooks.com

Contents

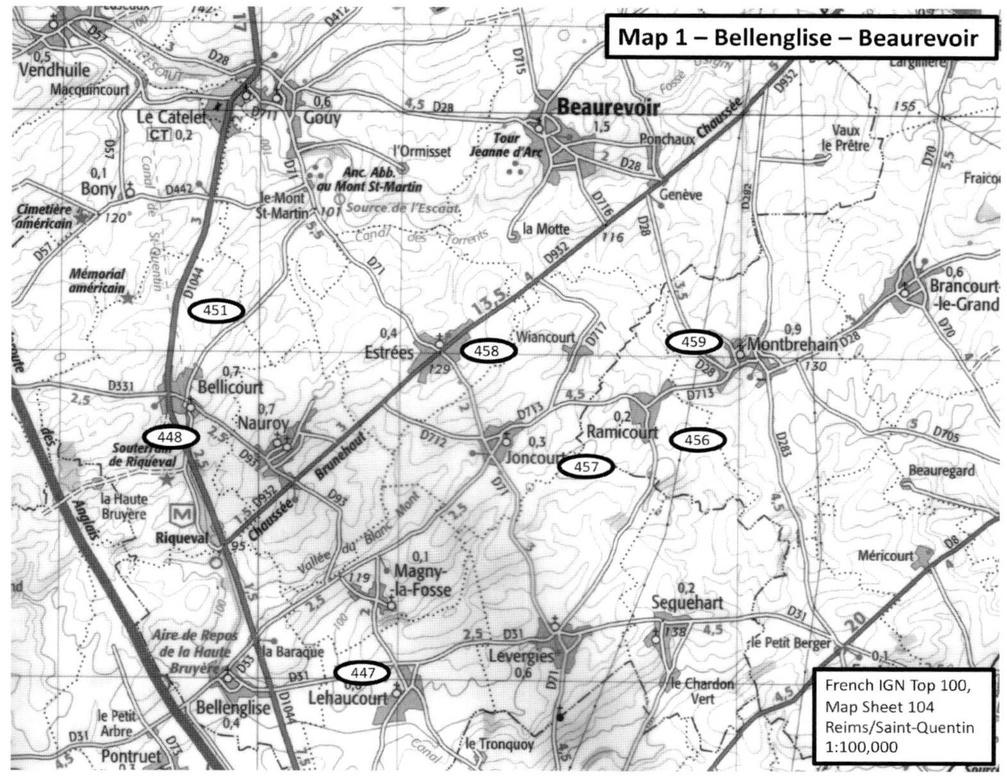
Map 1 – Bellenglise – Beaurevoir
451
458
459
448
457
456
447
Vendhuile
Le Catelet
Gouy
Beaurevoir
Bony
Bellicourt
Nauroy
Estrées
Joncourt
Ramicourt
Montbrehain
Brancourt-le-Grand
Magny-la-Fosse
Levergies
Sequehart
Lehaucourt
Bellenglise
Riqueval
French IGN Top 100,
Map Sheet 104
Reims/Saint-Quentin
1:100,000

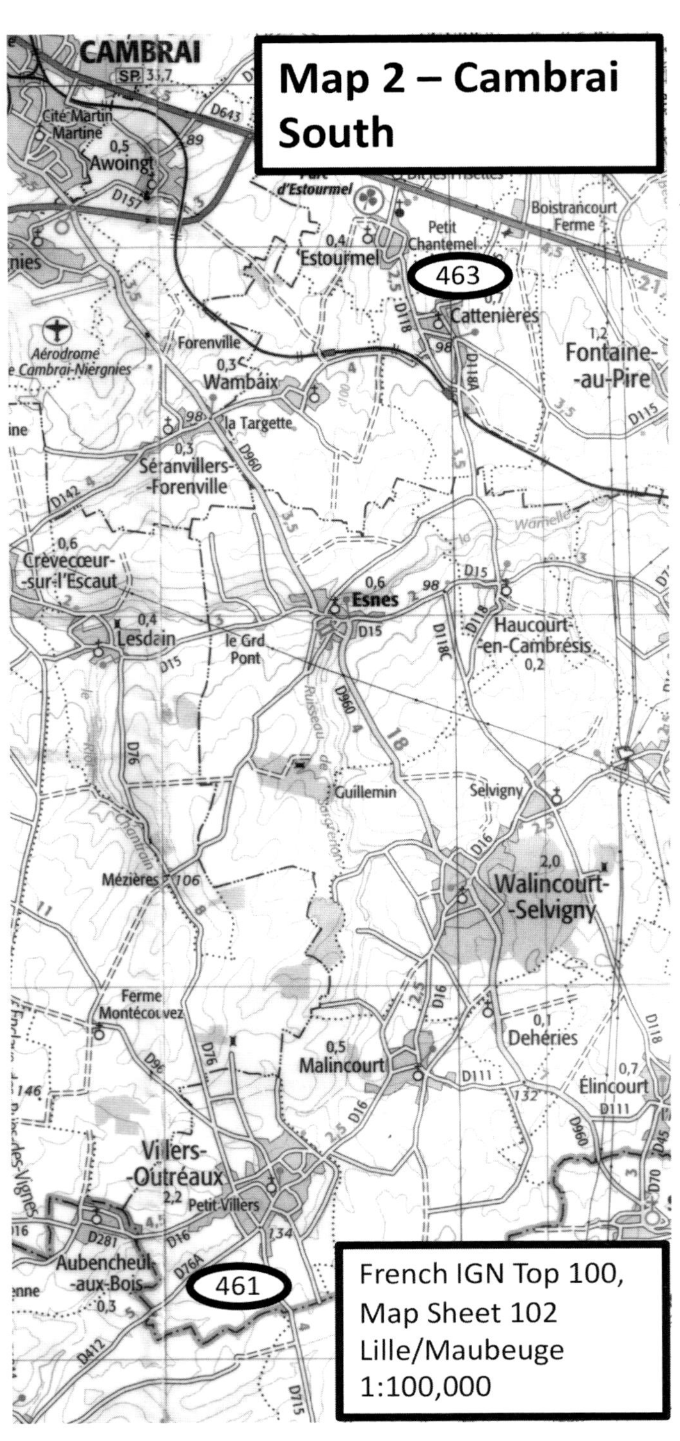
Map 2 – Cambrai South
French IGN Top 100, Map Sheet 102 Lille/Maubeuge 1:100,000
463
461
CAMBRAI
Cité Martin Martine
Awoingt
D643
D157
d'Estourmel
Boistrancourt Ferme
Petit Chantemel
Estourmel
Cattenières
Fontaine-au-Pire
D118
D115
Aérodrome de Cambrai-Niergnies
Forenville
Wambaix
la Targette
Séranvillers-Forenville
D960
D142
Crèvecœur-sur-l'Escaut
Esnes
D15
Haucourt-en-Cambrésis
Lesdain
le Grd Pont
D76
Guillemin
Selvigny
D16
Walincourt-Selvigny
Mézières
Ferme Montécouvez
Dehéries
D96
Malincourt
D111
Élincourt
Villers-Outréaux
Petit Villers
D281
Aubencheul-aux-Bois
D76A
D412
D715
D70

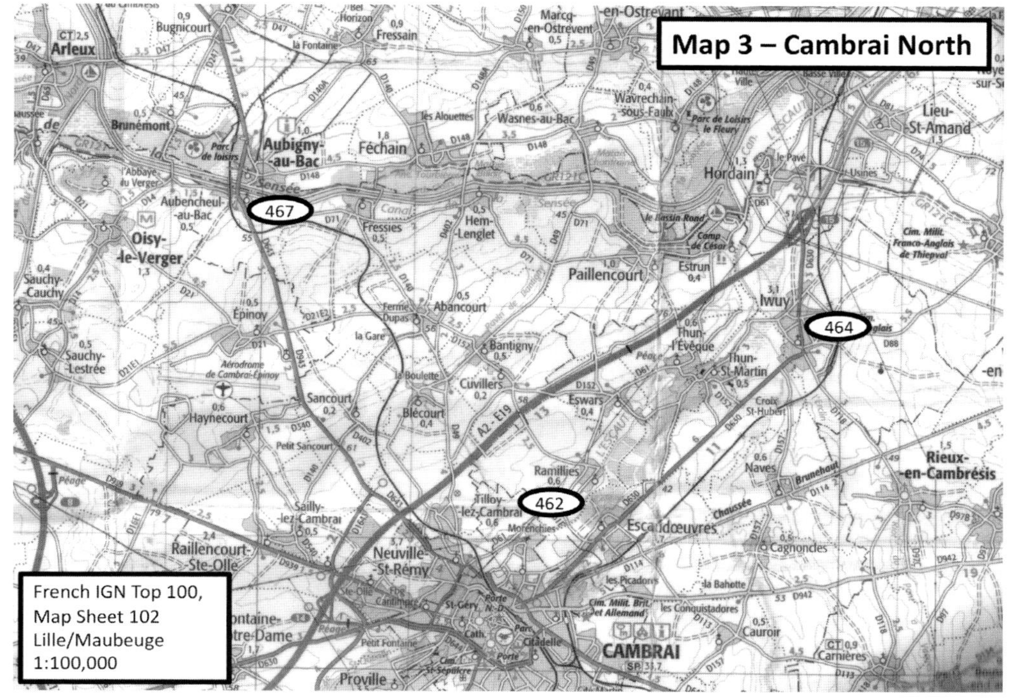
Map 3 – Cambrai North
French IGN Top 100,
Map Sheet 102
Lille/Maubeuge
1:100,000
467
464
462
Arleux
Bugnicourt
Fressain
Marcq-en-Ostrevent
Brunémont
Aubigny-au-Bac
Féchain
Wasnes-au-Bac
Wavrechain-sous-Faulx
Hordain
Lieu-St-Amand
Aubencheul-au-Bac
Oisy-le-Verger
Fressies
Hem-Lenglet
Paillencourt
Estrun
Iwuy
Sauchy-Cauchy
Sauchy-Lestrée
Épinoy
Abancourt
Bantigny
Thun-l'Évêque
Thun-St-Martin
Cuvillers
Sancourt
Haynecourt
Blécourt
Eswars
Ramillies
Naves
Rieux-en-Cambrésis
Tilloy-lez-Cambrai
Escaudœuvres
Cagnoncles
Sailly-lez-Cambrai
Raillencourt-Ste-Olle
Neuville-St-Rémy
Cauroir
Carnières
CAMBRAI
Proville
A2 - E19

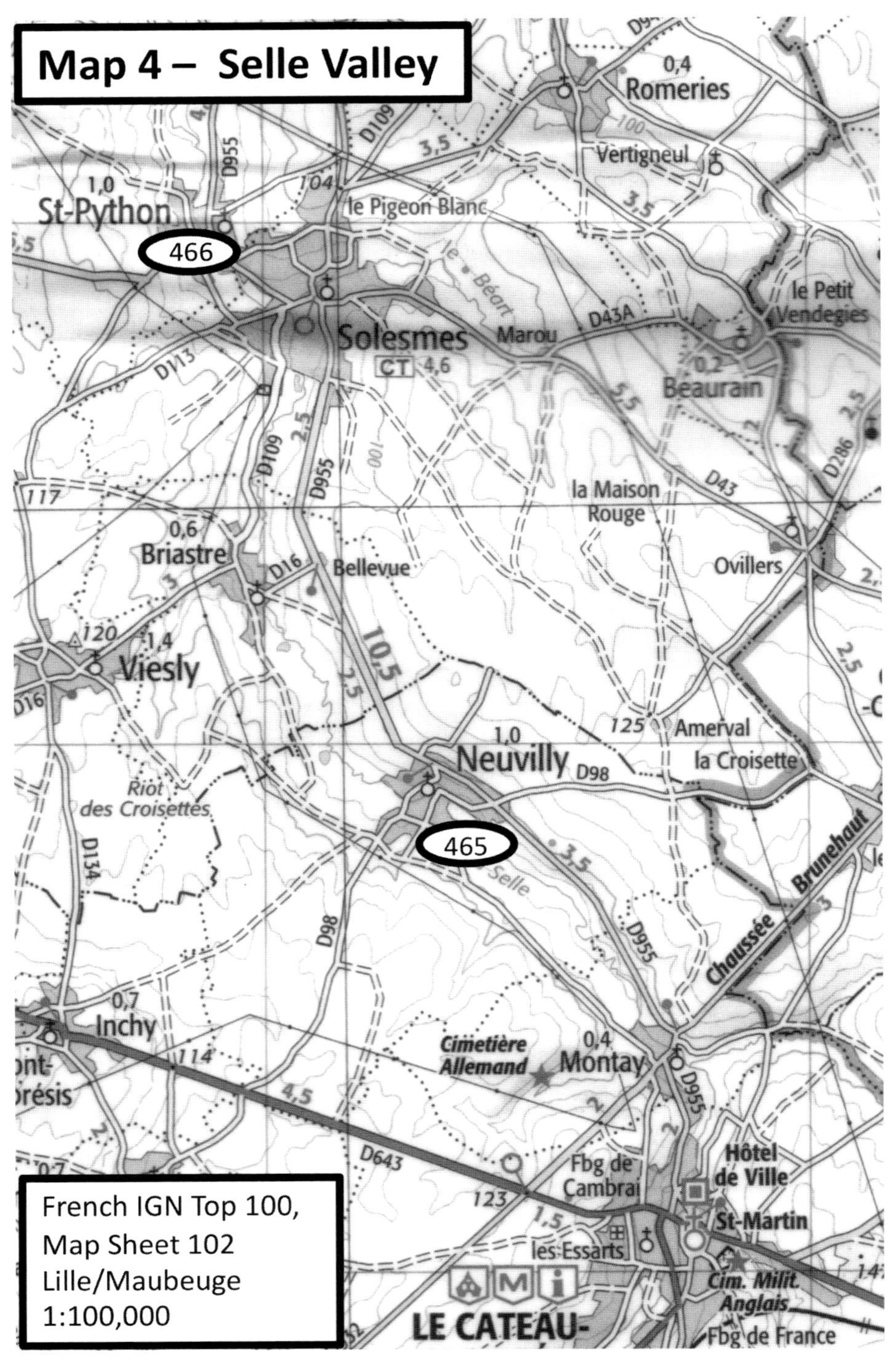
Map 4 – Selle Valley
Romeries
Vertigneul
St-Python
466
le Pigeon Blanc
Solesmes
Marou
le Petit Vendegies
Beaurain
la Maison Rouge
Briastre
Bellevue
Ovillers
Viesly
Neuvilly
Amerval
la Croisette
Riot des Croisettes
465
Selle
Chaussée Brunehaut
Inchy
Cimetière Allemand
Montay
Fbg de Cambrai
Hôtel de Ville
St-Martin
les Essarts
Cim. Milit. Anglais
LE CATEAU-
Fbg de France
French IGN Top 100,
Map Sheet 102
Lille/Maubeuge
1:100,000

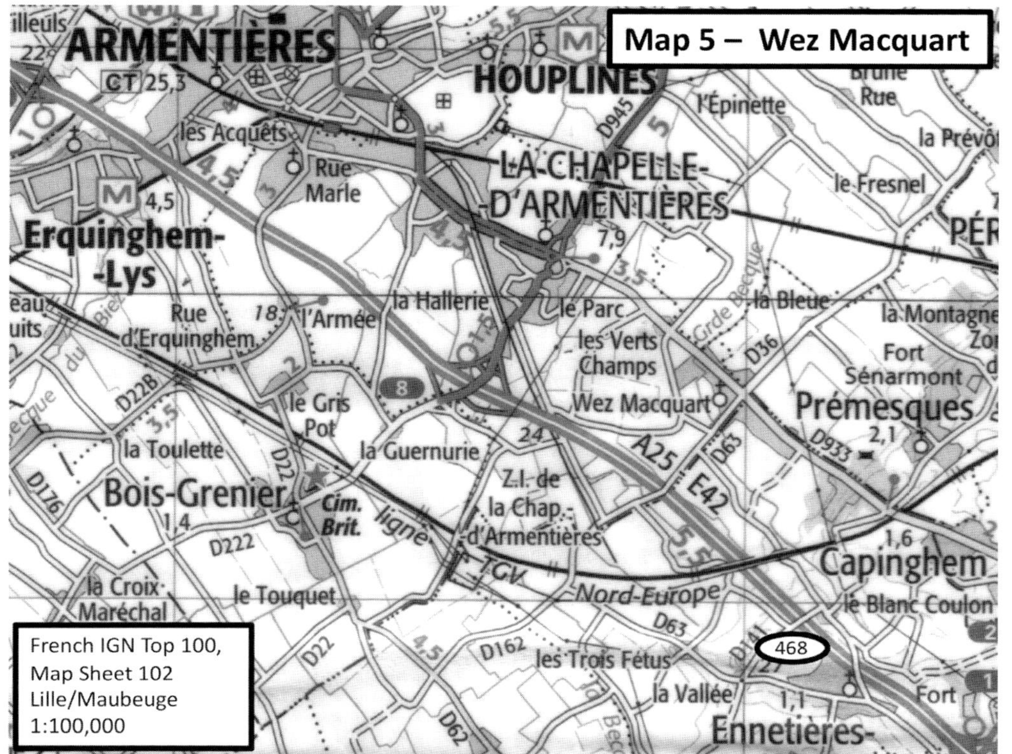
Map 5 – Wez Macquart
French IGN Top 100,
Map Sheet 102
Lille/Maubeuge
1:100,000
ARMENTIÈRES
HOUPLINES
LA-CHAPELLE-
-D'ARMENTIÈRES
Erquinghem-
-Lys
les Acquêts
Rue
Marle
l'Épinette
le Fresnel
la Prévôt
Rue
d'Erquinghem
l'Armée
la Hallerie
le Parc
les Verts
Champs
Wez Macquart
la Bleue
la Montagne
Fort
Sénarmont
Prémesques
le Gris
Pot
la Toulette
la Guernurie
Bois-Grenier
Cim.
Brit.
Z.I. de
la Chap.-
d'Armentières
Capinghem
le Blanc Coulon
la Croix
Maréchal
le Touquet
ligne TGV Nord-Europe
les Trois Fétus
la Vallée
Ennetières-
Fort
A25
E42
D945
D36
D63
D933
D22
D22B
D222
D176
D162
D62
468

Abbreviations

ACF	Army Cadet Force
ACT	Australian Capital Territory
AE	Australian Engineers
AFA	Australian Field Artillery
AFC	Australian Flying Corps
AIF	Australian Imperial Force
APM	Assistant Provost Marshal
ARP	Air Raid Precautions
ASC	Army Service Corps
AT	Auxiliary Transport
Att'd	Attached
BD	Bachelor of Divinity
BEF	British Expeditionary Force
Bty	Battery (artillery unit of 4–8 guns)
Capt	Captain
CCS	Casualty Clearing Station
CE	Canadian Engineers
CEF	Canadian Expeditionary Force
CFB	Canadian Forces Base
CFC	Canadian Forestry Corps
Co	County/company
C-in-C	Commander-in-Chief
CO	Commanding Officer
Col	Colonel
Cpl	Corporal
CQMS	Company Quartermaster Sergeant
CSgt	Colour Sergeant
CSM	Company Sergeant Major
Cty	Cemetery
CWGC	Commonwealth War Graves Commission
DCM	Distinguished Conduct Medal
DSO	Distinguished Service Order
ESM	Emergency Service Medal
FA	Football Association

GAF	Group of Armies in Flanders
GHQ	General Headquarters
GOC	General Officer Commanding
GOC-in-C	General Officer Commanding-in-Chief
GSO1, 2 or 3	General Staff Officer Grade 1 (Lt Col), 2 (Maj) or 3 (Capt)
HE	High Explosive
HMAT	Her/His Majesty's Australian Transport/Troopship
HMHS	Her/His Majesty's Hospital Ship
HMS	Her/His Majesty's Ship
HMT	Her/His Majesty's Transport/Troopship/Hired Military Transport
HQ	Headquarters
HT	Hired Transport
JP	Justice of the Peace
Kms	Kilometres
LCpl	Lance Corporal
LG	London Gazette
LL.B	Legum Baccalaureus
LNER	London and North Eastern Railway
Lt	Lieutenant
Lt Col	Lieutenant Colonel
Lt Gen	Lieutenant General
Maj	Major
Maj Gen	Major General
MC	Military Cross
M.Inst.CE	Member of the institute of Civil Engineers
MLC	Member of the Legislative Council
MM	Military Medal
MO	Medical Officer
MOD	Ministry of Defence
MP	Member of Parliament
NSW	New South Wales
OC	Officer Commanding
P&O	The Peninsular and Oriental Steam Navigation Co
Pte	Private
Pty	Proprietary company
RAAF	Royal Australian Air Force
RAE	Royal Australian Engineers
RAF	Royal Air Force
RAMC	Royal Army Medical Corps
RAP	Regimental Aid Post
RE	Royal Engineers
RFA	Royal Field Artillery

RFC	Royal Flying Corps
RGA	Royal Garrison Artillery
RHA	Royal Horse Artillery
RNAS	Royal Naval Air Service
RQMS	Regimental Quartermaster Sergeant
RSL	Returned Services League
RSM	Regimental Sergeant Major
Sgt	Sergeant
SS	Steam Ship
SV	Sailing Vessel
TF	Territorial Force
UEFA	Union of European Football Associations
VC	Victoria Cross
WA	Western Australia
WO1 or 2	Warrant Officer Class 1 or 2
YMCI	Young Men's Christian Institute

Introduction

The fourteenth book in this series covers the end of the Battles of the Hindenburg Line, specifically the Battles of the St Quentin Canal, Beaurevoir, Cambrai 1918 and the Pursuit to the Selle in September and October 1918. The book tells the story of fifteen Victoria Crosses, six of which were awarded to Dominion troops.

As with previous books in the series, it is written for the battlefield visitor as well as the armchair reader. Each account provides background information to explain the broad strategic and tactical situation, before focusing on the VC action in detail. Each is supported by a map to allow a visitor to stand on, or close to, the spot and at least one photograph of the site. Detailed biographies help to understand the man behind the Cross.

As far as possible chapters and sections within them follow the titles of battles, actions and affairs as decided by the post-war Battle Nomenclature Committee. VCs are numbered chronologically 447, 448, etc and, as far as possible, they are described in the same order. However, when a number of actions were fought simultaneously, the VCs are covered out of sequence on a geographical basis in accordance with the official battle nomenclature. As a result, it may appear that 449–450, 452–455 and 460 are missing. However, 449 and 452–454 appear in the previous volume and 450, 455 and 460 will be included in the next volume.

Refer to the master maps to find the general area for each VC. If visiting the battlefields it is advisable to purchase maps from the respective French and Belgian 'Institut Géographique National'. The French IGN Top 100 and Belgian IGN Provinciekaart at 1:100,000 scale are ideal for motoring, but 1:50,000, 1:25,000 or 1:20,000 scale maps are necessary for more detailed work, e.g. French IGN Serie Bleue and Belgian IGN Topografische Kaart. They are obtainable from the respective IGN or through reputable map suppliers on-line.

Ranks are as used on the day. Grave references have been shortened, e.g. 'Plot II, Row A, Grave 10' will appear as 'II A 10'. There are some abbreviations, many in common usage, but if unsure refer to the list provided.

I endeavour to include memorials to each VC in their biographies. However, every VC is commemorated in the VC Diary and on memorial panels at the Union Jack Club, Sandell Street, Waterloo, London. To include this in every biography would be unnecessarily repetitive.

In any work of this scale, it is almost inevitable that some errors will be included unintentionally. Every effort is made to cross-check facts. If mistakes occur, I apologise for them and urge readers to let me know so that future revisions can be made.

Thanks are due to too many people and organisations to mention here. They are acknowledged in 'Sources' and any omissions are my fault and not intentional. However, I make no apology for mentioning again the contribution made by fellow members of the 'Victoria Cross Database Users Group', Doug and Richard Arman, and those no longer with us, without whom these books would never be completed. The work of Steve Lee and the Memorials to Valour website team is also invaluable.

Paul Oldfield
Wiltshire
December 2023

Battle of the St Quentin Canal

447 Lt Col Bernard Vann, 8th attached 6th Battalion, The Sherwood Foresters (Nottinghamshire and Derbyshire Regiment) (139th Brigade, 46th Division), Bellenglise, France
448 Maj Blair Wark, 32nd Battalion AIF (8th Australian Brigade, 5th Australian Division), Bellicourt, France

29th September 1918

On 29th September the final piece of the great Allied offensive fell into place north of St Quentin, when the British Fourth Army joined forces with Third and First Armies. Almost the whole Allied front was then on the offensive. Fourth Army was to breach the Hindenburg Main System, including crossing the St Quentin Canal. The only part of the nineteen kilometres long attack frontage not covered by the canal was where it ran through the Bellicourt Tunnel. However, in that sector the defences were even stronger than the rest of the line, including five lines of trenches, each covered by thick belts of wire. The line of the tunnel was marked on the surface by a linear mound about three metres high, where the spoil had been deposited having been hauled to the surface through various access shafts.

Having broken through the Hindenburg Main System, Fourth Army would face the Hindenburg Support System (le Catelet–Nauroy Line) and the Hindenburg Reserve System (Masnières–Beaurevoir–Fonsomme Line). Each system, which consisted of two trenches, was well wired in front and had numerous concrete pillboxes, although the Support and Reserve were less complete than the Main.

Fourth Army had IX, Australian–American and III Corps in the line, with XIII and Cavalry Corps in reserve. There were fifteen infantry divisions available, together with two cavalry divisions, three tank brigades and a RAF brigade in support. It was estimated that Fourth Army faced seven enemy divisions, with six more available from reserve within three days.

The American II Corps (27th and 30th Divisions) had trained with the British Second Army and joined the Australian Corps to form the Australian–American Corps. American divisions had double the infantry of a British division, three times the number of machine guns and twice as many engineers. However, they lacked artillery. In addition, these two divisions had not been engaged previously in a major action and were very inexperienced, but they did have the advantage of being fresh. The plan was for the IX and Australian–American Corps to make the main attack, while III Corps held a defensive left flank between the Australian–American Corps and Third Army. The Germans knew that the attack was coming, but everything possible was done to conceal the precise date and time. General Rawlinson's orders to Fourth Army were issued on 22nd September.

A preliminary bombardment commenced at 10.30 p.m. on 26th September, with 1,637 field, medium and heavy guns and howitzers taking part. Gas was fired into battery positions and headquarters until 6.00 a.m. on the 27th. Sustained high

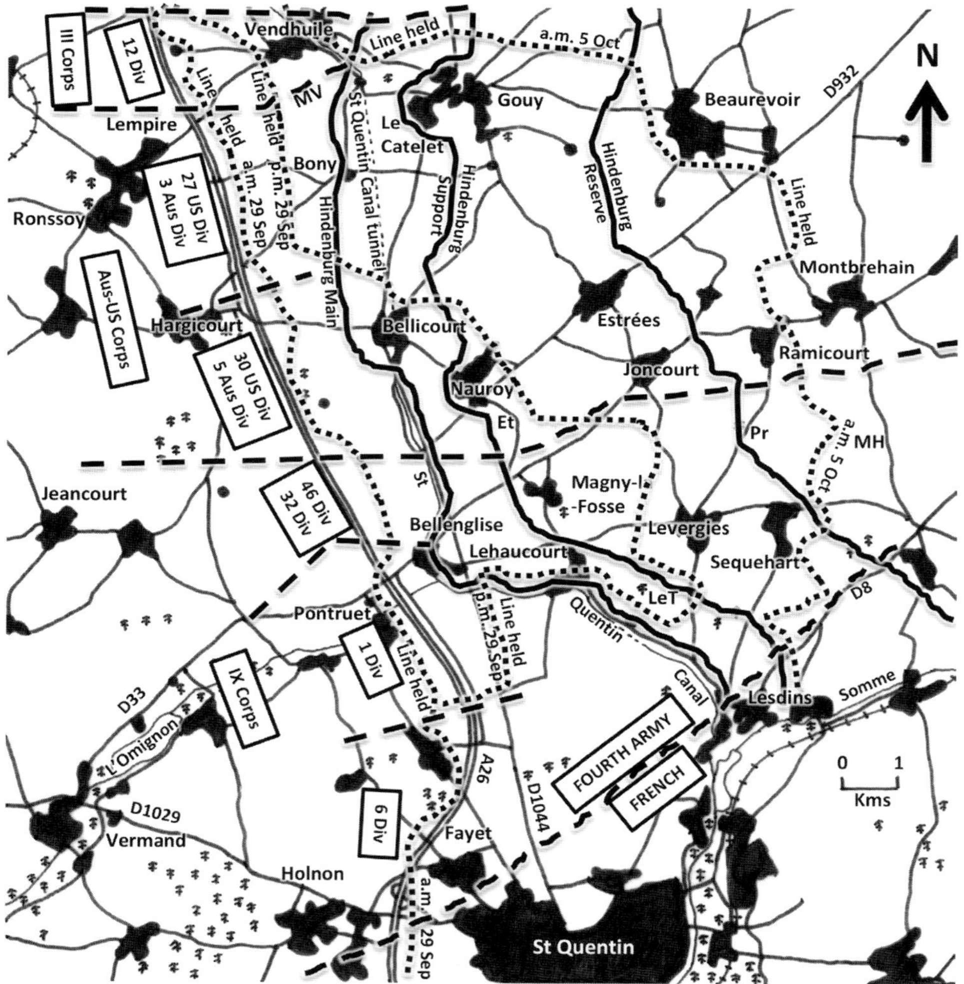

Fourth Army's sector 29th September–5th October 1918. The boundaries and formations are as for 29th September. There are a number of abbreviations – Et = Etricourt Farm, LeT = Le Tronquoy, MH = Mannequin Hill, MV = Macquincourt Valley, Pr = Preselles.

explosive and shrapnel shelling of strongpoints followed and gaps were cut in the wire defences. However, an attempt to lower the water level in the canal by cutting the embankment with artillery fire was unsuccessful.

On the right of Fourth Army, IX Corps had the difficult task of forcing crossings over the St Quentin Canal. On the left of the Corps, 46th Division was to make the initial crossing to secure the Green Line, a total advance of 3,650–5,600m. It would be followed by 32nd Division, which was to pass through to seize the Red Line in the Hindenburg Reserve System, some 1,800–3,650m further on. In the centre, 1st Division's task was to advance on the right of 46th Division to form a defensive flank and to maintain pressure on the enemy in front. 6th Division on the right was not involved in the initial assault, except to maintain contact with the enemy by patrols and to make diversionary demonstrations with gas and smoke.

The 46th Division's front overlooked the German defences west of the canal, which consisted of a line of trenches, well wired and furnished with numerous strongpoints. The canal was fifteen metres wide and three metres deep, with sheer brick wall sides and very steep banks running down to the water. It was also covered by belts of wire on the banks and in the water. Altogether it presented a formidable obstacle. In the Division's southern sector there was not much water in the canal, but the mud was just as impenetrable. The Germans dammed the canal at Bellenglise and north of the village the water level had been kept up in the deep ravine through which the canal ran. Three thousand lifebelts from Channel steamers were supplied to the assault troops. The sappers produced a variety of devices to get over the water, including man-portable floating piers made of petrol tins or slabs of cork, light collapsible boats, mats laid over the mud and scaling ladders. A rehearsal was held on the Somme to ensure that the devices worked and the men knew how to use them. As soon as crossings had been made twelve field companies of sappers stood by to repair the damaged bridges and build new ones.

The night of 28th/29th September was dark and stormy. Early in the morning a ground fog developed which, when combined with the smoke of battle, made air cooperation all but impossible. The rain had made the ground surface soft and slippery but below was still hard. The tanks reached their start positions overnight and set off just before zero to pass through the waiting assault infantry. Their noise was covered by the artillery and aircraft flying overhead.

The 137th Brigade, commanded by Brigadier General JV Campbell VC, was to make the initial crossing by rushing the canal with three battalions in line. The rate of advance was set at double the norm. The defences west of the Canal had been very badly battered by artillery. The mist at zero hour, 5.50 a.m., gave the balance of advantage to the attackers.

The German barrage came down five minutes after zero but caused very few casualties. The trench on the west bank was overcome without difficulty and 120 prisoners were taken. The advance swept on to the canal through the mist and smoke. In the southern sector men got across on rafts and a single plank bridge

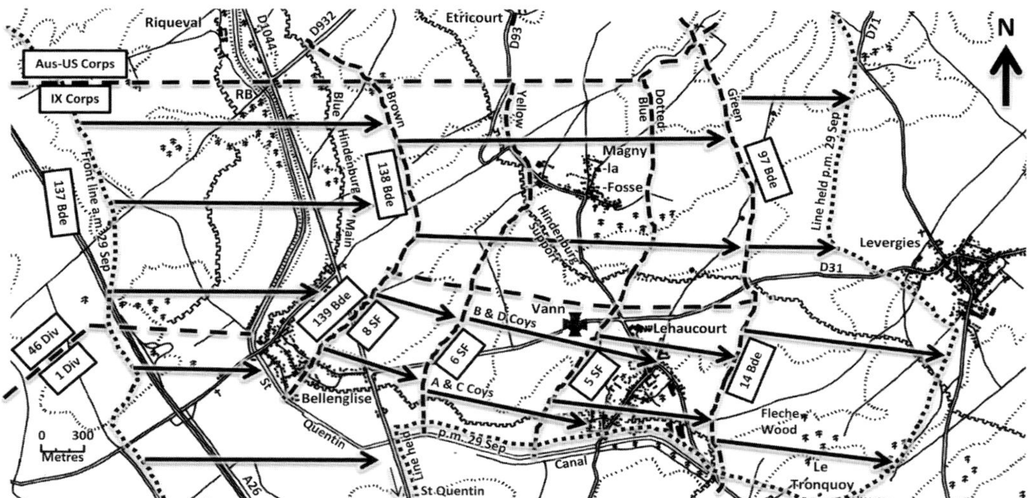

Approach Lehaucourt from the west along the D31 to where the ground rises to the top of a ridge. Just before the top there are hard standings either side of the road on which to park. Beware as you walk along the roadside as it is fast. RB = Riqueval Bridge.

left by the Germans. In the north they had to use the lifebelts and some men were hauled over on planks. Riqueval Bridge was seized intact by Captain Arthur Humphrey Charlton (DSO for this action and was later awarded the MC) and nine men of 6th North Staffordshire. They rushed the defending machine gun position

The D31, with Lehaucourt to the right of the road. On the far right the line of trees marks the course of the St Quentin Canal. This is the area where B and D Companies ran into heavy fire and the attack was about to stall until Vann reorganized the men and led the line forward again.

and overcame the demolition party before it could explode the charges. Another 130 prisoners were taken on the far side, including a battalion staff.

After a short pause to reorganise behind a standing barrage, the three battalions went forward again at 7.30 a.m. to the first intermediate line (Blue Line). After another short pause the support companies passed through for deeper objectives. The second intermediate line (Brown Line) was held by 8.20 a.m. and the barrage paused there for three hours.

The 139th and 138th Brigades, on the right and left respectively, were moving over the canal by 8.30 a.m. When the barrage lifted at 11.20 a.m., both Brigades advanced through 137th Brigade, each with eight tanks of 9th Tank Battalion attached. However, the tanks were late, as they had been diverted to assist the Americans at Riqueval crossing, north of the captured bridge. Each brigade had two intermediate objective lines (Yellow and Dotted Blue). The barrage would pause for thirty minutes on each, before the advance to the final objective (Green Line), about 2,500m away, commenced. Both brigades allocated one battalion for each objective. In 139th Brigade these were: 8th Sherwood Foresters (Yellow), 6th Sherwood Foresters (Dotted Blue) and 5th Sherwood Foresters (Green).

The 139th Brigade's leading battalion, 8th Sherwood Foresters, mopped up in Bellenglise and caught up with 137th Brigade on the Brown Line. The barrage commenced at 11.20 a.m. and, despite some hostile shelling, 8th Sherwood Foresters reached the Yellow Line at 12.15 p.m.

The 6th Sherwood Foresters, commanded by **Lieutenant Colonel Bernard Vann**, which was to pass through to seize the Dotted Blue Line west of Lehaucourt, set off at 9.30 a.m. with A Company on the right and B Company on the left. Gas shells caused a few casualties in B Company, but otherwise the advance began well. The canal was reached and B Company crossed by a broken wooden bridge, while

the rest of the Battalion used the main bridge north of Bellenglise. The heavy enemy fire was largely ineffective at that time due to the mist and smoke. By 11.15 a.m. the Battalion was in position behind 8th Sherwood Foresters on the Brown Line, ready for the advance.

The Battalion wasted no time and passed straight through 8th Sherwood Foresters on the Yellow Line. By then the mist and smoke were clearing. Heavy fire was encountered from machine guns and field guns, particularly from south of the canal in 1st Division's area, and by 1 p.m. five tanks had been knocked out. A party of 6th Sherwood Foresters re-crossed the canal and dealt with these field guns.

B and D Companies on the left ran into heavy fire from field guns and machine guns between Lehaucourt and Magny-la-Fosse. With no support there was a danger that the barrage might be lost and the advance would stall. Vann dashed over to this flank, reorganised the men with no thought for his own safety and then led the line forward again. The Dotted Blue Line was reached without difficulty once the artillery and other opposition had been overcome. On the right, A and C Companies were heavily engaged in the Hindenburg Main Line, which at that point swung sharply eastwards. A flanking attack into the strongly built and well defended enemy positions resulted in some hard fighting, until the enemy saw the troops in their rear being overcome by B and D Companies. At this they broke and fled to the rear, leaving 400 prisoners, eight field guns and fifteen machine guns.

By 1.15 p.m. the Battalion had taken its objective and beaten off a counterattack. Vann took a small party of signallers (Lance Corporal Whitworth and Privates Broughton and Charles Hufton) and charged on towards Lehaucourt, where the enemy was setting up a number of guns. The signallers struggled to keep up, encumbered as they were with their equipment. However, many Germans surrendered to them and were sent to the rear without escort. As one man pointed out, the Germans knew where they were going anyway! Vann made straight for the guns and the Germans tried to bring up horse teams to rescue them. The gunners fought bravely to the end. Vann tackled the crew of one gun on his own. Having emptied his revolver, he kicked a man down a dugout steps before setting about two others with a riding crop. At the same time A Company headed for the south of the village to cut off the enemy's retreat, while 5th Sherwood Foresters did the same to the north.

The objective was secured by both brigades by 3.30 p.m., with the enemy surrendering freely everywhere. Magny-la-Fosse was cleared and Lehaucourt a little later. The 139th Brigade had captured about 1,200 prisoners, thirty-four guns and numerous machine guns and mortars. As both flanking formations, 1st Division on the right and the American 30th Division on the left, were behind, defensive flanks were formed.

The 46th Division assault had been a splendid feat of arms, accomplished for only 800 casualties; remarkably light in the circumstances. The Division took 4,200 prisoners and seventy-two guns. The 6th Sherwood Foresters had only eight men killed and fifty-two others were wounded or missing.

At dusk, 32nd Division continued the advance. On the right, 14th Brigade took le Tronquoy and Fleche Wood, along with 300 prisoners and a number of guns and howitzers. On the left, 97th Brigade did not advance as far because it was checked by fire from Levergies. With no friendly troops on either side, 32nd Division formed defensive flanks.

On the right, 1st Division protected the right flank of 46th Division but was prevented from advancing to protect 32nd Division by heavy flanking fire from the south. The Division did advance 1,200m to the St Quentin–Bellicourt road and took one hundred prisoners. In total, IX Corps took 5,100 prisoners, ninety guns and hundreds of machine guns and mortars.

In the centre of Fourth Army was the Australian–American Corps, with twenty-three field and ten heavy artillery brigades in support, plus five siege batteries, a total of 818 guns and howitzers. In addition there were elements of three tank brigades. The 4th Tank Brigade provided eight-four machines and 5th Tank Brigade between seventy and eighty, both brigades including a proportion of Mark Vs and Mark V Stars. Part of 3rd Tank Brigade provided twenty-five Whippets and a battalion of armoured cars. The 13th Australian Light Horse was also stood by and a number of special companies RE were to produce smoke screens. Air support was provided by 3rd Squadron AFC and No.8 Squadron RAF, with assistance from 5th Brigade RAF also available. For subsequent operations and exploitation, 5th Cavalry Brigade and B Battery, 84th Army Brigade RFA, were attached to the Corps.

During the operations to seize the Hindenburg Outpost Line in the middle of September, III Corps had been unable to take this objective and had handed over to the Australian–American Corps. However, the Hindenburg Outpost Line had been seized in other areas and was to be the start line for the attack on 29th September. The American 27th Division was therefore tasked to undertake a preliminary operation on 27th September to close up to the start line. This entailed advancing 900–1,375m on a frontage of 3,650m.

The attack was made by 106th Regiment (53rd Brigade), supported by twelve tanks of 4th Tank Battalion and a creeping barrage fired by nine field artillery brigades, including fifteen percent smoke shell. The right flank was covered by patrols of the American 30th Division and the left flank by 12th Division (III Corps). Although parts of the objective were reached, most notably the Knoll on the left, they could not be held and the troops were almost back in their start positions that night. This had implications for the barrage on 29th September. There was insufficient time to make extensive changes to the artillery plan, without risking massive confusion. As a result the Americans faced an advance of 800m before reaching the barrage line. Rawlinson allocated additional tanks to assist them in fighting forward before the barrage came down at zero hour.

On 29th September, 27th Division, on the left of the Australian–American Corps, had the furthest distance to cover to reach the start line and set off at 4.50 a.m. A number of resistance points were encountered as expected – Quennet Copse,

Gillemont Farm, the Knoll and other positions. Of the forty supporting tanks, twelve fell victim to field guns, seven ditched and others ran into an unmarked minefield left by Fifth Army during the retreat in March 1918. Inexperienced but enthusiastic, the Americans pressed on through heavy machine gun and artillery fire. Another disadvantage suffered by the Americans was the lack of company officers, as many had been sent to training schools for courses. By 11.00 a.m. the leading troops had almost reached the start line but, in doing so, they had overlooked many Germans in the fog. Some men reached the Hindenburg Main System but were either killed or forced to surrender there.

On the right, 30th Division was much closer to the start line. The left came under fire from 27th Division's area and had to face northwards. However, the right took Bellicourt and the southern entrance to the canal tunnel. Mopping up was overlooked as the troops pressed on and some parties reached the first objective. About 9.00 a.m. nine machines of 17th Armoured Car Battalion and eight Whippets moved along the Hargicourt–Bony road to engage the Germans in Bony. Half of the force was knocked out before the survivors withdrew.

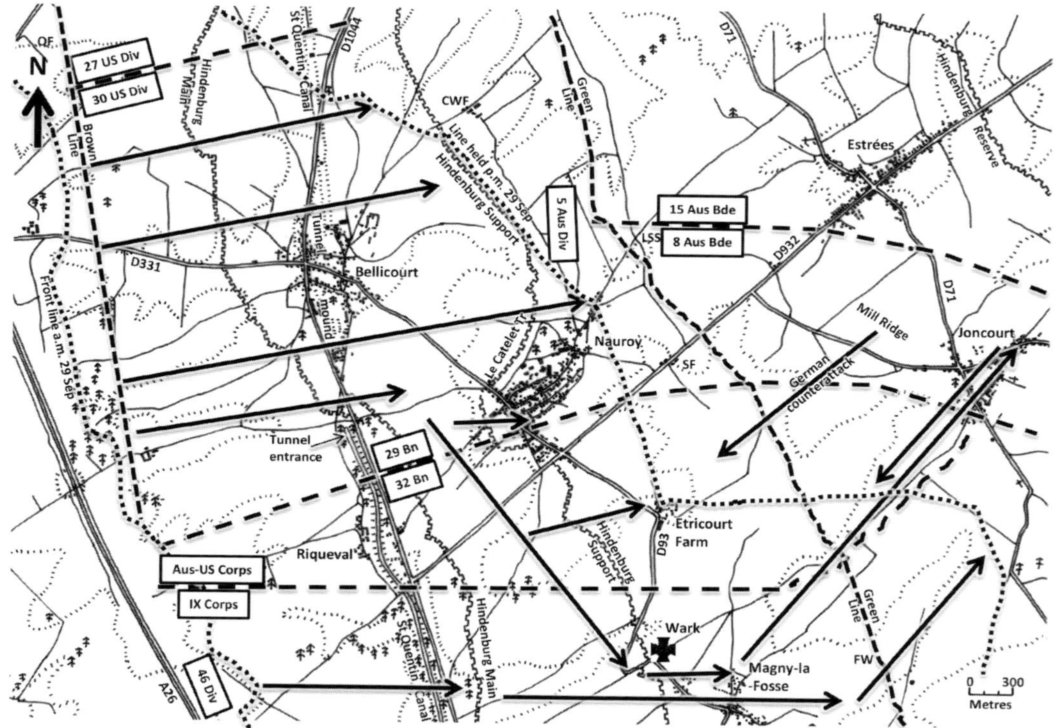

Wark's VC action took place over a long distance. The position marked on the map is in the vicinity of the Hindenburg Support Line. The following abbreviations are used – CWF = Cabaret Wood Farm, FW = site of Fosse Wood, LSS = lamp signal station, QF = site of Quennemont Farm, SF = sugar factory.

At the Green Line, 5th and 3rd Australian Divisions were to pass through 30th and 27th American Divisions respectively and continue the advance to the Red Line. They left their assembly areas at 7.00 a.m. and were scheduled to pass through the Americans at 11.00 a.m.

On the right, 5th Australian Division was led by 8th Australian Brigade on the right and 15th Australian Brigade on the left, with 14th Australian Brigade in reserve. The 8th Australian Brigade had eight tanks of B Company, 8th Tank Battalion attached, four each with 32nd and 29th Battalions, which were the leading assault battalions on the right and left respectively. There were also four Whippets for dealing with the Hindenburg Reserve Line, in addition to one and a half companies of 5th Australian Machine Gun Battalion, 13th Brigade AFA, two troops of 13th Australian Light Horse, 8th Field Company AE and a bearer division of 8th Australian Field Ambulance. The 31st Battalion was in support on the right, to fill any gaps as they occurred, and 30th Battalion was in reserve. The Brigade left its bivouac area at Hesbecourt at 7.00 a.m. and moved cross-country so as to cross the Brown Line at 9.00 a.m.

As the Brigade descended towards Bellicourt it ran into dense fog and smoke. American wounded coming back reported that the Hindenburg Main System and Bellicourt had been taken. Less optimistically other parties of soldiers were encountered retiring with slung rifles. They appeared to have no orders and did not know what to do. Because of the density of the fog the Australians had to close up and advance in very close order, visibility at times being reduced to five metres. On the left, 29th Battalion cleared some overlooked machine gun posts on the edge of Bellicourt, assisted by a couple of tanks and some Australian and American engineers. The village was crowded with Allied troops, which could have spelled disaster if the fog had lifted and presented the enemy gunners with such a rich target. The 29th and 31st Battalions therefore pushed through the village to the trenches to the east.

When the mist thinned twenty Americans appeared, reporting that there were no friendly troops ahead. A 29th Battalion patrol reported that Nauroy, on the next rise, was held by the Germans. About 11.00 a.m., 32nd Battalion came up some distance to the right. Although there were no friendly troops on the left flank, it was decided to press on to the Hindenburg Support Line. At 11.15 a.m. the battalions were reported to be moving up the ridge towards Nauroy, supported by tanks. As the visibility cleared, German fire from Nauroy increased and three of the four tanks allocated to 29th Battalion were knocked out. Some Australian guns that had moved too far ahead had to pull back. German artillery fire also forced Australian batteries west of Bellicourt to take up positions west of the Hindenburg Outpost Line. The 14th Brigade in reserve had to scatter to avoid this fire as it moved forward.

At 11.50 a.m., 29th Battalion advanced again along two sunken roads and an east-west communications trench, to pass through the American line. It reached Le Catelet Trench (Hindenburg Support Line) and captured an anti-tank gun position

The D93 runs through the centre of this view. In the left distance surrounded by trees is Etricourt Farm. Magny-la-Fosse is on the right. This is the area where Wark rushed a gun battery and then captured fifty Germans near the village.

(two field guns, two mortars, anti-tank rifles, machine guns and thirteen frightened Germans), before being halted by fire from Cabaret Wood Farm 900m to the north. By 3.00 p.m. 29th Battalion had reached the Green Line but, because there was no support on the left, it had to pull back to the Hindenburg Support Line. Meanwhile unknown to 29th Battalion, 32nd Battalion had fought its way forward through the mist south of Bellicourt.

On the eve of this great battle, GOC 5th Australian Division, Major General Sir Joseph John Talbot Hobbs was away on leave, and GOC 8th Australian Brigade, Brigadier General Edwin Tivey, was in command. Lieutenant Colonel Charles Stewart Davies, CO 32nd Battalion, was in command of the Brigade and **Major Blair Wark** was in temporary command of 32nd Battalion. At the last moment Major General Hobbs returned and Tivey resumed command of 8th Australian Brigade. However, as the troops were in position and Wark had issued his orders, Tivey decided to give him a chance of leading the Battalion.

When 32nd Battalion came upon its first opposition, the acting CO, Major Blair Wark, who was often ahead of his men reconnoitering the way forward, gained the cooperation of a tank and captured two machine gun posts. West of the tunnel mound he found 200 leaderless men of the American 117th Regiment, who should have crossed to the east of the tunnel and swung south. Wark attached these men to his force. Hearing engines in the fog, he found the tanks that had been attached to 117th Regiment. With the tanks leading, he advanced again at 10.00 a.m. between Bellicourt and the canal tunnel entrance. A number of enemy machine gun posts that had been missed were cleared. About 10.30 a.m., Wark found the tanks that had been allocated to his own Battalion south of Bellicourt. However, only two had survived that far. It was clear that the Americans had not taken their objectives and Wark decided that he had to seize them before his own.

With two tanks leading and two companies following in line, he headed south of Nauroy. As the visibility improved the German guns in Nauroy hit one tank. Wark

sent the other with his two rear companies to the southern end of the village. The tank was hit soon afterwards but D Company swept into the village at 11.30 a.m. and took fifty prisoners. It then followed the rest of the Battalion to the southeast. Ahead of the Battalion all seemed to be empty, except for a few isolated machine guns and field guns. There was no sign of any American troops.

Close by a 30th Battalion patrol found some tanks and persuaded one to go into Nauroy to discover where the Germans were. About 12.45 p.m. two tanks and patrols entered the village and cleared it and part of the Hindenburg Support Line to the west. Posts were established east of the village.

Meanwhile Wark pressed on to the southeast, despite not having support on his left flank. Scattered machine gun and field gun teams continued firing until the Australians were about 350m away and then tended to surrender. At 11.30 a.m., as the Battalion climbed up the second ridge past Nauroy, it linked up with 4th Leicestershire (138th Brigade, 46th Division), which had crossed the canal to the south. By noon the Magny-la-Fosse–Etricourt road had been reached, with the left flank held up at Etricourt Farm. Wark sent one company through Magny-la-Fosse, in 46th Division's area, and another through Etricourt Farm, which was mopped up, with twenty prisoners, four guns and three machine guns being taken. Wark personally collected a few men and rushed a battery of four guns, capturing them and ten of the gunners. He then rushed forward with two NCOs and surprised and captured fifty Germans near Magny-la-Fosse.

A defensive left flank was formed. With his right flank secured by 46th Division, Wark reported at 12.20 p.m. that he was waiting for the barrage to lift before advancing to his final objective. He pressed on through the northern half of Magny-la-Fosse against weak machine gun fire, alongside a battalion of 32nd Division, and headed northeast towards Joncourt. There were still no friendly troops on the left flank. By 3.00 p.m. Wark's men were very tired and he halted them on the spur southwest of Joncourt.

On the left of 5th Australian Division, 15th Australian Brigade reached the start line at 9.00 a.m., largely without incident, but beyond came under machine gun fire from positions missed by the Americans. However, the Hindenburg Main System was crossed and the line of the canal tunnel was reached by 11.00 a.m. Several hundred Americans found there reported that something had gone wrong ahead. The western side of the tunnel mound was occupied by 57th and 58th Battalions (right and left respectively), the latter having been in support. However, on the left 59th Battalion was mixed up with the right of 3rd Australian Division and could not advance as quickly. It came under fire from Quennemont Farm to the north and had difficulty reaching the Hindenburg Main System. The open flank resulted in 57th and 58th Battalions coming under fire from the left rear. The front and support trenches were eventually cleared and enemy bombing attacks down the trenches from the north were repulsed. Bombing blocks were established in both trenches of the Hindenburg Main System.

During the morning 3rd Australian Division, on the left, had run into strong resistance before reaching the appointed start line. It led with 11th and 10th Australian Brigades, right and left respectively, each supported by eight tanks, all of which were put out of action by direct fire or mines. As they approached the American start positions they encountered parties of soldiers retiring, often leaderless and confused by the smoke and fog. They were followed by German infantry, particularly along the Macquincourt valley, and were engaged by German anti-tank and field guns. The brigades had strict instructions not to become entangled in the Americans' tasks but some battalion commanders felt compelled to do so in order to save the situation from becoming worse.

As the brigades crossed the American start line at 9.00 a.m., they came under heavy fire from Gillemont Farm Ridge. The fog prevented observation of what was going on and there was little accurate information to be had. Both brigades were sent immediately to assist the Americans. However, visibility improved and enemy shelling increased from the north. By noon only a little progress had been made. Quennet Copse had been taken and the Knoll, on the left flank, was held by 54th Brigade (18th Division, III Corps). However, the enemy still held Quennemont and Gillemont Farms and was working up the Macquincourt valley to make repeated counterattacks against the Knoll. Fierce bombing battles developed and forces combined to push the Germans back and to stop them regaining the Knoll.

In contrast, south of Quennemont Farm, 5th Australian Division had advanced about 1,600m further, where the Americans had been able to clear the Germans from the Hindenburg Outpost Line, Hindenburg Main System and the tunnel mound. Had the troops to the north been able to advance alongside, the final objective could have been reached. An obvious solution was to attack northwards from 5th Australian Division's area into the rear of the enemy opposing 3rd Australian Division. At 11.50 a.m. 9th Australian Brigade, 3rd Australian Division's reserve, originally intended to guard the northern flank, was warned to be ready to attack on the southern flank instead.

A renewed attack was arranged for both divisions at 3.00 p.m. In 5th Australian Division, 15th Australian Brigade had four Mark V tanks and eight Whippets remaining in support. The 57th and 58th Battalions were tasked to press on to clear Estrées but the supporting barrage was very light and did little more than warn the enemy that the attack had restarted. All Mark V tanks and five of the Whippets were put out of action within fifteen minutes. Machine gun fire from the Hindenburg Support System slowed progress but both battalions managed to secure footings there, although there were Germans holding out between them. Heavy enfilade fire from 3rd Australian Division's area on the left necessitated establishing a defensive flank facing north.

In 8th Australian Brigade, 32nd Battalion was already in line with 32nd Division (IX Corps) to the south. Strong patrols were sent through Joncourt and towards the sugar factory east of Nauroy, both of which were found to be held by the Germans. Four Mark V tanks still with the Brigade were disabled. One company of 31st Battalion pushed through Nauroy to the eastern outskirts and two companies of 32nd Battalion were extended back for 1,600m towards Etricourt Farm to guard the left flank. The 32nd Battalion was then in a deep salient in enemy territory, with no support on its left flank. It was isolated and also under fire from the sugar factory to its rear. As a result, at 5.00 p.m., the patrols east of Joncourt were pulled back and the Battalion retired 900m to the main line, in contact with 46th Division (IX Corps) on the right.

At 5.30 p.m., a force of 400 Germans counterattacked from the high ground of Mill Ridge towards Etricourt Farm, about 1,800m to the southwest. They came under fire from 31st and 32nd Battalions, the British on the right and a RHA battery. The nearest the Germans came to 32nd Battalion was 450m, before the survivors took cover in shell holes. Despite this success, with 31st Battalion held up east of Nauroy by fire from the sugar factory, 32nd Battalion's flank remained exposed. Contact was made with 31st Battalion on the left at 6.00 p.m. During the night, 29th Battalion on the left gained a footing on the high ground northeast of Nauroy. The 8th Australian Brigade had suffered 250 casualties but had inflicted numerous casualties on the Germans. It had also taken 250 prisoners, six field guns and sixteen machine guns.

At 7.00 a.m. next day, 32nd Battalion attacked again through heavy shell and machine gun fire. An advance of 1,500m was made and a line was consolidated between Joncourt and Etricourt Farm. At 6.00 a.m. on 1st October, the Battalion and a company of 30th Battalion pushed through Joncourt and a little beyond. Wark again rushed forward to silence machine gun posts that were causing heavy casualties. General Sir Henry Rawlinson, CinC Fourth Army, concluded, ... *It is beyond doubt that the success achieved by the brigade during the heavy fighting was due to this officer's gallantry, determination, skill and great courage.*

The 3rd Australian Division attacked without artillery support again because of continuing uncertainty over the position of the Americans. The advance was met by a hail of fire and it was clear that the objective could not be taken in daylight. However, an advance of 325m was made, resulting in the capture of Quennemont and Gillemont Farms and the ridge between them. The Germans regained the eastern side of the Knoll and a battalion of 9th Australian Brigade was sent to the head of Macquincourt valley. On the right, contact was made with 5th Australian Division in the Hindenburg Main System south of Bony.

On the left, III Corps' short front was held by 12th Division. It was to gain ground as the formations on either side advanced. 18th Division, less 53rd Brigade in Corps reserve, formed up behind the American 27th Division. The 54th Brigade was to advance alongside the Americans to guard the left flank. For this purpose a special liaison force was created, consisting of two infantry companies, a machine gun company, an engineer field company and a signal section. The 55th Brigade was stood by from 8.00 a.m. to protect the left of 54th Brigade and to mop up Vendhuille as the opportunity arose.

The 54th Brigade reached its first objective, Macquincourt Trench, 650m east of the Knoll, but the Americans had drifted to the south and the Brigade could advance no further. It halted and repelled German counterattacks. Meanwhile reports indicated that the Americans were progressing well and 55th Brigade was ordered to move forward at 8.45 a.m. After advancing about 900m, the slopes in front were seen to be swept by machine gun fire and this Brigade also halted. Later, a battalion sent against the Germans northeast of Gillemont Farm was halted by heavy fire. Eventually a line was established in contact with 54th Brigade at the Knoll.

Overall the results of the day were disappointing for Fourth Army, except on the right where an advance of five kilometres had been made. More positively, most of the Hindenburg Main System had been taken and there was a 7,500m long breach in the Hindenburg Support System. The continuous Allied offensives were having their effect; at 10.00 a.m. on the morning of 29th September, Generals Hindenburg and Ludendorff concluded that an armistice must be requested immediately. Unknown to all concerned, after over four years of conflict, the war had just seven weeks left to run.

30th September 1918

451 Pte John Ryan, 55th Battalion AIF (14th Australian Brigade, 5th Australian Division), Hindenburg Defences, France

Although 46th Division had performed outstandingly on 29th September, elsewhere the advance of Fourth Army had not lived up to expectations. Much of this was due to the failure of II American Corps to secure the start line on the 27th, leaving it with an almost impossible task on the 29th.

General Rawlinson decided to withdraw the II American Corps and to continue the attack with IX, Australian and XIII Corps, the latter replacing the exhausted III Corps on the right, which had been in action since 8th August. The IX Corps was to press northeastwards to Joncourt and eastwards to Preselles and Sequehart, in order to assist the Australian Corps on the left and the French XV Corps on the right. The Australian Corps was to get in touch with the Americans that were still believed to be holding out in front. The attack was to be to the north and east to breach the Beaurevoir Line at Estrées, Folemprise Farm and Gouy. This included the northern canal tunnel entrance near Vendhuille and parts of the Hindenburg Main and Support Systems. On the left, III Corps would occupy Vendhuille if possible and assist the Australians with artillery support. The XIII Corps was to take over from III Corps at noon and would later take over the part of the Australian Corps front that faced north. It was then to advance northeastwards to assist Third Army. The 5th Cavalry Brigade was transferred from the Australian Corps to IX Corps.

On the right of IX Corps, 1st Division advanced at 8.00 a.m. to clear the triangle between the canal and the Corps southern boundary. By 8.35 a.m. Thorigny and Talana Hill had been captured, along with 300 prisoners. Later the whole area up to the boundary with 32nd Division at le Tronquoy was secured. On the left, 32nd Division also advanced at 8.00 a.m. Its right pushed out patrols and waited for the French to appear on the flank but it was unable to reach Sequehart. The centre eventually took Levergies in the evening and 400 prisoners. The left reached the outskirts of Joncourt in contact with 5th Australian Division to the north.

The Australian Corps was to clear the remainder of the Hindenburg Main and Support Systems. However, it had limited call on artillery support because it was feared that American troops were still holding out in front. Exceptions were made for the Hindenburg Main System, which was clearly held by the enemy, and for the tunnel mound and Hindenburg Support System. Heavy rain set in on the evening of 29th September, making the resupply of food and ammunition difficult and flooding trenches and dugouts. On the 30th poor weather limited air cooperation and attempts to find the Americans and drop food to them were unsuccessful. The Australians planned to attack at 6.00 a.m. with 8th and 14th Australian Brigades in 5th Australian Division and 11th, 9th and 10th Australian Brigades in 3rd Australian Division. Two brigades, the 14th (5th Australian Division) and the 11th (3rd Australian Division), would attack northwards, leading with one battalion each. As 14th Australian Brigade seized Le Catelet Line (Hindenburg Support System), 15th Australian Brigade behind would extend its garrison up the line and attack eastwards later.

On the right of 5th Australian Division at Nauroy, 8th Australian Brigade had been ordered to cooperate with 32nd Division (IX Corps) to the south. It sent patrols onto Mill Ridge but fire from the sugar factory and the lamp signal station on the left flank stopped every effort. On the far right, 32nd Battalion advanced in the morning towards Joncourt. Even though it was unsupported by tanks or artillery, and under heavy, long distance, machine gun fire, it managed to gain 900m and later went on to within a few hundred metres of the village.

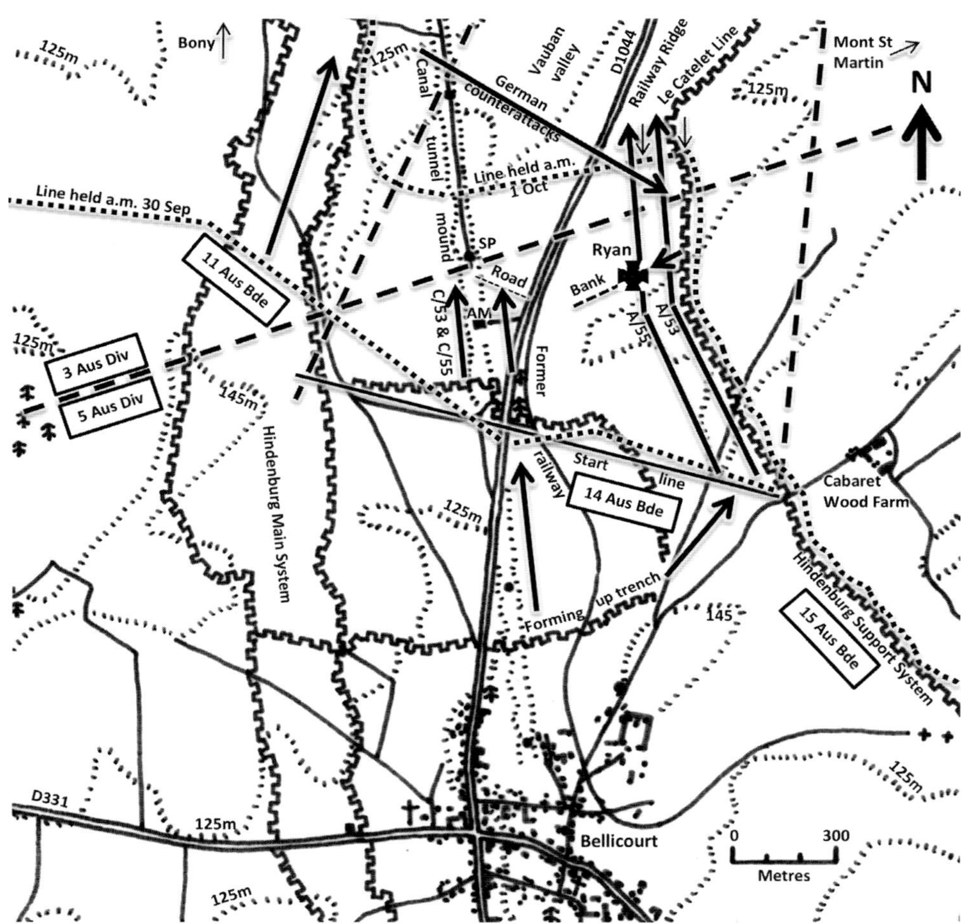

Park in the Bellicourt American Monument car park and walk back to the road. Cross over carefully and look eastwards to the site of the bank cleared by Ryan on the far side of the former railway line. The American Monument sits atop the tunnel mound. AM = American Monument, SP = strongpoint.

On the left of 8th Australian Brigade, 29th Battalion advanced at 4.00 p.m. However, the barrage was weak and on the flanks it fell behind the Battalion. One company made a little ground but on the left enfilade fire poured from Cabaret Farm Wood and frontally from the lamp signal station. Machine guns in concrete shelters and field guns also fired point blank. As a result there was little progress.

On the left, 14th Australian Brigade was to advance northwards at 6.00 a.m, between the tunnel mound and the Le Catelet Line, to support 3rd Australian Division's attack on the left. The aim was to clear Railway Ridge and the Le Catelet Line to the high ground overlooking Le Catelet village. This involved an advance of over 2,000m. The 53rd Battalion was to lead, with 55th Battalion following to attack eastwards later with 15th Australian Brigade. As 14th Australian Brigade advanced, 58th Battalion (15th Australian Brigade) was to follow and take over the Le Catelet Line as far north as the divisional boundary. The attack was to be covered by a barrage fired by two field artillery brigades, starting 275m in front of the start line and advancing ninety metres every five minutes.

Most Australian units were under-strength due to casualties and a shortage of replacements. In addition, the men of 1914 were withdrawn for leave in Australia. As a result, both 53rd and 55th Battalions had been reorganised into two rifle companies each, known as A and C Companies. In 55th Battalion both companies numbered just ninety men each.

In 53rd Battalion, A Company was to advance along the Le Catelet Line on the right, while C Company cleared along the tunnel mound on the left. Behind, 55th Battalion was to mop up the Le Catelet Line, whilst maintaining contact with 53rd Battalion in front and 58th Battalion (14th Australian Brigade) behind. Patrols were to be sent towards Mont St Martin to the east.

The 53rd Battalion did not find its guides. The CO, Lieutenant Colonel WJR Cheeseman MC, led it to the start line but it was still 450m short when the ineffective barrage fell. The CO formed up the Battalion in a trench and set off for the start line, where it deployed into attack formation. As a result, the Battalion was fifteen minutes late and met with intense fire from Cabaret Wood Farm, the Le Catelet Line, Bony and the tunnel mound.

The right of 53rd Battalion forced the Germans back 275m northwards to a road crossing in the Le Catelet Line. The enemy counterattacked. On the left, beside the tunnel mound, fire was received from the Hindenburg Main and Support Systems as well as from the front, making progress extremely difficult. The fighting in the Le Catelet Line flowed to and fro and eventually the Germans were forced further northwards. By 10.00 a.m., 53rd Battalion had cleared as far north as the bend in the Le Catelet Line. A small party also pushed along the tunnel mound from where the Germans were enfilading the Le Catelet Line. The mound was cleared to the railway crossing but the advance was held there by a strongpoint.

The acting CO of 55th Battalion, Major Eric William Stutchbury MC, had returned from the Brigade HQ planning conference at 3.15 a.m., leaving only three hours to plan the attack and get into position. The Battalion had already made a difficult move that night and faced another four kilometres through a confusion of barbed wire, trenches and shell holes on a particularly dark and rainy night. The Intelligence Officer led the move brilliantly, avoiding Bellicourt, which was under enemy shellfire. The Battalion arrived at the same trench in which 53rd Battalion had formed up, a few hundred metres behind the start line, at 5.45 a.m. Once 53rd Battalion crossed the start line, 55th Battalion followed about 450m behind. A Company followed along the Le Catelet Line, while C Company moved to the left, where the tunnel mound provided some protection from enemy fire.

C Company reached another trench, where some men of 58th Battalion were found and C Company, 53rd Battalion had paused before continuing. As the latter moved off, it was covered by fire from C Company, 55th Battalion as it crossed a shallow valley to the north. Enemy fire continued, particularly from Cabaret Wood Farm. The OC of C Company intended moving out of the trench to a railway cutting to the north from where he intended attacking eastwards towards the Le Catelet Line. A party of 53rd Battalion arrived having been halted where a road cut through the tunnel mound. The Germans had a strongpoint just beyond. This party then made its way to join the rest of 53rd Battalion in the Le Catelet Line. OC C Company, 55th Battalion realised that the strongpoint would enfilade his planned attack to the east and set about dealing with the strongpoint instead.

The platoon on the right maintained supporting fire towards the Le Catelet Line. A Lewis gun was moved so as to be able to fire on the German machine gunners holding up A Company. Several were killed and the remainder were pinned down, allowing A Company to close with and destroy them. Another platoon made its way along the trench and crossed to the western side of the mound to see if a covered approach existed on that side. The platoon came under sustained machine gun fire from Bony and the Hindenburg Main System. The platoon commander and his batman crawled forward to the road junction without being seen. They could see the enemy machine guns, but not the gunners, and returned. Three other men arrived and they decided to attack the strongpoint immediately. They reached the bottom of the bank below the strongpoint unseen but, as they inched forward to attack, they were hit by another machine gun twenty metres to the left and two men were killed. C Company sent a Lewis gun team and four other men but they were stopped by the same machine gun, which the Lewis gun was unable to neutralise. Other enemy machine guns to the left also opened fire, making a flanking move in that direction impossible. They returned over the mound to report to the OC. Lack of progress on this flank meant that A Company on the right had pulled ahead.

Orders were issued for C Company to advance either side of the mound. There was no specific objective, other than to keep pushing ahead. C Company advanced in line down the slope and for the first 200m all went well. Then it came under heavy small arms fire from a line of Germans lying in the grass ahead. The Australians dived for cover and returned fire. After a while the OC ordered, *Come on C Company, charge the bastards*. The men leapt up and charged forward, screaming and shouting. The Germans fled down the slope, hotly pursued by C Company, until they jumped into a trench and the garrison opened fire. C Company dived for cover again about where the road crossed the mound. It was under fire from various points on the mound, including the strongpoint, and also from Bony, the Hindenburg Main System and Railway Ridge. Some minenwerfers and artillery were also brought to bear. However, despite the heavy fire, the strongpoint was captured. The OC was wounded and all other officers east of the mound were also casualties. A sergeant took over. The advance continued and a number of machine gun posts were cleared but only a handful of men arrived at the German trench. The survivors took cover wherever possible but it soon became clear that they were in an impossible situation. A retirement was ordered back to the start trench.

West of the mound the advance also ran out of steam. The survivors pulled back several hundred metres to the trench from where they had launched the attack. The officer in command was badly concussed by a shell and took no further part in the action. By then about half of C Company had become casualties and there was only one uninjured officer remaining. The men were exhausted and orders were issued to the survivors to reorganise and hold where they were.

On the right, as 53rd Battalion bombed its way along the Le Catelet Line, A Company, 55th Battalion cleared the low ground to the left of the trench system. It came under heavy fire but reached the same trench that caused C Company so much trouble on the left and paused there. By 8.30 a.m., 53rd Battalion had made sufficient progress to allow A Company to resume its advance. Resistance was ferocious. The structure of A Company broke down and groups of men gravitated to a leader, often a man with no rank, to continue the advance and attack strongpoints and trenches. The officers moved amongst the groups, rallying scattered parties and encouraging the men to move on. Some positions were overcome in headlong frontal charges, a tactic that was totally unexpected by the Germans. The men were in no mood for prisoners and none were taken at this stage. After four hours the Company had advanced almost 1,000m and a 77mm field gun was captured. Thus far the Company had been quite fortunate, suffering only three fatalities.

Enemy resistance then stiffened considerably and the fire of machine guns, minenwerfers and artillery intensified. Casualties mounted and a strong counterattack was launched from the Hindenburg Main System at 10.00 a.m. A Company sought cover in the Le Catelet Line and a chaotic retirement to it followed, with the men involved in running skirmishes with the advancing enemy. Once in the Le Catelet Line they took up positions behind 53rd Battalion, which was still attempting to advance along it.

The Germans surged ahead and into the trench in many places, which was held too thinly by A Company to prevent this. Frenzied and vicious hand-to-hand fighting followed in which bayonets, knives, spades, grenades and pistols were the most useful weapons. Despite having suffered heavy casualties in reaching the trench, the Germans began bombing down the Le Catelet Line and the Australians were driven back. At the same time a large party of Germans established itself on an open bank to the southwest. As a result, 53rd and 55th Battalions faced the prospect of being cut off while under attack from front and rear.

The situation was critical. However, a hitherto unremarkable soldier, **Private Jack Ryan**, immediately appreciated the situation. In the initial assault, he had advanced with great dash and determination and was one of the first to reach the enemy trench. His skill and daring inspired his comrades and, despite heavy fire, the hostile garrison was overcome and the trench occupied. When the enemy

On the right is the American Monument on top of the tunnel mound. In front of the monument is the D1044 Bellicourt–Le Catelet road. To the left of the road and parallel with it, is a track on the line of the former railway. In the centre of the picture in the middle ground are a few slight undulations. The bank, of which nothing can now be discerned, was in that area. The main attack was towards the camera and Jack Ryan's attack came from the high ground just left of centre. In the centre distance is Bellicourt. The Hindenburg Support System/Le Catelet Line ran along the high ground on the left in front of Cabaret Wood Farm, which is surrounded by trees on the far left of the picture.

counterattack established a bombing party in the rear of the position, he organised the few men near him and rushed with them into the flank of the Germans at the bank. A few were hit in the charge but Ryan and three others made it. Undeterred by being outnumbered many times over, they threw themselves amongst the Germans, bayoneting three and causing chaos and confusion amongst the others. Ryan moved alone along the bank, throwing bombs at the remaining enemy, and forced them to break back across no man's land, where they provided easy targets for the Lewis gunners. Ryan was wounded in the shoulder as he returned and took no further part in the battle. However, his action had removed the threat to the Battalion's rear and enabled others to recapture lost parts of the Le Catelet Line.

The German attack down the Le Catelet Line was also halted and individuals and small groups gradually cleared the lost sections. The Germans held on to the trench to the north and the Australian attack was halted several hundred metres south of the bend. A bombing block was erected. Taking stock, the Brigade Commander, Brigadier General James Campbell Stewart DSO, realised that 53rd Battalion had been reduced to 180 men and 55th Battalion to only 120. The two battalions amounted to the strength of two companies. In its position around the tunnel mound, C Company, 55th Battalion offered no tactical advantage and it was ordered to join the rest of the Battalion in the Le Catelet Line.

Attempts by 53rd Battalion to link up with 3rd Australian Division on the left, failed due to heavy machine gun fire. However, despite not being able to attain its objectives, 14th Australian Brigade had cleared about 1,100m of the Hindenburg Support System up to the northern divisional boundary and had repulsed several counterattacks. This posed a serious problem to the Germans in maintaining their

hold in the Hindenburg Main System to the west. All resupply and communications links ran from east to west and many had been cut by the Brigade's successes.

In pouring rain at 3.00 p.m., the Germans launched an intensely savage counterattack down the Le Catelet Line and also from the tunnel mound. 53rd Battalion lost the bombing block and fell back 200m down the Le Catelet Line. The Lewis gunners did great damage to the advancing enemy in the open, mowing down many of the attackers before they could close with the Australian positions. About 200 Germans were killed and many more were wounded before the attack stalled and fell back. Pushing north again, some lost ground was retaken by the Australians. Another bombing block was established but not as far north as previously. At 4.30 p.m. a concentration of Germans appeared to be massing for another attempt but they were broken up by the artillery. Fighting then descended into the maze of trenches and saps around the Le Catelet Line.

Stretcher-bearers were very active at this time, moving about in the open to deal with the wounded, including several Americans from the previous day. Four bearers were awarded the MM but 2143 Corporal Ernest 'Ernie' Albert Corey stood out from the rest. In charge of the Battalion's bearer party, he was in the thick of it with his men, rescuing the wounded from seemingly impossible situations. Corey received a third bar to his MM, the only man ever to be so honoured.

At 6.00 p.m., 53rd and 55th Battalions were combined under CO 53rd Battalion. The 55th Battalion war diary says that this arrangement was made in the morning, which seems unlikely. At 9.00 p.m. this ad hoc unit was ordered to establish a line joining the northernmost point held in the Le Catelet Line with 44th Battalion (3rd Australian Division) to the west. Due to the darkness of the night this could not be completed until 4.30 a.m. on 1st October. There were a number of firefights with isolated parties of Germans and some prisoners were taken. The following morning dawned with Australians, Americans and Germans intermingled in places along an ill-defined front line. During the operations on 30th September, 55th Battalion captured eighteen prisoners, two guns (77mm and 4.2″) and twenty-nine machine guns. The Battalion suffered seventy-two casualties (eighteen killed and fifty-four wounded, two of whom remained at duty).

Ernest Albert Corey (20th December 1891–25th August 1972), born at Numeralla, NSW, the eighth child of his parents, was educated at Thubergal Lake Public School before becoming a blacksmith's striker. In January 1916 he marched from Cooma to Goulburn as a member of the *Men from Snowy River* recruiting march. He enlisted in 55th Battalion AIF on 13th January 1916 and trained at Goulburn before embarking on 4th September aboard HMAT A15 *Port Sydney* with the 4th Reinforcements. In England, he spent three months with 14th Training Battalion, Hurdcott Camp, Wiltshire, before joining 55th Battalion on 8th February 1917 at Montauban, France. He joined the grenade section in C Company and took part in the capture of Doignies in April. On 15th May near Quéant, CO 55th Battalion called for volunteers to assist the stretcher bearers. Ernie was one of thirty men who volunteered and for seventeen hours he assisted in carrying the wounded two kilometres back to a dressing station. He was awarded the MM. He became a regular stretcher bearer and was awarded a Bar to the MM for his actions on 26th September during the Battle of Polygon Wood, near Ypres. In that action, whilst under heavy artillery and machine gun fire, he frequently went out into no man's land to assist the wounded. In February 1918 he was granted leave to Britain, where he fell ill and spent ninety days in hospital. Rejoining the Battalion in July, he took part in the capture of Péronne and received a second Bar to the MM for assisting the wounded on 1st-2nd September, under heavy machine gun and artillery fire. On 21st September he was promoted corporal in charge of the Battalion's stretcher bearers. While leading them in the battle north of Bellicourt on 30th September, he attended to the wounded while exposed to fire, but continued to direct other bearer parties throughout the action. At about 11.00 a.m. he went out to bring in a wounded officer, whom he had previously bandaged, when he was seriously wounded in the right groin and thigh by a shell burst. He crawled to his aid bag and applied a tourniquet to his femoral artery, before crawling 300m to the rear, where he was picked up by an officer and a sergeant and taken to a casualty clearing station. He was operated on there before being transferred to a general hospital at Le Havre. After another operation, he was evacuated to hospital in Bristol, England. Ernie was repatriated to Australia on 30th April 1919 and was discharged on medical grounds.

Returning to Cooma, Ernie worked as a contract rabbiter before moving to Canberra in 1922, where he was employed as a camp caretaker. On 23rd September 1924 he married Sarah Jane Fisher at St Gregory's Catholic Church, Queanbeyan and they had a daughter, Patricia, before the marriage ended in divorce in 1935. Ernie was an office cleaner for the Department of the Interior 1927–40. He re-enlisted in the Australian Military Forces on 23rd September 1941 and joined 2nd Garrison Battalion. He was medically discharged on 11th October 1943. He had a number of jobs, including caretaker, cook for a departmental survey party and leading hand at the Canberra incinerator. He died on 25 August 1972 and is buried in the Ex-Servicemen's section of Woden Cemetery, ACT.

The 3rd Australian Division faced Bony, which was bristling with machine guns. In addition, German batteries north of Vendhuille were able to enfilade the ground over which the Division was to advance. Eighteen tanks were allocated but only seven arrived at the start line and they were fifty minutes late. These tanks set off alone without the infantry, who were not ready. They came under heavy machine gun and anti-tank rifle fire at Bony, which was returned. The tanks skirted the village but only one survived undamaged and, without infantry support, it fell back.

The Hindenburg Outpost Line was to be taken by 9th and 10th Australian Brigades at 6.00 a.m. While these brigades moved to the east, 11th Australian Brigade was to progress northwards along the Hindenburg Main System. Scouts

Ernie Corey's unique medal group displayed in the First World War gallery at the Australian War Memorial.

probing forward at dawn discovered that the Germans had already fallen back to the Hindenburg Main System.

Ground conditions were such that 9th Australian Brigade could not get into position in time. As a result, 11th Australian Brigade, which was on the spot, was ordered to attack up the Hindenburg Main System instead, allowing time for 9th Australian Brigade's battalions to get into position for the latter part of the attack. Meanwhile, 9th Australian Brigade would clear the Hindenburg Outpost Line and the area east of it for 900m. It was also to keep connection between the other two brigades. To the north, 10th Australian Brigade was to attack eastwards between Bony and the northern tunnel entrance.

In 11th Australian Brigade, 44th Battalion attacked with 42nd and 43rd Battalions following. However, 44th Battalion, exhausted from the fighting the day before, did not receive the orders by the time that the barrage opened. The other battalions were also delayed or received the orders late. Advancing over the open was not possible due to the weight of fire from Bony and the flanks. An attempt to bomb up the trenches by 44th Battalion also failed.

On the right flank, 14th Australian Brigade had by then pushed beyond the alignment of 11th Australian Brigade. However, 43rd Battalion arrived and at 11.00 a.m. advanced along both trenches. When the machine guns in the western trench had been suppressed, parties in the eastern trench were able to make progress. However, the ground then sloped towards Bony and the advance was stopped there. The Germans counterattacked and pushed all battalions back and they were pinned down by machine guns in Bony and Vauban Valley. Despite the setbacks, by nightfall, 11th Australian Brigade had cleared 900m of the Hindenburg Main System and had a foothold in the outskirts of Bony.

On the right of Fourth Army, III Corps was ordered to hold on to the high ground overlooking Vendhuille and, where possible, to press on to gain greater security in depth and better observation. In the morning, patrols of 18th Division discovered that the Germans had pulled back from Vendhuille west of the canal. In the afternoon, 54th Brigade moved into the village and began mopping up. After dark, patrols were sent over the canal to locate the enemy. On the right, 55th Brigade formed a defensive flank to connect with 3rd Australian Division. On the left, 12th Division closed up to the canal and that night it was relieved by 18th Division, which then held the entire Corps frontage.

Battle of Beaurevoir

456 LCpl William Coltman, 1/6th Battalion, The Prince of Wales's (North Staffordshire Regiment) (137th Brigade, 46th Division), Sequehart, France
457 Sgt William Johnson, 1/5th Battalion, The Sherwood Foresters (Nottinghamshire & Derbyshire Regiment) (139th Brigade, 46th Division), Ramicourt, France
458 Lt Joseph Maxwell, 18th Battalion AIF (5th Australian Brigade, 2nd Australian Division), Beaurevoir, France

3rd October 1918

Fourth Army attacked on 3rd October to seize the last element of the Hindenburg System, the Reserve System or Beaurevoir–Fonsomme Line. This consisted of the familiar two lines of trenches with concrete emplacements, well protected by wire in front. The Germans also sited isolated machine gun posts behind the Line and in groups in villages. The ground was rolling and open, with small woods and sunken lanes, but there were no natural obstacles to movement. The Army objective was the high ground around Montbrehain and Beaurevoir. The IX Corps, on the right, and the Australian Corps, in the centre, were to make the main attack, while XIII Corps, on the left, formed a defensive flank.

On the right of IX Corps, 1st Division was to fill the gap between the French on its right and 32nd Division in the centre of the Corps. On the left of the Corps, 46th Division took over most of the front from 32nd Division in order to make the main attack. The 6th Division was in reserve and 5th Cavalry Brigade was in close support.

The 32nd Division attacked Sequehart with its 14th Brigade. At the same time a detachment of 97th Brigade advanced through 46th Division's area to the north, before swinging south to roll up the trench system and link up with 14th Brigade. The village was taken after heavy fighting and was almost immediately lost in a counterattack against the weakened companies. However, the situation was restored and the lost ground was recovered. Another counterattack at 6.00 p.m. was driven off.

The first objective of 46th Division was between Sequehart and Ramicourt, before pressing on to Mannequin Hill and Montbrehain. The Division had the added difficulty of taking over part of the line from 32nd Division in the dark, on ground that had not been reconnoitred previously. Despite this, it was achieved on time

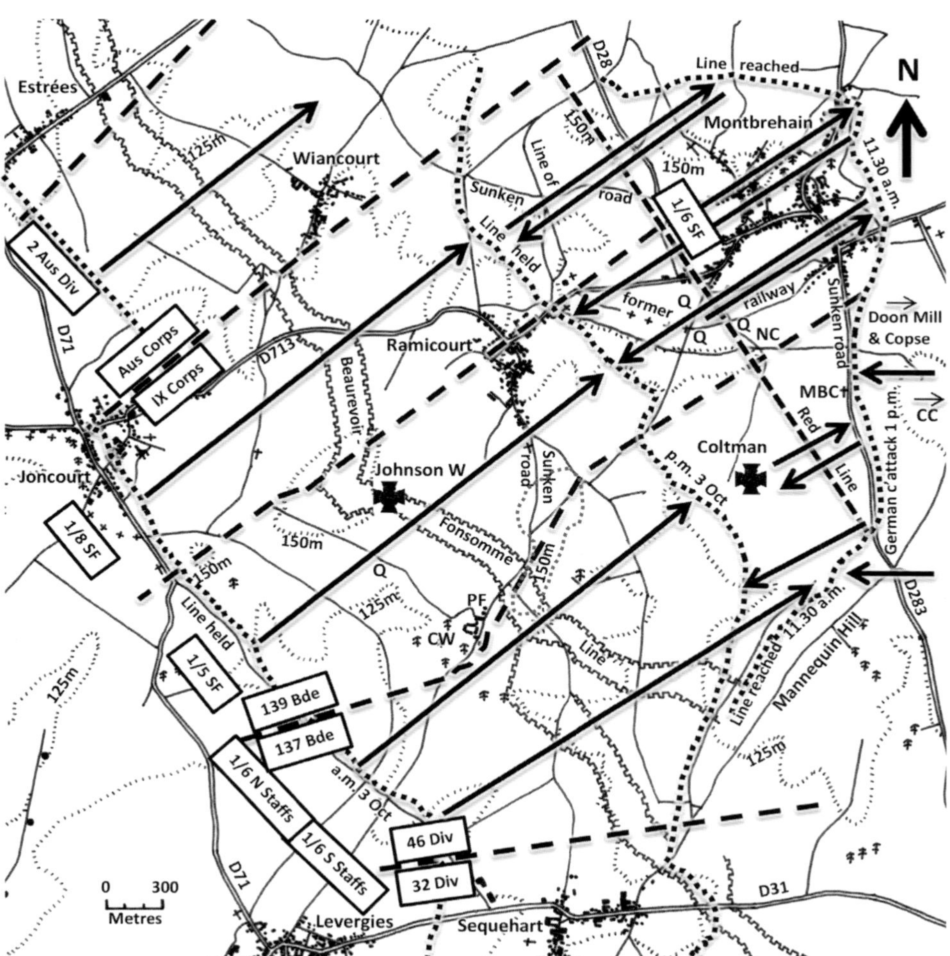

CC = Champignons Copse, CW = Chataigniers Wood, MBC = Montbrehain British Cemetery, NC = Nevilles Cross, PF = Preselles Farm, Q = quarry. The line reached by 11.30 a.m. in the top right corner is almost the same as the Blue Line, which had been omitted for clarity. To reach the site of Coltman's VC action, leave Montbrehain on the D283 southwards towards Fontaine-Uterte. Park on the right at Montbrehain British Cemetery. Look to the southwest, from where 137th Brigade attacked towards you. Coltman made the daring rescues of the wounded men in the shallow valley below the cemetery. There are tracks that will allow you to walk into the valley and get closer to the site of Coltman's VC action. However, the best view is probably from the cemetery wall. To reach the site of Johnson's VC action, leave Levergies north-easterly on an unclassified road. Follow for 2,000m and just after Preselles Farm, park on the left, where there is a weighbridge. Walk along the track to the northwest around a couple of bends north of Chataigniers Wood. After 800m there are the remains of a small quarry on the left. Johnson's VC action was about 300m north of here in the Beaurevoir-Fonsomme Line.

and in good order. The Division was supported by twenty-two tanks, eight brigades of field artillery, one of RHA and another of RGA. The advance commenced at 6.05 a.m., with 137th and 139th Brigades, on the right and left respectively, leading from the Joncourt–Sequehart road. The brigades had a number of tanks allocated to them to flatten lanes through the wire. Overall the Beaurevoir–Fonsomme Line fell relatively easily. However, the success could not be exploited due to difficulties over internal cooperation within the Division, the French making no progress to the south and Third Army being held up on the St Quentin Canal to the north.

The 137th Brigade advanced with 1/6th South Staffordshire on the right, 1/6th North Staffordshire on the left and 1/5th South Staffordshire in support in the centre. The Brigade was allocated seven tanks, three with the right battalion and four with the left. Each leading battalion had two guns of 137th Light Trench Mortar Battery attached. In the advance they engaged a number of enemy positions successfully and were then positioned where they could best support the infantry against counterattacks.

On the right, 1/6th South Staffordshire moved forward against almost no opposition until reaching the high ground in front of the Beaurevoir–Fonsomme Line north of Sequehart. This was overcome and the surviving defenders fled, losing heavily to the Lewis guns. Several concrete machine gun posts were encountered next. They were silenced at bayonet point with tank support. Two of the three tanks were hit but only one was disabled. As the advance progressed there was uncertainty about what was happening in Sequehart. As a result, the Battalion dropped off companies on the right flank as it progressed, and this had the effect of drawing the whole Brigade to the right. Inevitably this resulted in creating a gap on the left flank of the Brigade. The Battalion reached its final objective at 8.10 a.m. and posts were pushed forward towards the top of Mannequin Hill. However, 32nd Division on the right was forced back and the Battalion was subjected to heavy flanking fire from the high ground just east of Sequehart. In this situation it was not possible to hold the top of Mannequin Hill and a withdrawal was conducted back to the final objective.

On the left, 1/6th North Staffordshire advanced as planned. At Chataigniers Wood it split, with the companies on the right skirting around to the south and those on the left to the north. A tank fired into the Wood to clear out some of the enemy. A platoon of 1/5th South Staffordshire, following in support 550m behind the leading battalions, reinforced 1/6th North Staffordshire and mopped up Chataigniers Wood. There was stiff fighting in the Beaurevoir–Fonsomme Line before the advance progressed to Nevilles Cross, where two field guns were firing point blank over open sights. A party of Lewis gunners moved around to a flank and put the enemy gunners out of action. The advance then continued towards Doon Mill. About twenty men arrived there, with another twelve from the Sherwood Foresters of 139th Brigade. Being so far ahead of the flanking units, including the Battalion's right company, and with the enemy advancing in strength at 1.00 p.m., it was decided to pull back to Nevilles Cross and the road running south from it. After

From the wall of Montbrehain British Cemetery with the D283 Montbrehain–Fontaine–Uterte road on the far right. Montbrehain is in the right distance. Just left of centre is a tall grain silo on the D713 road northeast of Ramicourt. Coltman rescued the three wounded men from the low ground in the centre and left of picture. The western edge of Mannequin Hill is in the left distance.

two hours there, whilst under heavy fire from Mannequin Hill, a further retirement was carried out to the southeast of Ramicourt and this was the line that was consolidated. During the afternoon the CO, Lieutenant Colonel Thomas Richard Evans DSO RWF, was killed (Bellicourt British Cemetery – III D 5) and Major Dowding, Second-in-Command of 1/5th South Staffordshire, took command.

During the course of its advance 1/6th North Staffordshire had slipped to the right and created a gap between it and 139th Brigade on the left. C Company,

From the track west of Preselles Farm looking to the northwest. The Beaurevoir–Fonsomme Line ran along the high ground on the right towards the centre of the picture. Follow the line of the track from the left diagonally towards the centre, where there is a slight dip with a bush above. This is the site of the quarry. The 1/5th Sherwood Foresters attacked from left to right. The approximate site of Johnson's VC action is on the high ground just right of centre.

1/5th South Staffordshire was sent to deal with the enemy in this gap and seized the Beaurevoir–Fonsomme Line, together with a number of prisoners and machine guns. Another platoon of 1/5th South Staffordshire was sent north-eastwards to try to maintain contact with 139th Brigade but it also came under heavy fire from Mannequin Hill.

During the retirement, three severely wounded men had to be abandoned, but **Lance Corporal William Coltman**, of 1/6th North Staffordshire thought otherwise. This remarkable man, already the holder of the DCM and Bar and MM and Bar, went forward alone into the shallow valley to the north of Mannequin Hill and found them. He dressed their wounds on his own and, one at a time, he carried the three men back to where his stretcher-bearer team could take them to safety. He was under heavy artillery and machine gun fire throughout. Coltman spent the next two days tending other wounded and evacuating them, until the last men had been attended to.

At 6.00 p.m. the Germans attacked again and forced 137th Brigade further down the slope of Mannequin Hill. However, the British artillery and a counterattack stopped further loss of ground. For the time being, the British held the western slopes and the Germans the eastern but the intensity of fire meant that no one held the summit.

The 139th Brigade's advance was led by 1/5th Sherwood Foresters on the right and 1/8th Sherwood Foresters on the left, with 1/6th Sherwood Foresters in support up to the first objective (Red Line). Then, after a pause of twenty minutes, 1/6th Sherwood Foresters was to advance to the final objective, from where posts were to be pushed forward for observation. The other battalions were to follow to mop up Montbrehain. Six tanks were attached to the Brigade. All units were in position by 5.15 a.m.

There was strong resistance from machine gun posts in the Beaurevoir – Fonsomme Line. The 1/5th Sherwood Foresters, led by B Company on the right and D Company on the left, sustained heavy casualties. C Company came forward to fill a gap that formed when B Company slipped to the right in order to avoid the fire. **Sergeant William Johnson**'s platoon in D Company was held up by one of the machine gun posts. He worked his way towards it under heavy fire, closed in and charged the post, bayoneted several gunners and captured two machine guns.

The advance resumed down the slope towards Ramicourt. A number of machine posts were encountered behind the Beaurevoir – Fonsomme Line and the crews were prepared to fight it out to the end. It was estimated that 150–200 of the enemy were killed in this area and only a few surrendered. Despite a serious wound from a grenade, Johnson led his men forward until they were once more pinned down. Unhesitatingly he rushed another post and bombed it from close range, putting two machine guns out of action and capturing the crews.

The leading battalions lost direction slightly on the way to Ramicourt. The advance of 137th Brigade on the right had resulted in a gap opening between the two

The reverse view from the approximate site of Johnson's VC action looking back towards Preselles Farm, which is hidden by the trees on the left of Chataigniers Wood in the centre distance.

formations, which allowed heavy enfilade fire to be directed upon 139th Brigade. The 1/5th Sherwood Foresters swung right to deal with the enemy south of Ramicourt, while 1/8th Sherwood Foresters swept around the village to the north. There was some fighting in Ramicourt and in the sunken road to the south but it was less intense than before. A company of 1/6th Sherwood Foresters, commanded by Lieutenant Colonel Bernard Vann VC, was pushed forward to mop up the village and later the support companies of the leading battalions assisted. About 400 prisoners were taken there. Vann was killed shortly after crossing the Beaurevoir–Fonsomme Line and Major Sheddon MC took command.

On the left, a company of 1/8th Sherwood Foresters moved through Wiancourt, as the Australians had yet to come up on that flank and took a few prisoners. German resistance stiffened as they fought it out in sunken lanes and along the railway. The tanks were invaluable in smashing concentrations of machine guns and the Red Line was reached on time. The barrage throughout was very effective, although more than the usual number of guns firing short were noted. With no Australians on the left flank, 1/8th Sherwood Foresters formed a defensive flank along the line of a sunken road running east to west from Montbrehain.

When the barrage resumed, 1/6th Sherwood Foresters passed through the leading battalions and continued the advance. Initially the enemy defended the village well and it took a series of small attacks to clear the area around the cemetery. However, it was not possible to occupy it due to intense machine gun fire from the high ground to the north. The western edge of Montbrehain was reached on time but four of the tanks either broke down or were knocked out there.

Within the village there was considerable opposition from machine guns and snipers. Two houses near the church in the centre of the village were blown up. As the support battalions pushed companies into the village to assist in mopping up, the defenders became more inclined to surrender. Montbrehain was mopped up by 11.30 a.m. Over 1,000 prisoners were taken, as well as a battery of field guns. A number of inhabitants were still living in the village and they rushed out to give their liberators coffee. The Blue Line was reached on time, except for the

high ground to the north of the village. Several attempts to take it were met with extremely heavy fire and failed. If a tank had been available, the situation may have been different. Attempts to push posts forwards to the east were forced back by heavy fire from Doon Copse and positions to the east and northeast of the village. Nevertheless, the line was consolidated and the troops reorganised.

The enemy appeared to be in disarray at this time and calls went back to send the cavalry forward in order to exploit the situation. However, the moment passed before any serious action could be taken and 5th Cavalry Brigade occupied the Beaurevoir–Fonsomme Line dismounted instead. At midday 139th Brigade's position remained exposed, with both flanks in the air. The Australians to the north were some way behind and 137th Brigade to the south had run into difficulties, causing a gap of 1,600m to open between the two formations. A battalion of the reserve brigade (138th) was sent to fill the void on the left.

On 139th Brigade's right, 1/5th Sherwood Foresters crossed the Sequehart–Ramicourt road but was held up there by concrete machine gun posts. Three tanks assisted in getting the advance restarted but about 12.30 p.m. enemy scouts were seen moving through Champignons Copse. They were followed by other troops in artillery formation, who formed up about the sunken road south of Montbrehain. The troops in the southeast corner of the village were unable to deal with this threat due to the shape of the ground and trees obscuring their field of fire. A strong counterattack was launched and the British protective barrage was late in responding, due to the telephone line being cut. The weight of defending infantry fire was also much reduced because of earlier casualties. As a result, the Germans advanced as far as the road running south from Nevilles Cross and also infiltrated into the next road to the southwest, where they were behind the right flank of 139th Brigade. However, the counterattack came under heavy machine gun and Lewis gun fire from the troops east of Ramicourt. They changed direction to get into the quarries south of Montbrehain and were lost to view in the southwest corner of the village. Reports were received that the Germans also appeared to be massing to attack north of Montbrehain. With both flanks wide open, the situation was serious and it was decided to pull back and abandon Montbrehain.

A difficult but successful withdrawal was conducted to a line covering Ramicourt, where the Brigade was in contact with 137th Brigade and also with the Australians on the left. However, in the confusion units had become mixed up and a company of 4th Leicestershire (138th Brigade) had also come forward to assist. The Germans retook Montbrehain but were unable to advance further than the western edge. They shelled Ramicourt heavily and the troops there were dispersed to the north and south to avoid it.

At the end of the day, 139th Brigade held a line east of Ramicourt and Wiancourt and had captured about 1,400 prisoners and hundreds of machine guns. It had suffered about 670 casualties. That night 138th Brigade took over and the units of 139th Brigade fell back into reserve south and southeast of Joncourt.

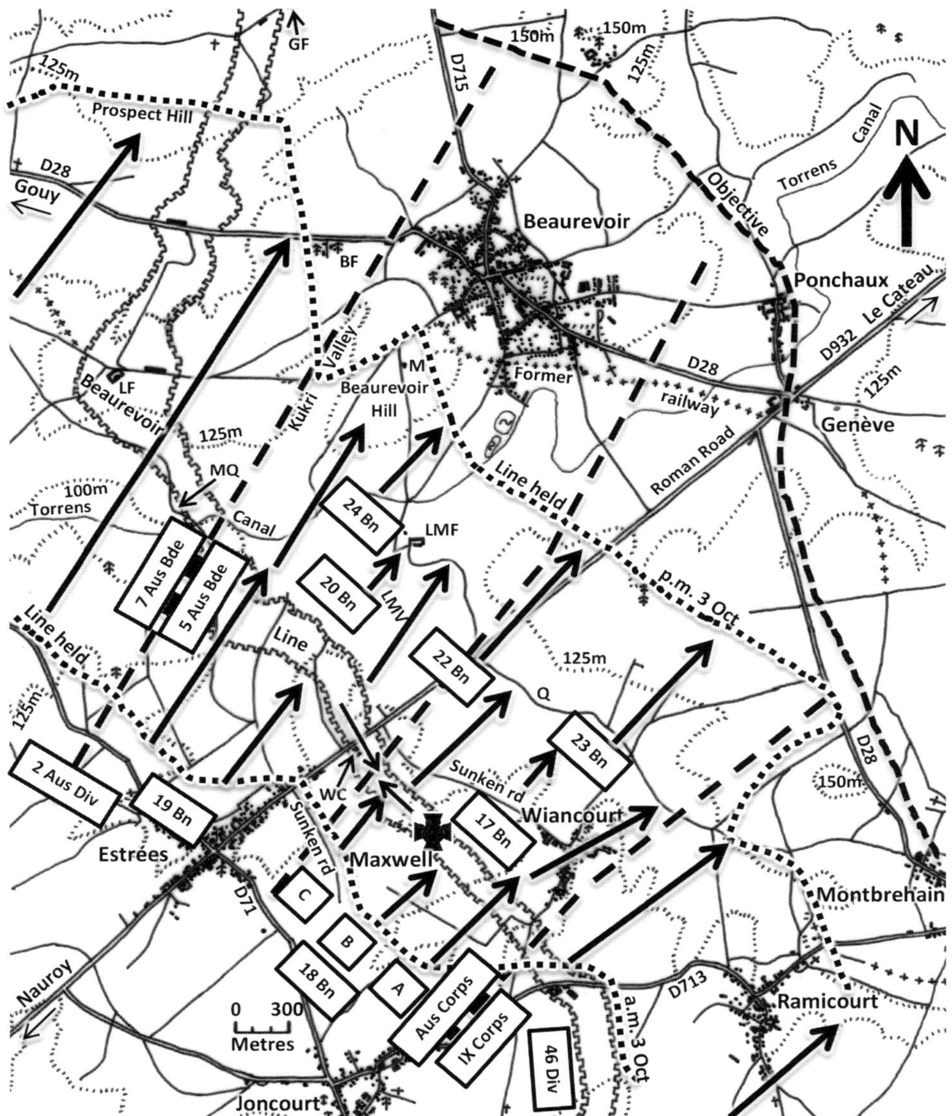

BF = Bellevue Farm, GF = Guisancourt Farm, LF = Lormisset Farm, LMF = La Motte Farm, LMV = La Motte Valley, M = ruined mill, MQ = Mushroom Quarry, Q = quarry, WC = White Cottage. It is difficult to get a decent view of the area where the Maxwell VC action took place. About the best option is from the water tower on the D71 Joncourt–Estrées road, just south of the latter.

To the north, the Australian Corps only had 2nd Australian Division in the line, with 5th Australian Brigade on the right and 7th Australian Brigade on the left. During the night, 25th Battalion (7th Australian Brigade) relieved 20th Battalion in 5th Australian Brigade, allowing the latter to move into position behind 19th Battalion. Within 5th Australian Brigade, 18th Battalion took over the line from 17th Battalion to allow it to withdraw into its assembly position. The 6th Australian Brigade was in reserve behind Nauroy, with its 23rd Battalion in reserve to 5th Australian Brigade south of Joncourt. The first objective was the Beaurevoir Line and the second was Beaurevoir village and the high ground around it. The attack would start on a frontage of 4,600m, widening to 6,000m at the final objective. It was not known if XIII Corps would attack on the left and therefore a defensive flank was planned, adding another 4,100m to the final frontage.

In addition to its own guns and the Corps artillery, the Division was supported by the artillery of 1st, 4th and 5th Australian Divisions. The heavy guns of XIII Corps were to protect the Australian left flank by firing on the high ground (Prospect Hill) east and northeast of Gouy. Each brigade was to lead with two battalions to the Beaurevoir Line, where the two support battalions would pass through to the final objective. Each brigade had eight Mark V tanks attached and 5th Australian Brigade also had eight Whippets to assist in capturing Beaurevoir. However, because the ground was badly cut up by trenches and shell holes and the roads were congested, the tanks were late arriving and were not available immediately to crush the wire in front of the Beaurevoir Line. In places this consisted of six belts, each up to nine metres wide.

The 5th Australian Brigade was led by 18th and 19th Battalions, on the right and left respectively, each supported by four tanks. They were to capture the Beaurevoir Line, which involved an advance of 600–900m. Without pausing there, 17th and 20th Battalions, on the right and left, were to pass through to the final objective east of Beaurevoir, Ponchaux and Genève. Each battalion was allocated four Whippets, which were to remain in their assembly area near Nauroy until the Beaurevoir Line had been captured. A section of the Brigade Machine Gun Company was to accompany 20th Battalion, while the remainder of the Company was to move forward after the final objective had been taken. The 22nd Australian Machine Gun Company was to move onto the high ground south of Beaurevoir. Having cleared the Beaurevoir Line, 18th and 19th Battalions were to follow in support of 17th and 20th Battalions. A barrage by five field artillery brigades would precede the assault troops until the top of the slope behind the Beaurevoir Line. Thereafter the guns would fire on selected targets. A squadron of 13th Australian Light Horse was attached to the Brigade for prisoner escort, and to form a Brigade reserve. Three gallopers were also attached to each battalion HQ as mounted despatch riders. Shortly before midnight on 2nd October the Germans commenced firing gas shells into the Brigade's area. This coincided with the attacking troops being briefed, having a hot meal and moving into position. Many men were affected by the gas well into the next day.

All units were in position by 5.30 a.m. At 6.05 a.m. the barrage opened, and 18th and 19th Battalions advanced on time either side of Estrées. The 18th Battalion, which had been reorganised into three companies each of three platoons, crossed the start line with thirteen officers and 249 others ranks. All three companies were in line with A Company on the right, B in the centre and C on the left. The barrage was reported to be consistently effective, although a few guns on the left appeared to be falling short and caused some casualties. However, this may have been due to the men closing up too quickly as the barrage paused on its start line for six minutes before moving ahead, longer than was the usual practice. The enemy counter-barrage was not effective but heavy machine gun fire was encountered from the outset. The tanks experienced great difficulty in getting forward in time due to the condition of the road and the congestion upon it. As a result, they were late and only three of the eight allocated crossed the Beaurevoir Line. The remainder were either knocked out or ditched. Two of the three accompanied 17th Battalion and the third was with 20th Battalion.

The wire in front of the Beaurevoir Line was very thick and the troops were halted by a machine gun post beyond it. However, by 7.15 a.m. the right company of 18th Battalion and the left and left centre companies of 19th Battalion, had got through the wire, where a tank caught up and the Beaurevoir Line support trench was taken. The right of 18th Battalion was also in contact with 46th Division at this time.

In the centre of the Brigade, the inner companies of both battalions were checked. They were also fired upon from the rear from the last few houses in Estrées, which was eventually suppressed by a tank. As the tanks and infantry moved on, they came under fire from a field gun in the White Cottage on the main Estrées–Le Cateau (Roman) road, between the two trench lines. They were also engaged by several anti-tank rifles and about twenty machine guns, most of which were in concrete pillboxes along the trench line. The left of 18th Battalion and the two right companies of 19th Battalion were pinned down in front of the wire 300m either side of the Roman road, as was 17th Battalion moving up behind the forward battalions. It was discovered that the Beaurevoir Line was only complete astride the Roman road. Elsewhere, although there were pillboxes with short lengths of trench either side of them, the trenches had only been dug down about forty centimetres and were less than one and half metres wide. Parties of both battalions facing the completed sections tried to bomb the enemy out.

On the left of 18th Battalion, Lieutenant Robert Edward Dryden DCM (MC for this action) and twelve men of C Company succeeded in climbing over the wire just behind the barrage. They managed to penetrate to a point between the two trench lines just south of the Roman road. They were held up there through lack of Lewis guns and rifle grenades. Most of the other troops on the left were unable to get further than the sunken road east of Estrées. Meanwhile B Company had managed to work through the wire, suffering considerable casualties in doing so. Dryden observed a large German force north of the Roman road in both trenches. He was joined by Second Lieutenant George Frederick Foote MC (Bar for this action) and a few men with a Lewis gun. Dryden went back to bring up more troops and Lewis guns. While he was away, Foote and five men captured seventy prisoners by bluff. They were then attacked by a force of about one hundred Germans and were driven back into the trench system but held there. With a larger force, Dryden was able to establish a position in the second line trench just south of the road.

South of Dryden, **Lieutenant Joseph Maxwell MC DCM** in B Company reported at 6.45 a.m. that they were held up south of the Roman road by a strongpoint in the Beaurevoir Line. Maxwell managed to get through the wire and killed three and captured four of the crew of one machine gun, which allowed his company to move through. Maxwell took over command of the Company when Lieutenant Alexander William Irvine MC was wounded. The Company then made some progress before being stopped. Dryden could see no progress north of the road so decided to form a flank facing northwest towards the road. Maxwell realised that there was no threat from the northeast and went to the assistance of C Company. The fighting fluctuated constantly. Maxwell charged and silenced another machine gun that was holding up C Company. Because the force was small and the defences were scattered, it was impossible to mop up an area and then deal with another whilst also ensuring that the first area remained clear.

After a few ineffectual attempts to get forward by small parties, the four companies held up in front of the wire pulled back at 8.45 a.m. to the sunken road just east of Estrées. A coordinated attempt was then made to clear the trench by 19th Battalion working along it southwards from the north, while 18th Battalion worked northwards from the south. A tank that had been sent to support this move was put out of action. The attempts to bomb along the trench from north and south

The view looking northeast over the D71 road from the water tower. On the left is Estrées, with the houses on the right of the village marking the D932 Le Catelet road. The sunken road northeast of Estrées is marked by a line of low bushes in the low ground in the middle distance, just left of centre. Beyond it the Beaurevoir Line ran across the top of the next ridge of high ground from right to left. This is where Maxwell cleared the trenches to meet up with the troops fighting down the trenches from the north.

made no progress. At 9.40 a.m. the companies lying in front of the wire were pulled back, while arrangements were made for the trench system to be shelled intensely for five minutes at 10.30 a.m. Then the two withdrawn companies of 19th Battalion bombed down the Beaurevoir Line from the north. There was little resistance and the trench fell at about 11.30 a.m., when contact was made with 18th Battalion. About 200 prisoners, three trench mortars, three anti-tank rifles and eighteen machine guns were taken.

Maxwell had been involved in the earlier attempt to advance northwards along the Beaurevoir Line. In this action a captured German sergeant major told him that the soldiers in the next bay were keen to surrender but were afraid to give themselves up. Maxwell took two men and went over to the German post, where they were surrounded by about twenty of the enemy. Their weapons were seized but, when the first shells of the bombardment fell in the trench, Maxwell took advantage of the confusion. He drew a pistol that he kept hidden in his respirator, shot two of the enemy and the three men escaped.

In the meantime, parts of 17th and 20th Battalions had passed through on the flanks and into La Motte Valley between Wiancourt and La Motte Farm. However, much time had been lost in capturing the trench and the whole right flank was delayed, resulting in a gap in the centre of the advance. The right of 17th Battalion passed through Wiancourt, not knowing that it had already been cleared by elements of 46th Division to the south. Pushing on with a tank, the right company reached the slope below the objective but was hit there by a battery further along the objective ridge. With both flanks in the air, the company dug in with A Company, 18th Battalion coming up in support. Both units had contact with 46th Division to the south by 11.00 a.m. Strong German resistance was encountered from La Motte Farm and a ruined mill on Beaurevoir Hill, southwest of Beaurevoir. The left of 17th Battalion, south of the Roman road, was held up by fire from the Farm. The mill held a field gun firing point blank, as well as a number of machine guns, and

there were two other field guns behind it. The 20th Battalion was prevented from reaching the crest of the ridge. A mixed party from several companies held on in a sunken road and silenced the fire from the mill using two captured machine guns. Although not far apart the two Australian brigades were not at this stage in contact with each other.

Having assisted C Company to secure the Beaurevoir Line south of the Roman road, B Company, 18th Battalion, moved to the sunken road northwest of Wiancourt, where it supported 17th Battalion, in accordance with the original plan. B Company had by then been reduced to Maxwell and just twenty men. They were pinned down in the road by machine guns to the northeast. C Company's attempts to move forward and connect with troops on its flanks were met by heavy machine gun fire. However, on the left a few men of 19th Battalion were found in the trench system north of the road. Around noon Dryden decided to try rushing forward to join 20th Battalion, reported to be around La Motte Farm. This move was also met by heavy fire, but a line of posts was established just north of the Roman road.

On the left, 20th Battalion got through the Beaurevoir Line with few casualties. Soon afterwards machine gun fire, from the uncaptured portion of the Line astride the Roman road and from the railway in front of Beaurevoir, deflected the Battalion's advance along Kukri Valley on the northern boundary, southwest of Beaurevoir. Despite the heavy fire, the Battalion managed to reach the crossroads at the northern end of Beaurevoir Hill. However, it came under fire from a 77mm Gun near the railway southwest of Beaurevoir and was forced to pull back down the slope. The Battalion's Lewis gunners managed to put a battery of 77mm guns out of action that was holding up 7th Australian Brigade on the left.

Because the situation in the centre of the Brigade was still obscure, at 9.00 a.m. 20th Battalion was told to consolidate on the line of the Torrens Canal. There it managed to link up with the left and part of the centre left companies of 19th Battalion, which had moved forward from the Beaurevoir Line once it had been mopped up. A party of 20th Battalion worked along Torrens Canal to close up to La Motte Farm. In addition to the defences at the Farm, machine guns were firing from the hill behind, and reinforcements were seen arriving along the Roman road. A tank attempted to close with the Farm, firing as it moved, but a shell broke a track, killed the driver and set the tank on fire when it was about one hundred metres from the Farm.

Both flanks of 5th Australian Brigade had pushed on, leaving a gap in the centre, which was still held up astride the Roman road. A company of 23rd Battalion in reserve was ordered forward in case it was needed to fill the gap. At 11.45 a.m. the rest of 23rd Battalion was ordered to move to the sunken road east of Estrées in preparation to continue the line held by 20th Battalion north of La Motte Farm.

About this time GOC 2nd Australian Division realised that the Germans were hanging on to Prospect Hill on the left flank and Montbrehain on the right, although the latter had been seized temporarily by 46th Division. He therefore decided to be satisfied with securing a foothold on the heights in front of Beaurevoir. With 7th Australian Brigade already on this line, 5th Australian Brigade was ordered at 12.10 p.m. to secure the line in its area using, from right to left, the 23rd, 22nd and 24th Battalions of 6th Australian Brigade, which were to pass through 17th, 18th, 19th and 20th Battalions. A creeping barrage would commence at 4.15 p.m., but it was not until 3.00 p.m. that 22nd and 24th Battalions received orders to move from Nauroy to the start line in the Beaurevoir Line. The 23rd Battalion was already in the Beaurevoir Line near Wiancourt.

In the meantime, 20th Battalion discovered that most of the Germans at La Motte Farm had pulled out and those remaining were overcome. The mill was bombarded, as was the hill behind La Motte Farm. Germans, massing in Beaurevoir and the Torrens valley to the southeast, were also shelled. The 20th Battalion positioned three posts beyond La Motte Farm and astride the Torrens. Once the Farm had been cleared this allowed the four companies of 18th and 19th Battalions in the Brigade centre astride the Roman road, to establish a line of posts between 17th and 20th Battalions at about 2.00 p.m. By 4.00 p.m. the four battalions were holding a line roughly along the Wiancourt–La Motte Farm road.

It was clear that 22nd and 24th Battalions could not be in position for the attack by 4.15 p.m. and it was rescheduled for 6.30 p.m. The attack started well and the flank battalions met little opposition as the enemy surrendered freely. The main resistance was in the centre against 22nd Battalion around the Roman road. There was stiff fighting on the way to the quarry south of the road. A battery of four 77mm Guns was captured and a 5.9″ Howitzer was found intact on the road. By 7.50 p.m. all three battalions had achieved their objectives and were in contact with each other, although not with the brigades on either flank until later. Casualties had been light, with nine killed and nineteen wounded. One hundred and forty prisoners were taken, together with six artillery pieces, a minenwerfer, thirty-eight machine guns and four messenger pigeons. At 10.30 p.m. command of the sector passed to HQ 6th Australian Brigade and the 5th Australian Brigade's battalions withdrew.

The 5th Australian Brigade suffered 601 casualties in the period 1st-3rd October, including 122 in 18th Battalion, although the latter's war diary records only 112 (eleven killed, ninety-one wounded and ten missing). The Brigade captured 634 prisoners, together with a 5.9″ Howitzer, two 4.2″ Guns, eight 77mm Guns, seven minenwerfers, six anti-tank rifles and about seventy machine guns. It was estimated that about 450 enemy had been killed. The 18th Battalion claimed to have captured 330 prisoners, including the CO of 2nd Battalion, 80th Infantry Regiment.

7th Australian Brigade had a slightly narrower frontage than 5th Australian Brigade. Initially 25th Battalion faced an advance of 1,100m to seize the Beaurevoir Line, where 26th Battalion was to pass through to the final objective between Beaurevoir and Guisancourt Farm, including the section of the Beaurevoir Line on the left flank. The 28th Battalion was to take over most of that flank, while 27th Battalion wheeled left and formed part of the flank. Five field artillery brigades fired the supporting barrage. Unlike in 5th Australian Brigade's sector, the Line here was complete and in places there was a third trench. All were thickly wired, particularly around Mushroom Quarry, and there were numerous pillboxes. There were at least fifty machine gun posts in the Brigade area. The Brigade had to cross a significant drainage channel, the Torrens Canal, to reach the Beaurevoir Line on the left. Fortunately the channel was almost dry and passable to infantry.

The Lewis gunners managed to suppress much of the enemy fire and two tanks arrived to crush paths through the wire. German regimental and battalion commanders were captured in Mushroom Quarry. The enemy outposts were overcome, by when three tanks had caught up and the Line was captured at 8.00 a.m. The 26th and 28th Battalions passed through to capture Bellevue Farm, west of Beaurevoir, and the Gouy–Bellevue Farm road, with almost no opposition. However, the advance was checked at 9.30 a.m. The left of 26th Battalion crossed the wire of the Beaurevoir Line while the barrage was still in support. Three pillboxes at Lormisset Farm were rushed. Progress was made from pillbox to pillbox and there were many captures, while other Germans fled to the rear. The 28th Battalion came up, after subduing several posts, and took up its assigned position on the left flank. The 27th Battalion also swung into position. A platoon from 50th Division to the north was encountered. Field guns firing over open sights from north of Beaurevoir forced 26th Battalion back to Bellevue Farm. However, the right flank there was raked by fire from the high ground to the north and the mill southwest of Beaurevoir. As a result, the Farm had to be abandoned later. A machine gun position at the Farm was engaged by a tank until both of its guns jammed and it had to retreat under anti-tank gun fire. On the far left, the eastern slopes of Prospect Hill could not be taken, although 50th Division (XIII Corps) to the north had outposts on it.

Enemy troops were seen massing for a counterattack. In order to meet this threat, a withdrawal was made to the Torrens valley and 7th Australian Brigade was reinforced by a battalion of 6th Australian Brigade. Together with the three reserve battalions of 5th Australian Brigade on the right, the advance was resumed at 6.30 p.m., following a short barrage. The crest of the high ground beyond the Wiancourt–La Motte Farm valley was reached but an assault on Beaurevoir had to be postponed. The 7th Australian Brigade suffered 388 casualties in the period 1st–3rd October. In the same period 2nd Australian Division suffered about one thousand casualties but captured 1,192 prisoners, 163 machine guns and eleven field guns.

The XIII Corps had only 50th Division in the line, supported by thirteen brigades of field artillery. Prospect Hill was captured about 8.00 a.m. and Gouy and Le Catelet by 9.00 a.m. A strong counterattack from the north, about Aubencheul aux Bois, was launched at 2.00 p.m. by at least five battalions. This resulted in Le Catelet being lost but the rest of the line held and secured the left flank of Fourth Army.

Although not all objectives had been reached, the overall result of the day was a considerable tactical success for Fourth Army. However, it did not force the Germans to pull back in front of Third Army to the north as had been hoped. Despite this, indications were that the Germans were preparing bridges for demolition in their rear in preparation to pull back. The emphasis turned to taking Beaurevoir, in order to speed up the German withdrawal. That night the French 47th Division relieved 1st Division and Chardon Vert, just south of Sequehart, became the new boundary between the British and the French.

459 Lt George Ingram, 24th Battalion AIF (6th Australian Brigade, 2nd Australian Division), Montbrehain, France

4th–5th October 1918

Fourth Army's orders for 4th October assumed that the French XV Corps would be attacking to the south, with the support of IX Corps' artillery. The boundary between the French and British was shifted northwards to just south of Sequehart at Chardon Vert. The IX Corps was to seize Mannequin Hill and the ground to the north. The Australian Corps was to assist IX Corps and was also to seize the high ground northwest of Montbrehain. To the north a new boundary with XIII Corps on the Torrens Canal was effective from 6.00 a.m. The XIII Corps was to attack Beaurevoir and capture Prospect Hill, Guisancourt Farm and the high ground La Pannerie–Harguival Farm. A reorganisation of the artillery also took effect from 6.00 a.m. and resulted in some batteries transferring from the Australian to XIII Corps.

Despite the expectation, the French First Army did nothing to help that day. The IX Corps' frontage had been reduced by about 1,500m by the change of boundary. Despite being reinforced by 3rd Brigade (1st Division), the Corps Cyclist Battalion and 2nd Life Guards Machine Gun Battalion, no progress was made against enemy counterattacks from Mannequin Hill. During the night, 137th Brigade was relieved by 3rd Brigade.

In the Australian Corps sector, 20th Manchester (7th Brigade, 25th Division) relieved 24th Battalion at 4.25 a.m. The attack along the reduced Australian Corps frontage was launched in fog at 6.00 a.m. by 6th Australian Brigade (2nd Australian Division), which had to swing forward its left in contact with 25th Division (XIII Corps) at Genève. The barrage was stationary for twenty-five minutes after zero hour to allow 20th Manchester on the left to draw level, before the advance commenced.

On the right, 23rd Battalion discovered overnight that an apparently elaborate trench system ahead of its right company was only dug down about thirty centimetres. The position was occupied quickly when the attack commenced and the company dug in there, with a view of the ridge north of Montbrehain. The left company was held up on the Montbrehain–Genève road and every attempt to get forward was stopped by fire from the ridge ahead. Germans were seen pulling back but, due to poor communications with the artillery, many targets escaped before they could be engaged.

On the left, 22nd Battalion advanced 900m before encountering resistance. A machine gun was cleared from a hedge as Genève was approached. Thereafter resistance intensified from Genève and from Ponchaux, beyond the Torrens. The barrage, which was not very strong, moved ahead and left the assault troops on a grassy slope with no cover. Despite the difficulties, the CO ordered the advance to continue, which was done at heavy cost in casualties. Genève factory and crossroads could not be taken. At the end of the day, 6th Australian Brigade had pushed forward a small salient between it and Montbrehain to the south. It was in contact with 25th Division, 500m west of Genève. The Brigade suffered 116 casualties (twenty-three killed, ninety-one wounded and two missing). Captures included twenty-one prisoners and twenty-four machine guns.

On the night of 3rd/4th October in XIII Corps' extended area, 7th Brigade (25th Division) took over the front on the right from the Australians. However, the decision to carry out this relief had been made late the previous day, leaving little time to effect it. After a long march in full kit, 7th Brigade relieved 7th Australian Brigade at 2.00 a.m.

The German positions at Beaurevoir were strong and the village commanded the surrounding country. There were also numerous farms and other buildings, in addition to the railway embankment, for small enemy parties to conceal themselves. The barrage was fired by six field artillery brigades (25th Division's own, two Army brigades and two Australian). Beaurevoir was to be shelled until half an hour after the attack reached the railway. The village was then to be mopped up from north and south. The attack got into Ponchaux and Beaurevoir and a counterattack was pushed back about midday. However, heavy casualties in 20th Manchester, on the right of the Brigade, led to a withdrawal at 1.10 p.m. The line occupied thereafter was held for the rest of the day and was in contact with the Australians. On the left of the Brigade, 9th Devonshire did not receive its orders until 5.15 a.m. The barrage was lost and the Battalion came under heavy fire. Despite this, Bellevue Farm was taken, although it had to be abandoned. It was not possible to reach Guisancourt Farm. As a result, the line held that night was only a little advanced from the morning. Preparations were made to attack again on the 5th with a larger force.

On the left of XIII Corps, 150th Brigade (50th Division), with two battalions of 149th Brigade, attacked at 6.00 a.m. The barrage was fired by eleven field artillery brigades. The enemy reacted strongly but 2nd Royal Munster Fusiliers fought its way into Le Catelet. By 9.45 a.m. the Battalion had reached La Pannerie. On the left, 3rd Royal Fusiliers had gained some high ground on the west of Le Catelet the previous night. It reached the high ground north of the town but, having lost heavily, and with 2nd Royal Dublin Fusiliers unable to make further progress, it was forced to retire almost back to its start line and La Pannerie was abandoned.

The 2nd Northumberland Fusiliers then swung around the north of Le Catelet and captured a strongpoint that had been holding up the advance earlier. Two hundred and fifty prisoners were taken. At the same time 7th Wiltshire, holding the top of Prospect Hill, captured a trench on its northern slope. Another attack was organised after a two hours' bombardment. On the right, 2nd Royal Munster Fusiliers, with part of 1st King's Own Yorkshire Light Infantry (151st Brigade), advanced on La Pannerie, while 4th King's Royal Rifle Corps (also 151st Brigade) advanced on Hargival Farm, with the remnants of 3rd Royal Fusiliers. The objectives were seized, and these posts were taken over by 38th Division (Third Army). All 150th Brigade units were then withdrawn, except for 7th Wiltshire on Prospect Hill.

Although some progress had been made by the Australian and XIII Corps, Montbrehain and Beaurevoir remained in enemy hands and IX Corps had failed completely. General Rawlinson issued his orders for 5th October. The advance was to continue in order to give the enemy no time for rest and reorganisation. The objectives remained essentially the same as for 4th October. The IX Corps was to seize the high ground southeast and south of Montbrehain on Mannequin and Doon Hills. Because of a boundary change between corps, Montbrehain became the objective of the Australian Corps. The XIII Corps was to capture Beaurevoir, while 38th Division (Third Army) on the left passed through to occupy the high ground near Guisancourt Farm and la Sablonnière. Meanwhile the artillery was to move forward in preparation for another major effort that was envisaged to commence on 6th October.

The 46th Division took over command of IX Corps' reduced line at 6.00 a.m. The line was held by 14th, 97th and 3rd Brigades, plus IX Corps Cyclist Battalion. The Division's task was to engage the enemy on Mannequin and Doon Hills to assist the Australians by covering their right flank as they moved on Montbrehain. The artillery was to barrage the ground, while patrols of 3rd Brigade were to occupy the two hills. Resistance encountered in this area was strong, with ten enemy regiments from four divisions identified from prisoners. The 1st Gloucestershire attacked Mannequin Hill and took twenty-six prisoners and six machine guns. However, it was unable to hold the crest under a deluge of fire. On the left, the Cyclist Battalion maintained contact with the Australians at Nevilles Cross. A counterattack drove back all the gains, except on the extreme left of the IX Corps area.

In the Australian Corps, 2nd Australian Division was due to be withdrawn for rest but that could not take place until the night of 5th/6th October. The 6th Australian Brigade had all four battalions in line, although only 21st and 24th Battalions on the right, which had thus far been little used, were to attack. On the left, 23rd and 22nd Battalions were to stand fast. The first move was 2nd Australian Pioneer Battalion taking over the front from 138th Brigade (46th Division) at dusk, in accordance with the boundary change. The plan was for 21st and 24th Battalions, on the right and left respectively, to form up behind the Pioneers by 5.05 a.m. At 5.50 a.m. the Pioneers would withdraw behind the assault battalions and the barrage

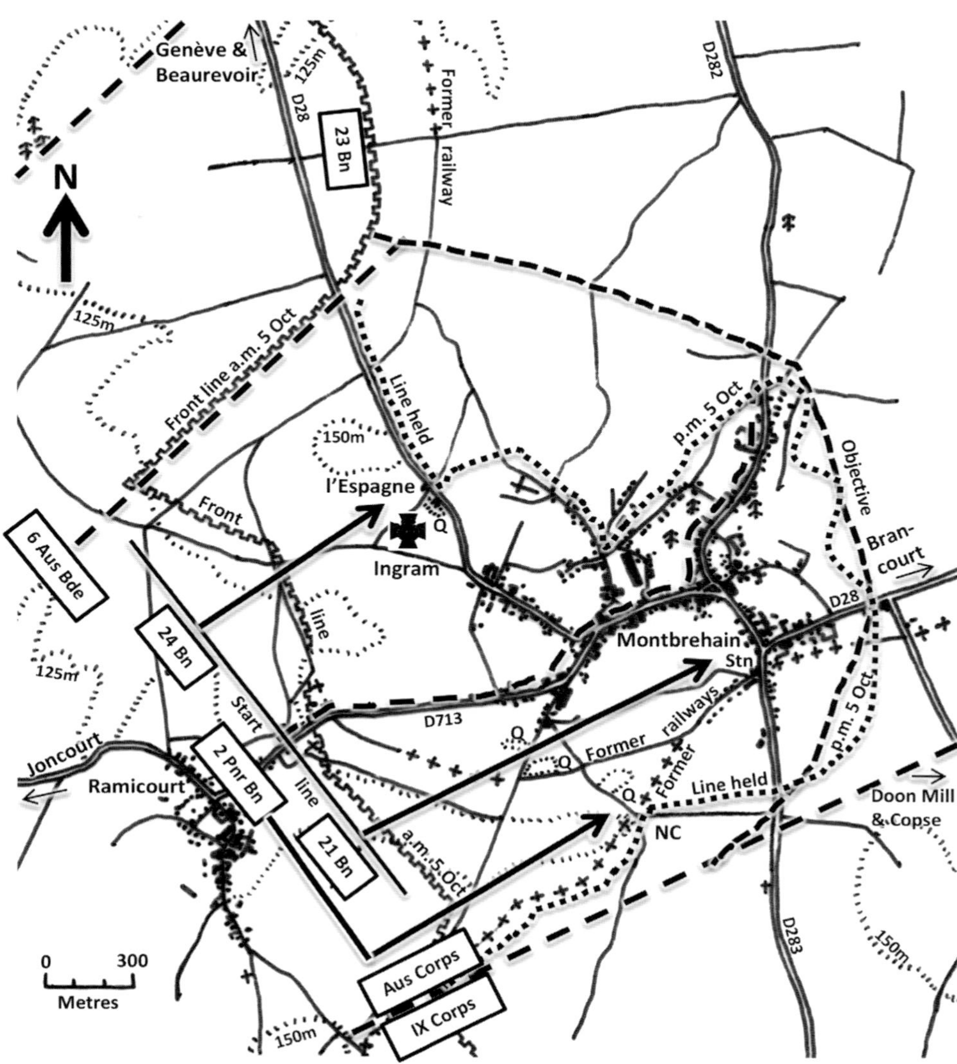

The various accounts, official histories and historical maps do not agree precisely where the various lines held ran, or which sections were held by which units. This map is the best estimate of reality. NC = Nevilles Cross, Q = quarry, Stn = railway station. Ingram's VC action took place at a tiny collection of buildings on the D28 Montbrehain–Beaurevoir road, now known as l'Espagne. There is very limited parking on the grass verges alongside the houses on the southwest side of the road. For a long-distance view, leave Montbrehain on the D713 road westwards towards Ramicourt. There is a concrete sileage store on the right with just enough room to park. Look north just left of the power lines to the quarry and houses on the D28, with a wind turbine beyond.

would come down at 6.05 a.m. It would start to creep forward at 6.09 a.m. and 21st and 24th Battalions would follow it through Montbrehain to the objective on the eastern and northern sides of the village. The 2nd Australian Pioneer Battalion was to follow and hold a flanking position beyond the southern outskirts of the village. The 18th Battalion (5th Australian Brigade) and 27th Battalion (7th Australian Brigade) were in reserve in case of a major enemy counterattack.

The start line was about 800m from the first German trenches. Each assault battalion had four Mark V tanks from 16th Tank Battalion attached, with another four to be allocated to 2nd Pioneer Battalion if available, or to be held in reserve. A barrage, fired by six of the eight available field artillery brigades, was to precede the advance. Two Vickers machine guns were allocated to each of the three battalions from 6th Australian Machine Gun Company, as were two mortars from 6th Australian Light Trench Mortar Battery. To facilitate coordination a combined HQ of 21st, 24th and 2nd Pioneer Battalions was established in a sunken road (D713) just east of Joncourt. The various moves took place as planned and the assault battalions assembled either side of the Ramicourt–Montbrehain road. Each battalion was organised into three companies.

The tanks were late due to a difficult approach march conducted under heavy shell fire. The advance started without them, but they soon caught up. The barrage was weak on the right, where some batteries were late opening fire. When they did join in, they fell short and caused casualties in 21st Battalion. With unregistered artillery such accidents were almost inevitable. The Battalion reached the old front line by the railway before the German barrage fell. The advance continued in the half light, dust and smoke until machine guns opened fire close on the right flank. They were engaged by the Lewis guns, while sections advanced in short rushes. The fire was coming mainly from two quarries. As the Australians closed in, both positions surrendered with eight machine guns. Fire was then received from a sunken road, which caused some casualties. The German barrage shortened as the advance continued and took no account of where their own troops were located. It continued until the Australians were in the village and then fell back onto the old front line, where it remained until 5.00 p.m.

On the left a machine gun opened fire from the first house in the village. The window through which it was fired was shot up by two Lewis guns. A small party then began working up the main street and drove out groups of Germans in the cellars. It turned south to the railway station, where the men were greeted by twenty French women and children, from whom they found it difficult to disengage. A tank arrived and accompanied the infantry to the south of the village. A position was established along a spur to the southeast but any movement in this area brought point blank fire from enemy guns on Doon Hill, in Doon Copse and Brancourt. The Battalion tried getting around Doon Mill and some men reached the sunken road in the gully leading to it. German infantry, led by an officer on a white horse, repeatedly reached the crest beside the Mill, but each attempt was forced back by fire from the Australian posts. Another party of 21st Battalion pressed on through the village eastwards, in conjunction with 24th Battalion, and established three posts there. A line was established by 21st Battalion around the eastern edge of the village.

The 2nd Pioneer Battalion swung to the south of 21st Battalion. Several posts were cleared and the right company established a line on the flank as planned, bringing five captured enemy machine guns into action. As the centre company advanced towards the railway south of the village, it came under heavy fire from a sunken road, the quarries and the railway. The men took cover in some crops, while Lieutenant Norman Francis Wilkinson, in command of the attached machine guns, with 102 Sergeant John Peter Adam MM, crept up to the embankment and made their way along it to the left. Ahead were about one hundred German machine gunners manning a line of guns on the embankment. Wilkinson and Adam were not seen and sent back for the gun teams. As they approached, two other German machine guns opened fire from a rise ahead of them and appeared to be the flank guard for the guns on the embankment. They were captured by Wilkinson's men, who set up their own guns unseen by the enemy. They then opened fire with two full belts each. Wilkinson and his men rushed the German position to find fourteen machine guns out of action, about thirty enemy dead and fifty wounded. The remainder had fled, including two guns guarding the other flank. The objective was then reached without further incident. A party of pioneers advanced a little further and took some prisoners but, due to the failure of IX Corps to the south, it was attacked by Germans coming out of a depression on the right. The party was extracted from this difficult situation and Wilkinson withdrew to Nevilles Cross.

The left company of the Pioneers came under very heavy machine gun fire from three posts west of Nevilles Cross. These were silenced with the assistance of two tanks and the company established itself on the left of the Pioneer Battalion's line. However, the whole of this flank remained under heavy machine gun fire from Doon Hill. Gaps in the line were filled with Lewis gun teams. The fourth company, following 24th Battalion, was to mop up in the village and then swing south behind 21st Battalion to take up a supporting position behind the rest of 2nd Pioneer Battalion. However, it came up against the same fire encountered by the left and centre of 24th Battalion. A strongpoint with eight machine guns was captured with the assistance of a tank, before the company continued into the village and captured a 4.2″ Howitzer. In accordance with its orders, the company was returning when it came under heavy artillery fire and suffered a number of casualties. Instead of turning south, the company commander took up a position behind the hard pressed 24th Battalion.

The left company of 21st Battalion and A Company on the right of 24th Battalion encountered strong resistance from enemy posts in hedges, houses and trenches along the western edge of the village. The German barrage appeared to be controlled from the right flank and moved closely with the Australian advance until it reached the village, causing many casualties. A tank firing cannister shot arrived in A Company's area and four enemy posts were captured. A Company entered the village to mop up various enemy posts and, although having suffered heavy casualties, pushed through and established posts on the far side, in contact with 21st Battalion on the right. It had a strength of just twelve men. When the enemy began to work forward again, A Company and the 21st Battalion posts next to it had to fall back. The lost ground was later made up and a series of posts were established in contact with 21st Battalion.

B Company in the centre met even stiffer resistance. It first encountered a German post that was so advanced that it was missed by the barrage. It then came under fire from four strongpoints, which were rushed and a number of prisoners taken. Immediately afterwards the Company came up against a trench system east of the railway and southwest of the quarry. One strongpoint south of the quarry, with forty-two defenders and numerous machine guns, resisted fiercely until the assault troops were within three metres. The position was overcome and there were no survivors. Two minenwerfer and a machine gun were captured in another strongpoint nearby.

B Company continued to receive heavy fire but pushed on and overcame a series of groups of riflemen in shell holes. Eventually the men were forced into the cover of a small trench and any attempt to move out was met by heavy and accurate fire. The situation looked hopeless until Sergeant DW Witherden DCM MM dashed to a point about twenty metres from the enemy with a Lewis gun and opened fire. **Lieutenant George Ingram MM** led a charge from one flank, while the company commander, Captain George David Pollington MM (MC for this action), led from the other flank. Forty Germans were killed or captured and six (possibly nine) machine guns were taken. The Company reorganised behind a bank but was pinned down by machine guns. Ingram rushed several posts but Pollington was wounded and intense fire met all attempts to leave the bank. The fire was thought to be coming from a house near the crossroads 275m northwest of the village at l'Espagne. A Stokes mortar crew fired all five of its rounds and hit the house but the fire did not stop. Witherden used a German machine gun to good effect in reducing the enemy fire. A tank was called over by waving helmets on rifles. As it passed on the way to the house, Ingram jumped up and called on the Company to follow him. It was only then that the fire was seen to be coming from the edge of the quarry. The tank circled it while Ingram jumped in and shot several Germans. The total strength of the garrison there was well over one hundred. From one dugout alone there were sixty-three prisoners and forty machine guns were found in the quarry. The Company mopped up while Ingram went to investigate some houses to the north of the quarry. A machine gun fired from one and he shot the gunner through the cellar ventilator, then held up the rest of the garrison of thirty in the cellar. Seeing some Germans escaping from a window, he burst into the back of the house and took the entire garrison prisoner, along with four machine guns. Another strongpoint at the southwestern corner of the cemetery was overcome as were three

L'Espagne from the southwest, looking in the direction of 24th Battalion's attack. The quarry is the grassy depression on the right. The houses are on the D28, which runs across the picture but cannot be seen due to the shape of the ground and the buildings and vegetation.

posts to the north of it. A heavy enemy barrage running southwest to northeast through the northwestern edge of the village effectively separated the right and centre companies. B Company also came under heavy flanking fire from the north. A line of posts was established and efforts were made to regain contact with A and D Companies on the flanks.

Reverse of the previous view, looking southwest over the D28.

On the left, D Company was held up on the western edge of the hill under terrific fire from the north, northeast and east. The artillery support in this area was ragged and had no effect on the defenders. A tank came up and dealt with one strongpoint before it was knocked out by a field gun. All the officers were casualties and the CSM held the Company where it was. When B Company made contact, Lieutenant Newton Rae Calvert came across and took command of D Company. Touch was later gained with 23rd Battalion on the left. Ingram went back with the tank that had supported the centre company. Despite the success at the quarry, the northwest corner of the village was not yet secure, including the cemetery and a small trench system just north of it. Numerous enemy posts were cleared with the assistance of the tank. The centre of the village was mopped up and many civilians came out to greet their liberators.

At 8.55 a.m. two machine gun teams were sent to 21st Battalion to replace the two attached that had been knocked out by German artillery. Six guns were also sent to 24th Battalion in case of a major counterattack on the northern flank. From about 9.00 a.m. the Germans began to infiltrate back from the low ground ahead, from Brancourt and also on the left. The Germans got back into the cemetery. With ammunition running low, it was decided to pull back the advanced posts to a sunken road on the northeastern edge of the village.

The company of 21st Battalion southeast of the village was also attacked and two platoons of the reserve company on the railway west of the village were sent up. Rather than withdraw, this company hung on. At 11.00 a.m. the Australian artillery helped by driving the Germans away from their field gun at Doon Mill. Meanwhile at 10.15 a.m. the CO had ordered the two remaining platoons of the reserve company to advance, collecting any men that they found on the way. They set off around the west and north of the village, where they had to dash across the open under heavy fire. They managed to eject the enemy from the orchards in this area and by noon were holding the northeastern edge of Montbrehain in contact with 24th Battalion. The Germans withdrew again under fire. Two companies of

27th Battalion in reserve assisted 24th Battalion in consolidating some posts and in carrying up ammunition. However, they were not required further and were sent back. Two companies of 18th Battalion, each about fifty strong, arrived on the eastern edge of the village bringing much needed ammunition to 21st Battalion. One company reinforced the line astride the Montbrehain–Brancourt road, while the other established communications between posts along the line to the north of the road, up to the northeastern corner of the village.

Another company of 18th Battalion at the disposal of 2nd Pioneer Battalion reinforced existing posts and established a new one. Just after midday, four machine guns of 7th Army Company arrived and were sent two each to 21st Battalion and 2nd Pioneer Battalion. The artillery fired protective barrages throughout the afternoon against enemy concentrations. At 5.00 p.m. Doon Mill was again bombarded and all German activity in that area ceased.

During the night 117th and 118th Regiments, 59th Infantry Brigade, 30th American Division came forward to take over from the Australian Corps. However, the Americans were unsure of themselves and a number of Australian officers and NCOs were left behind for twenty-four hours to assist the newcomers. The leading American battalions in 117th Regiment deployed without Lewis guns and telephones, which had to be transferred from the departing Australian units. Command of the front was handed over at 2.45 a.m. and 6th Australian Brigade began to withdraw, initially to Nauroy. At least 400 enemy were killed in and around the village on 5th October and many more beyond it. In the period 3rd–6th October, the Brigade had taken 765 prisoners, together with 212 machine guns, nine minenwerfer and eight artillery pieces. The cost to 6th Australian Brigade, 2nd Pioneer Battalion and 6th Australian Machine Gun Company in the same period (mainly on the 5th) was 461 casualties (127 killed, 408 wounded and twenty-

Looking north from the D713 west of Montbrehain. The sileage store is on the right with the outskirts of the village beyond. L'Espagne is on the crest on the left with a wind turbine beyond it.

six missing). Within 24th Battalion there were 143 casualties (forty-seven killed, eighty wounded, eight missing and eight died of wounds). Tragically some of the dead had been with the Battalion since the first actions at Gallipoli in 1915.

This proved to be the last action fought by the Australians on the Western Front. The Corps had been in almost continuous action since 8th August. It had come up against thirty German divisions and captured 22,854 prisoners and 332 guns. However, the cost had been great, with 24,163 killed, wounded, missing or prisoners. The Australian Corps had gained a deservedly impressive reputation. It had avoided the reductions imposed on British formations early in 1918 and retained its unique identity and esprit. The 2nd Australian Division joined the other four Australian divisions in a rest area at Yzeux, between Amiens and Abbeville.

The XIII Corps was to gain the line Genève–Ponchaux–la Sablonnière–Guisancourt Farm, which included the capture of Beaurevoir. The 25th Division carried out the attack, supported by eight tanks of IV Tank Brigade, six field artillery brigades and No.35 Squadron RAF. Beaurevoir was to receive the attention of the heavy artillery for eighty minutes after zero hour (6.00 a.m.) prior to being mopped up. The tanks, although in support, were to operate independently. Four were to clear Bellevue Farm and then help to clear Beaurevoir, while the other four moved along the Torrens valley to enter Beaurevoir from the south.

The attack was delivered by 7th and 74th Brigades. Bellevue Farm and part of the Beaurevoir–Guisancourt Farm road were captured but, when the fog lifted, the Farm had to be given up. The bombardment of Beaurevoir appeared to have little effect as fire continued to pour from it. However, five tanks creeping along the Torrens valley entered the village from the south and shot up the machine gun crews. When the infantry did not arrive, the tanks were forced to withdraw, having lost one machine. On the extreme left there was less resistance and 11th Sherwood Foresters captured Guisancourt Farm, together with 191 prisoners. The Battalion was hit by enfilade fire from the right and had to fall back a little on that flank. The left remained secure, with 50th Division on Prospect Hill. A battalion of 75th Brigade in reserve was split, with half heading towards Bellevue and the other half towards Guisancourt Farm. Due to intense fire, no change occurred in the ground held.

Patrols of 50th Division found Vendhuile, east of the St Quentin Canal, had been evacuated and the line moved forward. The 150th Brigade established a line north to Vauxhall Quarry and to the Army boundary south of Aubencheul aux Bois, which was occupied by 115th Brigade (38th Division).

A fresh attack by 75th and 7th Brigades was ordered. The barrage was to open at 6.15 p.m. and the attack was to commence at 6.40 p.m. Every available machine gun was to cooperate, including 100th Machine Gun Battalion, and the heavy artillery was to bombard Beaurevoir again. The Germans appeared to be surprised. The 7th Brigade captured the cemetery but could get no further. At 6.25 p.m., while the barrage was still coming down, 1/5th Gloucestershire (75th Brigade) climbed the railway embankment west of Beaurevoir and cleared the machine guns on the other side. The leading companies passed through the village, encountering only isolated resistance, and the Battalion occupied a line beyond. On the left, a platoon of 1/8th Worcestershire cleared machine guns on the railway and in houses and pits west of Beaurevoir. Two companies of the Battalion joined 1/5th Gloucestershire in the village.

At 3.00 a.m. next morning, 7th Brigade made another unsuccessful attempt to gain the trenches between Ponchaux and Beaurevoir. The 74th Brigade on the left failed to capture Guisancourt Farm. However, at 4.10 a.m., 11th Sherwood Foresters, with two companies of 8th Royal Warwickshire attached, captured Guisancourt Farm. The rest of the Brigade pushed up the valley to the high ground west of la Sablonnière.

This action marked the end of the Battle of Beaurevoir. Over three days the twelve divisions in Fourth Army had encountered twenty enemy divisions. Just about all the objectives had been taken, albeit with hard fighting over an extended period. Between 29th September and 5th October, the Army had taken 14,664 prisoners.

Battle of Cambrai 1918 and Subsequent Operations

461 CSM John Williams, 10th Battalion, The South Wales Borderers (115th Brigade, 38th Division), Villers-Outréaux, France

7th–8th October 1918

While Fourth Army continued to reduce the German defences in and around the Beaurevoir Line, orders were issued for a renewed offensive. The intention had been to launch it on 7th October, but a shortage of

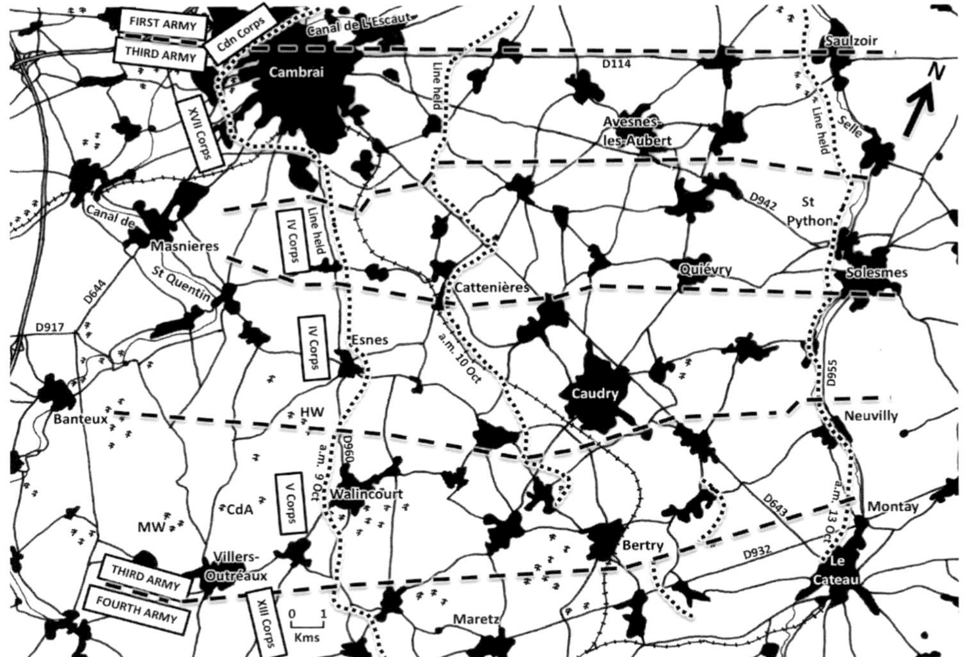

Third Army 8th–14th October.
CdA = Chateau des Angles, HW = Hurtebise Wood, MW = Mortho Wood.

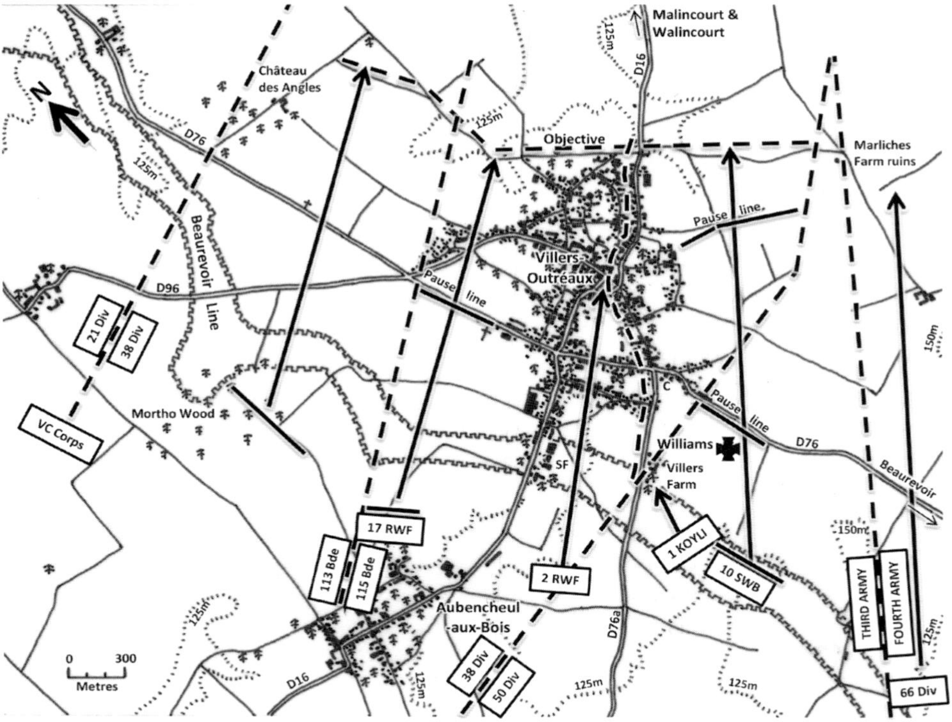

C = crucifix, SF = sugar factory. Approach Villers-Outréaux from the south on the D76 from Beaurevoir. About 450m south of the village on the left is a track and a grassy area on which to park. Look to the west-southwest 600m along the track to 10th South Wales Borderers' start line. The advance crossed the track from left to right about halfway to the pause line on the D76. Williams' VC action was in the area west of the D76.

Williams' VC action took place in this field in the centre, with Villers Farm in the background. The track leading off the D76, which is behind the camera position, is on the left of picture. Follow the line of the track down into the low ground to where the start line for 10th South Wales Borderers straddled the track. Villers-Outréaux is on the right.

ammunition forced a delay until the 8th. Third and Fourth Armies were to attack, while First Army demonstrated to pin down German reserves and reduce their scope for manoeuvre. When Third Army reached the high ground southeast of Cambrai, First Army was to secure crossings over the Schelde northeast of the town and protect Third Army's left flank. The Cavalry Corps was to be used when its commander saw opportunities.

On 5th October the Germans informed their troops that they were seeking peace, but at the front there was no respite. By the end of that day, Fourth Army had all but concluded the reduction of the Beaurevoir Line, setting the scene for the next stage of the relentless offensive.

Fourth Army attacked at 5.10 a.m. on 8th October to seize objectives 2,700m away and a line of exploitation another 2,700m beyond. A defensive flank on the right at Doon and Mannequin Hills was allowed for in case the French did not advance as rapidly. In the event the advance was a complete success. The Army Commander, Rawlinson, ordered the line of exploitation to be crossed but within set limits as the artillery was still struggling forward. Four thousand prisoners were taken.

Third Army attacked forty minutes earlier. Its general objective was the Hermann Line between Le Cateau and Solesmes, some thirty-two kilometres distant, but the immediate objective was 5,000m from the start line. Although Fourth Army held the Beaurevoir Line, the northern part was still in enemy hands and V Corps was ordered to capture it in a preliminary operation prior to the main attack.

The preliminary operation was allocated to 38th and 21st Divisions, with zero hour set for 1.00 a.m. Having carried the Beaurevoir Line they were to press on to the line Villers-Outréaux – Chateau des Angles – Hurtebise Wood. There they were to establish themselves in a trench line running north to south just east of Villers-Outréaux and gain contact with Fourth Army. This flank was to advance again at 8.00 a.m. in conjunction with the second phase of Fourth Army's attack. However, coordinating the details of the attack took so long that 38th Division was not able to issue its orders until 3.00 p.m. on the 7th. As a result, there was only sufficient time for verbal orders to allow the assault troops to reach their start positions on time.

The 21st Division achieved its objectives with relative ease. In 38th Division, 113th Brigade on the left was to advance north of Villers-Outréaux through Mortho Wood until reaching east of Chateau des Angles. On the right, 115th Brigade's leading battalions were to split to the west (17th Royal Welsh Fusiliers) and east (10th South Wales Borderers) of Villers-Outréaux and join up to the north. One company of the support battalion, 2nd Royal Welsh Fusiliers, was to follow 17th Royal Welsh Fusiliers to mop up the Beaurevoir Line from the south. Once it had been cut off, the village was to be mopped up at dawn by the other three companies of 2nd Royal Welsh Fusiliers, assisted by four tanks. The creeping barrage was to stand on the German forward positions for fifteen minutes in order to allow time for the leading assault troops to get through the wire. The barrage would then advance ninety metres every five minutes to the final objective, pausing for ten minutes each on two intermediate objectives.

The operation was more complicated for 10th South Wales Borderers as it started the attack within 50th Division's area to the south. This Division allocated 1st King's Own Yorkshire Light Infantry to capture Villers Farm at 1.00 a.m., which would protect 10th South Wales Borderers' flank during the preliminary operation. Another 50th Division battalion, 4th King's Royal Rifle Corps, was to protect the left flank of 66th Division to the south. The 50th Division would be pinched out of the line on the first objective at Marliches Farm, where 38th and 66th Divisions would converge.

The 113th Brigade made a little progress and penetrated the Beaurevoir Line on its flanks, but the centre was held at Mortho Wood and could make no progress until 115th Brigade came up on the right. The 1st King's Own Yorkshire Light Infantry (50th Division) captured Villers Farm to plan. In 115th Brigade, 10th South Wales Borderers reached its assembly position with just five minutes to spare. Its advance was led by A and B Companies with C and D in support. Both 10th South Wales Borderers and 17th Royal Welsh Fusiliers ran into numerous belts of unseen wire and heavy machine gun fire, despite the considerable efforts of the artillery the previous day. There were many casualties. In the confusion men lost direction in the dark.

In B Company, 10th South Wales Borderers, **CSM John Williams** saw a machine gun that was pinning his men down and causing heavy casualties. He ordered a Lewis gun to engage it while he, accompanied by 21315 Private Rees Evans (DCM for this action), went forward and outflanked the post. He captured fifteen Germans but, when they realised that he was alone, turned on him. One grabbed his rifle and tried to wrench it away. Williams broke free and bayoneted five before the rest surrendered again. He brought back eleven prisoners.

Williams' action allowed part of his Company to reach its objective, but the rest of the Battalion was scattered and disorganised. The 17th Royal Welsh Fusiliers attack also stalled. At 5.00 a.m., 2nd Royal Welsh Fusiliers arrived in front of Villers-Outréaux and came under a hail of fire. However, with excellent artillery support the attack went ahead, supported by 2nd Royal Dublin Fusiliers and the Scottish Horse, who headed for the sugar factory and crucifix respectively. Following two tanks through the wire at the southwest corner of the village, 2nd Royal Welsh Fusiliers stormed the defences, which allowed 10th South Wales Borderers and 17th Royal Welsh Fusiliers to advance on the flanks. The elements of 10th South Wales Borderers that had been held up surged forward and joined the small detachment that had managed to reach the objective following CSM Williams' exploits. The Brigade took 130 prisoners and numerous machine guns.

The 114th Brigade has been scheduled to advance through the leading brigades at 8.00 a.m., but its attack from the first objective east of Villers-Outréaux had to be delayed until 11.30 a.m. It was involved in the fighting for the Beaurevoir Line well before it should have been in action, but the advance got away at the revised time. The Brigade was well supported by artillery and reached the final objective near Walincourt. At 4.00 p.m., 10th South Wales Borderers followed and dug in 1,600m southeast of Walincourt. The Battalion had suffered over 200 casualties. However, by the end of the day the British had seized the last remnants of the Beaurevoir Line and were preparing to exploit their success next day.

Further north, in Third Army, IV Corps advanced 4,600m and took over 1,400 prisoners. The VI Corps had some hard fighting before reaching its objectives. The XVII Corps advanced northeasterly from the left of VI Corps area. The intention was to encircle Cambrai from the south and force the Germans to abandon the town. The advance was subjected to a number of counterattacks, including by captured British tanks, some of which ironically were knocked out using German anti-tank rifles. At the end of the day, although the full advance had not been made, Cambrai had been outflanked and more than 1,200 prisoners were taken.

During 8th October, the Canadian Corps, on the right of First Army, cooperated with the attack by Third Army by artillery fire and aggressive patrolling to simulate attacks. The aim was to obscure the limits of the main attack and thereby tie up German reserves.

462 Capt Coulson Mitchell, 1st Tunnelling Company, 4th Canadian Engineers (4th Canadian Division), Canal de L'Escaut, France

8th–9th October 1918

On the afternoon of 8th October, Field Marshal Haig ordered the advance of Fourth and Third Armies to continue next day. In addition, First Army was to support the left of Third Army in its advance. When XVII Corps, on the left of Third Army, had captured the Niergnies–Awoingt ridge southeast of Cambrai, the Canadian Corps on the right of First Army was to secure crossings over the Schelde (Escaut) Canal between Cambrai and Ramillies. Overall, the intention was to push ahead where the enemy gave way and to attack where he resisted.

The right of First Army's sector 8th–12th October.

The XVII Corps did not reach the intended area of Niergnies–Awoingt on 8th October. However, in view of Third Army continuing the advance early on the 9th, Lieutenant General Arthur Currie, commanding the Canadian Corps, decided to begin his operations at 1.30 a.m.

During the night the German Eighteenth, Second and Seventeenth Armies opposite the French First and British Fourth, Third and right wing of First Armies pulled back to the Hermann Position, abandoning Cambrai in the process. A line of rearguards was established about five kilometres in front of the Allied front. When the advance recommenced in the dark, there was almost no resistance at first, but by first light the enemy outposts had been reached.

On the right, Fourth Army resumed the advance at 5.20 a.m. Opposition was minimal and the Army Commander, Rawlinson, ordered the Cavalry Corps forward at 11.45 a.m. and assigned more distant objectives. However, the opportunity passed and in general the second objective, about 6,400m from the start, was reached instead. Third Army also advanced at 5.20 a.m. and made considerable progress.

On the left of Third Army in XVII Corps, 24th Division was to attack with a smokescreen on its left flank. The objective was Awoingt and the railway to the north and east. A flank was to be thrown back to connect with 57th Division. At the objective, 73rd Brigade was to be ready to pass through. Early in the advance it was learned that the Canadians to the north had crossed the canal at Pont d'Aire. About 5.00 a.m. patrols of 57th Division entered Cambrai and met up with Canadian patrols. The 72nd Brigade captured all objectives against little opposition and, instead of pausing, pressed on at 9.30 a.m. Cauroir was reached but the advance was then halted by machine gun fire from a ridge east of the village. The 73rd Brigade was ordered to form an advanced guard with a cavalry troop, two field artillery brigades, a company of engineers and two companies of machine guns. It was to probe forward as far as St Aubert. The ridge east of Cauroir was taken but, without heavy artillery support, Cagnoncles was too strongly held and the line settled on the ridge.

On XVII Corps' left flank, 57th Division ordered all three brigades, which were in line, to push ahead with patrols to the railway southwest and south of Cambrai. This was achieved and by 4.00 p.m. the southern suburbs had also been cleared. At

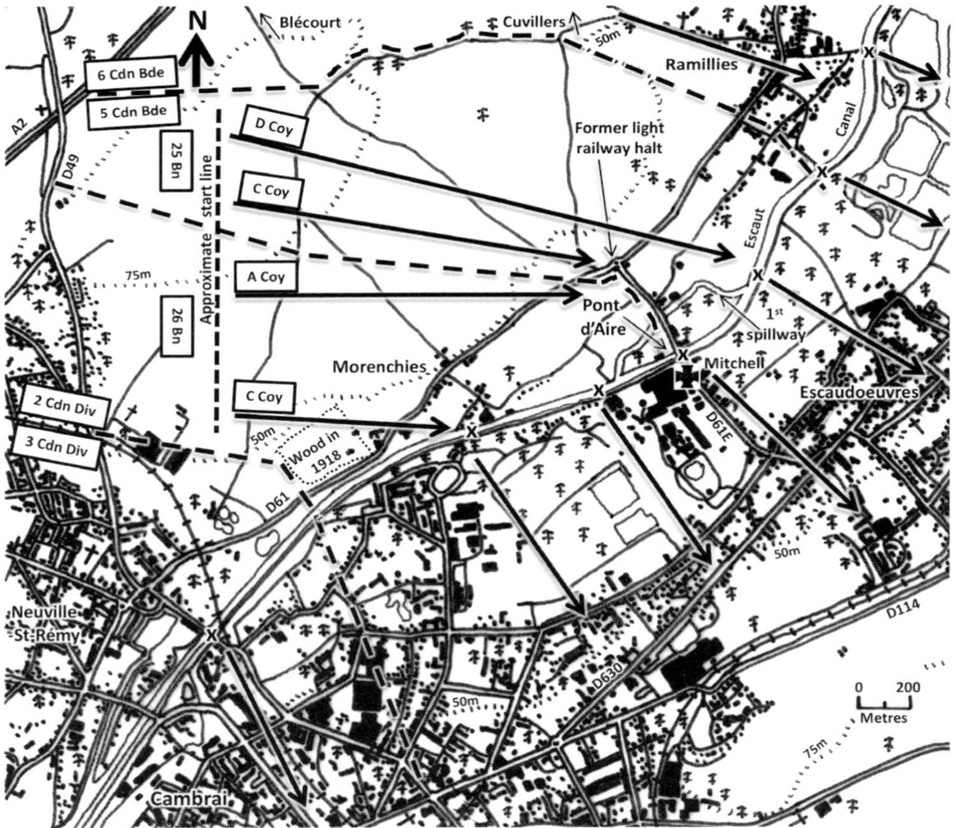

X = crossing point. Leave Escaudoeuvres on the D61E towards the northwest. Pass the enormous sugar factory on the left and cross the Canal de l'Escaut. After 50m turn right into a layby for lorries delivering sugar beet to the factory and park tidily. The southern entrance to the layby is where the second spillway crossed the road but nothing remains today. Walk back to the canal bridge and the site of Mitchell's VC action. On the south side of the canal on the left side of the road is a memorial to Mitchell. Return to the layby and look north to the Escaut crossing (first spillway) and the road junction beyond it, which was the light railway halt in 1918.

that point 57th Division was squeezed out of the line by 24th Division on the right and withdrew to move to Fifth Army's area.

On the right of First Army, the Canadian Corps' zero hour was set for 1.30 a.m. The 2nd Canadian Division on the left of the Corps was to cross the Schelde Canal between Morenchies and Ramillies, establish itself on the high ground behind Escaudoeuvres and make contact with XVII Corps in Third Army to the southeast. Once a crossing had been established, 3rd Canadian Division on the Corps right was to cross the canal and enter Cambrai.

The 2nd Canadian Division faced advancing over the same ground that 3rd Canadian Division had attempted a week earlier and suffered heavy casualties. It was therefore decided to attack in darkness at 9.30 p.m. on the day that XVII Corps reached its objective. On the left, 6th Canadian Brigade was to advance first to capture Ramillies and then form a flank guard back to Bantigny Ravine. On the right, 5th Canadian Brigade was to seize bridges at Morenchies, Pont d'Aire and immediately south of Ramillies, then establish a bridgehead at Escaudoeuvres. The 4th Canadian Brigade in reserve was then to pass through and advance with its right flank on the Cambrai–Le Cateau road, in order to establish contact with XVII Corps. It was also to establish a defensive flank facing northeast in contact with 5th Canadian Brigade east of Escaudoeuvres. During the night of 7th/8th October British engineers projected 1,000 drums of phosgene and chloropicrin gas into Bantigny Ravine to deny its use to the Germans. Units of 6th Canadian Brigade pushed forward a screen of posts between Blécourt and Cuvillers. The 7th Canadian Brigade (3rd Canadian Division) was at the disposal of 2nd Canadian Division in the event of an enemy counterattack on the left flank.

It was a dark and windy night with cold showers but the conditions did not delay preparations and all troops were in position by 1.15 a.m. Because the attack was to set off in the dark, every man wore a white calico armband on each arm for identification. These were to be removed at first light. The 2nd Brigade CE constructed three floating cork bridges to cross the canal between Morenchies and Ramillies. Eight brigades of field artillery fired various barrages, with two more brigades kept in reserve.

The 26th and 25th Battalions led 5th Canadian Brigade, on the right and left respectively, with parties of engineers attached. The 22nd Battalion was to follow to form a defensive flank on the right, while 24th Battalion remained in reserve. At Pont d'Aire, in addition to the canal and lock, there were also two spillways to the northwest (only the most north-westerly remains today), making a total of three waterways to be crossed and, if necessary, bridged.

On the right, 26th Battalion was led by C Company on the right, supported by D Company, and A Company on the left, supported by B Company. The right was responsible for the bridgehead at Morenchies and the left the bridgehead at Pont d'Aire. When C Company was twenty metres from Morenchies Wood (no longer exists) a machine gun opened fire. It was engaged by a Lewis gun section and the

From the layby on the D61E looking north, with the bridge over the Escaut (first spillway) in the foreground. This had been blown by the time that Mitchell and his men arrived but they found a crossing further to the right. The buildings in the middle distance are at the road junction, the location of the light railway halt in 1918.

post was rushed. The gunner was killed and two prisoners were taken. The canal was reached and the engineers came forward to construct a bridge. Once over the canal, the troops swept on to their objectives.

At Pont d'Aire the bridge over the first spillway had been destroyed by the Germans but the bridges over the other two waterways were intact. A Company met Captain Moggs and some engineers with cork bridges at the light railway halt in case they were needed to cross the canal. Accompanying A Company was a party of D Company, 4th Battalion CE, commanded by **Captain Coulson Mitchell**. They had the task of preventing the enemy demolishing the bridges in this area. Covered by a platoon under Lieutenant Clarke, Mitchell led his party to the first bridge, which was found to have been blown. However, another bridge was discovered further up the spillway and the party crossed over under artillery fire. Word was sent back and A Company also crossed over to take up positions in buildings nearby. Clarke's platoon overcame four machine gun posts and killed ten of the enemy.

Meanwhile Mitchell's party had continued to the bridge over the second spillway and cut the wires leading to the demolition charges under the bridge. Having made the charges safe, they continued to the canal bridge in almost total darkness. That bridge was also found to be prepared for immediate demolition. Mitchell and 464107 Sergeant Edward Jackson (DCM for this action) dashed over and began cutting the charge leads just as an enemy party attempted to rush the bridge and initiate the charges. 501257 Private Lloyd George Brewer (DCM for this action), Mitchell's sentry, was wounded. While the rest of the party continued to render the demolition charges safe, Mitchell rushed to assist the sentry in holding off the enemy party. He killed three of them, captured another twelve and thereby held the

Looking south over the canal bridge, with the sugar factory on the far bank on the right. The double lock on the canal is below the factory to the right of the bridge. The second spillway, since filled in, crossed the road (D61E) at this point on the left of picture.

bridgehead. He then returned to deal with the rest of the demolition charges under heavy fire.

Word was sent back that all was clear and Lieutenant Roland Colton's platoon was the first over to clear the opposition on the eastern bank. When this had been achieved the remainder of A Company crossed. Considerable resistance was encountered and overcome. The Company halted at 2.30 a.m. and waited for the barrage to lift at 4.30 a.m. Artillery firing short was a problem for both battalions throughout the day, despite messages being sent to lift.

The modern canal bridge from the southeast with the double lock below and beyond. Mitchell and his men stormed over the bridge from right to left.

On the left, 25th Battalion was led by C Company on the right and D Company on the left, supported by A and B Companies respectively. C Company appears to have drifted slightly to the left in the dark and A Company following met some resistance on the road near the railway halt. Casualties were such that two of the platoons were amalgamated into one. Forty prisoners were taken. Another post was overcome along the road to the canal and many Germans were killed or wounded in that action. Meanwhile C Company also met with some resistance at the railway halt, where several enemy were killed and eight prisoners were taken. The canal was reached at Pont d'Aire and two platoons crossed in single file over a German footbridge to occupy trenches on the far side. This crossing was shared with 26th Battalion. Later the two other platoons were sent forward to fill a gap between A and B Companies, which had leapfrogged through C and D Companies.

On the left D Company met no opposition until reaching the light railway southwest of Ramillies and the canal, where the barrage failed to lift on time. Green flares were fired as the signal for the artillery to cease firing but not before there were some casualties. The Company was then able to close up to the canal 600m north of Pont d'Aire at 5.15 a.m. and crossed over.

By 3.20 a.m. a bridgehead had been established at Pont d'Aire. By then one company of 26th Battalion had crossed the canal and the engineers were reported to be working on the bridges. By 4.15 a.m. 25th Battalion had two companies across the canal at Pont d'Aire and 26th Battalion had one and a half companies across.

By 6.00 a.m. 25th Battalion had captured Escaudoeuvres and the objective on the railway had been secured. It was learned that the Germans had been planning to pull back from 2.30 a.m. onwards and the Canadian attack had pre-empted this move. The 5th Canadian Brigade then mopped up the north-eastern outskirts of Cambrai.

In 6th Canadian Brigade, 27th Battalion occupied Ramillies at 2.25 a.m. after subduing some opposition. On the left, 31st Battalion established a defensive flank north of Ramillies to the south of Blécourt. Patrols from 29th and 31st Battalions followed up and, having established that the Germans had retired, occupied Blécourt, Bantigny and Cuvillers.

In 3rd Canadian Division, 4th Canadian Mounted Rifles (8th Canadian Brigade), on the left, took the railway embankment against almost no opposition. At 2.30 a.m. it was clear that the Germans had pulled back and the brigade commander decided to dispense with the barrage and ordered 4th and 5th Canadian Mounted Rifles to establish bridgeheads across the canal. These battalions advanced through Neuville St Rémy and crossed the canal on partially demolished bridges to enter Cambrai. There was almost no resistance, except from occasional enemy shelling and a few small rearguards. By 7.00 a.m. these battalions had pushed halfway through the deserted Cambrai. By midday they were on the railway to the east.

Behind the advancing infantry, the engineers immediately commenced building more bridges. By 7.00 a.m. 4th Battalion CE had completed a light trestle bridge and a pontoon bridge at Escaudoeuvres and Morenchies respectively. A heavy traffic bridge was ready by 3.00 p.m. at Escaudoeuvres. The 6th Battalion CE constructed two pontoon bridges at Ramillies. The 7th Battalion CE had a pontoon bridge on the Douai road northwest of Cambrai by 11.15 a.m. and a heavy bridge by 6.15 p.m. the XVII Corps engineers constructed another alongside the latter to allow for two-way traffic. Engineers were also heavily involved in searching for booby traps and delayed action explosive charges.

By 10.45 a.m. it was clear to HQ First Army that the enemy was conducting a general withdrawal. It immediately ordered the Canadian Corps to occupy the angle between the Schelde and Sensée canals and advance east of the Schelde, in order to cover the left flank of Third Army. On the left, XXII Corps was to relieve the Canadians as far east as Fressies on the Sensée Canal on the night of 9th/10th October, to allow the whole of the Canadian Corps to follow the retreating Germans. HQ Canadian Corps issued its orders at 12.25 p.m. for an advance of about six and half kilometres across the whole Corps frontage. The 3rd Canadian Division was to establish posts on the railway east of Cambrai. The 2nd Canadian Division was to make contact with XVII Corps to the south around Cauroir. When this had been achieved, 3rd Canadian Division was to withdraw. Then the two corps were to advance together to Naves–Thun Levêque. On the left, in XXII Corps, 11th Division was to continue the line from Thun Levêque to Paillencourt.

Brutinel's Brigade was ordered forward to exploit success along the line of the Cambrai–Iwuy road. The Canadian Light Horse was to press ahead to seize successive objectives on high ground northwest of Naves and beyond the Selle. However, as the cavalry rode along the Cambrai–Iwuy road it was stopped on the first objective south of Thun St Martin by machine gun fire from Iwuy and Naves. The attempt to get over the Selle had to be abandoned.

In 2nd Canadian Division, 5th Canadian Brigade switched direction to the northeast, with its boundaries being the Cambrai–Naves and Cambrai–Iwuy roads. It did not attack until 5.00 p.m. and was held up 2,750m short of Naves. The 6th Canadian Brigade started earlier at 3.00 p.m. and passed through Eswars but was held up by fire from Thun St Martin and Thun Levêque. In 11th Division, 34th Brigade on the right advanced at 2.45 p.m., supported by Canadian artillery. There was some resistance from Abancourt and Paillencourt but it had been taken by 5.30 p.m. On the left, 33rd Brigade was being relieved by 168th Brigade when the orders to advance arrived. It set off at 3.30 p.m. and established a defensive flank from Paillencourt back to the old front line. Just after midnight two platoons of 32nd Brigade, which had been in reserve, arrived and found Thun Levêque had been evacuated. Posts were established beyond it.

Further north VIII Corps found that the enemy were falling back to the Drocourt-Queant Line. Elsewhere the British Fifth and Second Armies in Flanders were preparing to launch a new offensive, whilst the US First and French Fourth Armies in the Argonne continued to attack, albeit with little progress since 4th October. However, in the centre the Germans in front of the French First and British Fourth, Third and First Armies were in retreat.

464 Lt Wallace Algie, 20th Battalion (Central Ontario) (4th Canadian Brigade, 2nd Canadian Division), Cambrai, France

11th October 1918

On 10th October Field Marshal Haig was informed by Marshal Foch that he intended allocating new boundaries between the Allied armies. He wished the BEF to change direction and advance eastwards rather than north-eastwards as hitherto. The BEF was making steady progress and Haig believed that, if it continued north-eastwards, there was every expectation that the German lateral lines of communications between Valenciennes and Mézières would be severed. Continuing to advance north-eastwards would also allow the BEF's Fourth, Third and First Armies to cooperate with the Allied armies in Flanders. Elsewhere on the Western Front the Americans were attacking vigorously in the Argonne but were making little progress. The French were doing little better. The French First Army on the right of the British Fourth Army, despite constant urging, had failed to attack with any commitment and remained well behind the British. By turning eastwards the BEF would increase the length of its frontage and the converse was true for the French to the south. Haig requested reinforcement by six American divisions but Foch refused, although he conceded other points. As a result the BEF main effort was to be towards the line Wassigny – Solesmes. At the same time operations were to develop between the Schelde and Sambre north-easterly, in combination with the BEF armies and the Belgians on the left. To allow the BEF to extend its attacks to the north, the boundary between it and the French was prolonged to the south of Wassigny and Avesnes, i.e. almost north-easterly. This remained the boundary until the end of the war.

The period 10th-12th October saw Fourth, Third and the right of First Armies close up to the German Hermann Position on the east bank of the Selle. Advanced guards probed forward, often against negligible opposition from German rearguards. Little work had been carried out on the Hermann defences but, as the line was approached, it became clear that it was held in strength. Fourth Army and the right of Third Army were the first to reach the new position. The left of Third and right of First Army had further to cover. It was clear that the Germans had brought up reinforcements and the line of the Selle would not be breached without heavy artillery support. The river was up to five and a half metres wide and over two metres deep in places, with marshes on both banks up to 200m wide. The whole therefore presented a considerable obstacle.

First Army's orders for 10th October were to continue clearing between the canals and to cover Third Army's left flank. The Canadian Corps underwent a series of reliefs at this time:

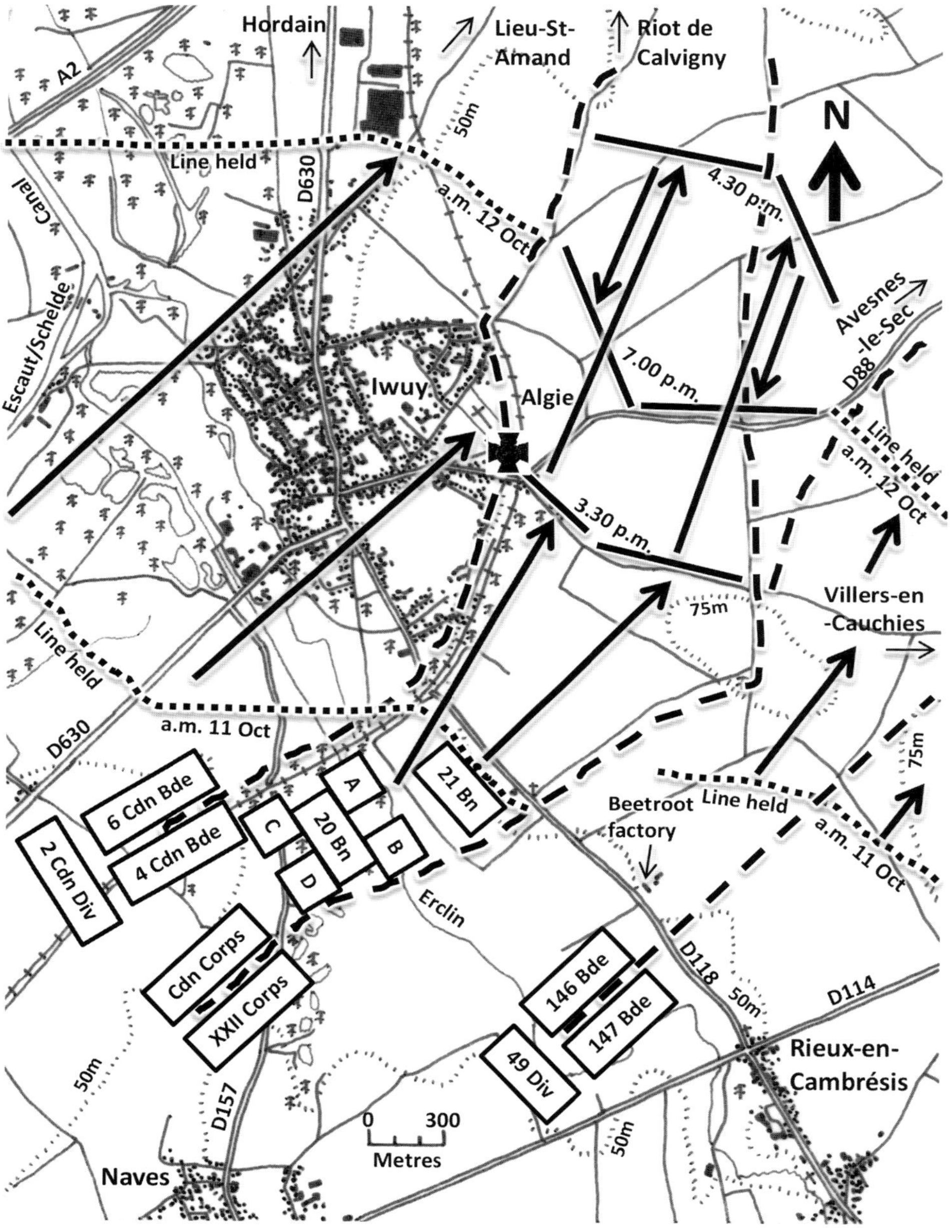

Enter Iwuy from the east on the D88 and park near the railway crossing to consider Algie's VC action in this area. An alternative view can be had from the cemetery. Continue along the D88 for 475m and turn sharp right onto Rue du Quatre Septembre. The cemetery is 400m along this road on the right, but parking is on the left. Cross the road and enter the cemetery by the gate on the right. Walk the length of the cemetery to the gate at the bottom left to look over the railway crossing. Some of Algie's men were deployed in this part of the cemetery.

order to move first and swing to the right, while 20th Battalion behind swung left along the railway, eventually to come up on the left of 21st Battalion.

In 20th Battalion, B Company was on the right and A Company was on the left, supported by D and C Companies respectively. The objective for the Battalion was Riot de Calvigny. The attack commenced at 9.00 a.m., supported by a light barrage. The German artillery responded quickly and effectively and shortened as the companies advanced. It was supported by intense machine gun fire from Iwuy on the left. There were many casualties but the advance continued to the first objective, which was reached at 10.30 a.m. While a reorganisation was taking place before the advance to the next objective, the Germans launched a counterattack from the direction of Avesnes-le-Sec, supported by six or seven tanks (mainly captured British machines) and heavy artillery and machine gun fire. The brunt of this attack was borne by the two brigades of 49th Division on the right and the whole line was forced back 1,800m to the ridge west of the Villers-en-Cauchies–Iwuy

road. The 21st Battalion also had to fall back 700m to the sunken Villers-en-Cauchies–Iwuy road and 20th Battalion had to conform. The German tanks were forced back by batteries of artillery rushed forward and the infantry by small arms fire, particularly from 2nd Canadian Machine Gun Battalion. In this retirement 147th and 146th Brigades suffered losses of about 900 each and 4th Canadian Brigade almost 700.

On 20th Battalion's left, 27th Battalion (6th Canadian Brigade), which had met stiff opposition in Iwuy, was behind when the counterattack was launched and thus avoided it. However, as a result 20th Battalion suffered many casualties from enfilade fire from the village. While the Battalion was reorganising, the Germans were seen bringing more machine guns from the village into positions from where they could enfilade the whole of 4th Canadian Brigade's frontage along the sunken road.

Lieutenant Wallace Algie, commanding B Company, was determined to prevent the enemy setting up more machine guns by denying them the east end of the village. He led a small party of nine volunteers to the left across the brigade boundary. If successful, this move would also threaten the defenders of the village and force them to abandon it. In the first rush Algie's party captured two machine guns, one on the railway and the other in a building on the eastern edge of the village. The crews were killed and the Canadians brought the machine guns into action, along with their Lewis guns, against other enemy machine gun teams advancing from the village. Before they could recover, Algie led his men forward again and, after a brief fight, the survivors, an officer and ten men, were captured. Algie disposed his men in positions from where they could deny the enemy the eastern part of the village, including firing from the gravestones in the cemetery. He then returned to the Battalion to bring up reinforcements but was killed as he guided them across the railway.

The reinforcements continued to help Algie's original party to hold on. As they spread to the north, the enemy began pulling back towards Hordain, allowing 6th Canadian Brigade to get forward and seize the village. An hour later 27th Battalion relieved the 20th Battalion posts, which returned to the 4th Canadian Brigade area. The 20th Battalion then held the sunken road from the railway near the cemetery 600m to the southeast to the junction with 21st Battalion.

Having reorganised, the assault brigades advanced again at 3.30 p.m. under a light barrage. There was less opposition and the next ridge was reached by 4th Canadian Brigade, where contact was made with 146th Brigade on the right and a little later with 27th Battalion on the left. However, 21st Battalion was 1,100m behind to the right rear. It had been ordered to pull back about a kilometre to a sunken road. The right of 20th Battalion had no option other than to conform and joined with 21st Battalion at the sunken road. The left pulled back 650m in contact with 27th Battalion and the new position was occupied by 5.15 p.m. At 7.00 p.m. 20th Battalion took over some posts held by 27th Battalion and also established other posts about 450m in advance of the main line. At the end of the day 4th Canadian

resistance on the railway and the high ground beyond. The Battalion stalled on the line of the Neuvilly–Montay road, short of the railway, and suffered severe casualties from machine guns in the village and on the right flank. The support companies managed to cross the river before the enemy barrage fell but were unable to progress much beyond a road just east of the river. Due to casualties amongst the officers, Second Lieutenant Marsden took command of the Battalion temporarily. After two hours fighting, a row of houses was captured on the Montay road on the eastern outskirts of Neuvilly. Posts were formed there to cover the Battalion's left flank.

The two right companies of 10th Lancashire Fusiliers (A and C) were fired upon from houses west of the Selle that had been reported clear. The footbridges were also swept by machine guns. A Company was stalled behind the support companies of 9th Duke of Wellington's and was unable to cross the river before the enemy barrage fell. The OC was wounded and Second Lieutenant W Davidson MC was sent from Battalion HQ to take over.

Meanwhile at 5.48 a.m. Second Lieutenant R Graham, commanding C Company, had been ordered by the CO to clear the village west of the river. **Corporal Frank Lester** was in a party of seven led by an officer. He was the first to enter a house from the rear and shot two of the enemy as they tried to exit through the front door. Shortly after the party entered the house a fall of masonry blocked their exit to the rear, but the street to the front was swept by heavy point-blank machine gun fire. A sniper was causing casualties to another party in a house across the street and it faced the choice of being picked off one by one or chancing a dash across the street. Lester shouted, *I'll settle him* and, although he must have realised it meant certain death, dashed out into the street. He shot the sniper at close range but was himself shot down at the same time.

C Company forced the Germans back over the bridge near the church after severe fighting. An attempt to follow the retreating enemy over the bridge was halted by heavy machine gun fire.

Contemporary houses along Rue de Montay, which may be the road in which Lester's VC action took place.

Meanwhile A Company on the right attempted to cross the footbridges south of the village but was also held up by machine gun fire and suffered considerable casualties. The Company dug in on a road west of the Selle facing east to protect 9th Duke of Wellington's right rear flank. By 8.30 a.m. it was evident that 9th Duke of Wellington's could not cross the railway.

D Company, 10th Lancashire Fusiliers, the left support company, was placed at the disposal of 12th Manchester to be used on the Battalion's right flank. However, an enemy pocket on the railway northwest of Neuvilly was causing considerable trouble and D Company was used to secure the left flank instead. The factory and cemetery were cleared and two platoons reached the railway behind 12th Manchester. Contact was made with 63rd Brigade north of the town. However, the right flank remained open and of concern.

The situation worsened at 9.00 a.m., when the Germans counterattacked into 33rd Division's exposed right flank, where Fourth Army was not as well advanced. The forward battalion was driven off the high ground to the east of Neuvilly but held the railway line for a while. The 9th Duke of Wellington's opened effective fire against this attack. A refused flank had to be formed close to the Selle on the right by Battalion HQ details. The Battalion maintained contact with 33rd Division. Having reached the railway cutting, the enemy was able to use it to infiltrate back into the village.

At about midday, Major Thompson arrived from B Echelon to take command of 9th Duke of Wellington's. A renewal of the attack was envisaged for 4.15 p.m. During it 10th Lancashire Fusiliers was to clear the village from northwest to southeast until contact was made with 9th Duke of Wellington's. Two companies of 7th East Yorkshire (50th Brigade attached to 52nd Brigade) were ordered to move in small groups to form up north of the railway. They were to advance to the southeast, keeping the railway on their right. At the same time, 9th Duke of Wellington's was to occupy the railway and link up with 12th Manchester. Once this had been achieved, the 7th East Yorkshire companies were to become the reserve.

The left of 10th Lancashire Fusiliers was ordered to clear Neuvilly north of the Selle. At 12.50 p.m. A and C Companies on the right were ordered to move round to the south and cross the river by the bridges north of the village. They were to assist B Company in mopping up. They set off at 1.15 p.m. led by A Company. At first no bridges could be found intact and most of the men waded over the river. The fighting strength of the four companies at this time amounted to just 230 men. About 3.00 p.m. B Company began to clear the village from the northwest again. By then A and C Companies had crossed the river and were ready to follow B Company. Two of D Company's platoons advanced on the factory and the other two were at the quarry southwest of the cemetery. Strong opposition was met from the Germans who had filtered back into the village from the railway cutting and sunken road to the east.

However, the renewal of the main attack was forestalled by an enemy counterattack at 3.00 p.m. from the north and northwest against 37th Division and 12th Manchester. The enemy barrage was intense and a counter-barrage was called for. The German attack was pushed forward, despite heavy losses to small arms fire, and the line of the railway was lost. The 37th Division was pushed back to the Selle and 12th Manchester to within 200m of it, having suffered heavy casualties. The section of four machine guns on the right managed to get away, losing just one gun when the man carrying it was hit. The left section was lost completely due to heavy casualties in the withdrawal. All the forward trench mortars were brought back intact. The 10th Lancashire Fusiliers on the west bank helped to prevent the Germans crossing the river.

HQ V Corps ordered the line to be consolidated where it would best lend itself to a resumption of the offensive at an early date. At 5.00 p.m., A and C Companies, 10th Lancashire Fusiliers started to clear the village south of the river once again and, although no enemy were encountered, heavy fire was received from the north bank. By last light C, B and A Companies were holding the river crossings for 12th Manchester. They were relieved early on 13th October and marched back to Inchy. After dark the remainder of 9th Duke of Wellington's was also withdrawn from its isolated position by elements of 51st Brigade, which had relieved the whole of 52nd Brigade by 3.50 a.m. During this action 52nd Brigade captured ninety-three prisoners and suffered 679 casualties (102 killed, 521 wounded and fifty-six missing), including 198 in 10th Lancashire Fusiliers (thirty-five killed, 159 wounded and four missing). However, the Battalion's war diary records forty-nine prisoners and 186 casualties (thirty-three killed, 138 wounded and fifteen missing).

466 LSgt Harry Wood, 2nd Battalion, Scots Guards (3rd Guards Brigade, Guards Division), St Python, France

13th October 1918

The general move forward to the Selle continued on 13th October. Third Army had already secured crossings and thrown some bridges over in preparation for a further advance, but nowhere did it have a substantial foothold to the east. During the course of 13th October only two incidents of note took place in Third Army: the loss of Belle Vue, taken by IV Corps the previous day; and the clearance of the western part of St Python.

In the Guards Division the three battalions of 3rd Guards Brigade edged forward towards the Selle from the high ground to the west. Each battalion led with two companies, one in support and the fourth in reserve. During the previous night each battalion had been tasked with pushing forward up to a company each. This was in preparation for sending patrols at dawn to establish where the enemy positions were on the high ground east of St Python. If little enemy opposition was encountered, D Squadron, Oxfordshire Hussars was to be ready to advance rapidly onto the high ground. If this was gained, 1st and 2nd Guards Brigades would pass through 3rd Guards Brigade and continue the advance on the 14th. If not, they would relieve 3rd Guards Brigade on whatever line had been reached.

On the right was 125th Brigade (42nd Division). It was to hold in its existing positions unless the Guards reached the high ground east of St Python. In that event 125th Brigade would also push forward. On the left, 17th Brigade (24th Division) was to advance to the northeast of Haussy.

In 3rd Guards Brigade, 1st Grenadier Guards was on the right, 2nd Scots Guards in the centre and on the left was 1st Welsh Guards. The Welsh and Scots Guards had been allocated three bridges each, should they be needed when the line of the river was gained. The 2nd Scots Guards faced St Python, which straddled the Selle. Patrols of the Battalion entered the village just after midnight to clear it west of the river and, if possible, to gain a foothold on the east bank. About the same time 1st Grenadier Guards established posts along the railway south of St Python. On the left, 1st Welsh Guards reported that it was on its objective on the spur just west of the railway by 6.20 a.m.

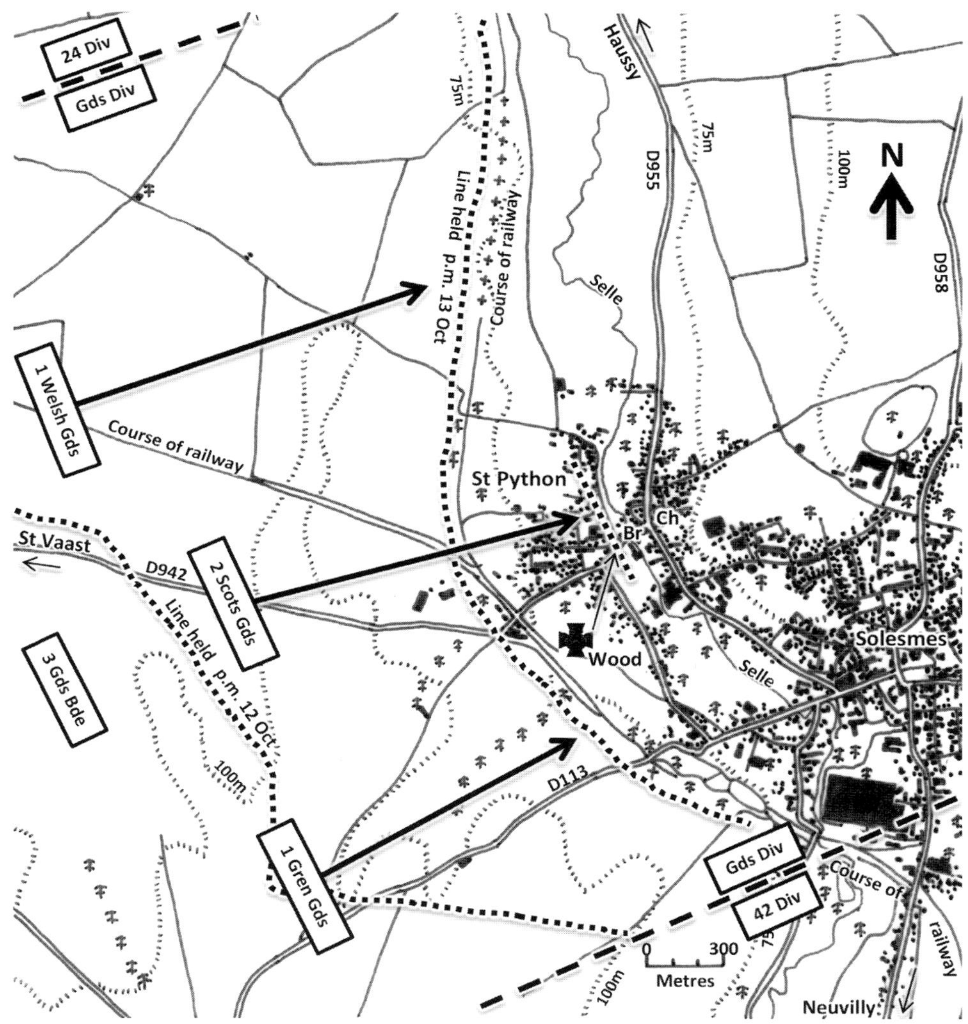

Br = bridge, Ch = church. From the centre of Solesmes follow the D955 northwards. At the church in St Python turn left, cross the Selle and turn right to park in the Mairie car park. Walk back to the road, which is where Wood's VC action took place.

St Python was strongly held and, to complicate matters, a large number of civilians remained. Right Flank (RF) Company, 2nd Scots Guards passed through the two forward companies. By 4.10 a.m. it had pushed into the north of the village and reached the river. An enemy patrol was defeated near the church. However, the main road bridge over the river there was found to have been demolished. A ford north of the village was discovered. On the right, Left Flank (LF) Company captured the railway junction, cleared the railway and entered the village. Both companies did well against considerable resistance in pitch darkness.

The east bank was found to be held in strength and there were many concealed machine guns. After dawn movement became even more difficult. By 6.30 a.m. there were three platoons north of the village and two platoons in the south and west, where the demolished main road bridge crossed the river opposite the church. The remainder of the Battalion dug in along the crest on the railway line.

On reaching the river it was found that debris from the destroyed bridges had blocked the flow and created several dams. Patrols of the Oxfordshire Hussars and the Cyclist Corps made great efforts to get over but eventually withdrew. The ford to the north was found to be passable, being just one metre deep, but machine guns on the far side made a crossing impossible. Elsewhere the river proved to be a more formidable obstacle, being about ten metres wide and one and half metres deep. The only dry crossing remaining was a footbridge in 1st Welsh Guards' area and that was also under machine gun and artillery fire. While the German snipers and machine guns dominated possible crossing points from the east bank, it was not possible to cross in daylight.

In 2nd Scots Guards, RF Company and a platoon of F Company gradually cleared the north of the village, while LF Company had hand to hand fighting in the southwest. Two mortars were sent forward into St Python, where they had some success in supporting the infantry and stopping enemy mortar fire.

In attempting to get over the main road bridge, **Lance Sergeant Harry Wood**'s platoon in LF Company came under a hail of fire. The platoon sergeant was killed and Wood took over (13229 Lance Sergeant Ellis Frederick Merryweather is buried in Romeries Communal Cemetery Extension – IV B 17). There was very little space for manoeuvre and the approach to the bridge was covered by machine guns and snipers. Before a crossing could succeed, the area had to be dominated by fire. Wood carried a large piece of masonry into the open street, lay down behind it and calmly engaged the snipers to cover his men. He remained fully exposed to well-aimed fire

St Python church from the west. The bridge over the Selle is marked by the railings on both sides of the road at the end of the long brick wall on the right of picture. The turning into the Mairie car park is on the left.

while his men gained their objective. Later in the day he led his platoon in driving off repeated counterattacks.

One platoon was driven back by shellfire at 2.30 p.m., but by evening the village west of the river had been cleared. A number of casualties were caused during a thirty-minute enemy barrage on the railway, commencing at 4.00 p.m.

Attempts to secure a more substantial bridgehead in this area failed and the sappers made preparations to cross that night. The Germans thinned out their positions later in the day and many were hit by machine guns and artillery from the west bank. There was at least one incident of a German trying to escape disguised as a civilian. One account states that the man was discovered and shot. However, another says that a civilian identified him to the British but the German shot him and Corporal Lindekvist of LF Company (14426 Lance Corporal Harold Lindekvist is buried in St Vaast Communal Cemetery Extension – B4).

The 3rd Guards Brigade was relieved by 1st and 2nd Guards Brigades that night, with 2nd Scots Guards being relieved by 3rd Grenadier Guards (2nd Guards Brigade) at 10.45 p.m. The Battalion marched back to billets in St Hilaire before midnight, having suffered seventy-two casualties (fifteen killed and fifty-seven wounded).

Local Operations

467 Cpl James Brennan McPhie, 416th (1st Edinburgh) Field Company Royal Engineers (56th Division), Aubencheul-au-Bac, France

13th October 1918

On 13th October, 56th Division was in the process of handing over to 4th Canadian Division before leaving the Canadian Corps (First Army). Despite the general calm a number of sharp actions were fought, one of which involved 1/2nd London (Royal Fusiliers), 169th Brigade, crossing the Sensée Canal east of Aubencheul-au-Bac.

The 169th Brigade had taken over the right sector of the Division's front from 168th Brigade on 11th October. An attack was planned against Aubigny-au-Bac on the north bank of the canal. The aim was to ascertain the enemy's strength and either to interfere with his retirement or hasten it. Having crossed the canal silently, the attack was to be launched from southeast of the village through it to the northwest.

The Brigade front was held by 1/16th London (Queen's Westminster Rifles) on the left and 1/5th London (London Rifle Brigade) on the right. Both battalions were widely extended and so it was decided to use D Company of the reserve battalion, 1/2nd London, for the operation, with C Company in support.

The canal was twenty metres wide (about half the current width) and all the bridges had been destroyed. Two of the downed bridges were south of Aubigny, about 1,150m apart. Each was closely covered by a German post and it was therefore decided not to attempt crossing at either point initially. Instead there would be a new crossing between the two and a site was reconnoitred on the night of 9th/10th October. The original plan was for 416th Field Company RE to construct rafts to carry over a strong patrol of 1/16th London after dark. The patrol was to check that a sufficiently large area, free of the enemy, existed in which to assemble the assault company prior to the attack. While the reconnaissance was going on, the engineers would construct a floating footbridge for D Company, 1/2nd London to gain the north bank. The 1/2nd London set up an advanced HQ at Aubencheul Chateau, with the HQ of D Company and the RE Section being co-located.

In view of the limited time and resources available, Second Lieutenant Arthur Edward Arnold (MC for this action), commanding No.1 Section, 416th Field

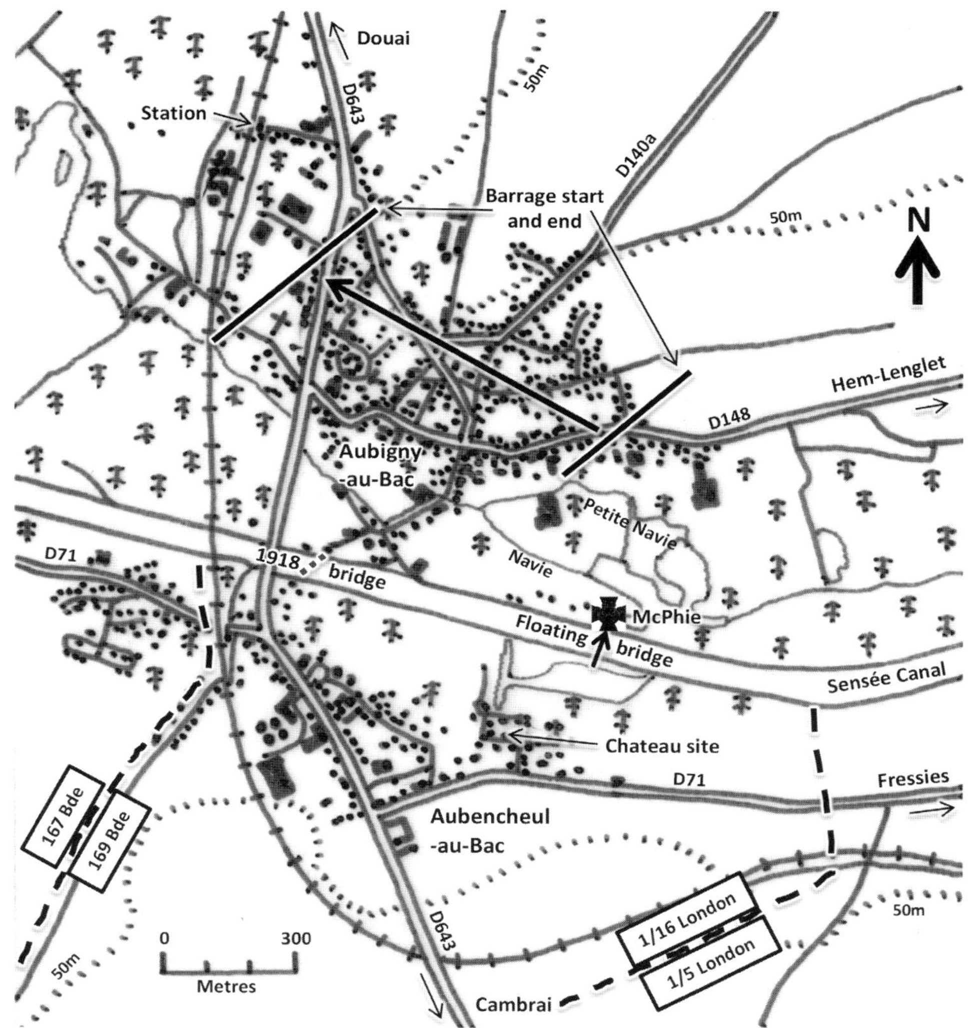

Approach Aubencheul-au-Bac from the south along the D643. Just before reaching the bridge over the Canal de la Sensée, turn right into Rue Leo Lagrange and park. Walk back to the D643, turn right and after 100m turn right again along a path to the canal bank. Follow the tow path with the canal on the left for 700m to the site of the floating bridge.

Company, decided to dispense with the rafts and to construct the floating bridge straight away. The bridge was constructed on the night of the 12th/13th, the work having to be carried out in silence. Due to the darkness and rain it took longer than expected but the rain helped to cover any noise made by the sappers. The bridge was completed by 3.00 a.m. Work commenced on a second bridge at the site of the former road bridge south of Aubigny until Arnold was wounded and later killed

The floating bridge crossing site was on the right of picture. The canal in 1918 was about half the width today. The white house on the far bank left of centre may be the one in which the German sniper was positioned. On the far left is the D643 road bridge.

(Sauchy-Cauchy Communal Cemetery Extension). The requirement for the second bridge was then cancelled.

The 1/16th London patrol crossed over and found that it could not move more than ten metres in any direction without being challenged by one of three German posts. However, the posts did not open fire and orders were issued to attempt capturing the posts without raising the alarm. At 4.00 a.m. a platoon of 1/2nd London was ordered over the canal and captured two Germans. The rest of the company followed under Captain D Sloan.

No.2 Section, 416th Field Company had relieved No.1 Section at 7.30 p.m. the previous evening. **Corporal James McPhie** and five men were responsible for the maintenance of the floating bridge. When the main body of the infantry began crossing at 4.50 a.m., enemy shells falling into the Canal threatened to damage the flimsy cork floats. McPhie crossed to the far bank. As the infantry crossed, they closed up and the floats broke apart. McPhie and 169995 Sapper Charles Arthur Cox were thrown into the water, where they tried to hold the bridge together. Cox's hands were badly injured by being repeatedly trodden on and he had to let go. He and McPhie swam ashore and reported to CO 1/2nd London, who made it clear that it was imperative to keep the bridge open.

McPhie went into Aubencheul-au-Bac to collect more stores and made his way back to the canal, but dawn had broken before he reached the bridge. He quickly briefed his men that death or glory work was required if the infantry north of the Canal were to make it back. Equipped with an axe, he and Cox dashed onto the bridge and started to cut away the broken cleats. A sniper in a house only seventy-

five metres away shot McPhie in the face and he fell into the water. At the same time Cox was hit in the arm and leg. Despite his wounds, Cox grabbed McPhie and partly pulled him onto the bridge. A machine gun opened fire, hitting McPhie in the back and Cox was shot another four or fives times in the thigh, but he held onto McPhie until he was sure that the Corporal was dead. Sapper Hawkins then dashed onto the bridge, threw a rope to Cox and pulled him back to the friendly shore. Later that morning 10th Battalion CE relieved 416th Field Company RE.

Once over the canal, D Company faced the difficult task of assembling for the attack in the dark. It was complicated by two streams across the assembly area, La Navie and La Petite Navie. La Navie was found to be six metres wide and up to two and a half metres deep. Fortunately a crossing was found thirty metres north of the canal crossing and the Company was in position half an hour before zero hour, which was set for 5.15 a.m.

It was not possible to follow the barrage in the usual way due to the nature of the ground. The barrage was directed against the flank of the enemy positions to creep north-westerly. Platoons were directed to make their own way to the points allocated to them. Despite the huge difficulties encountered, the attack was a success. It hit the Germans from a totally unexpected direction. Two machine guns were overcome and about 160 prisoners were taken in the village without causing any trouble. Pre-planned posts were occupied by 6.30 a.m. Meanwhile at 6.00 a.m. two platoons of C Company had crossed over to reinforce various posts.

About 7.00 a.m. two machine gun posts that were causing problems were engaged with rifle grenades before being rushed. Another twelve prisoners were taken. By 9.30 a.m. the other two platoons of C Company had crossed the canal with the intention of establishing three posts at the station northwest of the village. However, due to the strength of the enemy force there, this was not possible.

At 10.00 a.m. the Germans laid down a heavy barrage on the village with machine guns in support. Half an hour later an enemy battalion counterattacked. Heavy losses were sustained from the German barrage and British small arms fire. However, the attack was pressed with great determination and one by one the 1/2nd London posts were outflanked. They were pushed back to La Petite Navie, where a line was held and the Germans were prevented from debouching from the village. However, machine gun and sniper fire eventually forced the companies back to the line of the canal. The crossing over La Navie was held for an hour and a small bridgehead was maintained north of the canal. However, by 5.00 p.m. all troops had recrossed the canal and were behind the south bank. During the night a small bridgehead was re-established on the north bank. In total 171 officers and men of 1/2nd London had crossed the canal, of whom 143 became casualties (twenty killed, ninety-two wounded and thirty-one missing). Three enemy machine guns were brought back and another ten were either damaged or thrown into streams. The Battalion captured 207 prisoners.

Charles Cox's grave in Bucquoy Road Cemetery, Ficheux. He was born on 24th April 1890.

McPhie was buried in the chateau grounds at Aubencheul. Later his remains were moved to Naves Communal Cemetery Extension. Cox lived until 17th October and is buried in Bucquoy Road Cemetery, Ficheux (III J 10). There is no doubt that McPhie thoroughly deserved his posthumous award by setting a magnificent example in circumstances where death was almost inevitable. But why did Cox not receive the same award? He did as much on the bridge and in the water as McPhie, arguably more, but received nothing for his incredible bravery.

The date of this action is often quoted as 14th October 1918. However, the Battalion and Brigade war diaries are quite clear that it started on the evening of 12th October and was completed by the evening of the following day.

468 2Lt James Johnson, 2nd attached 36th Battalion, The Northumberland Fusiliers (178th Brigade, 59th Division), Wez Macquart, France

14th October 1918

The main event on 14th October was the renewal of the offensive by the Group of Armies in Flanders, including the British Second Army. This is the subject of the next book in the series – *The Final Advance in Flanders and Artois*.

Further south activity was confined to intense local patrol actions to keep the Germans off balance. Fifth Army continued to connect the GAF with the BEF Armies to the south. In the next phase Fifth Army faced low lying and waterlogged ground, but on the left was the huge urban area of Lille. The plan was to pinch it out by Second Army to the north driving eastwards, while Fourth, Third and First Armies converged to the east of Lille in a thrust from the southwest. There were signs that the enemy opposite Fifth Army was preparing to withdraw from the general line of the Haute-Deûle Canal, west of Lille, to a new position east of the city. From there they were expected to conduct a fighting withdrawal to the Schelde, where the next stand would be made, to comply with the line to north and south. British preparations were therefore made for rapidly moving advance guards.

There was little activity in Fifth Army's area on 14th October, except for a sharp action fought by two battalions of 178th Brigade in 59th Division. There

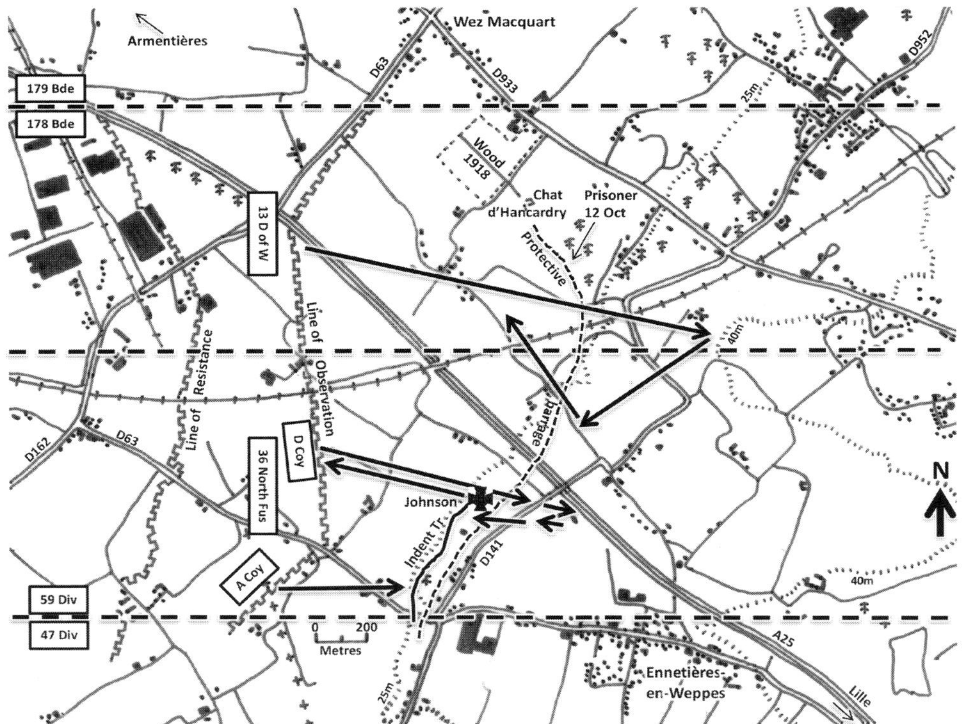

Leave Ennetières-en-Weppes on the D63 westwards. The road descends a gentle ridge. At the D141 crossroads continue straight ahead, signed for Bois Grenier. After 600m turn right onto Rue des Trois Fetus. Follow this road for about 600m and park at the junction on the left. Look southeast to the ridge line where the patrol action took place. Continue for 150m to a T-junction and follow the route to the right along Rue Aubry to head back towards the ridge. Pass some farm buildings on the right and 150m beyond look right along a deep ditch. This is the northern continuation of the stream in which the patrol sheltered prior to retiring back to their lines. Continue another 275m to a T-junction and turn right onto the D141. About 150m along this road is where the 36th Northumberland Fusiliers patrol crossed before being forced back.

are discrepancies over the date of this action, which is variously quoted as 13th, 14th or even as late as 20th October in the 59th Division history. However, the body of evidence indicates it occurred on the 14th. The 178th Brigade had taken over the front from 177th Brigade on the night of 10th/11th October. On the right was 36th Northumberland Fusiliers and 13th Duke of Wellington's was on the left, with 11th Royal Scots Fusiliers in Brigade reserve. Battalions were ordered to send out patrols early every morning to check that the enemy was still holding his positions on the ridge in front.

On 12th October a patrol, led by Lieutenant AT Bradley, captured a prisoner who stated that the enemy was to withdraw on the night of 12th/13th October. The 178th Brigade and 36th Northumberland Fusiliers' war diaries state that it was a Northumberland Fusiliers patrol, but the prisoner was taken well inside 13th Duke of Wellington's area. The withdrawal did not occur that night and HQ 178th Brigade ordered two fighting patrols, one from each forward battalion, to advance at 5.00 a.m. on 14th October. Each patrol was to consist of one platoon, covered by a screen and supported by a second platoon. The aim was to ascertain if the ridge southeast of Wez Macquart had been abandoned. Every effort was to be made to take a prisoner. The remainder of each battalion was warned to be ready to advance at short notice.

For an unspecified reason 36th Northumberland Fusiliers sent out two patrols, one each from A and D Companies. B and C Companies were to move forward

From the junction on Rue des Trois Fetus looking east. The A25 Autoroute is on the far left. Johnson's patrol advanced up the ridge from the right of picture towards the wood on the skyline in the centre. The stream is marked by a line of dark bushes across the centre of the picture in the middle ground at the base of the ridge.

to occupy the positions vacated by the forward companies if they advanced. The patrols were to report progress every half hour. A Company on the right ran into heavy machine gun fire from the ridge and, as the battalion on that flank was not to advance, a protective flank had to be formed from the ridge to the junction with the flanking battalion.

The platoon commanders in D Company on the left were Second Lieutenant Robert Woodward (14 Platoon attached from 5th Battalion) and **Second Lieutenant James Johnson** (13 Platoon). The enemy appeared to be demoralised and six surrendered immediately, together with a machine gun. They were sent back and another fifteen prisoners were taken. They were also sent back but drifted into 13th Duke of Wellington's hands. A sunken road was occupied on top of the ridge.

Meanwhile 13th Duke of Wellington's had penetrated a considerable distance into the enemy lines. The patrol's left flank was open and a covering party was sent out to face a small wood immediately south of Wez Macquart. This party suffered heavy casualties from machine guns on a light railway just north of d'Hancardry Chateau. The fighting patrol noticed enemy parties working around its flanks. They were held off by two Lewis guns and the patrol retired to a road in 36th Northumberland Fusiliers' area, close to its patrol. More enemy parties tried to get around the flanks and the 13th Duke of Wellington's patrol dispersed them with Lewis gun fire before withdrawing further to the northwest, i.e. away from the 36th Northumberland Fusiliers' patrol.

The Brigade post action report and 13th Duke of Wellington's war diary suggest that the two fighting patrols were separate and made their own way back to their

lines. However, other accounts, particularly that by former 79118 Acting Corporal Edward Foulkes DCM MM, and 36th Northumberland Fusiliers' war diary are clear that the two fighting patrols became mixed up. As a result, many in the 13th Duke of Wellington's patrol acted under orders from the 36th Northumberland Fusiliers officers in the withdrawal. Except where stated otherwise, the remainder of this account is based upon the 36th Northumberland Fusiliers' sources.

A party of the enemy, including three officers, emerged from a pillbox and surrendered, except for a machine gunner, who had to be dealt with by a grenade. The advance proceeded another one hundred metres eastwards from the sunken road. A German officer was seen leading a party along a hedge before taking up positions on a road. From there it poured enfilade fire into the patrol, which was forced to retire back to the sunken road.

Corporal Foulkes was not initially chosen for the patrol. He had spent days observing the ridge and believed that his knowledge would be valuable. He soon caught up with his pockets stuffed with Mills bombs. Johnson called him a bloody fool and then ordered him to deal with some machine guns, which he did and then held on to an advanced position for some time. Foulkes wisely reconnoitred a possible escape route along a trench that ran down the ridge and joined a ditch at right angles. He distributed a stock of German stick grenades to ward off counterattacks.

A German pillbox on top of the ridge, possibly the one from which the enemy surrendered. It is certainly on the line of advance of the 36th Northumberland Fusiliers patrol. The prominent tree on the right is on the side of the D141, which runs left to right across the picture just out of sight in a slight dip. It was described as a sunken road in the post operation reports. The pillbox could also possibly be the one bombed by Corporal Foulkes when he went to look for Lance Corporal Wilkinson and two other men.

The northern end of the ditch/stream used by the patrol for shelter before attempting the hazardous retirement back to their lines on the far right of picture.

Lieutenant Woodward arrived. His batman, Private Stevenson was wounded on the way. Woodward was pleased with Foulkes' dispositions and followed his escape route down the ridge, promising to send word when the position was to be withdrawn. The Germans had by this time outflanked the patrol and another withdrawal took place to just east of Indent Trench. No man's land was covered by enemy machine guns on the flanks, making retirement to the British lines extremely hazardous.

At 6.30 a.m. the Germans cheered and launched a strong counterattack over the ridge. Five Lewis guns were brought to bear and the Germans were forced back. They then made a number of attempts to infiltrate around both flanks of the small party but were repulsed on each occasion. Enemy snipers in trees picked off the unwary. Any walking wounded who tried to return over no man's land were invariably shot down. At 7.00 a.m. a German box barrage fell around the party and another loud cheer was heard.

Foulkes waited for some time in his exposed forward position but eventually went back with a runner to see what the officers were planning. He was not pleased with Woodward and told him so! The four officers (two from each Battalion) had conferred and decided that they would eventually have to make a run for it back to the British lines. Foulkes sent his runner to bring in his men and they came running back. As they were about to move off, Foulkes realised that Lance Corporal Wilkinson and two other men were missing because they had not been informed by the runner. Foulkes received Johnson's consent to return and went to warn the three men in their isolated post. He set off, with the pin of a grenade already extracted. On the way he heard German voices and, peering into a side trench, saw a German officer and a party of soldiers setting up two machine guns under a concrete cupola. Foulkes threw the grenade, which killed or injured the entire party, except for one man. Foulkes tried to take him prisoner but he went for him and Foulkes choked him to death. Foulkes then picked up the German officer's pistol and binoculars and

Looking north-easterly along the D141. A bridge on the A25 Autoroute is in the left background. Johnson's patrol ascended the ridge on the left and crossed the road just right of the centre of picture before returning by roughly the same route.

rushed off to find Wilkinson. His party was firing at a German machine gun post and was unaware how isolated he had been for about an hour. Foulkes guided them back at a run to the main party.

Foulkes then went back to rescue Private Stevenson, Lieutenant Woodward's batman, from an exposed position, while Corporal Williams covered him. Foulkes dashed into the open and got Stevenson into cover. He then rescued a Duke of Wellington's NCO with a shattered leg and another man, on his own, while exposed to enemy fire. Back in the trench he realised that Williams had either been captured or had already withdrawn (it was the latter). On his own, Foulkes brought in all three men, the last taking him twenty minutes to cover about twenty metres with the wounded man strapped to his back with a rifle sling. He was also blown up by a shell while dragging the last man into cover. Utterly exhausted after this enormous effort, he rejoined the main party.

However, there was to be no respite. Johnson told Foulkes to get eleven walking wounded back and the Duke of Wellington's NCO, who was on a stretcher, while the able bodied covered them. After one hundred metres they reached a stream filled with barbed wire and attempted to cross by a tree trunk bridge. They came under close-range machine gun fire. The man that Foulkes was supporting was hit twice more and killed. The survivors took cover in the stream. The machine gun continued to engage any movement. Foulkes had his head against the log and spent most of the time singing the Wesley hymn, *Jesu, lover of my soul*, which includes the appropriate line, *Hide me, O my Saviour, hide till the storm of life be past*.

One of the Duke of Wellington's officers volunteered to go back to describe their plight, but he was killed crossing the stream. Meanwhile the main party was under constant attack. The Germans shouted, *Tea up Tommy*, as they threw grenades in response to the British, *Stir your tea with this Fritz*. 316318 Private (later Acting

Corporal) Cyril Henry Clark broke up another attack with a Lewis gun (DCM for this action). The Germans called upon the party to give up and three men went to surrender, but Johnson was having none of it. Grabbing a rifle, he ran along the outside of the ditch in which his small force was sheltering, jumped into the next trench, shot a German officer and drove the three back. His response was simple and uncompromising, *I'll shoot any bastard, officer or man, that offers to surrender.*

Eventually an airman flying over the scene reported the situation, having broken up an attack with his own machine gun. A protective barrage was arranged to last for ten minutes, during which it was every man for himself. The Duke of Wellington's company commander managed to get through to the beleaguered party with the details, but he was killed just after delivering the message.

The barrage came down at 12.15 p.m. and, under cover of this and the Brigade's machine guns, they started running back, while Johnson kept the enemy at bay. Foulkes checked the men around him, but they had all been killed. Having emptied his revolver, Johnson threw it into a German officers' face, picked up his wounded batman and carried him back towards the British lines. The man was hit in the head and killed as Johnson crossed the log bridge guided by Foulkes. Johnson carried the dead man back for a decent burial. Many others were hit in the mad scramble over no man's land. Foulkes covered Johnson with a rifle picked up from one of the dead. The two of them were the last into the line held by 11th Royal Scots Fusiliers.

Johnson noticed some men moving in no man's land and with Foulkes went back and carried them to the shelter of a shell hole. They were made as comfortable as possible, their wounds were dressed and they were left with rum and water. On returning to the British lines Johnson was assured that the wounded would be recovered after dark by the relieving unit. Only seventeen Northumberland Fusiliers returned unharmed of the forty-two who set out. Five were killed, nine wounded and eleven were unaccounted for (CWGC record seven fatalities). Four Lewis guns were also lost. However, heavy losses had been inflicted on an already demoralised enemy and twenty-one prisoners were brought in along with a machine gun.

The members of 36th Battalion engaged in this action were awarded a VC (Johnson), a DSO, two DCMs (Foulkes and Clark), a MC Bar, two MCs (Captain Robert William Wright, attached from 25th Battalion, and Lieutenant Woodward) and twelve MMs (including 315911 Sergeant James Stirton, 62396 Corporal Robert Fingland, 316355 Private (later Lance Corporal) GW Dawson, Private Maxwell/Gladwell and 316717 Private E Green), which was quite a feat. News of the award of the VC to Johnson came through on Christmas Eve and, in a touching gesture, the GOC gave Foulkes the job of telling him. Edward Foulkes (1895–1989) was recommended for the VC but it was downgraded to the DCM. He also served during the Second World War, during which he was wounded five times. He was awarded the MBE for services to the Dunkirk Veterans' Association in 1981.

The 13th Duke of Wellington's war diary makes no mention of its patrol being mixed up with that of 36th Northumberland Fusiliers. It says that its patrol was counterattacked three times before the final withdrawal. The British artillery barrage came down from 11.45 a.m. until 12.15 p.m. A British airman was also brought down around this time. The patrol returned having suffered thirty-one casualties – two officers (Acting Captain Arnold Fairbairns, attached from 10th Yorkshire, and Second Lieutenant JA Lamb, attached from 4th West Yorkshire) and four other ranks killed (CWGC record ten fatalities), nineteen wounded and six missing, including Lieutenant Herbert Ernest Lewis Priday (he does not appear in CWGC records). A barrage was put down for half an hour from 8.00 p.m. to cover patrols sent out to recover the bodies in no man's land.

By 8.30 p.m. on 14th October 36th Northumberland Fusiliers had been relieved by 11th Royal Scots Fusiliers. Three days later, when the area had been evacuated by the Germans, the ground was checked. Foulkes came upon the body of Stevenson, the man he had rescued. He was in the process of ripping the identity disks from Stevenson's neck, when the 'corpse' opened its eyes and in no uncertain terms asked Foulkes where he had been! He was sent back with the stretcher bearers. Johnson had a less happy outcome. He found seven men dead of exposure in the shell hole where he left the wounded and had to be restrained in his anger from going after the Royal Scots Fusiliers.

Biographies

LIEUTENANT WALLACE LLOYD ALGIE
20th Battalion (Central Ontario), Canadian Expeditionary Force

Wallace Algie was born on 10th June 1891 at Alton, Peel Co, Ontario, Canada. His father, James Algie MD (8th April 1858–16th January 1928), was born at Dumfries Township, Ontario. He graduated from Trinity Medical College, Toronto, Ontario and was licensed to practice as a physician and surgeon in 1878 at Ayr, North Dumfries, Ontario. He moved the following year to Alton, near Caledon Township, Peel Co. He married Rachel (also seen as Rachael) née Jago (10th July 1857–3rd December 1917), born at Camelford, Cornwall, England, on 13th October 1880 at Rockwood, Eramosa Township, Wellington Co, Ontario. She had emigrated to Canada in 1875. James purchased Archibald Dick House, 1581 Queen Street East, Alton in 1883. In 1884 he was appointed Medical Officer for Caledon Township and his first action was to rebuke the inhabitants of Alton, Caledon East, Charleston (Caledon Village), Mono Mills and Belfountain for their unsanitary habits. James went on to pioneer the establishment of public health standards. He was also a novelist and published several works under the pen name 'Wallace Lloyd' including, *The Sword of Glenvohr*, *Houses of Glass: A Philosophical Romance* in 1898 and *Bergan Worth*. The family moved to Cardwell, Ontario in 1891 and to Toronto in 1908, living at 1155 King Street. He was appointed surgeon to the Central Prison and the Hospital for the Insane, both in Toronto. By 1916 they had moved to 75 Dewson Street. James lived at 1 Mulgrave Apartments, 378 Markham Street, Toronto from August 1917 and at 57 MacPherson Avenue, Toronto from May 1918. He spent time at St Petersburg, Florida, USA, where he met Cordelia Shelby Thornton (14th April 1885–1945), born in Georgia, USA, and they married on 12th June 1923

Wallace's father, James Algie.

Camelford, in north Cornwall on the River Camel, is sixteen kilometres north of Bodmin, close to Bodmin Moor. It has been linked to the legendary Camelot, the Battle of Camlann and another battle at Gafulford but other evidence suggests the two battles took place elsewhere. The town elected two members to Parliament from 1552 but it was a rotten borough. In 1832 the constituency was abolished and the town became part of East Cornwall constituency. The parish church is at Lanteglos by Camelford, dedicated to St Julitta. A chapel of St Thomas was recorded in 1312. John Wesley, founder of Methodism, visited Camelford on several occasions.

There was a Medical Faculty at Trinity College from 1850 but, despite its success, all six founding members resigned in 1856. The re-establishment of a medical school at Trinity was considered in 1863, 1866 and 1867 but nothing came of it. In 1870 four of the founding members of the former medical faculty were appointed provisionally as a board of medical examiners for Trinity College. In 1871 they were appointed the first professors of the new Trinity Medical Faculty. By the end of the year a new building had been constructed close to Toronto General Hospital. Trinity Medical Faculty developed a strong reputation for quality medical education and training. In 1877 the Faculty became an independent teaching body as Trinity Medical School. By 1879 a new wing had been built but there was a growing view within the provincial government that competing medical schools could no longer provide satisfactory medical education and a single publicly financed medical teaching faculty in Toronto was the way ahead. As a result, in 1887 Trinity Medical School and Toronto School of Medicine were invited to join as the medical faculty of the University of Toronto. The Toronto School of Medicine accepted. Trinity Medical School refused and the Corporation of Trinity provided some funds to improve teaching facilities and purchase equipment in order to raise the faculty to college status in 1888, when Trinity Medical School became Trinity Medical College. However, during the 1890s there were mounting deficits and falling registration and in April 1903 Trinity Medical College surrendered its charter to Trinity University and in July the Corporation of Trinity College formally constituted the Corporation of Trinity Medical College as the medical faculty of Trinity University. Federation with the University of Toronto was finally agreed in October 1904.

at Clarke Co, Georgia. She was the sister of Eunice Thornton, who married the VCs uncle, Dr Thomas Jago. James committed suicide at St Petersburg by consuming potassium cyanide. Cordelia stated that he had been troubled by financial matters and had previously threatened to end his life. Cordelia married John Boyd Jones (c.1870–23rd January 1946), born at Beaufort Co, North Carolina, USA, on 26th May 1934 at Hillsborough Co, Florida. John had married Hattie Cook Hord (10th August 1877–20th October 1926), born at Mason Co, Kentucky, USA. She died at Chicago, Illinois. Wallace had three sisters:

- Ada Esme Algie (7th February 1882–15th February 1955), born at Brampton, Peel Co, was a stenographer in 1901. She married

John Stewart Skeaff (8th December 1863–16th February 1941), born at Cromdale, Morayshire, Scotland, on 8th October 1919 at Toronto. He was a banker and emigrated to Canada in 1882. They were living in Cardwell, Caledon Township in 1891 and 1901, at Toronto in 1911 and at 26 St Andrew's Gardens, Toronto by 1921. John returned to Canada aboard SS *Letitia*, embarking at Glasgow on 7th September 1928 after a visit to Scotland and disembarked at Québec on 16th September. They moved to St Petersburg, Florida, USA in 1929 and were known to have lived there until at least 1937. They returned to 26 St Andrew's Gardens, Toronto. They had two sons:

1581 Queen Street East, Alton was purchased by James Algie in 1883.

- Lloyd John Murray Skeaff (born 6th April 1921) was an engineer educated at Springfield College, Springfield, Massachusetts, USA. He married Mary Elizabeth Wemp (born 4th July 1924). He was a supervisor in 1957, when they were living at 34 Tangmere Road, Scarborough, York Co, Ontario and at 5 Whitefriars Drive, Scarborough in 1965. By 1972 he was a coordinator, living at 39 Dalton Crescent, Simcoe North, Ontario.
- Forbes Mowat Skeaff (1922–13th May 2003) married Thelma Reeves. He served in the Royal Canadian Air Force and was stationed at Falconbridge, Nickel Belt, Ontario in 1958. Thelma was on the electoral roll for Lac St-Denis, Québec in 1963.

John Skeaff had married Edith Alice Polson Murray (6th April 1871–15th October 1917) on 6th May 1895 at Montréal. She was the daughter of

Toronto Central Prison, also known as the Central Prison for Men or Toronto Jail, was a 336-bed facility at the intersection of King Street and Strachan Avenue. It opened in 1873 as an industrial facility, manufacturing railway cars for the Canada Car Co. Although it was an example of a modern penal facility, by the 1880s it had gained a reputation for brutality. In 1915 the prison was closed to be replaced by the Ontario Reformatory in Guelph. During the Great War it was used by the Army and was also a processing centre for immigrants. In 1920 the main prison building was demolished and today all that remains are the RC chapel and a wall of the prison's paint shop, which is part of the east wall of AR Williams Co Liberty Storage Warehouse.

In 1846 construction began on the first Provincial Lunatic Asylum, the largest and most modern building in British North America at the time. The Asylum opened on 26th January 1850 with 250 beds and the first 211 patients were transferred from a temporary asylum in a former jail. In 1852 a brick wall on the north, east and west sides of the property was completed and in 1860 along the south side. Between 1866 and 1869 new east and west wings were added to ease severe overcrowding. The facility changed its name in 1871 to Asylum for the Insane, Toronto. In 1889 two brick workshop buildings were constructed for use by skilled trades. In 1905 the name changed to Hospital for the Insane, Toronto and in 1966 to Queen Street Mental Health Centre. By 1974 four new Active Treatment Units had been constructed, each with 250 beds. As each of the four new units was completed, the patients were moved over from the 1850 asylum building, which was demolished in 1976, followed in 1978 by the former Superintendent's Residence, later the Nurses' Residence. The 1970s saw the inpatient population decline from 1,600 to 4–500. In 1998 the Centre for Addiction and Mental Health was formed by merging the Queen Street Mental Health Centre, the Clarke Institute of Psychiatry, the Addiction Research Foundation and the Donwood Institute. Between 2006 and 2008 new buildings were constructed in a major Queen Street Redevelopment Project.

James Clark Murray (1836–1917) and Margaret Smith Polson (1844–1927), of 340 Wood Avenue, Montréal. John Clark Murray FRSC was educated at Paisley Grammar School, Renfrewshire and the Universities of Glasgow, Edinburgh, Heidelberg and Göttingen. He was Professor of Philosophy and Chair of Mental and Moral Philosophy at Queen's College, Kingston, Ontario 1862–72. He was then appointed Frothingham Professor of Mental and Moral Philosophy at McGill University, Montréal 1872–1903. He also lectured at Montréal Ladies' Educational Association, Kingston Ladies Educational Association, Glenmore Summer School of Philosophy, the Cooper Union, the People's Institute in New York City and the Presbyterian College of Montréal. His advocacy of equality for women caused friction with McGill's Principal, John William Dawson, and Murray was forced to retire in 1903. He was one of the original members of the Royal Society of Canada and his wife, Margaret, founded the Imperial Order Daughters of the Empire in 1900. Edith was living at 3 Cotswold Court Apartments, 164 Cumberland Street, Toronto when her sons, James and John, enlisted in 1915. She died at Muskoka Cottage Sanitorium, Gravenhurst, Ontario. John and Edith had three sons:

- John Murray Skeaff (14th April 1896–24th January 1916) was a banker when he enlisted in the CEF on 28th August 1915 at Toronto, having previously served for two weeks in 92nd Highlanders and one month in 48th Highlanders, attached to 198th Battalion. He was described as 5′ 10″ tall, with fair complexion, brown eyes, red hair and his religious denomination was Presbyterian. He was commissioned as a lieutenant in 92nd Battalion and died of pneumonia (Toronto (Mount Pleasant) Cemetery, Ontario – Lot 10, Section 22, Plot G, Grave 1).

The grave of John Murray Skeaff and other members of the family in Toronto (Mount Pleasant) Cemetery.

- ◦ James Michie Skeaff (11th January 1899–19th March 1976) was a clerk when he enlisted in the CEF at Ottawa on 15th March 1917 and was commissioned as a lieutenant in 235th Battalion the same day. He was described as 5′ 10¾″ tall and his religious denomination was Presbyterian. He had served previously in 48th Regiment (Militia) and was attached for five months to 198th Battalion for training. He transferred to the Forestry Department CEF in Toronto on 23rd April. At Camp Borden he made a will on 31st July, leaving his estate to his mother. He embarked for England aboard SS *Missanabie* at Halifax, Nova Scotia with a Canadian Railway Troops Draft on 11th August and disembarked at Liverpool on 23rd August. James was taken on the strength of Canadian Railway Troops Depot, Purfleet next day but was returned to Canada on 15th September surplus to establishment. He was taken on the strength of Forestry and Railway Construction Depot No.2 on 27th September. On 19th November he made a new will at Exhibition Camp, Toronto, leaving his estate split equally between his father and brother, Stewart. James embarked aboard SS *Grampian* with a Forestry Draft at St John, New Brunswick on 18th December, disembarked at Glasgow on 31st December and was taken on the strength of the Canadian Forestry Corps Base Depot, Sunningdale. On 28th January 1918 he was posted to HQ Canadians, Shorncliffe, Kent and attached to 8th Reserve Battalion there until 19th February. On 22nd February he was struck off the strength of the CEF and resigned his commission to accept a commission in the Oxfordshire & Buckinghamshire Light Infantry as a lieutenant on 28th February 1918. He appears under the Regular and Service Battalions in the Army List until May 1920. On returning to Canada he became a stockbroker, living at 584 Church Street, York, Ontario. He married Estelle Margaret Milne (30th April 1900–19th January 1991), born at St Machar, Aberdeen, Aberdeenshire, Scotland, on 5th January 1928 at York. Estelle was living at 282 Jarvis Street, York at the time.
- ◦ Stewart Munroe Skeaff (25th February 1904–28th May 1982).

- Ethel Algie (18th April 1885–10th May 1973), born at Alton, Peel Co, married Vernon Robert Ide (28th April 1876–27th January 1938), a cashier, born at Etobicoke Township, York Co, on 25th October 1911 at Toronto. He was an

accountant in 1921 when they were living at Etobicoke Township. She was living with her children at 14 Sunnybrook Road, York West, Ontario in 1945. They had two children:
  - Audrey Velma Ide (born 28th January 1913) was a librarian in 1945.
  - Robert W Ide (26th July 1916–10th August 2007) was on active service in 1945. He married Catherine W Maver (7th December 1917–2nd December 2008).
- Bessie Algie (18th December 1887–6th December 1980) was a nurse at the General Hospital, Toronto, living at 481 Shaw Street, Toronto. She married Alexander McPhee Maver (26th March 1886–30th March 1937), a commercial traveller, born at Wentworth, Ontario, on 28th June 1924 at Toronto. He was living at 579 Sherbourne Street, Toronto at the time.

Wallace's paternal grandfather, Matthew Algie (c.1821–12th February 1905), born at Glasgow, Lanarkshire, Scotland, was a cotton hand loom weaver in 1841, living with his family at Shawhill Street, Eastwood, Renfrewshire. He married Janet née Wallace (born c.1822) at Glasgow, Lanarkshire, on 10th December 1845 at Eastwood, Renfrewshire and they emigrated to Ontario c.1851. By 1871 he was a miller, living with his family at North Dumfries, Waterloo South, Ontario. By 1891 he was an oatmeal miller and they were living at Cardwell, Caledon, Ontario. He was living at Alton, Peel Co at the time of his death there. In addition to James they had six other children:

- Elizabeth Algie (5th May 1848–9th May 1904), born in Scotland, was a dressmaker in 1871, living with her parents. She married William Henry Thuresson (c.1838–16th December 1898), born at Picton, Prince Edward Co, Ontario of Swedish origin, on 21st October 1876 at Paris, Brant Co, Ontario. He was a manufacturer in 1881, when they were living at Ancaster, Wentworth South, Ontario. By 1889 he was a hotel keeper at Owen Sound, Grey Co, Ontario. Elizabeth was living with her children at Cardwell, Caledon in 1891 but her husband was not with them. William died at Bridgeburg, Welland Co, Ontario and Elizabeth at Peel Co, Ontario. They had six children:
  - Jennie Maud Thuresson (1878–1933).
  - Twins Lulu May 'Agnes' Thuresson and Mabel Clare Thuresson (1880).
  - Jane Brandon Thuresson (1882).
  - Robert Matthew Thuresson (1885–1909).
  - Jesse Henderson Thuresson (John in his British Army service record) (1890–1938), born at Owen Sound, Ontario, was an insurance agent living at 373 Broadway, Winnipeg, Manitoba when he enlisted in the Winnipeg Company, 196th Battalion CEF at Camp Hughes on 26th May 1916 (910215). He was attested and taken on strength at St Vital, Manitoba on 19th June. His next of kin was his sister, Mrs Forbes Davidson, living at corner of Osler &

Balfour Avenue, Vancouver, British Columbia. He was described as 5′ 7½″ tall, weighing 154 lbs, with fair complexion, blue eyes, fair hair and his religious denomination was Presbyterian. He was appointed acting corporal on 1st September. On 11th October he made a will leaving everything to Mrs Ralph L Netherby, 223 Fern Avenue, Toronto. Jesse embarked aboard SS *Southland* at Halifax, Nova Scotia on 31st October and disembarked in Liverpool, England on 11th November. He was promoted lance corporal on 19th November and joined 19th Reserve Battalion, Seaford, Sussex on 31st December. Appointed acting sergeant on 2nd March 1917 and applied for a commission on 27th June, by when 19th Reserve Battalion had moved to Bramshott, Hampshire. He was 5′8½″ tall and weighed 160 lbs. He joined No.16 Officer Cadet Battalion, Kinmel Park, Rhyl, Denbighshire on 1st September. Jesse was appointed to a commission in 8th London Regiment on 29th January 1918. He served in France from 30th April and was treated at 2nd General Hospital, Le Havre for influenza for five days and was discharged to the Base Depot on 9th May. A medical board at the Base Depot, Harfleur, Le Havre on 14th May found him fit for General Service. Jesse was attached to 2/10th London when he was seriously wounded at Morlancourt on 24th August by a gunshot to the right shoulder and shrapnel to the right ribs/side and back. He was evacuated to Britain on 26th August from Le Havre and disembarked at Southampton next day. A medical board at Empress Eugenie's Officers' Hospital, Farnborough, Hampshire on 2nd September found him unfit for service for two months. A medical board at Cambridge Military Hospital, Aldershot on 1st November also found him unfit for service for two months. He was treated at Cliff Hydro Auxiliary Hospital, Ilfracombe, Devon. He was granted leave to 31st December and a wound gratuity of £83/6/8. He was admitted to 3rd London General Hospital, Wandsworth, London on 4th February 1919. A medical board there on 6th February found him fit and he reported to the dispersal officer there. He was released from the Repatriation Camp, Winchester, Hampshire on 10th April 1919 and his service ended on 28th April. He gave his address as 1092 Broughton Street, Vancouver, British Columbia, Canada. He received a gratuity of £97/13/- and was belatedly promoted lieutenant on 30th July 1919.

- William Wallace Algie (16th February 1850–1st February 1914), born at Alton, Caledon, Peel Co, Ontario, was a carder and spinner living with his parents at the time of the 1871 Census. He married Phoebe Ann Ward (18th September 1852–1942), a wool manufacturer born at Watertown, Massachusetts, USA, on 25th December 1871 at Ancaster, Wentworth, Ontario. William played for the Alton Aetnas Baseball Team in 1890. They were living at Cardwell, Caledon in 1891. William died at Alton. Phoebe was living at 91 Hadwen Road, Worcester,

Massachusetts in 1939, where she subsequently died. They had six children – Janet Algie (1874–1945), William Algie (1877), James Algie (1880–1947), Constance Algie (1882), Cordelia Algie (1885) and Phoebe Algie (1889).

- Janet Algie (1853–85), born at Ayr, Waterloo, Ontario, married James Wellington Culligan (1st May 1860–4th July 1934), a spinner born at Streetsville, Chinquacousy, Peel Co, Ontario on 4th January 1881 at Waterloo, Ontario. Janet died at Caledon, Peel Co. They had three children – William Algie Culligan (1881–1951), Janet 'Nettie' Culligan (1883–1962) and Charles August Culligan (1885–1950). James married Elizabeth Ann Algie née Little (11th May 1861–10th March 1945), born at Caledon, Peel Co, on 1st January 1889 at Dundalk, Southgate, Grey Co, Ontario. She had been married previously to Janet Algie's brother, Mathew Algie, in 1882. James was a spinner in a woollen mill in 1911, when they were living at Alton. Both James and Elizabeth subsequently died there. They had three daughters – Irene Culligan (1889–1930), Ethel Culligan (1891–1975) and Edith Myrrel Culligan (1903–40).
- Agnes 'Aggie' Algie (12th November 1854–22nd April 1911) was a weaver in 1871, living with her parents and was still with them in 1891. Her death at 31 Havelock Road, Parkdale, Toronto was certified by her brother, James.
- Mathew Algie (c.1855–13th October 1884) married Elizabeth 'Lizzie' Ann Little (11th May 1861–10th March 1945) on 25th December 1882 at Caledon, Peel Co, where she was born. They had a daughter, Lucinda May Algie (1883–1980). Matthew died at Alton and Elizabeth married James Wellington Culligan on 1st January 1889 at Dundalk, Southgate, Grey, Ontario. He had been married previously to Mathew Algie's sister, Janet Algie.
- Robert Algie (17th July 1862–3rd April 1944) married Harriet 'Hattie' Beatrice Sells (11th May 1865–30th December 1930), born at Vienna, Ontario, on 5th December 1885 at Toronto. He was the coach of the Alton Aetnas Basketball Team in 1890. In 1891 he was a merchant and they were living at Cardwell, Caledon. In 1911 he was a real estate agent and they were living at 31 Havelock Street, Parkdale, Toronto. By 1921 he was an accountant and was still at 31 Havelock Street. They had eight children:
  - Gertrude 'Gertie' Algie (1887–1945).
  - Harriet 'Hattie' Algie (1890–1952).
  - Jessie Algie (1892).
  - Robert Laird Algie (1893–1965) was a clerk when he enlisted in 3rd Canadian Division Cyclists Company at Toronto on 15th November 1915 (540501). He had served previously for three years in the Queen's Own Rifles of Canada. He was described as 5′ 8½″ tall, weighing 161 lbs, with fresh complexion, blue eyes, fair hair and his religious denomination was Presbyterian. Promoted lance corporal on 29th November. On 22nd January 1916 he embarked with the unit aboard SS *Missanabie* at Halifax, Nova Scotia and disembarked at Plymouth, Devon on 30th January. The unit was attached to the Canadian

Reserve Cyclist Company, Chiseldon Camp, Swindon, Wiltshire and arrived in France on 27th March. Robert assigned $20 per month from his Army pay to his sister, Hattie, from 1st April and was promoted corporal on 17th May. He transferred to 4th Divisional Cyclist Company on 18th May, to 74th Battalion at Bramshott, Hampshire on 9th June and to 102nd Battalion on 15th July. He embarked for France on 11th August and landed at Le Havre next day. On 15th February 1917 he was promoted lance sergeant and sergeant on 19th April. He was granted ten days leave 29th July–9th August and fourteen days in Paris 8th-23rd March 1918. He returned to England on 31st October and was taken on the strength of 1st Reserve Battalion, British Columbia Regiment Depot, Seaford on 2nd November, pending officer training. However, the war ended before this commenced and he transferred to 8th Reserve Battalion on 26th November. He was granted leave in Edinburgh 3rd-17th December and transferred to 3rd Reserve Battalion on 20th December. On 19th January 1919 he had a medical at Witley, Surrey. He embarked aboard RMS *Grampian* at Liverpool on 24th January and disembarked at St John, New Brunswick on 2nd February. Having had a discharge medical at Exhibition Camp, Toronto on 18th February, he was discharged from No.2 District Depot on 22nd February 1919.
  - Marie Agnes Algie (1896).
  - Grace Sells Algie (1898).
  - Jean Alexandria Algie (1900).
  - Nellie Elizabeth Algie (1907).

His maternal grandfather, William Henry Jago (8th June 1824–11th September 1907), born at Bodmin, Cornwall, England, was a woolcomber in 1854, living at Callington. He married Elizabeth née Nichols/Nicholls (15th July 1832–27th March 1908), born at Lanteglos, near Camelford, Cornwall, on 25th December 1854 at Lanteglos Parish Church. William was a fishmonger and Elizabeth was a dressmaker in 1861, when they were living at Tregoodwell Village, Lanteglos. By 1881 he was a glove manufacturer and they were living at Eramosa Township, Wellington Co, Ontario and were still there in 1901. He died at Simcoe, Norfolk, Ontario and she at Toronto, Ontario. In addition to Rachel they had seven other children:

- Sarah Jane Jago (10th May 1855–23rd February 1935), born at Lanteglos, married Richard Arthur Algernon Dunbar (6th December 1849–8th September 1917), a book agent, on 9th February 1874 at Eramosa Township. They lived at Caledon, Bardwell, Ontario and by April 1917 they were living at 22 Glasgow Street, Guelph, Ontario. Richard died at St Joseph's Hospital, Guelph and Sarah at York, Ontario. She was living at 308 Glenayr Avenue, Toronto at the time. They had seven children:
  - Mary Dunbar (1876).
  - Dorothy 'Dora' J Dunbar (1878).

Bodmin was formerly the county town of Cornwall and for most of its history the tin industry was the mainstay of its economy. St Peroc founded a monastery there in the 6th century, which lost some of its lands at the time of the Norman Conquest. Despite this, Bodmin is the only large Cornish settlement recorded in the Domesday Book in 1086. The Black Death killed half of the population in the 14th century. The Norman church of St Petroc was rebuilt in 1469–72 and is one of the largest churches in Cornwall. The tower, which remains from the original Norman church, lost its spire in 1699. There have been three Cornish uprisings centred on Bodmin. In the 1497 Cornish Rebellion an army marched to Blackheath, London, where it was defeated by the King's army. That autumn Perkin Warbeck was proclaimed King Richard IV in Bodmin and tried to usurp Henry VII, who had little difficulty in crushing the uprising. In 1549 the lower classes of Cornwall and Devon, who were strongly Roman Catholic, rose up when the Protestant Edward VI tried to impose a new Prayer Book. A Cornish army formed in Bodmin and lay siege to Exeter in Devon, in what became known as the Prayer Book Rebellion. In putting it down, 4,000 people were killed.

Bodmin Jail, built in the late 18th century, was the first British prison to hold prisoners in separate cells, up to ten in each, rather than communally. Over fifty prisoners were hanged at the prison and it also held prisoners prior to transportation. During the Great War it held some of Britain's national treasures, including the Domesday Book and the Crown Jewels.

Victoria Barracks, former depot of the Duke of Cornwall's Light Infantry, is now the regimental museum. In 1966 the *Finn VC Estate* was named in honour of James Henry Finn VC, who had lived in the town.

- Ernest Maltravers Dunbar (1879–1915).
- Randolph Churchill Dunbar (1883).
- William Henry Vivian Dunbar (1891).
- Lillian Marguerite Dunbar (1893).
- Roger Arthur Algernon Dunbar (1899–1930) was a bank clerk when he enlisted in 64th Depot Battery CFA CEF at Guelph on 17th April 1917 (335115). He was described as 5′9¼″ tall, with fair complexion, brown eyes, fair hair and his religious denomination was Church of England. He

assigned $17 per month to his mother from his Army pay from 1st June. On 28th May he embarked aboard RMS *Olympic* and disembarked in England on 9th June, where he joined the Reserve Brigade CFA, Shorncliffe, Kent next day. He was struck off strength to 2nd Canadian Reserve Artillery on absorption on 22nd June. He was detached to No.1 Detachment Canadian Army Pay Corps, London on 3rd October and was appointed clerk class II on 3rd November and class I on 1st December. He rejoined the Reserve Brigade on 18th November. On 29th April 1918 he ceased to be attached to the Canadian Reserve Artillery. He was struck off strength to 16th Brigade CFA, Witley on 7th September and proceeded overseas to North Russia aboard HMT *Stephen* on 20th September. Roger joined the unit at Archangel on 1st October and was awarded the MM for gallantry in the field on 27th October. He was appointed paid acting bombardier on 1st December. On 11th June 1919 he embarked aboard HMT *Czaritza* and returned to England on 18th June. He had a discharge medical at Ripon, Yorkshire on 2nd July, embarked aboard RMS *Carmania* at Liverpool on 5th July and disembarked in Canada on 13th July. Roger was demobilised on 15th July from Dispersal Station F, Military District No.4, Montréal as a gunner 1st class clerk/signaller and was issued War Service Badge Class A No.295818.

- John Jago (1859–6th September 1944), born at Camelford, was a glove cutter when he married Florence Sarah Roome (16th June 1860–8th September 1939), born at Toronto, on 25th November 1885 at Rockwood, Wellington Co, Ontario. They were living at Sydenham Street, Simcoe Town, Ontario in 1911. He was a commercial traveller in 1921, when they were living at 363 Cassells Street, North Bay, Nipissing, Ontario. They had two daughters – Irene Florence Jago (1887) and Violet Elizabeth Jago (1894–1943).
- Thomas Edward Jago (2nd July 1862–16th August 1936) was a farmer in 1881, living with his parents. He married Eunice Thornton (6th April 1872–6th January 1934) on 19th November 1901 at Clarke Co, Georgia, USA, where she was born. He was a veterinary surgeon and she was a teacher in a public school, living at Thomas Street, Athens, Clarke Co in 1910 and at 465 College Avenue, Athens in 1928. Eunice was living with her brother, Prince D Thornton and family, in Athens City at the time of the 1930 Census. Eunice and Thomas had three children – William Henry Jago (1902–73), Edward Thornton Jago (1904–05) and Anne 'Annie' R Jago (1906–87).
- Annie Jago (2nd November 1865–6th May 1943) married James Alvin Hamilton (9th February 1866–18th April 1938), born at Fairview, Eramosa Township, Wellington Co, Ontario, on 21st September 1892 at Rockwood, Wellington Co. He was a hotelkeeper and they lived at 999 Queen Street, West Toronto. They had eight children – Claude Wilford Hamilton (1894–1933), Blanche Elizabeth Hamilton (1895–1966), Henry Hamilton (1896), Alva Burnett Hamilton (1897–

1977), Alvin Hamilton (1898), unnamed female (1900), William Frederick Earl Hamilton (1902–78) and Harry Livingstone Hamilton (1906–75).

- Mary Elizabeth Jago (4th July 1869–12th January 1950), born at Rockwood, Wellington Co, was living with his sister Rachel and family in 1891. She married Charles Edward Shaw (31st October 1868–3rd December 1943), born in Ontario, on 21st December 1893 at Fergus, Wellington Co. He was a chemist/druggist in 1901, when they were living at Boissevain Village, Brandon, Manitoba. They had moved to Assiniboia East, Saskatchewan by 1906 and to Queen Street, Victoria, Alberta by 1916. They both died at Vegreville, Alberta. They had eight children:
  - Winifred 'Wynn' Edith Shaw (1894–1985).
  - William Frederick Floyd Shaw (1896–1979) was a farmer when he enlisted at Vegreville on 2nd January 1915 (108531). He had served previously for two years in 19th Alberta Dragoons. He was described as 5′ 8½″ tall, weighing 160 lbs, with light complexion, grey eyes, red hair and his religious denomination was Presbyterian. He sailed from Montréal aboard SS *Megantic* on 12th June and went to France on 22nd September with 3rd Canadian Mounted Rifles. He was admitted to 4th Canadian Field Ambulance on 9th October and transferred to Rawalpindi British General Hospital, Wimereux with a contused left foot on 11th October. He was transferred to No.1 Convalescent Depot, Boulogne on 14th October and whilst there was awarded ten days Field Punishment No.1 for disobeying a lawful command on 12th November. William was discharged to the Base Depot on 22nd November and rejoined the Battalion on 1st December. Promoted lance corporal on 3rd December and transferred to 1st Canadian Mounted Rifles on reorganisation on 2nd January 1916. He was granted ten days leave in England 13th-26th December. He assigned $20 per month from his Army pay to his mother from 1st March 1917 and was appointed CQMS on 9th April. William was treated at 9th Canadian Field Ambulance for an accidental wound to the upper lip 29th September–4th October and was admitted to No.42 Casualty Clearing Station with pyrexia of unknown origin on 11th October. He was transferred to 1st Australian General Hospital, Rouen on 17th October and was evacuated to England with trench fever on 23rd October on the strength of the Saskatchewan Regiment Depot, Bramshott. Next day he was admitted to Reading War Hospital, transferred to the Military Convalescent Hospital, Woodcote Park, Epsom on 22nd November and was discharged to 2nd Canadian Command Depot, Bramshott on 19th December. He joined 15th Reserve Battalion on 22nd February 1918 and was on overseas conducting duty 1st-5th June. On 26th August he joined Syren Party (Special Mission), Witley, attached to 4th Reserve Battalion. He proceeded to the North Russian Expeditionary Force on 17th September and disembarked at Murmansk on 28th September. William returned to England aboard SS *Toloa* on 21st August 1919 and

joined the Canadian Discharge Depot, Buxton, Derbyshire on 29th August. He was struck off strength to Discharge Station I in Canada on embarking aboard SS *Royal George* at Southampton on 20th September, disembarking at Halifax, Nova Scotia on 29th September. William was demobilised from No.2 District Depot, Toronto on 4th October and was issued War Service Badge Class A No.400106.

- Herbert Jago Shaw (1897–1921) was a student when he enlisted in 151st Battalion CEF on 3rd January 1916 at Vegreville (624268). He had served for two years in 19th Alberta Dragoons. He was described as 5′ 6½″ tall, weighing 140 lbs, with sandy/fair complexion, blue eyes, red hair and his religious denomination was Presbyterian. The unit sailed aboard SS *California* on 3rd October and disembarked at Liverpool on 13th October. Herbert transferred to 9th Reserve Battalion, Shorncliffe, Kent the same day and was appointed acting corporal. He went to the Canadian Base Depot, Le Havre, France on 15th November, reverting to private at his own request, and joined 50th Battalion on 21st November. He attended a Lewis gun course 11th-18th February 1917. He was admitted to 11th Canadian Field Ambulance on 22nd May and transferred to 7th General Hospital, St Omer with mumps on 23rd May. On 10th June he was discharged to Details St Omer and rejoined 50th Battalion on 12th June. He was gassed on 21st June and admitted to No.22 Casualty Clearing Station. Next day he was transferred to 24th General Hospital, Étaples, with slight gas poisoning, and was evacuated to Britain aboard HMHS *St Patrick* on 8th July, on the strength of the Alberta Regiment Depot, Bramshott. He was admitted to Dublin Castle Red Cross Hospital next day and was transferred to the Canadian Convalescent Hospital, Bromley, Kent on 11th August. On 17th August he was discharged and joined 2nd Canadian Command Depot, Bramshott. He joined 21st Reserve Battalion on 19th October and was taken on the strength of 50th Battalion in France on 8th December. Next day he joined the Canadian Infantry Base Depot and the Canadian Corps Reinforcement Camp on 15th December. Herbert was granted the Good Conduct Badge on 3rd January 1918 and rejoined 50th Battalion on 10th January. He attended courses at the Canadian Corps Reinforcement Camp 24th-26th March and 3rd May–3rd June. He assigned $15 per month to his mother from his Army pay from 1st April. He was appointed paid acting lance corporal on 3rd September and paid acting corporal on 28th September, later substantive from the same date. Herbert was granted fourteen days' leave to Britain 6th-24th November. On 3rd April 1919 he was promoted lance sergeant at Le Havre and joined the Canadian Concentration Camp, Bramshott on 4th May. On 31st May he was taken on the strength of No.2 District Depot, Toronto on embarking aboard HMT *Mauretania*, disembarked at Halifax,

Nova Scotia on 6th June. Herbert was demobilised on 12th June and was issued War Service Badge Class A No.133153.
  - Algie 'Buster' Wilford Shaw (1899–1974).
  - Mary 'Madge' Marjorie Nicol Shaw (1901–81).
  - Helen Jago Shaw (1903).
  - Mary Elizabeth Shaw (1907).
  - Kathleen Jago Shaw (1908).
- William Henry Jago (10th February 1874–13th December 1943), born at Crewson's Corner, Wellington Co, was a dry goods clerk, living with his sister Rachel and family in 1891. He was a glove maker when he married Jane 'Jean/Jennie' Beattie Croft (12th November 1872–27th April 1932), born at Eramosa Township, on 29th July 1896 at Wellington Co. By 1901 he was a farmer and they were living at Huntsville, Muskoka Co, Ontario. By 1911 he was a liveryman in a stable. They moved to Nugget Block, Klock Avenue, North Bay, Nipissing, Ontario about September 1921 and she subsequently died there. They had three children – Edythe Madelson Jago 1900, Wilfred Jago 1902 and Floyd Jago 1905. William was a salesman when he married Mary Adeline Richard née Laing (born 28th June 1886), his housekeeper born at Puslinch, Wellington Co, on 29th April 1933. They lived at 444 Runnymede Road, Toronto. They were living at 50 High Street, Barrie, Simcoe at the time of his death at the Royal Victoria Hospital, Barrie. Mary had married William Ernest Richard (16th May 1878–6th March 1923), a salesman born at Elgin Co, Ontario, on 11th September 1912 at Huntsville, Muskoka Co. They were living at Brunel Street, Huntsville, Ontario in 1921. They had three children including, Donald Alexander Richard (born and died 1918) and Ernest Dean Richard (1921–2002).
- Richard Frederick Jago (12th February 1876–5th September 1961), a tanner born at Rockwood, Wellington Co, married Alice Grace Elsworth (21st November 1873–14th December 1940), on 4th April 1901 at Toronto, where she was born. He was a lathe worker in a factory in 1911, when they were living at 70 Dagmar Avenue, Toronto. They were living at 134 Bertmount Avenue, Toronto at the time of her death there. They had three children – twins Norman Edward Jago and Gladys Lillian Jago 1903 and Margery Jago 1905.

Wallace was educated at Alton Public School, Peel Co, Ontario. He worked as a bank teller at the Elm Street Branch of the Bank of Toronto, Ontario. He spent two months with the Queen's Own Rifles of Canada before being commissioned as a lieutenant in 40th Regiment (Militia) in late 1915. He attested in 198th Battalion CEF and applied for a commission in the CEF on 19th April 1916 (916711). He was appointed provisional sergeant on 24th April and was commissioned (General List) in 20th Battalion CEF at Toronto, backdated to 19th April 1916. He had a medical at Camp Borden on 19th September and also made a will that day, leaving everything to his sisters, Ada and Bessie. On 25th September he embarked aboard RMS

Borden Military Camp opened during the Great War west of Barrie, Ontario to train units for the CEF. It was named after Sir Frederick William Borden, former Minister of Militia. Camp Borden became the first flying station of the Royal Flying Corps Canada in 1917. In the interwar period, the airfield became the training location for the nascent Royal Canadian Air Force and was renamed RCAF Station Borden. In 1938 Camp Borden was expanded to house the Canadian Tank School. During the Second World War Camp Borden and RCAF Station Borden became the most important training facility in Canada. The British Commonwealth Air Training Plan's No.1 Service Flying Training School was located there until 1946. During the Cold War Borden's importance as a RCAF facility declined in favour of other bases. It remained an important Army facility until 1970, when the Infantry School and Armoured School moved to Gagetown, New Brunswick. However, other training establishments moved in, including the Canadian Forces School of Administration and Logistics, the School of Aerospace Ordnance Engineering and the Canadian Forces Health Service Training Centre. With the unification of all Army, Navy and Air forces into the Canadian Forces in 1968, all military facilities were grouped under Canadian Forces Base Borden. The airfield closed in 1970. Eight surviving Royal Flying Corps hangars have been designated a National Historic Site of Canada.

Laconia at Halifax, Nova Scotia and disembarked at Liverpool on 6th October. The same day he proceeded to the Canadian Military School, Shorncliffe, Kent with the 198th Battalion Officers Draft for the 19th Course. He qualified on 23rd December and was posted to 95th Battalion.

On 25th January 1917 Wallace was attached to 5th Reserve Battalion, Bramshott, Hampshire and transferred to 5th Battalion on 31st January. He assigned $50 per month from his Army pay to his sister, Ada, from 1st February. He attended a bombing course at Aldershot, Hampshire, qualifying 1st class on 23 February, and an anti-gas measures course at Eastern Command School 2nd-7th April, qualifying 2nd class. Wallace went to France with reinforcements for 20th Battalion on 28th May. He departed the Canadian Base Depot on 31st May and joined 20th Battalion on 3rd June. He attended a course at the First Army School of Mortars on 14th June and a general course at the Canadian Corps School 2nd-19th September. On 5th November he was appointed Battalion Lewis Gun Officer and was granted fourteen days leave 10th-26th December.

On 24th April 1918 Wallace was admitted to 6th Canadian Field Ambulance and No.45 Casualty Clearing Station with pyrexia of unknown origin. He was transferred by 42 Ambulance Train to 2nd British Red Cross Hospital, Rouen on 26th April with

RMS *Laconia*, a Cunard liner built by Swan Hunter & Wigham Richardson, was launched on 27th July 1911. She entered service on 20th January 1912 on the Liverpool – Boston route. On the outbreak of the Great War she was converted into an armed merchant cruiser, with eight 6″ Guns and two seaplanes housed on the quarterdeck. Based at Simon's Town, South Africa, she patrolled the South Atlantic and Indian Ocean until April 1915, when she was used as a headquarters ship at Zanzibar, engaged in operations to capture Tanga and German East Africa. *Laconia* returned to Britain in June 1916, carrying a large shipment of gold ingots from Cape Town. She was returned to Cunard in July and resumed service in September. On 25th February 1917 she was torpedoed by U-*50* about eleven kilometres west-northwest of Fastnet returning from the United States with seventy-five passengers and 217 crew aboard. The first torpedo struck the starboard side just abaft the engine room. Twenty minutes later a second torpedo exploded in the engine room on the starboard side and she sank at 10.20 p.m. Twelve people were killed, including two of the American passengers, which stirred up public opinion in the USA against Germany and increased support to enter the war. The graphic account of the sinking by *Chicago Tribune* reporter Floyd Gibbons, who was aboard *Laconia*, was read to both Houses of Congress and helped to bring the United States into the war. The wreck of *Laconia* was located in November 2008 and 852 bars of silver and 132 boxes of silver coins worth c.£3M have been recovered. The second RMS *Laconia* was launched on 9th April 1921. At the outbreak of the Second World War she was also converted into an armed merchant cruiser and was sunk by U-*156*. When *Kapitänleutnant* Werner Hartenstein realised that civilians and prisoners of war were on board, he surfaced to rescue survivors and requested assistance. Several U-boats were dispatched flying Red Cross flags and signalling by radio that a rescue operation was underway. Next morning an American *Liberator* flew over and Hartenstein signaled the aircraft for assistance. The pilot consulted the American base on Ascension Island, where the senior officer on duty, who later claimed to have been unaware of the German radio message, ordered the U-boats to be attacked. Despite the *Liberator* crew clearly seeing the Red Cross flags, they pressed home their attack, although survivors were crowded on the submarines' decks and in towed lifeboats. The German submarines dived, abandoning many survivors. Vichy French ships rescued 1,083 from lifeboats and took aboard those picked up by the four German submarines, a total of about 1,500 survivors. An estimated 1,658 persons died. As a result of the incident, Admiral Karl Dönitz issued the Laconia Order, forbidding his commanders from rescuing survivors after attacks.

trench fever. On 4th May he was transferred to the Canadian Infantry Base Depot and classified 'A' by a medical board on 6th May. He joined 2nd Canadian Corps Reinforcement Camp on 22nd May and returned to 20th Battalion on 30th May. He attended a Lewis gun course at VI Corps School 17th-24th June and was granted fourteen days leave in Britain 17th-30th August.

Awarded the VC for his actions at Iwuy, France on 11th October 1918, LG 31st January 1919. Wallace was killed during the VC action at Iwuy and is buried in Niagara Cemetery, Iwuy (C 7). His batman, 412878 Private Alfred Saunders, was killed in the same action. He was born on 15th January 1881 and was the son of Mrs Elizabeth Castle, 16 Anderson's Row, Florence Street, Hitchin, Hertfordshire, England. Alfred is also buried in Niagara Cemetery, Iwuy (B 29). The VC was presented to Wallace's father by Sir John Strathearn Hendrie, Lieutenant Governor of Ontario, in Toronto on 28th March 1919.

Wallace is commemorated in a number of other places:

- Ontario
  - Lt Algie VC Branch No.449, Royal Canadian Legion (Ontario Command), 1267 Queen Street, Alton.

2nd Red Cross Hospital at Rouen.

The graves of Wallace Algie and his batman, Alfred Saunders, in Niagara Cemetery, Iwuy.

Sir John Strathearn Hendrie KCMG CVO (1857–1923), 11th Lieutenant Governor of Ontario 1914–19.

Lt Algie VC Branch No.449, Royal Canadian Legion, Alton, with the War Memorial in front.

The Alton War Memorial.

- ◦ Named on the War Memorial, Alton, outside Lt Algie VC Branch No.449, Royal Canadian Legion.
- ◦ Algie Avenue, Etobicoke, Toronto.
- ◦ A wooden plaque bearing fifty-six maple leaves each inscribed with the name of a Canadian-born VC holder was dedicated at the Canadian Forces College, Toronto on Remembrance Day 1999.
- ◦ Victoria Cross obelisk to all Canadian VCs at Military Heritage Park, Barrie dedicated by Princess Royal on 22nd October 2013.
- ◦ Named on one of eleven plaques honouring 175 men from overseas awarded the VC for the Great War. The plaques were unveiled by the Senior Minister of State at the Foreign & Commonwealth Office and Minister for Faith and Communities, Baroness Warsi, at a reception at Lancaster House, London on 26th June 2014 attended by The Duke of Kent and relatives of the VC recipients. The Canadian plaque was unveiled outside the British High Commission in Elgin Street, Ottawa on 10th November 2014 by The Princess Royal in the presence of British High Commissioner Howard Drake, Canadian Minister of Veterans Affairs Julian Fantino and Canadian Chief of the Defence Staff General Thomas James Lawson.
- ◦ Plaque No.3 on the York Cemetery VC Memorial, West Don River Valley, Toronto dedicated on 25th June 2017.
- ◦ Commemorated in the Canadian Books of Remembrance in the memorial Chamber in the Peace Tower of the Parliament Buildings in Ottawa.

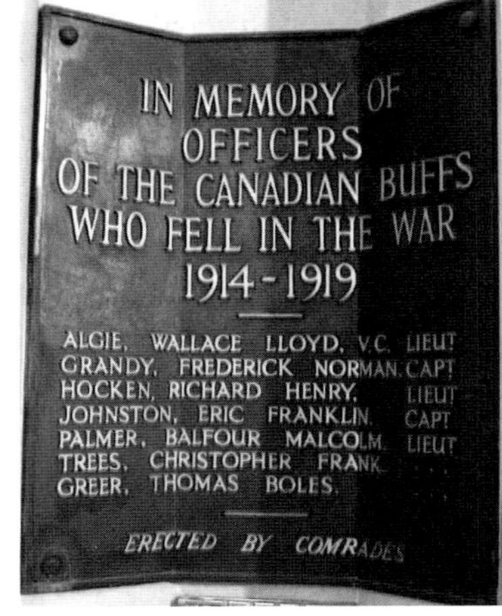

The Canadian Buffs War Memorial in Canterbury Cathedral was dedicated on 1st July 1923.

- Two 49 cents postage stamps in honour of the ninety-four Canadian VC winners were issued by Canada Post on 21st October 2004 on the 150th Anniversary of the first Canadian VC's action, Alexander Roberts Dunn VC.
- Communities and Local Government commemorative paving stones for the 145 VCs born in Australia, Belgium, Canada, China, Denmark, Egypt, France, Germany, India, Iraq, Japan, Nepal, Netherlands, New Zealand, Newfoundland, Pakistan, South Africa, Sri Lanka, Ukraine and United States of America

were unveiled at the National Memorial Arboretum, Alrewas, Staffordshire by Prime Minister David Cameron MP and Sergeant Johnson Beharry VC on 5th March 2015.

- Named on the Canadian Buffs War Memorial, Canterbury Cathedral, Kent, England.
- Named on The Ring of Remembrance (L'Anneau de la Mémoire or Ring of Memory) at Ablain-Saint-Nazaire, France, inaugurated on 11th November 2014. The Ring commemorates the 576,606 soldiers of forty nationalities who died in Nord-Pas-de-Calais in the Great War.

The Memorial Cross, awarded to the next of kin of a member of the Canadian armed forces who lost their life on active service, was created on 1st December 1919 by King George V.

In addition to the VC he was awarded the British War Medal 1914–20 and Victory Medal 1914–19. His next-of-kin was eligible to receive the Canadian Memorial Cross. The VC was sold for £16,800 at Glendining's on 22nd March 1995 and was purchased by Lord Ashcroft. It is held by the Michael Ashcroft Trust, the holding institution for the Lord Ashcroft Victoria Cross Collection, and is displayed in the Imperial War Museum's Lord Ashcroft Gallery.

241028 LANCE CORPORAL WILLIAM HAROLD COLTMAN 1/6th Battalion, The Prince of Wales's (North Staffordshire Regiment)

William Coltman was born on 17th November 1891 at Tatenhill Common, Rangemore, near Burton upon Trent, Staffordshire. His father, Charles Coltman (1851–1903), an agricultural labourer born at Hanbury, Staffordshire, married Emma Green (1851–27th January 1880), born at Potters Marston, Leicestershire, in 1870 at Penkridge, Staffordshire. They were living at Hanbury in 1871. She died there, almost certainly due to complications with the birth of her son Charley. Charles married Annie née Gopsill (1861–1930), born at Tutbury, Staffordshire, on 24th February 1881 at St Peter's Church, Birmingham, Warwickshire. They lived at 19 Dale End, Birmingham before moving to a tied cottage at Rangemore belonging to the estate of Lord Burton. Charles was a garden labourer by 1891. They were living at 62 Tatenhill Lane, Tatenhill, near Burton upon Trent in 1891 and 1901. After Charles died, Annie provided for her family by delivering milk with a horse and trap. She married Frederick Bannister (22nd July 1872–1957), a brewer's wagoner, born at Horninglow, Burton upon Trent, in 1909 at Burton upon Trent. They were living at 60 Forest Road, Burton upon Trent in 1911. Frederick was living with his mother, Alice Bannister (1844–1946), and his sister, Fanny Bannister (1879–1954), at 33 Dover Road, Burton upon Trent in 1939. William had ten siblings from his father's two marriages:

Rangemore is about six kilometres west of Burton upon Trent. Rangemore Hall was rebuilt in the late 1850s for Michael Bass, head of the brewing firm Bass, Ratcliff & Gretton. His son, Lord Burton, extended the house for the visit of King Edward VII in 1902. The King also visited in January 1907. The National Football Centre at St George's Park was built in 2012 as the home of England's national football teams.

- Sarah Eliza Coltman (28th July 1872–13th December 1947), born at Rolleston, near Burton upon Trent, was living at Rangemoor when she married Isaac Sherrard (25th March 1864–1940), born at Linton, Derbyshire, on 30th December 1891 at St Peter's Church, Stapenhill, Staffordshire. He was a garden labourer

Tutbury, eight kilometres north of Burton upon Trent, has been inhabited for over 3,000 years. There are Iron Age defensive ditches within which the Norman castle was built. One of the Royal Studs was established there by Henry VIII and Mary, Queen of Scots, was imprisoned in Tutbury Castle in 1569. Quarries nearby produced Nottingham alabaster and the Priory Church of the Blessed Virgin Mary has a unique west door with the only known alabaster arch (c.1160) in the country. Tutbury and Hatton railway station was opened by the North Staffordshire Railway in September 1848 on the Crewe to Derby Line. It closed in the 1960s but reopened in 1989. Tutbury Crystal, manufacturers of quality cut glass, was based in the village until 2006, when it transferred to Stoke-on-Trent. Amongst the notable people who were born or lived there are:

- William de Ferrers, 3rd Earl of Derby (died 1190), lived in Tutbury Castle, and Robert de Ferrers, 6th Earl of Derby (1239–79), was born there.
- Ann Moore (1761–1813), the 'fasting-woman of Tutbury', claimed to have eaten nothing from 1807 to 1813, but her claims were eventually proved to be a hoax.
- John Henry Davies (c.1864–1927), a wealthy brewery owner born in Tutbury, was one of four businessmen who took over the running of struggling Newton Heath Football Club in 1902. On 24th April 1902 the club changed its name to Manchester United. Davies became the club president.
- Air Vice Marshal William Staton CB DSO & Bar MC DFC & Bar (1898–1983), a Great War airman with twenty-six victories, pioneered the pathfinder bombing technique before serving in the Far East and becoming a prisoner of the Japanese in the Second World War. Post-war he captained the British Olympic Shooting Team in 1948 and 1952.

in 1901, when they were living at Tatenhill Common, Staffordshire. By 1911 he was a cowman and Sarah was a laundress and they were living at Cliff Lodge, Newton Solney, Derbyshire. They were living at 143 Station Street, Burton upon Trent in 1939. There were no children.

Dale End, Birmingham.

- Henry Coltman (1874–92), born at Hanbury, was an agricultural labourer in 1891.
- George Coltman (born and died 1876).
- Joseph Coltman (20th October 1877–16th February 1954) was a servant at Yew Tree Farm, Little Cubley, Derbyshire in 1891. He married Maude Mary Geraldine Smith (1878–1949) on 21st July 1897 at Willington, Derbyshire, where she was born. She was the illegitimate daughter of Mary Jane Smith (born October 1862) and the brother of Ernest William Dick Smith, who married Joseph's sister, Annie. Maude was living with her mother at her grandparent's home at Twyford Road, Willington in 1881 and was still with her grandparents in 1891, recorded as their daughter. Joseph was a coal carter in 1901 and 1911, when they were living at Baptist Chapel Cottage, Twyford Road, Willington. By 1939 he was a general labourer and they were living at 47 Humberstone Lane, Barrow upon Soar, Leicestershire. They had ten children, all born at Willington:
  - Frances Annie Coltman (26th September 1898–9th January 1931) married Alfred Draper (5th May 1892–15th February 1940), born at Gosberton, Lincolnshire, on 27th December 1922 at Averham, Nottinghamshire. He was living with his uncle, George, a farm wagoner, and aunt, Sarah Draper at Westhorpe, Gosberton in 1901. Alfred was serving as a driver in the Army Service Corps in 1911. Frances died at Church Street, Sutton-on-Trent, Nottinghamshire. Alfred was a blind pensioner living at 5 Archdale Street, Barrow-upon-Soar in 1939. He died at Syston, Leicestershire. They had five children – Gerald Alfred Draper (1923–76), Audrey Mary May Draper 1925, Frances J Draper 1927, Maurice A Draper 1928 and Derek A Draper 1930.
  - Maud Mary Elizabeth Coltman (born 2nd September 1900) was living with her uncle, Isaac Sherrard, and aunt, Sarah Sherrard, at Cliff Lodge, Newton Solney, Derbyshire in 1911. She married Thomas Scott (born 5th May 1898) on 30th March 1929 at Newton Solney Church. They had moved to Greenwich, London by 1933 and lived there at 60 Victoria Road. By 1939 they had moved to 54 Wolfe Crescent and he was a tool maker. They

are believed to have had three children – Dennis T Scott 1930, Sylvia M Scott 1931 and Peter Scott 1933.

- May Coltman (7th August 1902–January 1998) married John Harry Whitwell (11th November 1902–1975), born at Kettering, Northamptonshire, in 1929 at Leicester. He was a public service driver in 1939, when they were living at 43 Humberstone Lane, Barrow-upon-Soar. He died in Leicestershire and she at Coventry, Warwickshire. They had two children – Josephine M Whitwell (1931–2016) and Walter SJ Whitwell 1936.
- Joseph Coltman (30th December 1904–24th June 1984), a twin with Harry, married Rachel Alice Naylor (29th November 1906–8th March 1990), born at Preston, Rutland, in 1932 at Uppingham, Rutland. He was a mill feeder in a brickworks in 1939, when they were living at Rosegarth, Rosedene Avenue, Barrow-upon-Soar. He died at Leicester and she at Thurmaston, Leicestershire. They had two children – Malcolm J Coltman 1934 and Gwenyth Coltman 1940.
- Harry Coltman (30th December 1904–1969), a twin with Joseph, married Alice Mahala Pacey (29th August 1904–1978) in 1925 at Newark, Nottinghamshire, where she was born. He was a coal lorry driver and deliveryman and she was a tailor's finisher in 1939, when they were living at 81 Main Street, Barrow-upon-Soar. They had two sons – Ronald H Coltman (born and died 1925) and Derek Alan Coltman (1930–2013).
- Charles 'Charley' William Coltman (18th March 1907–1985) married Mary Green (13th October 1922–1984) in 1949 at Barrow-upon-Soar. Mary was a packer of celluloid goods in 1939, living with her parents at 149 Wanlip Lane, Barrow-upon-Soar.
- Marjorie Coltman (14th December 1910–1944) married Joseph Neale (12th September 1913–February 1996) in 1934 at Barrow-upon-Soar. He was a hosiery counterman in 1939, when they were living at 7 House, Manor Road, Barrow-upon-Soar. Her death probably followed complications with the birth of her son Rodney. They had three children – Norma M Neale 1934, Barry EA Neale 1937 and Rodney O Neale 1944.
- Samuel Coltman (21st April 1913–28th September 1990) was a greengrocery shopkeeper in 1939, boarding at 151 Dunton Street, Leicester with a widow, Lizzie Eugenie Brookes (1888–1963), and her daughter of the same name (7th July 1916–February 1986). Samuel married the daughter later in 1939 at Leicester. Her father, 27560 Private George Henry Brookes, 8th Leicestershire, died on active service on 11th June 1917 (St Leger British Cemetery – D25). Samuel was living at Forest View, 65 St George's Hill, Swannington, Leicestershire at the time of his death there. They are believed to have had a son, Cedric S Coltman, in 1945.
- Walter Herbert Coltman (24th March 1916–8th August 1979) was a motor van salesman in 1939, living with his parents. He married Louisa Bowering

(13th March 1920–26th April 2003), born at Sculcoates, Yorkshire, on 22nd September 1943 at Kingston-upon-Hull, Yorkshire. She was living with her parents at 5 John's Terrace, Spyvee Street, Kingston-upon-Hull. They had four children – Geraldine M Coltman 1949, Jacqueline A Coltman 1950, Michael J Coltman 1956 and Geoffrey W Coltman 1958.
    - Grace Coltman (4th September 1918–10th June 1994) was a fancy goods packer in 1939, living with her parents. She married Ronald Frederick Warren (13th June 1914–28th February 2006), born at Lyddington, Uppingham, Rutland, in 1940 at Barrow-upon-Soar. He was a motor mechanic in 1939, living at 33 Front Street, Birstall, Barrow-upon-Soar. She died in Leicester and he at Nottingham. They had two children – Diann Warren 1942 and Patricia Warren 1944.
- Charley Coltman (16th January 1880–1944) was living with his maternal grandparents in 1891. He was a labourer when he married Ada Richardson (9th January 1877–1952), born at Unstone Green, Derbyshire, on 3rd December 1899 at Dronfield Parish Church, Derbyshire. They were visiting William H and Olive R Jackson at 121 Sheffield Road, Derby at the time of the 1901 Census. Charley and Ada were living at 2 Potter Hill, Greasbrough, Rotherham, Yorkshire in 1911. They were living in retirement at 15 Lyme Street, Rotherham in 1939. They had four children:
    - Charles Henry Coltman (1900–05) was born at Rotherham.
    - Sarah Emma Coltman (27th October 1901–24th April 1972) married Mark Morley (1900–68) at Rotherham in 1924. They had a son, Eric Coltman, in 1930.
    - Clara Coltman (9th March 1904–1970), born at Hillsborough, Sheffield, married George K Hobson (1904–64) at Rotherham in 1924. They had two sons – George W Hobson 1926 and Brian Hobson 1933.
    - Eliza/Liza Coltman (born 11th January 1908), born at Dronfield.
- George Coltman (9th December 1881–6th February 1954) was a brewer's labourer in 1901. He married Elizabeth Yeomans (2nd June 1884–1st January 1986), born at Tatenhill, Staffordshire, in 1906 at Burton upon Trent. They were living at 40 Church Street, Tutbury, Burton upon Trent in 1911, by when he was a domestic gardener. They both died at Barton-under-Needwood, Staffordshire. They had a daughter:
    - Evelyn Daisy Coltman (29th July 1909–18th April 1983) married Samuel Thomas Brien (7th September 1908–9th May 1987), born at Dublin, Ireland, at Tatenhill in 1932. He was an assistant superintendent for an insurance company and an ARP Warden in 1939, when they were living at Killiney, Market Street, Hoyland Nether, Yorkshire. They were living at 88 Costock Avenue, Sherwood, Nottingham at the time of her death there. He was living at Halcro, Derby Road, Stenson, Derbyshire at the time of his death there. They had two children – Barbara P Brien 1934 and Kenneth S Brien 1946.

- Annie Coltman (born 21st August 1883), born at Hanbury, was a general domestic servant in 1901 and a cook in a boarding house at Shaftesbury House, Burton upon Trent in 1911. She married Ernest William Dick Smith (21st or 29th September 1881–1961) there in 1914. He was known as Dick and was the illegitimate son of Mary Jane Smith (born October 1862) and the brother of Maude Mary Geraldine Smith, who married Annie's brother, Joseph. Dick was living with his grandparents at Twyford Road, Willington in 1891. In 1911 he was a coal carter living with his sister, Maude, and husband, at Baptist Chapel Cottage, Twyford Road. Dick was on the repair staff at a railway engineering works in 1939, when they were living at Rose Cottage, Twyford Road, Willington. They had four children, all registered at Burton upon Trent:
    - Kathleen A Smith (born 31st March 1915) married Thomas Peet (born 29th March 1911), born at Derby, in 1936 at Burton upon Trent. They were living at Ecton House, Repton, Derbyshire in 1939. They had four children – Dennis T Peet 1937, Barbara Peet 1938, Mavis A Peet 1945 and Veronica Peet 1946.
    - William IG Smith (1917–21).
    - Frederick A Smith (born 1923).
    - Ruby Evelyn Smith (13th June 1924–7th March 1984) was an apprentice tailoress in 1939, living with her parents. She married Alfred Thomas Webster (1924–27th January 2010), born at Derby, in 1949 at Shardlow, Derbyshire. He was living with his parents at 39 Mount Street, Derby in 1939. Ruby and Alfred were living at 6 The Oval, Bicton, Shrewsbury, Shropshire at the time of her death there. He died at Wallingford, Oxfordshire. They are believed to have had a child.
- Samuel Coltman (30th August 1886–6th May 1956) was a traveler for a drapery in 1911. He married Nellie Stableford (23rd January 1887–10th March 1974), born at Tilton on the Hill, Staffordshire, in 1927 at Leicester. She was a parlour maid in 1911, living with her brother at Tugby, Leicester. Samuel was a chimney sweep in 1939, when they were living at 190 Shobnall Road, Burton upon Trent. She was living at 68 Bury Edge Lane, Winshill, Burton upon Trent at the time of her death there.
- Frances Coltman (1888–1918), born at Tatenhill Lane, Tatenhill, Rangemore, Burton upon Trent, married John Bull in 1914 at Burton upon Trent. They had two children:
    - Doris Bull (28th February 1915–August 1987) was a maid in 1939 at Burton upon Trent General Infirmary on New Street. She married Edward Harrison L Jones (26th September 1913–November 1987) in 1945. He was a rubber worker in 1939, living with his parents at 28 Park Street, Burton upon Trent. They had two children – Donald Jones 1948 and David K Jones 1951.
    - Frances Annie Bull (14th August 1917–October 1982) was a domestic servant living with her uncle, Samuel Coltman, in 1939. She never married.

- Herbert Leonard Coltman (9th July 1890–4th December 1954) was living with his sister, Sarah and family, and his brother, William, in 1901. He married Bertha Brittain (1894–1916) in 1915 at Hanbury, where she was born. Herbert married Harriet Eliza Rivett (21st August 1894–1979), born at Stow, Suffolk, in 1919 at Burton upon Trent. Herbert was a general labourer and Harriet was a charwoman in 1939, when they were living at 192 Shobnall Road, Burton upon Trent. Herbert and Harriet had three children:
    - Marjorie A Coltman (1921–25).
    - Ronald Leonard Coltman (17th September 1926–15th February 1994) married Doreen Maud Baxter (31st January 1926–20th July 2002) on 27th August 1947 at Burton upon Trent. She was living with her parents at Lawns Farm Cottages, Tutbury, Staffordshire in 1939. They had eight children – Michael J Coltman 1948, David C Coltman 1949, Christine A Coltman 1951, Brian A Coltman 1952, Howard A Coltman 1954, Dorothy M Coltman 1957, Ian S Coltman 1961 and Nigel Graham Coltman 1968.
    - Edward H Coltman (1928–30th May 2012) married Ida Laura Bagnall née Glover (7th December 1925–October 1973), born at Birmingham, Warwickshire, in 1949 at Burton upon Trent. They had eight children – Richard NEC Coltman 1950, Bert S Coltman 1952, Barry LA Coltman 1954, Paul GG Coltman 1957, Faith D Coltman 1959, twins Glenn and Wendy Coltman 1963 and Annette Christine Coltman 1971. Ida had married Francis H Bagnall (born 1923) in 1944 at Birmingham. The marriage ended in divorce. Francis married Beryl Bown in 1949.

William's paternal grandfather, George Coltman (1821–95), born at Hanbury, Staffordshire, was an agricultural labourer. He married Sarah née Merry

Hanbury's most significant building is the Church of St Werburgh, which dates back to the 12th century. Nearby was RAF Fauld, a huge underground bomb and ammunition storage facility in old gypsum mine workings. At 11.11 a.m. on 27th November 1944 it was devastated by the largest explosion ever in the United Kingdom. Up to 4,400 tons of ordnance exploded, resulting in a crater thirty metres deep and up to 270m wide. The precise death toll is uncertain but seventy people are known to have died, including twenty six RAF personnel, civilians workers and Italian prisoners of war in the tunnels. Another thirty-seven were drowned or missing at a nearby gypsum mine as a result of a nearby reservoir, containing 450,000 cubic metres of water, being obliterated. Seven workers died at Upper Castle Hayes Farm, which was destroyed completely. Eighteen bodies were never recovered and a diver was killed in the search and rescue operations. Despite the devastation, the rest of the site was used by the RAF until 1966, when it was taken over by the US Army. It finally closed in 1973. Recovery of the remaining explosives would be impractical and too expensive. The site has therefore been fenced off. The crater, which covers twelve acres, is now a haven for wildlife.

(c.1821–84), also born at Hanbury, in 1848 at Burton upon Trent. They lived at Hanbury Woodend. He was living with his daughter, Sarah, and her family in 1891. He died at Uttoxeter, Staffordshire. In addition to Charles they had six other children, all born at Hanbury:

- Thomas Coltman (1848–54).
- John Coltman (1854–1918) was a farm servant, living with his sister, Hannah, and family in 1891. By 1901 he was an alabaster miner, living with his sister, Sarah Lloyd, and family.
- Hannah Coltman (1857–1939) was a nursemaid in 1871 for Ralph and Elizabeth Bullock at Hanbury. She married Thomas Tipper (born 21st December 1848) on 10th December 1876 at Hanbury. He was a general labourer in 1881, living with his family at Hanbury Woodend, Staffordshire. By 1901 he was an alabaster miner and by 1911 he was a farm labourer. There were deaths of Thomas Tippers of the correct age in 1931 and 1933. They had eleven children including:
    - Joseph Tipper (1879–1962).
    - Annie Elizabeth Tipper (born 1881).
    - Sarah Tipper (1885–1965) is believed to have married Alfred Page (1883–1954) in 1906. Both their deaths were registered at Lichfield. They had at least five children – Linda N Page 1912, Kenneth C Page 1913, Arthur J Page 1914, Lucy Page 1916 and Leslie C Page 1918.
    - Louisa Tipper (1887–1980) is believed to have married Arthur Wood Jeffery (1882–1940) in 1908 at Uttoxeter. They both died at Ashbourne. They had at least three children – Ida M Jeffery 1912, Mary Jeffery 1922 and Constance A Jeffery 1924.
    - William George Tipper (1889–1951) is understood to have married Lydia Woolley (1890–1960) at Burton in 1920. They had two children – Reginald Tipper 1923 and Leslie Tipper 1930.
    - Eva Tipper (26th January 1891–1972) married Francis H Abberley (c.1891–1950) in 1913. They had seven children – twins Frank and John Abberley 1914, Hannah M Abberley 1915, Francis H Abberley 1920, Anthony F Abberley 1921, Samuel Abberley 1923 and Audrey Abberley 1925.
    - John Thomas Tipper (1893–1914) was a general farm servant in 1911, living with Arthur William and Louisa Tatlow at Daisy Bank, Thorney Lanes, Newborough, Burton upon Trent.
    - Tom Tipper (1895–1930).
    - Lucy Emily Tipper (born 5th May 1896) married George Gretton (probably 1889–1934) in 1924. They had twins Jack and Tom Gretton in 1928. She was a widow living at Brickyard Cottage, Tutbury in 1939. She is understood to have married Cyril F Hawkins in 1946.
- Sarah Ann Coltman (1859–1932) married Thomas Lloyd (April 1856–1932), an alabaster miner born at Newborough, Staffordshire, in 1878. They were

living at Hanbury Woodend in 1891 and 1901. By 1911 he was a foreman in an alabaster works and they were living at Purse Cottages, Hanbury. They had eleven children, including – Thomas Lloyd 1880, Hannah Lloyd (1881–1973), Martha Lloyd 1884, Mary Ann Lloyd 1886, Rose/Rosa Ann Lloyd (1890–1958), May Lloyd 1892, Sarah Lloyd 1893, George Coltman Lloyd (1897–1976) and Edith Lloyd (1899–1904).

- Mary Ann Coltman (born and died 1860).
- Martha Coltman (10th September 1866–6th September 1943) married Edwin Eastaff (12th May 1867–1931), born at Milton Bryan, Woburn, Bedfordshire, at Hanbury on 27th November 1890. He was a wagoner on a farm in 1901, when they were living at Alrewas, Staffordshire. By 1911 he was a colliery labourer above ground, living with his family at 24 Smith Street, Woodend, Hurley, near Atherstone, Warwickshire. His death was registered at Tamworth, Staffordshire. Martha was living at 13 Garden School Lane, Tamworth in 1939. She died at Sutton Coldfield, Warwickshire. They had nine children:
  - Edwin Joseph Eastaff (11th January 1891–1958).
  - Eli George Eastaff (1893–1920) was a colliery screen labourer in 1911, living with his parents. He married Daisy Catherine Thompson (1899–1937) at Tamworth in 1919. Daisy married Thomas Sturrock in 1920. They had a son, Thomas D Sturrock, in 1921. Daisy married William T Cook in 1936.
  - Mary Ann Eastaff (3rd September 1895–1985) married John H Hollick (14th November 1893–1972) in 1917. They had six children – Ivy Hollick 1921, Marjorie Hollick 1925, Ronald T Hollick 1927, Kenneth Hollick 1931, Raymond Hollick 1935 and Stanley Hollick 1937. They both died at Lichfield.
  - John Henry Eastaff (17th April 1898–1987) married Margaret Bates (1900–51) at Atherstone in 1921. They had a daughter, Margaret J Eastaff, in 1924.
  - Alice Louisa Eastaff (3rd July 1900–1984) married Thomas Buckley (c.1897–1967) in 1921. They had a daughter, Mary L Buckley, in 1923.
  - Albert Eastaff (1903–69) married Hilda M Clarke (18th July 1906–1973) in 1928. They had five children – Millicent M Eastaff 1930, Thelma Eastaff 1933, Derek R Eastaff 1935, Hilda M Eastaff 1936 and Trevor J Eastaff 1942.
  - Ernest Henry Eastaff (28th April 1906–1975) married Florence M Boonham (4th July 1906–1988) in 1931. They had three children – Brenda M Eastaff 1936, Barbara Eastaff 1937 and Dorothy Eastaff 1939.
  - Herbert Arthur Eastaff (1908–11).
  - Violet A Eastaff (1911–13).

His maternal grandfather, Samuel Gopsill (22nd September 1823–1894), born at Solihull, Warwickshire, was a cooper. He married Elizabeth née Hickman (c.1823–1901), born at Daventry, Northamptonshire, on 24th August 1851 at St Paul's

Solihull, an ancient market town, lies twelve kilometres southeast of Birmingham. The town dates back to the 1st century BC. When Mercia became part of England, the Manor of Ulverlei passed to the Earls of Mercia, the first of whom, Leofric, was the husband of Lady Godiva. Leofric's great-nephew, Thorkell of Arden, was one of the few Anglo-Saxons to retain their land after the Norman Conquest. In 1086 the Manor of Ulverlei was held by Cristina, great-granddaughter of Ethelred the Unready, daughter of Edward the Exile, and sister of the last Anglo-Saxon King, Edgar Aetheling. Christina entered the nunnery of Romsey Abbey in Hampshire and her lands were granted to the Norman Ralph de Limesy. The de Limsey (sic) family founded the settlement of Solihull and by the reign of Edward I, Ulverlie was known as the Old Town, shortened to its present name of Olton, to distinguish it from the New Town of Solihull. Solihull absorbed Shirley and Olton and by 1242 the Manor of Solihull had been established and was granted a Royal charter. By the 14th century the town was known for its blacksmiths, with the nearby Forest of Arden providing the necessary fuel. In 1400 the Crown took over the Manor and it was granted to the Duke of Norfolk, who, in 1530, passed it to the Throckmortons. Solihull was owned by the Throckmortons during the planning of the 1605 Gunpowder Plot. Their co-conspiritors included the Catesbys of Lapworth, which was then part of the borough of Solihull. Solihull survived the English Civil War 1642–51, although a number of important engagements and battles were fought nearby, including the Battle of Edgehill. In the modern era, Solihull became a centre of textile and iron working. In the early 1800s former Prime Minister Sir Robert Peel bought the Manor of Hampton in Arden. The Manor of Longdon came to Lord Byron in 1815 through his marriage to Anne, daughter of Sir Ralph Milbanke Noel. In 1936 two Solihull farms were bought for the construction of a shadow factory, which after the Second World War became the home of the Land Rover company. On 8th July 1939 Prime Minister Neville Chamberlain and the Duchess of Kent opened Solihull's airport, which was RAF Elmdon during the Second World War. In July 1946 it reopened for civilian operations and in 1960 became Birmingham International Airport. During the Second World War Solihull received evacuated children from Coventry and London. There was a military convalescent hospital in Tudor Grange House and the town adopted HMS *Vivacious* in 1942. An American Army headquarters was also established in the town. In 1954 Solihull became a Municipal Borough and ten years later a County Borough. Amongst the famous people born or resident in the town are:

- Sir Alfred Bird, 1st Baronet (1849–1922), chemist and politician, who founded the Bird's Custard company, bought Tudor Grange Hall.
- WH Auden (1907–73), the Anglo-American poet, lived on Homer Road.
- Actresses Stephanie Cole (born 1941) and Felicity Kendal (born 1946).
- Matthew Croucher (born 1983) Royal Marine George Cross holder.
- Martin Johnson CBE (born 1970), captain of the 2003 England rugby union team that won the 2003 World Cup.
- Mandy Rice-Davies (1944–2014), who was involved in the Profumo Affair in the early 1960s, attended school in Solihull.
- William Wilberforce (1759–1833), politician, philanthropist and leader of the movement to abolish the slave trade, moved to Elmdon following his marriage to Barbara Spooner, of the Spooner banking family, owners of Elmdon Hall.
- Poets Richard Jago (1715–81) and William Shenstone (1714–63) attended Solihull School and two houses are named after them.
- John Wyndham (1903–69) the science fiction author.

The Grade I listed St Paul's Church, originally Chapel, is in the centre of St Paul's Square. The area was laid out in a grid pattern around 1778 as part of the Colmores Newhall estate, a residential area for the affluent. The church was consecrated in 1779 and manufacturers and merchants, Matthew Boulton and James Watt had their own pews there. The upper part of the tower and spire were added in 1822–24. By the 1840s the wealthy industrialists had moved further out of town and the area degenerated into slums. In 1841 St Paul's became a parish in its own right. In 1947 the parish of St Mark's joined it, when the latter church was demolished. St Paul's was badly damaged in the bombing during the Second World War and was repaired between 1949 and 1951. Another major restoration took place between 1985 and 1994.

Chapel, Birmingham. She was a servant at 72 Caroline Street, Birmingham at the time of the 1851 Census. They were living at Anslow, Staffordshire in 1871. By 1881 they had moved to 201 Shobnall Street, Horninglow, Burton upon Trent and were still there in 1891. In addition to Annie they had nine other children:

- John Gopsill (12th October 1851–1937), a cooper born at Solihull, Warwickshire, married Agnes Petty (5th August 1851–1935), born at New Street, Burton upon Trent, on 13th July 1876 at Christ Church, Burton upon Trent. They were living at Burton upon Trent at 36 Ordish Street in 1881, at 187 Uxbridge Street in 1891, at 93 Branston Road in 1901 and with their daughter, Mary Agnes Brockwell and family, at 35 Castle Road, Castle Gresley, Derbyshire in 1911. They had four children:
    - Mary Agnes Gopsill (1877–1947) was a dressmaker in 1891 and 1901 living with her parents. She married Albert Victor Brockwell (1876–1968) in 1901. They were living at 35 Castle Road, Castle Gresley, Derbyshire in 1911. They had six children, including – Beatrice Brockwell 1901, Gladys May Brockwell 1905, Agnes Mary Brockwell 1907, John Victor Brockwell 1909 and Cyril J Brockwell 1914.
    - Isabella Gopsill (25th November 1878–1st July 1912) was a tailoress in 1901 living with her parents.

Shobnall Street in Horninglow.

She married William Henry Dolman (1880–1965) in 1902. She died at Guildford, Surrey.
  - Sydney John Gopsill (1881–1955), a machine fitter, married Martha E Howkins (March 1889–1971) in 1910. They had four children – Sydney J Gopsill 1913, Raymond H Gopsill 1914, Enid M Gopsill 1924 and Trevor E Gopsill 1929.
  - Leslie Gopsill (born 1891) was living with his sister, Mary, and his parents in 1911. He married Frances M Lovatt (14th January 1894–1977) in 1919. They had two sons – Douglas Gopsill 1921 and John T Gopsill 1923.
- Charles Henry Gopsill (1857–1919), a cooper, married Elizabeth Ann Botham (1855–1928), born at Burton upon Trent, at St John's Church, Derby in June 1876. They were living at Anslow, Staffordshire in 1881 and at 32 South Broadway Street, Burton upon Trent in 1901 and 1911. They had twelve children:
  - Samuel Thomas Gopsill (born 1876).
  - Mary Elizabeth Gopsill (1878–1943) married Walter Whiteland (1876–1950) in 1902. They had a number of children including – Sidney A Whiteland 1916 and Beryl E Whiteland 1920.
  - William Charles Gopsill (1879–1927) married Elizabeth Ann Stroud (1878–1946) in 1898.
  - Arthur Botham Gopsill (1881–1900).
  - Mary Jane Gopsill (born 1882).
  - Percy John Gopsill (1885–1916).
  - Frances Edith Gopsill (1887–1902).
  - Robert Ernest Gopsill (1888–89).
  - Ernest Charles Gopsill (born and died 1890) was a twin with Harold.
  - Harold Gopsill (1890–1951), a twin with Ernest.
  - Daisy Ethel Gopsill (1891–1967) is believed to have married Arthur Elliott at Leicester in 1919.
  - Ivy Amelia Gopsill (10th February 1895–1972) married Leslie G Dunnicliff (14th July 1892–1971) in 1915. They had two children – Leslie H Dunnicliff 1916 and Frederick C Dunnicliff 1919.
- William Thomas Gopsill (born 1863) was a cooper in 1881.
- Lewis/Louis Gopsill (1864–6th June 1937) was a cooper in 1881. He married Elizabeth Ann Sutton (16th February 1861–5th June 1949) in 1887. They were living at 466 Anglesey Road, Burton upon Trent in 1911 and both subsequently died there. They had four children, including:
  - Louis Samuel Gopsill (1890–1911).
  - Edith Harriet Gopsill (23rd December 1892–1973) registered at birth as Edgar Harriet and at death in Scarborough, Yorkshire as Edith Harriet. She never married.
  - Annie Elizabeth Gopsill (29th March 1898–1977) married Robert E Dove (1903–51) at Scarborough, Yorkshire in 1926. They had three children – Joan M Dove 1927, Graham AL Dove 1930 and Nancy C Dove 1932.

- Sarah Lily Gopsill (1866–June 1937), born at Yardley Wood, Worcestershire, was a domestic servant at St John Street, Ashbourne, Derbyshire at the time of her marriage to John Thomas Turner (January 1866–1898) on 24th February 1892 at Ashbourne Church, Derbyshire. He was born at Mayfield, Staffordshire and was living at Mayfield Road, Ashbourne when he married. He died at Tissington, Derbyshire. They had four children – John Turner 1892, Arthur Turner 1894, Harry Turner 1896 and Harold Turner 1898, all born at Tissington. Sarah married John Davies (born c.1872), a gas mains labourer with Derby Gaslight & Coke Co born at Chester, Cheshire, on 22nd May 1899 at Tissington Church. They were living at 64 Parliament Street, Derby in 1901 and at Eden Cottages, Normanton Lane, Littleover, Derbyshire in 1911. She was living at 60 Uttoxeter Road, Mickleover, Derbyshire at the time of her death there. They had five children, including:
    - Nellie Elizabeth Davies (born 1901) married Ernest GE Noble (1902–64), born at Bristol, in 1927. Nellie married Arnold Newbery (1886–1967) in 1964.
    - Dorothy May Davies (2nd April 1902–1979) married Alexander W Stevenson (11th March 1893–1971) in 1922.
    - William Ernest Davies (1904–67) married Doris Evelyn Riley (19th March 1900–1977) in 1927. They had a daughter, Joyce Davies.
    - Mary Ellen Davies (born 1907) married Eric Headlam Field (13th January 1901–1976), born at Bridlington, Yorkshire, in 1936. They had a daughter, Valerie M Field, in 1937.
- Alice Elizabeth Gopsill (19th September 1867–1955) was a domestic servant in 1881, living at the home of William and Ann Briggs, Hoar Cross, near Yoxall, Staffordshire. She married Arthur Baxter (26th December 1874–1944), born at Mutford, Suffolk, in 1896. He was a blacksmith's striker in 1911, when they were living at 94 Princess Street, Burton upon Trent. By 1939 they were living at 45 Victoria Crescent, Burton upon Trent, when Alice was an office cleaner. They had two children:
    - Reginald Arthur Baxter (11th October 1896–1972) was an errand boy in 1911. He married Alice Barnett in 1919. They had four children – Leslie A Baxter 1920, twins Kenneth C and Ronald A Baxter 1925 and Doris Baxter 1931.
    - Constance Annie Baxter (4th February 1900–1983) married Cecil A Gormer (9th August 1897–1972) in 1921. They had six children – twins Gladys and Joyce Gormer 1921, Raymond A Gormer 1923, Gwendoline A Gormer 1926, Reginald A Gormer 1928 and Janet Gormer 1932.
- Samuel George Gopsill (19th January 1870–1946), born at Anslow, Staffordshire, was a blacksmith. He married Lavinia Elizabeth Adams (2nd January 1870–April 1912), born at Burslem, Staffordshire, on 25th December 1891 at St Peter's Church, Stapenhill, Staffordshire. They were living at 119 Uxbridge Street,

Burton upon Trent in 1891 and were lodging at 8 Horninglow Street, Burton upon Trent in 1911. He was living as a retired master blacksmith at 93 Wood Street, Burton upon Trent in 1939 with Emily Brombruss, single (born 18th June 1867). Samuel and Lavinia had eight children:

  - Alice Gopsill (13th June 1893–1979) married Albert Percy Graves (1887–1932) at Leicester in 1914. They had four children – Betsy A Graves 1914, Margaret L Graves 1917, Muriel E Graves 1921 and Barbara E Graves 1929. Alice married Henry E Goodhead (2nd June 1905–1979) in 1935. Their deaths were registered with the same reference in the 4th quarter of 1979, indicating that they died at the same time and place.
  - Leonard Gopsill (12th June 1897–1974) was a newsboy in 1911. He married Elsie Lamb (15th January 1899–1988) in 1925. They had a daughter, Eileen Gopsill, in 1929.
  - Lavinia (also seen as Lavena/Lavina) Gopsill (19th July 1900–1985) married James Henry Reed (2nd August 1900–1976) in 1924. They had three children – James A Reed 1925, Joan A Reed 1928 and Beryl A Reed 1935. They both died at Grimsby, Lincolnshire.
  - George Gopsill (30th March 1903–1975) married Doris Grace Hamp (19th July 1904–1983) in 1936. They had a son, Garth H Gopsill, in 1943.
  - Ada Gopsill (31st July 1905–1976) married Albert William Wayling (1904–60) in 1926. They had four children – Robert W Wayling 1927, Renee Wayling 1928, Patricia A Wayling 1934 and Pamela Wayling 1938.
  - Samuel Gopsill (10th November 1907–21st September 1980) married Mary Magdalene Shaw (13th November 1905–1975) in 1932. They had a son, David Gopsill, in 1933.
  - Lucy Gopsill (1910) married Reginald Thomas Ratcliff (1905–62) in 1930. They had two sons – John T Ratcliff 1940 and William J Ratcliff 1942.
  - Arthur Gopsill (1912–13).

- Catherine Gopsill (born c.1872) was a tailoress in 1891, living with her parents. She married Harry William Sutton (born 6th April 1873), a gas fitter born at 49 Broad Street, Cambridge, on 13th April 1895 at St Peter's Church, Stapenhill. They were living at 69 Upper Boundary Road, Derby in 1901. By 1911 he was boarding on his own at 52 Burnside Street, Alvaston, Derbyshire. Catherine was living with William Brown (born c.1877) at 126 Minet Avenue, Harlesden, London in 1911. They had three children by 1911 – Reginald Sutton (sic) 1905, Dorothy Margaret Brown 1907 and Kathleen Brown 1911. Catherine and William moved to Derby and were living at 16 Dean Street at the time of their marriage there on 26th December 1912 at St Luke's Church.
- William Charles Gopsill (1879–1927) was a cooper in a brewery. He married Elizabeth Ann Stroud (5th June 1878–1946) in 1898. They were living at 55 Wellington Street, Burton upon Trent in 1911. There were no children. She was a brewery office cleaner in 1939, living at 53 Wellington Street, Burton upon Trent.

William and his brother, Herbert, were living with his sister, Sarah and family, in 1901. He was educated at Rangemore Council School, Burton upon Trent 1894–1904, where he had a reputation for being somewhat mischievous. He left school aged thirteen in order to help support the family and was employed as a gardener at Bleak House, Ashby Road, Burton upon Trent by Colonel CJ Goer. He then worked as a gardener at Repton and lived at 60 Forest Road, Burton upon Trent. William was a farm labourer in 1911, working for John Edward Chesman, a market gardener, at Springfield, Milton Road, Repton.

Rangemore Council School is now All Saints Rangemoor Church of England Primary School.

On 8th January 1913, William married Eleanor May Dolman (6th June 1893–24th December 1948), a domestic servant living at Park End, Repton, at Burton Registry Office. They lived on Churchill Street, Winshill, Burton upon Trent but later moved to Sequehart, 6 Wheatley Lane, Winshill, Burton upon Trent, where they lived for the rest of their lives. Eleanor subsequently died there. William and Eleanor were both members of the Plymouth Brethren non-conformist congregation. He became a Sunday School teacher at the Meeting House at Winshill. They had two children:

- Charles Henry Coltman (3rd March 1913–20th September 1979) was born at 49 Hawfield Lane, Burton upon Trent. He married Elizabeth Eunice Bown (17th August 1913–5th January 1999) in 1937 and they lived at 68 Berry Hedge Lane. Charles eventually inherited his father's medals. They were living at Wheatley Lane, Burton upon Trent at the time of his death there. They had two children:
    - John C Coltman (born 20th June 1945) married Marion J Kent (born 1946) on 22nd July 1967. They had two children – Philip Coltman 1968 and Timothy Coltman 1974.
    - David F Coltman (born 1st November 1949) married Jacqueline 'Jackie' A Mayne (born 1956) on 2nd June 1979. They had two children – Ashley Coltman 1981 and Jamie Coltman 1985.
- Dorothy Coltman (born 16th April 1923–30th April 1987) was a printing works puncher in 1939, living with her parents. She married Alan McMillan (born 13th January 1922) on 28th July 1944. He was a laundry salesman car driver in 1939, living with his parents at 3 Wheatley Lane, Burton upon Trent, a few doors from Dorothy. They shared the family home at 6 Wheatley Lane, Winshill with her father after 1948. They had two children:
    - Barbara McMillan (born 19th May 1947) married Derrick D Rankin (born 1944), born at Kingsclere, Hampshire, in 1973. They had two children

Repton village in South Derbyshire is seven kilometres northeast of Burton upon Trent. It is noted for St Wystan's Church, Repton School, Repton Abbey and Repton Priory. Some of the Mercian royal family were baptised there in 653. In 669 the Bishop of Mercia translated his see from Repton to Lichfield. Offa, King of Mercia, resented his bishops paying allegiance to the Archbishop of Canterbury in Kent and created his own Archdiocese of Lichfield, the third of the English church with Canterbury and York. However, sixteen years later Mercia returned to the Archbishopric of Canterbury. In 873–74 the Danish Great Heathen Army overwintered at Repton. Elsie Steele (1899–2010), the oldest documented person in Britain when she died, lived in a residential home at Repton during her final years. On his death in 1557, Sir John Port of Etwall left funds to create a grammar school at Repton Priory. For the first 400 years Repton School accepted only boys. Girls were admitted in the 1970s and the School was fully co-educational by the 1990s. Amongst its famous alumni are:

- Harold Abrahams CBE (1899–1978), 100m sprint champion in the 1924 Paris Olympics, whose story was depicted in the 1981 film *Chariots of Fire*.
- Henry Wilfred 'Bunny' Austin (1906–2000) was for seventy-four years the last Briton to reach a Wimbledon singles final until Andy Murray in 2012. He was part of the British team that won the Davis Cup in three consecutive years (1933–35).
- Roald Dahl (1916–90), novelist, poet, screenwriter and wartime fighter pilot.
- Charles Burgess Fry (1872–1956), sportsman, politician, diplomat, academic, teacher, writer and publisher. He represented England at cricket and football, made a Football Association Cup Final appearance for Southampton FC and equalled the then-world record for the long jump.
- Shona McCallin MBE (born 1992), England and Great Britain hockey player and Olympic gold medalist in 2016.
- Baron Arthur Michael Ramsey of Canterbury PC (1904–88), Bishop of Durham in 1952, Archbishop of York in 1956 and the 100th Archbishop of Canterbury 1961–74.
- Philip St John Basil Rathbone MC (1892–1967), a Shakespearean actor, who appeared in more than seventy films. His most famous role was Sherlock Holmes.

  – Rachel Rankin 1976 and Christina Edwards Rankin 1980. Derrick had married Patricia Ann Woodings (10th February 1947–3rd January 2007) in 1966 and they had a son, Steven McKenzie Rankin, in 1968. Patricia married Raymond A King (1937–31st January 2018) in 1975.
  - Linda May McMillan (born 29th April 1962).

Eleanor's father, Henry Dolman (1866–1938), born at Repton, Derbyshire, married Alice née Bamford (1873–October 1936), a servant, born at Milton Repton, Derbyshire, on 21st November 1891 at St Wystan's Parish Church, Repton. She gave her age as twenty-one, although she was only eighteen. Henry was a labourer in a water works in 1901, when they were living at Long Street, Repton. By 1911 he was a jobbing gardener and they were living at Wood End, Repton. In addition to Eleanor they had another five children, all born at Repton:

St Wystan's Church in Repton, with the entrance to Repton School on the right. In 653 Peada, a son of King Penda of Mercia, married the daughter of the King of Northumbria as a Christian, having been baptised on Lindisfarne. Peada brought Christianity to the Midlands and embarked on a campaign of conversion. About 660, Werburga, Penda's granddaughter, founded a double house (for men and women) Benedictine monastery in Repton. The Grade I listed St Wystan's Church is the burial place of two kings of Mercia in its 8th century crypt – King Æthelbald in 757 and King Wiglaf in 839. In 849 Wiglaf's grandson, Wystan, was murdered by a cousin seeking to replace him as king. Miracles are claimed to have occurred – a pillar of light shot up to heaven for thirty days and, on the anniversary of Wystan's death, human hair grew from the ground where he was killed. He was canonised and interred in the crypt c.840. Visits by pilgrims brought fame and wealth to the monastery and the church was extended. During the occupation of the town by the Danish Great Heathen Army in 873–74, the monastery was destroyed and the church was ransacked but St Wystan's remains were removed and survived. They were later moved to Evesham Abbey. Following the Norman Conquest, Repton was granted to the Earls of Chester, who built a castle near the church and the Priory was completed in 1254. The current church has medieval north and south aisles rebuilt in the 13th century and widened early in the 14th. The west tower and spire were added in 1340 and there were major alterations in the 15th century. The Priory was dissolved by Henry VIII in 1538 and soon afterwards it was demolished to prevent Queen Mary from re-opening it. In 1557 the Prior's guest house became a free grammar school, which evolved into the present Repton School. The masters and pupils attended services in St Wystan's until the School Chapel was built in the 1850s. The church crypt was forgotten until rediscovered in 1779, when a workman fell through the floor into it. There were major alterations to the church in 1792, which increased the seating capacity to 770 (double the current seating), and the first organ was installed in 1844. The church was restored in 1885–86 by Arthur Blomfield. There were repairs to the spire three times during the 20th century and in 2013.

- Edith Mary Dolman (10th March 1899–1941) married Francis William Failes (4th May 1892–1969), a gardener born at Newhall, Derbyshire, in 1919. Following the death of his father, Henry 'Harry' Failes, a railway signalman (1867–94), Francis was residing at The Railway Servants' Orphanage for the children of deceased railway employees at Ashbourne Road, Derby by 1901. By 1911 he was a collier living with his mother, Elizabeth Staley Asbury formerly Failes née Watson (1866–1944), and stepfather, Frances William Asbury (1875–1952), at 53 Main Street, Newhall. Francis and Edith were living at Mill Street, Repton in 1939. They had three children:
    - Harry Failes (born 30th March 1919) was a general farm labourer in 1939. He married Joan Stella E Fowers (25th March 1922–1983) in 1944. They had a daughter, Bridget J Failes, in 1952.
    - Doris M Failes (born 1930) married George A Paling (born 1928) in 1951. They had a son, Christopher J Paling, in 1953.
    - David W Failes (born 1934).

- Arthur Dolman (22nd July 1903–July 1969) married Ethel Hill (16th February 1904–1963), born at Derby in 1925. He was a builder's lorry driver in 1939, when they were living at 99 Empress Road, Derby. They had three children:
  - Freda Mary Dolman (25th August 1926–2002) married Edwin H Rogers (29th April 1925–1972) in 1946. They had four children – Paul A Rogers 1950, Jane Rogers 1954, Mark A Rogers 1962 and Sally A Rogers 1965.
  - Sheila M Dolman (born 1928) married Dennis William Shunburne (15th October 1927–1972) in 1959. They had three children – Trudy Shunburne 1960, Mandy Shunburne 1961 and Richard Shunburne 1972.
  - John Arthur Dolman (3rd August 1934–1993) married June E Hobson (born 1934) in 1955. They had two children – Neil W Dolman 1965 and Tracey Dolman 1968.
- Sidney Dolman (30th March 1908–1980) was a land worker in 1939, living with his sister, Ethel, and her family, at Wood End, Repton. He married Florence Lilian Cooke (23rd November 1905–1983) in 1940 at Repton, where she was born. Florence was a laundry sorter and packer in 1939, living with her mother at High Street, Repton. There were no children.
- Ethel Dolman (25th January 1910–1988) married Leslie Cecil Sarson (11th November 1909–1979), a plumber, in January 1938 at Repton. They were living with her brother, Sidney Dolman, at Wood End, Repton in 1939. They had two children:
  - Michael Sarson (born 1943) married Jessie Saxton (born 1946) in 1967. They had two daughters – Caroline Jill Sarson 1973 and Analie Jane Sarson 1976.
  - Lesley A Sarson (born 1949).
- Harry Dolman (25th June 1913–1977) was a joiner in the building trade. He married Kathleen Morley (3rd June 1914–5th November 2015) in 1938. They were living with her parents at 117 Lower Dale Road, Derby in 1939, when she was a temporary clerk. They had three daughters:
  - Anne Dolman (born 1942) married Keith McIntyre in 1966. They had two children – Benjamin McIntyre 1968 and Catherine McIntyre 1971.
  - Judith Dolman (born 1944) married Patrick D Bourne (born 1945) in 1978.
  - Jane E Dolman (born 1951).

William enlisted in 2/6th North Staffordshire in January 1915 (3585 & 241028). He was only 5′4″ tall. He went to France on 28th June and joined 1/6th Battalion in October. It is unclear what he was doing in the three months between but is understood to have been training at Rouen. Because of his religious beliefs he became a stretcher-bearer in A Company. The Battalion proceeded to Egypt in January 1916 and returned to France the following month. It was involved in the disastrous attack on Gommecourt on 1st July in which the Battalion suffered 305 casualties out of the 763 who went into action. William was noted for great gallantry that day but no award was made. The Battalion moved to the Ransart area, where William carried six wounded men in from the battlefield on his back. He was told of another casualty and went out to recover the wounded man under heavy fire. Later the same day he crawled out again under very heavy machine gun fire to bring in three others. On a final search he brought in an enemy machine gun. For this he is reported to have been mentioned-in-despatches but no London Gazette entry has been found.

Awarded the MM for his gallantry on 17th February 1917 near Monchy-le-Preux. An officer took advantage of misty conditions to take out a party to repair damaged wire in front of the Battalion's trenches. The mist cleared suddenly and the party was fired upon. The officer sent the party back and was the last to withdraw. As he passed through the wire, he was shot through the thigh and fell. William immediately went to his aid and, under enemy rifle fire, succeeded in bringing him in, placing himself between the wounded officer and the enemy, who were only eighty metres away, LG 26th March 1917.

The Military Medal, seen here with a Bar, was awarded to other ranks of the British Army (later extended to other services) and Commonwealth countries for bravery on land. It was established on 25th March 1916 as the other ranks equivalent of the Military Cross, which was awarded to commissioned officers and warrant officers. It was the third level gallantry award, ranking below the Distinguished Conduct Medal. Over 115,000 MMs were awarded during the Great War, as well as 5,700 bars and 180 second bars. Private Ernest Corey, a stretcher-bearer with 55th Australian Infantry Battalion, was awarded three bars. Over 15,000 MMs were awarded during the Second World War. It was discontinued in 1993, since when the Military Cross has been awarded to all ranks within the British honours system. Most Commonwealth nations established their own honours systems after the Second World War and award their own gallantry decorations.

The Battalion moved to the Lens sector. During a daylight operation to bomb the enemy's deep dugouts, William was told to leave his platoon and proceed to the dugouts. He was caught by the blast of a German mortar bomb and, although his helmet was blown off, he escaped unscathed. After administering first aid to the wounded, he set off to the dugouts in search of other casualties. The shelter was hit again but he remained unhurt. Discovering a number of serious cases, he volunteered to return to HQ for help under sniper fire and then crawled back, guiding the medical officer to the scene. He was promoted lance corporal in June.

Awarded a Bar to the MM for three separate acts of courage. On 6th June 1917 a trench mortar bomb set fire to the Company dump containing bombs and Very light flares. William

immediately set about removing the ordnance to safety. Next day another mortar bomb set fire to the Company HQ, resulting in several casualties, which William tended and he bandaged the broken legs of one man. On 14th June a tunnel through an embankment was blown in and twelve men were buried. William organised a party to dig them out and supervised their evacuation. This action undoubtedly saved the lives of several men, LG 16th August 1917.

The Battalion was relieved on 28th June but the stretcher-bearers remained until all the wounded had been successfully evacuated on 2nd July. **Awarded the DCM for his actions during this period. He assisted in evacuating several badly wounded men from the front line and worked untiringly until every wounded man had been taken out. This undoubtedly saved the lives of several men. During the night he searched the ground between and in front of the captured trenches. Under shell and machine gun fire he brought in many men who had been wounded. He displayed absolute indifference to danger. His gallant conduct had an inspiring effect on the rest of the men and was a splendid example to all, LG 25th August 1917.**

When a British gas mortar shell dump was hit by an enemy artillery barrage, William provided assistance to a number of men who suffered from the resultant gas cloud. He was also affected by the gas and was evacuated to a field hospital. This was the only injury he suffered throughout the war. On one occasion a battalion runner brought a message that the CO wanted William to guide a visiting officer around the trenches. William replied, *Ay, and there's some wounded men out there who want me too. Tell him I can't come*. With that he picked up a stretcher and set off. Fortunately, the CO understood the reason for this insubordination. There were no hard feelings as the two would joke about the incident at reunions. When Colonel Tomlinson died in 1959, he left a small legacy *to my old friend and comrade*.

The Distinguished Conduct Medal, seen here with a Bar, was instituted by Royal Warrant on 4th December 1854 for warrant officers and below for 'distinguished, gallant and good conduct in the field'. It ranked second only to the Victoria Cross and equated to the Distinguished Service Order for officers when awarded for gallantry. It was the first official decoration awarded by the British to recognise acts of individual gallantry in the Army. During the First World War there was concern that the number of medals being awarded would devalue it. As a result the Military Medal was instituted on 25th March 1916, as a lesser award for bravery. Nevertheless 24,591 DCMs were awarded during the First World War plus 472 Bars and nine second Bars. In 1942 other ranks of the Royal Navy and Royal Air Force also became eligible. In 1993 the DCM was discontinued after a major review of the honours system, which removed distinctions of rank in respect of awards for bravery. With the Conspicuous Gallantry Medal and the Distinguished Service Order when awarded for gallantry, these three decorations were replaced by the Conspicuous Gallantry Cross as the second highest award for gallantry for all ranks of all services.

Awarded a Bar to the DCM for his actions near Bellenglise, France on 28th-29th September. He worked for forty-eight hours without rest to dress and carry in numerous wounded men from no man's land, often under heavy enemy fire. He also provided valuable and accurate updates on the advance every time he returned with a casualty. In spite of very thick smoke and fog he always found his way and, as far as his work allowed, served as a guide. He never rested until he was sure that the sector was clear of wounded. He set the very highest example of fearlessness and devotion to duty, LG 2nd December 1919.

William Coltman leaving Buckingham Palace wearing all three gallantry medals on 22nd May 1919. With him is his brother George.

Awarded the VC for his actions northeast of Sequehart, France on 3rd-4th October 1918, LG 6th January 1919. He was the most highly decorated other rank of the Great War. Despite his multiple decorations, he never caused another human being to suffer injury or death. William was demobilised on 12th March 1919 and was presented with the VC by the King in the quadrangle of Buckingham Palace on 22nd May. He was a very modest man and on the way home from the investiture heard that a reception committee had assembled to greet him. He slipped off the train at an earlier station and walked home. William was a member of the VC Guard at the interment of the Unknown Warrior on 11th November 1920.

William Coltman in later life.

William was employed as a gardener by Mr and Mrs Yeomans in Ashby Road, Burton upon Trent. He was also a special constable with Staffordshire Police Force and became a lay preacher and later an overseer. During the Second World War he was commissioned in the Staffordshire ACF (272578), LG 26th March 1943, and rose to captain in 1945. In the 1960s he was a groundsman

The Coltman Trench at the Staffordshire Regiment Museum.

The grave of Eleanor and William Coltman in St Mark's Churchyard, Winshill.

for Burton Parks and Gardens at Wheatley Recreation Ground. He enjoyed beekeeping in his extensive garden at 6 Wheatley Lane, Winshill.

William attended a number of VC Reunions – the VC Garden Party at Buckingham Palace on 26th June 1920, the VC Dinner at the Royal Gallery of the House of Lords, London on 9th November 1929, the Victory Day Celebration Dinner & Reception at The Dorchester, London on 8th June 1946, the VC Centenary Celebrations at Hyde Park, London on 26th June 1956 and the first four VC & GC Association Reunions at the Café Royal, London on 24th July 1958, 7th July 1960, 18th July 1962 and 16th July 1964. In September 1968, William took the salute at the 1st North Staffordshire Regiment Arnhem Day parade at Lichfield Cathedral, alongside Robert Henry Cain VC and the Mayor, Councillor GW Beacon. Shortly before his death he said, *I sincerely hope that future generations will know nothing of war – only what they read in books – and that never again will there come a time when a Victoria Cross can be won.* William Coltman died at Burton District Hospital Centre (Outwoods Branch) on 29th June 1974. He is buried with his wife in St Mark's Churchyard, Winshill. The grave

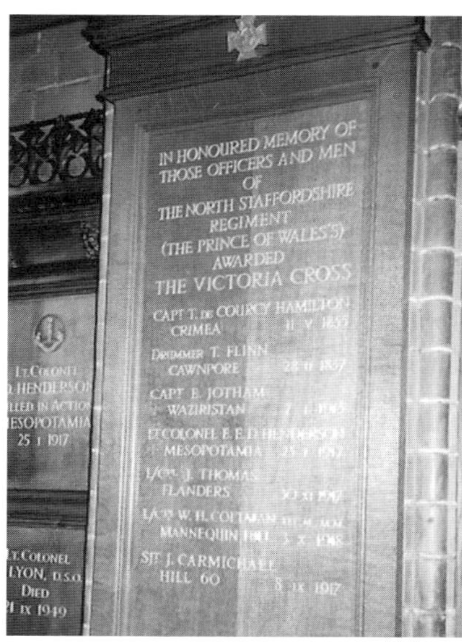

The memorial to the North Staffordshire Regiment's VCs in the Garrison Church, Whittington Barracks, Lichfield.

was refurbished in April 2010 and again in January 2014. He is commemorated in a number of other places:

- Lichfield
  - Coltman Close, Boley Park.
  - The Coltman Trench at the Staffordshire Regiment Museum, opened in 1993 by Jack Staley, a South Staffordshire Regiment veteran of the Great War and Second World War.
  - Memorial to the North Staffordshire Regiment VCs in the Garrison Church, Whittington Barracks.
  - Coltman House, Defence Medical Services, Whittington Barracks opened in 2008.
- Burton upon Trent
  - Coltman House, Hawkins Lane houses the Burton ACF and Army Reserve Centre.
  - Coltman VC Peace Wood, Mill Hill Lane, Winshill. A memorial plaque was unveiled on 17th November 2014. The wood also commemorates the ninety-four men from the area who did not return from the Great War. A silver birch tree was planted for each man.
  - Named on a memorial adjacent to Burton upon Trent War Memorial, unveiled by Sir Arthur Bryan, Lord Lieutenant of Staffordshire on 21st May 1977.
  - A Department for Communities and Local Government commemorative paving stone was dedicated at Stapenhill Gardens, Stapenhill Road on 4th October 2018.

The memorial to William Coltman close to Burton upon Trent War Memorial.

The Department for Communities and Local Government commemorative paving stone at Stapenhill Gardens (Memorials to Valour).

William Coltman's unique set of medals.

The Defence Medal was instituted in May 1945 for non-operational military and certain types of civilian war service (Home Guard, Civil Defence, Royal Observer Corps, Fire Service and other approved civilian services) from 3rd September 1939 to 8th May 1945 and for the Pacific Theatre until 2nd September 1945. In the United Kingdom military personnel in headquarters, training units and airfields were eligible for the award. Qualifying service varied. In the United Kingdom the requirement was three years or three months in a Mine and Bomb Disposal Unit. In a non-operational area, not subjected to air attack and not closely threatened, the requirement was one year's service overseas outside the individual's country of residence. In a non-operational area subjected to air attack or closely threatened, the requirement was six months.

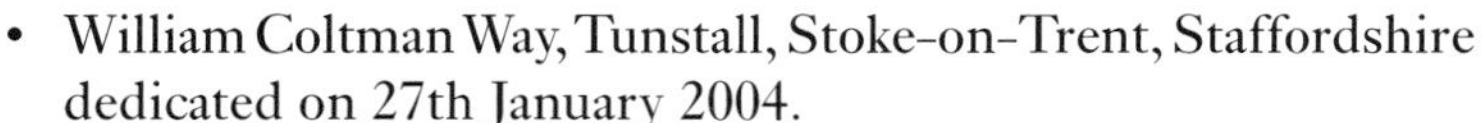

- William Coltman Way, Tunstall, Stoke-on-Trent, Staffordshire dedicated on 27th January 2004.
- Plaque in the Staffordshire Regiment Grove at the National Memorial Arboretum, Alrewas, Staffordshire.
- Coltman Stretcher Race held annually over a ten-mile course across the Malvern Hills, Worcestershire since 2014 to raise money for the Royal British Legion.
- The Staffordshire Regiment commissioned a painting of him by Mr AR Todd.

The Staffordshire Regiment Museum at Whittington Barracks, Lichfield.

In addition to the VC, DCM & Bar and MM & Bar he was awarded the 1914–15 Star, British War Medal 1914–20, Victory Medal 1914–19 with Mentioned-in-Despatches Oakleaf, Defence Medal, George VI Coronation Medal 1937, Elizabeth II Coronation Medal 1953 and

The Special Constabulary Long Service Medal was established on 30th August 1919 by King George V. Initially it was to recognise three years' service, involving at least 150 police duties, during the Great War and was known as the Special Constabulary Medal. Various changes to the Royal Warrant followed to recognise nine years of service and to change the name to the Special Constabulary Long Service Medal. Service during both World Wars counted as triple. Special Constables who complete an additional period of ten years' service are eligible for a clasp.

Special Constabulary Long Service Medal. When his son, Charles, died, the VC group was presented to the Staffordshire Regiment. The VC is held by the Staffordshire Regiment Museum, Whittington Barracks, Lichfield, Staffordshire.

16796 PRIVATE WILLIAM EDGAR HOLMES
2nd Battalion, Grenadier Guards

William Holmes was born on 5th June 1895 at Wood Stanway, near Winchcombe, Gloucestershire. His father, Edward Holmes (14th July 1865–9th August 1961), born at Stanton, Cheltenham, Gloucestershire, was a carter's boy in 1881, before becoming a timber feller on the Stanway Estate, living at Winchcombe, Gloucestershire. He was a labourer living with his parents in 1891. He married Ellen Elizabeth née Stanley (24th August 1867–9th March 1941), a domestic servant born at Bretforton, Worcestershire, on 9th May 1891 at the Parish Church, Stanton, Gloucestershire. At the time of the 1891 Census she was a visitor at the home of Alfred Holmes, her future father-in-law. They were living at Wood Stanway in 1901, at 65 Didbrook, near Cheltenham, Gloucestershire by 1911 and were still there in 1939. Ellen died at the District Hospital, Winchcombe and Edward at Westbury-on-Severn, Gloucestershire. Ellen had a son before they married:

- Arthur Stanley (29th September 1884–11th February 1966), born at Willersey, Gloucestershire, was living with his grandparents in 1891 as their son. By 1901 he was boarding at Sanatorium Road, Worcester and by 1911 was a builder's labourer, again living with his grandparents as their son. Arthur enlisted in the Grenadier Guards on 28th December 1914 at Stratford-upon-Avon, Warwickshire (21388). He was assigned to 14th Company at Caterham Barracks, Surrey, joining on 31st December, described as a labourer, 5′ 10″ tall, with fresh complexion, brown eyes and black hair. He was discharged on 6th April 1915 as not likely to become

Stanton is one of the most idyllic and unspoiled villages in the north Cotswolds area. The church, which dates back to c.1100, probably on the site of an earlier Saxon building, is Grade I listed. The manor of Stanway was owned by Tewkesbury Abbey for 800 years and by the Tracy family and their descendants, the Earls of Wemyss and March, for another 500 years. The House was constructed in the late 16th and early 17th century on the site of an earlier Tudor house and is also Grade I listed, as are the gardens. The main entrance gate may have been designed by Inigo Jones (1573–1652). JM Barrie, creator of *Peter Pan*, was a frequent visitor in the 1920s and early 1930s. The house has appeared in a number of television series and films. The tithe barn was built c.1370 for Tewkesbury Abbey and the Estate watermill has been restored and still produces flour. The Stanway Fountain, opened on 5th June 2004, rises to over ninety metres and is the tallest in Britain.

an efficient soldier. He was a timber feller in 1920, living at Shaftesbury Cottage, Charlton Kings, Gloucestershire. Arthur lived with his half-sister, Mabel Clark née Holmes (see below). They were living at 16 Derby Road, Worcester in 1939, by when he was a gardener and she was listed as Mabel Stanley, although no marriage has been found. Arthur died at 16 Derby Road, Worcester. Arthur and Mabel are believed to have had eight children including:

- Kathleen Violet Stanley (16th November 1920–25th December 2009), born at Tyndale, Clarence Square, Cheltenham. She was a general and domestic servant at 8 Warwick Road, Ealing, London in 1939. She married Henry Gilbert Vickers (4th October 1917–8th August 1984), born at Mansfield Woodhouse, Nottinghamshire, on 20th May 1961 at Haverfordwest, Pembrokeshire. He was a colliery haulage hand in 1939, when they were living with his mother and stepfather, Ernest Betts (1892–1966), at 19 Booth Crescent, Mansfield. By 1961 he was a platelayer on a private railway, living at 83 North Road, Milford Haven. They had a son, Alan K Vickers in 1962.
- Cynthia Jean Stanley (born 18th August 1928), born at Pershore, Worcestershire, married Douglas Harry Sheppard (2nd March 1925–September 1991), born at Ledbury, Herefordshire, in 1955 at Worcester. He was a roadstone quarry labourer in 1939, when they were living with his parents at Longstone Cottage, Martley, Worcestershire. They had a son, Ashley David Sheppard in 1961.

The Stanway parish church of St Peter was rebuilt in the 12th century and was restored in 1896. The tower, which was added in the 13th century, contains five bells dating from 1625 to 2014.

  - Betty Stanley (born 1929).
  - Edna Muriel Stanley (26th January 1931–December 2004) married Thomas J Clarke in 1957 at Worcester. They had a son, Martin K Clarke in 1960.
  - Kenneth R Stanley (born 20th February 1934) married Margaret Simpson in 1965 at Evesham, Worcestershire.

William had nine full siblings:

- Ivy Dora Holmes (21st June 1892–1983) was a servant at The Rectory, Buckland, Broadway, Winchcombe in 1911. She married Edgar Frederick Jones (born 1889), a coachman born at Woodford, Essex, on 27th October 1913 at Didbrook Parish Church. They lived at Berkeley House, Berkeley Street, Cheltenham, Gloucestershire. Edgar served in 2nd Worcestershire (24188) and died of wounds on 24th April 1918 (Boulogne Eastern Cemetery, France – IX A 18). Ivy married Walter Nicholas Bichard (9th March 1892–1971), born at Barry, Glamorgan, on 1st September 1918 at Winchcombe. He was the son of Nicholas Bichard (1870–1955) and Amelia Holmes (1871–1958), Ivy's paternal aunt. Walter was living with his parents at Towy Villa, Oldcastle, Bridgend, South Glamorgan in 1901. He was a stock taker living at 45 Lombard Street, Barry, Glamorgan when he enlisted in the Glamorgan & Pembroke Garrison Artillery on 3rd April 1908 at Barry (152), described as 5′6″ tall. He transferred on 22nd February 1909 to the Royal Field Artillery. He was mobilised on 10th January 1915 (55909) and had risen to sergeant by 1918. Ivy was issued with a re-marriage gratuity of £35/15/-. Walter was a chargeman pipe layer on the docks in 1939, when they were living at

William's brother-in-law, Edgar Frederick Jones, is buried in Boulogne Eastern Cemetery.

74 Jenner Road, Barry. A Mrs Norah A Holmes was living with them. Ivy had two sons from her two marriages:

   - Dennis William Frederick Jones (10th February 1914–May 1994), an enamel furnace fireman, married Olive May Lilian Clark (born 31st May 1917), born at Cardiff, Glamorgan, in 1939 and they lived at 71 Kingsland Crescent, Barry.
   - Douglas Walter C Bichard (4th April 1920–January 2002) married Gladys Amy Bowen (23rd November 1921–February 1994), born at Cardiff, in 1946. They had three children – Nicholas Bichard 1947 and twins Helena F and Judith V Bichard 1958.

- Harold Holmes (26th October 1893–5th July 1973), born at Wood Stanway, Gloucestershire was a farm labourer in 1911 and later a railway platelayer. He served in 9th Gloucestershire during the Great War, rising to corporal, and married Rosina Curnock (21st March 1896–29th October 1984) on 12th April 1915 at the Wesleyan Chapel, Winchcombe, where she was born. Rosina was living with her parents at Gloucester Street, Winchcombe in 1911 and was working in a jam factory. Harold was working on the railways in 1935, when they were living at 26 Gloucester Street, Winchcombe. By 1939 they were living at 3 Council Houses, Langley Road, Cheltenham. He was working on the permanent way and repair staff on the railways and Rosina was working in a paper mill. They were living at 1 Binyon Road, Winchcombe when they travelled aboard RMS *Mauretania* from Southampton, arriving at New York on 30th September 1958. Harold died at his home at 107 Binyon Road, Winchcombe. They had ten children:
   - Kathleen 'Kay' Rachel Holmes (2nd April 1916–10th February 2009) married Frederick Keith Penny (10th December 1913–27th February 2009), a Prudential Assurance Co agent born at Marlborough, Wiltshire, on 17th August 1935 at Winchcombe Parish Church. He was living at 31 Wallingford Street, Wantage, Berkshire. His father, Frederick Penny (1885–1966), enlisted in the Coldstream Guards (24091) at Marlborough on 10th December 1915, described as 5′7¼″ tall and weighing 133 lbs. He transferred to the Army Reserve the same day. He was a motor driver for W James Duck, Dairy, High Street, Marlborough, living at 31 London Road, Marlborough. A medical at Devizes on 9th May 1916 found that he had enlarged tonsils, slight varicose veins in both legs and he required dental attention. He was mobilised on 11th April 1918 and joined the reserve battalion at Caterham on 14th April. He embarked at Folkestone and disembarked at Boulogne on 7th September, joined the Base Depot on 14th September and 3rd Battalion on 18th September. He transferred to 1st Battalion on 28th October. On 26th November he suffered a strained heart and was admitted to No.53 Casualty Clearing Station next day. He was transferred to 12th General Hospital, Rouen on 30th November and joined

the Guards Division Base Depot at Le Havre on 10th December. A medical board at Harfleur on 6th January 1919 graded him B II. He was attached to 3rd Composite Guards Garrison Company. At a discharge medical at 5th Stationary Hospital, Dieppe on 5th February he claimed to have suffered a strained heart while carrying a pack in October 1918. No sign of disease was found. Frederick returned to Britain on 8th February and transferred to the Class Z Army Reserve on demobilisation at Fovant, Wiltshire on 11th March 1919. Frederick junior and Kay were living at 76 Newbury Street, Wantage in 1939. They both died at Devizes, Wiltshire. They had two children – Pauline R Penny 1936 and Yvette 'Betsy' Penny 1937.

- Harold Charles Holmes (26th November 1919–1992) married Catherine Ruby Jane Mills (8th November 1920–1981) in 1939 at Cheltenham, where she was born. Her mother, Johanna Harrington (1893–1975), married George Mills (1889–1917) in 1911 at Cheltenham. George served in 2/4th (City of Bristol) Battalion, Gloucestershire Regiment (202579) and died on active service on 3rd December 1917 (Cambrai Memorial, Louverval, France). Catherine was a chamber maid and her mother was a charwoman in 1939, living together with Catherine's siblings at Rosewood House, New Street, Cheltenham. Harold and Catherine were living at 14 Rowanfield Exchange, Cheltenham in 1973. Catherine died at Cheltenham and Harold at Havering, Essex. They had two sons – Kenneth G Holmes 1941 and Darrell WJ Holmes 1948.
- Betty Cynthia Holmes (born 1921) married Leslie Charles William Palmer (8th August 1920–20th February 1989), born at Northleach, Gloucestershire, in 1940 at Cheltenham. He was a bus conductor in 1939, boarding at 13 Lower Park Street, Cheltenham. He served in the Royal Air Force during the Second World War and she may also have served in the forces. They were living at 33 Cotswold Road, Prestbury, Gloucestershire in 1949 and at 63 New Barn Lane, Prestbury at the time of his death there. They had four children – David John Palmer 1941, Anthony K Palmer 1946, Creina E Palmer 1948 and Lesley E Palmer 1960.
- Kenneth Ronald Holmes (30th June 1922–22nd April 1974) served in the Gloucestershire Regiment during the Second

George Mills is commemorated on the Cambrai Memorial at Louverval.

World War (5186027). He transferred to 37th Anti-Aircraft Regiment, Royal Artillery on 29th February 1940 and to 123rd Light Anti-Aircraft Battery on 4th December 1942. He was in hospital in the Middle East from 11th January 1944 and returned to his unit on 26th February. He joined the Base Depot Royal Artillery on the X (IV) List on 22nd October. He was on the strength of Bellahouston Transit Camp, Glasgow 12th March–16th April 1945 for 'Leave in Addition to Python' (a points-based scheme for the repatriation and leave for soldiers who had served overseas for a long period). He joined C Royal Artillery Depot on 18th September, 16th Holding Regiment on 9th November and was released from service on 22nd May 1946. Kenneth married Enid Nancy Alethia Critchley (23rd September 1925–5th November 2000) in 1949 at Cheltenham, where she was born. Her brother, Reginald, married Kenneth's sister, Vivien. Kenneth and Enid emigrated to Canada and they both died at Calgary, Alberta. They had two children – Joanna L Holmes 1950 and Kenneth A Holmes 1956.

- Eddie Holmes (23rd August 1923–28th January 2009) was a grocer's assistant in 1939, living with his parents. He married Betty Winn (c.1924–28th January 2009) in 1945 at Cheltenham. They had eight children – Paul Holmes 1948, Peter Holmes 1949, Barry Holmes 1950, Christopher Holmes 1952, Richard Holmes 1953, Mark Holmes 1956, Jonathan Holmes 1958 and Neil Holmes 1961.
- Creina R Holmes (11th March 1926–7th May 2013) married James J Ehrig (20th June 1920–27th December 1983), born at Buffalo, Erie, New York, USA, in 1945 at Cheltenham. He was a semi-skilled switchman on the railroads when he enlisted in the US Army on 5th January 1942 at Fort Niagara, Youngstown, New York. He was discharged on 3rd December 1945. She was living at 3 Enfield Villas, Winchcombe before joining her husband at 111 Hollywood Avenue, Buffalo. Creina and her daughter, Dana, flew to London, England from New York on 8th October 1949 and returned later aboard SS *De Grasse* from Southampton to New York. James and Creina had moved to 55 Shenandoah Road, Buffalo by 1950. They had four children, including Dana L Ehrig.
- Merthys Beryl G Holmes (18th July 1927–1980) was known as Beryl. She married Konrad Siller (30th October 1926–27th May 1978), born at Georgshausen (now *Györgyháza),* Yugoslavia (formerly Austria-Hungary, now Serbia). His father, Georg Siller (23rd August 1890–October 1944), married Susanne Frank (1898–3rd May 1933) on 4th August 1920 at Erneszthaza (now Erneszthâza), Yugoslavia. Georg, also born at Georgshausen, served in the Imperial Austro-Hungarian Army as a hussar during the Great War and was decorated. They had four children, including Konrad. Georg was living at 140 Neue Gasse, Georgshausen in March 1941. The Yugoslavian police authorities carried out mass arrests of Danube

Konrad Siller, third from the left, in Hitler Youth uniform.

Swabian men beginning on 3rd October 1944. Georg was taken to Camp Sjokowitsch, where he was executed with numerous others by Yugoslav partisans. Konrad was a member of the Hitler Youth as a teenager. Konrad and Beryl were living at 87 Binyon Road, Winchcombe in 1955. They had two children – Stephen J Siller 1950 and Rosina J Siller 1957.

  - Vivien Mavis Holmes (11th August 1929 – in July 2000), known as Mavis, married Reginald Eric Critchley (18th November 1920–6th July 2005) in 1948 at Cheltenham. Her name was recorded as Mavis Vivien and his as Eric Reginald. They had five children – Michael E Critchley 1949, Gordon R Critchley 1951, Andrew N Critchley 1953, Betty A Critchley 1956 and Stella J Critchley 1958.
  - Anita Velma Holmes (1931–34).
  - Peggy Holmes (27th October 1932–December 2005) married Vladimir 'Vlade' Jerkovic (20th July 1927–July 1990) in 1949 at Cheltenham. They had three children – Maria Jerkovic 1949, Peter V Jerkovic 1951 and Alexander Jerkovic 1961.

- Mabel Holmes (born 26th December 1896) married John Seymour Clark (born c.1897) on 29th October 1917 at Didbrook Church, Gloucestershire. He enlisted in 2nd Grenadier Guards on 9th August 1914 (17203) and went to France on 19th January 1915, where he was wounded. He was discharged on 24th February 1919, surplus to military requirements, having suffered impairment, and was awarded Silver War Badge No.B.265853. The marriage failed and she moved in with Arthur Stanley, her half-brother (see above).
- Mark Stanley Holmes (24th July 1900–18th May 1970) was living at 6 Glyn Street, Ogmore Vale, Bridgend, Glamorgan at the time of his death there.

- Harry Holmes (born 18th June 1902), a chauffeur living at Tarderbigge, Worcestershire, married Norah Amelia Beszant (10th June 1916–6th December 2010), a needle viewer, on 2nd January 1937 at Headless Cross Parish Church, Worcestershire, where she was living. Norah was living with Harry's sister, Ivy and husband Walter Nicholas Bichard, at the time of the 1939 Register at 74 Jenner Road, Barry. Norah married Harold Hutchinson, registered at Richmond upon Thames in 1987. Norah and Harry Holmes had five children:
    - Pamela ID Holmes (born 1937), registered at Bromsgrove, married George E Hughes in 1957 and Peter L Wright in 1984.
    - Linda M Holmes (1940–41).
    - Nicholas S Holmes (born 1943).
    - Gillian Holmes (born 1949), registered at Surrey North.
    - Martin E Holmes (1956–57).
- Cynthia Holmes (8th April 1904–January 1996) married Edward Arthur Tredwell (17th June 1902–26th October 1994), born at Broadway, Worcestershire, on 1st November 1924 at Didbrook Church. He was a signalman with the Great Western Railway in 1939, when they were living at Holly View, Ledbury, Herefordshire. They both died at Evesham, Gloucestershire. They had three children:
    - Megan B Tredwell (born 1925) married Raymond Francis James (2nd October 1924–13th November 1985), born at Worcester, in 1944 at Martley, Worcestershire. He was a gardener in 1939, living with Thomas and Harriet James, probably his grandparents, at Great House Cottages, Leigh, Worcestershire. He worked for the Great Western Railway at Worcester as an engine cleaner from 2nd June 1941 and a fireman from 8th December 1941. He resigned on 23rd August 1947 and joined Rackstraws, furniture manufacturers of Worcester. They were living at 8 Knapp Way, Malvern, Worcestershire at the time of his death there. They had three children – Marilyn F James 1948, Jayne E James 1957 and Kevin C James 1959.
    - Josephine Marjorie Tredwell (born 1928) married Douglas W Richardson (15th June 1926–December 1988), born at Marlcliff, Warwickshire, in 1948. He was living with his parents at 14 Winterway Estate. North Cotswold, Gloucestershire in 1939. They had two children – Brian K Richardson 1949 and Susan J Richardson 1955.
    - Edgar A Tredwell (born 1931) married Lynette K Jones (born 1947) in 1967 at Leicester, where she was born. They had a son, Hayden Murray Tredwell, in 1970. The marriage ended in divorce. Lynette married John E Holland (born 1943) in 1974 at Leicester. John and Lynnette had at least two children – Corinne Rachel Holland 1975 and Miriam Eleanor F Holland 1984. An Edgar Arthur Tredwell (born January 1931), living at 57 East 3300 South, Bountiful, Utah, USA 1984–91, married Margaretha Elisabeth Zemlicka, born in Sweden, on 25th June 1979 at Davis, Utah.

- Leonard Holmes (11th November 1906 -1965) was living with his parents at 65 Didbrook, Cheltenham in 1939, recorded as an invalid.
- Horace Holmes (9th February 1909–28th October 2009) married Hannah Lewis (12th February 1911–24th July 2003), born in Glamorgan, on 2nd May 1936 at St George Church, Didbrook. He was an estate labourer (lorry driver) in 1939, when they were living at 62 Didbrook. They had twin daughters:
  - Ann Holmes (born 10th May 1937) married Ronald J Lyon in 1962.
  - Elizabeth Holmes (born 10th May 1937) is believed to have married John Fenton in 1964.
- Dorothy Holmes (14th September 1910–June 2005) married Ernest Frederick Lander (3rd December 1910–16th February 1981), born at Swindon, Wiltshire, in 1939 at Cheltenham. He was living with his parents at 41 Rolleston Street, Swindon in 1911. Ernest was a carpenter and joiner in 1939, when they were living at 45 Lansdown Crescent, Cheltenham. They were living at 40 Liddington Road, Gloucester at the time of his death there. She was residing at Magdalen House Nursing Home, 98a London Road, Gloucester at the time of her death there. They had three children:
  - Joan D Lander (1940–45).
  - Wendy A Lander (born 1944) married Graham H Middleton (born 1940), born at Gloucester, in 1965. They had two children – Sarah Jane Middleton 1966 and Kevin Henry Middleton 1968.
  - Allan P Lander (born 1946), born at Bristol, Gloucestershire, married June P Taylor (born 1947), born at Cheltenham, at Bristol in 1970. They had at least one son.

His paternal grandfather, Alfred Holmes (14th October 1838–20th December 1912), married Rose 'Rosetta' Anne née Porter (18th July 1839–1921) at Stanton Parish Church, Gloucestershire on 15th November 1859. They were both born at Stanton and lived the rest of their lives there. She was a gloveress in 1861 and Alfred was a shepherd in 1881. By 1891 he was an agricultural labourer. In addition to Edward they had seven other children:

- Frank Holmes (born 1860), born at Buckland, Gloucestershire, was an agricultural labourer in 1881.
- Ada 'Minnie' Holmes (21st March 1863–1951), born at Stanton, Gloucestershire, married William David Shergold (25th February 1862–15th June 1936) on 14th July 1883 at Toddington Manor Church, Toddington, Gloucestershire, where he was born. He was a plumber in 1901, when they were living at 2 Highfield Road, Barnwood, Gloucestershire. They had moved to 66 Victoria Street, Gloucester by 1911. Minnie was living at 50 Victoria Street in 1939. Living with her was Norman Shergold (born 9th December 1924), a printer. They had eight children:

  - Harold Francis Shergold (12th September 1884–7th March 1948) married Mary Evelyn Scrivens (1883–1959) at Gloucester in 1910. They had three children – Albert A Shergold 1911, Alfred W Shergold 1913 and Grace EM Shergold 1916.
  - Calvin Shergold (25th March 1886–1966).
  - Olive Edith Shergold (born 1890) is believed to have married Frederick W Kitson at Gloucester in 1916. They had a son, Alfred G Kitson, in 1917.
  - Mabel Edith Shergold (30th September 1892–1949), birth registered at Pontyridd, married Bertie Mortimer (3rd August 1896–1976) at Gloucester in 1916. They had a son, Edwin WA Mortimer, in 1918.
  - Maud Minnie Shergold (1895) married Frederick G Lee in 1918. They had two children – Francis WJ Lee 1918 and Dorothy M Lee 1934.
  - Blanche Hilda Shergold (28th October 1896–1983) married Herbert C Paisley (1892–1940) at Kingston upon Thames in 1924. They had two children – Ian P Paisley 1927 and Janet Paisley 1933.
  - Thyrza Beatrice Shergold (25th April 1900–1969) married Reginald Owen Shurmer (8th August 1896–1972) at Gloucester in 1936. They had two children – Graham R Shurmer 1936 and Janet B Shurmer 1938.
  - May Phyllis Shergold (born 1902).
- Oliver Holmes (14th August 1868–1941) was a carter in 1881. He was a painter when he married Florence Amelia Hunt (1869–1948), born at Clifton, Gloucestershire, on 13th January 1892 at Guiting Power Church, Gloucestershire. Oliver was a police constable in 1901, when they were living at Mangotsfield, Gloucestershire. In 1911 they were living at Winterbourne Police Station, Gloucestershire. He was living with his son, Roderick and family, in 1939. They had four children:
  - Oliver William Holmes (10th July 1892–16th May 1944) was a motor driver when he enlisted in the Army Service Corps at Bristol (M2/131627) on 13th October 1915 and joined at Grove Park next day, described as 5′ 6¼″ tall and weighing 140 lbs. He joined the Mediterranean Expeditionary Force, embarking at Avonmouth on 26th October and disembarking at Alexandria, Egypt on 13th November. He was posted to 596th Company and transferred to Mesopotamia, embarking at Alexandria on 22nd December and disembarking at Basrah on 17th January 1916. Oliver was admitted to hospital in Basrah on 18th September and was evacuated to India aboard HMHS *Oxfordshire* on 23rd September. Appointed acting lance corporal unpaid on 1st May 1919 and acting corporal with pay 11th June – 8th July, whilst in charge of stores. He transferred to No.8 Company on 31st July and arrived at Lahore, India on 15th August. He returned to Britain aboard SS *Soudan*, embarking on 22nd September and arriving on 1st November. He was demobilised from No.1 Dispersal Unit, Fovant, Wiltshire to the Class Z Reserve on 24th December 1919 and was discharged on 21st January 1920. Oliver married Rossanna Short in 1920. They had a son, John OS Holmes, in 1921.

 - Lily Ethel Holmes (11th December 1893–1974) married Elijah Matthews in 1918. They had three children – Roderick C Matthews 1920, Jack EI Matthews 1924 and Eileen M Matthews 1934.
 - Roderick Frank Holmes (14th September 1895–7th November 1969), married Nellie Bushell in 1922. They had two daughters – Evelyn Holmes (1923–25) and Evelyn P Holmes 1926. He was a station master with the Great Western Railway, living at Station House, Yeovil, Somerset in 1939.
 - George Edward Downs Holmes (November 1899–17th May 1969) married Elsie May Blanchard (8th December 1893–1981) in 1928.
- Amelia Holmes (4th August 1871–1958) married Nicholas Bichard (8th February 1871–1955), born at Bedwas, Monmouthshire, in 1891 at Cardiff, Glamorgan. He was a railway guard in 1901, when they were living at Towy Villa, Oldcastle, Bridgend, Glamorgan and at 45 Lombard Street, Barry by 1911. They were living at 4 Lombard Street by 1939. Also living with them was Nicholas's brother, Charles John Bichard (1875–1946), a general labourer on the docks. They had seven children:
 - Walter Nicholas Bichard (9th March 1892–1971) enlisted in the Glamorgan & Pembrokeshire RGA at Barry Dock on 3rd April 1908, described as a stock taker with Barry Railway Co and 5′ 6″ tall. He attended annual training 1st-15th August 1908. He transferred to the RFA on 22nd February 1909 and was later promoted bombardier (125 & 55909). He went to France on 10th January 1915. Walter married Ivy Dora Jones (21st June 1892–1983) in 1918.
 - Alfred Frank Bichard (21st December 1893–25th June 1961).
 - Nicholas Percy Bichard (26th July 1895–1949).
 - George Oliver Bichard (27th April 1897–31st October 1966) married Grace Smith (28th May 1893–1970) in 1922, registered at Thanet, Kent. They had two sons – Norman S Bichard 1924 and Peter A Bichard 1931.
 - Hubert Bichard (31st October 1900–1963) married Edith M Brookes in 1925, registered at Brentford, Middlesex.
 - Ivor Bichard (12th October 1907–1986) married Edith M Evans in 1926, registered at Cardiff. They had a daughter, Cynthia M Bichard, in 1927.
 - Leonard Charles Bichard (1909–18).
- Hudson Holmes (6th April 1876–19th March 1955) married Sarah Ann Simmonds (13th November 1879–19th December 1962), born at Lewes, Sussex, in 1897, registered at Swansea, Glamorgan. He was a labourer at Portsmouth Dockyard, Hampshire in 1911, when they were living at 77 Strode Road, North End, Portsmouth. He was later a crane driver. They were living at 55 Drayton Gardens, West Drayton, Middlesex in 1939, when he was unemployed. He subsequently died there. Sarah was living at 207 The Causeway, Petersfield, Hampshire at the time of her death there. They had five children:
 - Bertie Holmes (18th June 1898–1969).
 - Rose Elizabeth Holmes (1899).

  - Alfred George Holmes (1902).
  - Leonard Hudson Holmes (26th May 1904–1979).
  - Ivy Joyce Holmes (11th June 1907–10th December 1989) married Alexander FG Collard in 1929, registered at Uxbridge, Middlesex.
- Hilda Beatrice Holmes (born 1880) married Henry 'Harry' Beman Walker (born 1881) in 1906 at Evesham, Worcestershire, where his birth was registered. Harry was a bus driver in 1911, when they were living at Broadway, Worcestershire. They had two children:
  - Percy Oliver Graham Walker (7th July 1907–1981).
  - Hilda F Walker (1912).
- Leonard Holmes (11th October 1883–1938), a domestic gardener/labourer, married Ellen Mary/Helen Mary Hedges (1878–1927), birth registered at Oxford, on 7th September 1907 at South Banbury Parish Church, Banbury, Oxfordshire. She was living with her parents at 27 North Street, Grimsbury, Oxfordshire in 1901 and at 113 West Street, Grimsbury at the time of her marriage. She died at Bishop's Itchington, Warwickshire and he at Coventry, Warwickshire. They had four children:
  - Hubert Holmes (21st January 1908–1989) married Lavinia G Barclay (born 1910), birth registered at Greenwich, London, in 1935 at Coventry. They had three sons – Alan J Holmes 1935, Hubert D Holmes 1938 and Frank L Holmes 1945.
  - May Holmes (23rd June 1909–1998) married Ronald George Hirons (20th February 1908–1988), registered at Stratford upon Avon, Warwickshire, where his birth was also registered, in 1935. They had two daughters – Audrey M Hirons 1936 and Margaret J Hirons 1943.
  - Wilfred Holmes (16th September 1911–1967) married Margaret V Booth, registered at Coventry in 1942.
  - Dorothy Holmes (4th June 1918–1976).

Bretforton, Worcestershire, about seven kilometres east of Evesham, is recorded in a charter of 709. The village was owned by Evesham Abbey until the Dissolution of the Monasteries. The village school opened in 1877 as Bretforton Board School. The 1993 BBC production of Dicken's *Martin Chuzzlewit* used the Fleece Inn, renamed the Green Dragon, and village green. The Grade II listed manor house was rebuilt in 1105 and remodelled in 1177. It has a priest-hole in the library. Bretforton Hall, also Grade II listed, was built in 1785. St Leonard's Church, Grade I listed, dates from the late 13th century.

Willersey, Gloucestershire is five kilometres southwest of Evesham. The Church of St Peter, built in the 12th century, is Grade I listed.

His maternal grandfather, Henry Stanley (2nd January 1842–24 December 1913), born at Bretforton, Worcestershire, married Sarah née Collett (27th December 1842–29th October 1911), born at Willersey, Gloucestershire, at Saintbury, Gloucestershire on 29th July 1865. Henry was an agricultural labourer in 1871, when they were living at Saintbury Village and at Village Street, Willersey in 1881. By 1891 he was a carter and they were living at 31 Paul's Cottage, Mickleton, Gloucestershire and at Littlebrook, Evesham, Worcestershire by 1901. By 1911 he was an agricultural labourer and they were living at Willersey, Broadway, Worcestershire. They both died at Willersey. In addition to Ellen they had six other children:

- Harry Stanley (1869–75).
- William George Stanley (1871–5th March 1892) was a shepherd in 1891, living with his parents. He died at Pearls Cottage, Mickleton, Gloucestershire.
- Thomas Collett Stanley (1875–14th February 1885) died of tubercular meningitis at Broadway.
- Bertha Stanley (1878–1932) married Charles Jordan (1868–10th February 1935), a labourer born at Hampton, on 11th September 1897 at Badsey, Worcestershire. They were living at Village Street, Willersey, Gloucestershire in 1901 and at Colletts Fields, Broadway, Worcestershire in 1911. Charles was living at 58 Limetree Avenue, Broadway at the time of his death there. They had five children:
    - Walter Jordan (1897–31st July 1917) was serving in 1st Worcestershire (202406) when he died (Perth Cemetery (China Wall), Belgium – I E 12).

William's cousin, Walter Jordan, is buried in Perth Cemetery (China Wall), southeast of Ypres, Belgium.

- Charles Jordan (1899–1954) married Violet Primrose Gilder (19th April 1900–1977), registered at Evesham in 1922, where her birth was registered. They had five children – Eileen M Jordan 1924, Alfred Jordan 1926, Peter CE Jordan 1927, David W Jordan 1934 and Leslie A Jordan 1938.
- George Stanley Jordan (6th August 1900–1975) married Dorothy Harriet E Close (29th August 1900–1985), birth registered at Chard, Somerset, in 1926 registered at Evesham. They had four children – twins Jean M and Joan D Jordan 1928, John C Jordan 1935 and Jill D Jordan 1938.
- Elsie Jordan (born and died 1902).
- Dora Violet Jordan (28th November 1905–25th August 1988) married James H Garwood (9th December 1911–1979) in 1929 registered at Evesham, where their births were also registered. They had eight children – Joyce D Garwood 1929, Muriel V Garwood 1931, Rosaleen D Garwood 1932, Pauline D Garwood 1934, Brian J Garwood 1935, Graham G Garwood 1937, Dawn V Garwood 1940 and Averill D Garwood 1941.

- Jim Stanley (3rd August 1881–23rd December 1953) was a railway platelayer with the Great Western Railway in 1911. He married Amy Norris Shergold née Barrett (16th December 1879–1940), birth registered at Alderbury, Wiltshire, in 1919 at Bradford on Avon, Wiltshire. She lived with her parents on Exeter Street, Salisbury, Wiltshire. Jim and Amy lived at Dudley Cottage, Broadway, Worcestershire and had moved to 11 Cheltenham Road, Broadway by 1939. Amy had married 4761 Corporal Henry William Shergold, 2nd Wiltshire (1879–24th October 1914), birth registered at Wilton, Wiltshire, at Southbroom Church, Southbroom, Devizes, Wiltshire on 24th May 1911. They were both living at The Barracks, Devizes at the time, although he was serving with his Battalion at Le Marchant Barracks, Roundway, Derbyshire at the time of the 1911 Census. Henry's parents lived at Under Old Sarum, Stratford-sub-Castle, Alderbury, Wiltshire. Henry was promoted sergeant and went to France on 7th October 1914. He was killed in action later in October (Ypres (Menin Gate) Memorial, Belgium – Panel 53). Jim married Flora E Davis in 1946 at Upton, Worcestershire. He was still living at 11 Cheltenham Road, Broadway at the time of his death at Horseway, Springfield Lane, Broadway.
- Rose Mary Stanley (23rd February 1885–29th August 1975) married Alexander Deebank (23rd December 1877–10th November 1922), a foreman born at Hendon Union Infirmary, Middlesex, on 11th June 1904 at Broadway Parish Church, Worcestershire. He was living with his parents at 3 Lorne Terrace, Kent Road, Tottenham, London in 1881. By 1911 he was a bricklayer and railway contractor and they were living at 113 Whippindell Road, Watford, Hertfordshire. Alexander enlisted as a driver in the Army Service Corps on 10th November 1914 (T3/024062) and went to France on 22nd July 1915. He was discharged on 24th August 1918 no longer physically fit for war service and was awarded the Silver War Badge No.441247. Alexander died at 130 Camden Street, Pancras,

The Ypres (Menin Gate) Memorial is one of four memorials to the missing in the Ypres Salient. The Menin Gate was chosen because it was the closest exit of the town to the battlefront. In reality the Menin Gate was subjected to shellfire so frequently that most troops left through other gates. Commemorated on it are 54,395 missing servicemen of Australia, Canada, India, South Africa and the United Kingdom. For the latter only those prior to 16th August 1917 are commemorated. After that date the missing of the United Kingdom and New Zealand are named on the Tyne Cot Memorial, which carries another 34,984 names. Some New Zealanders from the Polygon Wood area are commemorated on a separate memorial there. The Menin Gate Memorial was designed by Reginald Blomfield, with sculpture by Sir William Reid-Dick. The Memorial was unveiled by Field Marshal Lord Plumer on 24th July 1927. Since 2nd July 1928 every evening at 8.00 p.m. the buglers of the Last Post Association sound the Last Post. During the German occupation in the Second World War the daily ceremony was conducted at Brookwood Cemetery in Surrey. The ceremony resumed at the Menin Gate on the evening that Polish forces liberated Ypres on 6th September 1944, despite fighting still taking place in other parts of the town.

London. Rose married Thomas Chappell (24th April 1873–1951), a solicitor's clerk and widower, born at Chepstow, Monmouthshire, on 17th December 1928 at St Pancras Register Office, London. They were both living at 17 Wellington Street, St Pancras at the time. Thomas was a county court clerk in 1891, living with his parents at 10 House, Back Hawker Hill, Chepstow. He was recorded as married in 1901 but his wife was not with him and no marriage record has been found. He was living with his parents at Hocker Hill House, Chepstow at the time. Thomas and Rose were living at 45 Mornington Terrace, St Pancras, London in 1939. His death was registered at Islington, London and she died at 25 Mackworth House, Stanhope Street, Camden, London. Rose had six children from her first marriage:

- Rose Dorothy Deebank (16th May 1905–25th March 1907).
- Violet Deebank (16th March 1907–11th March 1992) married Lewis W Porter in 1925 registered at Evesham, Worcestershire. They had a daughter, Dorothy R Porter, in 1926.
- Vera Deebank (22nd July 1909–1990) married Albert Edward J Lambarth (born 1904) in 1928 registered at Pancras, London. They had a daughter, Patricia J Lambarth, in 1949, registered at Islington, London. Albert married Thelma J Baldock-Apps in 1950, registered at Surrey Mid Eastern. Thelma married Douglas L Johnson in 1982 registered at Waltham Forest, London.
- Alexander Deebank (12th April 1912–12th April 1914).
- Maisie Deebank (4th May 1914–26th August 1985) is believed to have married Charles W Willis in 1935, registered at West Ham, London. They

had two children – Brenda E Willis 1938 and John C Willis 1942. They divorced and Maisie married Richard H Butler in 1951 registered at Pancras, London. Charles married Bridget E Hennessy later the same year and they had a son, John C Hennessy, in 1953.
- John Henry Deebank (17th February 1922–2004) married Josephine D Pickl (sic) in 1947, registered at Ilford, Essex. They had a daughter, Diane R Deebank, in 1948.

William was educated at Church Stanway School, near Winchcombe, Gloucestershire. He worked initially as a groom for Mr CH Smith and the Reverend HB Allen before assisting his father as a tree feller on the Stanway Estate. He enlisted in the Gloucestershire Regiment in July 1913 and transferred to 2nd Grenadier Guards on 21st October. He went to France on 8th November 1914. William suffered frostbite and had two toes amputated. He returned to France in July 1915 and was subsequently wounded twice.

William Holmes' grave in Carnières Communal Cemetery.

Awarded the VC for his actions at Catteniéres, France on 9th October 1918, LG 26th December 1918. He was killed during the VC action and is buried in Carnières Communal Cemetery, France (I B 3). The VC was presented to his parents by the King at Buckingham Palace on 29th March 1919. He is commemorated in a number of other places:

- St George's Church, Didbrook, Gloucestershire.
  - War Memorial.
  - Memorial bench.

Memorial bench in the grounds of St George's Church, Didbrook.

The St George's Church War Memorial, Didbrook William's name is at the bottom.

The Ring of Remembrance (L'Anneau de la Mémoire), designed by Philippe Prost, was inaugurated on 11th November 2014 by French President Hollande, Nord-Pas-de-Calais région président, Daniel Percheron, and German Minister of Defense, Ursula von der Leyen. The inspiration is a human ring holding hands, a sign of fellowship and unity among countries that were enemies. It commemorates 576,606 soldiers of forty nations who died in Nord-Pas-de-Calais in the Great War. It is co-located with the largest French national cemetery of Notre-Dame-de-Lorette, which can be seen in the background. The Ring is a 345m ellipse, including a raised section of sixty-one metres. Although the ring is a symbol of peace in Europe, the overhang reminds visitors that peace is not guaranteed and conflict can return at any time. Within the Ring are 500 stainless steel panels facing inwards arranged like the pages of a book. Each is three metres tall and has c.1,200 names listed alphabetically by surname regardless of nationality, gender, religion or rank. The first name is 'A' and the last is 'Zschiesche'. The 500th panel is blank for newly discovered names. There are four panels of Smiths alone.

    - A Department for Communities and Local Government commemorative paving stone was dedicated on 9th October 2018.
- Named on The Household Division (Foot Guards) Honour Roll for the Victoria Cross at the Sergeants' Mess, Wellington Barracks, London.
- Named on The Ring of Remembrance (L'Anneau de la Mémoire or Ring of Memory) at Ablain-Saint-Nazaire, France, inaugurated on 11th November 2014, which commemorates the 576,606 soldiers of forty nationalities who died in Nord-Pas-de-Calais in the Great War.

In addition to the VC he was awarded the 1914 Star, British War Medal 1914–20 and Victory Medal 1914–19. His medals were purchased by the Grenadier Guards

The 1914 Star was authorised for the Army in 1917 and for the Royal Navy in 1918. It was awarded to officers and men who served in France and Belgium between 5th August and midnight on 22nd-23rd November 1914. The closing date was the formal end of the First Battle of Ypres. The recipient's number, rank, name and unit are stamped on the reverse. In October 1919 a clasp was authorised, '5th Aug – 22nd Nov. 1914', for those who had been under fire or within range of enemy artillery during the period. A total of 365,622 medals were awarded. Approximately 145,000 clasps were awarded but the precise number is unknown as it had to be claimed personally and many of those eligible died before 1919 or simply failed to apply. Some Royal Navy personnel qualified by landing at Antwerp. A few women also qualified, serving as nurses or auxiliaries. However, the majority of recipients were members of the pre-war regular British Army and its reservists, the Old Contemptibles, and the medal became known as the 'Mons Star'. A small number were awarded to Canadians, mainly members of 2nd Canadian Stationary Hospital, which served with the BEF from 6th November 1914. The 1914 Star was always awarded with the British War Medal and Victory Medal. Anyone awarded the 1914 Star did not also qualify for the 1914–15 Star.

Wilfred Pickles OBE (1904–78), actor and radio presenter, initially worked with his father as a builder. His first professional appearance was as an extra in *Julius Caesar* at the Theatre Royal, Halifax in the 1920s. Later he became a radio celebrity and also pursued an acting career in London's West End and in films and on television. His most significant work was hosting BBC Radio's *Have A Go* 1946–67, which he co-presented with his wife Mabel. They travelled around the country speaking to members of the public, who were invited to answer quiz questions in the hope of winning a small amount of money. It was the first quiz show in Britain to offer such a prize and at its peak attracted an audience of over twenty million. He also hosted the show on television as *Ask Pickles* 1954–56. In 1955 he published an anthology of poetry and prose, *My North Countrie*. In 1950 he was awarded the OBE for services to broadcasting and in 1955 opened the Wilfred Pickles' School for Spastics in Rutland. Pickles appeared in the 1963 film *Billy Liar* as his father.

in 1985 and the VC is held by the Guards Museum, Wellington Barracks, London. His father told the story of his son's deed on the BBC radio programme *Have A Go* with Wilfred Pickles on 8th December 1959.

SECOND LIEUTENANT GEORGE MAWBY INGRAM
24th Australian Infantry Battalion AIF

George Ingram was born on 18th March 1889 at Huntly, Sandhurst (Bendigo from 1891) Victoria, Australia. His middle name has also been seen as Morby. His father, George Ronald Ingram (1855–December 1935), born at Sandhurst, Victoria, was a farmer. He married Charlotte née Hubbard (1854–1929), born at Prahran,

Victoria, in 1885 at Dandenong, Victoria. By 1912 George was a gardener and they were living at Seville, Lilydale, Victoria. By January 1917 they had moved to 39 Brougham Street, Box Hill, Victoria, by 1927 to Gladstone Road, Dandenong and to 74 Walker Street, Dandenong the following year. George senior was living with his son, George, at 659 St Kilda Road, Balaclava, Victoria in 1931. Both George senior and Charlotte died at Dandenong. George junior had three siblings:

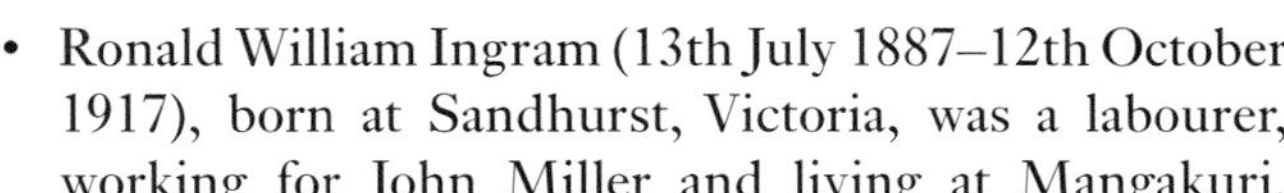

- Ronald William Ingram (13th July 1887–12th October 1917), born at Sandhurst, Victoria, was a labourer, working for John Miller and living at Mangakuri, Hawkes Bay, when he enlisted in 1st Battalion, Otago Regiment, New Zealand Expeditionary Force (25250) on 18th March 1916. He was described as 5′9″ tall, weighing 154 lbs, with fresh complexion, grey eyes, brown hair and his religious denomination was Presbyterian. He joined 14th Reinforcements on 21st March and J Company on 5th April. Ronald was admitted to hospital at Featherston with measles 19th April–3rd May. He embarked at Wellington on 26th June and disembarked at Devonport, England on 22nd August. Next day he joined Otago Company, Reserve Battalion, 2nd Brigade at Sling Camp, Bulford, Wiltshire. On 26th September Ronald went to France and joined the New Zealand Infantry & General Base Depot, Étaples next day. He joined 1st Otago on 12th October. On 19th May 1917 he was admitted to 1st New Zealand Field Ambulance and

Prahan, known locally as Pran, in 1909. It is a suburb of Melbourne and was originally named Pur-ra-ran. However, the Surveyor General recorded it as Prahran and so it remained. The Post Office opened in April 1853 and by the 1930s the area had developed commercially to rival the centre of Melbourne. Amongst the famous people who were born and lived there are:

- Graham Berry (1822–1904), 11th Premier of Victoria.
- Major General Sir Walter Joseph Cawthorn CB CIE CBE (1896–1970) head of the Australian Secret Intelligence Service.
- Air Commodore Arthur Henry Cobby CBE DSO DFC & two Bars GM (1894–1955), the leading Australian Flying Corps ace of the Great War, with twenty-nine victories.
- Frederick Anthony Owen Gaze DFC & two Bars OAM (1920–2013) flew with the RAF in the Second World War and was credited with twelve and a half victories. He was the first Australian to take part in a Formula One Grand Prix in Belgium in 1951.
- Gertrude Emily Johnson OBE (1894–1973), an opera soprano, enjoyed an international career before returning to Australia to found the National Theatre in Melbourne. (Victorian Places).

Lilydale was named after Lilly de Castella née Anderson. The Post Office opened in September 1860 as Brushy Creek and was renamed Lillydale in 1861 and Lilydale c.1872. The railway reached the town in 1882.

transferred to 7th General Hospital, St Omer on 27th May. Having joined the Base Depot on 6th June, he rejoined the Battalion on 12th June and was promoted lance corporal on 7th July. He was detached to the Divisional Gas School 1st–8th August. Two months later Ronald was killed in action (Panel 4, Tyne Cot Memorial, Zonnebeke, Belgium).

- Alexander 'Alex' Hales Ingram (1891–3rd January 1917), born at Bendigo, Victoria, was an electrical mechanic. He married Agnes Estella Wright (10th July 1891–26th October 1979), a tailoress born at Dimboola, Victoria, in 1916. They were living at 41 Margaret Street, South Yarra, Victoria in 1916. Alex enlisted as a driver in 3rd Pioneer Battalion AIF at Prahran, Melbourne, Victoria on 21st January 1916 (221) and joined A Company on 1st March. He was described as 5′10″ tall, weighing 146 lbs, with fresh complexion, blue eyes, light brown hair (curly) and his religious denomination was Methodist. His next of kin was his wife living at 39 Brougham Street, Box Hill, Victoria. He embarked aboard HMAT A62 *Wandilla* at Melbourne on 6th June, arriving at Plymouth, Devon, England on 26th July. While aboard he was treated for measles 9th–17th July. Alex embarked for France from Southampton, Hampshire on 24th November and joined the

Ronald William Ingram is commemorated in the New Zealand Apse on the Tyne Cot Memorial. His name appears bottom left.

Transport Section in A Company. He was killed by a shell at Houplines, near Armentières (Cité Bonjean Military Cemetery, Armentières, France – IV C 9). Agnes was living with her parents at 41 Margaret Street, South Yarra, Victoria and was granted a pension of £2/3/- per fortnight from 18th March 1917. She was still living there in 1924. By 1931 she had moved to 268 Whitehorse Road, Mitcham, Victoria, to 80 Glen Iris Road, Camberwell, Victoria by 1933, to Thistle Street, Canterbury, Victoria by 1937 and to 11 Monteath Avenue, Auburn, Victoria by 1943. Agnes married George Hastie (1892–17th August 1971), born at Kelvin, Glasgow, Scotland, on 17th June 1958. George enlisted at Melbourne on 14th March 1916 (2668). He was described as a grocer, 5′ 9¼″ tall, weighing 148 lbs, with fresh complexion, blue eyes, light brown hair and his religious denomination was Presbyterian. His next of kin was his father, David Hastie, Presbyterian Soldiers' Institute, Military Camp, Seymour, Victoria and later c/o A Bethune, Bonnie Doon, Seville. George joined 19th Depot Battalion at Geelong on 1st May, transferred to 3rd Reinforcements, 58th Battalion at Broadmeadows on 24th May and to 6th Reinforcements, 58th Battalion as a corporal on 1st August. He embarked aboard HMAT A71 *Nestor* at Melbourne on 2nd October and was appointed voyage only sergeant. He disembarked at Plymouth on 16th November and reverted to the ranks of 15th Training Battalion at Hurdcott, Wiltshire the same day. He went to France on 30th December aboard SS *Princess Clementine* from Folkestone and joined 5th Australian Divisional Base Depot, Étaples next day. He was appointed acting sergeant on 2nd January 1917 and joined 58th Battalion on 7th February, when he reverted to the ranks. He was taken sick with rheumatism on 21st February and was admitted to 14th Australian Field Ambulance and South Midlands Casualty Clearing Station. On 23rd February he was admitted to 22nd General Hospital, Camiers, was evacuated to England aboard HMHS *Grantully Castle* from Le Havre on 9th March and was admitted to 3rd London General Hospital, Wandsworth next day. He was transferred to Bermondsey Military Hospital on 23rd March and to 1st Australian Auxiliary Hospital, Harefield on 20th June. He was granted leave on 26th June to report to No.3 Command Depot, Hurdcott on 10th July. George returned to France via Folkestone from the Overseas Training Depot, Perham Down, Wiltshire on 6th August and joined 5th Australian Divisional Base Depot, Étaples on 8th August. He rejoined the Battalion on 27th August and was promoted corporal on 4th October and sergeant on 20th October. He was granted leave in France 12th-27th January 1918 and in Britain 20th March – 11th April. On 31st May he was admitted to 14th Australian Field Ambulance, transferred to No.6 Casualty Clearing Station and by 41 Ambulance Train on 7th June to 12th General Hospital, Rouen, arriving next day. He was transferred to No.2 Convalescent Depot on 10th June, to 6th General Hospital on 13th June with pyrexia of unknown origin, to No.2 Convalescent Depot on 17th June with influenza and to No.11 Convalescent Depot on 26th June. He returned to No.2 Convalescent

Depot on 17th August and was discharged to the Australian Infantry Base Depot, Le Havre on 24th September. He rejoined the Battalion on 15th October. George was granted leave in Britain 19th January–1st February 1919 and was detached to 5th Company, Graves Registration Detachment on 23rd March. He was appointed temporary WO2/CSM on 27th March and was granted leave in Britain 27th June–11th July. He rejoined 58th Battalion on 19th August, embarked aboard SS *Port Denison* at Devonport on 25th September and disembarked at Melbourne on 13th November. On the journey he was appointed voyage only RSM from 22nd September. Agnes and George were living at 5 Queen Street, South Ballarat, Victoria at the time of his death there. George had married Jessie Catherine Bethune (1893–8th April 1958), born at Wycheproof, Victoria, in 1919. He was a gripman (cable car operator) in 1921, when they were living at 19 Orford Street, Moonee Ponds, Victoria. Jessie remained there for the rest of her life but by 1931 George was living at 185 Richardson Street, Middle Park, Melbourne. She died at Footscray, Victoria. George and Jessie had two children – Gordon George Hastie 1920 and Douglas Bethune Hastie 1922.

Alex Ingram's grave in Cité Bonjean Military Cemetery.

- Elsie Joan Ingram (1896–January 1902) was born at Wandin Yallock, Victoria and died at Wandin Yallock, Victoria.

George's paternal grandfather, Alexander Ingram (c.1806–4th September 1886), born at Aberdeen, Scotland, emigrated to Australia. He married Joan née Ronald (c.1818–4th March 1884), born at Crail, Fife, Scotland, in 1852 at Geelong, Victoria. They both died at Huntly, Victoria.

His maternal grandfather, David Hubbard (1818–3rd May 1893), born at Uggeshall, Suffolk, England, married Elizabeth 'Betsy' née Mawby (1829–9th November 1900) in 1847 at Melbourne, Victoria. Her surname has also been seen as Morby or Mawbry. They both died at Prahran, Victoria. In addition to Charlotte, they had five other children:

Crail was first recorded in 1148 as Cherel. There is evidence of occupation on the site of the parish church from the 8th century. The church was dedicated in the 13th century to St Maelrubha. Crail became a Royal Burgh in 1178 and Robert the Bruce granted permission to hold markets. John Knox delivered a sermon in the parish church in 1559.

- Robert Hubbard (1849–11th September 1922), born at Richmond, Victoria, married Ellen Ryan (c.1846–7th July 1909), born at Limerick, Ireland, in 1871. She died at Erindale, Granville Street, Hampton, Victoria and he at Sandringham, Victoria. They had five children:
    - Amy Hubbard (1873–29th May 1877).
    - Mary Ann Hubbard (1874–1952) married James Patrick Thresher (1858–1916) in 1906. They had three children – Robert Francis Thresher 1908, Ellen Thresher 1909 and Veronica Agnes Thresher 1911. James had married Margaret Frances Lennon (1872–1903) in 1894. They had three children – Phillip John Thresher 1895, Mary Margaret Thresher 1896 and James Francis Thresher 1898.
    - Robert Francis Hubbard (1st April 1876–27th February 1959) married Alvena Florence 'Florry' Susan Corneille (1879–1960) in 1899. They had five children – Florence May Hubbard 1899, Ida Margaret Hubbard 1902, Francis Hubbard 1904, Allen Stanley Hubbard 1914 and Joseph Roy Hubbard 1917.
    - Charlotte Margaret Hubbard (1880–14th May 1919) married Thomas Henry Dent in 1907. They had three children – Henry Gordon Dent 1907, Alan Thomas Dent 1910 and Eric Jonathan Dent 1913.
    - David William Hubbard (1882–1962) married Mary Catherine Carroll (1880–1972), born in Tasmania, in 1910. They had five children – Patrick Thomas Hubbard 1912, Ellen Charlotte Hubbard 1913, David Robert Hubbard 1914, Bernard James Hubbard 1916 and Leo Joseph Hubbard 1919.
- Mary Anne Hubbard (1851–1939), married William Skinner (1847–September 1923), born at Comberton, Cambridgeshire, England, in 1875 at Windsor, Victoria. They had four children:
    - William John Skinner (1876–1956).
    - Frank Skinner (born and died 1878).
    - Herbert Henry Skinner (1879–1958).
    - Percival George Skinner (1887–1972) married Ruby Amelia Lamb (1888–1975) in 1913. They had at least two children – Clarence Percival Skinner 1915, Clive Percival Skinner 1916.
- Kezia Hubbard (1856–58), born and died at Prahan.
- David Hubbard (12th February 1861–1944) married Susan Baxter (30th March 1860–1941), born at Damper Creek, Boroondara, Victoria, in 1883 at Boroondara. He was a fruit grower in 1903, when they were living at Seville, Victoria. By 1908 he was a fencer and they were living at 9 Camberwell Road. By 1914 they had moved to 9 Prospect Hill and were still there in 1937. They both died at Hawthorn, Victoria. They had nine children:
    - Alice Mary Ann Hubbard (1884–1957) married Joseph McTaggart Blair in 1912. They had at least two children – Alan McTaggart Blair 1912 and Bruce Athol Blair 1919.

    - Keziah May Hubbard (1885–1951) never married.
    - Alfred Irwin Hubbard (1887–1961) married Delia Josine Payne (c.1886–1956) in 1914.
    - Eva Charlotte Hubbard (1889–1973) married Robert Pine (1873–1954) in 1911. They had a son, Robert Alfred Pine, the same year.
    - Fanny Louisa Hubbard (1891–1975) never married.
    - Mabel Jessie Hubbard (1893–1969) married Clive Fraser Fraser in 1919. They had at least one child, Hector David Fraser in 1920.
    - Frances Hannah Hubbard (1895–1977) married Arthur Erskine McMillan (1890–1987) in 1922.
    - Percy Hubbard (1899–1967) married Annie Edna May Lodwick (1899–1966) in 1923.
    - Stella Hubbard (1901–75) married William Thomas Morgan in 1923.
- William Hubbard (1862–30th January 1924) married Millicent Baxter (1864–12th June 1927) in 1881 at Boroondara, where she was born. She was the sister of Susan Baxter, who married William's brother David. He died at Prahran and she at Epworth Hospital, Richmond, Victoria. They had seven children:
    - Albert William Hubbard (15th November 1882–3rd August 1963).
    - Leslie Hubbard (1884–6th February 1946) married Florence Lillian Taylor (c.1884–1971), born at Bradford, England, in 1903. They had four children – Edith Maud Hubbard 1903, Florence Lillian Hubbard 1905, Leslie Albert Harry Hubbard 1909 and Edward William Hubbard 1911.
    - Norman Frederick Hubbard (born and died 1887).
    - Harold Reuben Hubbard (1889–7th March 1941) married Flora May Woodruff (1888–1948) in 1911. They had four children – Alma May Hubbard 1912, Reuben Henry Hubbard 1914, Olive Irene Hubbard 1915 and Ethel Muriel Hubbard 1918. Flora married Alfred William Bickerton (1884–1969) in 1948. He had married Elizabeth Chivers in 1908.
    - Ethel May Hubbard (1891–15th December 1917).
    - Alice Myrtle Hubbard (1893–5th October 1923) married John Walter Gould in 1920.
    - Ivy Elizabeth Hubbard (1897–5th July 1930) married John William Gould in 1926.

George was educated at Lilydale State School and Seville State School. He was apprenticed as a carpenter and joiner aged ten and, on completion, went into business as a building contractor at Caulfield, Melbourne. He joined the Militia in 1903, enlisting in No.7 Company, Australian Garrison Artillery and in 1906 went to New Zealand in an Australian military contingent for the opening of an exhibition.

George married Jane 'Jean' Frances Nichols (1889–November 1972), born at East Prahran, Victoria, at 29 Bay View Street, East Prahran on 19th January 1910.

Lilydale Common School opened on 1st July 1866 and in 1872 a number of small schools in the area joined to become Lilydale State School No.876. The main building was built in 1876, a second storey was added in 1927 and a new wing in time for the School's centenary. The wing was destroyed in a fire in 1980 and the replacement also burned down in 1991. A new section was opened in 1995. The 150th anniversary was celebrated in 2016.

Seville Primary School (formerly State School) celebrated its centenary in 1987. A memorial plaque to George Ingram is on the wall to the left of the left gatepost (Sandra Brown).

George purchased a property at Carnegie, Victoria and Jean remained there for twelve months but the payments fell into arrears and she had to leave. In 1916 their address was Chestnut Street, Murrumbeena, Victoria.

Jean's father, Edward Nichols (25th March 1853–21st December 1937), born at Tank Hill, Launceston, Tasmania, was a labourer and later a butcher. The surname has also been seen as Nicholls. He married Elizabeth Hall (1852–24th July 1937), born at Brighton, Victoria, on 10th September 1874 at St James' Church, Dandenong, Victoria. They lived at Narre Warren for four years, Berwick for two years, and then at Prahan and East Prahan until February 1913, according to the evidence she presented in the divorce papers. By 1909 he was a contractor and asphalter, living with his family at 70 Chomley Street, Armadale, Victoria. They later moved to 62 Chomley Street. In addition, Edward owned a house and land in Point Nepean Road, Elsternwick, Victoria, a block of land in New Street, Elsternwick, another piece of land at Malvern, Victoria and a half-share in a weekend residence at Aspendale, Victoria. He began an affair with a Miss Bottomley, which Elizabeth found out about. He repeatedly promised that he would have nothing more to do with Miss Bottomley but the affair continued. Elizabeth refused to share the same bedroom with him from about June 1912. Elizabeth moved to High Street, Prahran, with her daughter Florence, on 14th February 1913. She filed for divorce on 7th April 1913 on the grounds of her husband's adultery and moved in with her son, William, and his family. The court awarded her £1/10/- per week alimony from 28th July, and £0/15/- per week maintenance for Florence. Court costs of £3/3/- were also awarded against Edward. On 22nd August the marriage was annulled. Custody of Florence was awarded to Elizabeth. In addition to Jean, they had eleven other children:

- Edward 'Ted' Henry Nichols (18th September 1875–1948), born at Narre Warren, Victoria, married Louisa York (c.1873–1935) in 1896. They had two children – Dorothy Margaret Ezelpher Nichols 1898 and Edward Henry York Nichols 1901.
- Henry George Nichols (1876–78), born at Berwick, Victoria.
- James Nichols (1879–3rd July 1949), born at Melbourne, Victoria, married Margaret Jane Upton (1883–16th March 1929), also born at Melbourne, in 1900. He was an asphalter in 1914, when they were living at 67A Union Street, Windsor, Victoria. James was living with his son, Harry, at 15 Halstead Street, Caulfield, Victoria in 1943. They had four children – Muriel Elizabeth Nichols 1900, James Nichols 1902, William Henry Nichols 1904 and Harry Hall Edward Nichols 1910.
- William Nichols (1880–1957), a carter born at Prahran, married Violet Victoria Hill (12th November 1882–27th December 1960), a dressmaker born at North Melbourne, on 8th February 1908 at the Congregational Church, Market Street, St Kilda. They lived on Charles Street, Prahran until moving to Earl Street, Windsor, Victoria in 1909 and then briefly to Chomley Street, East Prahran for six weeks, then Tooronga Road, Malvern for two months before 6 Point Nepean Road, Elsternwick. William became an asphalter about 1912. They moved to 8 Point Nepean Road in April 1913. On 19th July 1917 he purchased a farm at Garfield, Victoria. He visited the family once a month but claimed that he was in difficulties with his creditors and had mounting debts. He had still not sold the business by July 1919. William had begun an affair with Doris 'Nellie' Rose Edwards in July 1916. They co-habited as man and wife from July 1917, with him being known as Bill Johnson, and they had a son. Violet found out about the affair and confronted William on 23rd June 1919 at his works at 10 Point Nepean Road. She filed for divorce on 5th September 1919. In his defence William claimed that Violet had been conducting an affair with Joseph Henry Beadle, a labourer, between February and April 1919. This was denied by Violet and the court found against William, who was living at 31 Trinian Street, Prahan at the time. Decree nisi was issued on 21st April 1920 and Violet was granted custody of the children. William was ordered to pay £1/5/- per week to maintain the children. Decree absolute was issued on 16th October 1920. William and Violet had two daughters – Marjorie Alma Nichols 1909 and Thelma Eileen Nichols 1913. William married Doris Rose

Port Moresby was a key objective of the Japanese in March 1942. However, the amphibious force was intercepted and suffered a heavy defeat by the Americans in the Coral Sea in May. The Japanese then advanced on Port Moresby overland in September. Those who died in the fighting in Papua and Bougainville are buried in Port Moresby (Bomana) War Cemetery. The unidentified Royal Artillery soldiers were captured by the Japanese at Singapore and died in captivity on Bailale, in the Solomons. They were re-buried in a temporary war cemetery at Torokina on Bougainville Island before being transferred to Port Moresby. The cemetery, which contains 3,824 Second World War burials, including 699 unidentified, was dedicated by the Governor-General of Australia, Field Marshal Slim, on 19th October 1953. The Port Moresby Memorial behind the cemetery commemorates almost 750 men of the Australian Army (including Papua and New Guinea local forces), the Australian Merchant Navy and the Royal Australian Air Force who died on operations in Papua and have no known grave. The missing of the Royal Australian Navy from the southwest Pacific are commemorated on the Plymouth Naval Memorial, Devon, England.

Edwards (20th January 1897–July 1969), born at Brighton, Victoria, later in 1920. They were living at 27 Rothesay Avenue, Balaclava, Victoria in 1921 and had moved to 3 Knight Street, St Kilda by 1924. William and Doris had a son, William Henry Nichols (18th February 1918–28th October 1942), who enlisted in the Australian Imperial Force on 18th July 1940 at Elwood, Victoria (VX29741). He was commissioned and promoted to lieutenant. He married Violet Constance Keating (born 1918) in May 1942 at St Kilda. William was serving in 2/6th Independent Company at Port Moresby, Papua New Guinea when he was killed in action (Port Moresby Memorial). Violet married Reuben Matthew Hart (27th March 1886–19th May 1966), a labourer born at Avoca, in 1929. She died at Rowena Private Hospital, Ivanhoe, Victoria and he at Heidelberg, Victoria.

- Frederick Nichols (1882–1st June 1964), born at Toorak, Victoria, married Florence Annie Stewart (13th October 1890–14th June 1949), born at Wangaratta, Victoria, on 25th September 1912 at Prahran. Florence had a daughter, Ruby May Stewart, in 1911. Florence died at Ferntree Gully, Victoria and Frederick at Prahran. They had eight children, some registered as Nicholls at birth – Frederick Lennard Nichols 1913, Arthur James Nelson Nichols 1915, Ronald Stewart Nichols 1916, William Keith Nichols 1919, Albert Ernest Nichols 1917, Robert Gibton Nicholls 1920, George Nicholls 1922 and Leslie Guthrie Nichols 1924.
- Ezelfer Elizabeth Nichols (5 June 1884–8th May 1913) married Patrick Joseph Kelly on 26th January 1907 at 448 Queen Street, Melbourne. She died at

Elsternwick, Victoria. They had two children – Walt Daniel Kelly 1907 and Stella Ezelfer Kelly 1909.
- Ann Charlotte Nichols (July–9th November 1886), born at Armadale, Victoria.
- John 'Jack' Henry Nichols (1887–1978).
- George Chomley Nichols (1892–1965) married Margaret 'Mags' Elizabeth Morris (1893–1957), born at Prahran, in 1911. She died at Melbourne and he at Prahran. They had eleven children, some were registered as Nicholls at birth – Dorothy Florence Elizabeth Nichols 1911, Stella May Nichols 1913, John Henry Nichols 1914, Daphne Elizabeth Nichols 1917, Pearl Margaret Nichols 1919, George Chomley Nichols 1922, Edward Nichols 1923, Norman Nichols 1925, Herbert Nichols 1926, Jean Mavis Nichols 1927 and Lorraine Sylvia Nichols 1936.
- Maude Nichols (June 1893–10th February 1894).
- Florence 'Florrie' Daisy Nichols (1897–29th January 1914).

On 10th December 1914 George enlisted at South Yarra in 3rd Battalion, Australian Naval & Military Expeditionary Force (233). He gave his age as thirty years and ten months but was actually twenty-six years and ten months. He embarked aboard SS *Eastern* with G Company at Sydney, New South Wales on 25th January 1915 for service at Matupi, Rabaul, Bougainville Island and German New Guinea. He transferred from Rabaul to Matupi for permanent duty at the Battery on 22nd February. He was appointed provisional corporal on 5th July and served in German New Guinea until 6th December. He returned to Australia suffering from malaria aboard SS *Te Anau*, disembarking at Melbourne, Victoria on 6th December.

A Royal Australian Navy 4.7" Gun position on Matupi Island (Australian War Memorial).

George was discharged in Melbourne on 19th January 1916 and the same day enlisted in the AIF at Royal Park, Melbourne (5919). He was described as 5′ 10½″ tall, weighing 173 lbs, with dark complexion, grey eyes, brown hair and his religious denomination was Wesleyan. He underwent training with 11th/22nd Reinforcements in B Company, 10th Depot Battalion at Langwarrin, Victoria from 1st February. He was in hospital at

SS *Te Anau* (1,652 tons) was built for the Union Steam Ship Co by William Denny & Bros at Dumbarton, Scotland in 1879. She was sold to Todd & Borlase, Dunedin, New Zealand and was stripped out at Port Chalmers in June 1924, before being sunk as a breakwater at Wanganui in August. The captain's cabin was removed, restored to its original condition and is displayed at Wellington Museum.

In 1845 Governor Charles La Trobe set aside a reservation of four square miles for parkland and open space. However, by the time of its formal proclamation in 1854 this had been reduced by almost half. It was later further reduced to just over one square mile due to the rapid increase in population due to the Victorian gold rush. In 1860 the Burke and Wills expedition to cross Australia from south to north set out from Royal Park. In 1861 the Royal Melbourne Zoological Gardens was formed there. Further losses of land resulted from road, tram and railway line construction and also the building of University High School in 1929, the Royal Melbourne Hospital in 1944, the Royal Children's Hospital in 1957 and the Royal Dental Hospital in 1963. The Park was used for military camps during both World Wars.

Langwarrin from 3rd March and on discharge transferred to C Company at Royal Park on 27th March. He rejoined B Company on 8th April, transferred to A Company, 23rd Depot Battalion at Royal Park on 1st May and to that Battalion's D Company on 26th May. George was allocated to 16th Reinforcements of A Company, 24th Depot Battalion at Royal Park on 13th June and transferred to B Company next day. On 2nd October he embarked with the Battalion aboard HMAT A71 *Nestor* at Melbourne. He was appointed voyage only acting sergeant and disembarked at Plymouth, Devon on

The entrance to Langwarrin Camp with the hospital on the left (Museums Victoria Collections).

SS *Nestor* (14,501 tons) was built by Workman Clark & Co, Belfast, Ireland for the Ocean Steam Ship Co. She commenced her maiden voyage on 19th May 1913 from Liverpool to Brisbane, calling at Cape Town, Adelaide, Melbourne and Sydney. She was used as a troopship throughout the Great War and was under Australian control from September 1915 until 1918. She resumed commercial service on 22nd April 1920. In 1936 *Nestor* fired a towline aboard SS *Mungana*, which was drifting towards Cape Jaffa, with her last rocket and then towed the disabled ship 275 kms to Adelaide. She was requisitioned for government service again in 1940 but continued on the Liverpool–Brisbane route, including evacuating children to Australia. Her final voyage to Australia commenced on 23rd December 1949. On 8th August 1950 she arrived at Faslane, Scotland where she was broken up, having completed sixty-eight round voyages and steamed 3,398,302 kms (Australian War Memorial).

16th November. He reverted to private on joining 6th Training Battalion, Tidworth, Wiltshire. He was appointed extra duties pay sergeant on 17th November and was reduced to extra duties pay corporal on 29th December.

On 1st January 1917 George was appointed temporary sergeant on the permanent cadre of 6th Training Battalion. He reverted to acting corporal on 12th January and embarked at Folkestone, Kent aboard HT *Princess Clementine* for France on 16th January. On joining 2nd Australian Divisional Base Depot, Étaples next day, he reverted to private. He was taken on the strength of 24th Battalion on 20th January, which was at Ribemont for a month of rest and training. George was promoted lance corporal on 20th February and spent a day in hospital on 23rd February.

Awarded the MM for his actions in the Bapaume sector on 15th/16th March 1917 – he was part of a bombing section that held off a superior enemy force, mainly due to his accurate bomb throwing. When the enemy counterattacked, he, with two other men, covered the retirement, holding the enemy at bay with accurate sniping and averted any loss to the bombing party, LG 11th May 1917. George was promoted corporal on 17th March and temporary sergeant on 18th March. He was evacuated to 2nd Australian Field Ambulance on 21st March, reverting to corporal, and then to 2nd Divisional Rest Station with cellulitis of the face, rejoining the Battalion on 29th March. On 14th April he was evacuated to 6th Australian Field Ambulance with 'pyrexia of unknown origin'. He was transferred to No.45 Casualty Clearing Station near Bullecourt the following day, by ambulance train to 2nd Australian General Hospital, Boulogne on 19th April and embarked aboard SS *Princess Elizabeth* at Boulogne on 20th April. He had a slight case of influenza and was admitted to Summerdown Camp Military Convalescent Hospital, Eastbourne,

Summerdown Camp Military Convalescent Hospital, Eastbourne.

Orchard Hospital opened in Joyce Green Lane, Dartford in the spring of 1902 as another temporary hospital for smallpox patients. It had 800 beds. As smallpox declined, the facility became a fever hospital in 1910. Much of the time it was closed, opening only in times of epidemics, particularly of scarlet fever and diphtheria. In 1915 it became the Orchard Military Hospital and, on 16th October 1916, 3rd Australian Auxiliary Hospital, which had previously been 1st Australian Stationary Hospital on Lemnos and in Egypt. The Australians added an operating theatre and increased the bed capacity to 1,200. From October 1915 to December 1918, 56,441 casualties were treated there.

8th General Hospital was based to the south of Rouen from August 1914 until May 1919 and was the largest of the base hospitals in the area. It occupied a combination of buildings, huts and tents. Due to its isolated position, there was some unrest among the nursing staff, who felt cut off.

Sussex the following day. On 2nd May he was transferred to 3rd Australian Auxiliary Hospital, Dartford, Kent and was discharged on furlough on 9th May, to report to the Infantry Reinforcement Depot, Perham Down, Wiltshire on 24th May.

George embarked at Southampton for France on 29th May and joined 2nd Australian Divisional Base Depot, Harfleur, near Le Havre the following day. He rejoined the Battalion on 21st June and was appointed temporary sergeant on 23rd June (later substantive from the same date). On 22nd September he dislocated a knee in an accident and was evacuated to 6th Australian Field Ambulance. He was transferred the same day to No.3 Canadian Casualty Clearing Station and next day travelled by ambulance train to 35th General Hospital, Calais. He was discharged from hospital on 3rd October and returned to 2nd Australian Divisional Base Depot the following day. On 10th October he rejoined the Battalion near Bellewaarde Ridge near Ypres and was appointed temporary company sergeant major (later substantive from the same date). He was appointed temporary regimental sergeant major on 28th January 1918 and reverted to company sergeant major on 9th June.

George was commissioned on 20th June 1918 and joined B Company. He was evacuated to 6th Australian Field Ambulance and No.5 Casualty Clearing Station with 'pyrexia of unknown origin' on 24th June. He was transferred to 8th General Hospital, Rouen on 28th June. On being discharged from hospital on 1st July, he joined the Australian Infantry Base Depot, Harfleur on 4th July, marched out on 6th July and rejoined the Battalion on 12th July. He was granted leave to England 9th-28th August. **Awarded the VC for his actions at Montbrehain, France on 5th October 1918, LG 6th January 1919.**

On 24th October, George was promoted lieutenant and transferred to 37th Battalion. He attended two special courses at the School of Musketry, Bisley Camp, Surrey 11th November–13th December and was granted fourteen days' leave on termination of the courses. He returned to France via Folkestone, Kent on 28th December. George left the Battalion on 7th February 1919 and disembarked at Folkestone on 10th February. The VC was presented by the King in the ballroom of Buckingham Palace on 15th February. George embarked aboard HMT *Nevasa* at Portland on 5th March and disembarked at Melbourne, Victoria on 25th April. His appointment with the AIF was terminated on 2nd June 1919 and he transferred to the Militia. On 31st March 1921 he transferred to 37th Battalion, on 1st July 1922 to the Reserve of Officers and on 1st August 1930 to the Regimental List of Officers for 24th Battalion, from which he was removed on 1st May 1938.

George Ingram, second from left, at the end of the Mall outside Buckingham Palace, London in February 1919.

While George was away, Jean ran a pork and butchery business in High Street, Armadale with a man named Cox. She stopped corresponding with her husband in early 1918 and refused to answer his letters. Her address in October 1918 was 1 Moore Street, South Yarra, Victoria. George and Jean reunited after his discharge and rented 10 Newry Street, Prahran. However, she frequented theatres and went on motor rides with other men and their relationship disintegrated. By February 1922 she was refusing to share his bed. Jean was operated on at St Alban's Private Hospital, Oakleigh for a back complaint in December 1922, which was paid for by George. She stayed with her mother during recuperation and refused to rejoin her husband in February 1923. He filed for divorce on the grounds of her desertion over three years on 1st July 1926, when she was living at 27 Osborne Street, South Yarra, having recovered from another operation. Decree Nisi was issued on 29th September 1926 on the grounds of Jean's desertion but her court costs of £46/13/4 were awarded against him. He was unable to pay and attempted to get the court to agree to paying the sum out of her share of selling their farmland. On 27th June 1927 the court ordered him to make the payment within two months. He was also to pay the cost of the hearing of £10/10/-. There were no children.

Jean was living alone at 19 Commercial Road, South Yarra, Victoria in 1931. She married Thomas Leslie Ashdown (9th November 1894–16th December 1965), born at South Yarra, in 1933. Thomas was a chauffeur when he enlisted in 4th Reinforcements, 29th Battalion on 20th July 1915 at Melbourne (2445), with his mother's consent, having previously served for two years in 29th Australian Light Horse at Albert Park, Victoria. He undertook basic training at the Depot, Seymour, Victoria from 2nd August and was assigned to C Company on 12th August but transferred to B Company on 30th September. He sailed for Suez, disembarking on 15th April 1916 from HMAT A68 *Anchises*. On 21st March he embarked at Alexandria, Egypt aboard HT *Ivernia*, disembarking in France on 29th March. He transferred to the Pioneer Training Battalion on 28th May and was appointed paid acting sergeant at 5th Australian Division Base Depot, Étaples on 1st July. He reverted to the ranks at his own request on 22nd August and joined 5th Pioneer Battalion on 25th August. Thomas was promoted lance corporal on 23rd October, temporary corporal on 17th January 1917 and reverted to lance corporal on 28th January. He reported sick on 25th January with suspected gonorrhoea and was transferred to 13th Australian Field Ambulance on 28th January and to No.45 Casualty Clearing Station the following day. He travelled by ambulance train to 1st Stationary Hospital, Étaples on 12 February as a non-venereal case and returned to duty at 5th Australian Division Base Depot, Étaples on 18th February. He rejoined 5th Pioneer Battalion on 21st April. Thomas reverted to the ranks at his own request and transferred to 1st Australian Ammunition Supply Park on 21st May. He was appointed driver MT, HQ Australian Corps MT Column on 24th May, joined K Supply Column the same day and was attached to HQ 5th Australian Division on 29th May. He transferred to 5th Australian Division Train Supply Column on 13th November and remained detached to HQ 5th Australian Division. He joined 5th Australian Division Base Depot on 18th February 1918, was taken on the strength of 5th Division Motor Transport Company on 12th March and returned to 5th Pioneer Battalion on 15th October. On 7th March 1919 he was admitted to 11th Australian Field Ambulance with epididymitis and was transferred to 3rd Australian General Hospital, Abbeville the same day. He was transferred to 39th General Hospital, Le Havre on 8th March and was evacuated to 1st Australian Dermatological Hospital, Bulford, Wiltshire on 11th March. He transferred to the Training Depot, Parkhouse Camp, Tidworth, Wiltshire on 11th June and was admitted to the Military Hospital, Tidworth with inflammation of the soft part of the nose on 24th June, while on the strength of the Australian Army Service Corps Training Depot, which he joined on 1st July. He was granted leave to attend Belgrave Motor Company, Wilton Crescent Mews, London 23rd July–31st October. The leave was cancelled on 1st October and he joined No.2 Group, Sutton Veny, Wiltshire on 3rd October. He embarked aboard HT *Ypiranga* on 15th November and disembarked at Melbourne on 4th January 1920. He was discharged on 30th April 1920. Thomas was an auctioneer in 1936, when they were living at Pearcedale, Frankston, Victoria. She was living at 12 Portland Place, South Yarra in 1954 and he at Ladds Road, Dewhurst, Victoria as a farmer. Jean was still at 12 Portland Place in 1967. She died at Elwood, Victoria.

George joined the building contractor firm of EA and Frank Watts Pty Ltd, Melbourne as a general foreman in April 1919. He was appointed Inspector of the War Service Homes Department in August 1920 and was in business at Murrumbeena, Victoria as a wood and coal merchant from April 1921. On 5th January 1923 he became a farmer with twenty-three acres at Gladstone Road, Dandenong.

On 10th February 1927, George married Ivy Lillian Wakeling née Hart (2nd October 1889–25th May 1951), born at Lorquon, Victoria, at the Methodist parsonage, Malvern, Victoria. They were living at 659 St Kilda Road, Balaclava, Victoria in 1931 and had moved to 7 North Street, Maribyrnong by 1949. Ivy died at Middle Brighton, Victoria. Ivy had married Arthur Wakeling (1883–3rd September 1969), a coachbuilder born at Brunswick, Victoria, on 14th November 1907 in Melbourne. They lived at Stewart Street, Brunswick, Victoria before moving to Lemon Avenue, Mildura, Victoria. Arthur is understood to have come home intoxicated frequently and neglected her. They moved to 313 Edward Street, Brunswick, followed by O'Connor Street, Brunswick and later to Arthurton Road, Northcote, Victoria. Arthur deserted Ivy in May 1914 and she moved to St George's Road, North Fitzroy, where she ran a confectionery shop. She ran into financial difficulties, sold the business and moved to Clarke Street, Northcote with her children. While she and two of the children were in hospital with diphtheria in December 1914, Arthur took away the third child and later the other two, refusing her access to them. They were neglected and in July 1915 he asked her to take them back and promised to pay maintenance of 7/6 per child per week, which he did irregularly. She moved to 125 Hope Street, South Yarra on 16th July 1916, where she ran a boarding house. Ivy was living alone at 33 Martin Street, South Yarra by 1917. She filed for divorce on the grounds of his desertion for three years on 4th February 1920, when she was living at 20 Martin Street. Arthur was living at Dawson Street, Brunswick. He claimed that Ivy had committed adultery with William J Martin of 80 Bent Street, Northcote from 1914 to 1920. They had been seen by private investigators and by himself and his brother at 38 Rokeby Street, Collingwood in February and March 1921. Arthur claimed £1,000 in damages against William Martin. On 20th April 1922 the court found against Ivy and dissolved the marriage on the grounds of her adultery. Custody of the children was awarded to Arthur, with £450 damages against William Martin and court costs of £74/9/10 against Ivy. Decree Nisi was issued on 20th April 1922. Arthur and Ivy had three children – Vera Allison Wakeling 1908, Arthur Harrison Hart Wakeling 1909 and Austen Lyle Charles Wakeling 1911. Arthur married three more times. In 1925 he married Mary Kathleen Wilson (1884–1934), who had married Hedley Herbert Robbins (1881–1920) in 1912 and had two children – Charles Robbins 1914 and Gladys May Robbins 1918. Arthur married Edna Mary James née Baker (1884–1945) in 1937. She had married Thomas Edward James (1878–1947) c.1908 and they had five children – Thomas Edward James 1909, Lillian Gwendoline James 1913, Raymond George James 1914, Ernest William James 1917 and May James 1919. Edna also had a daughter prior to her first marriage, Iris May Baker, in 1906. Arthur married Ada May Nelms née Thompson (1896–1976) in 1946. Ada had married Henry James Nelms (1881–1945) in 1919. George and Ivy had two children:

- George Mawby Ingram (18th January 1928–6th December 2007), born at 229 Dandenong Road, St Kilda East, Victoria, was a draftsman in 1949, living with his parents at 7 North Street, Maribyrnong., Victoria. He was later an architect. He married Patricia O'Shannassy (1st December 1928–10th February 2000) in 1952. They had two sons:
    - Phillip Gerard Ingram (born 1956) was appointed Deputy Senior Crown Prosecutor 12th June 2008–11th June 2015.
    - Bernard Francis Ingram (born 1958).
- Bettine Rosemary Ingram (1929–24th November 1931) born at Carlton, Victoria.

Ivy's father, Albert Francis Hart (31st October 1864–6th October 1948), born at Sellicks Hill, South Australia, married Helen Frances 'Fanny' Smith (1869–6th June 1943), born at Ashby de la Zouch, Leicestershire, England, on 23rd June 1885 at Willunga, South Australia. Helen entered into a relationship with James Henry McKeich in 1896, which led to the marriage ending in divorce in 1897 at Melbourne. Albert died at Port Vincent, South Australia. In addition to Ivy, Helen and Albert had four other children:

- Gertrude May Hart (27th May 1886–17th April 1958), born at Nhill, Victoria, married Edward Matthew Witherow (8th September 1887–18th August 1951), a plumber born at Crookston, Polk Co, Minnesota, USA (Emmerson, Canada in his service record), on 28th March 1910 at Collingwood, Victoria. Gertrude had a son, Laurence Hugh Hart (later Witherow), in 1904. They were in New South Wales for a period around 1911–13. They were living at 72 Little George Street, Fitzroy, Victoria in 1915 and her address was 33 McKenzie Street, Brunswick West, Victoria in June 1918. He enlisted as Edward Witherow in C Company, 23rd Battalion at Melbourne on 24th February 1915 (61), declaring that he had been apprenticed for five years to Great North B Works, Crookston, Minnesota, USA. He was described as 5′9″ tall, weighing 158 lbs, with dark complexion, brown eyes, black hair and his religious denomination was Roman Catholic. On 29th March he was appointed armourer sergeant and embarked aboard HMAT A14 *Euripides* on 8th May, disembarking at Alexandria, Egypt on 11th June. The Battalion embarked for Gallipoli on 30th August and landed there on 4th September. Edward disembarked from SS *Winifredian* at Alexandria from Mudros on 27th December. He embarked at Alexandria aboard SS *Lake Michigan* on 19th March 1916 and disembarked at Marseille, France on 26th March. He was attached to 16th Company, Australian Army Service Corps from 22nd December. He was granted leave 7th-21st July 1917. An Elsie Holbert of Bell View, Kangaroo Street, Raymond Terrace, NSW enquired in October 1917 if Edward had been killed in action. He was granted leave to Paris 1st-8th January 1918 and to England 1st-17th February. On 2nd September he was attached to the Divisional Armourers' Workshop and on 12th December transferred to the Australian Army Ordnance Corps, attached to 23rd Battalion as armourer sergeant. Edward left the unit on 24th January 1919, joined the Australian Infantry Base Depot on 27th January and returned to England on 29th January, where he joined 3rd Training Brigade next day. He embarked aboard HT *Trasos Monte* for return to Australia on 8th April and was discharged from 3rd Military District on 22nd July 1919. They were living at Gladstone Road, Dandenong, Victoria in 1924 and at 50 Nicholson Street, Fitzroy, Victoria in 1938. He was living at the last address when his discharge certificate was lost in a house fire. A nephew, Lester Bienek, of 506 Idaho Avenue, Grangeville, Idaho, USA enquired about his whereabouts in 1938, as nothing had been heard from him for about twelve years. The last known address was Valley Road, Gladstone, Queensland, Australia. In March 1951 Margret Appellof, daughter of Edward's sister, wrote from the Coos Bay Shoe Factory, 239 South 4th Street, Coos Bay, Oregon, USA, to the Veterans Bureau in Canberra, asking for his whereabouts as they had not heard anything about him for some time. By then Edward was a patient in Mont Park Mental Hospital, Melbourne, Victoria and was unable to understand any correspondence. They had five children – John 'Jack' Edward Witherow 1911, Norman Albert Witherow 1913, Dorothy 'Kerri' Eleanor Malta Witherow 1915, Maisie Marion Witherow 1920 and Alan Lester Witherow 1922. Alan enlisted in the Australian Army on 12th January 1942 at Mitcham, Victoria (VX72132) and was a sergeant at the time of his discharge on 12th October 1945 from 3rd Australian Mechanised Transport Training Depot.

- Elizabeth Olive Hart (2nd October 1887–16th February 1945), born at Woorak, Victoria, married James Ramsey Wardlow McFarlane (13th December 1876–1926), born at Geelong, Victoria, in 1906. They were living at 9 James Street, Fitzroy when he enlisted in 5th Battery, 2nd Field Artillery Brigade at Albert Park, Victoria on 17th August 1914 (1076). He claimed four and a half years previous service in the Australian Field Artillery Brigade, a year and a half with the New South Wales Bushmen and a year in the Scottish Horse as a corporal during the Second Boer War. He was described as 5′ 8¼″ tall, with fair complexion, blue eyes, black hair and his religious denomination was Presbyterian. James embarked aboard HMAT A9 *Shropshire* on 20th October. He was admitted to No.2 Australian General Hospital, Mena House, Cairo, Egypt on 3rd March 1915 and was diagnosed with a tumour in the epigastric region of the abdomen. He embarked aboard HMAT A38 *Ulysses* at Suez on 20th March and disembarked at Melbourne on 14th April. James was admitted to hospital on 3rd May and was discharged from the Army from there medically unfit on 5th March 1916. Elizabeth submitted a claim under the War Pensions Act 1914–16 in August 1917, but it was rejected because the condition was not caused by his military service. They were living at 3 Prentrice Street, West Brunswick at the time. She was living at 35 Margaret Street, Moonee Ponds, Victoria in 1931. They had at least five children – Ellen Ruby McFarlane 1907, Elizabeth McFarlane 1909, Olive Doreen McFarlane 1912, James Ramsay McFarlane 1915 and Mena McFarlane 1918.
- Rose Gladys Hart (12th September 1892–11th March 1990), born at Lorquon, Victoria, married Horace Owen Button (21st April 1888–30th November 1964), born at Brentwood, South Australia, on 26th October 1914 at Minlaton, South Australia. They both subsequently died there. They had five children – Gladys Button 1915, Leslie Horace Button 1917, Doreen F Button 1919, Colin Ernest Button 1920 and Mary Beth Button 1924. Colin served as a corporal in No.99 Squadron, Royal Australian Air Force 27th August 1940–16th November 1945.
- Mildred Hart (9th March 1894–31st October 1983), born at Netherby, Victoria, married Frederick John Herring (17th May 1873–3rd December 1938), born

at Willunga, South Australia, on 17th April 1915 at Minlaton. They had two children – Dulcie Louise Herring 1915 and Norman Frederick Herring 1918. Mildred married Norman Augustus Walter (9th October 1886–17th April 1967), a farmer born at Norwood, South Australia, in 1938. Norman had married Margaret Ellen Button (1885–14th December 1963) on 3rd December 1913 at Magill, South Australia. They were living at Lambert Road, Payneham, South Australia in 1915. Norman enlisted in the AIF on 21st June 1915 and was assigned to 5th Reinforcements, 27th Infantry (1824). He was described as 5′7″ tall, weighing 155 lbs, with fresh complexion, blue eyes, brown hair and his religious denomination was Church of England. He was discharged on 31st August 1915 as 'unlikely to become an efficient soldier'. Margaret and Norman had two children – Marion Elizabeth Walter 1914 and James 'Jim' Freeman Walter 1916.

Helen Frances 'Fanny' Hart née Smith married James Henry McKeich (6th May 1876–1961), born at Dunedin, New Zealand, on 14th September 1916 at Wellington, New Zealand. James' father, Robert McKeich (1855–4th June 1902) joined the New Zealand Mounted Rifles and served as a lieutenant in 2nd Brigade, 9th New Zealand Contingent during the Second Boer War. A peace treaty had been signed on 31st May 1902 and Robert and Lieutenant Henry Raynes rode out across the veldt to shoot springbok on 4th June. They were confronted by a party of three Boers, two of them armed, at Nitnengt, near Vereeniging, Gauteng Province. The Boers were unaware that peace had been declared and ordered the two to dismount and remove their uniforms. Raynes had a revolver in his hip pocket with just two rounds. After removing his jacket, he pulled out the revolver and shot one Boer through the head and another through the chest. He threw the empty revolver at the third Boer, crushing his skull and killing him. As they went to remount their horses, a wounded Boer crawled to a rifle and shot Robert dead. He was the last New Zealander to die in the Second Boer War and the last officer of the Empire to be killed. James was a miner, working for the Public Works Department, and was living with his family at 33 (later 35) Neville Street, Spreydon, Christchurch, Canterbury, when he enlisted in the New Zealand Expeditionary Force on 31st May 1916 at Trentham (27321). He had previously served in the Tuapeka Rifles, Dunedin Rifles, reaching the rank of corporal, and in the Victorian Rangers in Australia, reaching the rank of sergeant. He recorded his date of marriage to Helen falsely as 11th April 1896 at Gerang Gerung, Victoria, Australia, followed by a question mark and 14th September 1916. He was described as 5′8″ tall, weighing 154 lbs, with fresh complexion, brown hair, grey eyes and his religious denomination was Presbyterian. He was assigned to J Company, 17th Reinforcements on 31st May and was promoted lance corporal on 19th June, temporary corporal on 27th August and temporary sergeant on 18th September. He embarked aboard HMNZT 64 *Devon* on 25th September, disembarked at Devonport, Devon on 21st November and marched into Sling Camp, Bulford, Wiltshire the same day, reverting to temporary corporal. He was assigned to 2nd Canterbury Company next day and was promoted corporal on 28th December. James went to France and transferred to 2nd Canterbury Company on 1st February 1917. He joined the New Zealand Infantry and General Base Depot, Étaples on 5th February and was attached to the New Zealand Tunnelling Company on 24th February, transferring on 11th June. He was appointed temporary sergeant on 17th September and substantive on 7th October. James was detached to XVII Corps School on a musketry course 25th April–1st May 1918 and was granted leave to Britain 30th June–20th July. He was detached to Chief Engineer, HQ IV Corps 4th-14th September. On 9th December he was taken ill and was admitted to No.6 Casualty Clearing Station with diphtheria and debility on 23rd December. He was transferred to 25th General Hospital, Hardelot next day and was evacuated to England on 2nd January 1919. On 13th January he was transferred from the City of London Hospital to 2nd New Zealand General Hospital, Walton and was discharged on 31st January to report to Sling Camp on 13th February. He transferred to Codford, Wiltshire next day. James embarked aboard HMNZT 104 *Ionic* at London on 14th March and disembarked in New Zealand on 26th April. He was granted sick leave 27th April–3rd May, giving his home address as 188 Lyttleton Street, Spreydon. James was discharged no longer fit for war service due to bronchitis on 23rd July 1919. They were living at Tangarakau, Taranaki in 1935. Helen died at Whangarei and James at Levin, Horowhenua. They had seven children, all born before they married:

- Walter Royce Hart McKeich (5th February 1897–3rd April 1981), born at Nhill, Victoria, married Lilian Jones (22nd December 1896–3rd April 1982), born at Reading, Berkshire, on 5th June 1923 in New Zealand. They had three children – Walter Stanley McKeich 1923, Iris Muriel McKeich 1925 and Desmond Jack McKeich 1929.
- Ernest Gordon McKeich (22nd September 1898–5th January 1978), born at St Arnaud, Victoria, was a miner, working for the Public Works Department at

Lieutenant Robert McKeich and his grave in Maccaulvei Cemetery, Vereeniging, Orange Free State, South Africa. The year of death is incorrectly shown as 1901.

Bealey Flat, Canterbury, New Zealand at the time of his enlistment in C Company, 4th Reinforcements, Canterbury Infantry Battalion, New Zealand Expeditionary Force on 6th January 1915 at Trentham (6/1914). He was described as 5′7″ tall, weighing 145 lbs, with fresh complexion, hazel eyes, brown hair and his religious denomination was Church of England. He gave his year of birth as 1894. Promoted lance corporal on 15th February, he sailed from New Zealand on 17th April. On 27th April he was severely reprimanded for being absent from parade and for neglect of duty. He reverted to the ranks on 8th June, when he joined 1st Canterbury at Gallipoli. On 15th June he was admitted to No.2 Australian Stationary Hospital, Mudros with dysentery and was evacuated to Egypt aboard HMHS *Alnwick Castle* on 4th July, where he was admitted to the Egyptian Army Hospital, Cairo on 7th July. He transferred to the Convalescent Camp, Helouan on 12th July and to Lady Godley's Hospital, Alexandria on 7th August. He was sentenced to twenty-eight days' detention for being absent without leave on 22nd August. On 28th September he rejoined the Battalion at Mudros and returned to Alexandria, Egypt on 30th December. He was admitted to the New Zealand Field Ambulance, Ismailia on 21st January 1916 and rejoined the Battalion there on 27th January. Appointed temporary lance corporal on 4th March, substantive next day. Embarked for France aboard HMT *Franconia* at Port Said on 6th April. Appointed temporary corporal 9th August–25th September. Ernest was wounded in the left hand by shrapnel on 25th September and was admitted to XV Corps Collecting Station before being transferred to 6th General Hospital, Rouen on 26th September. He joined the New Zealand Infantry and General Base Depot on 8th October and was appointed temporary corporal next day. He rejoined the Battalion on 18th October and was attached to the Royal Engineers next day. On 26th December he was promoted corporal and rejoined the Battalion on 9th January 1917. On 22nd January he was admitted to No.2 New Zealand General Hospital, Walton-on-Thames while on leave, with debility. He was transferred to the New Zealand Convalescent Hospital, Hornchurch, Essex on 5th March. He was fined three days' pay for absence without leave from 10.00 p.m. on 7th April until 7.00 a.m. on 9th April. He was granted leave from 19th April, then to report to Codford, Wiltshire on 4th May. Ernest was admitted to No.3 New Zealand General Hospital, Codford on 7th June with renal calculus. He was discharged to the Command Depot, Codford on 2nd July and was granted ten days sick leave. He was re-admitted to No.3 New Zealand General Hospital with tonsillitis on 20th July, which were removed on 1st August. He was granted ten days leave then reported to the Depot at Codford on 16th August. He was attached to 3rd Hampshire at Portsmouth for a course 10th-29th October as a temporary sergeant. On 24th December he joined the New Zealand Discharge Depot, Torquay, Devon. Appointed CQMS on 7th January 1918 and was selected for duty in New Zealand. Ernest embarked aboard HMNZT 105 *Remuera* at Plymouth on 14th March 1918 and disembarked in New Zealand on 11th May.

He attended a medical board at Trentham and was granted three weeks leave. On 12th September he attended a medical board at Wellington and was found to be indefinitely incapable of active service and was discharged on 25th September 'no longer physically fit for war service due to illness contracted on active service'. Ernest married Winifred Gertrude Hollick (14th February 1902–10th June 1966) on 27th August 1917 at Romford, Essex, England. Her address was 2 Lucius Street, Torquay, Devon and also 10 King's Road, Gosport, Hampshire. She joined Ernest in New Zealand in 1918, where he working as an electrician. The marriage ended in divorce in 1919. Ernest was arrested on 2nd November 1921 and was jailed for two months in Auckland Prison. He was £21 in arrears on a maintenance order for the support of Winifred and their two children – James Henry McKeich 1917 (born at Gosport, Hampshire, England) and Dorothy Maud McKeich 1918. Ernest married Gladys Helen McLaughlin (16th September 1901–21st October 1978), born at Kaiapoi, Waimakariri, on 8th December 1920 at Christchurch. They were living at 19 Harwood Street, Whitiora, Hamilton in April 1923. He was an electrical contractor in 1942, when they were living at 6 Preston Avenue, Mount Albert, New Zealand. The marriage ended in divorce. Ernest and Gladys had three children – Douglas Gordon McKeich 1921, Douglas Gordon McKeich 1922 and Robert McKeich 1923. Ernest married Mary Lilian (surname unknown) in 1952 at Auckland. He was a company manager in 1954, when they were living at 35 Great South Road, Paptoetoe, Auckland and they were still there in 1972. Winfred married Mitchell Melville Martin (October 1902–3rd June 1964), born at Wellington, New Zealand, in 1923 at Rotorua. He was a storeman in 1963, when they were living at 67 Huxley Street, Canterbury. They both died at Christchurch.

- May McKeich (12th (also seen as 17th and 27th) January 1900–19th July 2001), married William Rowntree (born c.1895) on 31st May 1919 in New Zealand. They had two children – Royce William Rowntree 1919 and Rona Rowntree 1922. May married James Christopher Delich (24th October 1887–22nd June 1956), born at Zoastrog, Dalmatia, Austria, in 1924 in New Zealand. He became a naturalised British subject in 1911. He was a bushman when he enlisted in A Company, 6th Reinforcements on 16th April 1915 (12/2685). He was described as 5′ 10″ tall, weighing 190 lbs, with fresh complexion, brown eyes, dark brown hair and his religious denomination was Roman Catholic. James left New Zealand aboard HMNZT 21 *Willochra* on 14th August and disembarked in Egypt on 27th September. He joined the Auckland Infantry Regiment at Mudros on 29th September. On 27th December he returned to Alexandria, Egypt aboard HT *Ionian*. He transferred to 2nd Battalion from 1st Battalion on 14th March 1916 and marched into Moascar Garrison, Egypt the following day. On 8th April he embarked at Alexandria aboard HT *Ascania* for France and joined the New Zealand Infantry Brigade Base Depot, Étaples on 15th August. He joined the New Zealand Convalescent Camp, Hornchurch, Essex on 31st August, transferred to

No.3 Convalescent Camp on 1st September and joined the Canterbury Company on 3rd September. He was detailed for cookhouse duty at Group HQ on 9th October, on the strength of 3rd Reserve Canterbury and Otago Regiment. On 7th November he was admitted to 3rd New Zealand General Hospital, Codford, Wiltshire with scabies and on 2nd December with a sprained left ankle. He was transferred to the Convalescent Section, New Zealand Command Depot, Codford on 6th December. He was admitted to hospital at Codford with syphilis 12th January–9th March 1917 and was discharged to the Command Depot, Codford. On 9th May he joined the New Zealand Reserve Group, Sling Camp, Bulford and was taken on strength of 4th Reserve Auckland and Wellington Regiment. He was admitted to the New Zealand Isolation Hospital, Codford, Venereal Disease Section 14th-16th July and was discharged to the Command Depot, Codford but continued to be treated until 4th September, when he transferred to the Auckland Regiment, Reserve Group, Sling Camp. On 11th September he joined 4th Reserve Battalion, Auckland Regiment. James joined 4th Reserve Auckland Regiment, Sling Camp on 2nd February 1918. On 1st April he was admitted to 3rd New Zealand General Hospital, Venereal Disease Section with gonorrhoea, transferred to the Venereal Convalescent Section on 8th May and was discharged to the Command Depot, Codford on 15 May. James transferred to Sling Camp on 30th May and joined the New Zealand Machine Gun Depot, Grantham on 5th June. He was admitted to the Venereal Disease Convalescent Hospital, Codford 31st January–8th February 1919 and then returned to Sling Camp. He embarked at Southampton, Hampshire aboard HMNZT 21 *Willochra* on 8th March, disembarked at Wellington, New Zealand on 15th April and was discharged on 28th April 1920. May and James were living at 47 Cambridge Terrace, Wellington in 1942. He was an overseer in the Public Works Department, Ohakea when he enlisted in the New Zealand Defence Engineer Service Corps at Wellington on 1st September 1942 (805618) giving his date of birth as 26th November 1890. He was described as 5′ 11½″ tall, with ruddy complexion, brown eyes, grey hair and his religious denomination was Roman Catholic. He was not mobilised but was promoted lance sergeant on 1st November. He was transferred to Area 5 Pool on 1st January 1944. They were living at 11 Gower Street, Trentham in 1946 and at 9 Gower Street, Trentham in 1954, where James subsequently died. James and May had a son, James Sylvester Delich, in 1925. May married Joseph Noel Kitchen (19th December 1907–20th February 2002), born at Upper Hutt, New Zealand, in 1961. They both died at New Plymouth, Taranaki. Joseph had married Eileen Merle Hines (1908–58) in 1937.

- Robert Edward McKeich (20th July 1903–26th February 1904), born at Otago and died at Dunedin.
- James Henry McKeich (12th December 1905–28th July 1961), born at Dunedin, married Eva Ethel Hurst (born 1st November 1907), born at Daisy Hill, Westhoughton, Lancashire, England, in 1926. The marriage ended in divorce.

Eva married William Butler Mildenhall (born October 1904), a miner born at Wellington, in 1934. They were living at Glen Afton, Waikato in 1935.

- Robert McKeich (14th May 1908–1984), born at Christchurch, married Gladys Maud King (31st August 1910–14th May 2002) on 28th July 1934 at Burrowa, New South Wales, Australia, where she was born. He was an electrician in 1968, when they were living at 10 Frederick Street, Ryde, NSW. He died at Sydney, NSW and she at Perth, Western Australia.
- Rona Elsie McKeich (6th September 1912–27th September 1985), born at Burwood, Christchurch, was living with her mother in 1935. She married Harold Maugham Herdson Maugham (13th May 1899–21st January 1990), born at Auckland, New Zealand, in 1939. He was a dairy farmer, serving in 6th Hauraki Regiment (Territorial Force) and living at Kensington Road, Waihi, New Zealand when he enlisted in the New Zealand Rifle Brigade on 14th May 1918 (81586). He was described as 5′ 6¾″ tall, weighing 136 lbs, with dark complexion, blue eyes, black hair and his religious denomination was Church of England. He was discharged on 18th October 1919. They were living at Pukeatua Road, Maungatapere in 1972. They had two sons and two daughters.

An Anzac Dinner on 23rd April 1927, hosted by Lieutenant General Sir John Monash GCMG KCB VD, was attended by twenty-three VCs, including George Ingram. For an unknown reason the Duke of York (future King George VI) was not invited. George also attended the ANZAC Commemoration Service on 25th April 1927 at the Exhibition Building, Melbourne in the presence of the Duke of York, with twenty-three other VCs. George joined the Victoria Police as a probationary constable (PC 8987) on 8th April 1935. His appointment was confirmed on 8th October 1935 and he subsequently became one of the first fourteen Shrine Guards at the Shrine of Remembrance in Melbourne, selected from 250 applicants. He was superannuated on 18th March 1944 with exemplary conduct.

George was appointed a lieutenant in 5th Works & Parks Company, Royal Australian Engineers in Melbourne on 11th November 1939, from the Reserve of Officers (V82281). He was detached to Seymour, Victoria on 28th December 1939 (7th February 1940 in some documents) as OC 5th Works & Parks Company and was attached to Area Command as Garrison Engineer. He was appointed temporary captain on 17th May 1940 and was admitted to 7th Australian General Hospital 3rd-11th April. Having been granted leave 15th March–4th April 1941, he rejoined his unit from Seymour on 5th April. On 30th April 1942, he transferred from RAE (Militia) Services, 3rd Military District to Victoria Lines of Communications RAE Works and was acting OC from 14th June until 27th July, whilst serving with 13th Army Troops Company RAE. He was promoted captain on 17th October and was treated at 107th Australian General Hospital, Seymour 3rd-11th March 1943. His medical category changed from B1 to B on 5th April. George was detached to the RAE Training Depot, Wagga Wagga, New South Wales 6th April–22nd May

During the Second World War seven internment camps were set up around Tatura, Rushworth and Murchison, four for civilians and three for prisoners of war. The population was between 10,000 and 13,000. In 1939 there were about 73,000 Germans living in Britain, most of whom had left Germany due to the rise of the Nazis. On the outbreak of war most were shipped to Australia and Canada. In 1941, German Templers from Palestine were also interned and sent to Australia. The Templers were in Camp 3 at Tatura, where they established a school and a kindergarten. After the War, the majority of Templers remained in Australia. Many of the German Jews enlisted in the British or Australian Armies. Another 500 German civilians were detained following the invasion of Iran in August 1941, although they were housed in South Australia until being transferred to Tatura in 1945. Among the internees was the crew of the German auxiliary cruiser, *Kormoran*, following the battle with HMAS *Sydney* in November 1941. The Tatura camps housed many of the 'Dunera Boys', who were deported to Australia in 1940 aboard HMT *Dunera*. Over 2,500 men were crammed into the ship that was registered for 1,600. The majority were Jewish refugees but they were amongst German and Italian prisoners of war, some of whom were ardent Nazis and fascists. Conditions were appalling and were made worse by physical and verbal abuse from the British guards. The Dunera Boys included musicians, artists, philosophers, mathematicians, scientists and writers. Following their release many remained in Australia and made a significant contribution to the nation's economic, social and cultural life. Tatura German Military Cemetery contains the graves of 351 German civilians and servicemen who died during internment in both World Wars.

and was attached to 6th Workshop & Park Company 27th July–30th August. He was attached to 11th Australian CRE (Works) on 31st August and served as Garrison Engineer with 17th Australian Garrison Battalion from 14th October. On 26th October he transferred to Internment Camp Tatura near Murchison, Victoria as Garrison Engineer and was posted to 7th Engineer Works on 1st May 1944. George was placed on the Retired List on 6th May 1944 from General Details Depot Royal Park.

George married Myrtle Lydia Thomas née Cornell (6th July 1916–2nd May 2006), born at Hawthorn, Victoria, on 24th December 1951 at Brunswick Methodist Church, Melbourne. They were living at 7 North Street, Ascot Vale East in 1954. She was living at 52 Pinewood Drive, Hastings, Victoria in 1977 and had moved in with her son, Alex, at 36 Pinewood Drive by 1980. Myrtle had married William James Thomas in 1939. She was living at 26 Capel Street, Melbourne in 1943 and at 470 William Street, Melbourne in 1949. George and Myrtle had a son, Alexander 'Alex' Ronald Ingram (born c.1952). He was a bank clerk, living at 36 Pinewood

Drive, Hastings, Victoria in 1977 and was still there in 1980, by when his mother had moved in with him. Alex was working for Australia Post when he suffered a motor accident. He accepted a redundancy package in 1992 and was forced by concerns for security and some debts to sell his father's medals in 2008.

Myrtle's father, John 'Jack' Cornell (1st January 1892–1970), a market gardener born at Oakleigh, Victoria, was living at Waverley Road, Mount Waverley, Victoria in 1914. He married Kathleen Venticich (1884–21st July 1919), born at Burwood, Victoria, in 1915. Her father, Pietro Venticich, was born in Austria in 1851. She died at Exhibition Hospital, Carlton, Victoria and he at Prahran, Victoria. In addition to Myrtle, they had at least one other child:

Brunswick Methodist Church, Melbourne.

- William Horace Cornell (born 26th August 1918), born at Hawthorn, Victoria, enlisted in the Australian Army on 29th July 1941 at Camberwell, Victoria (VX60489) and was discharged from 147th Australian General Transport Company on 11th April 1944. He also served in 24/39th Battalion (V40634). William married Shirley Norma Leech (3rd November 1923–8th June 2008) in 1949. He was a driver in 1968, when they were living at 21 Lynden Street, Camberwell, Victoria and they were still there in 1980.

George attended the VC Centenary Celebrations at Hyde Park, London on 26th June 1956, travelling aboard SS *Orcades* along with other Australian VCs, who were part of the 301 VC recipients from across the Commonwealth to attend. George Ingram died at his home in Hastings, Victoria on 30th June 1961 and is buried in the Methodist Section B/80 of Frankston Cemetery, Melbourne. He is commemorated in a number of other places:

George's memorial in Frankston Cemetery, Melbourne.

- Australian Capital Territory
    - Australian Victoria Cross Recipients plaque on the Victoria Cross Memorial, Campbell, dedicated on 24th July 2000.

- Named on one of eleven plaques honouring 175 men from overseas awarded the VC for the Great War. The plaques were unveiled by the Senior Minister of State at the Foreign & Commonwealth Office and Minister for Faith and Communities, Baroness Warsi, at a reception at Lancaster House, London on 26th June 2014 attended by The Duke of Kent and relatives of the VC recipients. The Australian plaque is at the Australian War Memorial, Canberra.
- Ingram Street, Canberra, named on 8th February 1978.
- Commemorative display in the Hall of Valour at the Australian War Memorial, Canberra.

- Victoria
    - Named on a plaque on the Seville Primary School gate, School Road, Seville.
    - Named on a plaque unveiled at Marine Parade, Hastings on 25th April 2018.
    - Victoria Cross Memorial, Springvale Botanical Cemetery, Melbourne.

The memorial at Hastings.

- New South Wales
    - Victoria Cross Memorial, Queen Victoria Building, George Street, Sydney dedicated on 23rd February 1992 to commemorate the visit of Queen Elizabeth II and Prince Phillip on the occasion of the Sesquicentenary of the City of Sydney. Sir Roden Cutler VC AK KCMG, Edward Kenna VC and Keith Payne VC were in attendance.
    - Victoria Cross Memorial Wall, Ingleburn RSL, Liverpool, Sydney.
    - Victoria Cross Recipients Wall, North Bondi War Memorial donated to Waverley on 27th November 2011 by The Returned & Services League of Australia.
    - Victoria Cross Memorial, Peards Complex, East Albury.

Kerry Matthew Stokes AC (born John Patrick Alford 1940), a businessman with interests in a wide range of industries, including electronic and print media, property, mining and construction equipment. He was born in Melbourne and adopted by Matthew and Irene Stokes. He dropped out of school aged fourteen and started off installing TV antennas in Perth, before getting into property and other interests. He has been married four times, including to actress, Peta Toppano. Stokes is believed to be worth over A$3 billion. In 1995 he was appointed an Officer of the Order of Australia for service to business, commerce, the arts and the community. In 2008 Stokes became a Companion of the Order of Australia for service to business and commerce through strategic leadership and promotion of corporate social responsibility, to the arts through executive roles and philanthropy, and to the community, particularly through contributions to organisations supporting youth. He was chairman of the National Gallery of Australia for several years and has made multimillion-dollar donations to it. Stokes is a life member of the Returned and Services League of Australia. He has acquired three other VCs (Alfred Shout, Bernard Gordon and Peter Badcoe) and a GC (George Gosse), which he donated to the Australian War Memorial.

- Communities and Local Government commemorative paving stones for the 145 VCs born in Australia, Belgium, Canada, China, Denmark, Egypt, France, Germany, India, Iraq, Japan, Nepal, Netherlands, New Zealand, Newfoundland, Pakistan, South Africa, Sri Lanka, Ukraine and United States of America were unveiled at the National Memorial Arboretum, Alrewas, Staffordshire by Prime Minister David Cameron MP and Sergeant Johnson Beharry VC on 5th March 2015.

In addition to the VC and MM he was awarded the British War Medal 1914–20, Victory Medal 1914–19, War Medal 1939–45, Australia Service Medal 1939–45, George VI Coronation Medal 1937 and Elizabeth II Coronation Medal 1953. The medals were purchased by Australian media mogul, Kerry Stokes, at a Sotheby's auction in Melbourne, Victoria on 27th/28th May 2008 for A$468,000, who then donated them to the Australian War Memorial. The VC is held at the Hall of Valour, Australian War Memorial, Treloar Crescent, Campbell, Australian Capital Territory.

SECOND LIEUTENANT JAMES JOHNSON
2nd attached 36th Battalion, The Northumberland Fusiliers

James Johnson was born on 28th January 1882 at Widdrington, Northumberland. His name if often seen as James Bulmer Johnson. The only such birth was registered in 1895 at Scarborough, Yorkshire and that man served as a corporal in the Royal Field Artillery during the Great War. The middle name Bulmer does appear on the VC's death certificate but this is the only instance in his entire life. His father, Robert Johnson (born 1851), born at Tweedmouth, Northumberland, was a fireman on the railway in 1871, living with his mother at 5 Back John Street, Seaham Harbour, Co Durham. He married Elizabeth née Johnston (born 1851) in 1871 at Berwick-upon-Tweed, Northumberland, where she was born. He was an engineman in a colliery in 1891, when they were living at 5 Cement Row, Widdrington and at 29 Theodosia Street, Elswick, Northumberland in 1901. In 1911 he was an engineman in a factory by when they had moved to 103 Hugh Gardens, Benwell, Newcastle upon Tyne, Northumberland. James had nine siblings of whom eight are known:

- John Johnson (1872–1907), born at Tweedmouth, Northumberland, was a coal miner in 1891. He married Mary Telfer (born 1872), born at Earsdon, Northumberland, in 1894 registered at Morpeth, Northumberland. John's death

Widdrington was the seat of the Widdrington family. William Widdrington supported Charles I during the Civil War and his estates were confiscated by Parliament but he returned to support Charles II. The 4th Baron Widdrington was convicted of high treason for his part in the Jacobite rebellion in 1715 and forfeited his title and estates. The medieval Widdrington Castle was ruined by a fire in 1777 and was demolished in 1862. The Grade I listed parish church dates back to the 12th century. The village was the birthplace of Anne Hepple Dickinson née Batty (1877–1959), who wrote over twenty-five romantic novels as Anne Hepple, and was the first editor of *The Woman's Magazine* in London 1931–34.

Tweedmouth, on the south bank of the Tweed, is part of Berwick-upon-Tweed, Northumberland and is connected to it by two road and one railway bridges. Tweedmouth has always been part of England, whereas Berwick came under Scottish control several times in the Middle Ages. In an annual ceremony dating back to 1292, Tweedmouth schools elect a *Salmon Queen* to mark the start of *Salmon Week*, which celebrates Tweedmouth's long history of salmon fishing. The parish church dates from the late 18th century and is on the site of an earlier church built in 1145 and its 7th century predecessor. The Old Bridge was constructed in 1610 on the orders of King James VI & I, forming part of the Great North Road between London and Edinburgh. The Royal Border Railway Bridge was opened by Queen Victoria in 1850. The Tweed Dock opened in 1876, replacing the older port on the north bank of the river.

Seaham in Co Durham is on the coast ten kilometres south of Sunderland. Until the early 19th century it was a small farming community. Its only claim to fame then was the local landowner's daughter, Anne Isabella Milbanke, who married Lord Byron at Seaham Hall in January 1815. The Milbankes sold the estate to the 3rd Marquess of Londonderry who built a harbour in 1828. However, it could not deal with the volume of coal produced in the area and a deeper and extended dock opened in 1905. The town was called Seaham Harbour, to differentiate it from the ancient village, but over time it became known simply as Seaham. Seaham Colliery, one of three in the area, suffered an underground explosion in 1880 resulting in the loss of over 160 lives. By 1992 all three coal mines had closed and the local economy was hit extremely hard. Most of the Durham coastline is now a heritage coast and Seaham beach has been entirely restored. The film *Billy Elliot* (2000), set during the 1984–85 miners' strike in the fictional Co Durham town of Everington, was filmed in part around Seaham and Easington. The opening scene in *Alien 3* (1992) was filmed on Blast Beach.

was registered at Castle Ward, Northumberland. Mary was living with her sister, Elspeth, at West Chevington, Acklington, Morpeth in 1911.

- Robert Johnson (born 30th July 1874), born at Widdrington, Northumberland, was a coal miner in 1891. He married Isabella Ann Brown (5th October 1874–

20th April 1952) in 1900 at Newcastle upon Tyne, where she was born. They were living at 71 Durham Street, Newcastle upon Tyne in 1911, by when he was a bar manager. He was incapacitated through illness by 1939, when they were living at 47 Nuns Moor Road, Newcastle upon Tyne. Robert predeceased his wife. She was living at 10 Lancaster Street, Newcastle upon Tyne at the time of her death there. They had at least three children:

  - Gertrude Isabella Johnson (18th March 1905–1979) was a brewer's clerk in 1939, living with her parents. She died unmarried.
  - Ethel Florence Johnson (1910–12).
  - Robert Johnson (born 1st August 1912) was a furniture warehouseman in 1939, living with his parents.

- Esther Jane Johnson (13th May 1877–12th September 1958) married William Ruddick Dodd (29th October 1867–29th September 1957), a hospital porter born at Felling, Co Durham, in 1901 at Newcastle upon Tyne, Northumberland. William had married Martha Owens (1869–93), born at Heworth, Co Durham, in 1890. He was a cooper in 1891, when they were living at 12 Heworth Street, Heworth, Co Durham. Esther and William lived at 131 Salter's Road, Coxlodge, Northumberland and at the Royal Victoria Infirmary, Newcastle upon Tyne by 1911. They were still living there in 1939. They were both living at 12 Green Square, West Monkseaton, Whitley Bay, Northumberland at the time of their deaths at Preston Hospital, North Shields. They had a son:
  - William Ruddick Dodd (born 13th January 1902), birth registered at Castle Ward, Northumberland, was educated at Durham University. He was a cadet in the Senior Division of the Officers' Training Corps and was commissioned in 50th (Northumbrian) Division Engineers on 9th May 1923. Promoted lieutenant 1st August 1925. He served in the Royal Engineers again in the Second World War as a lieutenant from 24th August 1939 and was promoted captain on 18th April 1943 (27689). He last appears in the Army List in March 1946. He was appointed lieutenant in the Army Cadet Force (Kent) on 28th May 1952, with seniority from 1st June 1946. He was a schoolmaster in 1958.
- Ann 'Annie' Johnson (born 13th June 1880) was living with her parents in 1901.
- David Johnson (7th June 1884–7th January 1961) was an engine fitter in 1901. He married Mary Ann Grant (born 6th July 1883) in 1905 at Gateshead, Co Durham, where she was born. She was living with her parents at 79 St Cuthberts Road, Gateshead in 1891. David and Mary were living at 7 Chapel Street, New Shildon, Co Durham in 1911, by when he was a wagon builder in a railway company carriage works. He was a carriage wagon fitter for the London & North Eastern Railway in 1939, when they were still living at 7 Chapel Street. He subsequently died there. They had nine children, all born at Shildon:
  - David Johnson (born 17th January 1906) was an insurance agent for a friendly society in 1939, living with his parents.

  - John Robert Johnson (6th November 1907–April 1998) was a general labourer for the London & North Eastern Railway in 1939, living with his parents.
  - Elizabeth Johnson (born c.1910).
  - James Johnson (born 1912).
  - Frank Johnson (born 1914).
  - Alfred Johnson (born 6th March 1916–December 1981), a blacksmith striker, married Lynette Kirkbride (7th July 1917–July 1990) in 1939. She was living with her parents before the wedding at 2 Waverley Terrace, Shildon. They lived at 19 Short Street, Shildon. They had four children – Dorothy K Johnson 1940, Christine H Johnson 1946, Sheila M Johnson 1949 and Karen E Johnson 1956.
  - George Johnson (born 1918).
  - Henry Johnson (5th June 1920–November 1996) was a hammer driver for the LNER in 1939, living with his parents.
  - Lilian Johnson (8th December 1922–August 1994) married Thomas Appleby in 1959. They had a son, Leslie T Appleby, in 1960.
- Frank Johnson (born 2nd October 1886) was an engine fitter in 1901.
- Elizabeth Johnson (born 1890) was living with her parents in 1911.
- Christina Johnson (1893–1965), also seen as Christiana, married Frederick James Jordan (4th December 1893–7th July 1970) in 1914 at Newcastle upon Tyne, where he was born. He was a clerk in 1911, living with his parents at 86 Hamilton Street, Newcastle upon Tyne. Frederick was a cinema circuit general manager in 1939, living with Eva Jordan (25th February 1897–4th April 1992) as his wife at 38 Woodburn Avenue, Newcastle-upon-Tyne. She is believed to have been born Eva Gatiss and was living with her parents at 19 Durham Street, Newcastle upon Tyne in 1911. It is understood that the marriage between Frederick and Christina broke down before 1939 and he and Eva lived together as a married couple. They married after Christina's death in 1965, with Eva's surname recorded as Gatiss and Jordan. Frederick and Eva were living at 38 Woodburn Avenue, Newcastle upon Tyne at the time of their deaths there. Christina and Frederick had a son:
  - Albert Frederick Jordan (born 4th September 1916) later changed his surname to Johnson. He married Frances Jane Sankey (6th November 1917–16th October 1991), born at Gateshead, in 1936. He was steward of a gentleman's club in 1939, when they were living at 70 Condercum Road, Newcastle upon Tyne. He was also an Air Raid Precautions warden and a volunteer with the Ambulance Service. They had three children – Albert J Johnson 1937, Terry Johnson 1943 and Sheila C Johnson 1944. Frances married secondly as Welsh, possibly Peter Welsh, in 1982.

James' paternal grandfather is unknown. His grandmother, Jane Johnson (born 1820), born at Ford, Co Durham, was recorded as unmarried and her father's housekeeper in 1851, when they were living at West End, Tweedmouth. She was recorded as a widow in the 1861 Census and was still living with her father as his housekeeper at 5 Back John Street, Seaham Harbour, Co Durham. Jane was living at Kiln Hill, Tweedmouth in 1871, with her children, Robert and Mary Jane. In addition to Robert she had two other children:

- Christian Johnson (born c.1845), born at Ford, was living with her mother in 1861.
- Mary Jane Johnson (born 1856), born at Tweedmouth, Co Durham, was a general servant in 1871, living with her mother.

Nothing is known about his maternal grandparents. James was educated at Widdrington Colliery Village School, Northumberland. He was employed as a machine man in 1901 and then worked at the Royal Victoria Infirmary, Newcastle upon Tyne as a porter and clerk.

James enlisted in the Royal Horse Guards (1836) on 13th October 1914 at Newcastle-upon-Tyne. He was described as 5′10″ tall, weighing 157 lbs, with fresh complexion, hazel eyes, brown hair and his religious denomination was Presbyterian. He departed from Southampton, Hampshire on 18th May 1915, arriving at Rouen, France the following day, and joined his Regiment in the field on 23rd May. Promoted lance corporal on 11th August. He was admitted to 8th Cavalry

The Newcastle upon Tyne Infirmary at Forth Banks, funded by public subscription, opened in October 1752. Despite major extensions in 1855 and 1885, the infirmary was overcrowded by the end of the 19th century. A new hospital, the Royal Victoria Infirmary, built on ten acres of Town Moor, was opened by King Edward VII on 11th July 1906. The new hospital had seventeen wards, a nurses' home, chapel and five operating theatres. The infirmary was part of 1st Northern General Hospital, treating wounded military personnel during the Great War. Overcrowding remained a problem. The Dental Hospital and School was added in 1978 and the Medical School in 1985, plus other extensions in the 1990s. Many of the original Edwardian buildings were demolished to make way for the new structures. Consolidation of medical services transferred children's services to the RVI from the Fleming Memorial Hospital in 1988 and maternity services from the Princess Mary Maternity Hospital in 1993. A major expansion included the New Victoria Wing, which replaced the Newcastle General Hospital accident and emergency department. The Great North Children's Hospital opened in 2010.

No.8 Officer Cadet Battalion was based at Whittington Barracks, near Lichfield, on Whittington Heath, the site of the Lichfield races. The popularity of the races waned during the 19th century and military use of the heath grew. Construction commenced in 1877 and the newly built barracks became the Depot of 38th (1st Staffordshire) Regiment and 80th Regiment (Staffordshire Volunteers), which amalgamated to form the South Staffordshire Regiment in 1881. They were also intended to be the Depot of 64th (2nd Staffordshire) Regiment and 98th (Prince of Wales's) Regiment, which amalgamated to form the North Staffordshire Regiment in 1881. The last race meeting was held in 1895 and the old grandstand became a soldiers' home. It was purchased in 1957 by Whittington Heath Golf Course as its clubhouse. During The Second World War the barracks became the 10th US Army Replacement Depot and a US military prison, with a reputation for brutal and cruel punishments. Post war the barracks become the Mercian Brigade Depot in 1960, the home of the Staffordshire Regiment Museum in 1963 and Depot of the Prince of Wales' Division in 1968. The barracks was occupied by an Army Training Regiment 2002–08. In 2007 Whittington Barracks became the Headquarters of the Mercian Regiment. In 2008 the centralisation of all planning and training of Defence Medical Services was concentrated there and a new HQ, Coltman House (named after Bill Coltman VC DCM* MM*), was built. The barracks were renamed Defence Medical Services Whittington.

Field Ambulance with tonsillitis 13th-22nd April 1916 and with a wounded finger on 11th January 1917. He rejoined his unit on 10th March and reverted to trooper at his own request on 20th May. James returned to England on 21st October as a candidate for a commission and was posted to No.8 Officer Cadet Battalion, Lichfield on 7th December. He was treated at Lichfield Military Hospital 6th-15th January 1918 for lymphangitis. He was commissioned in the Northumberland Fusiliers on 29th May 1918 and returned to France on 29th September, disembarking at Boulogne. He joined E Infantry Base Depot on 3rd October and 36th Battalion on 9th October.

Awarded the VC for his actions southwest of Wez Macquart, France on 14th October 1918, LG 26th December 1918. When the GOC of 59th Division, Major General Sir Neville Maskelyne Smyth VC KCB, learned of the award on 24th December, he sent Corporal Foulkes to hand the telegram to James. When James read it, he waltzed Foulkes around his billet and then threw every piece of shaving kit through the window. A runner arrived with an invitation from the Brigade commander, Brigadier-General Thomas Wolryche Stansfeld CMG DSO, for James to join him for dinner that evening. James gave the runner ten Francs and told him to say that James could not be found. He then whisked Foulkes off to the photographers instead. The VC was presented by the King in the quadrangle of Buckingham Palace on 14th June 1919.

Major General Sir Nevill Maskelyne Smyth VC KCB (1868–1941) was the son of the geologist, Sir Warington Wilkinson Smyth, grandson of Admiral William Henry Smyth and a cousin of Robert Baden-Powell, founder of the Scout Movement. He was commissioned in 1888 and joined the Queen's Bays (2nd Dragoon Guards) in India. In 1890 he was attached to the Royal Engineers to assist with a railway survey during the Zhob Valley expedition. By 1896 he was with his Regiment in Cairo, Egypt. For his services during the Mahdist War he was Mentioned in Despatches on 3rd November 1896 and was awarded the Order of the Medjidieh, 4th Class in 1897. On 2nd September 1898, at the Battle of Omdurman, he rescued two war correspondents and was awarded the VC. In November 1899 he was Intelligence Officer and ADC to Colonel Lewis, commanding the Infantry Brigade during operations leading to the defeat of the Khalifa, for which he was Mentioned in Despatches for the third time and was awarded the Order of Osmanieh, 4th Class. He served with the Queen's Bays during the Second Boer War and was promoted brevet major on 22nd August 1902. Promoted substantive major in October 1903, transferred to the Carabiniers (6th Dragoon Guards) in India and returned to South Africa in 1908. He was promoted lieutenant colonel in May 1909 and became CO of the Carabiniers. He was promoted colonel in December 1912 and was seconded to the Egyptian Army, where he was commandant of the Khartoum District 1913–14 and was active in combating the slave trade. He commanded 1st Australian Infantry Brigade at Gallipoli as a temporary brigadier general and was one of the last officers to leave the peninsula. He also commanded the Brigade in France and on 28th December 1916 took command of 2nd Australian Division. He was promoted major general on 1st January 1918 and briefly commanded 58th Division before 59th Division from August 1918. Having learned to fly in 1913, he sometimes borrowed an aircraft to look at the lines for himself. During the war he was Mentioned in Despatches a number of times (eleven times in his career), was awarded the Belgian Croix de Guerre and the French Legion d'Honneur and was appointed KCB in the 1919 King's Birthday Honours. On 30th July 1919 he was appointed GOC 47th (1/2nd London) Division TF until 30th July 1923. He retired on 5th July 1924 and emigrated to Australia, where he farmed at Balmoral, Victoria. One of his sons, Dacre, served in the Royal Australian Navy, rising to the rank of commodore.

James returned to Britain from Boulogne on 9th October 1919 and was demobilised on 12th October 1919, giving his place of residence as 103 Hugh Gardens, Benwell, Newcastle upon Tyne. He relinquished his commission on 1st September 1921 and retained the rank of second lieutenant. James served in the Auxiliary Division of the Royal Irish Constabulary from 15th June 1921 (2066 & 2074) and joined the Depot on 18th June. He was granted leave 13th-26th August and was struck off strength as an absentee on 22nd August. He was unemployed and living at 72 Gerald Street, Benwell, Newcastle upon Tyne when he applied for the VC pension in February 1922 but at that time it was not paid to commissioned officers.

James was employed by the Northern Branch Racecourse Betting Control Board at Doncaster Racecourse until October 1933. While unemployed in March 1934 he asked for work at the War Office but no opportunities existed. He was living at 18 Essex Avenue, Doncaster at the time. He moved to Plymouth, Devon with his

Thomas Wolryche Stansfeld CMG DSO (1877–1935) joined the Army in 1897 and served during the Second Boer War 1899–1902. He was involved in operations near Colesberg, in the Relief of Kimberley and at Paardeberg. He was Mentioned in Despatches and awarded the DSO in 1900. He was wounded at Ypres in 1914 and was involved in many later battles, being awarded the French Legion d' Honneur and Croix de Guerre, the CMG and was Mentioned in Despatches a number of times. He was promoted to colonel in 1919. Post war he was Commandant of the Small Arms School, Hythe and commanded two brigades – 137th Staffordshire Infantry Brigade 1924–25 and 10th Infantry Brigade 1925–29, after which he retired. One of his sons, Lieutenant Colonel Thomas Wolrych Guy Stansfeld DSO (1906–87), served in the East Surrey Regiment during the Second World War.

landlord and lady, William Thomas Ramsey (1894–1979) and Gertrude Florence Ramsey (1900–61), and was living with them at 74 Fletemoor Road, Plymouth in 1939. At the time James was a civilian clerk working for the Army Recruiting Office. James was employed by Plymouth City Treasury from 28th July 1941 as a Rating Assessment Officer for buildings. He later lived at 2 Salisbury Road, Plymouth, probably because his previous residence had been damaged during the Blitz.

James attended two VC Reunions – the VC Garden Party at Buckingham Palace on 26th June 1920 and the VC Dinner at the Royal Gallery of the House of Lords,

James Johnson, seated second left, with some of the other medals recipients. Foulkes is standing far right.

Recruiting for the Auxiliaries began in July 1920 and the Division had grown to 1,900 strong by November 1921. Although part of the Royal Irish Constabulary, the Division operated independently in rural areas in companies about one hundred strong. They were heavily armed and highly mobile, under the command of Brigadier General FP Crozier. James Johnson was one of three VCs to serve in the Auxiliaries, the others being James Leach and George Onions. The Division was not suited for counterinsurgency, as it had been hurriedly recruited and was poorly trained. With an ill-defined role, it gained a reputation for drunkenness, ill-discipline and brutality. It was disbanded in 1922.

Doncaster is one of the oldest and largest horse racing centres in Britain, with regular meetings going back to the 16th century. The racecourse is home to two of the world's oldest horse races – the Doncaster Cup, first run in 1766, and the St Leger Stakes, founded in 1776 by Colonel Anthony St Leger, the world's oldest classic horse race. During the Great War the racecourse was used by the military and substitute races were run at Newmarket. Doncaster hosts the start and end of the flat season. In 1992 it staged the first Sunday meeting on a British racecourse.

London on 9th November 1929. He died at Plymouth City Hospital, Devon on 23rd March 1943. The informant was his landlady, Gertrude Florence Ramsey, 1 Evelyn Street, St Budeaux, Plymouth. His funeral was held on 26th March at St Boniface Church, St Budeaux, Plymouth, followed by cremation at Efford Crematorium, Plymouth, where there is a memorial plaque. His ashes were scattered in the Garden of Remembrance. Only one member of his family attended the

The Plymouth Workhouse, which opened in 1858, was enlarged several times and became Greenbank Infirmary in 1909. When the workhouse system ceased in 1930, it became the City Hospital and a new nurses' home was opened in 1936. It suffered damage in a number of air raids during the Second World War. Wards 6 and 7 were destroyed on the night of 13th January 1941 and a twelve year old girl was killed. On the night of 20th March the new maternity block, opened in February, received a direct hit, which killed four nurses, nineteen babies and one mother. In 1951 the City Hospital combined with The Prince of Wales's Hospital and was renamed Freedom Fields Hospital. The hospital closed in 1998 and the site has since been largely redeveloped for residential use.

The foundation stone of Saint Boniface Mission Hall was laid on 17th December 1900 and was dedicated by the Bishop of Exeter on Saint Boniface's Day, 5th June 1901. However, a proper church was required, and the Bishop of Exeter laid the foundation stone on 4th October 1911. The church was consecrated on 14th May 1913 as a chapel of ease to Saint Budeaux Church and the parish of Saint Boniface formed in 1916. The Anglican Church of Saint Boniface, Bishop and Martyr, in Victoria Road, Saint Budeaux, has since been demolished and replaced by a smaller modern building in Percy Street. At its entrance is a large cross made of ships' timber that was presented to the original church by the Royal Navy in 1965. A large stained-glass window was salvaged from the old building.

Plymouth City Crematorium, situated in Plymouth (Efford) Cemetery, opened in 1934. During the Second World War sixty-one service personnel were cremated there and are commemorated on a screen wall behind the Cross of Sacrifice in Efford Cemetery. The Cemetery contains 338 burials from the Great War and 109 from the Second World War, including five who are unknown. The CWGC also maintains twelve war graves of other nationalities, mainly Greek merchant seamen.

funeral, his brother-in-law, William Ruddick Dodd of Whitley Bay. James' sister, Chris, sent a wreath in the design of a Victoria Cross. Members of Plymouth City Council, the Old Contemptibles Association, British Legion and his former Regiment attended. A Department for Communities and Local Government commemorative paving stone was dedicated at Memorial Garden, Grangemoor Road, Widdrington, Northumberland on 14th October 2018.

The VC commemorative paving stone at Grangemoor Road, Widdrington, Northumberland (Memorials to Valour).

Alnwick Castle, the seat of the Dukes of Northumberland, was built following the Norman Conquest. The first part of the castle dates from c.1096 and was captured by King David I of Scotland in 1136. It was besieged in 1172 and 1174 and in 1212 King John ordered it to be demolished but this was not carried out. The castle and estates were sold to the Percys and have been owned by the family since. Henry Percy and his son, also Henry, turned the castle into a major fortress. The Abbot's Tower, Middle Gateway and Constable's Tower survive from this period. The Percys rebelled against King Richard II, helping to dethrone him, and later against King Henry IV, who, after the Battle of Shrewsbury, pursued the Earl and the castle surrendered under the threat of bombardment in 1403. During the Wars of the Roses, Alnwick held against King Edward IV until it was surrendered in 1461, after the Battle of Towton. The castle changed hands a few times and by May 1463 was in Lancastrian hands for the third time since Towton. During the next decade, the 4th Earl of Northumberland pledged loyalty to Edward IV and the castle was returned to the Percys. In 1650, Cromwell used the castle to house prisoners after the Battle of Dunbar. The castle was extensively restored in the second half of the 18th century by Robert Adam but much of his work was removed between 1854 and 1865. During the Second World War, Newcastle Church High School for Girls was evacuated to Alnwick Castle and post war parts of the castle continued in use by other educational establishments – Alnwick College of Education, a teacher training college, 1945–77, and since 1981, St Cloud State University of Minnesota, as a branch campus of its International Study Programme. The current Duke's family live in the castle but occupy only a part of it. The rest is open to the public throughout the summer. Special exhibitions are housed in three of the castle's perimeter towers. The Postern Tower has an exhibition about the Dukes of Northumberland and their interest in archaeology. Constable's Tower houses military displays such as the Percy Tenantry Volunteers exhibition, local volunteer soldiers raised to repel Naploeon's planned invasion of Britain 1798–1814. The Abbot's Tower houses the Royal Northumberland Fusiliers Regimental Museum. Alnwick Castle has been used as the setting of many films and television series, including:

Becket 1964.
Count Dracula 1977.
Black Adder 1983.
Robin Hood: Prince of Thieves 1991.
Elizabeth 1998.
Two *Harry Potter* films 2001–02.
The Virgin Queen 2005.
Downton Abbey 2014–15.
Transformers: The First Knight 2017.

In addition to the VC he was awarded the 1914–15 Star, British War Medal 1914–20, Victory Medal 1914–19 and George VI Coronation Medal 1937. The VC was lost when his home was destroyed in an air raid on Plymouth. The replacement VC is held by the Royal Northumberland Fusiliers Regimental Museum, The Abbot's Tower, Alnwick Castle, Alnwick, Northumberland.

306122 SERGEANT WILLIAM HENRY JOHNSON
1/5th Battalion, The Sherwood Foresters (Nottinghamshire & Derby Regiment)

William Johnson was born on 15th October 1890 at Court 1, Park Street, Worksop, Nottinghamshire. His father, William Edward/Edwin Johnson (1863–1904), born at Worksop, Nottinghamshire, was a groom in 1881. He married Harriet Elizabeth née Wing (12th February 1865–1915), born at Navenby, Lincolnshire, in 1887 at Worksop. She was known as Elizabeth. William senior was a house painter in 1891, when they were living at 3, Court 4, Park Street, Worksop. By 1901 they had moved to 8, Court 8, Bridge Street, Worksop. Elizabeth was a charwoman in 1911, living with her children, Edward, Mabel and Albert, plus her brother-in-law, Joseph Johnson, at 14 Forrest's Yard, Bridge Street, Lead Hill, Worksop. William junior had three siblings:

- Edward Henry Johnson (22nd February 1887–1983), a coalminer, married Keren Emma Milnes (11th November 1889–1953), born at South Wingfield,

Park Street, Worksop. Worksop is situated at the northern edge of Sherwood Forest, about thirty kilometres from Sheffield. It is known as the 'Gateway to The Dukeries' because of the four nearby ducal estates – Clumber House, Thoresby Hall, Welbeck Abbey and Worksop Manor. Worksop is mentioned in the Domesday Book of 1086. About 1103, William de Lovetot established a castle there and an Augustinian priory. A market town grew around them. A skirmish occurred in the area during the Wars of the Roses in 1460. The town grew in response to the construction of the Chesterfield Canal in 1777 and the Manchester, Sheffield and Lincolnshire Railway in 1849. The discovery of coal seams also brought expansion and provided the main employment for most of the 19th and 20th centuries. In the 1990s closure of the mines compounded employment problems caused earlier by the decline of the timber trade and other local industries.

Bridge Street, Worksop. Amongst the famous people from the town are:

- Donald Henry Pleasence OBE (1919–95) began his acting career on the stage in the West End. When war broke out in 1939, he initially refused to serve and registered as a conscientious objector. However, he changed his mind in autumn 1940 after bombing attacks on London. He volunteered for the RAF and flew on almost sixty missions over occupied Europe as a wireless operator with No.166 Squadron in Bomber Command. On 31st August 1944, his Lancaster was shot down and he was a prisoner of war for the rest of the conflict. He was held in Stalag Luft 1, where he produced and acted in many plays to entertain his fellow prisoners. After the war he embarked on a screen career, appearing appropriately as an RAF officer in *The Great Escape* 1963. Amongst his other roles was the villain Blofeld in the James Bond film, *You Only Live Twice* 1967.
- Graham Taylor OBE (1944–2017), football player and manager, was born in Worksop, but grew up in Scunthorpe. He played for Grimsby Town and Lincoln City before retiring through injury in 1972. He became a manager with Lincoln City before moving to Watford and took the club from the Fourth to the First Division in five years. Watford were First Division runners-up in 1982–83 and FA Cup finalists in 1984. Taylor took over Aston Villa in 1987, leading the club to promotion in 1988 and First Division runners-up in 1989–90. He was manager of the England team 1990–93 but resigned when England failed to qualify for the 1994 World Cup. He returned to club management with Wolverhampton Wanderers for a season, then back to Watford, leading the club into the Premiership in 1999 after back-to-back promotions. His last management appointment was with Aston Villa 2002–03. He served as Watford's chairman 2009–12.
- Lee John Westwood OBE (born 1973), golfer who has won tournaments on five continents in four decades. He was European Tour Golfer of the Year 1998, 2000, 2009 and 2020 and represented Europe in ten Ryder Cups. In October 2010 he replaced Tiger Woods as the world number one, the first British golfer to do so since Nick Faldo in 1994, despite never winning a major.

Navenby village is thirteen kilometres south of Lincoln. Remains in the area date back to the Bronze Age. The Romans had a small base there, as the village straddles Ermine Street, the Roman road from London to Lincoln and York. Navenby became a market town after receiving a charter from Edward the Confessor in the 11th century. The market fell into disuse in the early 19th century and Navenby lost its status as a market town. During the Great War there was a RFC/RNAS airfield at Wellingore Heath. It re-opened in 1935 as RAF Wellingore, a satellite for RAF Digby until 1944 and then a relief landing ground for RAF Cranwell until its closure in 1945. Guy Gibson and Douglas Bader were based there at various times.

Derbyshire, at Worksop in 1913. She was living with her parents at Church Lane, South Wingfield in 1891 and in Mansfield, Nottinghamshire in 1911, by when she was a cotton spinner. Edward and Keren were living at 298 Portland Road, Worksop in 1939. They had two children:

   - Marjorie Johnson (21st February 1914–1979) was a hairdresser in 1939, living with her parents. She married Raymond Lockhart Lupton (28th July 1915–May 1984), born at Bakewell, Derbyshire, in 1941 at Chesterfield, Derbyshire. He was a gamekeeper in 1939, living with his parents at Monsal Dale, Derbyshire. They are believed to have had a son, David J Lupton, in 1949.
   - Helen Johnson (born 1919) married Edwin Spowage (3rd August 1917–July 1997) in 1941 at Chesterfield. He was a plasterer's labourer in 1939, living with his widowed mother at Cotton Mill, Langwith, Nottinghamshire. They had a daughter, Karen Spowage, in 1943, and a son, Graham Spowage, in 1947.
- Albert Johnson (15th November 1894–1968) was a whitesmith in 1911, living with his mother. He served in the Sherwood Foresters (18323) and was discharged with a disability on 19th October 1918. He married Grace Wilkinson (17th March 1894–1974) in 1921. Albert was a colliery ripper in 1939, when they were living at 3 Ebenezer Terrace, Worksop. They had three children:
   - Margaret Johnson (14th September 1922–1997) was a drapers' shop assistant in 1939, living with her parents. She married Kenneth Westerby (24th July 1919–May 2002), born at Sculcoates, Yorkshire, in 1948. He was a horseman on a farm in 1939, living with his parents at Grange Cottage, East Retford, Nottinghamshire. They had a son, Paul Westerby, in 1958.
   - William Johnson (born and died 1924).
   - Grace E Johnson (born 1926).
- Mabel Alice Johnson (born 22nd September 1892), whose birth may have been registered at Worksop as Alice Anne M Johnson. She was a general domestic servant in 1911 and is understood to have married Ernest Goodacre (1888–23rd April 1917) later that year. He was a coal hewer at Shireoaks Colliery, living with his parents at 9 Dock Road, Worksop. Ernest enlisted in 1/8th Sherwood Foresters in January 1915 (3507 & 306098) and went to France on 28th June. He was reported missing on 23rd April 1917 and was later confirmed as being killed in action on that day. His remains were never recovered (Arras Memorial, France). Mabel was living with her two children at 12 Forrest's Yard, Bridge Street, Lead Hill, Worksop in 1917 and at 6 Forrest's Yard in 1939. She is believed to have died in 1977 but the year of birth is given as 1889. Mabel and Ernest had two children:
   - Edwin Ernest Goodacre (27th December 1911–July 1979) was a coalminer haulage hand in 1939, living with his mother and sister. He married Dorothy Brammar (21st July 1923–July 1978), born at Ecclesall Bierlow (Sheffield), Yorkshire, in 1945. She was living with her parents at 42 Furnival Street, Worksop in 1939. Edwin

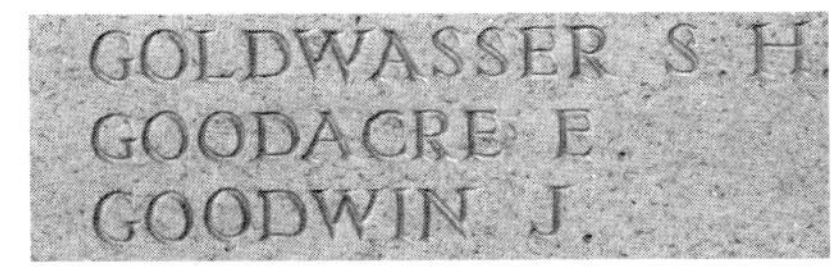

Ernest Goodacre's name on the Arras Memorial.

and Dorothy had three children – twins Terence and Trevor Goodacre in 1948 and Lawrence S Goodacre in 1958.
  - Hilda Elizabeth Goodacre (3rd July 1915–1995) married Charles W Shaw in 1935. Hilda and her daughter were living with Hilda's mother in 1939 but Charles was not with them. They had three children – Cynthia Shaw 1935, Maureen Shaw 1941 and Valerie E Shaw 1944.

William's paternal grandfather, Edwin Johnson (1841–88), born at Worksop, Nottinghamshire, married Anne née Audiss (born c.1837), born at Laceby, Lincolnshire, in 1861 at Sheffield, Yorkshire. She was baptised at Laceby on 4th November 1840 and was living with her parents at Brook Lane, Laceby in 1851. Anne had a daughter, Eleanor 'Ellen' Johnson Audiss, in 1861 at Worksop. Ellen was an unemployed general servant in 1881, living with her parents. Edwin was a house painter in 1861, when they were living at 2, Court 9, Bridge Street, Worksop. They later moved to 53 Park Street, Worksop. Anne was living with her three sons at 7, Court 8, Bridge Street, Worksop in 1891 and at 14 Lead Hill, Worksop in 1901. In addition to William, Edwin and Anne had four other children:

- Elizabeth Johnson (born 1866) was a general domestic servant at 47 Park Street, Worksop in 1881.
- Frank Johnson (31st July 1869–1945) was a tailor in 1891. He married Edith Hannah 'Anna' Hind (28th July 1869–1942), born at Whitwell, Derbyshire, in 1893. She was a domestic servant in 1891, living with her parents at Larpit Lane, Whitwell. Frank and Edith lived at Worksop at 7 Court, 8 Bridge Street in 1901, at 6 Court, 1 Potter Street in 1911 and at 99 Westgate in 1939. They had six children including – Winifred 'Winnie' Johnson 1893, Mary Ellen Johnson 1895, Minnie Johnson 1901 and Frank Reuben Johnson (1903–36).
- Albert Johnson (6th June 1873–1941) was a wood turner in 1891. He married Lilian Ginnever (17th February 1876–1949), born at Maltby, Yorkshire, in 1900 at Rotherham, Yorkshire. They were living at 3 South View, Cheapside, Worksop in 1911 and were still there in 1939. They had four children:
  - Florence Ethel Johnson (born 1903).
  - Frederick William Johnson (born 1904).
  - Probably Jessie Audess Johnson (1907–09).
  - Lucy Audiss Johnson (9th December 1910–1973) married John R Pennington

Laceby village is just outside Grimsby. Remains dating back to the Mesolithic period have been found there. There have also been Roman and Anglo-Saxon finds. At the time of the Domesday Book in 1086, the land passed to Bishop Odo of Bayeux. In 1234, Henry III granted John, son of Geoffrey de Nevill, the right to hold a fair at Laceby Manor.

(January 1910–1982) at Rotherham in 1942. They had three children – David J Pennington 1943 and twins Ann and Jean Pennington 1944.
- Joseph Johnson (1876–1928) was a paperboy in 1891 and a labourer in a coalmine in 1901, living with his mother. By 1911 he was living with his widowed sister-in-law, Elizabeth Johnson, at 14 Forrest's Yard, Bridge Street, Lead Hill, Worksop.

His maternal grandfather, John Wing (28th August 1836–1st February 1907), born at Navenby, Lincolnshire, was a shepherd. He married Sarah née Antcliff (10th April 1838–21st October 1896), born at Bathley, Nottinghamshire, on 6th September 1859 at Muskham, Nottinghamshire. They were living at 2 Blacksmith Lane, Navenby in 1881 and at 10 Blacksmith Lane in 1891. Sarah died at Boothby Graffoe, Lincolnshire. John married Ellen Wildy (21st July 1865–1931) there on 9th February 1899. She was the daughter of Thomas Wildy (1829–76) and Mary Ann Abley (1844–1905). However, Thomas Wildy was still married to his first wife, Mary Elizabeth McCarthy (1834–94), when Ellen was born to Mary Ann Abley, so she was baptised as Ellen Morgan. In 1891 Ellen was living with her mother, Mary, who by then had remarried as Smith and was a widow, at 5 Sincil Street, Lincoln. John and Ellen were living at Village Street, Boothby Graffoe in 1901. He died at Navenby. Ellen married John Williamson (born 1835), an agricultural labourer born at Snettisham, Norfolk, in 1908 at Lincoln. They were living at Holbeach Clough, Lincolnshire in 1911. John Williamson had married Mary Ann Fish née Clarke (1838–82), born at Whaplode, Lincolnshire, in 1867 at Holbeach, Lincolnshire. He was a ratcatcher in 1871, when they were living with their five children, the first four being born illegitimately – Mary Ann Williamson Fish 1859, Sarah Ann Williamson Fish 1861, Ellen Elizabeth Williamson Fish 1864, Matthew Williamson Fish 1866 and John Henry Williamson 1869. In addition to Harriet, John and Sarah Wing had another ten children:

- John Henry Wing (19th August 1859–25th January 1894), an agricultural labourer born at North Muskham, Nottinghamshire, married Elizabeth Burkitt (21st October 1856–3rd November 1936) on 1st June 1880 at Swinderby Parish Church, Lincolnshire. She had a son prior to her marriage, George Henry Burkitt (born 1879), birth registered as Birkett. George was an agricultural day boy in 1891. John and Elizabeth were living at Brewery Lane, Carlton le Moorland, Newark, Nottinghamshire in 1891, where he subsequently died. They had seven children:
    - Harriet Elizabeth Wing (29th September 1881–20th July 1969) was an unemployed waitress in 1901 living with her mother.
    - Walter Wing (1884–1913).
    - Alice Wing (5th February 1886–29th June 1967).
    - Arthur Wing (2nd November 1888–1964) was a farm labourer in 1911.
    - Rose Wing (born 1890).

- Elizabeth Wing (born 1891).
- Sarah Ann Wing (2nd September 1893–1976) married George W Hurst (16th October 1888–1978) in 1919.

Elizabeth had a daughter, Amelia Wing (born 1898), whose father is unknown. This girl may have married John W Wray in 1924 and had three children – Clarice P Wray 1924, Betty A Wray 1925 and John P Wray 1928. The death of an Amelia Wray aged sixty-two was registered in 1960 at Derby, as was the death of John W Wray in 1986, who was born in 1898. Elizabeth was a charwoman, living with her children, Harriet, Arthur, Sarah and Amelia at Carlton le Moorland Village, Lincolnshire in 1901. She married Tom Clawson Sibcy (19th July 1873–11th January 1963), a farm labourer born at Carlton le Moorland, in 1905. They were living at Carlton le Moorland in 1911 with her son, Arthur, and Tom's children from his first marriage. Elizabeth died at North Kesteven, Lincolnshire. Tom was living with his son, Frederick, a dealer in drapery and small ware, at 3 Church Lane, North Kesteven in 1939. Tom had married Elizabeth Saxby (1869–1904) on 20th July 1897 at Carlton le Moorland. They had two children – Frederick Bertie Sibcy (1898–1964) and Florence Anne Sibcy (1902–2000).

- William Anthony Wing (1861–11th January 1907), a coal porter, married Ellen Maria Copus (27th March 1865–20th May 1927), a domestic servant born at 5 James Street, Windsor, Berkshire, on 7th March 1886 at St George the Martyr, Battersea, London. She was living with her parents at 61 Haines Street, Battersea in 1881. William and Ellen were both living at 12 Ceylon Street, Battersea Park Road, London at the time of their marriage. They were living at 11 Haines Street, Battersea in 1891 and 1901. William later died there. Ellen was a hospital cleaner in 1911, living with her children at 6 Ceylon Street. She married Henry Latter (born 1857), born at Tunbridge, Kent, in 1914. They were living at 6 Ceylon Street in 1915. Henry had married Jeanie Russell Anderson née Cox (1865–5th November 1911), born at Tewkesbury, Gloucestershire, in 1895 at St George in the East, London. Henry and Jeanie were living at 56 Red Lion Street, St George in the East in 1901, by when he was an orange porter. By 1911 he was a church caretaker and they were living at Church House, Abbey Grove, Abbey Wood, Kent. Jeanie was a patient in a convalescent home at The Cottage, Westbrooke, Worthing, Sussex. Jeanie had married Arthur William Bonner Anderson (born c.1865) on 28th February 1885 at St Thomas's Church, Bethnal Green, London. Arthur was a short-hand clerk in 1885 and they were living at 25 Albert Road, Hackney, London. Jeanie and her daughter, Mary, were living with her widowed stepmother, Alice Cox (born c.1852) at 15 Lillian Street, Hackney, London in 1891. It is not known what became of Arthur. Arthur and Jeanie had two children – Arthur Alec Russell Anderson 1885 and Mary Russell Anderson 1887. William and Ellen had twelve children:

- ◦ Violet Wing (born 1st January 1887) was a ladies maid in 1911.
- ◦ John Wing (28th March 1888–20th December 1969) was a carman in 1911.
- ◦ William Wing (1889–21st July 1893).
- ◦ Bella Wing (1891–7th August 1962) was a dressmaker in 1911. She married Robert Meager (1873–1949) in 1918. They had two children – Robert G Meager 1919 and Frances A Meager 1920.
- ◦ Annie Wing (1892–1946) was a book folder in 1911. She is believed to have married Frederick AE Giles (1892–1964) in 1920. They had three children – Harry LG Giles 1923, Audrey J Giles 1924 and Stanley D Giles 1927. Frederick is understood to have married Beatrice A Welch (c.1892–1950) in Penzance, Cornwall in 1948 and Elizabeth A Spence in Wandsworth in 1951.
- ◦ Walter Wing (1893–15th February 1915) was a clerk in 1911. He was serving in 1/12th Battalion, London Regiment (The Rangers) (1591) when he was killed in action (Ypres (Menin Gate) Memorial, Belgium).
- ◦ Nellie Maria Wing (21st June 1895–1984) married William A Randall (5th October 1894–1985) in 1926.
- ◦ Arthur Wing (1897–14th March 1914) was an assistant milkman in 1911.
- ◦ Frederick Wing (1899–1962) is believed to have married Ethel B Hicks in 1923. They had a daughter, Ruby Wing, the same year.
- ◦ Ivy Wing (9th October 1900–1984) married Roland Bond (30th January 1898–1977) in 1925. They are understood to have had two children – Roy W Bond 1926 and Daphne G Bond 1928.
- ◦ George Wing (1902–65).
- ◦ Daisy Wing (27th November 1903–15th May 1978) married Albert Gulliver in 1926. They had eight children – Albert A Gulliver 1926, Maureen D Gulliver 1927, Leonard G Gulliver 1929, Norman S Gulliver 1931, Kathleen G Gulliver 1933, Kenneth D Gulliver 1934, Michael T Gulliver 1938 and Malcolm W Gulliver 1943.

- George Henry Wing (1863–72).
- Walter Joseph Wing (1867–14th March 1952), born at Navenby, Lincolnshire, emigrated to Australia, arriving at Brisbane, Queensland on 15th June 1887. He moved to Victoria and married Tamar Young (1865–27th July 1945), born at Newcastle, New South Wales, in Victoria in 1896. He was a Salvation Army officer in 1903, when they were living at Pakenham, Victoria. They moved to Moreton Bay, Queensland around 1913, by when Tamar was also a Salvation Army officer, before returning to Pakenham

Walter Wing's name, bottom right, on the Ypres (Menin Gate) Memorial.

by 1918. Walter was an orchardist in retirement. They were living at Army Road, Pakenham East in 1942. They had two children:

  - Evelyn Winifred Wing (1897–2nd March 1980) married James Joseph Priest (1889–1970) in 1917. They had at least three children – Jane Vera Priest 1917, Stanley Priest 1919 and Stella May Priest 1920.
  - Frederick Gordon Stanley Wing (1899–1978) married Ruth Alma Marion Lewis (born 1901) in 1929.

- Minnie Maria Wing (6th July 1868–5th March 1930) married William Farr (1862–29th April 1933), an agricultural labourer born at Owston Ferry, Lincolnshire, in 1888 at Gainsborough, Lincolnshire. They were living at Main Street, Owston Ferry in 1891. By 1901 he was a farm foreman, when they were living at Martin, Harworth, Nottinghamshire. They both died at Owston Ferry. They had five children:
  - John Harry Farr (19th December 1889–1971) married Amy E Lilly (11th September 1890–1969) in 1922. They had three children – Margaret Farr 1923, John D Farr 1925 and Malcolm S Farr 1929.
  - Lucy Bell Farr (1894–1915).
  - Mabel Annie Farr (1st February 1896–1972) married Willie Walker (14th August 1899–1977) in 1920. They are understood to have had at least two children – Audrey E Walker 1923 and George A Walker 1926. They both died at Dewsbury, Yorkshire.
  - Herbert Farr (1899–1918).
  - Violet Lilian Farr (27th March 1903–1980) married Richard A Clark (1890–1957) in 1938. They had a daughter, Enid M Clark in 1940. They both died at Scunthorpe.
- Mary Ann Wing (26th February 1870–1924) married Willie Donson (5th September 1863–1942), a farm labourer born at Navenby, in 1891 at Lincoln. He was a foreman on a farm by 1911, when they were living at 4 North Lane, Navenby. He was living at High Street, North Kesteven, Lincolnshire in 1939 with his nephew, Norman H Donson (1886–1956), a contractor's labourer and member of the Observer Corps. There were no children but they adopted a son, Arnold Smith Jackson (17th August 1901–1982).
- Arthur Wing (26th February 1871–30th March 1931), a farm labourer, married Ada Ann Brown (1868–1930), a dressmaker in 1891 born at Owston Ferry, in 1896. She was living with her parents on Main Street, Owston Ferry in 1891. They lived at West Street, Owston Ferry. Arthur was still living at West Street at the time of his death at Scunthorpe Hospital. They had five children:
  - John William Wing (1897–1958).
  - Dorothy Elizabeth Wing (1898–99).
  - Westoby Antcliffe Wing (1900–62) married Alice Spence (1904–92) registered at Thorne, where she was born, in 1925. They had two children –

Ronald A Wing 1926 and Sheila P Wing 1931. Their deaths were registered at Doncaster.
    - Walter Wing (1904–31).
    - Daisy Pearl Wing (16th June 1910–29th July 2003) married Herbert Sampson (31st May 1893–1969) in 1933.
- Herbert Wing (born c.1875), an agricultural labourer, married Elizabeth Higginbottom (1875–1917) on 17th May 1898 at Metheringham, Lincolnshire. They were living at Post Office Street, Ruskington, Lincolnshire in 1901 and at Roxholme and Leasingham, Lincolnshire in 1911. She died at Sleaford, Lincolnshire. They had six children:
    - William Edwin Wing (1899–1963) married Mabel Leonora N Roberts (6th February 1894–1986) in 1920. They had six children – Dorothy M Wing 1921, Edwin E Wing 1925, Betty M Wing 1928, Stanley W Wing 1929, June Wing 1932 and Eileen Wing 1936.
    - Gladys Mary Wing (1904–68) married Arthur Headland (1897–1969) in 1924. They had a daughter, Sylvia E Headland, in 1931.
    - Ernest Frank Wing (1905–69) married Louisa Ackroyd at Rotherham, Yorkshire in 1930. They had a daughter, Audrey L Wing, in 1932.
    - Hilda Mabel Wing (10th October 1906–1973) married Hubert Crossland (1897–1927) in 1926. They had a son, Hubert Crossland in 1927. Hilda married Anderson Tennant Day (2nd March 1896–1978) in 1929. They had five children – Edith M Day 1930, Raymond A Day 1937, Joan Day 1939, Arthur Day 1942 and Anthony M Day 1949. Anderson had married Ada Annie Doughty (1894–1928) in 1920. They had three children – Eric Day 1922, Ethel Day 1924 and Ada A Day 1928.
    - Margaret Elizabeth Wing (born 1909).
    - Agnes Lillah Wing (1910–12).
- Irvin Robert Wing (4th June 1876–1944), known as Robert, was a farm labourer. He married Florence Barlow (3rd September 1878–1940), born at Ragnall, Nottinghamshire, in 1896. They were living at Village Street, North Leverton and Hablesthorpe, Nottinghamshire in 1901. They moved to Rotherham, Yorkshire c.1902 and lived at 3 Eastwood Farm. In 1939 they were living at 54 Midland Road, Rotherham. They had the eleven children below, plus another two who died by 1911 and have not been identified:
    - Mary Pearl Wing (26th November 1897–1979) married George Edwin McCoy (1883–1942), born at Barnsley, in 1917 at Rotherham. They had two children – George E McCoy 1919 and Walter J McCoy 1920.
    - Walter Joseph Wing (6th May 1899–1967) married Lydia Limb (15th July 1900–1980) in 1923 at Doncaster. They had five children – Horace Wing 1924, Gladys Wing 1927, Walter J Wing 1928, Irvin Wing 1931 and Denis Wing 1931.

- Sally Wing (1900–61) married Ernest Rider (1884–1941) in 1925. They had five children – Harold FB Rider 1925, Natalie B Rider 1927, James E Rider 1929, Mary E Rider 1933 and Lillian DM Rider 1939. Ernest's death was registered at Scarborough. Sally is understood to have married Henry Woodworth (11th January 1901–1978) at Chester in 1945, where he was born and subsequently died. Her death was registered at Liverpool North. Henry had married Elizabeth A Hewson (c.1907–44) at Chester in 1931. Henry is understood to have married Mary AM Parker (1896–1978) in 1962.
- Daisy Wing (1901–61) married Ernest Rose (probably 1901–52) in 1921 at Rotherham. They had three children – Florence R Rose 1922, John E Rose 1923 and Doreen Rose 1926.
- Frank Wing (1903–47) married Mabel Read (19th June 1907–1971) in 1933 at Rotherham. Mabel is understood to have married Sydney L Ashley in 1956.
- Minnie Maria Wing (21st February 1905–1981) married Arthur Askew (2nd January 1906–1984) in 1932 at Rotherham. They had three children – Paul Askew 1939, Hazel Askew 1942 and Maureen Askew 1944.
- Sylvia Phyllis Wing (1908–60) married Percy Barraclough (probably 1909–37) in 1926. They had a daughter, Phyllis Barraclough in 1927.
- Herbert Wing (born and died 1911).
- Florence G Wing (1913–16).
- Horace Wing (1915–c.1917).
- Henry R Wing (28th October 1916–1966) was a fitter's labourer in 1939.

- Harriett Daisy Wing (31st May 1884–27th June 1960) was living with her aunt, Mary Ann Donson, in 1901. She married Isaac Stapleton (14th December 1880–19th July 1954), born at Washingborough, Lincolnshire, in 1907 at Worksop, Nottinghamshire. He was a drawing stores keeper in an engineering firm in 1911, when they were living at 5 Lord Street, Lincoln. In 1939 he was a general labourer and they were living at Back Street, North Kesteven. They were living at Blacksmith Cottages, Washingborough at the time of his death there. Harriett was living at Oak Hill Cottages, Washingborough at the time of her death at Beckfield Rest Home, Heighington, Lincolnshire. They had a son, George Albert Stapleton, in 1911.

William was probably educated at Priory Church School, Worksop and was a member of the Church Lads' Brigade. He worked as a clerk and a miner at Manton Colliery. In 1909 he married Gertrude Walton (19th October 1889–28th July 1961) at Worksop. They were living with her grandparents at 21 Prior Well Road, Worksop in 1911. By 1915 they were living at 1 Shelley Street, off Prior Well Road. William and Gertrude had four children:

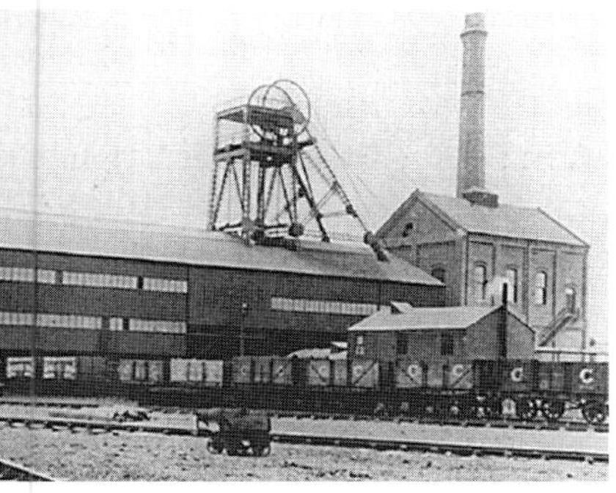

Manton (or Manton Wood) Colliery was in north Nottinghamshire. In 1897 the Wigan Coal & Iron Co began sinking a new colliery there on land owned by the Duke of Newcastle. The mine was to work the Top Hard or Barnsley seam at a depth of 718 yards (657m). A new model village was built to house the miners. Extraction began in June 1905 and continued until 1964. The Parkgate seam was worked between 1962 and 1994 and the Flockton seam from 1991. After nationalisation in 1947, Manton was put in the South Yorkshire Region rather than Nottinghamshire. In 1979, over a million tonnes of coal were extracted from the pit, most going to Cottam Power Station. When the electricity industry was privatised in 1990, power stations were not obliged to burn coal and many converted to gas, leading to a slump in the demand for coal. About 1,500 people were employed at the pit when it closed in February 1994. The area was restored as Manton Pit Wood in 1997.

- Mabel Annie Johnson (probably 19th October 1909–2nd April 1974) married Albert E Davis (probably 19th June 1907–1966) in 1930 at Basford, Nottinghamshire. He was a building contractor in 1939, when they were living at Bluehaven, Loughborough Road, West Bridgford, Nottinghamshire. They later moved to Norfolk. Albert may have died at Norwich. Mabel is understood to have died at Laburnham Hall Road, Hemsby, Norfolk. They had two daughters:
    - June J Davis (born 1930), born at Doncaster, Yorkshire, married Geoffrey W Brookes in 1952 at Acle, Norfolk. They had a child, Lindsay J Brookes, in 1955.
    - Wendy E Davis (born 1936), born at Basford, married Edward J Cooper in 1959 at Acle. They are believed to have had three children – Felicity A Cooper 1961, Alison J Cooper 1962 and Nicholas J Cooper 1964.

21 Prior Well Road, Worksop, now Priorswell Road, where William and Gertrude lived when they first married.

- William Albert Johnson (2nd July 1911–1976), known as Albert, married Lydia Elsie Scrivins/Scrivens (1st February 1912–30th June 1968) in 1936 at Basford, where she was born. Albert was a maltster's labourer in 1939, when they were living at 4 Acton Road, Arnold, Nottinghamshire. Albert served in the Royal Artillery in a searchlight unit during the Second World War and lost a leg and the opposite foot to frostbite in 1945. They were living at 164 Porchester Road, Carlton, Nottinghamshire at the time of her death there. They had a son:
    - William Keith Johnson (2nd June 1940–1st May 2013), known as Keith, married Janet Hutchings (23rd April 1942–18th April 2008) in 1964. They

had two daughters – Kathryn Lisa Johnson 1968 and Lesley Maria Johnson 1973.

- Gladys M Johnson (9th February 1916–1967) married John Arthur Nixon (6th January 1914–1998) in 1936. He was a builder's labourer in 1939, when they were living at 53 West Street, Arnold. They had two sons:
    - Ralph J Nixon (born 1937) married Betty Winifred Ross (22nd April 1937–17th December 2009), born at Mansfield, Nottinghamshire, in 1958. They had three children – Julia A Nixon 1962, Christopher Nixon 1964 and Talitha Victoria Nixon 1967.
    - Anthony 'Tony' Nixon (born 1943) is believed to have married Susan M Notman (born 1944) in 1961. They had a son, Philip A Nixon, in 1964.
- Victoria Jean Johnson (5th November 1929–8th January 2015) married Archibald Walter Romaine (20th August 1930–18th April 1998) in 1953. They emigrated to the USA and are known to have lived at Langhorne, Pennsylvania and Buford, Georgia. They had a son, Martyn Michael Romaine (born 1963), born at Nottingham, who is known to have lived in Pennsylvania, Florida and California.

Gertrude's father is not known. Her mother, Annie Walton (15th December 1868–1940), born at Worksop, married Henry 'Harry' Kipling (1871–1929), a colliery labourer below ground, there in 1893. He was living with his parents at 25 Westgate, Worksop in 1871 and with his mother and stepfather, Edward Pritchard, there in 1881. Harry and Annie were living at 25 Prior Well Road, Worksop in 1901 and at 23 Prior Well Road in 1911. Annie was living with her son, Harry, at 55 Prior Well Road in 1939, next door to her daughter Mary and her family. Annie and Harry had seven children, including four unknown who had died by 1911:

- Mary Jane Kipling (5th January 1894–1956) was a general domestic servant in 1911, living with her parents. She married James Grindle (6th October 1893–23rd July 1975) in 1919. James was a colliery screen labourer above ground in 1911, living with his parents at 37 Gladstone Street, Worksop. He was a railway wagon greaser in 1939, when they were living at 53 Prior Well Road, Worksop. He was living at 27 Prior Well Road at the time of his death there. They had a son, Eric Joseph Grindle (21st June 1923–1993), who was an accountant's clerk in 1939, living with his parents.

The French Médaille Militaire, established in 1852, is awarded for meritorious service or bravery in action and is the third highest award of the French Republic. During the First World War 230,000 medals were awarded. Foreign recipients include the black American fighter pilot Eugene Jacques Bullard, Winston Churchill, Dwight D Eisenhower, Field Marshal Bernard Montgomery, President Franklin D Roosevelt and President Josip Broz Tito (Fdutil).

- John Charles Kipling (1898–1927) served in the Sherwood Foresters (71360) and was discharged with a disability on 11th March 1919.
- Harry Kipling (10th October 1901–1972) was a colliery hewer in 1939.
- The four unknowns are probably amongst these, all born and died at Worksop – Nellie Kipling (1895–96), Frank Kipling (1895–96), Bernard Kipling (1899–1900), Albert Kipling (1903–06) and Lucy Annie Kipling (born and died 1907).

The Silver War Badge was issued to service personnel who had been honourably discharged due to wounds or sickness from September 1916. It was worn on the lapel badge in civilian clothes. They were individually numbered.

William enlisted in 2/8th Nottinghamshire and Derbyshire Regiment at Newark on 9th February 1915 (3538 & 306122) and immediately agreed to serve abroad. He was 5′9½″ tall. He was appointed unpaid lance corporal on 28th February 1916 and paid from 17th April. He was promoted unpaid lance sergeant on 1st February 1917 and went to France on 27th February. He was promoted corporal next day but reverted to lance corporal on 17th April. William was promoted sergeant on 15th January 1918. He transferred to 2/5th Battalion on 29th January, just prior to 2/8th Battalion disbanding on 6th February. 2/5th Battalion was reduced to cadre on 7th May and disbanded on 3rd August 1918. William transferred to 1/5th Battalion between May and August.

Awarded the VC for his actions at Ramicourt, France on 3rd October 1918, LG 14th December 1918. A special peal of honour, consisting of 2,160 changes (720 Kent Treble Bob), was rung following the announcement of his award. William received a gunshot wound to the back on 6th October and underwent at least two operations at one of the hospitals at Trouville, France. He was later infected with Spanish flu. William returned to England on 23rd January 1919. He joined the Depot next day, was demobilised on 10th March and discharged on 11th March 1919. He was issued Silver War Badge No.B199507. **Awarded the French Médaille Militaire in March 1919, LG 15th December 1919.** The VC was presented by the King at Buckingham Palace on 29th March 1919.

On his return to Worksop, William was paraded through the town with the church bells ringing. His work colleagues presented him with £100. William became a bellringer at Worksop Priory Church and later at St Paul's Church, Daybrook, Nottingham. He became a check weigh man for a coal and iron company. Later he become a deputy at Manton Colliery and was then the licensee at the Mason's Arms public house in Worksop. The family moved to Retford and then to Arnold, Nottingham in 1928, where he worked for the Home Brewery Co. Later he became the manager/steward of Arnold Ex-Servicemen's Club, Clinton Street, Arnold until the club burnt down. The family was living there in 1939 and had moved

William de Lovetot granted land and monies to establish the Augustinian priory at Worksop in 1103. The Worksop Bestiary, an illuminated manuscript donated by the Canon of Lincoln Cathedral in 1187, is now at the Morgan Library & Museum in New York. The priory was dissolved by Henry VIII in November 1539 and the property was granted to The Earl of Shrewsbury on condition that the Earl provided a glove for the right hand of the sovereign at the coronation. This tradition continues to this day. Most of the monastic buildings have been plundered for their stone, but the church was saved as a parish church and the early 14th century gatehouse became a school. There have been numerous additions and renovations to the church since.

Construction of St Paul's Church began in May 1893. It was completed in December 1895 and was consecrated on 4th February 1896. The spire and tower were added in 1897.

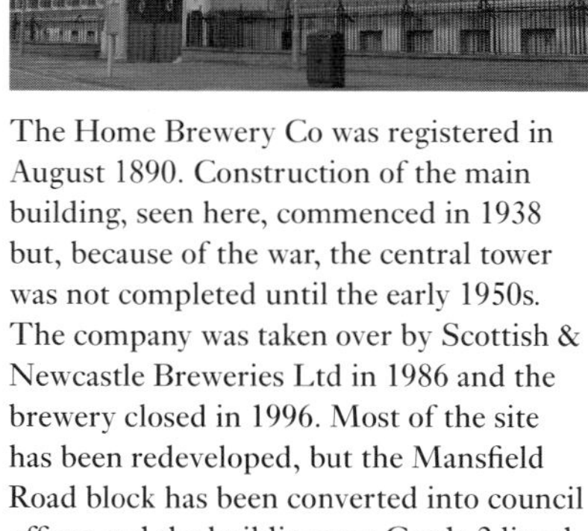

The Home Brewery Co was registered in August 1890. Construction of the main building, seen here, commenced in 1938 but, because of the war, the central tower was not completed until the early 1950s. The company was taken over by Scottish & Newcastle Breweries Ltd in 1986 and the brewery closed in 1996. Most of the site has been redeveloped, but the Mansfield Road block has been converted into council offices and the building was Grade 2 listed in 1993.

to 33 Nelson Road, Arnold by 1945. William worked as a packer for the John Players' tobacco company from 1941. He served in the Home Guard during the Second World War until ill-health forced him to retire.

Away from work William was involved with the local cadet force in Worksop. He was also a scoutmaster and a member of the Worksop British Legion, of which he became Chairman. He was present when General Sir Horace Smith-Dorien dedicated the Worksop War Memorial on

Worksop War Memorial was unveiled on 30th May 1925 by General Sir Horace Smith-Dorrien and was dedicated by The Right Reverend Edwyn Hoskyns, Bishop of Southwell. The memorial carries the names of 462 dead of the Great War and another 216 of the Second World War. Nottinghamshire County Council restored the Grade 2 listed structure in 2010, including replacing the spiked chain, which had been removed during the Second World War for scrap.

30th May 1925. On Armistice Day 1931, William took charge of the ex-servicemen at the war memorial at Arnold Hill Park and continued in this capacity for several years. He was the guest of honour at the 1934 reunion of 8th Battalion, The Sherwood Foresters at Worksop. William attended two VC reunions – the VC Garden Party at Buckingham Palace on 26th June 1920 and the VC Dinner at the Royal Gallery of the House of Lords, London on 9th November 1929.

William and Gertrude's grave in Redhill Cemetery, Arnold.

William died following a seizure while having breakfast at his home at 33 Nelson Road, Arnold, Nottinghamshire on 25th April 1945. He was very concerned about the health of his son, William, who had just lost a leg and the opposite foot. His funeral with full military honours took place at St Paul's, Daybrook, Nottinghamshire on 28th April. He is buried in Redhill Cemetery, Arnold (L4294). The ceremony was attended by John Caffrey VC. William is commemorated in a number of other places:

- Worksop
    - A tree with a plaque was planted in his honour by the local council in June 1991 in Memorial Avenue Gardens.
    - A foundation stone was laid by him, on behalf of the Worksop Branch of the British Legion, on 29th September 1923, for the extension to Victoria Hospital that was to be the town's war memorial. When it was demolished in 1996 the foundation stone and gable end stone were reset in a memorial wall in Memorial Avenue Gardens.
    - A Department for Communities and Local Government commemorative paving stone was dedicated at Memorial Gardens, The Canch Park, Priorswell Road on 3rd October 2018.
    - His portrait hangs in Worksop Town Library, Memorial Avenue.

- Twenty-two Berberis shrubs representing the twenty-two members of the Church Lads' Brigade who were awarded the VC were planted in the Church Lads & Church Girls Brigade Memorial Plot at the National Memorial Arboretum, Alrewas, Staffordshire.
- Named on a memorial to Nottingham and Nottinghamshire VCs in the grounds of Nottingham Castle dedicated on 7th May 2010.

The Church Lads & Church Girls Brigade Memorial Plot at the National Memorial Arboretum. The twenty-two Berberis shrubs are either side of the central walkway (Memorials to Valour).

In addition to the VC he was awarded the British War Medal 1914–20, Victory Medal 1914–19, George VI Coronation Medal 1937 and the French Médaille Militaire. His medals were donated to the Sherwood Foresters by his widow on 18th September 1948 and were received by Major General PN White CB CBE, Colonel of the Regiment. The VC is held by the Sherwood Foresters Museum, The Castle, Nottingham, Nottinghamshire. A VC and campaign medals were purchased by a Canadian, Dr Michael Smith, in 2006 on the understanding that they had been issued to William Johnson as a genuine replacement set. The group was supplied in an authentic box but no name was engraved on the reverse suspension bar of the VC and the date was inscribed in italics, with the month engraved in full.

The memorial to Nottingham and Nottinghamshire VCs at Nottingham Castle.

51674 CORPORAL FRANK LESTER
10th Battalion, The Lancashire Fusiliers

Frank Lester was born on 18th February 1896 at West View, Huyton Quarry, Liverpool, Lancashire. His father, John Lester (18th February 1868–27th April 1941), born at Whiston, Lancashire, married Ellen née Heyes (8th May 1870–22nd November 1947), a dressmaker born at Aughton, Ormskirk, Lancashire, on 29th September 1892 at Prescot Register Office, Lancashire. John was a general labourer in 1881 and a stoker with Pilkington Brothers, St Helens by 1891. By 1901 he

was a market gardener and horseman and they were living at 28 Rudd Street, Hoylake cum West Kirby, Cheshire. By 1911 they had moved to 37 Rudd Street, when he was a salesman and driver for a florist. The family moved to Miller's Hay, Mill Hill Road, Irby, Birkenhead, Cheshire in 1912. John was a market gardener again in 1939. Ellen was living at Burnside, 119 Mill Lane, Greasby, Cheshire at the time of her death at Arclid County Hospital, Sandbach, Cheshire. Frank had five siblings:

- Edwin Lester (15th August 1893–9th July 1917), born at Huyton, Lancashire, was an apprentice cabinet maker in 1911. He served as a sergeant in 1/4th Cheshire (2869 & 200851) in Egypt and in Sinai before taking part in the first two assaults against Gaza, Palestine. He died of syncope and his remains were later exhumed and reburied at Beersheba War Cemetery, Israel (O 22). He is also commemorated on the family headstone at Holy Trinity Churchyard, Trinity Road, Hoylake, Wirral Merseyside.
- Lucy Core Lester (23rd March 1901–16th July 1989) was a member of Irby Hill Primitive Methodist Chapel and played the piano for the choir. She married Tom Wilson (22nd September 1895–9th March 1989), born at Frankby, Cheshire, on 15th October 1924. He worked as a pattern maker at Cammell Laird's shipyard, Birkenhead. He enlisted in the Royal Naval Air Service (F40323) as an acting air mechanic I (C) on 24th October 1917, described as 5′ 3¾″ tall, with brown hair, grey eyes and fresh complexion. He was assigned to HMS *President II* at Crystal Palace, London and was posted to Cranwell, Lincolnshire on 26th October. Appointed acting air mechanic IRH (C) on 17th February 1918 and transferred to the Royal Air Force as air mechanic 2 on 1st April. Promoted air mechanic 1 on 25th June 1918. Reclassified as leading aircraftsman 1 on 1st January 1919. Posted to No.2 Flying School on 26th April and to 7 Wing Works Squadron on

Some of the Townfield Cottages that formed a square at the junction of West View and Hale View Road, Huyton Quarry. Living conditions in these cottages were poor and in 1933 they were demolished to be replaced with more modern housing.

The Huyton area was very boggy and there is little evidence of occupation until after the end of Roman rule. The first settlements were on slightly raised ground within the marshes. Huyton appears in the Domesday Book, valued at ten shillings and was a relatively wealthy area compared to settlements nearby. A fair was granted in 1304 but the market went into decline after the Plague, due to population decline and competition from other centres such as Prescot, Warrington and Liverpool. The Augustinian Burscough Priory was given Huyton Church c.1190 but this was probably more ceremonial than a profitable addition to the estate. Huyton was on the edge of a royal hunting forest and was therefore subject to some of the special laws of the forest. The Industrial Revolution brought major changes. Huyton Quarry expanded rapidly in the 19th century, with quarrying, coal mining, factories producing iron and gas and electric lamp works. A packhorse trail was developed into a major coaching route and became a turnpike under the 1726 Act. Huyton Quarry, initially called Bottom of Whiston Incline, was one of the original stations on George Stephenson's 1830 Liverpool and Manchester Railway, the world's first to cater for passengers. The station closed in September 1958. The railway allowed the wealthy to move away from the grime of the major industrial centres and in Huyton they built large houses, many of which survive. Liverpool Council bought land from Lord Derby in 1932 to build the first of three new housing estates. An internment camp was built in the residential streets of Huyton during the Second World War and the area suffered some damage from air raids on Liverpool. Post-war there was an even greater demand for new housing and more new estates were built. Prime Minister Harold Wilson was MP for Huyton 1950–83.

The Pilkington glass company was founded in 1826 by the Pilkington and Greenall families in St Helens, initially as *St Helens Crown Glass Company*. However, from 1845 it was run exclusively by the Pilkingtons as *Pilkington Brothers* and in 1894 became *Pilkington Brothers Ltd*. For many years it was the largest employer in the town. In the 1950s a revolutionary float glass process was invented to produce high-quality flat glass over a bath of molten tin, removing the need for costly grinding and polishing. The company had plants in several other countries including Argentina, Australia, Canada and Sweden and acquired existing plants in the USA, Germany and France. A two-months long strike in 1970 was the basis for Ken Loach's film, *The Rank and File*, although the BBC insisted on a change of location (West Midland) and company name (Wilkinsons). A hostile take-over bid in 1985 was successfully fought off with the assistance of the employees, the town and some government ministers. In 2006 the company was taken over by the Japanese NSG company, which had around half of the global market, to which it added Pilkington's 19% share. (Paul Nash).

Arclid Hospital was originally a workhouse built in 1844–45 for the Congleton Poor Law Union. In 1845 a separate fever ward was built, which was expanded twice. In 1899–1900 a new infirmary was built and during the Great War forty beds were allocated for military use. In 1929 it transferred to the County Council's Public Assistance Committee and was renamed Arclid Public Assistance Institution, certified for patients under the Mental Deficiency Acts. By 1945 the hospital had 291 beds and in 1948 it was taken over by the National Health Service. It closed in 1993.

Beersheba War Cemetery, where Frank's brother, Edwin, is buried. The cemetery was created immediately after the fall of Beersheba in November 1917, next to the Christian Cemetery. It was in use until July 1918, by when there were 139 burials. After the Armistice burials were brought in from a number of other sites and the cemetery now contains 1,239 Commonwealth burials of the Great War, of which sixty-six are unidentified. The cemetery was consecrated by the Bishop of Jerusalem on 22nd March 1923. Three VCs are buried there:

Major Alexander Malins Lafone VC, Middlesex Hussars, died 27th October 1917.
Lieutenant Colonel Leslie Cecil Maygar VC DSO VD, 8th Australian Light Horse, died 1st November 1917.
Captain John Fox Russell VC MC, Royal Army Medical Corps attached 1st/6th Royal Welsh Fusiliers, died 6th November 1917.

18th November. Tom transferred to the RAF Reserve on 28th November 1919. Tom and Lucy met when he later worked for his future father-in-law, John Lester, as a market gardener. They were living at Burnside, 119 Mill Lane, Greasby in 1939 and both subsequently died there. They had three children:

- Edna Lucy Wilson (1st December 1926–13th August 2019), born at Burnside, was delivered by her grandmother, Annie Wilson. She was educated at Dawpool School and attended the Sunday School at Irby Hill Primitive Methodist Chapel (Tin Chapel), where she met Cyril Hughes-Jones (2nd September 1925–2011). They married there on 26th July 1952 and moved to Croydon, Surrey shortly afterwards but returned to the Wirral a few years later. They lived at King's Drive, Pensby and later at Coome Road, Wirral. They retired to Lucy's childhood home at Burnside to care for her parents until their deaths. They had two children – Susan Hughes-Jones 1953 and David M Hughes-Jones 1955.
- Marjorie Wilson (26th November 1931–14th May 1933).

    - Frank Lester Wilson (born 1st April 1934) worked as a market gardener and served in the Army during the National Service period. He married Maureen A Harmer (born 1940) in 1962 at Birkenhead, Cheshire. Frank was appointed District Parks and Gardens Inspector with the local council. They had two sons – Stephen Wilson 1963 and Andrew Wilson 1967.
- George Lester (26th May 1903–24th September 1905).
- John 'Jack' Lester (21st February 1906–6th September 1929) died after his motorcycle struck a horse in Thingwall Road, Irby, Wirral, Cheshire.
- Ruth Lester (24th July 1908–12th November 1931), born at Hoylake, Cheshire, married William Hough Gray (25th April 1890–13th February 1972) on 19th September 1928 at St Bartholomew's, Thurstaston, Cheshire. William was a timber clerk in 1911, living with his mother at the home of his uncle, William Hough, and family at Hall Farm, Thurstaston. William married Margaret Agnes Cross née Kelly (3rd November 1885–7th January 1971), born at Liverpool, Lancashire, in 1935. William was a timber merchant in 1939, when they were living at 7 Woodlands Road, Irby. They both subsequently died there. William had a son with Ruth:
    - William Lester Gray (5th September 1931–10th November 2013) served in the Royal Navy during the Korean War. He married Betty M Taylor (born c.1928) at Sunbury-on-Thames, Middlesex in 1961. They lived at Abingdon, Oxfordshire. They had two daughters – Helen M Gray 1962 and Sally R Gray 1965.

  Margaret Kelly had married Rowland Cross (1884–10th October 1933) in 1910 at Wirral. They were living at the Anchor Inn, Irby at the time of his death there. Rowland and Margaret had two children:
    - Margaret Cross (1911–74) married George Eric Pessall (1906–72), born at St George's, Wellington, Shropshire, on 2nd January 1936 at Woodchurch, Birkenhead. He was a police constable in 1939, when they were living at 9 Orchard Green and Mottram Road, Alderley Edge, Cheshire.
    - Rowland James Cross (1912–39) married Nellie Killops (1914–2001) in 1936. He was a licensed victualler at the Anchor Inn, Irby in 1939 and died at the Royal Infirmary, Manchester, Lancashire. Nellie married Harry Bickley in 1968 at Wirral.

Frank's paternal grandfather, George Lester (1844–19th April 1929), born at St Helens, Lancashire, married Elizabeth née Davies (1846–1919), a midwife born at Whiston, Lancashire, on 14th March 1864 at St Thomas, Eccleston, Lancashire. George was a watchmaker in 1881, when they were living at The Pottery, Whiston. By 1891 they had moved to 37 Richardson's Lane, Huyton, Lancashire and he was described as a regulator maker for watches. By 1901 he was a coal yard labourer and they were living at Vale Cottage, Wood Lane, Huyton. In addition to John they had another twelve children including:

The first record of settlements in the St Helens area is in the Domesday Book in 1086. The earliest reference is in 1552 to a chapel of ease, dedicated to St Elyn, but there may have been a village there for centuries before. St Helens did not exist as a town until the mid 1700s and by 1838 it was formally responsible for administering nearby Eccleston, Parr, Sutton and Windle. The town was incorporated as a municipal borough in 1868, a county borough in 1887, with two MPs, and a metropolitan borough in 1974. During the Industrial Revolution it became a significant centre for coal mining, copper smelting, glassmaking and the cotton and linen industry, as well as other industries. The population grew accordingly from 5,825 in 1831 to 20,176 in 1861. Transport links were improved to carry goods, starting with a turnpike road. The Sankey Canal followed in 1757, linking St Helens to the Mersey and Liverpool. The Liverpool and Manchester Railway opened in 1830. After the Second World War industry began to decline and the last coal mine closed in May 1991. A notable family in the area were the Beechams. Thomas Beecham (1820–1907) founded Beechams, the pharmaceutical firm, in St Helens in 1880. His grandson was the conductor Sir Thomas Beecham. The Pilkingtons were another prominent local family, who built up the largest glass manufacturing business in Britain. Other famous people from the town include:

Bernie Clifton (born 1936), comedian and entertainer, known for his puppet costume, Oswald the Ostrich.

George Robert Groves (1901–76), Hollywood's first 'sound man', was the recording engineer on the Al Jolson film, *The Jazz Singer* in 1927. He became Warner Brothers Director of Sound and won two Academy Awards.

Rick Astley (born 1966) singer, songwriter and radio personality, who has received numerous musical awards.

Richard John Seddon PC (1845–1906) the fifteenth and longest serving New Zealand Prime Minister 1893–1906.

Lilian Parr (1905–78), professional footballer, who in 2002 was the only woman inaugural inductee into the English Football Hall of Fame.

Geoffrey Ernest Duke OBE (1923–2015) six times winner of the Grand Prix motorcycle world championship.

- Henry Lester (1864–65), birth registered at Prescot, Lancashire and death at Chorlton, Lancashire.
- Sarah Lester (born 1866) was a domestic servant in 1881. She married William Whitfield (1865–91) in 1889 registered at Chester, Cheshire. He was a general

labourer living with his parents at Hurst House Cottages, Whiston Lane, Huyton in 1881. He was a bricklayer in 1891, when they were living with his widowed mother, Margaret Whitfield (c1825–96), at 19 Devon Street, St Helens. Sarah was living with her parents in 1901.

Frank's paternal grandmother, Elizabeth, in 1914.

- Robert Lester (12th January 1871–20th May 1944), born at Whiston, was a coal miner in 1891. He married Margaret Bate (20th September 1872–30th December 1952) on 23rd May 1892 at St Peters, St Helens, Lancashire. He was a carter in 1901, when they were living at The Rooley, Huyton and at The Orchard, Huyton in 1911. He was a rock man in 1939, when they were living at Vale Cottage, Wood Lane, Huyton. They both subsequently died there. They had eleven children:
    - Elizabeth Lester (20th May 1893–1968) was a globe manufacturer filiment (sic) weigher in 1911.
    - John Lester (28th November 1894–1976) was an out porter for London & North Western Railway. He was a crane driver for British Insulated and Helsby Cables Ltd, Prescot, Lancashire, living at Hall Cottage, The Orchard, Huyton when he enlisted in 10th Battalion, King's Liverpool Regiment (Liverpool Scottish) (359283) at Seaforth on 10th December 1915. He transferred to the Army Reserve next day, described as 5′ 6¾″ tall and weighing 136 lbs. In a letter dated 10th January 1916 his employers claimed that he was exempt military service and was entitled to wear War Service Badge No.M15387. John was mobilised on 5th March 1917, went to France on 3rd June and joined 24th Infantry Base Depot. He was allocated to 9th Entrenching Battalion on 17th June and joined the unit on 3rd August. He transferred later to 10th Liverpool and was granted Class 1 Proficiency Pay on 4th December. He was granted leave 3rd-15th March 1918. Appointed unpaid lance corporal on 21st April and paid acting lance corporal on 13th January 1919. He was granted

The original church of St Thomas, Eccleston was built in 1839 and a new chancel was added in 1891. The original nave was demolished in 1908 and new one was built in 1910. It burned down in 1960 and was rebuilt.

leave 3rd–17th February. Appointed acting corporal on 4th February, acting lance sergeant 1st March, acting sergeant 12th March and acting company quartermaster sergeant on 9th September. Returned to Britain on 11th November and transferred to the Class Z Reserve on 10th December 1919. He died at Torrita, Victoria, Australia.

- George Lester (23rd March 1896–27th November 1915) was an assistant in a setting shop globe manufacture in 1911. He served in 1st Lancashire Fusiliers (5233) and drowned during the floods at Gallipoli (Helles Memorial, Turkey).
- Robert Lester (14th November 1897–7th November 1945).
- Ernest Lester (31st March 1899–1988) died at Heidelberg, Victoria, Australia.
- Peter Lester (1901–48).
- Ethel Lester (20th January 1903–c.1956).
- Edith Lester (15th May 1904–1948) was an invoice clerk in 1939.
- Wilfred Lester (7th November 1905–1976).
- Eva Lester (31st December 1907–1984) married William Houghton in 1932 and they had two children – Eva Houghton 1934 and June Houghton 1935. Eva married Stanley D Marks in 1960.
- Margaret Lester (born 25th September 1909).

- Mary Lester (born 25th August 1875) married John Clarke (born c.1876), a glassblower, on 25th November 1899. She was living with her children at her parents' home at Vale Cottage in 1911 but John was not with her. They had two children – Lily Clarke 1904 and John Clarke 1906.
- George Lester (2nd October 1878–21st October 1959) was a domestic gardener living with his parents in 1901. He married Ellen Stone (10th January 1876–13th August 1949), born at Radstock, Somerset, in 1904. They were living at 25 Groveland Avenue, Hoylake, Cheshire in 1911. He was Chief Officer of Hoylake

Frank's cousin, George Lester, is commemorated on the Helles Memorial, Gallipoli, Turkey. The Memorial has a dual function – Commonwealth battle memorial for the Gallipoli campaign and commemoration of many Commonwealth servicemen who have no known grave. British and Indian personnel named there died throughout the Peninsula and include troops lost at sea. However, the Australians named there were lost just at Helles. There are over 20,000 names. There are four other memorials to the missing at Gallipoli. The Lone Pine, Hill 60 and Chunuk Bair Memorials commemorate Australian and New Zealanders lost at Anzac, while the Twelve Tree Copse Memorial commemorates New Zealanders lost at Helles. Naval casualties are recorded on the Memorials at Portsmouth, Plymouth and Chatham in England.

Fire Brigade in 1939, when they were living at Fire Station House, Grosvenor Road, Hoylake. They were living at 35 Grove Road, Hoylake at the time of their deaths at The Cottage Hospital, Hoylake. They had a daughter:

  - Olive Lester (25th March 1907–26th September 1988) married Harry Corrin Day (19th December 1906–1973) in 1932. He was a ship's clerk in a victualling department and part time ARP service in 1939, when they were living at 18 Leighton Avenue, Birkenhead Road, Hoylake.

- Elizabeth Lester (1880–84).
- Ellen Lester (9th August 1884–1968) married John Wilkinson Hand (1886–19th August 1950) on 30th March 1907. He was a ship's patent floor layer in 1911, when they were living at 16 Dunstan Street, Wavertree, Lancashire and were still there in 1929. Ellen was an office cleaner in 1939, living with her daughters at 16 Dunstan Street. Wavertree. John and Ellen had four children:
  - John Lester Hand (28th February 1912–1915).
  - Elsie Hand (25th October 1914–1969) was a looper (hosiery) in 1939. She married Leonard N Sothcott (14th January 1919–1979), born at Portsmouth, Hampshire, in 1945 at Liverpool. They had a son, Raymond L Sothcott, in 1946. Elsie's death was registered at Portsmouth and Leonard's at Southampton.
  - Audrey Hand (27th April 1916–1998) was a brass cutter in 1939. She married Samuel F Bowerman (born 1924) at Liverpool in 1949. They had a daughter, Lynn Bowerman, in 1951.
  - Vera Hand (26th April 1920–1972) was a looper (hosiery) in 1939. She married William H Wood in 1941. They had two sons – Donald Wood 1945 and Andrew A Wood 1949.

  Circumstantial evidence indicates that John Hand had an affair with Helen/Ellen Owen (5th April 1894–23rd December 1948) and they had a daughter, Gwendoline Hand (19th June 1926–17th January 1974), born at 112 Edith Close, Chelsea, London. John and Helen/Ellen were living as man and wife at 56 Limerston Street, Chelsea in 1930. Helen/Ellen had another daughter, Megan Rowlands (27th November 1912–2002), at Corwen, Denbighshire, Wales. By 1939 John and Helen/Ellen were living together with Megan and Gwendoline at 445 Kings Road, Chelsea. Megan changed her name to Hand and married Frederick A Perkins in 1940. Gwendoline never married and died at St Stephens Hospital, Chelsea. Helen/Ellen died at Chelsea, registered as Hand. John died at 64 Wiltshire Close, Chelsea and was buried with Ellen in Brompton Cemetery.

- Lillie Lester (2nd May 1887–1984), born at Vale Cottage, Huyton, was working at the booking controls at the P Lamp Works in 1911 and was living with her parents. Lillie married Charles Wright Perkins (born 1882), a merchant seaman born at Montréal, Canada, in 1915. He served in the Merchant Navy during the Great War and was awarded the Mercantile Marine War and British War Medals.

The Mercantile Marine War Medal was established in 1919. It was awarded by the Board of Trade to mariners of the British Mercantile Marine (later Merchant Navy) for service at sea during the Great War. Qualification was one or more voyages through a danger zone or service at sea for six months between 4th August 1914 and 11th November 1918. Coastal mariners (pilots, fishermen, lightship and post office cable ship crews) could also qualify. There was no minimum qualifying period for those killed or wounded by enemy action, or those taken prisoner. All recipients also received the British War Medal but the award of the Mercantile Marine War Medal did not count for the award of the Victory Medal or either of the two Stars. Members of the Royal Navy, seconded to man defensive weapons on merchant ships, could also qualify. A total of 133,135 Mercantile Marine War Medals were awarded.

The ribbons were issued on 25th August 1919 to Canning Place, Liverpool and the medals in October 1925 to 9 Dales Row, Whiston, near Preston. Charles was 2nd Cook aboard SS *Calulu* sailing from Liverpool to New York in 1919. Lillie changed her name to Wright-Perkins. Charles died before 1939, by when Lillie was living with some of her children at 24 Windy Arbor Road, Whiston. Lillie had seven children, six of them with Charles:

- Evelyn Edwards Lester (22nd December 1910–January 2000) was born at Vale Cottage, Wood Lane in 1911. It is understood that her father was a Scotsman, possibly John Rorrison (born 1885 in Dumfries), a plumber boarding at 19 Cecil Road, Liscard, Cheshire in 1911. A man of that name and age was a farm servant, born at Castlemilk, Lockerbie, Dumfriesshire, when he enlisted in the King's Own Scottish Borderers (22755) at Lockerbie on 9th December 1915. He was described as twenty years and three months old, 5′ 5½″ tall and weighed 121 lbs. His parents were Thomas and Jane Rorrison, living at 28 River Side Terrace, Kirkconnel, Dumfriesshire. He was single with no children. John transferred to the Army Reserve next day and was mobilised on 7th February 1916. He joined 3rd Battalion on 11th February, embarked at Folkestone, Kent on 4th October and disembarked at Boulogne, France next day to join 21st Infantry Base Depot, Étaples. He was to join 7/8th King's Own Scottish Borderers but transferred to 2nd Royal Scots Fusiliers (40543) on 18th October and joined the Battalion on 20th October. He was missing on 23rd April 1917 and on 13th May was declared to be killed in action (Bootham Cemetery, Heninel, France – A 13). Evelyn married Isaac Yates (28th January 1908–April 1975) in 1930, registered at Prescot, Lancashire, where he was born. He was living with his parents at 1 Court, 5 Victoria Place, Prescot in 1911. He was a drum cable erector in 1939, when they were living at 22 Williams Street, Prescot. His death was registered at Crosby, Merseyside and hers at Knowsley,

Merseyside. They had at least one child, Mary E Yates (born 26th February 1931).
  - Georgina L Perkins (born 1916) married Leslie Compton at Bootle, Lancashire in 1937 and they had a daughter, Dena Compton, in 1938. Georgina married Henry A Matthews at Wrexham, Denbighshire in 1941 and Douglas H White at St Austell, Cornwall in 1947.
  - Hilda W Perkins (born 27th April 1918) was a twin with Victor.
  - Victor W Perkins (27th April 1918–1963), a twin with Hilda, was a general brickwork labourer in 1939. He married Gertrude E Young (born 1922) in 1944.
  - Geoffrey Perkins (23rd April 1920–1995).
  - Dorothea Perkins (born 1923).
  - Audrey Perkins (born 1926).
- Arthur Lester (14th July 1891–14th December 1958), born at Whiston, was working at the British Insulated Wire Works, Prescot in 1911. He married Elizabeth 'Lizzie' Annie Pountain (11th May 1894–May 1970), born at Alton, Staffordshire, on 22nd June 1912 at St Mary's, Prescot. She was living with her parents at 20 Cross Street, Prescot in 1911. Arthur and Lizzie emigrated to Canada. They both died at Leeds, Elizabethtown, Brockville, Ontario. They had two daughters – Irene Lester (11th January 1913–3rd November 1984) and Vera Lester (3rd April 1920–5th February 1990).
- Henry Lester (born c.1894) was only found in the 1901 Census.

His maternal grandfather, Henry Heyes (1844–78), born at Scarisbrick, Lancashire, married Lucy née Core (1845–1900), a dressmaker born at Halsall, near Ormskirk, Lancashire, on 6th August 1867 at St Cuthbert, Halsall. He was a labourer in a waterworks in 1871, when they were living at Halsall Lane, Aughton, near Ormskirk. By 1891 Lucy was living with her children, Ellen and Peter, at 225 Baker Street, Huyton, Lancashire. In addition to Ellen they had two other children:

- Elizabeth Heyes (born 1868) was a housekeeper in 1891 in the home of Thomas J Smith, solicitor of the Supreme Court, at St Agnes Road, Huyton.
- Peter Heyes (1872–1933) was a coalminer's labourer living with his mother in 1891. He

St Cuthbert's Church, Halsall dates from the 14th century, with a number of alterations and additions. The chancel was restored in 1873. In 1886 the nave, aisles and south porch were rebuilt and the church was re-roofed. It has been Grade I listed since 1950. Arthur Vaughn Williams, father of composer Ralph Vaughn Williams, served at St Cuthbert's before he was ordained in 1868.

married Margaret Davenport (1871–1955), born at Tarbock, Lancashire, in 1897. She was living with her parents at Naylors Road, Little Woolton, Lancashire in 1881. Peter was a coalminer's labourer in 1901, when they were living at Baker Street, Huyton. By 1911 he was a general labourer at a brickworks and they were living at 13 Baker Street. Margaret was living with her son, Albert and his wife Eliza, at Huyton-with-Roby in 1939. They had four sons:

- Harry Heyes (born 1898).
- Willie Heyes (born 1900).
- Peter Edward Heyes (born 1903).
- Albert Heyes (born 7th May 1907) married Eliza Garside (2nd May 1902–1941) in 1936. He was a house painter in 1939 living with his wife at his widowed mother's.

Frank was educated at Hoylake National School, Trinity Road, Hoylake, Cheshire, leaving in 1910. He played the organ at the Methodist Little Chapel, Irby Mill Hill and his parents sang with the Hoylake Temperance choir and the Congregationalist Church choir. Frank was a member of 1st Hoylake Company, Boy's Brigade. He worked as a trainee joiner with F Thomas at Oxton, Cheshire until the family moved to Irby in 1912. He then worked in his father's market garden business, moving produce across the Mersey on his father's horse and cart three times per week to sell at Cazneau Street Market, Liverpool.

Primitive Methodism was introduced to Irby in 1869 by Mr & Mrs George Cooke at their Irby Hill Farm. In 1881 a 'tin chapel' was built across the road from the farm. Two extensions were added, a small porch at the front and a vestry at the rear. A service was held at the chapel in memory of Frank Lester VC in August 1919. The congregation increased and in 1934 land was purchased in Mill Hill Road. The present church was built there in 1936. The vestry of the 'tin chapel' survived after the main structure was taken down. until it collapsed in bad weather in 2013.

Oxton was once one of the most affluent areas in England when it became a residential area for wealthy Liverpool merchants and tradesmen. As a result most of the village is mainly early Victorian and was designated a conservation area in 1979.

Cazneau Street market at the time of the 1911 Liverpool general transport strike.

Frank enlisted in 10th (Reserve) Battalion, South Lancashire Regiment on 30th March 1916 (27807). He trained as an instructor at Chelsea, London and was promoted sergeant. His unit was re-designated 51st Battalion, Training Reserve at Prees Heath Camp, Shropshire and Kinmel Park, near Abergele, North Wales and in May 1917 became 229th Graduated Battalion. Frank transferred to 10th Lancashire Fusiliers in June 1917 at his own request and reverted to private (51674) before sailing for France to join the Battalion there. He was granted leave in Britain 6th–13th December. He was wounded on 21st March 1918 at Havrincourt, near Cambrai. He was promoted corporal and returned to Cromer, Norfolk, England in July 1918, probably to join 24th Battalion, a training unit based on 2/7th Battalion, which had been reduced to cadre in April. Frank returned to 10th Battalion in France in September and joined A Company.

Awarded the VC for his actions at Neuvilly, France on 12th October 1918, LG 14th December 1918. He was killed during the VC action at Neuvilly

Prees Heath Camp was constructed to train new recruits as the British Army expanded on the outbreak of the Great War. It had a capacity for 30,000 men, with stores and its own branch line from the LNWR Crewe and Shrewsbury Railway. There were shops, a cinema and a military hospital with over 600 beds. One man based there was Norval Sinclair Marley, father of the reggae star Bob Marley. After the war the camp became a demobilisation centre before being dismantled. In 1940 the common became an internment camp for enemy aliens. It closed in the autumn when the internees who had not been released were transferred to the Isle of Man. The camp was then used for Italian prisoners-of-war, some of whom worked on local farms. The camp was closed in 1942 for the construction of a bomber training airfield, initially known as RAF Whitchurch Heath, but changed to RAF Tilstock to avoid confusion with RAF Whitchurch in southern England.

Kinmel Park Camp was built in 1915 in the grounds of Kinmel Hall, near Abergele, to train recruits for the Great War. Small shops opened nearby in what became known as Tintown. A railway served the camp and was later used for a nearby quarry until it closed in 1964. After the war the camp housed Canadian troops awaiting repatriation. A riot broke out in March 1919, resulting in the deaths of five soldiers. They were frustrated by basic living conditions and delays in travelling home due to a shortage of shipping. The camp was later reduced to around half its original size and continues as a military training facility.

on 12th October 1918. His body was recovered following a counterattack three days later and he is buried in Neuvilly Communal Cemetery Extension, near Le Cateau, France (B 15). The VC was presented to his mother by the King in the ballroom at Buckingham Palace on 22nd February 1919.

In addition to the VC, Frank was awarded the British War Medal 1914–20 and Victory Medal 1914–19. The VC passed to his sister Lucy and, on her death, to her son, Frank Wilson. It was sold to Lord Ashcroft at auction by Morton & Eden for £78,000 on 18th April 2002 at Westbury Hotel, New Bond Street, London. The VC is held by the Michael Ashcroft Trust, the holding institution for the Lord Ashcroft Victoria Cross Collection, and is displayed in the Imperial War Museum's Lord Ashcroft Gallery. Frank is commemorated in a number of other places:

Frank Lester's grave in Neuvilly Communal Cemetery Extension.

- Hoylake
  - Family headstone in Holy Trinity Churchyard (Church demolished 1976), Trinity Road, with his brothers George and Edwin, and his Aunt Ellen and Uncle George. John O'Neill VC MM is buried in the Churchyard.
  - Plaque at Hope Evangelical Church (former Congregationalist), Station Road, Hoylake.
  - Plaque at St Andrew's United Reformed Church (Hoylake with Meols), Greenwood Road, Meols, Wirral.
- West Kirby
  - Hoylake and West Kirby War Memorial, Grange Hill, West Kirby, Wirral, Merseyside, with his brother Edwin.

Frank's mother, Ellen, holding her son's VC. She appears to be standing outside Miller's Hay.

The Hoylake and West Kirby War Memorial stands on Grange Hill, West Kirby. It was designed by Charles Sargeant Jagger (1885–1934). Jagger also designed the Royal Artillery Memorial, Hyde Park Corner, London. The memorial was unveiled on 16th December 1922 by the Earl of Birkenhead.

Frank and Edwin Lester are commemorated on the Holy Cross Parish Church War Memorial, Woodchurch.

 - ◦ Hoylake, West Kirby, Meols, Caldy, Frankby, Newton, Irby, Greasby and Thurstaston Book of Remembrance at West Kirby Library, Grange Road.
- Birkenhead
  - War Memorial, Holy Cross Parish Church, Church Lane, Woodchurch.
  - A Department for Communities and Local Government commemorative paving stone was dedicated at Birkenhead War Memorial, Hamilton Square Gardens on 11th November 2018.
  - Wirral Peninsula Victoria Cross Memorial, at Birkenhead War Memorial.

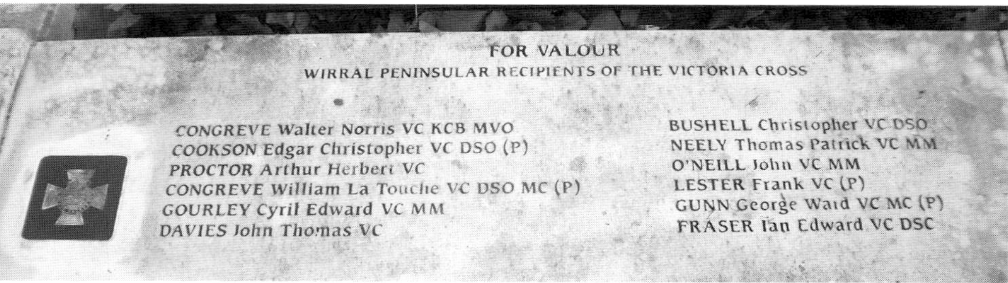

The Wirral Peninsula Victoria Cross Memorial at the base of Birkenhead War Memorial.

Blue Plaque at Millers Hay.

St Bartholomew Parish Church War Memorial, Thurstaston. Frank and Edwin Lester's names are on the right panel.

Hoylake Boys' Brigade with Frank Lester standing far left.

- Irby
  - Plaque at Methodist Chapel, Mill Hill.
  - Plaque at Irby Public Library, Thurstaston Road.
  - A Department for Communities and Local Government commemorative paving stone was dedicated at Millers Hay, Mill Hill Road on 10th October 2018.
  - Blue Plaque at his parent's former home at Millers Hay.
  - Lester Drive.
- Victoria Cross Roll of Honour, Victoria Cross Memorial Alcove, Wallasey Town Hall, Brighton Street.
- Plaque and War Memorial, St Bartholomew Parish Church, Church Lane, Thurstaston, Wirral, with his brother Edwin.

Victor Comic dated 6th January 1973 (DC Thompson).

- Book of Remembrance at Chester Cathedral, Cheshire.
- Boys' Brigade Memorial, National Memorial Arboretum, Alrewas, Staffordshire.
- Named on The Ring of Remembrance (L'Anneau de la Mémoire or Ring of Memory) at Ablain-Saint-Nazaire, France, inaugurated on 11th November 2014. The Ring commemorates 576,606 soldiers of forty nationalities who died in Nord-Pas-de-Calais in the Great War.
- His VC action was featured in Issue 620 of the Victor Comic entitled *The Village of Death*, dated 6th January 1973.

LIEUTENANT JOSEPH MAXWELL
18th Australian Infantry Battalion AIF

(Australian War Memorial)

Joseph 'Joe' Maxwell was born on 10th February 1896 at 268 Hereford Street, Forest Lodge, Annandale, Sydney, New South Wales, Australia. His father, John Maxwell (1866–28th February 1930), born at Glebe, New South Wales, was an engine cleaner. He married Elizabeth Alexandria née Stokes on 26th August 1885 at Bethel House, George Street, Sydney. She was living at 5 Nicholson Street, Maitland, NSW at the time. Elizabeth is reputed to have been born in Paris, France to British parents, at Maxwelltown, Scotland or Patrick's Plain, NSW. John found work at East Greta and North Rothbury in the Lower Hunter Valley coalfields, renting a property at West Maitland. They were living at 5 Nicholson Street, North Rothbury, Branxton, NSW by March 1917 and at Airlie, 35 Calvert Street, Marrickville, NSW by July 1918. They also lived at 8 Fairlight Street, Manly, NSW. John was recorded as a retired hotelkeeper when Joe married in 1928. John died at Granville, NSW. Joe is believed to have had nine siblings:

People boarding the Forest Lodge tram in the 1890s. Forest Lodge is a small suburb of Sydney, about four kilometres southwest of the central business district. It was named after a house built in 1836 by Ambrose Foss, which stood on Bridge Road until it was demolished in 1912. The University of Sydney Centre for Peace and Conflict Studies and the Medical Foundation are located there. A small park, *Lew Hoad Reserve*, is named after Lew Hoad (1934–94), who grew up in Forest Lodge. He was a member of Australia's four Davis Cup winning teams 1952–56. He also won Wimbledon twice and was the world's number one tennis player in 1956 before turning professional (Arthur Syer).

Joe's mother was living at 5 Nicholson Street, Maitland in 1885.

35 Calvert Street, Marrickville, where Joe's parents were living by July 1918.

- John Maxwell (1886–87), born at Sydney.
- Mary Maxwell (born and died 1887).
- Clarence Arthur Maxwell (1888–3rd October 1949) was a miner, working with his father in the Lower Hunter Valley coalfields. He married Margaret Schofield (10th March 1891–30th August 1971), born at Quirindi, NSW, in 1913 at West Maitland, NSW. They lived at 76 Mount View Road, Cessnock, NSW. They had five children, all born at Cessnock, including:
    - Leslie Clifford Maxwell (29th May 1914–11th May 1977) married Daphne Cecilia Rae (1915–2006), born at Gunnedah, in 1935. He was employed in a colliery and they were living at 7 Mills Crescent, Cessnock at the time of his death there. They had two children – Robert Rae Maxwell (died 1941) and Raymond John Maxwell (born 1943).
    - Clarence Arthur Maxwell (16th August 1917–17th March 1974) enlisted in the Australian Army on 13th August 1940 at Cessnock (N16631). He was tried by court martial on 1st March 1943 but the outcome is not known. He was serving as a gunner in 1st Australian Field Regiment at the time of his discharge on 12th January 1945. He died at Aberdare, NSW.
    - Cecil Maxwell (4th May 1925–8th September 2008), a miner, married Lillian Joan Walters (19th May 1926–4th October 2015), a shop assistant, in 1950 at Cessnock. Lillian was living at 38 Love Street, Cessnock in 1949. Cecil and Lillian were living at 14 Anzac Avenue, Cessnock by 1977. They had two children – Leanne Maxwell and Lorraine Maxwell.
    - John Henry Maxwell (24th July 1927–22nd March 1978) married Olga Jane Woseen (5th June 1928–28th December 2004), born at Bega, NSW, on 18th April 1953 at Boolaroo, NSW. Olga was a machinist in 1949, living alone at Cross Roads, Cardiff, Hunter, NSW. John was a process worker in 1958, when they were living at 44 Bruce Street, Glendale, NSW. He died at Cessnock and she at Newcastle, NSW.

- Irene Stella Maxwell (1891–12th August 1970), born at Newtown, NSW, married Enoch Elias Callaghan (23rd June 1889–11th August 1970), a miner born at Cessnock, NSW, in 1911 at West Maitland, NSW. They were living at 6 Lyell Street, Cessnock by 1936. They both died at Kogarah, NSW. They had four children:
    - Mary Eileen Callaghan (17th November 1912–31st July 1986) enlisted in the Royal Australian Air Force on 26th May 1941 at Cessnock (501105). She was discharged as a sister on 5th June 1944 at Richmond, NSW. She married William Joseph Scarff (7th November 1914–7th June 1954), a radio engineer born at Malvern, Victoria, in 1944. He was a student in 1936, living with his sisters Annie Mary, Margaret Mary and Mary Ellen Scarff at 9 Willis Street, Malvern, Victoria. William enlisted in the Australian Army on 8th October 1940 at Albert Park, Victoria (V27602). He was serving as a lieutenant in the Royal Australian Corps of Signals, with 2nd Cavalry Division, when he transferred to the Royal Australian Air Force on 12th October 1941 (25317). He was discharged as a squadron leader on 8th July 1946. William died as a result of a car crash at Wycheproof, Victoria. Mary was living with her daughter Anne, a solicitor, at 138 Tooronga Road, Glen Iris, Victoria in 1980. She was living at Boronia Park, NSW at the time of her death at Sydney. Mary and William had two daughters – Kristen Mary Scarff and Anne Maureen Scarff.
    - Edna Callaghan (31st July 1914–26th November 1991) was a nurse at the District Hospital, Cessnock in 1936. She enlisted in the Australian Army on 3rd September 1942 at Tamworth, NSW (NX112313 & N391899). She was commissioned as a lieutenant in the Australian Army Nursing Service and was discharged on 25th September 1946. Edna married Francis 'Frank' Joseph Byrne (died 29th November 1977) in 1943 at Sydney. Frank was a secretary in 1963, when they were living at 12 MacLaurin Street, Penshurst, NSW. They both died at Penshurst. Edna was living with their daughter, Elizabeth Mary Byrne, a teacher, at 12 MacLaurin Street in 1980.
    - John 'Jack' Joseph Callaghan (29th June 1917–12th February 2000) was a schoolteacher at Graman, NSW. He enrolled in the Royal Australian Air Force Reserve on 11th January 1941 and enlisted on 17th August at No.2 Recruiting Centre, Sydney (413342). He was posted to No.2 Initial Training School, Lindfield (later Bradfield Park), NSW. He was described as 5′6″ tall, weighing 134 lbs, with fair complexion, blue eyes, fair hair and his religious denomination was Roman Catholic. He was mustered to air crew V(O) on 6th October. Granted leave 5th-17th November. Promoted leading aircraftman and aircrew II(O) at No.2 Embarkation Depot, Bradfield Park on 8th November. He was attached to HQ Rathmines, NSW 27th December 1941–3rd March 1942. Granted leave 12th February–13th March. He attended courses at No.2 Air Observers School, Mount Gambier, South

Australia from 5th March, at No.3 Bombing Air Gunnery School, Sale, Victoria 1st June–23rd July and at No.2 Air Navigation School, Nhill, Victoria 24th July–20th August. He qualified as a Navigator B and received the Air Observers Badge. Appointed temporary sergeant and air observer on 20th August. He returned to No.2 Embarkation Depot, Bradfield Park on 21st August and was granted leave until 29th August. Posted to No.1 Operational Training Unit, Bairnsdale, Victoria on 8th September and attended No.4 Beaufort Operational Training Course there 6th October–8th December. He was involved in a crash in which six crew members were killed, leaving him shaken and uncertain of himself. On 18th December his CO reported that he was a good navigator but did not recommend him for a commission. Posted to No.14 Squadron, RAAF Pearce, Western Australia on 18th December. Appointed Navigator (B) on 25th January 1943. Granted leave 5th-12th February. Appointed temporary flight sergeant on 1st May. Granted leave 27th July–18th August and 13th December–7th January 1944. He was posted to No.1 Operational Training Unit on 29th February 1944 and attended No.19 Beaufort Operational Training Course there 1st March–8th May. Appointed temporary warrant officer on 1st May. Posted to No.4 Personnel Depot on 18th May, No.2 Initial Training School on 22nd May, No.55 Operational Base Unit, Birdum, Northern Territory on 27th May and No.1 Squadron, RAAF Amberley, Queensland on 29th May. Took part in an operational flight to sea on 9th June and went on to complete forty-three sorties, including four strike and attack missions, between 4th June and 27th December. Jack was commissioned as a pilot officer on 1st November. He was posted to No.2 Personnel Depot, Bradfield Park on 7th February 1945 and to No.1 Operational Training Unit on 12th April. Promoted flying officer on 1st May and was discharged at his own request, in order to return to teaching on 23rd August. Jack married Margaret Doris Meehan (7th April 1924–30th March 1976) on 18th December 1948 at St Mary of the Angels, Guyra, NSW. They were living at 3 Leeder Avenue, Penshurst in 1968. They had three children.

  - Joseph 'Joe' Maxwell Callaghan (28th August 1919–27th November 1991) enlisted in the Australian Army on 3rd December 1941 at Paddington, NSW (NX73646 & N130486). He was serving as a gunner in 2/1st Australian Field Regiment at the time of his discharge on 9th April 1946. He married Dorothy Ward (1925–26th January 2010) in 1947 at Cessnock, where she was born. Joe was a foreman in 1954, when they were living at 120 Gipps Street, Gwynneville, NSW.

- Myra Maxwell (1893–30th June 1974), born at Marrickville, married Walter McDonald in 1934 at Dubbo, NSW. They lived at 3/29 Macmahon Street, Hurstville, NSW. She ran a nursing home at Manly, NSW and a second one at Bondi Beach, at one time employing her brother Joe as a gardener.

The Beaufort was a twin-engine torpedo-bomber produced by the Bristol Aeroplane Co and was developed from the earlier Blenheim light bomber. Of the 1,180 Beauforts that were produced, more than 700 were Australian-built and saw service with the RAAF in the South-West Pacific theatre of operations. The Beaufort was later adapted as a long-range heavy fighter called the Beaufighter. No.1 Squadron RAAF was equipped with Beauforts from 1943. It formed in 1916 and saw action in Sinai and Palestine. It was commanded in 1917–18 by Major Richard Williams, known as the 'Father of the RAAF'. The Squadron disbanded in 1919 but reformed in 1922. After the Second World War the Squadron was reduced to cadre but was re-established at Amberley in 1948 with Avro Lincoln heavy bombers. It was based in Singapore 1950–58 and flew missions during the Malayan Emergency. Today the Squadron is equipped with Super Hornets.

- Possibly Mary Maxwell (born 1895), born at Young, NSW.
- Eileen V Maxwell (1898–1906), born at Gosford, NSW.
- Possibly Rebecca Maxwell (born 1901), born at Blayney, NSW.
- Possibly Aubrey Frank Maxwell (25th December 1903–20th July 1987) entered the Public Service on 8th March 1920 (BA LL.B). He married Mavis Dorothea Brady (18th January 1909–25th September 1980), a typist born at Grafton, NSW, in 1930 at Marrickville. She was living at 21 Shaw Avenue, Earlwood, NSW at the time. He was a clerk in the Deeds Branch of the Registrar General's Department in 1951. They were living at 71 Edward Street, Bexley North, NSW by 1958. They had a daughter:
    - Judith Elizabeth Maxwell (26th March 1941–11th September 2008) married Peter Kennedy Court, a law clerk, in 1962. They were living at 9 Mundarrah Street, Randwick, NSW in 1963.

Joe's paternal grandfather, John Maxwell (1841–13th December 1885), from Ardstraw, Co Tyrone, Ireland, was a baker. He emigrated to Australia aboard the *Sirocco*, departing Liverpool, Lancashire and arriving at Sydney, NSW on 28th January 1864. He married Mary Jane née Watson (1841–1921), also born in Ireland, on 8th February 1865 at the Presbyterian Church, Elizabeth Street, Sydney. He died at Sydney and she at Marrickville, NSW. In addition to John they had seven other children:

- Rebecca Jane Maxwell (1868–5th September 1942), born at Glebe, NSW, married Francis John Abigail (14th July 1867–24th December 1926) in 1888 at Sydney, where he was born. His father, Francis Abigail (1840–1921), was born in London, England and arrived in Sydney in 1860. With H Hilder he set up a boot manufacturing, leather and grindery business in Sydney c.1866. He entered the Legislative Assembly as a member for West Sydney in November 1880 and was Secretary for Mines January 1887–January 1889. He was elected Chairman of the Australian Banking Company of Sydney in July 1887, served on the New South Wales Commission for the Melbourne Centennial Exhibition of 1888 and for the Exhibition of Mining and Metallurgy held at the Crystal Palace, London in 1890. He was defeated in the elections of June 1891. In October 1892 he and six others were charged with falsely representing the affairs of the Australian Banking Company. He was found not guilty but at a second trial was convicted of conspiring to issue a false balance sheet with fraudulent intent. He was sentenced to five years hard labour in Darlinghurst Gaol on 3rd November 1892. Francis John Abigail worked on the railways and was a Freemason and Brother of Glebe Lodge No.1944, NSW. He died at 90 Hampton Court Road, Kogarah, NSW and Rebecca at Rockdale, NSW. They had six children:

  - Francis Harold Abigail (born 1889) is understood to have married Alma Beatrice Burgess (1894–1967) in 1913 at Hurstville, NSW. They had at least three children – Francis H Abigail 1914, Clement L Abigail 1916 and Raymond G Abigail 1919.
  - William Alfred Abigail (1891–1963) is understood to have married Elsie Louise Woodward (1891–1966) at Newtown, NSW in 1914.
  - Lydia Pearl Abigail (born 1894) married Sydney G Evans at Kogarah, NSW in 1916. They had at least one child – Maxwell G Evans in 1917.
  - Arthur S Abigail (1896–98).
  - Robert Abigail (born and died 1898).
  - Lillian Vera Abigail (1900–7th September 1972) married Athol Rupert Lennie (died 1947) at Sydney in 1926.

- Mary Maxwell (1870–1934) died at Lismore, NSW.
- William Maxwell (1871–27th May 1905), born at Balmain, NSW.
- Martha Maxwell (born and died 1873), born at Glebe.
- Joseph Maxwell (1876–1907), a driver, married Eva May Hall (16th November 1876 -1951), a tailoress born at Sydney, on 12th November 1898 at the Independent Presbyterian Church, 471 Pitt Street, Sydney. They were also Joe's parents-in-law. They lived at 85 Cowper Street, Glebe. Eva married James Joseph Crawshaw (1872–1944), a coach painter born at Queanbeyan, NSW, in 1910 at Sydney. They were living at 24 Calvert Street, Marrickville in 1930, at 257 Illawarra Road, Marrickville in 1935 and at 151 Windsor Street, Paddington, NSW in 1941. They both died at Marrickville. James had married Nellie Mason in 1898 at Sydney. Eva and Joseph had three children:

  - Joseph 'Joe' Ambrose Maxwell (28th May 1899–29th June 1976) was a baker living at 151 Windsor Street, Paddington, NSW when he enlisted in the Australian Imperial Force on 18th May 1918 at Liverpool, NSW (66242). He was described as 5′6″ tall, weighing 112 lbs, with dark complexion, brown eyes, brown hair and his religious denomination was Church of England. He

joined a recruit depot on 29th May and A Company, Composite Battalion, 20th General Service Reinforcements (New South Wales) on 29th August. He embarked at Melbourne, Victoria aboard SS *Zealandic* on 5th October, arriving on 5th December at London, England. Joe joined 14th Training Battalion and was allotted to Reinforcements, 57th Battalion. He was awarded five days Field Punishment No.2 and forfeited seven days' pay for being absent without leave from Hurdcott, Wiltshire from 12.01 a.m. on 24th January 1919 until 9.15 p.m. on 25th January. He was in hospital at Hurdcott 31st January – 15th February and went to France on 18th February from Southampton, Hampshire, arriving at le Havre. He joined the Australian Infantry Base Depot on 21st February and was taken on strength of 57th Battalion on 25th February. Joe was detached to 5th Australian Division Artillery 2nd-19th March, joined the Demobilisation Camp on 30th March and was detached to the Australian Base Reception Camp on 10th April. He returned to England on 6th June, arriving at Southampton the following day. On 22nd July he embarked aboard SS *Ulysses* and arrived in Australia on 5th September. He was discharged on 20th September 1919. He married Adelaide 'Addie' Dela Thirza Etherden (1903–32), born at Waterloo, NSW, at Marrickville in 1921. He married Alice M Lander at Marrickville in 1934. They were living at 64 Barden Street, Tempe, Sydney in 1941.
  - Mabel 'Mae' E Maxwell, Joe's cousin and first wife (see below).
  - William 'Bill' John Maxwell (1905–64).
- Margaret Ann Maxwell (1877–11th July 1947) married William Patrick Mulligan (c.1878–27th August 1955), a bookmaker, in 1902 at Leichhardt, NSW. They were living at 95 The Promenade, Sans Souci, NSW in 1930. They had at least seven children:
  - Sylvia May Mulligan (1904–27th May 1988).
  - Eileen 'Penny' Winifred Mulligan (1905–1st April 1987) married William Lancelot Penny (1906–72) at Kogarah in 1926.
  - William Patrick Mulligan (19th June 1908–21st December 1970) married Myrtle L Larsen (born 1909) at Kogarah in 1928.
  - Harold Maxwell Mulligan (11th April 1910–12th August 1979) married Marjorie L Allan at Rockdale, NSW in 1934.
  - Francis 'Frank' John Mulligan (1912–20th June 1964).
  - Ellen Margaret Mulligan (1916–27th February 1995).
  - Norma Kathleen Mulligan (6th January 1920–18th December 2002) married Francis Bruce MacCole (1917–88) at Kogarah in 1943.
- Eliza Maxwell (1880–14th April 1962) married Charles Lewis Smith (15th March 1877–26th April 1966), a clerk, in 1897 at Redfern, NSW, where he was born. They were living at 154 Rose Street, Darlington, NSW in 1918 and at 23 Acton

Street, Hurlstone Park, NSW in 1949. She died at Marrickville and he at Wentworth Convalescent Hospital, Randwick, NSW. They had nine children:

- Leslie Charles Smith (15th March 1898–1963) was a salesman when he enlisted at Sydney in 27th General Service Reinforcements (NSW) on 29th May 1918 (67937). He had served previously for four years in the Senior Cadets and two years with 5th Battalion, 53rd Infantry Regiment. He was described as 5′ 4½″ tall, weighing 128 lbs, with dark complexion, brown eyes, brown hair and his religious denomination was Church of England. He joined a composite battalion and embarked on HMAT A7 *Medic* at Sydney on 2nd November. The ship was recalled and returned to Australia on 12th December. He was discharged on 11th January 1919.
- Henry Smith (1900–68).
- Elsie Gladys Smith (1905–73).
- Emily Adelaide Smith (1906–84) married Albert Perry at Canterbury, NSW in 1932.
- Thelma Smith (1908–10).
- Cecil Smith (1911–90) married Esme Lila Florence Ross (born 1910), on 2nd October 1937 at All Saint's Church, Petersham. They were both clerks. He was living at 23 Achon Street, Hurlstone Park and she at 11 Neville Street, Marrickville at the time.
- Norman Maxwell Smith (13th September 1914–2008) enlisted in the Australian Army on 7th August 1943 at Hurlstone Park (NX162474 & N89368). He was discharged as a sergeant from No.4 Anti-Aircraft Operations Room on 3rd May 1946. Norman married Marion Louise Davidson (born 1924) on 12th October 1946.
- Francis William Smith (1917–2016).
- Kenneth George Smith (12th January 1924–1st November 2007) enlisted in the Australian Army at Hurlstone Park on 28th September 1943 (NX193310 & N256740). He was discharged from 160 Australian General Transport Company on 6th September 1946. He married Gladys Doreen Marshall (16th September 1921–17th August 2008).

Nothing is known about Joe's maternal grandparents. Joe was educated at Gillieston Public School, Ryan Road, Gillieston Heights, NSW and excelled as a cricketer. He completed a two-year post-primary technical course as a boilermaker at Maitland Superior Public School and was employed as a boilermaker's apprentice at Messrs James & Alexander Brown's engineering works at 100 Old Maitland Road, Hexham, near Newcastle, NSW (also known as Reliance Engineering). The outbreak of war caused disruption in the coal trade and a consequent reduction in engineering work. As a result the Hexham works closed temporarily, with 250 men being out of work.

Joe served for three years in the Senior Cadets and two years with the Militia. He enlisted in the Australian Imperial Force Infantry, N Company at Liverpool, NSW on 6th February 1915 (607) and was posted to 18th Battalion on 24th June, joining 8 Platoon in B Company. He was described as 5′4½″ tall, weighing 126 lbs, with dark complexion, brown eyes, black hair and his religious denomination was Church of England. He was promoted lance corporal on 29th March and embarked at Sydney aboard HMAT A40 *Ceramic* on 24th June, disembarking at Port Suez, Egypt. He narrowly avoided serious injury in Cairo when a piano, hurled out of a café second storey window by fellow Australians, missed him by a few centimetres. This almost certainly occurred in the 'second battle of Wazza' in the red light district of Cairo on 31st July. Joe sailed for Gallipoli on 16th August and landed on 18th August, where he took part in the attack on Hill 60 on 22nd August. He was admitted to 5th Field Ambulance on 28th November and embarked aboard a hospital ship bound for Egypt on 2nd December. On 5th December he was admitted to 3rd Auxiliary Hospital at Heliopolis with jaundice and transferred to Ras-el-Tin Convalescent Hospital, Alexandria on 11th December. Joe returned to duty at Overseas Base, Ghesireh on 5th January 1916 and rejoined the Battalion at Zeitoun on 28th January. He was admitted to 1st Australian Dermatological Hospital, Abbassia on 4th February, where he was diagnosed with venereal disease. He was discharged to duty on 11th March and rejoined his unit on 15th March.

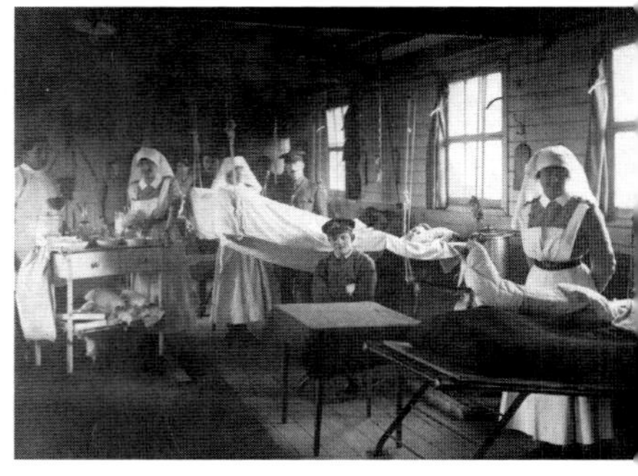

No.3 Canadian General Hospital was the first hospital unit created by a University (McGill) during the war. It mobilised in Montréal on 5th March 1915 under Colonel HS Birkett, McGill's Dean of Medicine 1914–21. After a short period in England, it moved to France on 16th June and opened at Dannes-Camiers on 19th June. From 6th January 1916 onwards it was in the old Jesuit College at Boulogne. Lieutenant Colonel John McCrae, who wrote *In Flanders Fields* was involved in setting it up and commanded the unit until his death from pneumonia on 28th January 1918 (McGill University).

Joe embarked at Alexandria on 18th March and disembarked at Marseille, France on 25th March. He reported sick with inguinal adenitis (non-venereal) and was admitted to 3rd Canadian General Hospital, Boulogne on 28th April. He was transferred to 1st Convalescence Depot on 2nd May and was discharged to Base Details on 13th May. Joe was reduced to private for breaking ranks on the 7.30 a.m. parade and absence from 8.00 a.m. until 1.00 p.m. on 24th May. He rejoined his Battalion on 1st June. Joe was appointed temporary corporal 4th – 27th August and was promoted sergeant on 11th October. He was treated at 6th Australian Field Ambulance with synovitis right knee 14th-16th October. Joe was posted to 5th Training Battalion, Rollestone Camp, Wiltshire, England as a bombing instructor on 28th October, arriving on 31st October.

On 1st January 1917 Joe was appointed to the permanent cadre of 5th Training Battalion. He departed Rollestone Camp for France on 9th May and rejoined

18th Battalion on 13th May. He returned to England to attend No.6 Officer Cadet Battalion, Trinity College, Oxford for officer training, commencing on 5th July. However, the day before he was involved in a brawl with civil and military police in London and was charged with being drunk and disorderly in Victoria Street, using obscene language and assaulting civil police. His case was heard at Westminster Police Court on 6th July and he was fined £20 or faced two months imprisonment. He paid the fine and returned to France on 11th July without undergoing officer training. Appointed temporary warrant officer class II and company sergeant major on 7th August. **Awarded the DCM for his actions in an attack near Westhoek during the Third Battle of Ypres on 25th September – he took command of a platoon, whose officer had been killed, and led it forward with great dash. Later, when he noticed that one of the newly captured positions was under heavy fire, he dashed to it and led the men to a safer and more tactically secure position, thus saving many lives, LG 19th November 1917.**

Rollestone Camp in Wiltshire is close to Larkhill. In the foreground are carriages on the railway built to service the various camps and airfields in the area during the Great War. Nothing remains of them today, although the course of the railway can be followed in places.

Joe was commissioned on 29th September 1917 and was promoted lieutenant on 1st January 1918. He was treated at 7th Australian Field Ambulance and No.2 Australian Casualty Clearing Station for scabies 10th–17th January and rejoined the Battalion on 20th January. **Awarded the MC for his actions while in command of a patrol at Pont Rouge, east of Ploegsteert Wood, on 8th March 1918 – having obtained the required information he ordered the patrol to withdraw and with three others covered the withdrawal. He observed a party of about fifty enemy entering a disused trench and recalled the patrol, then attacked the enemy with bombs and rifle fire, before assaulting the position. The Germans quickly withdrew, leaving three dead and one wounded, who was captured, LG 13th May 1918.** He was granted leave in England 17th July–1st August. **Awarded a Bar to the MC for his actions on 9th August – 18th Battalion was preparing to attack near Rainecourt when all officers in the company, except Maxwell, became casualties. Under his leadership he kept his men well in hand under heavy fire and the company attacked on time, still under heavy fire. A tank, which preceded the advance, was knocked out by a 77mm gun. Maxwell was close to it, rushed over and opened the hatch, freeing the occupants just before the tank burst into flames. After escorting the tank commander to comparative safety,**

Maxwell went forward again to lead the company in the attack and succeeded in reaching and consolidating the objective, LG 1st February 1919. Four other members of the party received the Military Medal, including Sergeant Dan Bishop.

Hotel Tortini opened in 1838 and was enlarged in 1858. It had its heyday between 1914 and 1918 but slowly declined thereafter. It closed in 1941 and was completely destroyed by Allied bombing in 1944.

Awarded the VC for his actions in the Beaurevoir–Fonsomme Line near Estrées, north of St Quentin, France on 3rd October 1918, LG 6th January 1919. Joe joined the Australian Base Depot, Le Havre on 27th January 1919 in preparation for returning to Australia. That evening he and several others visited Tortoni's Restaurant in Le Havre in a state of intoxication. A fracas followed in which chairs were thrown, glasses were broken and a disturbance resulted, which was eventually suppressed by the police. Due to the disgrace this brought on the AIF, the CO of the Depot returned Maxwell to his unit. The other officers were engaged in another disturbance and stood trial by field general court martial. Joe rejoined the Battalion on 6th February and demobilisation was delayed until April by order of the Corps Commander.

The VC was presented by the King in the ballroom of Buckingham Palace on 8th March 1919. Joe was escorted to a room in which were seated four others whose tunics displayed the VC ribbon. Leaning on the mantelpiece was a gentleman in the beribboned uniform of an admiral, who smiled at Joe, extended his hand and said, *You are here to be honoured: I am here merely to be knighted.* Joe laughed and replied, *I was under the impression that you were King George.* As the only officer to receive the VC that day, he was the first to be honoured. The King approached Joe and extended his hand, but Joe forgot to bow. He was prodded from behind as a reminder but, rather than accentuate the oversight, he decided to stand fast. When the King released Joe's hand, he bowed with such vigour that he almost butted the King's chest. As he strolled through the West End that afternoon, two immaculately dressed men in mufti approached and raised their hats. Joe felt embarrassed but returned the salute. Next day he saw an illustrated paper and realised that the two gentlemen were the Prince of Wales and Lord Louis Mountbatten. That night, after dinner at the Australian Officers' Club, he shared a room with Captain 'Birdie' Herron, who had an artificial eye. Joe awoke during the night feeling thirsty and fumbled in the dark to pour a whisky into a glass. He was surprised when something unusual touched his teeth and he spat it out. Next morning Joe spotted Birdie's artificial eye glaring at him from under his bed.

Joe rejoined the Battalion in France on 12th March. He was placed in open arrest from 1.00 p.m. on 16th March for disobeying a lawful command. This was the culmination of a series of disciplinary irregularities over a long period and the CO decided to recommend trial by field general court martial. The offences cited were:

> December 1917 – recalled from duty as officer in charge of picquet Bailleul at the request of the APM, who took strong exception to his conduct.
>
> January 1918 – paraded before CO when his company commander reported unfavourably on his conduct.
>
> March 1918 – paraded before GOC 5th Australian Brigade for being drunk and neglecting to carry out orders.
>
> Expelled from a riding class at Vignacourt owing to inattention to instruction.
>
> Paraded before GOC 5th Australian Brigade for, whilst drunk, galloping a horse on metalled roads rendering it unfit for work for seven days.
>
> Whilst detached as conducting officer for educational tours, his conduct in Charleroi twice came to the notice of the APM. The CO recalled him and placed him on draft for demobilisation. Two days before departure Maxwell grossly insulted the CO in the mess but, since he desired to be rid of Maxwell, accepted an apology.
>
> January 1919 – the incident described above at Le Havre.
>
> Failure to comply with movement restrictions imposed by his company commander. The CO personally ordered him to restrict his movements to the Battalion area but he disobeyed and visited Charleroi.

As a result, the CO referred Joe for trial but, following discussions with the Divisional Commander on 18th March, it was decided to return him to Australia without delay. He was released from open arrest on 20th March. Joe returned to England from Boulogne on 15th or 18th April and joined No.2 Group, Sutton Veny, Wiltshire on 20th April. He returned to Australia aboard HT *China*, embarking on 1st May. The ship arrived at Fremantle on 1st June. He disembarked at Melbourne on 8th June and moved to 2nd Military District, Sydney. On his return to Marrickville, he was welcomed by the Mayor, Alderman Richards. His appointment in the AIF was terminated on 10th August 1919. During the Great War he had a number of romances. One was with a Canadian nurse who helped treat him in Boulogne. Another was with a young lady in Shrewton, Wiltshire, when he was an instructor on Salisbury Plain. He also had an affair with Germaine in St Omer, France, where she lived, and later at Abbeville.

Joe was a difficult individual and his character is summed up in the words of his CO, Lieutenant Colonel George Francis Murphy CMG DSO (1883–1962), who wrote the Foreword to Joe's book, *Hell's Bells and Mademoiselles*:

The YMCA at Greenhill House used by Australian troops while training at Sutton Veny.

'Joe is a queer mixture. He had been brought up in a very hard school, and was well able to take care of himself in a rough and tumble....

In these pages he has openly confessed that he was way more than a handful 'behind the Line'. In the presence of the enemy, however, he became a different personage. On the several occasions that I accompanied him on patrol, I marked an utter change the moment he stepped over the sandbags into No Man's Land. I had an uncanny feeling of being accompanied by a descendant

George Francis Murphy (1883–1962) qualified as a teacher and later attended the University of Sydney as an evening student. In 1910 he was appointed a lieutenant in the New South Wales Cadets and in December 1914 was posted to Liverpool. On 5th May 1915 he joined the Australian Imperial Force, commanding A Company, 20th Battalion. He transferred to 18th Battalion at Gallipoli after the attack on Hill 60. He was the temporary CO in November and December 1915 and was second-in-command when the Battalion moved to France in March 1916. He was wounded at Pozières on 27th July, returned to duty in late October and on 7th November took command of the Battalion until the end of the war. During his time in command he was awarded the DSO & Bar, CMG and was mentioned five times. He proved to be 'a most competent commander and an able tactician' and commanded 7th Australian Brigade from mid-July to 24th August 1918. His AIF appointment terminated in January 1920 but he continued part-time service, commanding 17th Battalion 1921–22 and 1924–31. Murphy held a number of other prominent appointments – Under-Sheriff of New South Wales and Sheriff 1925–35, Custodian of the Sydney Cenotaph 1932–39, Deputy Marshal of the High Court 1935–39, Assistant Comptroller of New South Wales Prisons 1939 and Comptroller 1940, resuming the post after Second World War service in 1947. During the war he was a temporary colonel and Director of the Volunteer Defence Corps 1941–42, Provost Marshal at Army Headquarters 1941–43 and then Director of Military Prisons and Detention Barracks. He retired as an honorary colonel in November 1946.

of the Redskins of North America. To Maxwell, patrolling No Man's Land was as a chess problem: he balanced the objective to be attained against the risks to be run, and as the scales tipped so he acted. When the situation demanded he was reckless of his own life, but never of those of the men under his command. Back over the sandbags into our own territory he was again the devil-may-care, happy-go-lucky fellow depicted in his book.

I well remember one occasion when a number of newly-joined men were creating a disturbance in an estaminet. Maxwell was the orderly sergeant. They had heard of Maxwell and were ready to try conclusions with him. Without enlightening the sergeant, I instructed him to proceed to the estaminet to see whether he could induce the noisy ones to depart without the necessity of calling out the picket. Then I stood afar off to witness developments. Maxwell's quietly voiced request for all to leave the estaminet was greeted with derisive laughter. One asked the sergeant's name, and immediately led an attack upon him. Then there was one of the finest scraps it has ever been my lot to witness. Within a few minutes, five of the burliest were sorrowfully making their way from the middle of the adjacent midden. The remainder evacuated the estaminet without any further instructions. Sergeant Maxwell reported to me at orderly room some few minutes later that the disturbance had ceased. To my query as to whether any opposition had been offered to his orders he replied: *Oh, nothing much.*'

Joe worked in a variety of occupations in and around Sydney, Canberra and in the Moree and Maitland districts, mainly as a gardener, including with the Department of the Interior, Canberra in late 1930, and at some time for his sister, Myra, at one of her nursing homes in Manly. While there he lived at 8 Fairlight Street. He was later described as a journalist. He spent much of his time working for the Returned Services League and the Australian branch of the VC & GC Association. He was an active member of the Paddington-Woollahra and Malabar sub-branches of the Returned Sailors' and Soldiers' Imperial League of Australia. He lived at numerous addresses including:

June 1937 – c/o Mrs J Scott, Boston Street, Moree.
December 1937 – c/o Mrs E Callaghan, 6 Lyell Street, Cessnock.
July 1938 – c/o John O'Reilly at the hotel in Bradfordville near Goulburn.
November 1939 – 12 Yabsley Avenue, Marrickville.
March 1941 – Moss Vale, NSW.
May 1941 – Hillview via Liverpool.

On 11th November 1919 he was one of twenty-two VCs who attended a dinner at the Hotel Australia, Castlereagh Street, Sydney, provided by Hugh Donald McIntosh MLC of the New South Wales Legislative Council, in whose home Maxwell married in 1921. Joe joined thirteen other VCs of Irish descent to form a mounted guard of honour on grey horses to escort Daniel Patrick Mannix, Catholic Archbishop of Melbourne, who was leading the St Patrick's Day parade in Melbourne in an open car on 20th March 1920. The other VCs were – Thomas Axford, Maurice Buckley, John Carroll, George Cartwright, William Currey, John Dwyer, John Hamilton, George Howell, William Jackson, Lawrence McCarthy, Walter Peeler, John Ryan and John Whittle. He was one of ten VCs presented to the Prince of Wales at Farm Cove, Sydney, NSW on 7th June 1920. The other VCs were – Albert Borella, Walter Brown, George Cartwright, William Currey, John Hamilton, George Howell, Bede Kenny, Percy Storkey and Blair Wark.

Joe married Mabel 'Mae' Maxwell (1901–23rd December 1982), his cousin, a tailoress born at Newtown, NSW, on 14th February 1921 at Belhaven, 85 Victoria Road, Bellevue Hill, Sydney. Lieutenant Percy Storkey VC was the best man. Joe was living at Calvert Street near Marrickville railway station and Mae at Illawarra Road. Belhaven was owned by wealthy entrepreneur Hugh Donald McIntosh MLC. Harry Murray VC CMG DSO & Bar spent his honeymoon there. Murray was the most decorated Australian of the Great War and Joe Maxwell was the second. Details of the family appear above under Joe's uncle, Joseph Maxwell (1876–1907). Mae and Joe had a daughter:

- Jean Alma Maxwell (14th February 1922–3rd February 2008), married Raymond Edward Willett (3rd May 1925–13th February 1987), an electrical fitter born at Dubbo, NSW, in 1949 at Marrickville. Raymond enlisted in the Royal Australian Air Force on 28th April 1944 at Sydney (163262). He was discharged as a leading aircraftman from No.8 Operational Training Unit on 6th March 1946. They lived at various times at 9a Queens Avenue, Darlinghurst, NSW, at 78 Birriga Road, Bellevue Hill, NSW, at 25 Queen Street, Marrickville, NSW, and at 5a Beaconsfield Street, Revesby, NSW. He died at Budgewoi, NSW and she at Toukley, NSW. They had two sons – Gary Raymond Willett and John Gregory Willett.

Mae petitioned for divorce and the marriage was dissolved on 28th May 1925. Joe was ordered to provide financial support for Mae and Jean, who moved in with her parents at Marrickville. Joe moved to Lake Macquarie, NSW to live with his mother and brother, Aubrey. He failed to support Mae and Jean and a commitment warrant for £108/12/- was issued against him by the Children's Court Bench in June 1930. He was described as, '5′7″ tall, medium build, dark complexion and hair, clean shaven, usually dressed in a dark suit, grey felt hat and black boots, a journalist, a returned soldier, who was said to have gone to Queensland'. A magisterial order for the support of his wife (£22/8/- costs) was also issued and Joe was arrested by Detective Sergeant Keeble and Constables Haigh, Beveridge, Oldfield and Sharpe of the Sydney Police in August 1930. The charge was withdrawn but he was recharged with neglecting to pay the sum of £40/8/- and he was committed to Long Bay State Penitentiary until the order was complied with. A wartime comrade promised to pay the money owing to secure Joe's release.

Mae married Bertram Fraser, a carpenter, in 1929 at Sydney. They were living at 24 Calvert Place, Marrickville in 1930. The marriage ended in divorce and Bertram was living at 10 West Street, Crow's Nest, NSW in 1963. They had a son:

- Keith 'Mick' Bertram Fraser (died 1973) was a labourer in 1954, living with his mother and stepfather at 43 Kitchener Avenue, Earlwood. He married Nell Marie Saeter (7th October 1934–28th May 2007), a typist, on 1st December 1957. She was the daughter of Arne Johan Saeter (1902–74), born at Kristiansand, Norway and Marie Stella McDonnell-Kelly (1907–84) born at Tewkesbury, Gloucestershire, England. Keith was a barman in 1958, when they were living with her parents at 28 Water Street, Enfield. They are understood to have had a child but the marriage broke down later.

Mae married Frederick Charles Parker (died 1973) in 1940. He was a waiter in 1943, when they were living at 4 Spark Street, Earlwood. By 1954 he was a steward and they were living at 43 Kitchener Avenue, Earlwood. Mabel was still living there in 1980.

Joe was one of eleven VCs presented to the Duke of York (later King George VI), at Government House, Sydney on 26th March 1927. The others were Walter Brown, George Cartwright, Henry Dalziel, John Hamilton, George Howell, William Jackson, Bede Kenny, Percy Storkey, Blair Wark (in charge) and John Whittle.

Joe was described as a bachelor when he married Annie Ena Zoe Robinson (c.1907–1960), a nurse born at Dulwich Hill, NSW, on 1st December 1928 at St Clement's Church, Marrickville. The marriage ended in divorce in December 1937 on the grounds of desertion. Annie was living alone at 20 Shaw Street, Newington, NSW in 1933 and 1935. She married Victor James Rupert Woods (1907–81), born at Sunbury, Victoria, in 1941 at Marrickville. He was a striker and she was a nurse in 1943, when they were living at 34 Wardell Road, Lewisham, NSW. By 1972 Victor was a machinist and was still living at 34 Wardell Street in 1980.

St Clement's Church, where Joe married Annie Robinson in December 1928. The foundation stone was laid on 13th January 1883 (Trevor Bunning).

In November 1929 Joe was entertained at a luncheon at Government House by the Governor of New South Wales, Sir Dudley de Chair, together with thirteen other VCs – George Cartwright, William Currey, Arthur Evans, John Hamilton, George Howell, William Jackson, Bede Kenny, James Newland, John Ryan, Percy Storkey, Arthur Sullivan, Blair Wark and John Whittle. Joe published the book, *Hell's Bells and Mademoiselles* in 1932 in collaboration with reporter Hugh Buggy, who encouraged him and provided literary assistance. Buggy worked for the Sydney *Sun* and Joe occasionally wrote pieces for the paper about the war years. He also wrote for *Reveille*, *Sydney Morning Herald*, *Cairns Post* and others but the income from these articles was insufficient to sustain him. Buggy was General Douglas MacArthur's HQ chief operational censor 1942–44. The first edition of 10,000 copies of *Hell's Bells and Mademoiselles* sold out and negotiations took place for the sale of the American rights. There were at least six editions of the book, such was its popularity. Maxwell wrote a sequel, *From the Hindenburg Line to the Bread Line*, which was completed in the late 1930s by when the boom in war books had come to an end. The publisher decided not to proceed with it.

The cover of *Hell's Bells and Mademoiselles*.

In late 1932, Joe underwent a major operation on a kidney and convalesced at Glebe House (a boarding house for unmarried adults), Reid, Canberra. In 1933 he was a defence character witness in the trial of one of his former soldiers, Alfred Jamieson, who was accused of housebreaking. In November 1936 he was being treated as a mental patient for alcoholism and depression at Kenmore Hospital, Goulburn. In December 1938, Joe applied for a duplicate certificate of service, as another man had applied for a copy to impersonate him. His address at the time was still Kenmore Hospital. The certificate was issued. The other man appears to have been issued with the replacement certificate in January 1937 and was living at 46 Hutchinson Street, Surry Hills, Sydney. In August 1939 Joe was in the Prince of Wales Hospital, Randwick for extensive treatment. That November he requested another discharge certificate, as he had lost the replacement issued the previous year. He claimed he was too old to enlist in the AIF and was averse to *playing at soldiers in a garrison unit*. He intended going abroad to see if he could *wangle his way into an active service unit*. His address at the time was 12 Yabsley Avenue, Marrickville, NSW.

Joe made several attempts to re-enlist during the Second World War. He eventually went to Queensland to enlist as a private at Warwick on 27th June 1940, under the assumed name of Joseph Wells (QX11054). He gave his date of birth as 10th February 1904, his trade as a cook and listed his mother, Elizabeth Wells, St Kilda Road, Melbourne, Victoria as his next of kin. He was posted to 7th Australian Division Cavalry Regiment at Redbank, Queensland and was assigned duties in the cookhouse. He was transferred to 6th Infantry Training Battalion at the same location. On 13th July he was interviewed on national radio but declined to give his assumed name. Joe committed a series of offences:

Absent from 8.30 a.m. on 15th July to 4.00 p.m. on 16th July – confined to barracks for five days and forfeited two days' pay.

Absent from 2.00 p.m. on 17th July until 7.00 a.m. on 23rd July, losing by neglect articles issued to him valued at £3/10/3 – in detention for fourteen days and his pay was deducted to replace the lost items.

Wilful defiance of authority on 30th August – admonished.

Wilful defiance of authority on 2nd September – fined 20/-.

Absent from 3.15 p.m. to 10.00 p.m. on 2nd September – fined 10/-.

Drunkeness in Brisbane on 3rd September – , fined £3/10/-.

Joe was discharged from the Army on 19th September 1940 being 'unlikely to become an efficient soldier'. There is no evidence in his service record to indicate that his true identity was ever known to the authorities. In May 1941 he again requested a discharge certificate as he was having difficulty securing employment without one. He was living c/o J Raine, Hillview, via Liverpool, NSW at the time. That October he was in the Sanitorium, Waterfall with a lung problem. In 1943 he was working for Ansett Airways, which had been taken over by the Americans. In April 1949 he was set upon by three British sailors and a civilian in Hamilton Street, Sydney. An off duty plain clothes policeman came to his aid but he too was knocked down and beaten up. The attackers made off with Constable John Bywater's .32 pistol and handcuffs. Soon afterwards Bywater, with Detectives J Davis and M Kelly, arrested two of the naval ratings in Luna Park.

Joe married Anne 'Annie' Martin née Burton (12th November 1899–10th February 1981), born at Burton-upon-Trent, Staffordshire, England, on 6th March 1956 at the Registrar-General's Office, Sydney. She was also known as Nancy. She was working for Joe's sister, Myra, when they met. They were living at 17 Sir Thomas Mitchell Road, Bondi Beach, NSW in 1958 before moving to 12 Messines Crescent, Matraville, NSW by 1963. Annie was residing at Maroubra Junction Nursing Home,

Sydney in December 1979. She died at Malabar Heights, NSW.

Anne had married James William Martin (15th December 1891–23rd July 1951), also born at Burton-upon-Trent, in 1920 at Mosman, NSW. He was a bottler in an ale store in 1911, living with his parents at 13 St Paul's Street West, Burton-upon-Trent, and emigrated to Sydney, NSW aboard the *Nakool*, arriving on 19th October 1912. James enlisted in the Australian Light Horse Reserve AIF on 16th January 1915 at Liverpool Depot, NSW (566). He was described as a labourer, 5′ 4¼″ tall, weighing 127 lbs, with fair complexion, blue eyes, dark brown hair and his religious denomination was Church of England. He was assigned to 12th Australian Light Horse Regiment on 1st March and embarked at Sydney aboard HMAT A29 *Suevic* on 13th June. He transferred to D Squadron, 6th Australian Light Horse and sailed for Gallipoli from Alexandria, Egypt aboard HMT *Marquette*, arriving at Anzac Cove on 29th August. James returned to Alexandria aboard HMAT A72 *Beltana*, disembarking on 25th December. He transferred to 12th Australian Light Horse as a driver and joined at Oasis Camp, Heliopolis from Maadi on 22nd February 1916, moving to Tel-el-Kebir on 26th April. He was sent to the Rest Camp at Port Said 28th August–7th September 1917, then rejoined his unit. He was at Dump Shaluf, Belah 20th-23rd February 1918, then rejoined his unit. On 2nd November he was taken ill and was treated at 31st General Hospital, Abbassia 14th-22nd November and the Convalescent Depot, Boulaq until 2nd December. He was transferred to the Rest Camp, Port Said, where he was diagnosed with venereal disease on 19th December. He was treated at V Block Ward, No.2 Australian Stationary Hospital, Moascar Garrison 26th December–9th February 1919. James returned to his unit on 7th March and transferred to Details Camp on 25th March. James embarked aboard SS *Caledonia* at Port Said for Britain on 12th April. He returned to Australia aboard SS *Prinz Ludwig* on 9th July and was discharged at Sydney on 8th October 1919. James also enlisted on 15th June 1940 at Earlwood, NSW (N72664). He was discharged as a lance corporal on 30th March 1944 from 11th Australian Garrison Battalion. Anne and James were living at 21 Campbell Parade, Bondi Beach, NSW in June 1946. He died suddenly at 17 Sir Thomas Mitchell Road, Bondi Beach. Anne and James had six children:

Completed in 1913, the architecture of the Registrar General's building mirrored St Mary's Cathedral opposite. It was extended in 1930.

- George Walter Martin (5th January 1922–19th May 2004), born at Yenda, NSW, enlisted in the Australian Army on 8th October 1941 at Kingsford, NSW

(NX114127 & N228087). He was discharged as a corporal on 17th May 1944 from 1/45th Australian Infantry Battalion. He enlisted next day in the Royal Australian Air Force at Sydney, NSW (445119) and was discharged as a leading aircraftman on 24th July 1945 from 5th Aircraft Depot, Forest Hill, NSW. He married Mavis Morgan (9th October 1923–25th April 2005), born at Sydney, NSW, in 1944 at Randwick, NSW. He died at Canberra, ACT and she died in NSW.
- Marion Dorothy 'Dot' Martin (31st October 1926–15th July 1979), born at Kensington, NSW, married Reginald 'Reg' Arthur McGregor (5th March 1922–2012), born at Casino, NSW, on 8th April 1944 at Waverley, NSW. He enlisted in the Australian Army on 3rd April 1945 at Bondi Beach (NX206506) and was discharged on 16th July 1946 from 2/167th Transport Company. They were living at Oak Flats, Macarthur, NSW in 1963 and at Pagewood, Kingsford-Smith, NSW in 1977. They had two sons and two daughters.
- Michael 'Mick' James Martin (born 27th November 1926), born at Yenda, enlisted in the Australian Army on 16th January 1945 at Bondi Beach (NX205577) and was discharged on 10th November 1948 from HQ Eastern Command. He is understood to have married Margaret 'Peg' Angela Judge at Burwood, NSW in 1945. They were living at 37 Grey Street, Griffith, NSW in 1972, when he was an assistant manager.
- Philip J Martin (born and died 1935).
- William 'Bill' Martin (born c.1938) married Joy.
- Elizabeth Martin (1941–42).

Anne's father, Walter Burton (25th October 1876–30th November 1917), born at Burton-upon-Trent, Staffordshire, England, was living with his parents at 191 Waterloo Street there in 1881. He was employed as a labourer by the brewers, Messrs Bass & Co. He enlisted in 2nd Volunteer Battalion, North Staffordshire Regiment in 1894 and served during the Second Boer War in South Africa 1899–1902. Walter married Sarah née Gall (c.1879–1976), born at Marple, near Stockport, Cheshire, at St Paul's Church, Burton-upon-Trent in 1899, She was living with her father and siblings at 9 Morris's Cottages, Victoria Street, Horninglow, Burton-upon-Trent, Staffordshire in 1891 and at 12 Rosliston Road, Stapenhill, Staffordshire in 1901. Anne and Walter were living at 7 Ferry Street, Stapenhill, Burton-upon-Trent in 1911. He was mobilised in August 1914 with 6th North Staffordshire (567 & 240031) and was involved in suppressing the Easter Rising in Ireland in April 1916. He was promoted sergeant and went to France in February 1917. Walter was killed in action and was buried in Bourlon Wood but his remains were not recovered post-war (Cambrai Memorial). He was awarded the Queen's South Africa Medal 1899–1902 with three clasps, 1914–15 Star, British War Medal 1914–20, Victory Medal 1914–19, Army Long Service & Good Conduct Medal and Territorial Force Efficiency Medal. Sarah was living at 10 Spring Terrace Road, Stapenhill in 1927.

She emigrated to Sydney, NSW with her children aboard SS *Bendigo*, departing London on 28th April 1927, to join her daughter, Anne. In addition to Anne, Sarah and Walter had four other children, all born at Burton-upon-Trent:

- Philip Burton (born 21st December 1900) was a clerk in 1927. He married Edna M Hickey in 1934 at Petersham, NSW. He enlisted in the Australian Army on 9th March 1942 at Bankstown, NSW (N390493) and was discharged as a sergeant on 6th November 1945 from 5th Advanced Base Ordnance Depot.
- Mabel Burton (12th April 1906–1946) was a clerk shop assistant in 1927. She married Jesse Edwin Stephen Carter (born 25th December 1906), a battery process worker born at Herne Bay, Kent, England on 30th September 1932 at All Souls Church, Leichhardt, NSW. Jesse was a clerk when he enlisted in the Australian Army on 25th September 1942 at Bronte, NSW (NX116071 & N273152). He was discharged as a staff sergeant on 2nd November 1945 from Sydney Area Workshop, Australian Electrical and Mechanical Engineers. They were living at 70 Hewlett Street, Waverley in 1943. They had a son. Jesse married Marion Fettes (2nd June 1911–11th July 2007), born at Clydebank, Dunbartonshire, Scotland, in 1960 at Sydney. She emigrated from Glasgow, Lanarkshire on 27th February 1948 aboard SS *Ormonde*, giving her address as 62 Fleet Street, Carlton, Sydney. She was a corsetiere in 1958, living at 54 Bridge Street, King, West Sydney. They were living at 43 Gwendale Crescent, Eastwood, Parramatta, NSW in 1963 and at 26 Bourne Gardens, Canberra, ACT in 1980. They reportedly had a son.
- Edith Ann Burton (born and died 1902).
- Norman Frederick Burton (17th May 1917–1987) enlisted in the Australian Army on 24th January 1941 at Haberfield, NSW (N102858) and was discharged as a lance corporal on 27th April 1945 from 15th Australian Camp Hospital.

Joe attended the VC Centenary Celebrations at Hyde Park, London on 26th June 1956. He travelled aboard SS *Arcadia* with his wife, part of the 301 Victoria Cross recipients from across the Commonwealth to attend. Joe also visited France and Belgium on this trip. He was present at the official opening of VC Corner at the

SS *Arcadia*, a P&O passenger liner was built by John Brown & Co at Clydebank, Scotland and was launched on 14th May 1953. She was employed on the Britain to Australia route and also operated as a cruise ship. In February 1979 she was delivered to Taiwan to be scrapped. A ship of the same name featured in the 2023 TV series, *Ten Pound Poms*.

Joe Maxwell, on the left, with John Hamilton VC at the grave of Lewis McGee VC in Tyne Cot Cemetery, Passchendaele, Belgium (Australian War Memorial).

Lord De L'Isle. William Philip Sidney, 1st Viscount De L'Isle VC GCVO KG GCMG KStJ PC (1909–91), served as a British Army officer and politician. He was the fifteenth Governor-General of Australia 1961–65, the last non-Australian to hold the office and the last to wear the traditional viceregal uniform. He was educated at Eton College and Magdalene College, Cambridge before becoming a chartered accountant. He served in the TA and during the Second World War in the Grenadier Guards in France and Italy. He was awarded the VC in 1944 for his actions at Anzio. He became a Conservative MP. When he succeeded his father as Baron De L'Isle and Dudley, he was elevated to the House of Lords. He was Secretary of State for Air 1951–55 in Winston Churchill's government.

Australian War Memorial by the Governor General, Lord De L'Isle VC, in 1964 with seventeen other Australian VC's.

Joe submitted a statutory declaration on 17th October 1960, while living at 17 Sir Thomas Mitchell Road, Bondi Beach, NSW, stating that he had enlisted under the name of Joseph Wells (QX11054) and served as a trooper in 7th Division Cavalry. He claimed that he had lost his discharge certificate. In January 1962 he again applied for a discharge certificate, in order to join the local Returned Soldiers' Servicemens' Club (sic). He was living at 12 Messines Crescent, Matraville, NSW at the time. A basic resume of his service was issued by Central Army Records Office, Albert Park Barracks, Melbourne, Victoria in February, as it was not possible to provide another Certificate of Discharge under Army Regulations. In 1964 Joe appeared in the BBC's groundbreaking series *The Great War*.

Joe collapsed in a street in Matraville, Sydney and died of a heart attack on 6th July 1967. His funeral, with full military honours, was held at St Matthias Anglican Church, on the corner of Oxford Street and Moore Park Road, Paddington, NSW. He was cremated at Eastern Suburbs Crematorium, Botany, Sydney and his ashes were scattered in the Garden of Remembrance, with a plaque on Panel G, Niche 209. He is commemorated in a number of other places:

St Matthias Anglican Church, Paddington, where Joe's funeral was held in July 1967.

The memorial plaque at Eastern Suburbs Crematorium, Botany, Sydney (Memorials to Valour).

- New South Wales
  - The Maxwell VC Club, Holsworthy Barracks, opened by the Minister for Defence, Allen Fairhall, on 27th October 1967.
  - Maxwell Building, Macarthur Drive, Holsworthy Barracks, which houses a military bank.
  - Joseph Maxwell VC Park, Gillieston Heights, Maitland.
  - Victoria Cross Memorial, Queen Victoria Building, George Street, Sydney dedicated on 23rd February 1992 to commemorate the visit of Queen Elizabeth II and Prince Phillip on the occasion of the Sesquicentenary of the City of Sydney. Sir Roden Cutler VC AK KCMG, Edward Kenna VC and Keith Payne VC were in attendance.
  - Victoria Cross Recipients Wall, North Bondi War Memorial donated to Waverley on 27th November 2011 by The Returned & Services League of Australia.
  - Victoria Cross Memorial, Peards Complex, East Albury.
  - Victoria Cross Memorial Wall, Ingleburn RSL, Liverpool, Sydney.
  - Memorial in the public gardens of Matraville Soldiers' Settlement Estate.
  - Named on two rolls of honour in the vestibule of Maitland RSL Sub-Branch, Bulwer Street, Maitland from Hexham Workshop Employees and South Maitland and District Church of England Parish.
- Australian Capital Territory
  - Australian Victoria Cross Recipients plaque on the Victoria Cross Memorial, Campbell, dedicated on 24th July 2000.
  - Named on one of eleven plaques honouring 175 men from overseas awarded the VC for the Great War. The plaques were unveiled by the Senior Minister of State at the Foreign & Commonwealth Office and Minister for Faith and Communities, Baroness Warsi, at a reception at Lancaster House, London on 26th June 2014 attended by The Duke of Kent and relatives of the VC recipients. The Australian plaque is at the Australian War Memorial, Canberra.

 - ◦ Commemorative display in the Hall of Valour at the Australian War Memorial, Canberra.
- Communities and Local Government commemorative paving stones for the 145 VCs born in Australia, Belgium, Canada, China, Denmark, Egypt, France, Germany, India, Iraq, Japan, Nepal, Netherlands, New Zealand, Newfoundland, Pakistan, South Africa, Sri Lanka, Ukraine and United States of America were unveiled at the National Memorial Arboretum, Alrewas, Staffordshire by Prime Minister David Cameron MP and Sergeant Johnson Beharry VC on 5th March 2015.

In addition to the VC, MC & Bar and DCM he was awarded the 1914–15 Star, British War Medal 1914–20, Victory Medal 1914–19, War Medal 1939–45, Australia Service Medal 1939–45, George VI Coronation Medal 1937 and Elizabeth II Coronation Medal 1953. He qualified for the War Medal 1939–45 and the Australia Service Medal 1939–45 due to his service under the assumed name of Joseph Wells. He appears not to have claimed those medals. His widow, Anne, loaned her husband's medals to Paddington Returned and Services League Club, 220–232 Oxford Street, Paddington, NSW towards the end of July 1967. On 27th October 1967 she loaned them to the Maxwell VC Club, Holsworthy Barracks, NSW. On 24th September 1979 she and her son, George Martin, donated the medals to the Army Museum, Victoria Barracks, Paddington. The VC group was presented to the Australian War Memorial on 2nd April 2003 on long term loan, at a ceremony attended by Joe's daughter, Jean Willett. The VC is displayed in the Hall of Valour at the Australian War Memorial, Treloar Crescent, Campbell, ACT. However, not all the medals displayed there are originals.

The Queen Elizabeth II Coronation Medal 1953 was awarded immediately after the coronation on 2nd June 1953 as a personal souvenir from the Queen to members of the Royal Family, selected officers of state, members of the Royal Household, government and local government officials, mayors, public servants, members of the armed forces and police in Britain, the colonies and Dominions. It was also awarded to members of the Mount Everest expedition, two of whom reached the summit for the first time four days before the coronation. A total of 129,051 medals were awarded, including 11,561 to Australians.

In January 1928, Joe applied for a replacement VC, but no further action seems to have been taken. He claimed again in June 1934, when he also requested replacements for the campaign medal trio, which was available at a cost of £0/15/10. His address at the time was c/o The Sun Office, PO Box 2728, Sydney. Coincidentally Joe reportedly sold the MC & Bar and DCM to Sir William Dixson (1870–1952) in 1934. The Dixson Collection was bequeathed to the State Library of New South Wales in 1951. Joe applied again in October 1936, when his address was c/o Cummins & Wallace, Moree, NSW. He claimed that the war medals had been lost when a motor launch sank on Lake Macquarie in 1923. The other medals were lost a few years later in a house fire. The cost of replacing all six medals was quoted as £2/16/9 by the Department of Defence. Joe does not appear to have completed a statutory declaration and let the matter drop again. In September 1947 he again applied for replacement medals, while living at 8 Fairlight Street, Manly, NSW. He claimed five medals (MC & Bar, DCM and WWI trio) were lost in a boating accident on Lake Macquarie in 1927 (1923 in a previous claim). The VC and Coronation Medal were still in his possession, contrary to what he had claimed previously. The cost of replacements was quoted as £2/16/10 but a signed statutory declaration and form of undertaking were required before proceeding. He was advised that the campaign medals could be replaced immediately but the gallantry awards had to be dealt with by the War Office in London. The campaign medals were issued on 23rd January 1948 but no further action could be taken on the gallantry medals until he returned the signed forms. He returned the forms in March but they could not be acted upon as they had not been signed in the presence of a JP or commissioner for declarations. The forms were eventually signed on 10th April and the duplicate medals arrived from London in November 1948 at a cost of £2/3/-. As Joe had already paid £2/1/- for the medals he was requested to provide the extra £0/2/-. The replacement MC & Bar and DCM were issued on 18th January 1949. The MC was not engraved, as was the practice at that time. The current location of the various medals is understood to be:

- The Australian War Memorial group consists of the original VC and George VI and Elizabeth II Coronation Medals. The MC & Bar, DCM, 1914–15 Star, British War Medal and Victory Medal are the official replacements issued in 1948/49.
- The Dixson Library holds the original MC & Bar and DCM.
- Maryborough Military and Colonial Museum, Queensland has the original British War Medal, which was loaned by Warwick Cary ESM in 2009. It had been purchased by Michael Downey, with about twenty-five other medals, at a Sotheby's auction in London on 18th December 1990.
- The locations of the original 1914–15 Star and Victory Medal are not known.

422047 CORPORAL JAMES BRENNAN McPHIE
416th (Edinburgh) Field Company, Royal Engineers

James McPhie was born on 18th December 1894 at 21 Salisbury Place, Rose Street, Edinburgh, Midlothian, Scotland. His father, Allan McPhie (c.1848–4th September 1903), born at Canongate, Edinburgh, was an apprentice heraldic painter in 1861 and later a robber comb maker, living at 118 West Port, Edinburgh. He married Mary Barclay (c.1850–11th July 1886), a machine printer born at Edinburgh, on

25th March 1867 at 118 West Port. She was living at 4 Bruntsfield Place, Edinburgh. By 1881 Allan was a commercial clerk and they were living at 19 Fleshmarket Close, Edinburgh. Mary died at 10 South College Street, Edinburgh. By then Allan was a billiard room proprietor, living with his family at 56 Lothian Street, Edinburgh. He married Elizabeth née Brennan (c.1862–18th June 1932), born at Methil, Fife, on 11th January 1889 at 56 Lothian Street. Allan became a turf commission agent. They were living at 21 Salisbury Street, St Leonards, Edinburgh in 1901, where Allan subsequently died. By 1911 Elizabeth was an office cleaner, living at 112 Rose Street, Edinburgh. She died at 27 Rose Street. James had eleven siblings from his father's two marriages:

- Ann 'Annie' Barclay McPhie (6th May 1867–15th May 1909), born at 118 West Port, Edinburgh, was living at 10 South College Street, Edinburgh when she married Charles Albert Henderson (9th December 1861–1932), a clerk born at Newington, Edinburgh, on 26th February 1885 at 3 North St David Street, Edinburgh. By 1889 he was a shipping agent and they were living at 2 Dublin Lane Street, Edinburgh. They were living at 55 Albert Street, Leith in 1891 and at 6 Wardlaw Place, Edinburgh in 1901. By 1909 he was a shipping agent. Ann died at 9 Wardlaw Street, Edinburgh. Charles' death was registered at George Square, Edinburgh. They had eight children:

Rose Street runs parallel with and between Princes and George Streets in Edinburgh. It was built between 1770 and 1781 and was named Rose to represent England in a consciously unionist paring with Thistle Street representing Scotland. In 1789 Miss Margaret Burns moved into Rose Street and there were complaints that she kept, *...a very irregular and disorderly house*, and was threatened with jail. Robert Burns wrote a poem, *Under the portrait of Miss Burns*:

Cease, ye prudes, your envious railings,
Lovely Burns has charms: confess!
True it is that she had one failing:
Had a woman ever less.

Originally built as three-storey housing, by 1820 Rose Street was also a shopping street at ground level. In 1824 one of the first fire stations in the country was set up at No.66. In 1830 McVitie's opened at No.129, which later became the biscuit manufacturers famous for inventing the digestive. In the 19th century the street gained a bad reputation and was not a place for the respectable to be seen after dark. By the middle of the 20th century it was almost completely in use for shops and bars. In the 1950s and 60s Rose Street was known as the haunt of a new wave of Scottish poets. The street was pedestrianised, beginning in 1973. Because of the many drinking establishments, it is still known for the Rose Street Challenge.

Canongate, Edinburgh, where James' father was born.

West Port, Edinburgh.

- Allan McPhie Henderson (13th June 1885–7th May 1958), born at Riego Street, Edinburgh, married Elizabeth Maxwell Wilson (23rd May 1884–9th December 1960), born at 26 Simon Square, Edinburgh, on 17th July 1908 at 9 Wardlaw Street, Edinburgh. They both died at 4 Buller Street, Lochgelly, Fife. They had seven children – Ann McPhie Henderson 1908, James Wilson Henderson 1910, Elizabeth Maxwell Henderson 1913, Helen Murray Henderson 1914, Isabella Sharp Henderson 1917, Allan McPhie Henderson 1919 and John Layden Henderson 1922.
- Jessie McPhie Henderson (born 1887).
- Helen Henderson (born c.1889).
- John Henderson (born c.1891).
- Ada Henderson (born c.1893).
- Annie Henderson (born c.1895).
- Isabella Henderson (born c.1897).
- Agnes Barclay Henderson (born 1900).

Fleshmarket Close was named after the meat market which was situated there. It is the title of Ian Rankin's bestselling book in the *Rebus* series.

- Jessie McPhie (6th April 1870–12th May 1897) married William Ritchie, a commercial clerk, at St Giles, Edinburgh in 1887. She died at 14 Glen Street, Edinburgh.
- Allan Gordon McPhie (10th February 1873–15th November 1918), was a rubber worker, living at 190 Gorgie Road, Edinburgh. He died unmarried at the Royal Asylum, Edinburgh.

- Isabella Davie McPhie (born 3rd November 1874), born at 19 Fleshmarket Close, Cockburn Street, Edinburgh, was living at 21 Salisbury Place, Edinburgh, when she married James Rankine (born 1874), an engine fitter, on 25th April 1896 at 11 Marchall Crescent, Edinburgh.
- David McPhie (3rd April 1877–4th May 1902), born at 19 Fleshmarket Close, Cockburn Street, Edinburgh, was a hairdresser, living at Abbeyhill, Edinburgh. He married Jessie Gourlay Robertson (born 7th December 1867), a laundress born at St Giles, Edinburgh, on 9th October 1896 at All Saints Episcopal Church, Broughton Street, Edinburgh. Jessie was a bookkeeper in 1891, living with her uncle, William Dunlop, at 7 Ponton Street, Edinburgh. David and Jessie were living at 10 Nicholson Street, Edinburgh in 1901. David died at 17 Drummond Street, Edinburgh. They had four children:
    - Elizabeth Black McPhie (18th May 1897–1908), born at 10 Nicholson Street, Edinburgh.
    - Mary Barclay McPhie (16th May 1898–1898).
    - Alan McPhie (23rd December 1899–1995) married Sarah Louisa Koerber (1898–1986) in 1924 at Canongate, Midlothian.
    - Agnes Fleming Barclay McPhie (31st December 1901–1902), born at 17 Duncan Street, Edinburgh.
- William Ross McPhie (6th October 1880–24th October 1950) was a spirit merchant's assistant and later a general labourer, living at Whitefoord House, 44 Colinton Road, Edinburgh. He died unmarried at the Royal Infirmary Edinburgh.
- Adam Ferguson McPhie (10th June 1883–7th May 1905), born at 10 South College Street, Edinburgh, was an apprentice cycle maker, living at 14 Glen Street, Edinburgh. He died there unmarried.
- Agnes McPhie (6th December 1885–1888).
- Mary 'May' Ann McPhie (born 14th January 1893), born at 21 Salisbury Place, Edinburgh, married George Wilson Mein (born 1888), a bottle merchant, on 26th October 1909 at 47 George IV Bridge, Edinburgh. She was an office cleaner in 1911, living with her mother at 112 Rose Street, Edinburgh. George served as a corporal in the Seaforth Highlanders (S/17351) during the Great War. They had at least one son:
    - Philip McPhie Mein (21st December 1909–21st July 1915) born at 112 Rose Street, Edinburgh and died at City Hospital, Edinburgh.
- John Brennan McPhie (3rd December 1896–17th April 1977), born at 21 Salisbury Place, Edinburgh, was a message boy in 1911 living with his mother. He enlisted in 416th (Edinburgh) Field Company, Royal Engineers (422086) and served as a lance corporal. He helped to bury his older brother, James, on 15th October 1918. John married Janet McGillivray MacLean (1902–2nd October 1978), a clerk born at St Andrew, Edinburgh, on 20th September 1924 at St George's Parish Church, Edinburgh. She was living at 9 Bellevue Terrace, Edinburgh. John was a blacksmith, living at Meadowpark, Haddington, East Lothian. John

later became an assurance manager and was living at 6 Dobbie's View, Bonnyrigg, Midlothian. He died at the City Hospital, Edinburgh and Janet at the Western General Hospital, Edinburgh. They had three children:

- Iris McPhie (2nd September 1925–1st February 2007), born at Meadowpark, Haddington, was a registered nurse when she married Alexander Younger McKay (5th February 1913–23rd January 1985), a clerk, on 27th November 1975 at the Registry Office, Haymarket, Edinburgh. They were living at 57 Laburnum Road, Whitburn, West Lothian at the time of his death at Bangour Hospital, Broxburn, West Lothian. Iris died at St John's Hospital, Livingston, West Lothian. Alexander had married Jane Thom Crook Campbell (1909–53), at Dalziel, where she was born, in 1944.
- Allan Donald McPhie (30th August 1928–1981) was a wages clerk, living at 24 of 6 Dobbie's Road, Bonnyrigg, when he married Pamela Gardiner (born c.1935), a drapery assistant living at Tenth Street, Newtongrange, Midlothian, on 4th July 1953 at Strathesk Church, Lasswade, Midlothian.
- Sheila McPhie.

• Elizabeth Brennan McPhie (2nd September 1899–8th July 1995) emigrated to Edmonton, Alberta, Canada, where she married Fred Missingchuk/Misingchuk (22nd December 1897–1st April 1988), born in Saskatchewan. He was a farmer at Theodore, Saskatchewan when he enlisted in 188th Overseas Battalion CEF at Yorkton, Saskatchewan on 10th March 1916 (887474). He was described as 5′ 6″ tall, weighing 140 lbs, with dark complexion, grey eyes, brown hair and his religious denomination was Church of England. He transferred to 144th Battalion, Camp Hughes on 6th July but was identified as an enemy alien (Ukrainian) and discharged on 15th August. He re-enlisted in 251st Overseas Battalion at Winnipeg, Manitoba (1084146) on 23rd October, by when he had grown an inch and his religious denomination had changed to Roman Catholic. Fred sailed from Halifax, Nova Scotia aboard SS *Metagama* on 4th October 1917 and disembarked at Liverpool on 17th October. He transferred to 18th Reserve Battalion, Dibgate, St Martin's Plain, Folkestone, Kent next day and joined on 24th October. He was admitted to 11th Canadian General Hospital, Moore Barracks, Shorncliffe, Kent 31st October–26th November. He transferred to the Canadian Forestry Corps and joined the Base Depot CFC, Sunningdale, Berkshire on 3rd December and was posted to 52 District, 133 Company, Carlisle, Cumberland on 17th December. Fred was granted a good conduct stripe on 23rd October 1918 and was on leave 20th-28th December. On 31st March 1919 he was posted to 131 Company and on 27th May was struck off strength to Base Depot CFC, Sunningdale. He was struck off strength to P Wing, Canadian Concentration Camp, Witley, Surrey on 15th June. A discharge medical there on 18th June found him fit. He had grown another inch to 5′ 8″ and weighed 150 lbs. He sailed aboard HMT *Mauretania* from Southampton on 28th June, He was struck off strength Overseas Military Forces of Canada and taken on strength CEF Dispersal Station M, Military

District No.10 the same day. Fred was demobilised at Winnipeg on 8th July 1919. He was awarded the British War Medal. He is believed to have served in the CFC again, rising to company sergeant major (M15561). Elizabeth returned to Edinburgh briefly and was living at 5 Forth Street, Broughton in 1945. Fred was a labourer in 1963, when they were living at 12015 93rd Street, Edmonton. They both died at Edmonton.

James' paternal grandmother was living on Lauriston Street, Edinburgh in 1871.

James' paternal grandfather, Allan McPhie (c.1825–12th January 1864), born at St Giles, Edinburgh, married Ann 'Annie' née Jamieson (c.1830–11th February 1886) at St Cuthbert's, Edinburgh on 22nd June 1847. James was a butcher in 1851, when they were living at 4 Gilmore Street, Edinburgh. They were living at 1 Ponton Street, Edinburgh in 1861. Annie was a dressmaker in 1871, when she was living with her children at 6 Lauriston Street, Edinburgh. She died at 42 Home Street, Edinburgh. In addition to Allan they had seven other children:

- Ann 'Annie' McPhie (c.1849–17th January 1917), born at Canongate, died unmarried.
- Robert McPhie (1851–13th July 1855).
- Margaret McPhie (1853–18th June 1855).
- Jessie McPhie (26th May 1856–9th June 1916) was a rubber worker in 1871, living with her mother. She married Alexander Dawson (born c.1849), a jeweller, on 1st November 1872 at 24 Rankeillor Street, Edinburgh.
- William McPhie (17th December 1860–19th October 1936), a butcher's assistant, born at 1 Ponton Street, Edinburgh, married Annie Ferrie (6th January 1864–1st June 1950), a card box maker, on 23rd December 1881 at 12 Granville Terrace, Edinburgh. They both died at Linlithgow, West Lothian. They had ten children:
    - Hugh McPhie (17th May 1882–3rd March 1966) is believed to have married Mary Wardlaw Baxter (1894–1970) registered at St Andrew, Edinburgh in 1925.
    - Allan McPhie (4th June 1884–16th June 1960).
    - Annie Jamieson McPhie (1st March 1887–4th November 1956) married James Wright at Falkirk in 1905.
    - James McIntyre McPhie (26th May 1889–6th August 1957).
    - Frances Ferrie McPhie (21st October 1891–21st August 1956) married William Shannly (1891–1954) registered at St Giles, Edinburgh in 1911. They are believed to have had six children – Annie McPhie Shannly 1911, Margaret McPhie Shannly 1917, Frances McPhie Shannly 1921, George

McPhie Shannly 1925 and twins Thomas McPhie and Jeanie Ferrie Shannly 1928.
  - William McPhie (5th April 1893–27th August 1980).
  - George Ferrie McPhie (9th September 1896–3rd February 1990).
  - David McPhie (11th February 1900–22nd November 1984).
  - Margaret McIntyre McPhie (10th February 1903–29th December 1953) is believed to have married Andrew Ross Lindsay in 1950 registered at Haymarket, Edinburgh.
  - Thomas Stalker McPhie (6th June 1907–13th July 1968) married Janet Gardner Lidster (1909–82) at Linlithgow in 1932. They are believed to have had six children – Allan McPhie 1932, Janet Gardner McPhie 1932, Hugh McPhie 1933, Thomas Stalker McPhie 1934, Jeanetta McPhie 1936 and Allan McPhie 1937.
- David Jamieson McPhie (19th December 1863–14th December 1906) born at 3 Grassmarket, Edinburgh and died at Dunfermline, Fife.
- Isabella Hepburn McPhie (born 4th July 1868).

James' maternal grandmother was born at Pittenweem, Fife. The oldest known struc is St Fillan's Cave, dating from the 7th century. An Augustinian priory was establi in the 13th century, but there was already church in existence. The settlement grew a fishing village along the sheltered beache Later breakwaters were built, allowing larg boats to anchor rather than being beached. Pittenweem became a royal burgh under K James V in 1541. In 1779 John Paul Jones, founder of the American Navy, anchored offshore and bombarded Anstruther, but n Pittenweem. Despite reductions in the her catch, Pittenweem remains an active fishin port. There were two coal mines and salt production was also an important industry Pittenweem's most famous MP was the Li Prime Minister HH Asquith 1886–1918.

His maternal grandfather, James Brennan (c.1831–24th October 1907), born at Glasgow, Lanarkshire, married Mary Ann née Rodger (c.1824–8th January 1892), a seamstress born at Pittenweem, Fife, on 17th February 1854 at Markinch, Fife. He was a china merchant in 1861, when they were living at Wemyss, Fife. By 1881 he was a railway labourer and they were living at Craigside House, Edinburgh. James died at 112 Rose Street, Edinburgh. Mary was living with her children at 10 Rowan Street, Stirling in 1871. She also died at 112 Rose Street, Edinburgh. In addition to Elizabeth they had three other children:

The earliest human activity around Markinch dates back to 3,000 BC. The earliest written reference is a charter of c.1050. The Industrial Revolution led to spinning and weaving production. Water powered mills on the River Leven allowed paper and bleach mills to flourish as well as ironworks. The Haig Whisky bottling plant operated there for over a century until 1983.

- Agnes Brennan (11th January 1855–7th September 1923), born at Methil, Fife, was a dressmaker in 1871. She was living at 112 Rose Street, Edinburgh when she died unmarried at the Royal Infirmary, Perth.
- Philip Brennan (16th December 1856–16th March 1933), born at Methil, was a blacksmith in 1871. He emigrated to New Zealand and married Margaret Stobie Cockburn (30th March 1864–9th June 1898), born in Scotland, on 20th August 1885 at Knox Church, Dunedin. She emigrated to Otago, New Zealand, departing London on 12th October 1882. Margaret died at Otago, following complications with the birth of her daughter, Margaret. Philip married Margaret Love Bennie (16th July 1872–June 1949), born at Anderston, Glasgow, Lanarkshire, Scotland, in 1901. He died at Auckland and she at Oamaru, Otago. Philip had five children from his first marriage:
    - Mary Ann Lea Brennan (19th July 1886–18th January 1956) married William Sam Wakelin (c.1872–1910) in 1905. They had four children – William Tom Wakelin 1906, Mary Wakelin 1908, Phillip Wakelin 1909 and Margaret Nell Wakelin 1911. Mary married Walter Roderick Bennett (1894–1956), born in New Zealand, in 1911. They are believed to have had two children – Walter Sydney Bennett 1915 and May Evelyn Bennett 1917.
    - James Stobie Brennan (23rd July 1888–19th February 1964).
    - Georgina Brennan (14th March 1891–20th January 1974).
    - Muriel Stobie Brennan (1897–1969) married George Bower in 1916.
    - Margaret Brennan (6th-8th June 1898).
- John Brennan (born c.1865), born at Stirling, was a hotel waiter in 1881.

James was educated at South Bridge School, Edinburgh and was an apprentice upholsterer in 1911. He joined the Territorial Force early in 1912, and served in City of Edinburgh (Fortress), Royal Engineers (1204 later 422047). On the outbreak of war the unit mobilised to its war stations in the Forth Defences. During 1915 it formed 1/1st Edinburgh Field Company RE in 69th Division and embarked at Devonport, Devon on 19th December 1915. The Company arrived at Port Said, Egypt on 3rd-5th January 1916 and served as Army Troops on the Suez Canal defences 10th January–12th April 1916. The unit embarked at Alexandria, Egypt on 17th April and arrived at Marseille, France on 24th April to join 56th Division. The unit was renamed 416th (Edinburgh) Field Company on 30th January 1917. **Awarded the VC for his actions at the Canal de la Sensée, near Aubencheul-au-Bac, France on 13th October 1918, LG 31st January 1919.**

South Bridge School opened in 1886 and is now a community learning and development centre, the South Bridge Resource Centre.

James was killed during his VC action on the Canal de la Sensée, near Aubencheul-au-Bac, France on

13th October 1918. He was buried in the chateau grounds at Aubencheul on 15th October and his remains were moved later to Naves Communal Cemetery Extension (II E 4). The posthumous VC was presented to his mother by the King in the ballroom at Buckingham Palace on 3rd April 1919. James is commemorated in a number of other places:

James McPhie's grave in Naves Communal Cemetery Extension.

- A seat purchased by members of his Company in 1961 in Prince's Street Gardens, Edinburgh.
- Display at the Royal Engineers Museum, Brompton Barracks, Chatham, Kent, where he is also named on the For Valour board.
- A Department for Communities and Local Government commemorative paving stone was dedicated at the junction of Pleasance and Brown Street, opposite West Richmond Street, Edinburgh on 12th October 2018.
- Named on The Ring of Remembrance (L'Anneau de la Mémoire or Ring of Memory) at Ablain-Saint-Nazaire, France, inaugurated on 11th November 2014, which commemorates the 576,606 soldiers of forty nationalities who died in Nord-Pas-de-Calais in the Great War.
- Named on a scroll by the Edinburgh Union of Upholsterers now held in the archives of the Royal Engineers Museum, Chatham, Kent.
- Named on a memorial at the former St George's Church, Charlotte Square, Edinburgh, which was taken over by the Ministry of Public Buildings and Works as West Register House. The memorial was moved to St Andrew's and St George's Church, George Street, Edinburgh.

The Royal Engineers Museum, Library and Archive is in the Ravelin Building, completed in 1905 and originally used as an electrical engineers' school. The Museum was established there in 1987 and the building is Grade II listed. The Museum holds forty-eight VCs, in addition to over half a million other items and archives.

In addition to the VC he was awarded the British War Medal 1914–20, Victory Medal 1914–19 and Territorial Force War Medal 1919. The medals were loaned to the Imperial War Museum, Lambeth Road, London by his brother on 27th September 1963. In 1966 they were presented to the Museum by his sister, Elizabeth Missingchuk, of Edmonton, Alberta, Canada. It was the first VC group presented to the Museum, where it is currently held.

The public of Edinburgh raised £744 for James' mother. It was used to purchase an annuity bond to provide her with a weekly income of £1/2/3. The bond, and the balance of £14, was presented to her by the Lord Provost of Edinburgh.

The building of St George's Church, Charlotte Square, Edinburgh commenced in 1811, from a designed by Robert Adam in 1791. The church opened in 1814 but severe structural defects caused it to close in the 1960s. It was taken over by the Ministry of Public Buildings and Works as West Register House for use as archives for the National Archives of Scotland. James McPhie's name is fifth down on the right side.

The Territorial Force War Medal 1914–19 was established in April 1920 for members of the Territorial Force and Territorial Force Nursing Service who volunteered for service overseas. The award criteria were:

- To have been serving on 4th August 1914 or have completed four years' service with the Force before 4th August 1914 and rejoined on or before 30th September 1914.
- Undertook on or before 30th September 1914 to serve outside the United Kingdom.
- Served outside the United Kingdom between 5th August 1914 and 11th November 1918.
- Did not qualify for the 1914 Star or 1914–15 Star.

A total of 33,944 Territorial Force War Medals were awarded, including 227 to nurses of the Territorial Force Nursing Service.

CAPTAIN COULSON NORMAN MITCHELL
4th Canadian Engineers, Canadian Expeditionary Force

Norman, as he was known, Mitchell was born on 11th December 1889 at Ross Street, Winnipeg, Manitoba, Canada. His father, Coulson Nicholas Mitchell (12th June 1854–1st August 1950), born at Broughty Ferry, near Dundee, Forfarshire, Scotland, was living with his parents at Hilltown, Dundee in 1861. By 1871 the family had moved to 13 Alexander Street, St Andrew, Dundee and he was an unemployed shopman. He emigrated to Canada later that year as a merchant tailor

and married Mary Jane née Ptolemy (23rd March 1858–29th August 1943), a primary school principal born in Ontario, Canada, on 22nd November 1883 at Winnipeg. They moved to a terraced house in Edmonton Street, Winnipeg after 1889. By 1906 they were living at 310 Furby Street, Winnipeg. By 1921 they had moved to 25B Guelph Apartments and later to 3549, 40th Avenue, Vancouver, British Columbia. Coulson senior served as a captain in 90th Winnipeg Rifles and was in action during the Riel Rebellion of 1885. He was also a crack shot and was part of the Canadian Bisley Rifle Team with three of his brothers. Coulson was living at 3416 Oak Street, Vancouver, British Columbia at the time of his death. Norman had four siblings:

- Grace Love Mitchell (1st October 1884–9th February 1976) married George Richmond Kendall (16th June 1885–19th May 1944), born at Montréal, Québec, on 4th October 1911. The family was involved in equestrian activities, with thoroughbred racehorses and show jumpers. He died at Calgary, Alberta and she at Vancouver, British Columbia. They had three children:
    - Jean Mary Kendall (22nd March 1914–1992) married Gordon Peter Eligh (1917–May 2001), born at Ottawa. They had a daughter, Jane Leslie Eligh (born 4th July 1956).
    - Thomas Coulson Kendall (26th April 1916–28th November 1978) married Ruth Carolyne Wellwood (6th November 1915–2002) on 31st December 1934. He raced horses with his son, Thomas, all over North America but particularly on the west coast. He died at Burnaby, British Columbia. They had two children – Thomas George Kendall (1935–2000) and Joan Kendall.

Broughty Ferry, a suburb of Dundee on the north bank of the Firth of Tay, was a separate burgh from 1864 to 1913. Originally a fishing and whaling community, in the 19th century it became a haven for the wealthy, particularly owners of the nearby Dundee jute mills. A castle was built in 1495 and an English fort c.1548 but nothing remains of the latter. A roll on-off railway ferry, which gave the village its name, linked the Edinburgh to Aberdeen line until it was rendered redundant in 1878 by the Tay Railway Bridge. In December 1959 the town's lifeboat, RNLB *Mona*, was lost with all hands. Wing Commander Hugh Gordon Malcolm VC (2nd May 1917 – 4th December 1942) was born in Broughty Ferry.

- Dorothy Isabel Kendall (5th April 1922–2000) married Douglas 'Peter' George Buckley (30th August 1922–January 2001), born at Ottawa, Ontario. He was an assistant store manager in 1962, when they were living at 6309 Angus Drive, Vancouver. They had a son, Michael Kendall Buckley (1950–2012).

- Stanley Hall Mitchell (10th June 1886–8th April 1915) was a tailor, working with his father, and served in the Militia as a lieutenant in the Winnipeg Grenadiers.

Winnipeg, capital and largest city of Manitoba, lies at the confluence of the Red and Assiniboine Rivers and was a trading centre for the indigenous tribes before the arrival of Europeans. French traders built Fort Rouge in 1738 and many Frenchmen married First Nation women. Their descendants are known as the Métis. A settlement was founded by the Selkirk settlers of the Red River Colony in 1812. Winnipeg became a city in 1873, known as the 'Gateway to the West'.

In 1869–70 the Red River Rebellion, a conflict between the local provisional government of Métis, led by Louis Riel, and newcomers from eastern Canada, was put down by General Garnet Wolseley. Winnipeg developed rapidly after the coming of the Canadian Pacific Railway in 1881. However, its prosperity declined after 1914 when the opening of the Panama Canal reduced reliance on Canada's railways for international trade. In May 1919 more than 30,000 workers walked out on strike, a product of postwar recession, labour conditions, union agitation and the return of soldiers from the Great War seeking employment. The strike ended on 21st June 1919 when the Riot Act was read and the Royal Canadian Mounted Police charged a group of strikers, of whom two were killed and at least thirty were injured. The crash of 1929 and the Great Depression that followed caused widespread unemployment, which was worsened by drought and low agricultural prices. A consolidated metropolitan 'unicity' government of Winnipeg and surrounding municipalities was established on 27th July 1971. Amongst the city's famous are:

- 1970s pop group Bachman-Turner Overdrive.
- Neil Young (born 1945), singer-songwriter, musician and activist.
- Sir William Samuel Stephenson (23rd January 1897 – 31st January 1989) soldier, airman, businessman, inventor, spymaster and senior representative of British Security Coordination (BSC) during the Second World War, known as Intrepid, was born in Winnipeg. Ian Fleming wrote, *James Bond is a highly romanticized version of a true spy. The real thing is … William Stephenson.* The BSC operated out of the Rockefeller Center, New York and was known officially as the British Passport Control Office.
- Six other VCs:
  - Lionel 'Leo' Beaumaurice Clarke (1st December 1892 – 19th October 1916) lived there.
  - Robert Edward Cruickshank (17th June 1888 – 30th August 1961) born there but moved to England.
  - Frederick William Hall (21st February 1885 – 24th April 1915) born in Kilkenny, Ireland and lived in Winnipeg.
  - Andrew Charles Mynarski (14th October 1916 – 13th June 1944) born in Winnipeg to Polish immigrant parents.
  - Christopher Patrick John O'Kelly (18th November 1895 – 15th November 1922) born in the city.
  - Robert Shankland (10th October 1887 – 20th January 1968), born at Ayr, Scotland, was assistant cashier for the Crescent Creamery Co in Winnipeg.

He was a Freemason and member of Assiniboine Lodge No.114, Winnipeg. Stanley married Alice Lillian Holman (5th January 1887–15th July 1985) on 22nd June 1910 and they were living in an apartment block on Broadway in 1911. He was commissioned in 11th Battalion CEF as a lieutenant on 23rd September 1914 at Valcartier. He was described as 5′9½″ tall, weighing 165 lbs, with fair complexion, grey eyes, dark brown hair and his religious denomination was Presbyterian. He departed Québec on 4th October aboard SS *Royal Edward* and was appointed 11th Battalion Transport Officer at Tidworth, Wiltshire. He was promoted captain on 22nd January 1915 and returned to Canada aboard SS *Scandinavian*, departing on 26th March. Stanley was admitted to Royal Victoria Hospital, Montréal and died there while undergoing surgery for appendicitis. Alice moved in with her parents at 197 Mayfair, South Winnipeg. She married James Bloomer Carter (3rd March 1894–8th December 1982) on 10th May 1922. He was the founder and owner of James B Carter Ltd in 1920, which became Carter Temro Ltd in the 1970s and later Temro Automotive Division of Budd Co of Troy, Michigan, USA. He was a Freemason (Khartum Temple of the Shrine and Assiniboine Lodge No.114) and a member of the Kiwanis Club of Winnipeg. They were living at 1084 Wellington Crescent, Winnipeg at the time of his death. They had a daughter:

  - Shirley Ruth Carter (18th September 1926–12th June 2018) married William 'Bill' Grant Lugg (1924–28th June 2006), who served as a flying officer in Bomber Command in the Royal Canadian Air Force during the Second World War. They had at least four children – Grant Lugg, David Lugg, Barbara Lugg and Nancy Lugg.

- John Clifford Mitchell (13th October 1888–15th July 1889).
- Ivan 'Mike' Gladstone Mitchell (9th July 1893–8th May 1942) was a clerk and served in the Militia in 100th Winnipeg Grenadiers. He married Mabel Burnett (19th August 1895–29th August 1922) on 14th October 1913 at 1256 Fairfield Road, Victoria, British Columbia. Ivan was living at Suite 3, Cecil Court, Winnipeg when he attested for the CEF at Winnipeg on 7th August 1915 (service reckoned from 15th July). He gave his year of birth as 1892 and was described as 6′ tall, weighing 185 lbs, with fair complexion, blue eyes, brown hair and his religious denomination was Presbyterian. Mabel's address was 1256 Fairfield Road, Victoria at the time. From November 1917 she was living at 1030 Henry Building, Seattle, Washington, USA and from April 1918 at 616 Seneca Street, Seattle. Ivan sailed from Halifax, Nova Scotia aboard RMS *Empress of Britain* on 20th May 1916 and disembarked at Liverpool on 30th May. He was a lieutenant from the same date and assigned $45 per month to his wife from his Army pay. He went to France with 78th Battalion from Southampton on 12th August. He was granted leave 24th January–3rd February 1917 and was admitted to 11th Canadian Field Ambulance and No.23 Casualty Clearing Station with gonorrhea on 16th February. On 18th February he was admitted to the Duke of

Westminster's Hospital, Le Touquet and transferred to 39th General Hospital, Le Havre. He was discharged to OC Reinforcements, Canadian Base Depot, Le Havre on 7th March and joined 4th Entrenching Battalion on 25th March. On 10th April he was promoted captain and rejoined 78th Battalion on 12th April. He took part in the Corps Rifle Meet 21st-26th September. On 31st October he was wounded at Passchendaele, Belgium with slight gunshots to left shoulder and cheek. He was admitted to 11th Canadian Field Ambulance and No.2 Canadian Casualty Clearing Station the same day and transferred to 6th British Red Cross Hospital (Liverpool Merchants), Étaples on 1st November. On 10th November he was evacuated to Britain aboard HMHS *Stad Antwerpen* and was admitted to Prince of Wales's Hospital, Marylebone on the strength of the Manitoba Regiment Depot, Shorncliffe, Kent. A medical board at 13 Berners Street, London on 7th December found him unfit for any service for one month and he was granted leave. A medical board there on 8th January 1918 found him fit for light duties and he reported to the Manitoba Regiment Depot, Shorncliffe on 11th January. Medical boards at 23–25 Earls Avenue, Folkestone on 8th February and 8th March found him fit for Home Service and General Service respectively. He joined 11th Reserve Battalion, Dibgate on 9th March. He was treated at Westcliffe Canadian Eye and Ear Hospital, Folkestone for tonsilitis 16th April–29th May and then returned to 11th Reserve Battalion. Medical boards at Seaford on 3rd June and 24th August found him fit for Home Service and General Service respectively. Meanwhile he attended the School of Instruction, Stratford 15th-18th June. Having rejoined 11th Reserve Battalion on 24th August, he moved to Witley to join Syren Force (British North Russia Expeditionary Force) on 4th September. He was seconded to the War Office and departed for Murmansk, Russia to join the North Russian Relief Force aboard SS *Toloa* on 17th September, arriving on 28th September. Ivan returned to Britain on 21st August 1919 and his secondment to the War Office ceased on 27th August. Next day he joined 1st Canadian Discharge Depot, Buxton. He embarked aboard SS *Royal George* at Southampton on 20th September and disembarked at Halifax, Nova Scotia on 30th September. He was demobilised from Military District No.7 on 7th October, when his wife's address was 1220 McKenzie Street, Victoria, British Columbia. Ivan had played ice hockey for the Portland Rosebuds in 1914 and turned professional to play for Toronto St Patricks as a goaltender for three seasons in the National Hockey League. He was injured during the second game of the 1922 season and was sidelined for the rest of the season. Ivan and Mabel's marriage ended in divorce. Mabel married Alexander Lovie Meldrum (13th December 1893–18th December 1954), born in Aberdeenshire, Scotland, on 15th June 1921 at Winnipeg. He was the western representative for Johnson & Johnson, Montréal. They were living at 797 Dorchester Avenue, Winnipeg at the time of her death at Winnipeg General Hospital. Ivan married Jane 'Jean' Godfrey Dowd (10th June 1892–1st March 1973), born at Ballinacurra, Cloyne,

Middleton, Co Cork, Ireland, on 4th June 1925 at Winnipeg. They lived at 173 Woodhaven Boulevard, Sturgeon Creek, Winnipeg, Manitoba. Ivan died at Deer Lodge Hospital, Winnipeg. He had two children from his two marriages:

- Alma Pearl Mitchell (July 1914–28th September 1915).
- Charles Norman Mitchell (died 28th April 1974) married Mary Marguerite on 10th September 1949 at Winnipeg. He was a sales analyst in 1962, by when they were living at 164 Woodhaven Boulevard, Sturgeon Creek, Winnipeg.

Norman's paternal grandfather, Thomas Mitchell (c.1822–64), born at Blairgowrie, Perthshire, Scotland, married Helen 'Ellen' née Whitton (17th July 1822–29th April 1902) on 27th August 1842 at Dundee, Angus, where she was born. He was an iron founder in 1851, when they were living at 15 Princes Street, St Whittons Land, Dundee. By 1861 he was a machinist and they were living at Hilltown, Dundee. By 1871 Ellen was living at 13 Alexander Street, St Andrew, Dundee. By 1891 she was housekeeper for her brother, George Whitton (born c.1828), a house proprietor and factor, at Kinloch Street, Carnoustie, Angus. By 1901 she had moved to Hamilton, Ontario, Canada and was lodging with her son John. She died at 28 Gore Street, Wentworth, Hamilton. In addition to Coulson they had six other children:

- John Mitchell (4th June 1843–15th June 1917), born at Liverpool, Lancashire, was a shoemaker who emigrated to Canada. He married Margaret 'Maggie' Hardy (17th September 1855–22nd October 1909) on 17th June 1874 at Hamilton, Ontario. They had at least six children – Helen Guthrie Mitchell 1877, Henry Knight Mitchell 1879, Nicholas Coulson Mitchell 1880, Elvina May Mitchell

Blairgowrie and Rattray, at the crossroads of several historic routes, were united by Act of Parliament in 1928. Rattray is probably the older burgh, dating back to the 12th century, although there is evidence of the area around Blairgowrie being occupied continuously since the Neolithic period. The Roman legionary fort at Inchtuthil, six kilometres west-southwest of Blairgowrie, is one of the most important archaeological sites in Britain. Blairgowrie was made a barony in 1634 by Charles I. In 1724 the military road from Coupar to Fort George, which passes through the town, was completed. Blairgowrie became a free burgh in 1809. The town expanded hugely in the 19th century due to many textile mills being built along the River Ericht. By 1870 they employed nearly 2,000 men and women. Soft fruit growing developed in the 20th century and a cannery and jam factory were built. Large numbers of berry pickers were brought in and camps were set up on farms. Some pickers from Glasgow made this their annual holiday. More recently the pickers have been mainly eastern European students.

(1882–1953), John James Mitchell 1884 and Sadie Campbell Mitchell (1887–1956).

- David Mitchell (28th April 1849–20th March 1910), a shoemaker, married Isabella Storrier (7th April 1849–14th January 1908) on 31st December 1868. They emigrated to Canada c.1870 and settled at Hamilton, Ontario, where he became a violin maker. He was living at 14 Main Street, Hamilton when he suffered burns and died at Hamilton City Hospital. They had three children – Helen 'Nellie' Mitchell (1869–1957), Jessie Storrier Stacy Mitchell (1871–1955) and Thomas Storrier Mitchell (1873–1939).
- William E Mitchell (25th December 1850–1935) emigrated to Canada around 1864 and became a tailor. He married Margaret Jane McGowan (24th November 1855–1948). He formed part of the Canadian Bisley Rifle Team with three of his brothers. They were living at 528 Michigan Street, Victoria, British Columbia in 1921 and had eleven children – William Mitchell 1874, Edith Mitchell (1875–1966), Ethel Mary Mitchell (1878–1904), Archibald Coulson Mitchell (8th December 1880–16th September 1956), Russell Staite Mitchell (1883–1961), Edna Gertrude Mitchell (1884–1973), Beatrice Reed Mitchell 1886, James Boyd Mitchell 1888, Annie Mitchell (1890–1909), Clarence Ewart Mitchell (1892–1970) and Stewart Norman Mitchell (born 12th February 1895). Two of the sons served in the Army during the Great War:
    - Archibald Coulson Mitchell, born at Port Elgin, Ontario, was a machinist when he enlisted in 240th Battalion CEF (1042435) on 8th November 1916 at Renfrew, Ontario. He was described as 5′4½″ tall, weighing 155 lbs, with fair complexion, grey eyes, dark brown hair and his religious denomination was Presbyterian. He claimed three years previous service in the Royal Canadian Regiment, three years in the Queen's Own Rifles of Canada and three years in 48th Regiment. He embarked at Halifax, Nova Scotia aboard SS *Megantic* on 30th April 1917 and disembarked at Liverpool on 14th May. He joined 7th Reserve Battalion at Seaford and was appointed acting sergeant until reverting to private on 16th June. On 11th July he went to France and joined the Canadian Base Depot next day, 4th Entrenching Battalion on 31st July and 38th Battalion on 10th October. On 30th October he received a shrapnel wound to the left leg at Passchendaele, Belgium and was admitted to 11th Canadian Field Ambulance. He was transferred to 3rd Stationary Hospital, Rouen and was evacuated to Britain aboard HMHS *Aberdonian* on 5th November. Next day he was admitted to Richmond Military Hospital, Grove Road, Richmond, Surrey on the strength of the Eastern Ontario Regiment Depot, Seaford. He was treated at the Canadian Convalescent Hospital, Bromley, Kent 13th February–22nd March 1918, then to remedial training. He was admitted to 14th Canadian General Hospital, Eastbourne on 11th May from 3rd Canadian Command Depot, Seaford, with oedema of the left leg and foot due to the old gunshot wound. He was transferred to the

Canadian Convalescent Hospital, Woodcote Park, Epsom on 1st June and on 2nd August returned to 3rd Canadian Command Depot. He joined the Eastern Ontario Regiment Depot on 14th November and moved to Witley on 19th November. The same day he attended a medical board at Massey-Harris Canadian Convalescent Hospital, Kingswood, Dulwich. Archibald was struck off strength to CEF Canada on sailing on 7th December and was taken on the strength of District Depot, Military District No.11. He disembarked from RMS *Olympic* at Halifax, Nova Scotia on 14th December. A medical at New Westminster, British Columbia on 17th January 1919 found he was only fit for Home Service in Canada and a medical board on 21st January found he had weakness in his left leg. Archibald was demobilised in Vancouver on 30th January 1919.

- Stewart Norman Mitchell was a salesman when he enlisted in 15th Overseas Brigade Ammunition Column CFA (1260405) on 17th April 1916, described as 5′9″ tall, weighing 150 lbs, with fair complexion, grey eyes, brown hair and his religious denomination was Presbyterian. He gave his year of birth as 1897 and his mother as his next of kin. He was confined to barracks for three days and forfeited two days' pay for overstaying his pass and being absent without leave 5th-7th August. From September he assigned $20 per month from his Army pay to his mother. Stewart arrived in England aboard SS *Cameronia* on 22nd September. He joined 60th Battery, 14th Brigade CFA at Witley on 22nd January 1917 and was attached to 5th Canadian Division Train 10th July–16th August. He went to France on 22nd August with 60th Battery and was attached to 5th Canadian Division Train 3rd September–21st November. He was awarded seven days' Field Punishment No.1 for being absent from the 4.45 p.m. parade on 13th November. Stewart contracted scabies and was admitted to 14th then 12th Canadian Field Ambulance 14th-18th January 1918. He was admitted to 2nd and 4th Canadian Field Ambulances on 11th February and transferred to No.1 Canadian Casualty Clearing Station on 15th February. On 17th February he was transferred to St John's Ambulance Brigade Hospital, Étaples, with scabies and pyrexia of unknown origin (later diagnosed as tonsilitis and trench fever). He was evacuated to England aboard HMHS *Stad Antwerpen* on 23rd February and was admitted to Beaufort War Hospital, Bristol next day, on the strength of the Canadian Artillery Reinforcement Depot, Witley. On 2nd March he was transferred to the Canadian Convalescent Hospital, Bear Wood, Wokingham and was attached to 2nd Canadian Command Depot, Bramshott 28th March–23rd May, then joined the Composite Brigade, Canadian Royal Artillery, Witley. On 24th October he returned to France, joining the Canadian General Base Depot on 26th October and the Canadian Corps Reinforcement Camp on 29th October. He rejoined 14th Brigade CFA on 28th December and was attached to 5th Canadian Division Train 1st-21st January 1919. On 2nd February he was admitted to 3rd Canadian Field Ambulance with scabies and transferred to No.55 Casualty Clearing Station on 13th February. On 17th February he transferred to 8th Stationary Hospital, Wimereux with venereal warts and syphilis. Two days later he was moved to 7th General Hospital, Wimereux and to 3rd Canadian General Hospital, Boulogne on 28th March. Stewart was posted to 2nd Canadian Command Depot, Bramshott and his pay was stopped 19th February–28th March. On 11th May he was posted to the Canadian Artillery Pool, Le Havre but on 13th May transferred to the Canadian Convalescent Hospital, Woodcote Park, Epsom, where he remained until 5th June. He was posted to S Wing, Witley on 7th June and I Wing on 23rd June. He was struck off strength to No.2 District Depot, Toronto, Canada on 2nd July, embarking aboard RMS *Olympic* at Southampton and disembarking at Halifax, Nova Scotia on 8th July. He was demobilised on 11th July and issued with War Service Badge, Class A No.318276.

- Thomas Mitchell (born c.1852) was a boot closer in 1871, living with his mother.
- George Mitchell (born 12th June 1856) was a mill worker in 1871, living with his mother.
- Jane Glen Leach Mitchell (born 5th December 1858).

His maternal grandfather, John Ptolemy (4th March 1824–30th October 1898), born at Stewarton, Ayrshire, Scotland, emigrated to Canada where he became a farmer. He married Elizabeth née McWatters (16th November 1830–15th June 1880), born in Ireland, on 3rd July 1849 in Ontario, Canada. She died at 68 Walnut Street, Hamilton, Ontario. He was living with his daughter, Mary Mitchell, and her family at Winnipeg, Manitoba in 1891. He subsequently died there. In addition to Mary, they had seven other children:

- William John Ptolemy (29th March 1850–10th September 1920), born at Smithville, Ontario, married Isabella Muir (12th June 1856–8th December 1915), born at Islay, Argyll, Scotland, on 26th September 1877 at Winnipeg. William was living at 80 Colony Street, Winnipeg, Manitoba when his sons, John and David, enlisted. They had seven children – William George Ptolemy (1878–1927), Edna Isabella Ptolemy (1880–1949), David Allen Pilblado Ptolemy (26th September 1881–3rd October 1949), Thomas Bertram Ptolemy (1883–87), Annie Gertrude Maria Ptolemy (1887–1979), John Alexander Ptolemy (23rd December 1888–21st April 1948) and Laura Irene Ptolemy (1892–1950). Two of the sons, John and David, served in the Army during the Great War:
    - David Allen Pitblado Ptolemy was a bank assistant inspector when he enlisted at Winnipeg in 190th Overseas Battalion CEF on 27th May 1916 (892283). He was described as 6′ ½″ tall, weighing 150 lbs, with dark complexion, blue eyes, black hair and his religious denomination was Presbyterian. He had

There are Bronze Age remains in the area and Stewarton has existed since at least the 12th century. There are various non-historical references dating back to the early 11th century, the most famous of which is the legend of Máel Coluim III, son of Donnchad I of Scotland, who appears in Shakespeare's *Macbeth*. Two local powerful families, Cunninghame and Montgomery, were involved in a dispute over landholdings which came to a head in 1586. Hugh, 4th Earl of Eglinton, was attacked at the ford on the Annick Water, which flows through Stewarton, by about thirty of the Cunninghame clan and was shot dead by John Cunninghame of Clonbeith. In response the Montgomeries vowed to kill every Cunninghame involved and a series of tit for tat killings between the two families followed. Several of those responsible for the murder fled to Denmark and were eventually pardoned by King James (VI of Scotland and I of England) when he married Anne of Denmark.

served previously in 100th Winnipeg Grenadiers. He was promoted sergeant on 23rd June, CSM on 13th July and was commissioned as a lieutenant on 18th July. David sailed from Halifax, Nova Scotia aboard SS *Justica* on 3rd May 1917, disembarked at Liverpool on 14th May and was taken on the strength of 18th Reserve Battalion, Dibgate the same day. He was treated at Westcliffe Eye and Ear Hospital, Folkestone for Eustachian catarrh, which caused some deafness. He was admitted to Connaught Hospital, Aldershot 2nd-13th August with syphilis and treatment continued until 26th September. He went to France on 23rd December, joined 1st Canadian Infantry Base Depot next day and the Canadian Corps Reinforcement Camp on 26th December. David joined 107th Battalion on 1st January 1918 and transferred to 2nd Battalion CE on 24th May. He was granted leave to Britain 24th-31st August and Paris 31st August–7th September. On 20th March 1919 he returned to England and was taken on the strength of A Wing next day. On 4th April he was declared fit for General Service, having suffered Eustachian tube catarrh, syphilis and chronic indigestion. The former and the latter were due to service conditions. On 29th April he transferred to the Canadian Concentration Camp, Bramshott and sailed for Canada the same day from Liverpool aboard SS *Baltic*. He was demobilised on 13th May 1919 and was issued War Service Badge, Class A.

- John Alexander Ptolemy served from 29th August 1914, having enlisted at Winnipeg, and departed Canada on 3rd October. He was a law student when he attested in No.1 Automobile Machine Gun Brigade, 1st Contingent, Bustard Camp, Larkhill, Wiltshire, England on 22nd October (45646). He declared three months previous service in 90th Winnipeg Rifles but it is unclear why he was not formally attested until arriving in England. He was described as 5′9″ tall, with fresh complexion, blue eyes, yellow hair and his religious denomination was Presbyterian. John forfeited two days' pay at Bustard Camp on 28th January 1915. He went to France on 17th June. On 6th February 1916 he was struck off the strength of the Canadian Section, 3rd Echelon GHQ and was commissioned as a lieutenant in 8th Battalion. He joined next day and was granted leave in England, extended to 22nd February. He was attached to 2nd Canadian Brigade Machine Gun Company on 24th February. He suffered pyorrhea from April and eventually had all his teeth removed. He also suffered loose internal cartilage in the right knee from June, resulting from a shell fragment. The knee had also been injured by an axe cut to the patella eight years previously. He was admitted to 2nd General Hospital, Le Havre on 14th October with arthritis in the right knee. On 21st October he was evacuated to England aboard HMHS *Asturias* and was treated at Mrs Burn's Hospital for Officers', Stoodley Knowle, Torquay until 4th November. A medical board at 11–12 Charing Cross, London on 6th November found him unfit for service for six weeks and granted leave. A medical board at 86 Strand, London on 18th December found him unfit for General Service for two months and he was attached to the Canadian Machine Gun Depot, Crowborough. John was admitted to 2nd Eastern General Hospital, Brighton on 18th January 1917 with old knee trouble. A medical board at Hastings on 20th April found him unfit for service for one month and granted leave. He was transferred to Granville Canadian Special Hospital, Ramsgate on 21st May. On 1st June he was transferred to Westcliffe Eye & Ear Hospital, Folkestone, where his tonsils were removed. He returned to Granville Canadian Special Hospital, Ramsgate on 22nd June with arthritis in the right knee and transferred to the Canadian Convalescent Hospital for Officers, Broadstairs on 10th July. A medical board at Shorncliffe on 20th July found him unfit for Home Service for three months and permanently unfit for General Service. He was taken on the strength of the Canadian Machine Gun Corps Depot, Seaford on

22nd July. On 14th August he sailed for Canada aboard SS *Megantic* from Liverpool and disembarked on 28th August. He was attached to G Unit for treatment and on 3rd February 1918 he was admitted to Winnipeg General Hospital, where he had cartilage removed from his knee. He was a Deer Lodge Centre, Winnipeg outpatient from 28th February and was admitted to Manitoba Military Convalescent Hospital, Winnipeg on 25th March. He was granted leave 1st April–31st May and was on the strength of Details Company from 18th April. He transferred to Casualty Company on 16th June, to 1st Depot Battalion on 18th June and to Casualty Company again for duty on 26th September. A medical board at Winnipeg on 15th April 1919 found him fit for Home Service in Canada only. He was demobilised from No.10 District Depot on 30th April and transferred to the Reserve of Officers next day.

- Robert Allen (also seen as Allan/Alan) Ptolemy (2nd February 1852–12th June 1935), born at Binbrook, Wentworth, Ontario, was a bookkeeper. He married Mary Appleyard Dunwiddie McIntyre (8th December 1860–12th June 1922), born at Blythswood, Glasgow, Scotland, at Montréal on 18th June 1885. They were living at 117 East Avenue South, Hamilton in September 1914. He was living at 19 Homewood Avenue, Hamilton when he died. They had six children – Mary Appleyard Ptolemy (1886–1955), Alice Louise McWatters Ptolemy (1888–1955), Archibald Allen Ptolemy (20th October 1890–26th March 1943), Janet McIntyre Ptolemy (1891–1974), Robert Morice Ptolemy (1893–1986) and Irene Elizabeth Ptolemy (1899–1965).
    - Archibald was a teamster when he enlisted at Wolsley, Saskatchewan on 10th August 1914. He attested in 5th Battalion CEF (12882) at Valcartier on 18th September, declaring previous service in 21st Cavalry at Calgary. He was described as 5′ 8″ tall, with fair complexion, grey eyes, sandy hair and his religious denomination was Presbyterian. His next of kin was his mother, later his wife, living at 5 Waterworks Cottages, Friston, near Eastbourne, Sussex, England. He sailed to England aboard SS *Lapland*, departing Québec on 3rd October and arriving on 14th October. He forfeited one days' pay at Westdown Camp South, Wiltshire on 31st October. He assigned $20 per month from his Army pay to his mother until November 1917 and then to his wife. On 3rd February 1915 he transferred to Base Train Depot, Larkhill, Wiltshire, to 11th Battalion, Tidworth on 8th February, to 5th Battalion, Tidworth on 19th February and joined the Battalion in France on 9th March. On 28th November he transferred to HQ 2nd Canadian Brigade. Having been granted leave in Britain from 14th November 1916, he was admitted to Westcliffe Eye & Ear Hospital, Folkestone with conjunctivitis on 24th November and was treated until 20th December. As a result his eyesight was defective and he was graded medically B1. While in hospital he was posted as a deserter in error, although he was

on the strength of the Canadian Casualty Assembly Centre, Hastings. On 4th January 1917 he transferred to the Garrison Duty Company, Seaford. He transferred to 2nd Canadian Labour Battalion, Hastings on 10th January, to General Duties Company, 16th Reserve Battalion, Seaford on 23rd January and was attached to 3rd Reserve Battalion, British Columbia Regiment, Seaford on 3rd March. He transferred to the British Columbia Regiment Depot, Seaford on 17th March and was detached to the General Depot, Seaford 27th May–7th September. On 16th October he was granted permission to marry by HQ 3rd Canadian Reserve Brigade and soon afterwards married Jenny E Hall (born c.1893) at Eastbourne. They had a daughter, Irene W Ptolemy, in 1918. Archibald was admitted to 14th Canadian General Hospital, Eastbourne, Sussex with influenza 19th October–8th November 1918 and was appointed acting corporal while in charge of the HQ stables from 11th November. He was posted to H Wing, Canadian Concentration Camp, Witley on 16th July 1919 and transferred to the 1st Canadian Discharge Depot, Buxton on 15th August. He was struck off strength to Canada on embarking aboard SS *Adriatic* at Southampton on 3rd September and disembarked at Halifax, Nova Scotia on 10th September. On 15th September he was demobilised from Military District No.6 and was issued War Service Badge Class A. His intended address was 377 Barton Street East, Hamilton.

- Thomas Ptolemy (25th June 1854–29th April 1935), born at Hamilton, was a general merchant. He married Carolyn 'Carrie' Elizabeth Ott (26th April 1868–21st May 1961), born at Berlin, Waterloo, Ontario, in 1887 at Lethbridge, Alberta. They had five children – Franklin Percival Ptolemy (1888–1965), Edna Elizabeth Ptolemy (1889–1985), John Harold Glenny Ptolemy (born and died 1891), Clara Alma Ptolemy (1893–1971) and Vernon William Ptolemy (1895–99).
- Samuel Ptolemy (26th January–30th March 1857), born at Binbrook.
- Elizabeth Ptolemy (5th-27th March 1860).
- Sarah Maria Elizabeth Ptolemy (15th October 1866–11th September 1928), born at Tapley Town, Ontario, married Robert Hance Shanks (29th August 1858–24th April 1932), an accountant and financial agent born at Belleville, Ontario, on 10th June 1890 at St Andrew's Church, Winnipeg. They were living at 351 Assiniboine Avenue, Winnipeg at the time of her death aboard SS *Noronic* en route from Duluth to Fort William, Thunder Bay Co, Ontario. He died at Winnipeg. They had four children:
    - Gordon Lane Shanks (3rd April 1891–11th March 1983) was educated at the University of Manitoba, Winnipeg and became a civil engineer (member of the Canadian Society of Civil Engineers). His work appointments included:

      Three summers (fifteen months) with the Canadian Pacific Railway in western Canada on railway location and construction as a rodman and instrument man.

Nine months with Dominion Bridge Co at Winnipeg on structural steelwork as a draughtsman and shop inspector.

Two years with the Foundation Co of New York City on heavy constructional work in western Canada as timekeeper, contractor's civil engineer, job office manager and assistant to the Western Manager at Vancouver.

One and a half years with the Rural Municipality of Rockwood, Manitoba on highway work as Municipal Engineer.

Gordon enlisted at Winnipeg on 11th November 1914, declaring previous service in 100th Regiment and two weeks in 2nd Field Troop CE at Winnipeg (292459). He was described as $5'8\frac{3}{4}''$ tall, with fair complexion, blue eyes, brown hair and his religious denomination was Presbyterian. He was discharged at Ottawa as medically unfit on 30th November. Gordon departed Halifax, Nova Scotia on 14th November 1916 aboard RMS *Olympic*. He was attested and assigned to 222nd Overseas Battalion, Shoreham Camp, Sussex, England on 23rd November. By then he was $5'\ 10\frac{1}{2}''$ tall and weighed 152 lbs. He was passed fit for Home Service only. On 31st January 1917 he transferred to 19th Reserve Battalion and was attached to 2nd Canadian Discharge Depot, London for duty 20th February–19th August and to HQ Canadian Troops, London Area on 8th March. Appointed acting sergeant 23rd May–19th August, then reverted to acting corporal. He was posted to the Manitoba Regiment Depot on 19th August and was attached to the Royal Engineers Cadet Class of Instruction, RE Training Depot, Newark Park for officer training. Commissioned in the Royal Engineers on 17th November and went to France on 27th April 1918. Promoted lieutenant on 17th May 1919 and was demobilised on 6th June from the Officers' Wing, Repatriation Camp, Pirbright. He relinquished his commission on 20th June 1919.

- Jessie Eleanor Shanks (born 17th April 1893).
- Edith Grace Shanks (born 1st February 1897).
- Robert Arthur Shanks (born 2nd October 1899).

- Jessie Isabella Ptolemy (8th December 1868–1st February 1931), born at Saltfleet Township, Ontario, was a public school teacher in 1891, living with her father and brother-in-law, Coulson Nicholas Mitchell, at Winnipeg. She was still living there in 1901 by when she was principal of a public school.

Norman was educated at Mulvey Public School and Winnipeg Collegiate Institute, both in Winnipeg, Manitoba. He attended the University of Manitoba, Winnipeg and graduated as an engineer in 1912. He worked as a civil engineer with the Foundation Company of Canada in Manitoba and British Columbia. He was working on the Transcona Elevator when war broke out.

Norman enlisted in 2nd Field Troop CE at Winnipeg, Manitoba in November 1914, described as $5'9\frac{1}{4}''$ tall, with medium complexion, light blue eyes, brown

A view of the third Mulvey School building. The first, a two-classroom structure, opened in October 1884 with forty-seven pupils and was named after politician Stewart Mulvey. The second, built in 1893, had three-stories with ten classrooms, but burned down on 9th April 1895. While a replacement was being built, pupils were educated in Mulvey School No.1, which remained at the site, or at nearby Carlton School. The third structure, completed in late 1895, was similar to its predecessor and had twelve classrooms and an assembly hall. Mulvey School No. 1 was demolished in 1907. By 1908, Mulvey School No.3 was overcrowded and nine more classrooms were added. In 1922 the assembly hall was divided into two classrooms, resulting in the school being able to accommodate up to 900 pupils. The fourth and present Mulvey School was built in 1925 as Gordon Bell Junior High School and became a Senior High School in 1932. When a new building for senior students was erected in 1956, it was named Gordon Bell and the old Gordon Bell became Mulvey School.

hair and his religious denomination was Presbyterian. He was posted to 4th Field Company CE at Ottawa, qualified as a signaller and was posted to 2nd Divisional Signal Company. He transferred to the Canadian Overseas Railway Construction Corps CEF (596) at Ottawa on 21st January 1915. He departed St John, New Brunswick aboard SS *Herschel* on 14th June 1915, arriving at Plymouth, Devon on 25th June and was posted to Longmoor Camp, near Liphook, Hampshire. He went to France via Southampton on 25th August, arriving at Calais, and proceeded to Alveringen, Belgium, where the unit was attached to the Belgian Army. The

The first high school classes in Winnipeg were held in September 1882 for eight students in the upper room of a school building on Louise Street. The facility was inadequate in the winter and classes were moved to a room on the upper floor of the Central School. In 1891 the city's first dedicated high school building (seen here) was erected with an initial enrolment of 360 students. In September 1915 the collegiate transferred to the newly built Isaac Brock School and in 1922 to Daniel McIntyre Collegiate. Thereafter the building was used by Maple Leaf School until it was demolished in 1928. It was replaced on the same site by Hugh John Macdonald School.

The University of Manitoba, founded by Alexander Morris and established under the University of Manitoba Act on 28th February 1877, was the first university established in western Canada. It was formed by the federation of three existing denominational colleges. They were joined in 1882 by the Manitoba Medical College and in 1888 by the Wesley College (Methodist). Others followed, for example Manitoba College of Pharmacy 1902, Manitoba Agricultural College 1906, St Paul's College 1931, Brandon College 1938, Manitoba Law School 1966 and St Andrew's College 1981. In 1967 United College became the University of Winnipeg and Brandon College became Brandon University. The first woman student was admitted in 1886. Many students fought in the Great War and the University was used as a training ground. During this time enrollment reduced significantly from 925 students in 1914–15 to 662 in 1916–17. A total of 1,160 students and fourteen staff served of whom 123 were killed or died during the war and 142 received military awards. After the War, the university saw a large increase in students enrolling. During the Second World War the Army took over the Fort Garry residence and all fit male students were required to train for six hours per week. All students aged over twenty-one received two weeks military training. Ninety percent of women students enrolled on courses to aid the war effort. The University saw an influx of 3,125 war veterans in 1946, increasing registration to 9,514.

The Canadian Pacific Railway Co built the Transcona grain elevator near Winnipeg in 1913 to store grain from the wider area. The grain elevator was constructed of reinforced concrete with an engine room and five rows each of thirteen grain storage containers. The total volume was 36,000 m3. The construction was based on a reinforced concrete slab measuring 23.5m by 59.5m, the whole forming a very rigid foundation. Limited testing was carried out on the subsoil, as there was very little knowledge of the science at the time. Once construction was completed, the tanks were evenly filled with grain. When 87.5% full the building was seen to be settling and after twenty-four hours the foundation soil collapsed and the structure tilted over by twenty-seven degrees. Remediation action was carried out by the Foundation Co Ltd to build supporting structures, excavate the foundation slabs and build piles in order to return the building to its original upright position. The work was successful and the grain elevator is still in operation today.

SS *Herschel* (6,293 tons) was built in 1914 for Lamport & Holt Line. She was one of the ships hired to move the BEF to France 6th–28th August 1914.

unit built a narrow-gauge railway as far as the support line and then returned to Longmoor Camp on 5th October. Norman transferred to the HQ Sub Staff, Deputy Assistant Adjutant General, Garrison Training Division, Shorncliffe, Kent on 21st October and to the Infantry Depot, Shorncliffe to take up a commission on 17th November. Promoted sergeant on 24th November. He was commissioned as a lieutenant on 28th April 1916 and was attached to the Canadian Engineers Training Depot. He went to France as a conducting officer 8th–13th June. He returned to join 1st Canadian Tunnelling Company in Belgium on 1st July and was granted leave 6th–18th November.

Awarded the MC for his actions at the Bluff, near Ypres on 11th December 1916, where he worked almost thirty metres below ground. He displayed great courage and skill in countermining enemy galleries and on one occasion was cut off from his own lines for twelve hours, LG 13th February 1917. Norman was granted leave 26th June–6th July and 7th–17th October 1917, rejoining the unit on 23rd October. He was appointed acting captain on 23rd September and was granted leave in Nice, France 29th January–12th February 1918. Promoted captain on 24th May and was posted to D Company, 4th Battalion CE, 2nd Canadian Division on 11th July. **Awarded the VC for his actions on the Canal de l'Escaut, Pont d'Aire, northeast of Cambrai, France on 8th/9th October 1918, LG 31st January 1919.** Mitchell is the only Canadian Engineer to be awarded the VC.

He was granted leave 16th October–1st November and remained with 4th Battalion CE to the Armistice and in the march to the Rhine, which it crossed at Bonn on 13th December. He was granted

The camp at Shorncliffe was established in 1794 and in 1803 Sir John Moore trained the Light Division there. It became a staging post for the Western Front during the First World War and in April 1915 a Canadian Training Division formed there and Canadian hospitals from September 1917 onwards. The camp remains in use.

RMS *Olympic* (45,324 tons) arriving at New York on her maiden voyage on 21st June 1911. She was the lead transatlantic liner of the White Star line. Her sister ships, *Titanic* and *Britannic*, had short and tragic careers. *Titanic* sank after striking an iceberg in April 1912 with the loss of 1,514 lives. *Britannic* struck a mine and sank in the Mediterranean in November 1916 with the loss of thirty lives. *Olympic*'s first voyage from Belfast to Liverpool coincided with the launch of *Titanic* on 31st May 1911. On her maiden voyage on 14th June 1911 from Southampton to New York, *Britannic* was captained by Edward Smith, master of the *Titanic* on her maiden voyage the following year. On 27th October 1914, off the north coast of Ireland *Olympic* went to assist the battleship HMS *Audacious*, which had struck a mine. *Olympic* took off 250 of *Audacious*' crew, but on the way to Lough Swilly the towing cable parted and *Audacious* sank later. In May 1915, *Olympic* was requisitioned as a troop transport. On 12th May 1918, en route to France with US troops, she sighted U-*103* surfaced 500m ahead and opened fire. U-*103* crash-dived, but *Olympic*'s port propeller sliced through the pressure hull. U-*103* surfaced and was scuttled and abandoned by her crew. *Olympic* reached Southampton via Cherbourg with some damage, but her hull was not breached. USS *Davis* picked up thirty-one survivors from U-*103*. *Olympic*'s master, Captain Hayes, was awarded the DSO. During the war, *Olympic* carried 200,000 troops and travelled 184,000 miles. In 1920 she returned to passenger service, carrying many celebrities such as Charlie Chaplin, Mary Pickford and the Prince of Wales. The Depression and competition from new larger and faster liners had their effect and she left New York for the last time on 5th April 1935. She was broken up in 1936–37, having completed 257 Atlantic crossings, transporting 430,000 commercial passengers and travelling 1,800,000 miles.

fourteen days' leave in Britain from 18th March but was retained in England on 1st April to join the Canadian Engineers Regimental Depot. At that time he was described as 5′ 11″ tall and weighed 160 lbs. The VC was presented by the King in the ballroom at Buckingham Palace on 3rd April. On 14th April he sailed for Canada aboard RMS *Olympic*, arriving on 21st April, where he was demobilised on 28th April and transferred to the Reserve of Officers. His address was 25B Guelph Apartments, Winnipeg.

Norman returned to Winnipeg to continue employment with the Foundation Company of Canada. He was appointed manager of a high-power electrical station in British Columbia. In 1926 he joined the Power Corporation of Canada Ltd and was appointed General Superintendent, Construction and Development of Steam

Hamilton is a port city at the western end of Lake Ontario, about sixty kilometres southwest of Toronto. The area was first visited by the French in 1699. After the American Revolutionary War large numbers of Loyalists left the United States to settle in southern Ontario. In 1792, the Crown purchased the land on which Hamilton now stands and granted plots to the Loyalists to encourage settlement. During the War of 1812 an invading American force was defeated by British regulars and Canadian militia at Stoney Creek, now a park in Hamilton. After the war George Hamilton established a settlement and in 1832 a canal was cut through the outer sand bar enabling Hamilton to become a major port. Hamilton became a city on 13th February 1833. The first commercial telephone service in Canada, the first telephone exchange in the British Empire and the second in North America were established in the city 1877–78. Industry expanded and the population doubled between 1900 and 1914. In 1930 McMaster University moved there from Toronto. Many of the heavy industries have since moved or closed. On 1st January 2001, the new city of Hamilton was formed by amalgamating Hamilton and five neighbouring municipalities. Hamilton was the birthplace of General Henry Duncan Graham 'Harry' Crerar CH CB DSO CD PC (1888–1965), who commanded First Canadian Army during the Second World War.

and Hydro-electric Plants from Newfoundland to the Yukon. He was appointed Construction Manager of the Power Corporation after the Second World War and retired in 1957.

Norman married Gertrude Hazel 'Daisy' Bishop (4th January 1890–30th December 1985), born at Hamilton, Ontario, in 1922. They were living at 310 Furby Street, Winnipeg in 1924. By 1956 they had moved to 81 Woodland Avenue, Beaurepaire, Québec. She died at London, Ontario and was buried with her husband. They had two daughters:

- Marjorie Ruth Mitchell (27th April 1924–27th July 2010), born at St Joseph Hospital, Mishawaka, Indiana, USA, married Ronald Simpson Urquhart (8th January 1924–30th September 1991) on 8th September 1948 at First United Church, Mount Royal, Québec, where he was born. He was a supervisor in 1963, when they were living at 224 Braebrook Avenue, Jacques-Cartier-Lasalle, Québec. By 1974 Ronald was working for Bell Canada, Marjorie was a nurse and they were living at 174 Woodside Drive, St Catharine's, Ontario. She died at Bracebridge, Muskoka, Ontario. They had four children.
- Frances Mary Mitchell (born c.December 1919).

Daisy's father, Peter Francis Bishop (28th July 1860–24th October 1955), born in Ontario, married Frances Mary née Tressider (also seen as Tresedder) (30th August

1857–February 1942), born at St Austell, Cornwall, England, on 17th August 1883 at Montréal, Québec. She emigrated to Canada in 1872. He was a lithographer in 1901, when they were living at Hamilton, Ontario. They were living at Red Cottage, Winnipeg, Manitoba in 1916 and later at 517 Gertrude Avenue, Winnipeg. They also owned a summer home at 141 Kingston Row, St Vital, Manitoba. Peter was founder and President of Bishop Printing Co. In addition to Gertrude they had five other children:

- Frank Charles Bishop (7th August 1884–9th July 1936), born at London, Middlesex Co, Ontario, was a copperplate engraver before attending McKillop Veterinary College, Chicago, Illinois, USA for four years and then ran a veterinary practice at Invermay, Saskatchewan, Canada. He married Edna Mary Kemp (5th June 1890–November 1957), born at Peterborough, Ontario, on 26th June 1912 at Edmonton, Alberta. Frank was appointed to the government inspection staff in 1910, stationed at Edmonton and Winnipeg. He was appointed a field livestock inspector of the Dominion government in 1910, when they were living at Dauphin, Manitoba. He was a member of the Orange Order and served as a major in the Canadian Army Veterinary Corps, attached to the Manitoba Horse. He was living at Dearborn Street, Winnipeg in 1919. Frank and Edna brought up their nephew, William Crossley, following the death of William's mother, Emma, in March 1927. Frank died at his parent's summer home at St Vital, Manitoba. They had a daughter, Margaret Kemp Bishop (23rd May 1913–6th September 2010).
- Frances Myrtle Kate Bishop (29th July 1886–28th September 1971) married Robert Erie Nay (3rd September 1885–1st January 1976), a barrister-at-law born at Howick Township, Huron Co, Ontario on 29th March 1911 at Winnipeg. He was educated at Minga, Manitoba, at Manitoba University and studied law at Winnipeg and Saskatoon, Saskatchewan. He was called to the Saskatchewan bar in 1910 and went into practice at Scott. He was appointed agent of the Attorney General in 1914 and they moved to Wilkie in 1919 to join the judicial centre. He also served as school board chairman at Wilkie and as agent of the Attorney General for the Wilkie Judicial Centre until 1925 and 1935–45. He was appointed King's Counsel in 1926 and represented Wilkie in the Legislative Assembly of Saskatchewan as a Liberal 1925–29. In 1946 he was appointed judge for the judicial district of Kerrobert and transferred to Battleford, Saskatchewan in 1949 before retiring from the bench the following year. They had three children – Robert Bishop Nay (20th April 1913–29th November 1983), Dorothy Phyllis Nay (17th November 1916–6th January 1993) and Parkyn Bishop Nay (9th June 1919–2010).
- Emma Olive Bishop (30th June 1888–20th March 1927), born at Hamilton, Ontario, married Percival 'Percy' Frederick Crossley (12th July 1891–24th December 1955), born at Montréal, Québec, on 13th September 1924 at St Vital, Manitoba.

His parents, Frederick Crossley (1856–1924) and Mary Emma Shackleton (1858–1912), emigrated to Canada before 1891 and were living in Québec in 1901 and Winnipeg, Manitoba in 1906. Frederick returned to England aboard SS *Virginia*, arriving at Liverpool, Lancashire on 1st August 1914, and lived at 45 Gisburn Street, Keighley, Yorkshire, England. Percy was a bookkeeper, living at 140 Clarke Street, Winnipeg, when he attested as a driver in 5th Field Artillery Brigade CFA Ammunition Column, 2nd Canadian Division CEF on 29th December 1914 at Winnipeg (86213). He was described as 5′9″ tall, weighing 150 lbs, with dark complexion, brown eyes, dark hair and his religious denomination was Church of England. He claimed three years previous service in 90th Rifles. Percy embarked aboard SS *Metagama* on 5th August 1915 and landed at Plymouth, Devon on 18th August. He was admitted to 5th Field Ambulance Tent Hospital, Otterpool Camp, Kent with a suspected misplaced cartilage on 3rd September. No trace was found and he was discharged to duty on 6th September with a recommendation for light duties. He was confined to barracks for seven days for being drunk at Shorncliffe, Kent on 16th December. He went to France, landing at Le Havre, on 19th January 1916. On 2nd September he was posted to the Trench Mortar Battery, 2nd Canadian Division as batman to Lieutenant Robert Fitchie Craig, on the strength of 2nd Divisional Ammunition Column. Percy was granted leave 3rd-17th August 1917 and rejoined the Trench Mortar Battery on 2nd October. He was granted fourteen days' leave at Keighley, Yorkshire 9th-27th September 1918 and transferred to 2nd Divisional Ammunition Column on 20th November. He transferred to 15th Field Battery, 6th Brigade CFA on 1st January 1919 and joined on 8th February. On 15th April he was posted to H Wing, Canadian Concentration Camp, Witley, Surrey. He embarked aboard SS *Minnekahda* on 14th May and disembarked in Canada on 23rd May and was taken on the strength of No.2 District Depot, Toronto. He was demobilised from there on 27th May and was issued War Service Badge, Class A. Emma died at Winnipeg and Percy in Toronto, Ontario. They had a son, William Crossley.

- Parkyn Sydney Bishop (17th October 1890–30th November 1917), educated at Wesley College, Winnipeg, was working in transportation and living with his parents when he enlisted in 108th Battalion CEF on 28th March 1916 at Selkirk, Hamilton, Ontario (722233). He claimed three years previous service in 90th Militia and four months in the Fort Garry Horse. He was described as 5′7¼″ tall, weighing 148 lbs, with dark complexion, black eyes, dark hair and his religious denomination was Church of England. Promoted corporal on 18th April and attended the School of Instruction 30th April–11th June. Promoted provisional sergeant on 14th June. He departed Halifax, Nova Scotia aboard RMS *Olympic* on 18th September, arriving at Liverpool, Lancashire on 25th September. He was posted to Witley, Surrey and was appointed acting sergeant on 25th September, backdated to 18th September. He assigned $15 per month from his Army pay to his father September 1916–October 1917. Posted

Parkyn Sydney Bishop's name on the Cambrai Memorial.

to 14th Reserve Battalion (Manitoba), Dibgate Camp, Shorncliffe, Kent on 10th January 1917. He applied for a commission on 9th February. On 5th May he joined No.2 Officer Cadet Battalion, Pembroke College, Cambridge for instruction, while on the strength of the Manitoba Regiment Depot. He was discharged from No.2 Canadian Discharge Depot, London on 28th August and was commissioned next day in 1/8th Battalion, London Regiment (Post Office Rifles), joining on 24th September. He was killed in action at Cambrai, France and is commemorated on the Cambrai Memorial, Louverval, France.

- Dorothy Tressider Bishop (20th March 1895–April 1990) married Cyril 'Slim' Frederick Euseby (also seen as Eusaby and Ensaby) Armel Greene (1st January 1889–December 1963), born at Harlesden, Middlesex, England, on 8th October 1927 at Winnipeg. His parents were the Reverend Hugh Percy Armel Greene (1856–97) and Florence Mary Sanders (1860–1940), a professor of music living at Belle Vue, Harrow Road, Kensal Green, London, later at The Homestead, Hyde Heath, near Amersham, Buckinghamshire and at Great Missenden, Buckinghamshire. Cyril was living with his mother and sister, Clarice, at 30 Purves Road, Willesden, London in 1891. His father was living with a housekeeper at 17 Straits House, Sedgley, Staffordshire. Hugh stabbed himself seventeen times in the chest after breakfast at the Green Dragon Hotel, Hereford on 2nd March 1897 and died on 18th March. A verdict of 'suicide whilst temporarily insane' was returned by the coroner. By 1901 Cyril was attending St Edmund's College, Old Hall Green, near Standon, Hertfordshire. He emigrated to Canada in 1909 and was Secretary of the Winnipeg YMCA when he enlisted in the Canadian Officer Training Corps on 20th March 1917 at Winnipeg (2181311). He was described as 6′ 3½″ tall, weighing 164 lbs, with dark complexion, blue eyes, dark brown hair and his religious denomination was Church of England. He assigned $20 per month from his Army pay to his mother and was promoted corporal. He was discharged from Camp Fort Charles, Manitoba on 19th September 1917 in order to enlist in the Imperial Army. Cyril enlisted in the Devonshire Regiment at Oxford on 8th November 1917 (65019) and joined at Aylesbury the same day. He was described as 6′ 3¾″ tall and weighed 165 lbs. He joined No.2 Officer Cadet Battalion, Pembroke College, Cambridge on 9th November and was commissioned in the Wiltshire Regiment on 27th March 1918. Initially he was posted to 4th Reserve Battalion, Hampshire Regiment, Larkhill, Wiltshire and then served with 3rd Wiltshire, Sittingbourne, Kent. Cyril had suffered from pyorrhoea since January 1918. A medical board at Chatham, Kent on 30th July found him unfit for service for one month but fit for light duties and he returned to his unit. A medical board at Chatham on 30th August found him fit for General Service. He went abroad at some time but it is not clear where or when. However, no medal entitlement has been traced and so it is assumed that it was after 11th November 1918. He returned to Britain on 18th April 1919 and joined 9th Welsh Details on 23rd May. On 28th August 1919 he was demobilised from the Officers' Wing, Repatriation Camp, Pirbright and relinquished his commission on 30th November 1920. Cyril was lodging at 301 Vaughan Street, Winnipeg in 1921. Cyril and Dorothy were living at 541 Blair House, Rosslyn Road, Winnipeg in the late 1950s. He was the presenter of the Canadian Broadcasting Corporation's *Neighbourly News From the Prairies* radio programme broadcast each Sunday. They both died at Winnipeg.

Norman served with 16th Field Company, 4th Reserve Engineers (Militia) September 1930–March 1933 as a captain. He rejoined the Canadian Army at the outbreak of the Second World War as a major. He sailed to England in August 1940 and was posted to C Company, 2nd Pioneer Corps, Borden, Hampshire. He assumed command of 11th Field Company, Royal Canadian Engineers in July 1941. In February 1942 he was promoted lieutenant colonel and commanded No. 1 Training Wing, Canadian Engineers Reinforcement Unit. In September 1943 he returned to Canada and was appointed to the National Defence Headquarters in Ottawa. In April 1944 he assumed command of the Royal Canadian Engineers Training Centre at Petawawa and in August assumed command of the Royal School of Canadian Military Engineering, Chilliwack, British Columbia. He was involved in the building of a Legion Hall at Chilliwack and in raising money for a memorial in Vedder Crossing, near Chilliwack in memory of members of the Canadian Corps killed in battle. He also played a key role in a campaign to build the first permanent married quarters in the camp. Norman was discharged from the Army in October 1946.

On 16th July 1936, five liners departed Montréal for France, carrying 6,400 Canadian veterans and family members. Another 1,365 came from Britain for the dedication of the Canadian National Vimy Memorial on 26th July. Edward VIII led the ceremony in one of his few official engagements. Over 50,000 Canadian, British and French veterans and their families attended. The Memorial commemorates 11,284 Canadians who died in France and have no known grave. It stands on Hill 145, the highest point on the Vimy Ridge battlefield. The Memorial took eleven years to build. It sits on a bed of 11,000 tons of concrete and more than 6,000 tons of limestone were used in its construction.

Mount Royal United Church was founded in October 1925, just after the Methodist Church of Canada, the Congregational Union of Canada and most of the Presbyterian Church in Canada joined to form the United Church of Canada. It was moved to its current location in December 1951 and an extension was added in 1960. Other churches have since amalgamated with Mount Royal United Church – 1990 Fairmount-St Giles United Church, 2007 St-Andrews-Norwood United Church and 2010 Rosedale Queen Mary United Church.

Norman attended a number of VC Reunions – the VC Dinner at the Royal Gallery of the House of Lords, London on 9th November 1929, the VC Centenary Celebrations at Hyde Park, London on 26th June 1956 and the 7th and 9th VC & GC Association Reunions at the Connaught Rooms, Covent Garden, London on 18th June 1970 and the Café Royal, London on 23rd May 1974. In 1936 he attended the dedication of the Canadian National Vimy Memorial with his father. While in France he visited the site of his VC action at the Pont d'Aire bridges. He was an active member of the Mitchell VC Branch of the Royal Canadian Legion at Montréal. Norman also attended two dinners for VC recipients hosted by:

- Governor General of Canada, Daniel Roland Michener, at Government House, Ottawa on 16th June 1967. The other attendees were AP Brereton, DV Currie, TF Dinesen, JW Foote, FM Harvey, JK Mahony, CC Merritt, GR Pearkes, CS Rutherford, EA Smith, FA Tilston, P Triquet and RL Zengel.
- Royal Canadian Military Institute, Toronto, Ontario on 15th August 1975. The other attendees were AP Brereton, DV Currie, JW Foote, BH Geary, JK Mahony, GR Pearkes, CS Rutherford, EA Smith, FA Tilston, P Triquet and RL Zengel.

Norman died whilst watching television at his home at Mount Royal, Québec, Canada on 17th November 1978. His funeral took place at Mount Royal United Church on 21st November and he is buried in National Field of Honour Cemetery, 703 Donegani Avenue, Pointe-Claire, Mount Royal (Section M, Grave 3051). He is commemorated in a number of other places:

- Ontario
  - Victoria Cross obelisk to all Canadian VCs at Military Heritage Park, Barrie dedicated by Princess Royal on 22nd October 2013.
  - Plaque No.92 on the York Cemetery VC Memorial, West Don River Valley, Toronto dedicated on 25th June 2017.

Norman's gravestone in National Field of Honour Cemetery.

- ◦ A wooden plaque bearing fifty-six maple leaves each inscribed with the name of a Canadian-born VC holder was dedicated at the Canadian Forces College, Toronto on Remembrance Day 1999.
  ◦ Named on one of eleven plaques honouring 175 men from overseas awarded the VC for the Great War. The plaques were unveiled by the Senior Minister of State at the Foreign & Commonwealth Office and Minister for Faith and Communities, Baroness Warsi, at a reception at Lancaster House, London on 26th June 2014 attended by The Duke of Kent and relatives of the VC recipients. The Canadian plaque was unveiled outside the British High Commission in Elgin Street, Ottawa on 10th November 2014 by The Princess Royal in the presence of British High Commissioner Howard Drake, Canadian Minister of Veterans Affairs Julian Fantino and Canadian Chief of the Defence Staff General Thomas James Lawson.

The Victoria Cross obelisk in Military Heritage Park, Barrie, Ontario.

- British Columbia
  ◦ Mitchell Gardens, Chilliwack, named because of the significant role he played in the building of married quarters there. A memorial cairn was unveiled by him on 12th October 1973.
  ◦ A brass plaque at All Sappers' Memorial Park, CFB Chilliwack was dedicated in 2005 by the CFB Chilliwack Memorial Society. He played a significant role in building the memorial.
- Mitchell Street, Mount Royal, Québec, where he played a significant part in the building of a housing project.
- The main building of the Canadian Forces School of Military Engineering, CFB Gagetown, New Brunswick, is named after him.
- Coulson Mitchell Lake, Manitoba, about one hundred kilometres east of Thompson, named in November 2013 was renamed Norman Mitchell Lake at the request of his family, as that is how he was known.
- Two 49 cents postage stamps in honour of the ninety-four Canadian VC winners were

The York Cemetery VC Memorial.

The Canadian VC memorial plaque (back right) outside the British High Commission in Ottawa (Memorials to Valour).

issued by Canada Post on 21st October 2004 on the 150th Anniversary of the first Canadian VC's action, Alexander Roberts Dunn VC.

- Communities and Local Government commemorative paving stones for the 145 VCs born in Australia, Belgium, Canada, China, Denmark, Egypt, France, Germany, India, Iraq, Japan, Nepal, Netherlands, New Zealand, Newfoundland, Pakistan, South Africa, Sri Lanka, Ukraine and United States of America were unveiled at the National Memorial Arboretum, Alrewas, Staffordshire by Prime Minister David Cameron MP and Sergeant Johnson Beharry VC on 5th March 2015.
- Memorial at the site of the VC action, Pont d'Aire, Escaudoeuvres, France.

The dedication of the All Sappers' Memorial Park, CFB Chilliwack, in 1946.

The Canadian Centennial Medal commemorates the hundredth anniversary of the Canadian Confederation About 29,500 medals were issued, including 8,500 to Canadian military personnel.

The Canadian Volunteer Service Medal was awarded to military personnel who completed eighteen months voluntary active service between 3rd September 1939 and 1st March 1947. A silver clasp with a maple leaf was awarded for sixty days service outside Canada. Eligibility was extended in 2001 to members of the auxiliary services, merchant mariners, Corps of Canadian Fire Fighters who served in Britain during the Blitz, Overseas Welfare Workers, Voluntary Aid Detachments, Ferry Command pilots and British Commonwealth Air Training Plan instructors. Members of the Royal Canadian Mounted Police were added in 2003.

The memorial to Norman Mitchell at Pont d'Aire. The sugar factory is on the right and the Canal de l'Escaut is behind the camera position.

The Queen Elizabeth II Silver Jubilee Medal was created in 1977 to mark the 25th anniversary of the Queen's accession in the United Kingdom, Canada, Australia and New Zealand. Until 1977 the United Kingdom authorities decided on a total number for coronation and jubilee medals, which were then allocated to Empire, Dominion and Commonwealth countries. From 1977 the award was at the discretion of each national government – 30,000 in Britain, 1,507 in New Zealand, 6,870 in Australia and 30,000 in Canada.

The 49 Cent postage stamps issued by Canada Post on 21st October 2004.

In addition to the VC and MC he was awarded the 1914–15 Star, British War Medal 1914–20, Victory Medal 1914–19 with Mentioned-in-Despatches Oakleaf, Defence Medal 1939–45, War Medal 1939–45, Canadian Volunteer Service Medal 1939–45 with Maple Leaf clasp, George VI Coronation Medal 1937, Elizabeth II Coronation Medal 1953, Canadian Centennial Medal 1967 and Elizabeth II Silver Jubilee Medal 1977. The VC is held by the Canadian Military Engineers Museum, CFB Gagetown, New Brunswick.

1717 PRIVATE EDWARD JOHN FRANCIS RYAN
55th Australian Infantry Battalion AIF

John, or Jack, Ryan, as he was known, was born on 9th February 1890 at Tumut, New South Wales, Australia. His father, Michael Ryan (22nd April 1860–18th June 1922), born at Sydney, New South Wales, was a bullock cart driver and labourer. He married Eugenia Constance née Newman (18th December 1864–12th November 1940), born at Yass, NSW, in 1886 at Tumut. They were living at Russell Street, Tumut in 1918, where he subsequently died. She was living there in 1930 and subsequently died at Yass. John had six siblings:

- Harold Edward Mervyn Ryan (18th January 1888–3rd November 1926) was accepted as a teacher on probation on 30th October 1907. He had a heart condition, contracted rheumatic fever and died at Tumut and District Hospital.
- Leslie Hensfort Ryan (15th November 1891–1892) was born at Hay, NSW and died at Narrandera, NSW.
- Eileen Muriel Ryan (September 1893–30th August 1943) born at Tumut, married Orbert Albert Garland (1895–21st August 1939), her maternal cousin, in 1916 at Yass, NSW, where he was born. He was a carrier in 1930, when they were living at O'Brien Street, North Yass. They both died at Yass. They had five children:
    - Albert Philip Garland (1916–70) married Grace Adeline Mowll née Daw (15th December 1909–22nd May 1965), born at Waterloo, NSW, in 1959 at Sydney, NSW. She had married Richard Albert Mowll (26th May 1908–27th March 1958), a labourer, at Redfern, NSW in 1929. Richard and Grace were living at 103 Wilson Street, Botany in 1931, at 30 Government Road, Mascot, NSW

John Ryan's mother, Eugenia.

Tumut is 410 kms southwest of Sydney and 525 kms northeast of Melbourne. Hamilton Hume discovered the Tumut River in 1824 and the first white squatter, Benjamin Warby, arrived in 1828, although he and others who followed only became licensed leaseholders from 1839. More settlers arrived in the 1840s and a courthouse was established in 1845. The town was laid out in 1848 but for a while most buildings were just huts. The first Post Office operated from the Courthouse in 1849. After the 1852 floods, the town site moved uphill away from the Tumut River. In 1860 thousands of prospectors passed through on their way to the goldfields. With gold inevitably came bushrangers and Ned Kelly's brother operated in the district in the 1870s. In 1887 Tumut became a municipality and a public hospital opened in 1900. In 1903 the railway reached the town from Gundagai until it closed in January 1984. Dairy farming and forestry were the main employments in the 20th century. Blowering Dam was built above the town, with power stations on the Tumut River. In 1908 Tumut was one of the sites considered for the National Capital.

in 1933, at 34 Albert Street, Botany in 1936 and at 90 Rochford Street, Grayndler, NSW in 1943, where Richard subsequently died. Richard and Grace had three children – Beresford Albert Mowll (1930–72), Noelene Dorothy Mowll (1932–2007) and Richard John Mowll (died 2002). Albert and Grace were living at Camdenville, Grayndler, NSW in 1963 and at Unit 8, 6 Warilda Street, Bexley, NSW in 1965.

Yass, in the Southern Tablelands of New South Wales, is 280 kms southwest of Sydney and fifty-nine kilometres from Canberra. The historic main street has a number of well-preserved 19th century verandah post pubs, although most have since been converted to other uses. The area was first visited by Europeans in 1821, during an expedition led by Hamilton Hume. By 1830 a settlement had begun, where the Sydney to Melbourne road crossed the Yass River. Yass was incorporated as a District Council in 1843 and on 13th March 1873 the Municipal District of Yass was created. Sir Walter Merriman established Merryville, a famous sheep stud and fine wool establishment, in 1903. Yass was also a site considered for the Federal Capital. The Hume Highway passed through the town until it was bypassed in 1994. Many flourmills were set up and by 1842 the Yass Steam Mill was in operation. It continued until destroyed in a flood in 1870 but a new steam mill opened that June. In 1892 Yass was connected to the New South Wales Government Railways. The last trains operated in October 1988.

- ◦ Keith Garland (born and died 1917).
- ◦ Diana Madge Garland (c.1919–23rd May 1955) married Alexander 'Sandy' Wilson (11th August 1917–12th February 2004) in 1944 at Yass. He served as a sapper in the Royal Australian Engineers 19th December 1942–16th November 1945 (NX150032 & N242719). He was discharged from 59th Australian Corps Field Park Company. Sandy was a labourer in 1949, when he was living with his brother George Wilson (1892–1974) at Mountain View, Jeir. Diana was living at 46 Church Street, Yass at that time and they were both at the same addresses in 1954. They had three children.
- ◦ Jack Garland (21st February 1921–8th February 1985) served in the Australian Army 3rd August 1942–21st March 1946 (NX104155 & N4539). He was a private in 2/12th Australian Infantry Battalion at the time of his discharge. Jack married Clarice Ann Webb (1926–18th September 1972) in 1946 at Yass, where she was born. He was a labourer in 1949, when they were living at Upper Burrinjuck, Yass. By 1958 he was a station hand and they were living at Sugar Loaf Station, Wee Jasper, NSW and at Blackburn, Yass in 1968. Jack was living at Blackburn in 1977 and at 1/70 Rossi Street, Yass in 1980. They had two children, including Monica Ann Garland (1949–58).
- ◦ June Margaret Garland (12th April 1926–9th April 1990) married Norman 'Norm' William Parker (5th October 1912–28th February 1987), an electrician born at Mullumbimby, NSW, in 1947 at Yass. He had married Myrtle Eileen Williams McCabe (1914–2004), born at St Leonards, North Sydney, on 15th July 1933 at Christ Church, Lavender Bay, North Sydney, NSW. They were living at 58 Bolton Street, Newcastle, NSW in 1937 and had three children, including Gordon Graham Williams Parker (1935–90) and Myrtle Eileen Williams Parker (born 1937). The marriage ended in divorce. Myrtle married Almore David Andersen in 1944 at Balmain, NSW and they lived at 285 Waterloo Road, Bankstown East, NSW. Almore had married Ruby Celia James (1908–80) in 1929 at North Sydney and they had a son, Almore James Andersen (1929–30). The marriage ended in divorce and Ruby married twice more. Norm and June were living at Blacktown, Mitchell, NSW in 1949 and at Blacktown North, Chifley, NSW in 1980. Norm died at Leura, NSW and June at Seymour, Victoria. Norm and June had five children, including Mitchell Parker (born and died 1965).

- Malcolm 'Mack' Merlin Ryan (20th October 1896–14th August 1984) enlisted in the AIF at Cootamundra, NSW on 13th February 1918 (57347). He was described as 5′ 11″ tall, weighing 168 lbs, with fair complexion, blue eyes, fair hair and his religious denomination was Roman Catholic. He joined at Show Ground Camp, Sydney on 15th February and transferred to the Recruits Training Squadron, Menangle Camp. He transferred to the Australian Light Horse on 3rd July. On 17th August he embarked at Port Sydney and arrived at Suez, Egypt on 19th September. While aboard he was treated for gonorrhoea from 18th August and, on arrival at Suez, was admitted to hospital until 29th September. He was discharged to the Depot at Moascar and was allotted to 6th Light Horse Regiment on 13th October, joining on 16th October. He was admitted to the Light Horse Field Ambulance with pyrexia 20th-28th October and was detached to the ANZAC Mounted Division on 19th November. On 21st November, Mack was admitted to 2nd Australian Stationary Hospital, Moascar with gonorrhoea. He joined the Training Regiment on 13th December and rejoined 6th Light Horse Regiment at Rafa on 11th February 1919. On 3rd March he was admitted to 24th Stationary Hospital, Kantara with epistaris. He was transferred to 14th Australian General Hospital, Abbassia on 5th March, to the Military Hospital, Choulna with German measles on 10th March and back to 14th Australian General Hospital on 2nd April. He embarked aboard HT *Warwickshire* on 15th April and was admitted to hospital while aboard with gastritis 24th-25th April. He disembarked at Melbourne, Victoria on 28th May and was discharged from No.2 Military District on 5th April 1920. In 1930 he was a labourer, living at Mittagong, Werriwa, NSW. Mack married Dorothy Isobelle Hyams née Airey (1906–84) in 1951 at Melbourne, Victoria, where she was born. They were living in St Kilda, Victoria at 11a Alma Road in 1972, at 1/36 Eildon Road in 1977 and at 2/176 Barkly Street in 1980. He died at Caulfield and she at South Caulfield, Victoria. Dorothy had married Stanley John Airey (1898–1941), born at Perth, Western Australia, in 1927 at Melbourne. They were living at 115 Park Street, St Kilda in 1928 and had a daughter, Marlene Dorothy Airey (1933–88). Stanley had married Doris Eugene French (1895–1930), born at Barrington, Tasmania, in 1920 at Launceston, Tasmania. They were living at 6 Melvill Street, Hawthorn, Victoria in December 1921. They had twins, Margaret and Jeffery Airey, born prematurely in 1921, and neither survived. Doris went on holiday to Tasmania in February 1922 and never returned. Stanley filed for divorce on 26th June 1923, while living at 76 Osborne Street, South Yarra. The marriage was dissolved on 23rd May 1927.

- Phyllis Gertrude Ryan (1899–1974) married Harrington 'Henry/Harry' Alexander Grant (1894–21st September 1935), a horse trainer born at Tumut, in 1919 at Sydney. He contracted pneumonia at Wyalong, NSW in 1912, which developed into chronic bronchitis. Henry enlisted in 10th Reinforcements, 6th Australian Light Horse at Victoria Barracks, Sydney. NSW on 18th July 1915 and joined at Liverpool, NSW. He was diagnosed with chronic bronchitis and was discharged medically unfit for active service on 15th September. He attested again in the 10th Reinforcements, 53rd Battalion AIF as Henry Alexander Grant at Victoria Barracks on 4th July 1917 (3630). He was described as 5′9¾″ tall, weighing 154 lbs, with dark complexion, brown eyes, black hair and his religious denomination was Church of England. He reported for duty with E Company, 1st Depot Battalion at Show Ground Camp, Sydney on 6th July and embarked at Sydney aboard HMAT A28 *Miltiades* on 2nd August. He forfeited two days' pay for being absent without leave from 2.15 p.m. until 9.10 p.m. at Halifax, Nova Scotia on 20th September. Henry disembarked at Glasgow, Scotland on 2nd October and joined 14th Training Battalion, Hurdcott, Wiltshire the following day. He was confined to barracks for seven days for being absent from a night operation on 5th December. He went to France via Southampton on 12th February 1918 and joined the Australian Infantry Base Depot, Rouelles next day. On 19th February he joined 35th Battalion. Henry was taken ill on 14th July and was treated at 10th Australian Field Ambulance and to No.5 Casualty Clearing Station next day. He was transferred to 9th General Hospital, Rouen on 18th July and was evacuated to England on 21st August aboard the *Cornish Castle*. Next day he was admitted to 4th Southern General Hospital, Plymouth, Devon with chronic bronchitis. Henry was granted leave 12th-26th October and then reported to No.1 Command Depot, Sutton Veny, Wiltshire. He was admitted to 1st Australian General Hospital, Sutton Veny with pneumonia on 15th November and was discharged to No.2 Command Depot, Weymouth, Dorset on 3rd January 1919. He returned to Australia aboard HMT *Nevasa*, embarking on 5th March and disembarking at Sydney on 23rd April. Henry was discharged medically unfit for active service on 19th May 1919. They were living at 36 Houston Parade, Kensington, South Sydney in 1930. He died at Randwick, NSW and she later lived at 41 Doncaster Avenue, Kensington, NSW. She died at Queanbeyan, NSW.

- Reginald Leo Ryan (28th February 1904–17th September 1978), a railway fireman, married Nellie Josephine Doherty (7th November 1905–30th January 1980), born at Braidwood, NSW, in 1927 at Goulburn, NSW. They were living in Goulburn at 46 George Street in 1930, at 64 Kinghorne Street in 1937, at 54 Mulwarree Street in 1958 and at 162 Kinghorne Street in 1972. He died at Wollongong, NSW. They had a daughter:
    - Joyce Florence Ryan (16th July 1928–20th October 2000), born at Goulburn, was a clerk in 1954, living with her parents. She married Kevin Fisher McMahon (6th March 1928–5th February 2005), a police constable born at Werris Creek, NSW, at Goulburn in 1956. They were living at Bungonia Place, Goldsmith Street, Goulburn in 1958 and 1963, at 111 Albury Street, Harden by 1977 and at 26 Murray Place, Port Macquarie by 1980. They both died at Port Macquarie, NSW.

John's paternal grandfather, John Ryan (1841–20th January 1893), was born in Co Cork, Ireland. He married Margaret née Cross (1822–6th October 1915), born at Ennistymon, Co Clare, Ireland, in Ireland in 1857. They emigrated to Australia in the late 1850s. They both died at Tumut. In addition to Michael they had three other children:

- Bridget Ryan (19th February 1863–8th March 1945), born at Coolac, Cootamundra, NSW, married Francis James Dunstone (1860–16th August 1908), born at Batlow, NSW, in 1883 at Tumut. He died at Tumut and she at Narrandera, NSW. They had three children:
  - Hilda Alice Margaret Dunstone (1884–14th May 1945) married Henry F Hargreaves (1871–1952) at Sydney, NSW in 1907. They had two sons – Reginald W Hargreaves 1908 and George D Hargreaves 1911.
  - Mervyn Francis Dunstone (15th October 1886–3rd September 1947), a horse breaker, married Grace Ethel Gallard (1891–17th June 1963) at Granville, NSW in 1911 and they had a son, Laurence Jeffrey Dunstone (25th June 1912–5th February 1987). Mervyn enlisted in the AIF on 4th July 1918 at Sydney (124). At the time he was living with his family at Terminus Street, Liverpool, NSW. He gave his year of birth as 1888 and had previously been rejected for military service on medical grounds. He was described as 5′6″ tall, weighing 140 lbs, with fresh complexion, blue eyes, brown hair and his religious denomination was Roman Catholic. Mervyn joined 1st Remount Unit Reinforcements on 5th September. He was diagnosed with valvular disease of the heart on 11th October and was admitted to No.5 Australian General Hospital, St Kilda Road, Melbourne, Victoria on 22nd October. He stated that he had no complaints of any kind and had never felt better in his life. However, he was known to suffer from shortness of breath during exercise and was declared permanently unfit for service abroad. He returned to NSW for discharge on or about 26th October.
  - Reginald Harold Dunstone (15th July 1891–23rd May 1953).
- Edward Ryan (1864–89), born at Muttama, NSW and died at Tumut.
- John Ryan (1870–1910), born at Tumut, married Susannah Sarah Bridle (2nd August 1873–13th November 1961) at Tumut in 1900, where she was born. He died at Tumut and she at Casino, NSW. They had a daughter, Edna Ryan (19th February 1901–21st January 1984).

His maternal grandfather, Joseph Newman (23rd April 1830–1st October 1915), born at Rayleigh, Essex, England, emigrated to Australia with his parents aboard the *Upton Castle*, departing on 24th December 1837 and arriving on 24th February 1838. He married Susan née Fisher (1834–16th March 1903), born in Australia, in 1853 at Gundaroo, Gunning, NSW. She was living at Clifford Street, Goulburn in January 1901 and died at Boorowa, NSW. He was a farmer in 1913, when he was living with his son, Herbert and his family, at Flakney Creek, Rye Park, Woollahra, NSW. He died at Gunning, NSW. In addition to Eugenia they had eleven other children:

- Emma Newman (1855–19th May 1938), born at Yass, NSW, married Isaac Garland (1854–21st May 1914), born at Gunning, at Yass in 1881. They both died at Yass. They had seven children:

Gunning, between Goulburn and Yass in the Southern Tablelands of New South Wales, is 260 kms southwest of Sydney and seventy-five kilometers north of the national capital, Canberra. The region was first explored by Europeans in 1820 and was settled the following year by Hamilton Hume. In 1824 Hume and William Hovell left Gunning to discover the overland route to Port Phillip Bay, where Melbourne is now sited. Land sales began in 1838. In 1865, bushranger Ben Hall and his gang held up Kimberley's Inn, during which a constable was shot dead. By 1886 Gunning had a police station, courthouse, post office and school. Farming was the main economic activity. The Main South Railway from Sydney arrived in 1875 and was completed through to Albury in 1882. The Hume Highway through the town was bypassed in 1993.

  - Harriet Garland (1881–16th October 1945) married John Perceval at Yass in 1897. They had at least six children – Herbert AT Perceval 1900, John HM Perceval 1903, Clarence W Perceval 1906, Allen E Perceval 1910, Sylvia D Perceval 1917 and Iris J Perceval 1921. Harriet died at Temora, NSW.
  - Isaac Garland (1884–1962) married Ellen M Newood (died 1975) at Boorowa, NSW in 1904. He died at Sydney, NSW and she at Annandale, NSW. They had at least six children – Reginald P Garlan 1905, John HJ Garlan 1908, Jessie E Garlan 1910, Adeline M Garlan 1913, Amy M Garlan 1915 and Ethel V Garlan 1918.
  - Susan Garland (1886–15th February 1921) married George E Dunne at Yass in 1904, registered as Garlan. They had four children – Ethelina FA Dunne 1906, a stillborn boy 1908, Susan C Dunne 1910 and Gordon G Dunne 1913.
  - William 'Bill' Fisher Garland (1887–20th April 1965).
  - John J Garland (1889–91).
  - Harold Edward Garland (1893–1970).
  - Rupert Edgar Francis Garland (1st March 1895–19th June 1922) birth registered as Garlan. He was described as a carpenter, 5′ 8½″ tall, weighing 143 lbs, with fair hair, blue eyes, wearing a truss and his religious denomination was Church of England, when he was sentenced to two years' hard labour for perjury at Yass on 31st May 1917. He married Anastasia Murphy (1897–1987) at Yass in 1919. They had a daughter, Emma E Garland, in 1920. Anastasia married Percival Kirk at Boorowa in 1925.
- Sarah Newman (1857–65), born at Gunning and died at Yass.
- Lucy Newman (1858–1933) married John Wesley Bell (1851–5th December 1939) at Yass in 1876. They were living at East Street, Grenfell in May 1916. They had thirteen children:

- Mary 'Pearl' Frances Bell (30th April 1876–22nd April 1878).
- Aureola May Bell (born and died 1877).
- Charles EJ Bell (1878–81).
- Olive Marian Bell (1880–21st July 1924) married Charles H Mitton (1878–1931) at Grenfell in 1903. They had two children – Daisy M Mitton 1906 and Kenneth C Mitton 1914.
- Leonie Florence Bell (1882–14th November 1947) married Lachlan Donald Mitton in 1912. They had two sons – Donald K Mitton 1914 and Norman H Mitton 1916.
- Vernie Rowland 'Sonny' Bell (1884–25th March 1969).
- Cecil Newman Bell (1886–6th November 1955).
- Ina Geraldine Bell (1888–4th August 1970).
- Bertram 'Bertie' Norman Bell (1891–4th November 1955).
- Kenneth Roy Bell (1894–14th August 1968) was a labourer when he enlisted in the AIF on 27th May 1916 at Cootamundra, NSW. He was described as 5′6″ tall, weighing 140 lbs, with dark complexion, brown eyes, black hair and his religious denomination was Church of England. He joined 2nd Cootamundra Depot Battalion but was diagnosed with a large inguinal hernia on the right side on 5th June and was discharged on 8th June.
- Vera Gladys Bell (4th March 1896–18th December 1977) married Ernest Robert Hall (died 1964) at Grenfell in 1916. They had at least two children – Athol M Hall 1916 and Iris M Hall 1920.
- Muriel Fairlie Bell (1898–4th January 1984) married Thomas J Graham at Grenfell in 1922.
- Ruby Doris Bell (1901–17th February 1984).

• Martha Newman (1861–10th January 1941), born at Gundagai, NSW, married William Henry Garland (1858–28th May 1925) in 1881 at Yass, where he was born, registered as Garlan. He was a labourer in 1913, when they were living at O'Brien Street, Woollahra, NSW. He became a farmer later. They both died at Yass. They had nine children:
  - Janet Garland (1886–1967) married Edward A Bateup (1873–1949 or 1882–1927) in 1904. They had at least seven children – Ivy D Bateup 1905, Myrtle AR Bateup 1907, William E Bateup 1910, Ruby M Bateup 1912, Terence C Bateup 1914, Cecil C Bateup 1918 and Bede Bateup 1921.
  - William Henry Garland (27th February 1888–14th May 1956) married Elizabeth E Hatton (1885–1961) in 1906. They had at least five children – Phyllis G Garland 1912, Beryl C Garland 1914, Normal J Garland 1916, Rex Garland 1918 and Mervyn Garland 1920.
  - Mabel Adelaide Garland (1891–1940) married Alfred J Sheldrick in 1909. They had at least ten children – Dorothy M Sheldrick 1910, Mabel D Sheldrick 1911, Martha Sheldrick 1912, Choria Sheldrick 1914, Myrtle

Sheldrick 1916, twins Jack and Alfred Sheldrick 1918, twins May and Ray Sheldrick 1919 and Mary C Sheldrick 1921.
   - Edward Roy Adolphus Garland (1892–1938).
   - Orbert Albert Garland (1895–21st August 1939) married the VC's sister, Muriel.
   - Terence Claude Garland (1895–28th August 1967) married Ellen E Rayner in 1914. They had at least three children – Ellen C Garland 1915 and twins Dulcie M and Thelma M Garland 1920.
   - Cecil Joseph Garland (1897–1958).
   - Norman Clemence Garland (1900–8th February 1961) married Maud E Hearne in 1921.
   - Madeline D Garland (1907).
- David Newman (16th January 1863–14th June 1949) may have been David John Newman, who married Catherine Emma Susan Daly (24th October 1867–29th March 1945), born at Little Plain, NSW, in 1902 at Boorowa, NSW. He was a miner in 1913, when they were living at Rye Park, Woollahra. By 1930 he was a labourer and they were living at 1 Parry Street, Ryde, NSW. Catherine died at Smithfield, NSW and David 1949 at Rockdale, NSW. This couple had four children:
   - Minnie Iris Newman (1902–71) married Edwin Laurence Holman (died 1956) at Annandale, NSW in 1938. She died at Kogarah, NSW.
   - Mary Eileen Newman (13th March 1904–30th April 1977) married John Bitmead (died 1965) at Hornsby, NSW in 1944 He died at Burwood, NSW.
   - David D Newman (1907–09).
   - Dulcie H Newman (1910) married Bartholomew Keenan at Sydney in 1930.
- William Joseph Newman (13th September 1866–24th August 1961), a labourer, married Emma Jane Vitler (1874–8th May 1960), born at Carcoar, NSW, in 1891. He was a night watchman in 1930, when they were living at Willow Vale, Mittagong, NSW. They both subsequently died there. They had four daughters:
   - Lillian Beatrice Newman (1892–24th March 1963) married William E Brown in 1914. They had at least four children – Thelma Brown 1914, Elsie Brown 1916, William M Brown 1917 and Colin E Brown 1920.
   - Elsie May Mary Newman (1894–1957) married Spencer William Dowling (c.1888–1951) in 1910. They had at least three children – Alice M Dowling 1911, Cecil J Dowling 1913 and Lena J Dowling 1916.
   - Ivy Ann Elizabeth Newman (1897–1975) married Patrick J Feeney at Woollahra in 1918.
   - Kathleen Mona Marjorie Newman (1908–77) married Sidney William Clifford Smith (1905–74), a salesman born at Inverell, NSW, at All Saints' Church, Petersham, NSW on 25th February 1928.
- Henry Edwin Newman (1869–1942) was a labourer, living alone at West Dubbo, NSW in 1936. He later died there.

- Amy Jane Newman (26th June 1871–18th September 1957) married James Alexander McDonald (10th December 1865–31st October 1946) at Gunning on 16th September 1896. He died at Kingsford, NSW and she at Eastwood, NSW. They had seven children:
  - Aspasia Leila Lemercy McDonald (26th December 1898–1st November 1988) married John McCrory at Crookwell, NSW in 1928.
  - Dorothy Zilla Newman McDonald (11th November 1899–17th February 1972) married Henry M McDonald (sic) at Crookwell in 1927.
  - Thelma Eririta McDonald (17th June 1901–26th August 2000) married William H Stockton at Canterbury, NSW in 1932.
  - Glentworth James Lovell McDonald (17th August 1902–11th January 1903).
  - Hilfred Eric Glenn McDonald (27th January 1905–19th December 1960) married Ivy Myrtle Webster (1909–89) in 1930.
  - Thea Sybil McDonald (11th January 1909–21st February 2003) married Ronald Eric Leslie Hare at Chatswood, NSW in 1936.
  - Molly Constance McDonald (born 2nd February 1912) married John William MacNamara at Sydney, NSW in 1949.
- Harold Herbert Newman (1872–4th April 1956), a builder's labourer, married Ruby Mabel May Palmer (1888–1966), born at Rye Park, NSW, in 1907 at Boorowa, NSW. They were living at Flakney Creek, Rye Park, Woollahra in 1913. She issued a warrant at Yass for her nephew, Rupert Edgar Francis Garland, charged with committing perjury on 2nd February 1917. A warrant for Harold's arrest for deserting his wife and children was issued in 1926. He was described as 5′11″ tall, medium build, fair complexion, thin features, light brown hair, clean-shaven and with a dint on the side of his eye where the bone had been broken. The warrant was cancelled in 1928 and he was ordered to pay £1 per week to support his wife and £0/10/- per week for his two children. A warrant was issued by the Children's Court, Yass, for his arrest after disobeying a magisterial order for the support of his wife and children with £28 owing. Ruby was living at Orion Street, North Yass in 1930. Harold died at Liverpool, NSW, Ruby was living at 274 Lords Place, Orange, NSW in 1963 and died at Burwood, NSW. They had eight children:
  - Gladys Elsie Palmer (23rd July 1905–23rd May 1986) married Arthur S Johnson at Annandale, NSW in 1924.
  - Colin George Newman (1907).
  - Bertha M Newman (1908–09).
  - Edmund Joseph Newman (1909–85) married Kathleen MacMillan at Orange, NSW in 1938.
  - Vera Newman (born 1911).
  - Harold Edgar Newman (1913–16).
  - Rita P Newman (1914–16).
  - Sylvia Joyce Newman (born 1918).

- Jannett Newman (1874–7th November 1921) left home for Sydney in early January 1901 and her mother placed a missing person's report in the NSW Police Gazette on 30th January. Janet was described as 5' tall, slight build, sallow complexion and fair hair. She suffered from a hip disease and walked with a marked limp. Her mother believed that she may have gone to a maternity home in Sydney. Jannett was living with her brother, Harold and his family, at Flakney Creek, Rye Park in 1913. She died at Yass.
- Malcolm Wentworth Newman (born and died 1879).

West Blowering School in 1902. John Ryan is seated in the front row far left.

John was educated at West Blowering School, near Tumut until 1902 and then at Tumut Catholic Convent School. He worked at Tumut Post Office before becoming a labourer. He broke his right kneecap in an accident, which was wired and caused pain thereafter, although it did not affect his military service.

John enlisted as John Ryan in 2nd Reinforcements, 55th Battalion on 30th November 1915 at Wagga Wagga, NSW and was posted to Tiranna Camp, near Goulburn (1717). He was described as 5′7″ tall, weighing 154 lbs, with brown complexion, grey eyes, brown hair and his religious denomination was Roman Catholic. He was part of a group that became known as the Kangaroos. They marched 515 kms to

The old Tumut Catholic Convent School building.

Tumut Post Office opened on 1st January 1849.

The Kangaroo march in Yass.

Sydney, seeking recruits on the way. Nearly one hundred left Wagga on 1st December, but more than 220 completed the march at the Domain in Sydney on 7th January 1916. They were promised pay and leave in Sydney but on arrival were told to report to Goulburn before pay and allowances could commence. The group protested but obeyed. However, they caused 'disgraceful scenes' of drunkenness and disorder once leave was granted.

John embarked at Sydney aboard HMAT A40 *Ceramic* on 14th June 1916 and disembarked at Port Said, Egypt on 16th May. He was absent from muster parade on 26th July, while serving with 14th Training Battalion, and forfeited

HMAT A40 *Ceramic* loading in 1915. SS *Ceramic* was built in Belfast for the White Star Line 1912–13 and worked the Liverpool–Australia route. In 1914, she was requisitioned and survived a number of U-boat attacks. She returned to the White Star Line to resume civilian service in November 1920. When White Star merged with Cunard in 1934, *Ceramic* was sold to Shaw, Savill & Albion, but carried on working the same route. In February 1940, she was again requisitioned as a troopship. In the South Atlantic on 11th August, she collided at speed with the cargo ship *Testbank*. Both ships were damaged,but remain afloat. *Testbank* made Cape Town under her own power. *Ceramic*'s passengers were transferred to RMS *Viceroy* of *India* and she was assisted to Walvis Bay in South West Africa by a tug. After emergency repairs she went to Cape Town for renovation before resuming service. On 3rd November 1942, *Ceramic* left Liverpool for Australia. carrying 641 passengers and crew and 12,362 tons of cargo, as part of Convoy ON 149. When it dispersed, she continued unescorted and at midnight on 6th/7th December she was hit by a torpedo from U-*515* in mid-Atlantic. A few minutes later, two more torpedoes hit the engine room. However, she remained afloat and was abandoned in good order. Three hours later, U-*515* fired two more torpedoes, which sank her immediately. It was a stormy night and the heavy sea capsized some lifeboats. U-*515* returned to look for *Ceramic*'s Master, Herbert Elford, to ascertain the ship's destination. One lifeboat was sighted around noon, but with the storm raging, the U-boat crew seized the first available survivor, Sapper Eric Munday RE. Despite searches by neutral craft, no other survivors were picked up. Munday spent the rest of the war at Stalag VIII-B in Silesia (Australian War Memorial).

ten days' pay. On 29th July he embarked at Alexandria aboard HMT *Arcadian* and disembarked at Southampton, Hampshire on 9th August. He was late on parade at Larkhill, Wiltshire on 28th August and forfeited seven days' pay. On 9th September he embarked for France and joined 5th Australian Division Base Depot, Étaples on 11th September. He joined 55th Battalion on 23rd September 1916.

John was attached as a fettler to 17th ANZAC Light Railway Unit 8th January–12th June 1917. He overstayed leave from 8.00 p.m. on 2nd July until 3.30 p.m. on 3rd July and was awarded four days' Field Punishment No.2 and forfeited six days' pay. He was granted leave from 21st September and reported sick with gonorrhoea while returning. He was admitted at 7th Convalescence Depot on 4th October and transferred to 39th General Hospital, Boulogne on 6th October. On 11th November he was discharged to 5th Australian Division Base Depot, Étaples and rejoined his unit on 22nd November. He was absent without leave from 8.30 a.m. on 7th June 1918 until 5.00 p.m. on 9th June and was awarded seven days' Field Punishment No.2 and forfeited 10 days' pay.

Awarded the VC for his actions near Bellicourt, France on 30th September 1918, LG 26th December 1918. John was admitted to 13th Australian Field Ambulance and No.12 Casualty Clearing Station on 30th September and was transferred by Ambulance Train 20 to 74th General Hospital, Tronville on 2nd October. On 25th October he was transferred to No.1 Convalescent Depot, Tronville and was discharged to the Australian Infantry Base Depot on 15th November. He rejoined his unit on 7th December and was granted leave in Britain 17th December–10th January 1919.

John was transferred to the Depot in England on 16th April 1919. He was presented with the VC by the King in the quadrangle of Buckingham Palace on 22nd May. John reported sick at Weymouth, Dorset on 3rd June and was admitted to 1st Australian Dermatological Hospital, Bulford, Wiltshire later that day. On

1st Australian Dermatological Hospital at Bulford took over the facilities of an existing military hospital. Kiwi Primary School now stands on the same site.

Parkhouse Camp was between Bulford and Tidworth, on the edge of Salisbury Plain. Nothing remains today.

8th June he was discharged to the Convalescent Training Depot, Parkhouse, Tidworth, Hampshire where he was on the strength of 5 Platoon, B Company in No.1 Camp. On 30th July he appeared before a court martial at Bhurtpore Barracks, Tidworth for failing to appear at a place of parade on 15th and 16th July, disobeying a lawful command by failing to appear at the Battalion Orderly Room at 11.30 a.m. on 16th July when ordered to do so by Lieutenant JA Underwood and using insubordinate language, 'You are a fucking bastard', to 3074 RSM Charles Henry Beaconsfield Robson at 3.15 p.m. on 16th July. He pleaded guilty to missing the parade on 15th July and to swearing at the RSM but not guilty to the other charges. He was found guilty on all charges and forfeited one day's pay.

John transferred to No.2 Group Convalescent Training Depot, Sutton Veny, Wiltshire on 1st August. He embarked at Devonport on 7th September aboard HMAT A14 *Euripides* and was admitted to the ship's hospital on 4th October. When he disembarked in 2nd Military District on 24th October, he was carried shoulder high to a buffet where he met his mother and brother, Malcolm, who had returned from Palestine. He arrived at Tumut on 24th October, to be met at the station by a large crowd, including a representation of a kangaroo as he was one of the famous 'Kangaroos' in the march to Sydney. He was carried to a car and then to the Red Cross Rooms for a civic reception. On 4th November he was presented with an inscribed gold medal at Blowering and a wad of notes. He arrived at Wagga on 7th November and was greeted by a crowd of other soldiers, including his brother Malcolm, prominent citizens, representatives of patriotic bodies, the Council and the Soldiers' Welcome Committee. On the shoulders of other veterans he was carried to a car, which took him to the Town Hall and another civic reception. He was one of twenty-two VCs who attended a dinner at the Australia Hotel, Castlereagh Street, Sydney on 11th November, hosted by Hon Hugh Donald McIntosh MLC. On 10th December he attended a carnival at the Southern Cross Ground, Wagga and was presented with a wallet of notes. On

SS *Euripides* (14,947 tons), a passenger (140 first, 334 third and 750 steerage class) and cargo ship, was launched in January 1914 by Harland & Wolff in Belfast, Ireland for the Aberdeen Line. At the time she was the largest ship in the fleet and operated on the London – South Africa – Australia route. Her maiden voyage commenced in London on 1st July 1914. She was crossing the Indian Ocean to Australia when war broke out and was requisitioned as a troopship on 26th August. She made seven voyages carrying troops from Australia to Europe and, from February 1919, she repatriated troops to Australia. During the war *Euripides* covered 208,307 nautical miles and carried 38,349 troops. In November 1920 she resumed Aberdeen Line's service between London and Australia. From 1929, she was managed by White Star Line and in 1932 passed to Shaw, Savill & Albion Line. She was refitted, renamed *Akaroa* and transferred to the service between Southampton and New Zealand via the Panama Canal. On 1st September 1939, *Akaroa* left Southampton and reached Auckland on 8th October. On her return voyage, after calling at Curaçao on 30th November, she diverted to join Convoy HXF 12 from Halifax, Nova Scotia and arrived in London on 27th December. For the rest of the war *Akaroa* continued to trade between Britain and New Zealand, mainly sailing unescorted, having made the Atlantic crossings in convoy. In the second half of 1945 *Akaroa* was refitted and returned to service between Britain and New Zealand. She was scrapped in May 1954 at Antwerp, Belgium.

all these occasions he was cheerful but said little in response to welcoming speeches, except to thank people and request the children be given a holiday.

John Ryan was discharged from the AIF in Sydney on 10th January 1920. On 20th March he was one of fourteen VCs, who formed a mounted guard of honour on grey horses to escort Daniel Patrick Mannix, Catholic Archbishop of Melbourne, who was leading the St Patrick's Day parade in Melbourne in an open car. He went through bad times, struggling to find work, particularly during the depression, and also suffered a number of medical problems:

The Australia Hotel, on Castlereagh Stree Sydney, opened in 1891. The opening ceremony was performed by the French actress, Sarah Bernhardt. The hotel was described as 'the best-known hotel in Australia', 'the premier hotel in Sydney' a 'The Hotel of the Commonwealth'. It clos on 30th June 1971 prior to demolition and sixty-eight storey MLC Centre was built c the site.

1926 – thirty-four weeks in Queanbeyan Hospital and at Randwick Repatriation General Hospital with pleurisy.
1928 – broke his left ankle in May and was in Sydney Hospital with influenza in December.
1929 – head injury in a motor accident.
1930 – alcoholism, admitted to Casino Memorial Hospital.

Sir Dudley Rawson Stratford de Chair KCB KCMG MVO (1864–1958) outside Government House in 1925. He was born in Québec, Canada and the family returned to England in 1870. In 1878 he joined the Royal Navy and was held captive by Arabi Pasha for six weeks in 1882. In 1915–16 as a rear admiral he commanded the 10th Cruiser Squadron in the North Sea blockade of Germany. He was promoted to vice admiral to command 3rd Battle Squadron in 1917 but was relieved and placed on half pay when he refused a post on the Board of Admiralty and for criticising the treatment of Lord Jellicoe. In July 1918 he took command of Coastguard and Reserves and was President of the Inter-Allied Commission on enemy warships 1921–23 as an admiral. In October 1923 he was appointed Governor of New South Wales, arriving in Sydney with his wife on 28th February 1924. He retired on 8th April 1930 to London. His autobiography, *The Sea is Strong*, was published in 1961.

Government House, overlooking Sydney Harbour, was constructed between 1837 and 1843. It was temporarily the residence of the Governor-General of Australia 1901–14, until that office moved to Admiralty House, and it reverted to the residence of the Governor of New South Wales. From 1996 the Governor lived and worked elsewhere nearby, as the result of a political decision by the Premier of New South Wales. However, it was realised that it was more expensive than using Government House and the Governor returned there in 2011. On 13th December that year the building, its grounds and furnishings were listed on the New South Wales State Heritage Register.

John was a labourer for eighteen months from January 1927, then worked at Mitta Weir, Victoria for six months and in Canberra for another six months, where he was living at White City Camp in 1928. He worked at Cowra as a station hand for eight weeks and was a barman there for six weeks. Following that he became a ganger at Condobolin for six months. In November 1929 he was one of fourteen VCs entertained at a luncheon at Government House by the Governor of New South Wales, Sir Dudley de Chair. John was living at Casino, NSW in 1930.

Steady employment continued to elude him. In 1931–32 he was employed for just two months. In July 1932 he was a labourer at Davis Gelatine Works, Botany. He was a casual farm work in 1933 but was unemployed in 1934 and then worked at Woorina Packing Sheds as a packer. John may have been at Yarrawonga in 1934. He was living off Davidson Street, Deniliquin, NSW in 1935 with a Charles Ryan and appears in the electoral roll at Racecourse, Balranald, NSW in 1936. However, it is known that he walked the 130 kms from Balranald, NSW to Mildura, Victoria in August 1935. On the strength of his army discharge papers he was given temporary work by the local council from 15th August 1935. Colonel Wilfrid Kent Fethers DSO, former CO of 23rd Battalion AIF and manager of the Royal Insurance Co Ltd offices at 414 Collins Street, Melbourne, saw John's story in the Melbourne newspapers. He offered John a job as a commissionaire, which he accepted. John was assisted on his journey to Melbourne by the Mildura Returned Sailors' and

Soldiers' Imperial League of Australia. Money and clothing were also provided by the Mildura Carry On Club. He was living at 41 Albion Street in March 1936 and at 45 Ross Street, Richmond in December 1938.

John made a number of claims for treatment for pleurisy, sinusitis, bronchial catarrh and neurosis caused by his military service. The chest complaints he claimed were due to being gassed three times, although he was never evacuated and there is no record in his service papers. All the claims were rejected, as they were not due to war service, on 1st April 1927 and 29th July 1932, as were appeals on 21st and 28th September 1938. This was confirmed by the State Board on 18th November 1938. Disability of ten percent for the right shoulder gunshot wound was continued at 7/- per fortnight, in addition to the VC allowance of 6d per day.

An advertisement for the Davis Gelatine Company.

Years of depravation, drink and poor living conditions took their toll and he fell ill with pneumonia, while living in Victoria Street, Carlton. He was admitted to the Royal Melbourne Hospital, where he died on 3rd June 1941. Eight VC recipients were pallbearers at his funeral – HM Ervine-Andrews, WD Joynt, RV Moon, GM Ingram, W Ruthven, AC Borella, LD McCarthy and AD Lowerson. He is buried in the Roman Catholic Section, Springvale Botanical Cemetery, Melbourne, Victoria

The Royal Melbourne Hospital was established in 1848 as the Melbourne Hospital on the corner of Swanston and Lonsdale Streets, Melbourne. In 1935 it was renamed the Royal Melbourne Hospital and in 1944 it moved to Grattan Street, Parkville. The old buildings were then used by the Queen Victoria Hospital. During the Second World War, the Parkville hospital, although under construction, was occupied by the US 4th General Hospital 1942–44. The Royal Melbourne Hospital moved into the new premises when 4th General Hospital moved to New Guinea. In 1956, Australia's first kidney transplant was performed at the hospital. The cardiology and engineering teams developed and implanted Australia's first pacemaker in 1965 and in 1996 Australia's first keyhole coronary bypass was performed there. The hospital is internationally renowned for its research and education. Since opening in 1848, the Royal Melbourne has treated more than twenty million people.

and is also commemorated in the Victorian Garden of Remembrance there (Wall 12, Row A). John is commemorated in a number of other places:

John Ryan's grave in Springvale Botanical Cemetery, Melbourne (Memorials to Valour).

- Australian Capital Territory
  - Ryan Street, Canberra.
  - Australian Victoria Cross Recipients plaque on the Victoria Cross Memorial, Campbell, dedicated on 24th July 2000.
  - Named on one of eleven plaques honouring 175 men from overseas awarded the VC for the Great War. The plaques were unveiled by the Senior Minister of State at the Foreign & Commonwealth Office and Minister for Faith and Communities, Baroness Warsi, at a reception at Lancaster House, London on 26th June 2014 attended by The Duke of Kent and relatives of the VC recipients. The Australian plaque is at the Australian War Memorial, Canberra.
  - Commemorative display in the Hall of Valour, Australian War Memorial, Canberra.
- New South Wales
  - Victoria Cross Memorial, Queen Victoria Building, George Street, Sydney dedicated on 23rd February 1992 to commemorate the visit of Queen Elizabeth II and Prince Phillip on the occasion of the Sesquicentenary of the City of Sydney. Sir Roden Cutler VC AK KCMG, Edward Kenna VC and Keith Payne VC were in attendance.
  - Victoria Cross Recipients Wall, North Bondi War Memorial donated to Waverley on 27th November 2011 by The Returned & Services League of Australia.
  - VC Memorial, Borella Road, Peards Complex, East Albury.
  - Memorial Plaque on the Boer War Memorial, Richmond Park, Tumut.
  - VC Memorial, Ingleburn RSL Club, Sydney.
- Victoria Cross Memorial, Springvale Botanical Cemetery, Melbourne, Victoria dedicated on 10th November 2013.
- Communities and Local Government commemorative paving stones for the 145 VCs born in Australia, Belgium, Canada, China, Denmark, Egypt, France, Germany,

John Ryan's plaque on the base of the Boer War Memorial, Richmond Park, Tumut (Memorials to Valour).

The commemorative paving stones for the 145 VCs born outside the British Isles at the National Memorial Arboretum (Memorials to Valour).

The Victoria Cross Memorial, Springvale Botanical Cemetery, Melbourne.

The British War Medal was instituted on 26th July 1919 for all ranks who served for twenty-eight days in an operational theatre between 5th August 1914 and 11th November 1918 or died on active service before completing twenty-eight days. Eligibility was extended in 1919–20 to mine-clearing at sea and operations in North and South Russia, eastern Baltic, Siberia, Black Sea and Caspian Sea. Many veterans were awarded the 1914–15 Star, British War Medal and Victory Medal. They became known as Pip, Squeak and Wilfred after a strip cartoon published in the Daily Mirror from 1919 to 1956.

India, Iraq, Japan, Nepal, Netherlands, New Zealand, Newfoundland, Pakistan, South Africa, Sri Lanka, Ukraine and United States of America were unveiled at the National Memorial Arboretum, Alrewas, Staffordshire by Prime Minister David Cameron MP and Sergeant Johnson Beharry VC on 5th March 2015.

In addition to the VC he was awarded the British War Medal 1914–20, Victory Medal 1914–19 and George VI Coronation Medal 1937, although the latter appears not to have been claimed. The VC was presented to the Australian War Memorial, Treloar Crescent, Campbell, Australian Capital Territory by his sister, Phyllis Grant, on 8th November 1967 and is held in the Hall of Valour.

The King George VI Coronation Medal was awarded to the Royal Family, selected officers of state, officials, servants of the Royal Household, ministers, government and local government officials, mayors, public servants, members of the armed forces and police in Britain, the colonies and Dominions. A total of 90,279 medals were awarded.

LIEUTENANT COLONEL BERNARD WILLIAM VANN
1/8th attached 1/6th Battalion, The Sherwood Foresters (Nottinghamshire and Derbyshire Regiment)

Bernard Vann was born on 9th July 1887 at 46 High Street South, Rushden, Northamptonshire. His father, Alfred George Collins Vann MA (1st July 1859–2nd September 1906), born at Northampton and known as George, was a keen sportsman, playing rugby, tennis and cricket. He was a pupil teacher at St Edmund's National School, Northampton and in his spare time studied at Northampton College of Science. He and Hannah Elizabeth Simpson (1861–November 1924), his future wife born at Snaith, Yorkshire, applied for the posts of Headmaster and Mistress of Bugbrooke Board School, near Northampton and were accepted on 27th December 1881. George and Hannah married at St Edmund's Church, Northampton on 13th April 1882. Hannah was a pupil teacher at St Giles School, Northampton for five years. She was a schoolmistress at Braunston Girls School, boarding at High Street, Braunston, Northamptonshire in 1881. George was summoned to the Northampton Petty Sessions in November 1882 for common assault having caned a six year old twice on successive days. The magistrates believed that a child of six should not be caned but dismissed the case, with George paying costs. When a boy stole another boy's hat in October 1884, George asked the Board what would be an appropriate punishment. They decided on caning, which was administered but George was again summoned to court. The Board instructed a solicitor to defend George and the case was again dismissed. He was Master of South End Elementary School, Rushden, 5th January 1885–4th September 1899, and Hannah was a certified teacher there. All five of their sons attended the school at various times. Hannah often deputised for George while he attended various courses at Oxford. She was a member of the local St John's Ambulance Brigade and was later Lady Superintendent of the Nursing Sisters. By 1899 she was President of the Women's Cooperative Guild and a member of the School Board. George became the headmaster of Chichele Grammar School, Higham Ferrers, Northamptonshire in 1899. The school was in the former chapel of Chichele College, which was founded in 1422 and was disbanded during the Dissolution of the Monasteries. They were living at Church House, College Street, Higham Ferrers in 1901. George was taken ill on Christmas Eve 1903 and was operated on at Northampton General Hospital the next day. He was elected to the Town Council in November 1904 but for health reasons did not seek re-election a year later. George died at Church House. When Chichele College closed that year, the family had to vacate the property. Hannah was appointed Headmistress

South End Elementary School in 1897 and a class photograph c.1898, with Alfred Vann on the left. The cornerstone was laid by the Bishop of Peterborough on 11th October 1870. It was a Church of England School and later a National School. Its capacity was 250 pupils.

of Church Stowe National School, Northamptonshire on 27th April 1908 with an annual salary of £75. She was living at School House, Church Stowe, Weedon, Northamptonshire in 1911. She resigned on 28th February 1914 and went to live with her brother, the Reverend Thomas Crompton Simpson, as his housekeeper at Coates Rectory, near Cirencester, Gloucestershire. She died there and is buried in St Matthew's churchyard, Coates, the funeral being conducted by her brother. Bernard had four brothers:

- Alfred George Thomas Simpson Vann (21st March 1883–12th February 1949), born at Northampton, played for Northampton Town FC in 1906. He assisted his father as a teacher at Chichele College for seven years and, when he died, was appointed Headmaster there. However, the school was in financial difficulties and there were only twenty-three pupils. Alfred resigned to get himself properly qualified and the school closed. He married Heilda Lalouetta Guimerainessmythare (c.1880–18th December 1943) at St Margaret's Church, Ipswich, Suffolk on 27th August 1907. She is believed to have been born on a British ship in British waters, although the family home was in Algiers, Algeria. Heilda was a nurse at Northampton General Hospital 1903–06 and also qualified as a midwife. Alfred took a teaching post at Levitskaya private school, 12 Novoderevenskaya Ulitsa, Tsarskoye Zelo, near St Petersburg, Russia, site of the Tsar's favourite palace. The Tsar and family were held under house arrest at the Alexander Hotel there after the Revolution. Helida and her son, Rudolph, managed to get away across the frozen Baltic to Finland in March 1918 and then through Sweden to Kristiania (Oslo), Norway and from there to Aberdeen, Scotland. Alfred followed in April. He was commissioned on the General List during the latter stages of the Great War. His address at that time was Coates Rectory, Cirencester, Gloucestershire. He studied to enter the clergy at Queen's College, Birmingham and was ordained a deacon at Lichfield Cathedral in 1930 and a priest in 1931. He was a clergyman and schoolmaster, living with his cousin, Florence Annie

Higham Ferrers Grammar School was founded in 1422 by Archbishop Chichele. In the reign of Henry VIII, Robert Dacres was granted the estate on condition that he maintained a schoolmaster and kept the school in repair. In 1899 Alfred George Collins Vann became Headmaster of Chichele Grammar School and frequently attended courses at Oxford University (MA 1898). The Grammar School closed in 1906.

Simpson, at The Vicarage, Maryfield, St Germans, Cornwall in 1939. Heilda was living at 25 & 27 Hall Road, Handsworth, Birmingham, Warwickshire in 1940 and died there a few years later. Alfred converted to Roman Catholicism and was living at 43 Bridge Road, Chertsey, Surrey when he emigrated to Australia aboard RMS *Asturias*, departing Southampton, Hampshire in February 1947 for Fremantle, Western Australia. He was accompanied by his son and daughter-in-law and settled at Byron Bay, New South Wales, where he subsequently died. Alfred and Heilda had a son:

- Rudolph Douglas Grahame Vann (28th August 1912–1989) married Kate Evangeline Jones (born 21st February 1910), born at Longton, Staffordshire, in 1933 at Cirencester. He joined Birmingham University as a medical student on 2nd October 1933. Rudolph was still a medical student in 1939 and Kate was headmistress of Cherington School, Stourton, near Shipston-on-Stour, Warwickshire. Kate was also an Air Raid Precautions Warden. Rudolph was commissioned as a lieutenant in the South Staffordshire Regiment on 19th July 1940 (51303) and was promoted lieutenant on transfer to the Royal Army Medical Corps on 14th August 1940. He was

College Street in Higham Ferrers.

School House, Church Stowe, Weedon, where Hannah Vann was living in 1911.

promoted war substantive major and temporary lieutenant colonel on 11th March 1944. He relinquished his commission and was granted the honorary rank of lieutenant colonel on 8th April 1948. He was a medical practitioner at Northampton General Hospital when he and Kate emigrated to Australia, with his father, in February 1947. He was appointed to a short service commission on probation for twelve months in the Medical Branch of the Royal Australian Air Force as a squadron leader on 5th May 1951 (024187). They subsequently divorced and Kate travelled alone to Canada aboard SS *Lakemba*, departing Sydney, New South Wales on 9th November 1950, giving her address as 3003 Mathers Avenue, West Vancouver, British Colombia. Rudolph married Margaret Scott (26th August 1924–24th May 1985), a nurse born at Katanning, Western Australia, on 20th September 1952 at Sydney. They were living at Mary Street, Eden Monaro, NSW in 1958. They both died at Bunbury, WA. They had a son, Douglas David Vann (10th March 1960–23rd July 1999).

- Arthur Harrison 'Harry' Allard Vann (1st May 1884–25th September 1915) was a Sunday School teacher at St Mary's Parish Church, Higham Ferrers. He played nineteen League matches for Northampton Town FC in 1906–07 and scored three goals. He also played for Burton United FC. He took a teaching appointment in Doncaster, Yorkshire and whilst there he served as an officer in 5th King's Own Yorkshire Light Infantry (TF) 1909–11. Harry played hockey for Yorkshire and scored their only goal in the 6–1 defeat by Middlesex at Staines in January 1909. In 1909 he went up to Jesus College, Cambridge, living at 65 Jesus Lane. He played football and hockey there, captaining the College hockey team and gained a hockey blue, playing in the Varsity matches against Oxford in 1912 and 1913, the latter being a 7–2 win. He was also a member of the UOTC. He taught at a preparatory school at Dunchurch Hall, near Rugby and played hockey for Rugby and Warwickshire. On 31st August 1914, Harry enlisted with his brother, Bernard, in the Artists' Rifles (28th (County of London) Battalion, London Regiment) in London (1799). He was commissioned as a lieutenant in 12th West Yorkshire on 1st October. Harry was a captain and Adjutant of the Battalion when he was reported gassed and missing at Loos, France on 25th September 1915. Initial reports indicated that he may have been taken prisoner but, on 19th August 1916, as no further information had been received, the War Office concluded that he had been killed (Loos Memorial).
- Reginald Herbert Vann (born 12th December 1885), born at Wellingborough, Northamptonshire, was a member of the Rushden Church Old Boys' Association. He went to Canada in 1907. He married Elsie Edith Lack (7th November 1888–

Arthur Harrison Allard Vann is commemorated on the Loos Memorial at Dud Corner Cemetery.

28th May 1958) on 2nd March 1915 at Wellingborough, where she was born. They returned to Canada after honeymooning at Coates Rectory but later came back to England. Elsie was a widow and headmistress of a public elementary school on High Street, Rochford, Essex in 1939. She was living at 87 Bushland Road, Northampton at the time of her death at Mount Pleasant Nursing Home, Clevedon, Somerset. They had a daughter:

  - Elsie Margaret Vann (10th October 1917–October 2000) married Ian James McCulloch (29th January 1917–5th October 1994), born at Kensington, London, in 1941 at Edmonton, Middlesex. His father, Captain James Arthur McCulloch (1883–27th September 1918), 1/8th Lancashire Fusiliers, was killed in action and is buried in Ribecourt Road Cemetery, Trescault, France (II C 2). They were living at Flat 1, 90 Highbury New Park Road, London at the time of his death there. Elsie's death was registered at Chichester, Sussex. They had two sons – Michael C McCulloch 1943 and Colin J McCulloch 1945.

- Alban John 'Jack' Vann (4th April 1889–8th May 1941) was a member of the Rushden Church Old Boys' Association. He was a teacher at Higham Ferrers National School and enlisted in the Royal Gloucestershire Hussars on 19th October 1914. He was commissioned in 12th West Yorkshire on 23rd December 1914, was promoted lieutenant on 1st February 1915 and went to France, landing at Boulogne, on 10th September. Jack was wounded in a trench raid on 24th January 1916 and was wounded again on 27th March. He was evacuated to England and was Mentioned in Despatches (LG 15th June 1916). He was appointed musketry training officer with 2nd Training Reserve Brigade, Rugeley and later with the Humber Garrison and Lincolnshire Coast Defences at Alford. Jack was promoted captain on 23rd September and was seconded as a temporary lieutenant the same day to the Indian Army. He transferred to the General List on 17th October 1916 and was appointed temporary lieutenant Indian Army on probation on 6th November 1918, with seniority from 23rd September 1916. Jack arrived in India on 8th January 1919 and was promoted captain in the Indian Army on 15th September, as a company officer, and captain on the General List on 23rd September 1919. He was appointed to the Indian Army on 8th January 1920 with 19th Hyderabad Regiment, 1st Battalion (late 94th Russell's Infantry). Jack married Clarice Ella Sanders (20th February 1896–12th February 1992), born at Rushden, Northamptonshire, at Park Road Baptist Church, Rushden on 21st March 1917. Alban transferred to the Supplementary List and served in a variety of appointments in the Cantonments Department, Government of India, seconded from the Army/Defence Department. These included – Executive Officer Class I & Military Estates Officer 5th June 1922, Assistant Inspecting Officer Southern Command, Military Lands and Cantonments 6th March 1928, Executive Officer Class I at Nowshera 22nd October 1930, Military Estates Officer, Peshawar Circle 2nd January 1936 and Military Estates Officer, Meerut

Madras War Cemetery was created in 1952 to receive Second World War graves from civil cemeteries in the south and east of India whose maintenance could not be assured. It contains 856 Commonwealth burials. The Madras 1914–1918 Memorial, situated at the rear of the cemetery, bears the names of more than 1,000 servicemen who died during the Great War and who lie in many civil cemeteries in various parts of India, where it is not possible to maintain their graves.

& Agra Circles (Dehra Dun) 12th February 1938. He was transferred to the Supernumerary List as a major on 15th September 1933. Alban died in-service and is buried in Madras War Cemetery, Chennai, India (5 F 13). Although still on the Indian Army General List, he was working in the Civil Administration as President of the Cantonment Board in Secunderabad at the time of his death. Clarice was living at Charter House, Kimbolton Road, Bedford at the time of her death there. They had a son:

- John Noel Patrick Vann (21st January 1926–3rd August 1997), born in India, was a boarder at Northcliffe House School, Bognor Regis, Sussex in 1939. He served in the ranks for one year and twenty days and was granted an emergency commission in the Royal Engineers on 7th October 1945 (357172) and was promoted war substantive lieutenant 7th April 1946, acting captain 17th October 1946–16th January 1947 and temporary captain 17th January 1947–1st January 1953. He was granted a Regular Commission in the Royal Engineers 21st June 1947 (seniority as second lieutenant 2nd January 1947) and was promoted lieutenant 1st November 1947, captain 2nd January 1953, temporary major 20th November 1959–1st January 1960 and major 2nd January 1960. He retired on retired pay on 8th July 1971. John married Alma May Starling (10th May 1927–26th September 1982), born at Hackney, London, at Chatham, Kent in 1951. They had three children – Nicholas J Vann 1952, Paul W Vann 1953 and Antonia L Vann 1960. They were living at Leyclose, Weston-Subedge, Chipping Campden, Gloucestershire at the time of her death there. John married Mary Davidson (27th August 1930–3rd September 1998) in 1983. He died at Cheltenham, Gloucestershire.

Bernard's paternal grandfather, Thomas Collins Vann (30th October 1833–April 1904), born at Towcester, Northamptonshire, was a shoemaker. He married Mary Ann née Nobles (c.1836–1912), born at Rushden, Northamptonshire, on 27th May 1854 at the Church of the Holy Sepulchre, Northampton. Both gave their address as 1st Square, Todd's Lane (Grafton Street by 1861), Northampton. They were living at 7, 1st Square in 1861, at High Street, Towcester in 1871 and at 93 Talbot

Towcester was the Roman town of Lactodorum on Watling Street, the modern A5, which in Saxon times was the frontier between Wessex and the Danelaw. Edward the Elder fortified the town in 917 and in the 11th century the Normans built a motte and bailey castle there. Charles Dickens featured Towcester in his novel, *The Pickwick Papers*. In the 18th century, Towcester prospered as a stopping point for stagecoaches and the mail coach running along Watling Street from London to Holyhead. However, that ended in 1838 when the London and Birmingham railway opened and bypassed Towcester. By 1866 the town was on the national rail network and by 1892 was on four different routes. The last railway closed in 1964.

Road, Northampton St Giles, Northamptonshire in 1881. In addition to Alfred they had five other children:

- Thomas Collins Vann (1854–55) born and died at Northampton
- William Edward Collins Vann (1861–16th January 1937), a shoe clicker, married Maria Howlett (1863–3rd May 1936), a shoe fitter born at Brixworth, Northamptonshire, at St Edmund's, Northampton on 3rd April 1883. They were living at 39 Exeter Road, Northampton in 1891. By 1911 he was a newsagent and tobacconist and they were living at 60 Kettering Road, Northampton. They both died at 79 Derby Road, Northampton. They had seven children:
  - Albert Edward Rowland Vann (1883–17th August 1946) married Violet Lilian Rossiter (20th February 1885–1969) at Edmonton, Middlesex in 1908. He served in 6th and 20th Middlesex (G/33986) and 1st Wiltshire (40065) and transferred to the Class Z Reserve on 6th February 1919.
  - William Arthur Basil Vann (5th February 1888–25th January 1953) was a clerk for a shoe manufacturer in 1911. He married Florence Hanby (24th February 1890–2nd March 1967) at St Edmund, Northampton on 23rd February 1913. They had three children – Vavasour Olive Vann (1913–2004), Denis William Arthur Vann (1916–61) and Reginald Norman Horace Vann (1920–86). William was living at 103 Artizan Road, Northampton when he enlisted in 28th London at the Central London Recruiting Depot, Whitehall on 7th December 1915 (766822), described as 5′3″ tall and weighing 115 lbs. He transferred to the Army Reserve on 8th December and was called up to join E Company, 2nd Artist's Rifles OTC on 30th August 1917. He went to France on 22nd December, joined the Infantry Base Depot, Le Havre next day and 1/28th London on 10th January 1918. On 30th April he was wounded and admitted to 150th Field Ambulance and No.3 Casualty Clearing Station. He was transferred to 3rd Stationary Hospital, Rouen on 1st May and to 72nd General Hospital, Trouville next day. On 7th June he

joined the Infantry Base Depot, Le Havre and rejoined the Battalion on 9th July. William was demobilised from No.1 Dispersal Unit, Purfleet to the Class Z Reserve on 2nd March 1919. His address was 64 Cedar Road, Northampton. They were living at 30 Thursby Road, Abington Park, Northampton in December 1921.

- Thomas Cyril Vann (2nd August 1891–1973) was a shop assistant working with his father in 1911. He married Ethel Felce (1st April 1895–1987) in 1917.
- Beatrice May Vann (5th May 1898–1961) married Clement Pearcey Cockerill (15th June 1885–1978) in 1922. He had married Mary E Johnson (c.1892–1918) at Pottersbury, Northamptonshire in 1918.
- Kate Evelyn Vann (1899–1905).
- Sydney Frank Vann (9th April 1903–5th February 1960) married Emily Woodward in 1928. They had a daughter, Joy M Vann in 1929.
- Ivy Rose Phyllis Vann (2nd April 1909–1997) married Samuel Leggate in 1933. They had a son, Michael V V Leggate, in 1934.

• Mary Ann Elizabeth Collins Vann (1862–4th December 1931), born at Towcester, Northamptonshire, was a fitter in the shoe trade in 1881, living with her parents. She married Edward Stow (1861–27th October 1920), a butcher living at 34 Artizan Road, Northampton, on 3rd August 1885 at St Edmund's, Northampton, where he was born. They lived at 44 Whitworth Road, Northampton and both died there. They had six children including:
  - Florence Annie Stow (born 1887).
  - Albert Edward T Stow (1891–1944) was a clerk when he enlisted in the RAMC at Northampton on 25th October 1915 (72512), described as 5′ 10¾″ tall and weighing 136 lbs. He joined T Company on 28th October and transferred to P Company on 13th November as an acting corporal. He was appointed acting sergeant on 22nd January 1916. He fractured his left tibia while practicing the long jump at Colchester on 8th April 1918 in preparation for the 67th Divisional Recreational Training Scheme. He was in hospital at Colchester until 26th April and a medical board there classified him B1 on 10th June. He joined 50th Stationary Hospital as an acting corporal on 11th July. On 31st July he was appointed paid acting staff sergeant but reverted to the permanent rank of private when posted to K Company, RAMC Depot, Blackpool on the demobilisation of 50th Stationary Hospital on 29th November. He was demobilised to the Class Z Reserve as an acting sergeant from No.1 Dispersal Unit, Purfleet on 15th February 1919. Albert married Kathleen Elsie Burrows (1896–1923) in 1920. Albert married Winifred Bull in 1930. They had a daughter, Jean M Stow, in 1932.
  - Horace Arthur Stow (1892) married Mabel F Smith (c.1893–1967) in 1921. They had a son, Edward A Stow, in 1923.

  - Amy Elizabeth Stow (18th May 1894–1985) married Ernest A Berrisford (1892–1950) in 1920. They had a son, Peter W Berrisford in 1932.
  - Clara Agnes Stow (6th November 1895–1972) married Edward L Tibbs (9th January 1893–1972) in 1923. They had a son, Geoffrey T Tibbs, in 1927. They both died in Cheshire.
- Sarah Jane Collins Vann (1864–1929) was a fitter in the shoe trade in 1881, living with her parents. She married Harry Cory (16th December 1866–30th June 1917), a boot finisher born at Harpole, Northamptonshire, at St Edmund's, Northampton on 14th January 1889. They were living at 98 Lutterworth Road, Northampton in 1911 and were still there when he died. She died at Wellingborough, Northamptonshire. They had four children:
  - Mabel Jane Cory (5th October 1889–14th October 1984) never married.
  - Ellen Elizabeth Cory (23rd March 1891–29th January 1947) married Robert Thomas Timpson (1885–1949) at the same time as her cousin, Thomas C Vann, married Ethel Felce in 1917. Robert died at Worthing, Sussex.
  - Emma Cory (13th October 1895–1955) married William Arthur Scrimshaw (8th November 1896–1974) in 1921. They had a daughter, Freda J Scrimshaw, at Wellingborough in 1922. They both died there.
  - Winifred Zillah Cory (3rd January 1907–1994) married George R Freeman at Steyning, West Sussex in 1929. They had a son, Roy E Freeman, in 1926 (sic).
- Susannah Ellen Collins Vann (8th June 1866–6th June 1946) married Arthur Elwyn Wright (12th October 1868–31st March 1950), a shoe finisher, on 26th December 1890 at St Edmund's, Northampton, where he was born. They were living at 40 Florence Road, Northampton in 1911 and were still there when she died at 137a Wellingborough Road, Northampton. He also died there. They had four children:
  - Bertha Elizabeth Wright (1892–2nd March 1938) was a gold stamper in 1911. She married Ernest William Jarvis (10th January 1893–1971), born at Bedford, in 1917. They both died at Warwick.
  - Susannah Ellen Wright (14th December 1898–1990) married William Arthur Groves (born 1897) in 1925. They had a son, Gerald V Groves, in 1927.
  - Thomas Collins Wright (27th June 1904–6th December 1990) married Rose Minnie Groves (12th November 1906–1995) in 1931.
  - Dorothy Gwendolyn Wright (8th October 1908–19th January 1997) married Thomas William Bradshaw (5th October 1910–1980) in 1937. They had two children – Paul T E Bradshaw 1938 and Joy D Bradshaw 1942.

His maternal grandfather, Thomas Harrison Simpson (c.1836–20th April 1894), born at Skircoat, Halifax, Yorkshire, was a schoolmaster. He married Ellen née Crompton (c.1833–15th December 1880), born at Salford, Lancashire, on 1st May

1858 at St Catherine's Church, Manchester, Lancashire. They were living at Wesleyan Day School, Snaith, Yorkshire in 1861 and at 65 Erskine Street, West Derby, Liverpool, Lancashire in 1871. Ellen died at 25 Alfred Street, St Andrew, Northampton Priory. By 1881 Thomas was an assistant inspector of schools, still living at 25 Alfred Street, St Andrew. He married Jane Allard (4th October 1832–7th August 1902), born at Creaton, Northamptonshire, on 25th August 1888 at St Mary the Virgin with St John Church, Great Brington, Northamptonshire. Jane was a retired servant in 1881, living with her mother at 26 Alfred Street, Northampton. Thomas and Jane were living at 7 Trinity Street, Heigham, Norfolk by 1891, by when he was a sub inspector of education. He subsequently died there. Jane was living on her own at 3 Elysium Terrace, Northampton in 1901 and later died there. In addition to Hannah they had four other children:

- Mary Ellen Simpson (born 1859) was born at Snaith, Yorkshire. She was a single schoolmistress in 1891.
- Thomas Crompton Simpson (1864–17th August 1936), born at Liverpool, Lancashire, was a pupil teacher in 1881 and was ordained as a priest at Worcester Cathedral in 1889. He was living with his brother, Herbert, at High Street, Dorchester-on-Thames, Oxfordshire in 1891. In 1892 Thomas joined the Universities Mission to East Africa. For part of his time there he was Vice-Principal of Kiungani College in Zanzibar. After ten years he returned as Curate of St James' and St Michael's, Plymouth, Devon. In 1911 he was boarding at Hoe Garden House, Plymouth, Devon. Thomas was appointed Rector of Coates, near Cirencester, Gloucestershire in October 1913. He died at the Memorial Hospital, Cirencester.
- Florence Annie Simpson (29th November 1870–23rd August 1951), born at West Derby, Lancashire, was living with her maternal step-grandmother, Mary Crompton, at 24 Broughton Street, Cheetham at the time of the 1881 Census. She was a teacher at South End Elementary School, Rushden, where her sister, Hannah, was a certified teacher and her brother-in-law, Alfred Vann, was Master. She occasionally deputised for her sister while she was deputising for her husband. Florence was a head teacher with Northfield City Council, Worcestershire in 1911, living on her own at 89A Pershore Road, Selly Park, Birmingham, Warwickshire. She was living with her cousin, the Reverend Alfred Vann, at The Vicarage, Maryfield, St Germans, Cornwall in 1939. She was living at 25 Westbourne Road, Handsworth, Birmingham at the time of her death.
- Herbert Clayton Simpson (26th November 1872–4th May 1947), born at Northampton, was educated at Magdalene College School and Magdalene College, Oxford. He moved to Toronto, Ontario, Canada and was a lecturer in chemistry and physics at Trinity College in 1896. He was appointed lecturer in English Literature (sic) in 1900 and Professor and Head of Department in 1907. He married Nina Lawrence Rolph (born 9th November 1880), born at York,

Ontario, on 23rd April 1914. They were living at 71 Bernard Avenue, Toronto at the time of his death. They had a daughter, Elizabeth J Simpson 1916.

Bernard was educated at South End Elementary School, Rushden from 9th May 1892, where his parents taught, and later at Chichele Grammar School, Higham Ferrers, Northamptonshire, where his father was headmaster. While there Bernard played for the football, hockey and cricket teams. He went up to Jesus College, Cambridge in October 1907, where he was known as Bertie and lived at 30 New Square. He played for several football teams, including captaining the College team, which he led to promotion to the First Division of the University League. The College magazine described him as, 'a dashing forward, possessing both pace and weight… rather erratic in his passing… a good shot with either foot, he is always very dangerous in front of goal'. Bernard also played cricket and tennis and was Secretary of the College Football and Athletics teams. He and his brother, Harry, were selected to play hockey for the University against Surbiton on 30th October 1909. The University won 7–0, with Bernard scoring three goals and Harry two. The following week the University beat Mid Surrey 8–1, with Bernard scoring six and Harry one of the goals. Bernard was injured in a match against Hampstead Club, considered the best team in England that season. He became a Hockey Blue, representing Cambridge in the Varsity match against Oxford on 23rd February 1910. Oxford won 5–4 and Bernard scored one of the Cambridge goals. The Jesus hockey team finished second to Caius in the First Division of the University Hockey League in 1910. He went to St Petersburg, Russia in September 1910 as a vacation tutor and visited his brother Alfred and his wife Heilda there. At Cambridge he joined the University Officer Training Corps and reached the rank of sergeant. He was also the secretary of The Farragoes and a co-founder, vice-president and later president of The Roosters debating societies. After graduating (BD) he became an assistant master at Ashby de la Zouch Grammar School, Leicestershire in January 1906, with an annual salary of £85, rising to £95 in 1907. The head boy at the time was Philip Eric Bent, who was also awarded the VC during the Great War. Bernard was Housemaster of School House, where the boarders resided. He was boarding at 84 Uppingham Road, Leicester with Jane Wells and her daughter at the time of the 1911 Census.

Bernard was ordained deacon on 2nd October 1910 by the Bishop of Peterborough and was appointed junior assistant curate at St Barnabas Church, New Humberstone, Leicestershire. He also ran the Boys' Sunday School. He was ordained priest at Peterborough Cathedral on 21st December 1911 and in July 1912 he was acting chaplain at the Anglican Church in St-Jean-de-Luz, near Biarritz, France. In January 1913, Bernard was appointed chaplain and assistant master at Wellingborough Grammar School, where he taught history and theology. He helped coach the football and cricket teams and participated in the Debating Society. He was also a member of the Masters A Cricket XI, playing in the last match before

Jesus College was established in 1496 on the site of a 12th century Benedictine nunnery. The chapel is the oldest university building in Cambridge, predating the College by 350 years and the University by half a century. Three members of Jesus College have received the Nobel Prize and two have been appointed to the International Court of Justice. In 2019, forty years after the first women were admitted, Sonia Alleyne became the first black master of Jesus College. Amongst its numerous famous alumni are:

- Thomas Cranmer (1489–1556), a leader of the English Reformation and Archbishop of Canterbury under Henry VIII, Edward VI and Mary I. He helped build the case for the annulment of Henry's marriage to Catherine of Aragon, which led to the separation of the English Church from Rome. The Catholic Mary I had him tried for treason and heresy and he was ultimately executed.
- Samuel Taylor Coleridge (1772–1834) the poet, critic, philosopher and theologian.
- Lieutenant General Sir Harold Bridgwood Walker KCB KCMG DSO (1862–1934) commanded Australian and New Zealand forces during the Great War. He was highly regarded by his men but was replaced in 1918 when politics dictated that all Australian forces should be commanded by Australians. Walker did not challenge this and in July 1918 he was given command of 48th (South Midland) Division.
- Antony Charles Robert Armstrong-Jones, 1st Earl of Snowdon GCVO FRSA RDI (1930–2017) the photographer and filmmaker, who married Princess Margaret, sister of Queen Elizabeth II.
- Nicholas Rory Cellan-Jones (born 1958) the BBC technology correspondent.
- Prince Edward, Earl of Wessex KG GCVO CD ADC (born 1964), youngest child of Queen Elizabeth II and Prince Philip.

Ashby Grammar School was founded in 1567 by Henry Hastings, 3rd Earl of Huntingdon. A girls' grammar school opened in 1901 and the two merged in 1972 as the comprehensive Ashby School, which became an Academy in 2012.

Philip Eric Bent VC DSO (3rd January 1891 – 1st October 1917) was head boy. His story is related in a previous volume in this series, *Victoria Crosses on the Western Front: Third Ypres 1917: 31st July – 6th November 1917*. A notable former member of the girls' school was Clare Hollingworth OBE (1911–2017), a journalist and author. She was the first correspondent to report the outbreak of the Second World War, described as 'the scoop of the century', when she was working for the Daily Telegraph in 1939.

war broke out against Dallington on 18th July 1914, in which he scored just one run but took four wickets.

He was a keen sportsman who, in addition to his school, played football for High Ferrers YMCI and Irthlingborough Reserves, and cricket for Higham St Mary's. He was an amateur centre forward for Northampton Town Football Club in the

Bernard, standing on the left, outside Coates Rectory in 1914. The clergyman sitting is his uncle, the Reverend Thomas Crompton Simpson. Standing far right is Bernard's brother, Arthur Vann, and the lady sitting with the knitting is their mother, Hannah Elizabeth Vann. Bernard's sister, Florence, is sitting on the ground. The man standing at the rear wearing a boater is Hannah's brother, Herbert Simpson.

Southern League. In his first season in 1906 he appeared twice. In the second match, at Fulham, his brother Albert scored the visitors' only goal in a 3–1 defeat. Bernard, Harry and Alfred toured Austria-Hungary 11th April–1st May 1906 with the New Pilgrims FC, also known as the London Pilgrims. They played nine matches in Budapest, Prague, Vienna and Graz. In the 1906–07 season Bernard scored five times in three matches, including twice in the win against Swindon on 22nd December, the equalizer in a draw against Norwich City on 27th December and twice in the win against Crystal Palace on 31st December. He played his last of eight matches for

Wellingborough Grammar School was established in 1595 and the original school building still survives in the centre of the town. In January 1881 the school moved to its present site. During the Great War some 1,060 old boys served in the forces and 181 old boys and masters died. In 1929 a thatched pavilion was built on the playing fields. Its front doorstep was obtained from the former Bristol home of WG Grace when it was demolished in 1939. Another ninety-five old boys died in the Second World War. It became fully co-educational in 1979. Boarding ceased in 2000. Amongst the famous alumni are:

- Richard Keith Robert Coles FRSA FKC (born 26th March 1962) musician, journalist, broadcaster and Church of England parish priest. He was the multi-instrumentalist who partnered Jimmy Somerville in the 1980s band the *Communards*, achieving three Top Ten hits. He appears frequently on radio and television.
- Major George Drew (1918–2005) was a serial escaper, who spent most of the Second World War in Colditz.
- Group Captain James Brian Tait DSO and three Bars DFC and Bar (1916–2007) a bomber pilot who led the attack that sank the *Tirpitz* in 1944. He conducted a total of 101 bombing missions during the war and succeeded Leonard Cheshire VC as commander of 617 Squadron, the Dambusters.

Derby County Football Club, founded in 1884, was one of the twelve founder members of the Football League in 1888 and one of only ten clubs to have competed in every season of the English football league. The club began as an offshoot of Derbyshire County Cricket Club. The club's nickname, *The Rams*, is in tribute to its links with the First Regiment of Derby Militia, which had a ram as its mascot. The club played its home matches at the cricket club's Racecourse Ground until 1895, when it moved to a new stadium, the Baseball Ground seen here. The club was the winner of the first post-Second World War FA Cup in 1946, beating Charlton Athletic 4–1. A bleak period followed and by 1955 the club had been relegated to the Third Division. In 1967, Brian Clough and Peter Taylor took over the management and Derby County was promoted to the First Division in 1969, won its first Football League Championship in 1972 and reached the semi-finals of the European Cup the following year. Clough and Taylor fell out with the board and left in October 1973. However, their impact was such that thirty-seven years later a bronze statue of the pair was erected outside Pride Park. The club became League champions again in 1975 but was relegated to the Second Division in 1980 and to the Third Division in 1984. Back to back promotions saw the club back in the First Division for the 1987–88 season but in 1991 it was back down in the Second Division. In 1996 promotion was gained to the Premier League, by then the top flight of English football. At the end of that season, the club left the Baseball Ground after 102 years and moved into the new all-seater Pride Park Stadium. The Baseball Ground was demolished six years later. Derby County is the only club to have had three home grounds to host full England international matches. In 2002 Derby County was relegated to the Championship League and the club underwent a serious financial crisis. It survived and in 2006 returned to the Premiership but was relegated the following season, having equaled Loughborough's 108 year old record of winning just one match in an entire season. Amongst the club's many famous players are:

- Archibald Gemmill (born 24th March 1947) winner of the European Cup, three English league titles and captain of Scotland.
- Peter Leslie Shilton OBE (born 18th September 1949) the England goalkeeper with a record 125 caps. He also holds the record for the most competitive appearances in world football, playing 1,390 games. His thirty-year career included eleven clubs and he played over one hundred league matches for five of them. Amongst his many honours are a First Division championship, two European Cups, a UEFA Super Cup and the Football League Cup. He represented England in the 1980 and 1988 Euros and the 1982, 1986 and 1990 World Cups.
- Wayne Mark Rooney (born 24th October 1985) managed Derby County having previously been a player-manager. Rooney is the record goalscorer for England and Manchester United.

Northampton on 19th January 1907. He turned out for struggling Second Division side Burton United in February 1907 against Chelsea and Barnsley. He scored a goal in Burton's 4–1 victory over Wolverhampton Wanderers. An injury in that match, compounded by another when he returned not fully recovered, meant he missed a few matches and lost his edge. Although still an amateur, Bernard was recruited by Derby County in the First Division. He played against Aston Villa at Villa Park on 23rd March 1907, losing 2–0. His next match was against Notts County at Trent Bridge on 29th March, resulting in a 4–0 loss. His final match with Derby County was a 1–1 draw against Birmingham at the Baseball Ground, which resulted in Derby County being relegated. In June he signed for Leicester Fosse but never appeared in the senior team at Filbert Street as he went up to Cambridge University. Bernard was also a talented hockey player, playing for Woodville and Leicester in the 1906–07 season, scoring three times in the 6–0 victory against Nottinghamshire. While at St Barnabas Church he played rugby for Stonesgate RFC and continued after moving to Wellingborough, although he played only one match in the 1913/14 season. He was also a vice president of the St Barnabas Cricket Club. In October 1912 he was badly concussed in a rugby match at Oundle, Northamptonshire and was confined to bed for a week. He convalesced at Goscote Hall and returned to his duties but, while officiating at a funeral, he had a relapse and was forbidden from working again until the end of the year. He played hockey for Leicester and scored in the 3–2 victory over Bedford on 15th November 1913.

When war broke out Bernard was determined to serve as a combatant rather than a chaplain and obtained his Bishop's blessing to do so. There were far more clergymen volunteering to serve as chaplains than were needed but there was a shortage of officers. He enlisted in 28th (County of London) Battalion (Artists' Rifles) on 31st August 1914 (1800). He was described as 5′ 10½″ tall and served in E Company. On 2nd September he was commissioned in 1/8th Sherwood Foresters and joined the Battalion at Harpenden, Hertfordshire. Another clergyman, Egbert Melville Hacking, was serving as an officer in the Battalion. The Battalion moved to Bocking, Essex in October, with Bernard in B Company. He captained the Battalion football team, beating 1/6th Battalion 2–1 after extra time on Christmas Day. He proceeded to Southampton with the Battalion, embarking on 25th February 1915 aboard SS *Mount Temple*. After lying at anchor off Netley in Southampton Water for twenty-four hours, the men were taken off by tenders and camped on Southampton Common. On 27th February, 102 men of the Battalion embarked aboard SS *Caledonia* and the remainder aboard TS *King Edward*. Those on *Caledonia* remained aboard for three days before reaching France. Those aboard *King Edward* disembarked next morning and re-embarked the following evening before proceeding to France. Bernard first went into the trenches on 29th March.

Bernard was known for being outspoken and even had a heated exchange with Lieutenant General Edmund Allenby, the Army commander, who did not appear to resent it and was said to have enquired about him thereafter. Allenby often invited junior officers to dinner and Bernard attended one of these. **Awarded the MC for his actions at Kemmel on 24th April, when a small advanced trench was blown in by a trench mortar. The blast of another shell blew him eight metres. He was wounded and half-buried but organised the defence and rescued buried men under heavy fire. He refused to leave his post until ordered to do so. Also on 30th July and subsequent days at Hooge, near Ypres, Belgium, although slightly wounded, he assisted another officer hold the left trench of the line and led patrols up to the enemy trenches to gain valuable information, LG 15th September 1915.** After the Kemmel incident he was admitted to hospital at Locre for a week, suffering from a cut on the cheek, strained (sic) ankle and bad bruising to the neck and back. He was promoted lieutenant on 26th April and was granted leave on 1st July for a few days in England. By late July he was second-in-command of D Company and soon afterwards was commanding the company. The incident on 30th July refers to when he restored the situation in the trenches of 7th King's Royal Rifle Corps during the first liquid fire attack against the British, during which Sydney Woodroofe, 8th Rifle Brigade, was awarded the VC. When the brigade chaplain was not available, Bernard held services and on at least one occasion went into no man's land to read the burial service.

Second Lieutenant Sydney Clayton Woodroffe, 8th Rifle Brigade, who was awarded the VC for his actions at Hooge, Belgium on 30th July 1915. It was the first VC awarded to a unit of the New Armies. He was killed during this action and is commemorated on the Ypres (Menin Gate) Memorial. His story appears in the second volume of this series, *Victoria Crosses on the Western Front – April 1915–June 1916*.

On 6th June Bernard was appointed temporary captain and on 15th June he was promoted lieutenant. He was severely wounded in the left forearm at the Hohenzollern Redoubt near Loos, France on 14th October but continued throwing grenades until ordered to retire by his CO. He was evacuated to England aboard HMHS *Cambria* on 17th October. A medical board at Caxton Hall, London on 3rd November found him unfit for General Service for a month and a half and Home Service for one month. He was sent on leave for a month. A medical board at the Beaufort War Hospital, Bristol on 3rd December found him unfit for any service for a month and extended his leave over the Christmas period until 2nd January 1918. Part of that time was spent with his friend the Reverend Gerald Gurney and his wife Dorothy Frances. She is best known for writing the hymn *O Perfect Love* in 1883.

He was mentioned in Field Marshal Sir John French's despatch of 30th November 1915, LG 1st January 1916. The MC was presented by the

The Military Cross was created on 28th December 1914 for officers of the rank of captain and below and warrant officers. In August 1916 bars were awarded for further acts of gallantry. In 1931 the MC was extended to majors and to members of the RAF for ground actions. In the 1993 honours review the Military Medal for other ranks was discontinued and the MC became the third level decoration for all ranks of the British Armed Forces for acts of gallantry on land.

King at Buckingham Palace on 22nd December. A medical board at The Military Hospital, Devonport on 8th January 1916 found him fit for General Service. He joined 3/8th Sherwood Foresters at Grantham on 12th January. He had rejoined 1/8th Battalion in France by mid-March to command A Company and had attended a course at Third Army School by then. **Awarded a Bar to the MC for his actions on 21st/22nd September 1916 at Blairville, France, when leading A Company in a raid on Italy Sap, while suffering agony from neuritis. Finding a dugout full of Germans he ordered them out. Two charged him with fixed bayonets, so he killed one and wounded the other after which the remainder surrendered, LG 14th November 1916.** In this action eight British were wounded, five Germans were killed and five prisoners were taken.

Bernard returned to England from Boulogne to Folkestone on 25th September on leave and to attend the Senior Officers Course at Aldershot, Hampshire. He was slightly wounded during the raid and received electric treatment at Cambridge Military Hospital, Aldershot for neuritis at the back of the neck. The Bar to the MC was presented by the King at Buckingham Palace on 20th December. Bernard married Doris Victoria Strange Beck (29th November 1897–2nd November 1979), born at Port Arthur, Algoma, Ontario, Canada, on 27th December 1916 at St Paul's Church, Wilton Place, Knightsbridge, London. She was a nursing aide and they met in Paris. They gave their address as Alexandra Hotel, Hyde Park Corner, London. The service was conducted by his friend, the Reverend Gerald Gurney. Doris was given away by her uncle, Robert Maxwell Dennistoun KC, who was serving with the CEF. Doris was nursing at the Canadian Hospital, Beachborough Park, Shorncliffe, Kent. Bernard died never knowing that Doris had conceived. Doris and her son were living with her sister, Helen, and brother-in-law, Whiteford Bell, at 9 Beaumont Road, Toronto North in 1921. She moved to England and was living at Orchard Way Cottage, Knotty Green, Beaconsfield, Buckinghamshire in 1923 and later at Heatherdune, The Down, Bexhill-on-Sea, Sussex and at Coates Rectory, Cirencester, Gloucestershire. In 1939 she was living at The Old Vicarage, Penn, Buckinghamshire. She died at Circus Nursing Home, 718 Circus, Bath, Somerset. They had one son:

Bernard's wife, Doris, was born at Port Arthur on Lake Superior. Colonel Garnet Wolseley named the then tiny settlement as Prince Arthur's Landing, in honour of Prince Arthur. Port Arthur, to which the name was shortened, was the original eastern terminus of the Canadian Pacific Railway and was a major trans-shipment point for ships carrying cargo across the Great Lakes. It prospered as a result and was incorporated as a town in March 1884. Silver mining was the mainstay of the economy until the boom ended in October 1890. Dire economic circumstances followed until 1897–99, when Port Arthur was chosen as the Lake Superior headquarters for the Canadian Northern Railway. The town thrived as a grain handling port after the railway opened to Winnipeg, Manitoba in December 1901. Numerous grain silos were constructed. The Port Arthur Shipbuilding Co was a major employer for many years. Forestry, pulping and paper production were also important for the local economy. Port Arthur became a city in April 1907 but ceased to exist at the end of December 1969 when it joined other communities as the city of Thunder Bay.

- Bernard Geoffrey Vann (2nd June 1919–10th January 1994), born at The Rodney, Dalmeny Road, Bexhill-on-Sea, was educated at St Peter's Preparatory School, Seaford, Sussex and Marlborough College. He served in the Royal Navy and was appointed midshipman aboard HMS *Southampton*, while accommodated aboard HMS *Glasgow*, on 1st January 1938. He was a sub-lieutenant aboard the

Bernard and Doris married at St Paul's Church, Knightsbridge. The church, which is Grade II* listed, was founded in 1843, the first in London to champion the ideals of the Oxford Movement of the Anglo-Catholic tradition. A memorial outside commemorates fifty-two members of the First Aid Nursing Yeomanry who died on active service during the Second World War, either on clandestine intelligence work for the Special Operations Executive in occupied countries or as transport drivers for the Auxiliary Territorial Service. The memorial, which includes two holders of the George Cross, Noor Inyat Khan and Violette Szabo, was unveiled by Princess Alice on 7th May 1948. Amongst those present at the ceremony were Odette Hallowes GC and Tanya, daughter of Violette Szabo GC. A small memorial plaque was added in Odette Hallowes' memory in 1998.

At the time of their wedding, Bernard and Doris were living at the Alexandra Hotel on Knightsbridge, a short walk away from St Paul's Church. Originally the Wallace Hotel, it opened in 1858 on the site of the White Horse pub. It was bought in 1863 by the Alexandra Hotel Co Ltd and the enlarged and remodelled hotel opened in 1864. On the night of 11th May 1941, a bomb passed through five floors before exploding. Twenty-four people were killed and twenty-six were seriously injured. The hotel was demolished and was rebuilt as Agriculture House in 1954 and as 25–27 Knightsbridge in 1993–95.

minesweeper, HMS *Halcyon*, during the evacuation from Dunkirk. On 30th May 1940 he and Sub Lieutenant John Francis Worthington, with some crewmen, relieved the exhausted crew of a private motorboat, *Amblere*, which was bringing troops from the beaches to ships offshore. Worthington was awarded the DSC. On 27th June, while sweeping, the escort HMS *Wren* was sunk and HMS *Montrose* was damaged in an attack by fifteen enemy aircraft. *Halcyon* towed *Montrose* back to Harwich. During this attack, Bernard did excellent work in encouraging his gun's crew and getting the best results out of them during the action. In his new capacity as First Lieutenant he made excellent arrangements for the rescue and care of the survivors and was awarded the DSC (LG 4th October 1940). He continued to serve throughout the Second World War. HMS *Appledore* as lieutenant 6th January 1947. HMS *Drake* 1st April 1948. Promoted lieutenant commander 1st September 1948. HMS *President* 4th October. Appointed Flag Lieutenant Commander to Vice Admiral Sir Angus EMB Cunninghame Graham KBE CB, Flag Officer Scotland, HMS *Cochrane* on 19th September 1950. Appointed Flag Lieutenant Commander to Rear Admiral EM Evans-Lombre CB, Flag Officer Training Squadron, HMS *Vanguard* on 19th September 1949. HMS *Newcastle* 27th March 1952, including during the Korean War, for which he was awarded the MBE for blockade work (LG 10th November 1953). HMS *President* 23rd August 1954. Bernard married Bobyl Jane Hooper (1924–25th December 2008), born at Salford, Lancashire, on 7th April 1945 at St Martin in the Fields, London. She was the daughter of Sir Frederic Collins Hooper (1892–1963), Managing Director of Schweppes Group 1948–63 and Eglantine Irene Bland (1894–1957). Bobyl was living with her mother at 28 Drayton Court, Kensington prior to her marriage in 1945. Bernard and Bobyl were living at 38 Woodlands Avenue, Ruislip, Middlesex in 1949. Bernard retired from the Royal Navy in 1957

HMS *Halcyon* (815 tons) was the lead ship of a class of minesweepers built in the 1930s. She was built by John Brown at Clydebank and was launched on 20th December 1933, with a maximum speed of 16.5 knots and a range of 13,300 kms. *Halcyon* was armed with two QF 4″ guns and eight .303″ machine guns. Later the rear 4″ gun was removed, as were most of the .303″ machine guns, to be replaced by a quadruple mount Vickers .5″ machine gun and four 20mm Oerlikon anti-aircraft guns. On 26th May 1940 *Halcyon* arrived at Dover. Two days later she was off La Panne near Dunkirk on the first of several evacuation trips to Dover and Folkestone. A total of 2,271 Allied troops were recovered and three members of the crew were killed during the Dunkirk operation. On 5th June she was damaged in air attacks and sailed for Devonport for repairs. *Halcyon* returned to service with 6th Minesweeping Flotilla at Harwich on 15th June. On 27th June she was involved in an action during which HMS *Wren* was sunk and HMS *Montrose* was damaged in an air attack off Aldeburgh, Suffolk. *Halcyon* towed *Montrose* back to Harwich. Bernard was awarded the DSC for his part. *Halcyon* also saw service during the Arctic convoys and the Normandy landings. She was scrapped at Milford Haven in April 1950.

and became a cattle and sheep farmer at Woodhouse Lodge, Rodborough Lane, Butterrow, Stroud, Gloucestershire, where he subsequently died. They had two children:

- Michael Jeremy Bernard Vann (born 1946), born at Hammersmith, London, was educated at Oxford University (MA) and qualified as a land law consultant. He married Judith Pamela Preston-Rouse, a solicitor, in 1976 at Oxford. They were both partners in Preston-Rouse & Co, Solicitors at 6 Gray's Inn Square, London and were also directors in PR (Preston-Rouse) & Co Consultancy Ltd, Hart House, Priestley Road, Basingstoke, Hampshire. They had two daughters – Sophie Harriet Vann 1977 and Camilla Louise Vann 1981.
- James A Vann (born 1949), a doctor born at Harrow, Middlesex, married Yoma J Bolsover (born 1955), born at Oxford, at Witney, Oxfordshire in 1976. They had two daughters – Abigail Charlotte Vann 1979 and Georgina Jane Vann 1981.

Doris' father, Dr Geoffrey Strange Beck (6th June 1859–12th January 1914), born at Ashburnham, Ontario, married Lillias Margaret née Buchanan (21st August 1868–28th January 1953), born at Hillier, Prince Edward, Ontario, on 26th July 1886 at Port Arthur, Algoma, Ontario. He was the area medical officer for the Canadian Pacific Railway when the line was under construction on the northern shore of Lake Superior. In later life they spent half of the year in Monrovia, California, USA. They both died at Toronto, Ontario. In addition to Doris they had two other children:

- Georgina Agnes Beck (9th May 1887–22nd October 1888).
- Lillias Helen Sybil Beck (5th September 1893–22nd February 1980), known as Helen, studied medicine in Paris with her sister Doris and was a bridesmaid and witness at her wedding. She married Whiteford George Bell (8th August 1891–8th February 1975), a real estate broker born at Toronto, Ontario, on 19th February 1919 at Esclusham, Denbighshire, Wales. Whiteford attested in the CEF at Toronto on 14th August 1915, declaring four months previous service with 48th Highlanders. He was described as 5′ 8¾″ tall, weighing 160 lbs, with fair complexion, blue eyes, light brown hair and his religious denomination was Presbyterian. He was commissioned as a lieutenant with seniority from 12th July 1915. He embarked aboard SS *Empress of Britain* on 20th May 1916 and disembarked in England on 29th May. On 19th September he was posted to the permanent cadre of 92nd Battalion. He was shell-shocked on 19th October and was admitted to 4th London General Hospital, Denmark Hill on 24th October. He was discharged on 2nd November and attended 49th Class at the Canadian School of Musketry, Shorncliffe, Kent 1st-12th January 1917, qualifying 1st Class. He was transferred to the strength of 5th Reserve Battalion, East Sandling on 4th January and was granted sick leave 25th-31st January. On 15th March he was attached to RFC Reading on the strength of 1st Central Ontario Regimental Depot, West Sandling. Whiteford was seconded for duty with No.43 Squadron RFC in France from 8th April, while on the Canadian General List. He reported sick at Aire, France with right side abdominal pain on 14th April, was admitted to the Highland Clearing Station, Aire and then the Duchess of Westminster (1st British Red Cross) Hospital, Le Touquet on 20th April. He was evacuated to England on 23rd April aboard HMHS *Cambria*, on the strength of the Canadian General Depot, and was admitted to 4th London General Hospital with suspected appendicitis next day. No signs were found and an operation was not recommended. A medical board at 76 Strand, London on 1st May found him unfit for service for three weeks. His address was c/o Charles H Clover, Pentre Bycham Hall, Wrexham, Denbighshire. He was taken on the strength of 1st Central Ontario Regimental Depot on 14th June. On 6th July he was appointed flying officer (observer) with seniority from 8th April. On 2nd October he was admitted to 24th General Hospital, Étaples with syncope and was discharged to the Base Depot on 8th October. Whiteford ceased to be seconded to the RAF and was struck off strength of the CEF on 1st May 1919 and was demobilised the next day in England. They were living at Orchard Way Cottage, Knotty Green, Beaconsfield, Buckinghamshire in 1939. He was an insurance broker in 1945. He died at Blewbury, Oxfordshire. She died at Circus Nursing Home, 7 The Circus, Bath, Avon.

A medical board at The Connaught Hospital, Aldershot on 5th February 1917 examined the old gunshot wound to Bernard's left forearm and found him unfit for

The French Croix de Guerre was first awarded in 1915 to individuals or units distinguishing themselves by acts of heroism. Some notable recipients include:

- Josephine Baker – American born French dancer, singer and actress for her work in the Resistance.
- Jacques Cousteau – pioneer diver and underwater filmmaker.
- General Dwight D Eisenhower – Supreme Allied Commander during Operation OVERLORD.
- Noor Inayat Khan and Violette Szabo – British SOE agents awarded the George Cross and executed by the Nazis.
- Audie Murphy – actor and the most decorated US soldier of WW2, including the Medal of Honor.
- General George S Patton – commander of US Third Army in the Second World War.
- Theodore Roosevelt – son of President Theodore Roosevelt, awarded the Medal of Honor for 6th June 1944 on Utah Beach.
- James Stewart – actor, for his role in the liberation of France as a USAAF Colonel.
- Major Richard D Winters – Easy Company, 506th Parachute Infantry Regiment, made famous by the TV series and book *Band of Brothers*.
- Sergeant Alvin C York – American First World War Medal of Honor winner and subject of a film in 1941 starring Gary Cooper.

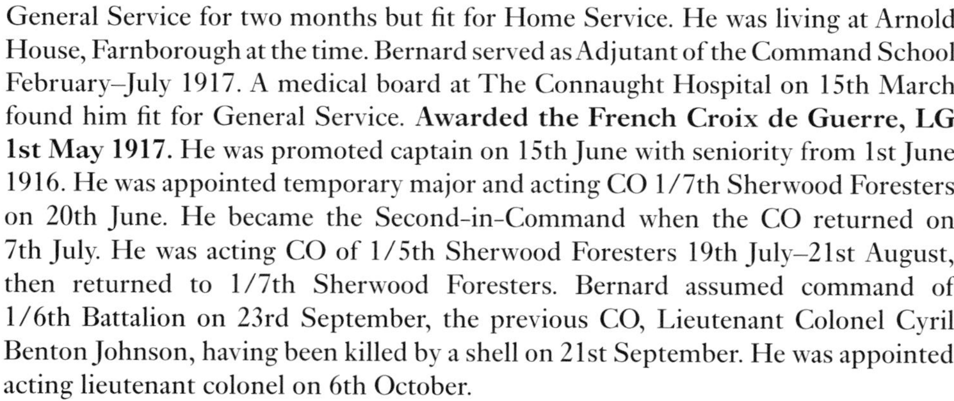

General Service for two months but fit for Home Service. He was living at Arnold House, Farnborough at the time. Bernard served as Adjutant of the Command School February–July 1917. A medical board at The Connaught Hospital on 15th March found him fit for General Service. **Awarded the French Croix de Guerre, LG 1st May 1917.** He was promoted captain on 15th June with seniority from 1st June 1916. He was appointed temporary major and acting CO 1/7th Sherwood Foresters on 20th June. He became the Second-in-Command when the CO returned on 7th July. He was acting CO of 1/5th Sherwood Foresters 19th July–21st August, then returned to 1/7th Sherwood Foresters. Bernard assumed command of 1/6th Battalion on 23rd September, the previous CO, Lieutenant Colonel Cyril Benton Johnson, having been killed by a shell on 21st September. He was appointed acting lieutenant colonel on 6th October.

Bernard was granted leave in England 21st-27th October, 3rd-18th December and 18th March–3rd April 1918. He was hospitalised 23rd May–10th June and was granted leave to Paris 1st-11th September, where he was joined by his wife. **Awarded the VC for his actions at Bellenglise and Lehaucourt, France on 29th September 1918, LG 14th December 1918.** This was the only VC to be awarded to an ordained Church of England clergyman as a combatant. About 500 Anglican clergymen served in the British and Imperial forces other than as chaplains. Of these, five commanded infantry battalions, including Bernard, and at least forty-six were killed. On 3rd October, while leading his Battalion in the attack on the Beaurevoir-Fonsomme Line near Ramicourt, he was shot through the heart and killed instantly by a German sniper. He was buried at Bellenglise British

The officers of 1/6th Sherwood Foresters in November 1917. Bernard Vann is in the centre of the front row.

Cemetery and his remains were moved in 1920 to Bellicourt British Cemetery (II O 1). His headstone bears the quotation, 'A great priest who in his days pleased God', which was written by the Bishop of Peterborough, who had ordained Bernard. **He was mentioned in Sir Douglas Haig's despatch of 8th November 1918, LG 28th December 1918.** Bernard was wounded possibly as many as thirteen times but only wore five wound stripes. The VC was presented to his widow by the King at Buckingham Palace on 26th November 1919. Bernard is commemorated in a number of other places:

Bernard Vann's grave in Bellicourt British Cemetery.

- Rushden, Northamptonshire
  - Bernard Vann Close, Lancaster Manor Estate dedicated on 3rd March 2016.
  - Heritage Blue Plaque, unveiled by his grandson, Michael Vann, on his former home at 46 High Street South on 14th October 2006.
  - Named on the War Memorial dedicated on 25th September 1921.
  - Named in St Mary's Church Memorial Chapel.
  - A Department for Communities and Local Government commemorative paving stone was dedicated at the War Memorial on 29th September 2018.
  - Plaque at Skew Bridge Lake.

Rushden War Memorial.

The Wellingborough War Memorial also commemorates Major Edward 'Mick' Mannock VC, DSO & two Bars, MC & Bar (24th May 1887–26th July 1918).

- Wellingborough, Northamptonshire
  - Named on the War Memorial dedicated on 11th November 1924.
  - Named on the War Memorial, All Saints Church, Midland Road.
  - Named on the Wellingborough School War memorial dedicated on 14th November 1924 and a plaque in Wellingborough School Chapel.
- Coates, Cirencester, Gloucestershire
  - Both Vann brothers are named on the War Memorial opposite the former National School.
  - Both Vann brothers are named on the Roll of Honour, St Matthews Church. There is also a small display to Bernard at the Old Rectory, adjacent to the church.
- Leicestershire
  - Named on the War Memorial, St Barnabas' Church (Barnabas Hall since July 2011), Leicester dedicated on 25th April 1920. There is also a memorial plaque and stained-glass window dedicated to his memory.
  - Named on the War Memorial and Roll of Honour, Ashby De La Zouch School.
  - Bernard Vann Crescent, Ashby-de-la-Zouch.
- University of Cambridge
  - Both Vann brothers are named on the Jesus College War Memorial.
  - Vann Club for past members of the Cambridge University Hockey Club.

The Great War Memorial in All Saints Church, Wellingborough.

- Plaque and chair in St George's Chapel, St Mary Magdalene Church, Newark, where the memorial to 8th Sherwood Foresters was dedicated on 30th October 1921.
- Named on the memorial to six members of Derby County Football Club who died in the Great War dedicated at Pride Park Stadium, Pride Parkway, Derby Derbyshire on 8th November 2014.
- The Vann Fellowship was established by Durham University in October 2016 for the study of the relationship between Christianity and the military.

The Derby County Football Club Great War Memorial at Pride Park Stadium.

In addition to the VC and MC & Bar he was awarded the 1914–15 Star, British War Medal 1914–20, Victory Medal 1914–19 with Mentioned-in-Despatches Oakleaf and the French Croix de Guerre 1914–18 with Bronze Palm. The VC, MC & Bar and Croix de Guerre were acquired by Lord Michael Ashcroft in 2010 but the Great War trio was not part of the group. The VC is held by the Michael Ashcroft Trust, the holding institution for the Lord Ashcroft Victoria Cross Collection, and is displayed in the Imperial War Museum's Lord Ashcroft Gallery.

The Victory Medal (or Inter-Allied Victory Medal) was first proposed by French Marshal Ferdinand Foch as a common award for all the nations allied against the Central Powers. Regardless of nationality, each medal is 36mm in diameter, the ribbon is a double rainbow and the obverse shows winged victory (except Japan and Siam where winged victory has no relevance). For British Empire forces the medal was issued to all who received the 1914 or 1914–15 Stars and to almost all who received the British War Medal. The British alone struck 6,335,000 Victory medals. These three medals were known as Pip, Squeak and Wilfred after a popular newspaper comic strip. To qualify for the Victory Medal recipients had to be mobilised for war service and have entered a theatre of war between 5th August 1914 and 11th November 1918, plus Russia 1919–20 and mine clearance in the North Sea until 30th November 1919. Those Mentioned in Despatches wore an oakleaf on the Victory Medal ribbon as shown here.

MAJOR BLAIR ANDERSON WARK
32nd Australian Infantry Battalion, AIF

Blair Wark was born on 27th July 1894 at Bathurst, New South Wales. His father, Alexander Wark (13th July 1858–1927), born at Blythswood, Glasgow, Lanarkshire, Scotland, was a gas engineer. He emigrated to Australia with his parents and settled at Bathurst. He married Blanche 'Ma' Adelaide Maria née Forde (16th March 1868–22nd August 1956), born at Collingwood, Victoria, at Bathurst, NSW on 19th November 1888. They lived at Roseville, 16 Princes Street, McMahon's Point, North Sydney and at various other addresses during the Great War:

Bathurst, 200 kilometres west-northwest of Sydney, is the oldest inland settlement in Australia. The first European arrived in 1813, after the first crossing of the Blue Mountains, and a road was pushed through by 1815. The site of the future town was named after the Secretary of State for War and the Colonies, Earl Henry Bathurst, on 7th May 1815. Settlers followed and, in the early years, Bathurst was a base for many explorations into the interior. Gold had been discovered in the Fish River in 1823, but it was not until February 1851 that payable quantities were discovered and Australia's first gold rush commenced. The Beyers Holtermann Specimen found on 20th October 1871 remains the largest single mass of gold ever discovered in the world, producing ninety-three kilograms of gold. The prosperity made the area a target for bushrangers. Bathurst became utterly reliant on the gold industry and it declined dramatically when the gold ran out late in the 19th century. It later became a centre for coal mining and manufacturing. The railway from Sydney reached the town in 1876.

Charles Edwin Woodrow Bean (1879–1968), war correspondent and historian, was born there. Bean edited the *Official History of Australia in the War of 1914–1918* and was instrumental in the creation of the Australian War Memorial. Also born at Bathurst was Joseph Benedict Chifley (1885–1951), leader of the Labor Party 1945–51 and the 16th Prime Minister of Australia 1945–49.

Collingwood, one of the oldest suburbs in Melbourne, three kilometres northeast of the central business district, is noted for its historical 19th century buildings. It is believed that the suburb was named after Admiral Collingwood in 1842. Collingwood became a municipality, separate from Melbourne, in 1855, a town in 1873 and a city in 1876. Its early development was dependent on the boom in Melbourne's economy during the Victorian Gold Rush in the 1850s and 1860s.

Princes Street, named after the Prince of Wales by Governor Macquarie in 1810, ran along the crown of the ridge to the west of Sydney Cove. By the 1830s it was in Sydney's most prestigious residential area, despite being surrounded by streets of some of the poorest residents. However, within a century, Princes Street had disappeared, to be replaced by the Bradfield Highway, the southern approach to Sydney Harbour Bridge.

Mascot, 113 Berry Street, North Sydney.
Warilda, 154 West Street, North Sydney.
28 Mount Street, North Sydney.
Greylands, Merrenburn Avenue, Crows Nest, Sydney.

Blair had four siblings:

- Alexander 'Alex' Newlands Wark (22nd January 1890–1956) was born at Lismore, NSW. He passed a medical at Victoria Barracks, NSW on 24th April 1918 and enlisted as Alexander Wark in 15th General Service Reinforcements at Sydney, NSW (60056). He joined on 27th May and was described as an orchardist, 5′ 7½″ tall, weighing 142 lbs, with fair complexion, blue eyes, fair hair and his religious denomination was Church of England. On 19th July he joined the Composite Battalion. He embarked aboard HMT *Gaika* at Sydney on 30th July and disembarked in London, England on 13th October. The same day he joined the reinforcements of 53rd Battalion with 14th Training Battalion, Hurdcott, Wiltshire. He was treated at Fovant Military Hospital for influenza 19th October–19th November. On 10th December he transferred to the reinforcements of 56th Battalion and was appointed acting corporal on 12th December. He was appointed extra regimental sergeant at Tidworth, Wiltshire on 21st January 1919 and transferred to 3rd Brigade Concentration Depot, Hurdcott on 8th February. Alexander returned to Australia aboard HT *Indarra* departing on 12th July and disembarking on 8th September. He was discharged from 2nd Military District on 24th September. In July 1923 he was living at Town Hall Hotel, Waratah, via Newcastle, NSW. That year he married Minnie Mackie (11th October 1900–1978), born at Stockton, NSW, in 1923 at Waratah, NSW. He died at Newcastle, NSW. They had a son:

  ◦ David John Wark (1927–2009), born at Newcastle, NSW, was known as John. He married Delma Joy Blanch at Hamilton, NSW in 1966. He was a general manager and she was a bank clerk in 1968, when they were living at 40 Conmurra Circuit, Shortland, NSW.

- Nellie/Nelly Anderson Wark (1st July 1891–18th April 1968) was born at Bathurst, NSW. She married Oliver Alfred 'Alfie' Godwin (19th December 1887–23rd July 1970), born at Amsterdam, New York, USA, on 1st October 1914 at St Mary's Church, Kangaroo Point, Brisbane, Queensland. Oliver joined the Merchant Navy and was an apprentice aboard the *Vincent* on a voyage from Hong Kong to Newcastle, NSW in 1906, during which there was a mutiny over conditions aboard. The captain armed the officers, and the mutineers were handed over to the police on arrival. He was Fourth Mate aboard SS *Star of Scotland* when he arrived in Melbourne, Australia from England on 25th July 1911. He then worked on coastal steamers of the Australasian United Steam Navigation Co and was Fourth Mate aboard SS *Levuka* in 1914 and SS *Indarra* in 1917. They were living at Bundarra, Ivory Street, Brisbane in July 1915. Oliver became a naturalised Australian on 11th August 1915 (Certificate No.22354). He became a captain with P&O Line for twenty years and served on a number of ships – *Emita* 1926, *Mareeba II* and *Mungana* 1927, *Mildura* and *Milora* 1928, *Maranoa* 1930, *Macumba* 1931 and *Ormiston* 1934. During his career he rounded Cape Horn, Chile six times in sailing ships. They were living at 3 Zeta Road, Lane Cove, NSW at the time of her death there. He also died at Lane Cove.
- Keith Newlands Wark (11th January 1893–9th February 1977) enlisted at Liverpool, NSW on 23rd May 1915 in 9th Reinforcements, 2nd Battalion (2895). He was described as an insurance clerk, 5′6¼″ tall, weighing 148 lbs, with fair complexion, blue eyes, fair hair and his religious denomination was Church of England. He embarked at Sydney aboard HMAT A8 *Argyllshire* on 30th September. On 6th January 1916 he joined 2nd Battalion at Tel-el-Kebir, Egypt. He was promoted lance corporal on 3rd February 1916 and transferred to 54th Battalion on 14th February. He was appointed temporary sergeant on

1st March and was later confirmed in the rank with effect from the same date. Keith attended the School of Instruction, Zeitoun 30th April–21st May. On 19th June he embarked aboard HT *Caledonian* at Alexandria and disembarked at Marseille, France on 29th June. He was reported wounded in error on 20th July. Awarded the DCM for his actions on 29th August, when he took charge of his platoon, after the officers became casualties, and did fine work under very heavy shell fire. He set a fine example and rendered great assistance in establishing the defences of the front line, LG 22nd September 1916. He was commissioned (dated 23rd August) and was granted leave in England 13th-27th December. On 26th December he was promoted lieutenant. Keith was admitted to 6th Australian Field Ambulance with a gunshot wound to the left chest on 30th March 1917. He was transferred to 14th General Hospital, Wimereux via a casualty clearing station on 4th April and to England aboard HMHS *Cambria* from Boulogne on 5th April, where he was admitted to 3rd London General Hospital, Wandsworth. On 18th April he was transferred to 5th Australian Auxiliary Hospital, Digswell House, Welwyn and joined No.1 Command Depot, Perham Down on 24th May. Keith returned to France, joining 5th Australian Division Base Depot, Le Havre on 17th June. He rejoined 54th Battalion on 23rd June but returned to England on 19th July and joined 14th Training Battalion, Hurdcott on 21st July. He qualified as an instructor in bombing on a course at the Southern Command Bombing School, Lyndhurst, Hampshire 13th-25th August. He was attached to 3rd Pioneer Training Battalion, Fovant on 30th August. Keith returned to France via Southampton on 15th January 1918, joined the Reinforcement Camp on 20th January and rejoined 54th Battalion on 24th January. He was appointed Battalion Bombing Officer on 15th March and was detached to HQ 14th Australian Brigade 7th-14th April. On 1st May he was appointed Battalion Intelligence Officer. Following leave in England 11th September–2nd October, he transferred to 56th Battalion on 11th October. He was mentioned in Sir Douglas Haig's Despatch of 8th November 1918, LG 27th December 1918. He was granted leave in France 10th-28th March 1919 and joined the Australian Infantry Base Depot, Le Havre on 9th April. Keith embarked at Le Havre on 16th April, disembarked at Southampton next day and joined 5 Group at Weymouth. He embarked aboard SS *Beltana* on 2nd June for return to Australia and disembarked in Australia on 19th July. His appointment was terminated on 13th September 1919. Keith married Dorothy Ruth Perdriau (1899–22nd November 1941), born at Burwood, NSW, in 1924 at Chatswood, NSW – see under paternal grandparents below. Dorothy died at Hawthorn, Victoria. Keith was living at Berkely Street, Hawthorn in 1949 and subsequently died at Hawthorn. They had a daughter:

- Margaret 'Mig' Ethelwynne Wark (12th June 1925–4th July 2002), born at Linfield, NSW, married Gavin Grant McDonald (25th June 1920–21st October 1994) on 30th September 1952 at Melbourne. He was educated at the University of Melbourne (BSc 1940, MSc 1941) and worked as a metallurgist at the Munitions Supply Laboratories, Maribyrnong, Victoria 1940–60. He was Superintendent at the South Australian Branch Defence Standards Laboratories 1960–63, Head of the Physics Metallurgy Group there 1963–66, Principal Research Scientist at the Commonwealth Department of Supply 1966–77 and Director of International Programmes at the Defence Science and Technology Organisation 1977–80. He published *Physics in Australia to 1945*. They had a child. The family lived at St Kilda, Hawthorn, at Higgins in Victoria and at Canberra, Australian Capital Territory, where they both died.

Old Monkland in Lanarkshire is now the town of Coatbridge, fourteen kilometres east of the centre of Glasgow. The earliest known settlement in the area was in the Stone Age but the town was founded in 1162 by Royal Charter to the monks of Newcastle Abbey by King Malcolm IV. It became known as Monklands. In 1641, the parish was divided into New Monkland, the present-day Airdrie, and Old Monkland, now Coatbridge. In 1745 Coatbridge was seized by Bonnie Prince Charlie in his march on Edinburgh. With its coal and ironstone deposits, Coatbridge became a major centre for iron works during the 19th century. It gained a reputation for air pollution and the worst excesses of industry. By 1885, the Monklands ironstone had been exhausted and it became increasingly expensive to produce iron in Coatbridge with imported raw materials. Living conditions remained very poor. By the 1920s coal had been exhausted and the iron industry was in serious decline. In 1934 many inhabitants moved to Corby in England to work in the steel works there. The decline in demand for steel for Clydeside shipbuilding in the 1950s caused the final collapse of the industry. The last blast furnace closed in 1967. Widespread unemployment followed, with appalling housing conditions and overcrowding. In the 1930s and 1950s state-sponsored programmes saw thousands of new homes and most of the slum housing was cleared. However, despite various initiatives to regenerate Coatbridge since the 1970s, the population has continued to fall. Amongst the famous people born or who lived there are:

- Admiral Sir James Stirling (1791–1865), who persuaded the British Government to establish the Swan River Colony and became the first Governor and Commander-in-Chief of Western Australia.
- Joseph Wallace 'Jock Cunningham (1902–69), a volunteer in the International Brigades during the Spanish Civil War, who became a battalion and brigade commander.
- John 'Jock' Stein CBE (1922–85) was the first manager of a British club to win the European Cup with Celtic in 1967. He also guided Celtic to nine successive Scottish League championships 1966–74. He played for Albion Rovers in Coatbridge from November 1942 and ironically his first match was a 4–4 draw against Celtic.
- George Graham (born 1944) had a successful playing career, making 455 appearances for Aston Villa, Chelsea, Arsenal, Manchester United, Portsmouth and Crystal Palace. About half of his appearances were for Arsenal and he was in the team that won the Football League Championship and FA Cup double in 1971. Graham was on the coaching staff of Crystal Palace and Queen's Park Rangers but it was his time as manager of Arsenal 1987–95 for which he is best known. During his tenure the club won numerous domestic and European honours, including two league titles, two Football League Cups and a European Cup Winners Cup.

- Lance Bathurst Wark (15th July 1896–21st December 1929) served in the Merchant Navy and was Second Mate on the Brig *Senorita* in 1918. He eventually became a captain. He married Annie Elizabeth Wells (born 1904), born at Sydney, in 1925 at Albury, NSW. He died at Blackheath, NSW. Annie married Reginald Hamilton (21st July 1896–17th August 1974), born at Wagga Wagga, in 1934 at Chatswood, NSW. They were living at 5/1 Morton Street, Crows Nest, NSW in 1972. They are believed to have had two children.

Blair's paternal grandfather, John Newlands Wark (29th December 1817–1st September 1884), born at Glasgow, Lanarkshire, Scotland, married Margaret née Anderson (12th September 1824–20th December 1879), born at Old Monkland, Lanarkshire, on 4th August 1847 at Dunoon, Argyllshire. John was a gas surveyor in 1851, when they were living at 78 Rose Street, Glasgow. By 1861 he was a muslin merchant and they were living at 43 Sea Shore, Dunoon. They emigrated to New

Dunoon is located on the western shore of the upper Firth of Clyde. Dunoon Castle, built in the 12th century, became a royal castle. Mary, Queen of Scots visited on 26th July 1563 and granted several charters. In 1646 members of Clan Lamont were massacred there by members of Clan Campbell. The castle was destroyed during Argyll's Rising in 1685. In the late 19th and early 20th centuries, Dunoon became a popular destination for steamships. However, this declined with the advent of improved road and rail travel and cheap overseas holidays. Gun emplacements around the town were part of the Clyde defences and in the Second World War covered an anti-submarine boom. At the height of the Cold War there was a United States Navy ballistic nuclear submarine base there. Its closure in 1992 resulted in an economic downturn for the area. Since then, the town has turned again to tourism, particularly for outdoor and wildlife lovers. Amongst the town's famous alumni are:

- Baroness Virginia Hilda Brunette Maxwell Bottomley of Nettlestone PC DL (born 1948) was a Conservative MP 1984–2005. She was appointed Minister of State for Health in 1989, Secretary of State for Health in 1992 and was Secretary of State for National Heritage 1995–97.
- Baron George Islay MacNeill Robertson of Port Ellen KT GCMG PC FRSA FRSE (born 1946) was a Labour MP, who was Secretary of State for Defence 1997–99 and the tenth Secretary General of NATO 1999–2004.
- John Smith QC (1938–1994) was Leader of the Labour Party from July 1992 until his death. He was appointed Minister of State for Energy 1975–76 and for the Privy Council Office 1976–78. He served as Secretary of State for Trade and President of the Board of Trade 1978–79. In Opposition he was Shadow Secretary of State for Trade 1979–82, for Energy 1982–83, for Employment 1983–84, for Trade and Industry 1984–87 and was Shadow Chancellor 1987–92.
- Sisters Arabella (1886–1980) and Muriel Eleanor Scott (1888–1963) were suffragette campaigners. Arabella underwent hunger and thirst strikes when she was sent to jail and was force-fed many times.

Zealand in 1863, where he was the manager of Auckland Gas Works. He moved to Sydney, New South Wales, Australia aboard the *Hero*, arriving on 30th December 1868. He was the engineer at Sydney Gasworks but in 1872 an Act enabled him to supply gas to Bathurst, NSW and he moved there in 1874. The venture was successful and he provided the first gas lighting to the city. John took a keen interest in Bathurst Hospital and the School of Arts and was on the Commission of Peace. He returned to Scotland for two years and on his return was appointed valuator for the Government in purchasing the gasworks in connection with the railways. He was appointed manager of Tamworth Gas and Coke Co Ltd in 1881. Margaret died at Bathurst, NSW. John married Annie Janet Fraser (1840–1913) in 1882 at Hawthorn, Victoria. They both died at Bathurst. In addition to Alexander, Blair and Margaret had seven other children:

- John Anderson Wark (26th December 1847–4th December 1930), born at Glasgow, Lanarkshire, studied analytical chemistry at Glasgow University. He worked for the Glasgow Corporation Gasworks and emigrated to Sydney, NSW in 1870. He erected Bathurst Gas Works the following year. John married Ellen Litster (1854–31st December 1876), born at Glasgow, on 13th March 1873 at Liverpool Street, Darlinghurst, NSW. John married Mary Gibbs Palmer (18th November 1855–6th July 1943), born at Hill End, NSW, on 9th August 1877 at Bathurst. He erected the gasworks at Wagga Wagga, NSW in 1880–81 and commenced building the Tamworth Gas and Coke Co the following year. They were living at Dundonald, Lovell Street, Leura, NSW in 1915. They both died at Katoomba, NSW. John had nine children from his two marriages:
    - Ethelwynne Mary Wark (1874–20th May 1919) married Edgar Martin Perdriau (2nd January 1873–24th October 1945) at Burwood in 1898. They had a daughter, Dorothy Ruth Perdriau (1899–22nd November 1941).
    - Maurice John James Wark (1876–12th May 1961).
    - Edith Palmer Wark (1878–31st March 1936) never married.
    - Aubrey George Wark (16th August 1881–8th March 1958) married Grace Kerr (1882–1974), born at Burwood, at Sydney in 1900. They had three children – Gordon Aubrey Wark (1901–77), Donald Stuart Wark (1906–79) and Dorothy Grace Wark (born 1908).
    - Roy Anderson Wark (1885–18th January 1887).
    - Athol Anderson Wark (1889–17th June 1908).
    - Olga Elaine Wark (12th June 1891–4th April 1972) never married.
    - Kenneth Stuart Wark (1893–15th March 1921) enlisted in C Company, 19th Battalion at Holdsworthy on 30th September 1915 (17234). He had served in the Senior Cadets in 1904 for eleven months. He was described as a salesman clerk, 5′ 5″ tall, weighing 113 lbs, with fair complexion, blue eyes, light brown hair and his religious denomination was Presbyterian. On 16th January 1916 he transferred to 6th Reinforcements, 5th Field Artillery

Brigade and to 6th Reinforcements, 2nd Division Ammunition Column on 1st April. Kenneth embarked aboard HMAT A69 *Warilda* at Sydney on 22nd May and disembarked at Plymouth, Devon on 18th July. He joined the Australian Artillery Training Depot, Bulford, Wiltshire on 12th August and was admitted to Bulford Hospital with bronchitis 14th-29th September. He transferred to 21st Field Artillery Brigade, Boyton on 26th October and was treated for scabies at Codford 4th-9th November. He went to France via Southampton on 20th March 1917, joined 116th Howitzer Battery on 29th March and was taken on the strength of 1st Field Artillery Brigade next day. Kenneth was wounded by a gunshot to the left wrist/arm in Belgium on 23rd October, whilst serving in 101st Australian (Howitzer) Battery AFA. He was admitted to 3rd Australian Field Ambulance and No.17 Casualty Clearing Station next day and was transferred by 36 Ambulance Train to 7th Canadian General Hospital, Étaples later on 24th October. He embarked aboard HMHS *Ville de Liege* for England on 9th December and was admitted to Northampton War Hospital, Duston. On 4th March 1918 he transferred to 3rd Australian Auxiliary Hospital, Dartford. A medical board there next day found him permanently unfit for General Service and for Home Service for six months. It was recommended that he be returned to Australia. He joined No.2 Command Depot, Weymouth on 12th March, embarked aboard HMAT A30 *Borda* on 5th April and disembarked in Australia on 1st June. He was treated at 4th Australian General Hospital from 25th June and was discharged from 2nd Military District on 30th November. Kenneth married Jean Gow Wallace (1895–1971), born at Petersham, NSW, at Sydney in 1919. They had a son, Ross K Wark, in 1920. Jean married Edward W Cooney at Randwick, NSW in 1925. Kenneth's British War and Victory Medals were issued to Jean living at 321 Liverpool Road, Enfield, NSW in February 1933.
    - Colin Clifford Wark (28th November 1901–16th October 1968) married Beryl Muriel Farran (1904–94) at Manly on 28th December 1923. He served in the Australian Army Service Corps 2nd July 1940–16th November 1944 (NX51537) and was discharged as a staff sergeant. They had a son, Alistair Malcolm Wark (1925–2012).
- Mary Wark (26th November 1849–30th December 1932) married James Henry Simson (1st June 1848–24th October 1890), also born at Glasgow, Scotland, on 23rd August 1881 at West MacQuarrie, Sydney. He drowned accidentally near Lady Robinson's Beach, Brighton-le-Sands in Botany Bay, Sydney. She died at Ashfield, NSW. They had six children:
    - Henry John Simson (22nd June 1882–6th May 1951), a doctor, married Christine Edgar Redpath (1881–22nd July 1924) at Sydney on 22nd January 1908. They were living in Vancouver, British Columbia, Canada later in 1908, in Edinburgh, Scotland by 1910 and Southampton, England by 1919. Henry was commissioned as a temporary lieutenant in the Royal Army

Medical Corps on 7th October 1916 and went to France on 20th October. He was promoted temporary captain and relinquished his commission due to ill health contracted on active service on 11th September 1918 (Silver War Badge No.B13506). They were living at 1 East Park Terrace, Southampton in 1920. Henry and Christine had four children – Edyth Mary Simson (1908–77), Henry 'Keith' Simson DFC (1910–92), Elma Vivien Simson (1916–2002) and Marjorie Simson (1919–2001). Henry married Hilda Dorothy Jeffrey (2nd November 1900–1977) in Surrey in September 1935.

- Frank 'Francis' William Simson (1st August 1883–17th December 1948) was a doctor and an expert on silicosis and tuberculosis. He married Elsie 'Bobbie' Robertson Murphy (born 25th March 1901), born at Belfast, Antrim, Northern Ireland, in 1929 at Durban, South Africa. They had two children. Frank died at Durban.
- Constance Mary Simson (30th April 1886–31st December 1887).
- Frederick Alexander Simson (1887–25th July 1945) enlisted in 8th Reinforcements, 22nd Howitzer Brigade at RA Show Grounds, Moore Park, Sydney on 1st August 1916 (30331). He was described as an orchardist, 5′7¼″ tall, weighing 120 lbs, with fair complexion, blue eyes, fair hair and his religious denomination was Presbyterian. He remustered as a driver on 1st November. On 9th November he embarked aboard HMAT A24 *Benalla* at Sydney and disembarked at Devonport on 9th January 1917. Frederick joined 120th Howitzer Battery, Artillery Reserve Brigade at Larkhill, Wiltshire on 10th January and moved to Boyton Camp, Wiltshire on 16th March. He went to France via Southampton on 26th March and transferred to 13th Field Artillery Brigade on 31st March. He was granted leave 17th February–7th March 1918, in England 4th-19th January 1919 and in Brussels, Belgium 18th-22nd March. On 23rd April he was appointed temporary bombardier and returned to England from the Artillery General Base Depot on 22nd May to join 5 Group, Weymouth next day. Frederick embarked aboard SS *Friedrichsruh* on 8th July and disembarked in Australia on 4th September. He was discharged from 2nd Military District on 12th October 1919. Frederick married Mary Sharpe Troup (1890–1941) at Chatswood, NSW in 1916. She was living at White Rock, Bathurst, NSW in August and later at 19 Orwell Street, Darlinghurst, Sydney, NSW. They had at least two children – Enid A Simson (born 1921) and James Henry Simson (died 1976). Frederick married Margaret Hannah Arnold (1901–97) in 1944 at Sydney.
- Margaret Dorothy Simson (1889–14th July 1951) married her cousin, Russell George Stanger (1887–1973), at Sydney in 1935. She died at Tamworth, NSW.
- Mary Elma Simson (1891–31st May 1972) married Desmond A Williams (1891–1973), born at St Leonards, NSW, at Sydney in 1915. They both died

at St Leonards. They had two children – Desmond C Williams (born 1917) and Desiree Elma Williams (1919–2002).

- William Wark (9th May 1852–12th January 1931) M.Inst.CE, a civil engineer, married Janet Jane Lamrock (23rd February 1854–30th October 1937), born at Kurrajong, on 6th February 1878 at Lemon Forest, Kurrajong Heights, NSW. He designed and constructed Bathurst Gas Works 1879–82 and was the proprietor 1885–97. He designed Wagga Wagga and Grafton Gas Works and designed and erected Tamworth Gas Works in 1883 and Hay Gas Works the following year. He was a director of Messrs Parkinson and W & B Cowan Ltd, manufacturers of gas appliances, a director of Manly Gas Co Ltd, attorney for International Lighting Association of Edinburgh and an engineer to the Colonial Lighting Syndicate in 1897. William remodelled the New Plymouth Gas Works in New Zealand. He was appointed JP for NSW in 1894. William and Janet lived at The Ridge, Kurrajong Heights, where they both subsequently died. They had five children:
  - William Nicol Wark (23rd January 1879–30th December 1944).
  - Florence Helen Wark (12th December 1880–18th January 1964) never married.
  - Jessie Constance Wark (16th May 1883–21st March 1955) married John Murray Campbell (1892–1954), born at Lismore, NSW, at North Sydney on 14th March 1933. They both died at Chatswood, NSW. They had a daughter, Laura Margaret Campbell, who died in 1988.
  - Gertrude Margaret Wark (17th October 1885–13th November 1968) married Burton Batley Sampson (1891–1969), born at Tamworth, NSW, at Waverley, NSW on 16th October 1917. They both died at St Leonards. They had a son, Burton James Mark Sampson (1918–2000).
  - Frederick Newlands Wark (27th November 1888–9th October 1911).
- Bethia Wark (24th June 1854–17th March 1946) married Alfred George Stanger (17th July 1855–24th September 1937) in 1880 at Bathurst, where he was born. He died at Quirindi, NSW. They had four children:
  - Muriel Margaret Stanger (1881–23rd April 1971) never married.
  - Mildred Newlands Stanger (1882–30th July 1903) never married.
  - Russell George Stanger (1887 -1973) married his cousin, Margaret Dorothy Simson (1889–1951) at Sydney in 1935.
  - Norman Alfred Stanger (21st November 1891–15th February 1936) married Zaidie Rebecca Budden (1900–58) in 1927 at Wollongong, where she was born.
- Margaret Wark (10th July 1856–28th April 1924) born at Blythswood, Lanarkshire, never married and died at Quirinsi, NSW.
- James Wark (18th October 1860–25th April 1909), born at Anderton, Lanarkshire, married Eveline/Evelyn Gertrude Dargin (1863–20th February 1951) in 1883 at Bathurst, NSW, where she was born. He died at Bathurst and she at Cremorne, NSW. They had two sons:

Kitty McSpedden while serving in the Australian Army Nursing Service.

  - Eric Robin Wark (born 21st September 1884) married Jessie 'Oovie' Robinson (2nd August 1889–24th June 1970), born at Petersham, NSW, at Marrickville, NSW on 23rd June 1917. They had a son, John Mervyn Wark (1920–2010). She died at Hornsby, NSW.
  - Alan Wark (9th September 1886–11th August 1965).
- Henry Simson Wark (2nd April 1864–23rd July 1929), born at Auckland, New Zealand, married Ellen Bessie Moynahan (1869–8th September 1926), born at Launceston, Tasmania, on 5th February 1890 at Launceston, Tasmania. They were living at White Rock, NSW in July 1916. She died at Bathurst. Henry married Catherine 'Kitty' Christina McSpedden (17th September 1880–11th May 1944) on 24th January 1928 at St Stephen's Church, Bathurst. Kitty enlisted as a staff nurse in the Australian Army Nursing Service on 19th June 1915 at Sydney. She was described as 5′6″ tall, weighing 128 lbs, with fair complexion, blue eyes, dark brown hair and her religious denomination was Presbyterian. She embarked aboard HMAT A67 *Orsova*, departing Melbourne, Victoria on 16th July and commenced duty at Tooting Military Hospital, London, England on 30th September. She was attached to 3rd Australian Auxiliary Hospital, Dartford, Kent on 19th October but was detached next day to 3rd Australian General Hospital, Brighton, Sussex. Kitty was granted leave 2nd-15th February 1917 and was detached to 2nd Australian Auxiliary Hospital, Southall, Middlesex on 9th April, proceeding to France the same day. Two days later she reported to 1st Australian General Hospital, Rouen. She was granted leave to Britain 1st-20th January 1918. Having been promoted to sister on 1st October, she proceeded to England on leave until 18th October. On 21st December she disembarked at Southampton and reported to Sutton Veny, Wiltshire. She was granted leave again on 23rd April 1919 and was detached to 2nd Australian Auxiliary Hospital, Southall on 13th May. On 21st May she embarked aboard HMT *Osterley* and disembarked at Sydney on 7th July. She was discharged on 6th September 1919. Kitty qualified as a State Registered Nurse on 3rd March 1927, when she was living with her father at The Lagoon, Bathurst. Henry was described as an orchardist at the time of his death. Kitty died at 11 Bromborough Road, Roseville, NSW. Henry had three children with Ellen:
  - John Newlands Wark (27th December 1890–2nd September 1982), born at Latrobe, Tasmania, passed a medical at Bathurst on 17th March 1916 and enlisted as a gunner in 7th Reinforcements, 22nd Howitzers at RA Show

Grounds, Moore Park, Sydney, NSW on 3rd July (29376). He was described as an orchardist, 5′ 10¼″ tall, weighing 140 lbs, with fresh complexion, hazel eyes, brown hair and his religious denomination was Presbyterian. He transferred to 11th Reinforcements, 5th Brigade on 1st August and to 117th Howitzer Battery on 1st September. He embarked aboard HMAT A60 *Aeneas* at Melbourne on 2nd October and disembarked at Plymouth, Devon on 19th November. Whilst aboard he was treated for mumps 23rd October–7th November. John joined the Australian Artillery Training Depot, Larkhill, Wiltshire. He went to France aboard SS *Princess Henrietta* from Folkestone on 8th January 1917 and joined the Artillery General Base Depot, Étaples. On 27th January he transferred to 2nd Division Ammunition Column and remustered as a driver on 1st March. He was granted leave in England 27th January–13th February 1918, in Paris 14th-22nd March and in England again 15th-29th December, although including travel he was away from 12th December until 8th January 1919. He embarked for England on 22nd February and joined 3rd Training Brigade on 3rd March. John returned to Australia aboard SS *Port Denison*, embarking on 25th March and disembarking on 13th May. He was discharged from 2nd Military District on 20th June 1919. John married Adelaide Dorothy Bullock (1893–1968) in 1922 at Bathurst, where she was born. They had at least two children – Barbara Mary Wark (died 1982) and Henry Newlands Wark (died 1973).

- Evelyn Nellie Wark (1892–5th October 1974) married Ralph W Goddard (1893–1959), born at Braintree, Essex, England, at Bathurst in 1925.
- Elvie Mollie Wark (3rd September 1894–23rd July 1972) married John Hilton Winterbottom (17th February 1893–16th June 1963) at Bathurst on 23rd March 1918. They had three children – John Robert Winterbottom (1919–60), Ellen Bessie Winterbottom (1924–1990) and an unknown.

His maternal grandfather, Joseph Michael Forde (c.1840–3rd May 1929), born at Dublin, Ireland, emigrated to Australia aboard SV *General Windham*, arriving at Melbourne, Victoria in September 1857. He married Ellen née Creeden (c.1841–23rd August 1918), born in Co Cork, Ireland, on 10th May 1862 at St Francis Catholic Church, Melbourne. He moved to Sydney, NSW with his son, Leonard, aboard the *City of Adelaide* on 23rd December 1877. The rest of the family followed later. Joseph died at Railway Parade, Hazelbrook, NSW. In addition to Blanche they had six other children:

- Mary Rose Forde (1863–67).
- Ellen Rachel Forde (1864–1953).
- Leonard Joseph Forde (1865–29th November 1954) married Anna Thomasina Doyle (1858–19th July 1892), born at Melbourne, in 1891 in Victoria. She died at Collingwood, Victoria.

- James Harcourt Forde (November–2nd December 1866).
- David Herbert Forde (August 1873–1878), born in Sydney and died at Hereford Street, Glebe Point, NSW.
- Joseph Michael Burton Forde (born 30th December 1874), born at Gorcreigha Cottage, Roslyn Street, Darlinghurst, NSW, was a clerk. He either lost his left hand or it was badly deformed. He married Louisa Frances Rose Richardson (31st January 1877–10th November 1958), born in Paris, France, on 5th January 1898 at St Barnabas Church, South Bathurst, NSW. She was known as Rose and they lived at 88 Falcon Street, North Sydney. He was a grocer when he became insolvent in 1910. At the time the family was living at Emmett Street, North Sydney. A warrant for his arrest was issued by the North Sydney Bench for deserting his wife in April 1913. He was described as 5′ 5/6″ tall, thin build, fair hair and complexion, clean shaven, generally dressed in a navy blue sac (sic) suit and white straw boater hat. He was last heard of at Deniliquin, NSW in February 1913 and is believed to have died before 1936. Rose had moved to 4 Lillis Street, Sydney by 1926 and to King Street, Sydney by 1933. She died at the home of her daughter, Daphne Shatford, at Kemp Street, Mortdale, NSW. Joseph and Louisa had five children:
  - Francis Wentworth Forde (11th July 1898–31st July 1956) married Doris T McDonald/MacDonald at Sydney in 1934. He died at Campsie, NSW.
  - Dorothy Rose Forde (1903–20th March 1989) never married.
  - Ellen Daphne Forde (1906–31st July 1973) married David Roland Shatford (died 1989) in 1940. She died at Kogarah, NSW.
  - John 'Jack' Joseph Forde (16th September 1908–25th February 1991).
  - Daisy Louisa 'Bid' Forde (9th September 1911–c.1993), also seen as Louisa Daisy, married Herbert Riley Woodrow (c.1911–85), at St Thomas' Church, North Sydney on 9th May 1936. She was a schoolteacher and he a clerk.

St Francis' Church, Melbourne is the oldest Catholic church in Victoria, one of very few buildings in Melbourne built before the 1851 Victorian Gold Rush. The foundation stone was laid on 4th October 1841, the feast day of St Francis of Assisi. The first mass was held on 22nd May 1842 and the completed church was blessed on 23rd October 1845. In 1848, St Francis' became the cathedral church of the first Catholic Bishop of Melbourne and continued as a cathedral until 1868, when the diocesan seat was moved to St Patrick's Cathedral. A new sanctuary was added in 1878–79 and a front in 1956. Today it is the busiest church in Australia, with more than 10,000 worshippers each week.

Blair was educated at Fairleigh Grammar School, Bathurst for six years, at St Leonard's Superior Public School (North Sydney High) for two years and at

SV *City of Adelaide*, a clipper ship, built in Sunderland by William Pile, Hay & Co, was launched on 7th May 1864 for transporting passengers and goods between Britain and Australia. From 1869 to 1885 she was part of Harrold Bros Adelaide Line of clippers. Between 1864 and 1887 she made twenty-three return voyages from London and Plymouth to Adelaide, South Australia, playing an important part in the early immigration to Australia. About a quarter of a million South Australians can trace their origins to passengers on *City of Adelaide*. On the return voyages she carried passengers, wool and copper. After 1887, *City of Adelaide* carried coal around the British coast and timber and immigrants across the Atlantic. In 1893 she became a floating isolation hospital in Southampton and in 2009 a new hospital at Millbrook, Southampton was named the Adelaide Health Centre in honour of the ship. In 1923 she was purchased by the Royal Navy as a training ship for the RNVR at Greenock and was renamed HMS *Carrick* to avoid confusion with the newly commissioned HMAS *Adelaide*. In 1948 she was decommissioned and donated to the Royal Naval Volunteer Reserve Club on the River Clyde until 1989, when she was damaged by flooding. Although unusually having protection as a listed building, in 1991 she sank at her mooring. *Carrick* was recovered by the Scottish Maritime Museum the following year and was moved to a slipway adjacent to the Museum in Irvine. Restoration funding ran out in 1999 and the ship's future was in doubt. The Duke of Edinburgh convened a conference in 2001, at which it was concluded that *City of Adelaide* was one of the most important historic vessels in the UK but that resources in Scotland were insufficient to ensure her survival. As a result the aim of the Maritime Trust and the Scottish Maritime Museum was to transfer the ship to either the Sunderland Maritime Trust or the Save the *City of Adelaide* 1864 Group as quickly as possible. In 2010, the Scottish Government decided that the ship would be moved to Adelaide. That September and October, she was moved by barge to the Netherlands via Chatham, Kent and Greenwich, close to *Cutty Sark*, where the Duke of Edinburgh formally renamed her *City of Adelaide*. She was loaded onto the deck of a cargo ship at Rotterdam and on 26th November she commenced her final journey. *City of Adelaide* arrived at Port Adelaide on 3rd February 2014. A celebration of the ship's 150th anniversary was held on 17th May 2014. On 29th November 2019, *City of Adelaide* was towed to her permanent home in Dock 2, Port Adelaide. She is the world's oldest of two surviving clipper ships, the other being the tea clipper *Cutty Sark*, built in 1869, now a museum ship and tourist attraction in Greenwich, London. *City of Adelaide* is also one of only three surviving sailing ships, and the only surviving purpose-built passenger ship, to have taken immigrants from Britain to Australia.

Sydney Technical College. He qualified as a quantity surveyor. He was a Senior Cadet from July 1911 until July 1912 as a sergeant. He also served with 18th North Sydney Infantry Regiment (Militia) and was promoted corporal in 1913. Blair was commissioned on 16th August 1913 in Neutral Bay Company. From August 1914 he was engaged on full time Home Service defending the Port of Sydney. He attended training at the Infantry Depot, Liverpool, NSW and passed a military topography course at Sydney University. He also attended a course at the Royal Military College, Duntroon June – July 1915 and was appointed a provisional lieutenant on 1st July.

On 5th August Blair enlisted in 30th Battalion AIF, although his application for a commission in the AIF was not approved until 19th November, which seems rather

The Sydney Technical College, established in 1878, superseded the Sydney Mechanics' School of Arts, founded in 1833, and is one of Australia's oldest technical education institutions. In 1911 the College became the Sydney Technical High School, known as Ultimo College due to its location. It became part of the Sydney Institute of Technology and is now the New South Wales Sydney Institute. In 1949, the separate New South Wales University of Technology was founded on the main site.

a long time. He was described as 5′ 7½″ tall, weighing 155 lbs and his religious denomination was Church of England. He embarked aboard HMAT A72 *Beltana* at Sydney on 9th November, with C Company, 30th Battalion, and disembarked at Suez, Egypt on 11th December. He moved to Heliopolis and Tel el Kebir to undertake Canal defence duties and was promoted captain on 20th February 1916.

Blair embarked aboard HMAT A20 *Hororata* at Alexandria on 16th June, arriving at Marseille, France on 23rd June. He received a gunshot wound to the leg on 20th July at Fromelles and was admitted to 7th Stationery Hospital, Boulogne, before being evacuated to England aboard HMHS *St George* from Boulogne on 22nd July. He was admitted to 3rd London General Hospital, Wandsworth next day and was transferred to 5th Australian Auxiliary Hospital, Digswell House, Welwyn, Hertfordshire on 7th August. On 1st September he was discharged and granted leave. On 16th September he joined No.1 Command Depot, Perham Down, Wiltshire and returned to France on 22nd September to join 5th Australian Division Base Depot, Étaples. He rejoined 30th Battalion on 24th September. On 9th October he was attached to 32nd Battalion and transferred on 18th November. Blair was detached to the Army Infantry School 2nd-11th January 1917.

SS *Beltana* was owned by the Peninsular & Orient Steam Navigation Co Ltd and operated on the London–Cape Town–Melbourne and Sydney route. She was leased by the Commonwealth of Australia as HMAT A72 *Beltana* until 14th September 1917, when she was taken over by the British Admiralty. In 1919 she resumed the Australian service via Suez. In 1930 she was sold to Japan with the intention of being turned into a whale factory ship but was laid up instead and scrapped in 1933.

SS *Horarata* was owned by the New Zealand Shipping Co Ltd and serviced the New Zealand emigrant trade, with five first and 1,066 steerage class berths. She was leased by the Commonwealth of Australia until 11th September 1917, when she was taken over by the British Admiralty as part of the Liner Requisition Scheme. As HMAT A20 *Horarata* she completed six voyages from Australia, including as part of the First Convoy in October 1914. Having been laid up from August 1930 until February 1933, *Horarata* served as a Cadet Training Ship 1934–39. She was sold to the British India Steam Navigation Co Ltd and was renamed *Waroonga* before being taken over again on 7th March 1940 for the Liner Requisition Scheme. On 5th April 1943 she was in a convoy from New York to London when she was torpedoed by a U-boat and sank next day.

HMHS *St George* was built for the Great Western Railway to operate on the Rosslare to Fishguard route until 1913. She was sold to Canadian Pacific and was requisitioned as a hospital ship until 1919. *St George* was later purchased by the Great Eastern Railway for the Harwich to Hook of Holland route and was scrapped in 1929.

3rd London General Hospital in Wandsworth. Before the war it was the Royal Victoria Patriotic School for orphans. By May 1917, the Hospital had almost 2,000 beds, many in hutted wards behind the main building. It closed in August 1920, having treated 62,708 patients, and became an orphanage again until the Second World War, when the children were evacuated. During the war, MI6 used it as a clearing, detention and interrogation centre. Post-war it became a teacher training college and later a school. By the 1970s the building was badly run-down. In 1980, the Greater London Council sold it for £1 on condition that it was properly restored. It has since been divided into apartments. At least two other VCs were treated there:

Arthur Blackburn – see the third book in this series, *Victoria Crosses on the Western Front – Somme 1916 – 1st July 1916 – 13th November 1916*.

William Donovan Joynt – see the ninth book in this series, *Victoria Crosses on the Western Front – Battle of Albert 21st – 27th August 1918*.

5th Australian Auxiliary Hospital opened on 16th June 1915 at Digswell House, Welwyn and closed on 31st January 1919.

Blair was recommended for the DSO for displaying great gallantry and devotion to duty at all times. At Fromelles in July 1916 he continued to direct his company after being severely wounded and his thoroughness and personal courage influenced his men with the utmost confidence. At Sunray Trench near Le Transloy in March 1917 his position was heavily shelled for two days but he walked around the trenches encouraging his men. By his untiring efforts all ranks were kept in a cheery state and withstood the intense bombardment. However, the award was not granted. He was promoted major on 27th April and was granted leave in Paris 2nd–8th June. **Awarded the DSO for his actions near Polygon Wood, east of Ypres from 27th September to 1st October. While in command of the front line, the enemy massed for counterattacks three times and attacked once. He made excellent arrangements for the protection of his area and, by vigorous patrolling and personal reconnaissance, was able to advise on the enemy's movements from time to time. His company dispersed the first wave of the counterattack on the evening of 29th September and the artillery barrage dealt with the remainder. He pushed out patrols and found the enemy once more massing in Cameron Covert but dispersed them with Stokes mortars and rifle grenades. He had never missed a turn in the front line with the Brigade since its formation in July 1915. He set a splendid example to all ranks and showed great courage and devotion to duty, LG 3rd June 1918.**

Blair was granted leave in Britain 3rd–19th November. He returned to England on 2nd January 1918 and attended

The Distinguished Service Order, instituted by Queen Victoria on 6th September 1886, is usually awarded to majors (or equivalent) or above. In the past it was occasionally awarded to valorous junior officers. There were 8,981 awards in the Great War. The order recognised meritorious or distinguished service in war. Prior to 1943 the order could only be given to someone mentioned in despatches. Since 1993 the order has been restricted solely to distinguished service and not for gallantry. Although the DSO is now open to all ranks, it has yet to be awarded to a non-commissioned rank.

Edwin Tivey (19th September 1866–19th May 1947) was born at Inglewood, Victoria to Joseph Tivey, an English-born storekeeper who arrived in Australia in 1848, and his wife Margaret née Hayes, from Tasmania. He was educated at All Saints Grammar School, St Kilda, and at Wesley College, Melbourne before returning to Inglewood as an accountant. He was commissioned as a lieutenant in the Victorian Rangers in 1889 and was a member of Inglewood Borough Council 1894–99. In 1899 he was a founder and first president of the local branch of the Australian Natives' Association. He served in South Africa in 1900 as a captain in the Victorian 4th (Imperial) Contingent and was mentioned in dispatches and awarded the DSO. In 1903 he became a member of the Melbourne Stock Exchange. On 26th September 1906 he married Annie Bird Robb, who died in 1921. Tivey also continued military service as a captain in 9th Light Horse Regiment and in 1906 was appointed Brigade Major, Victorian 3rd Light Horse Brigade. He became its commander in 1911 as a lieutenant colonel. When the Great War broke out, Tivey was a successful stockbroker and temporary colonel commanding the Victorian 5th Light Horse Brigade. He was promoted colonel in January 1915 and was appointed Commandant of the Officers' School at Broadmeadows. In July he was appointed commander of 8th Australian Infantry Brigade and quickly endeared himself to the men with his sincerity and concern for their welfare. The Brigade served on the Suez Canal defences in Egypt. He was appointed temporary brigadier general in February 1916 and in June the Brigade moved to France. Its first action was at Fromelles in July. For brief periods in 1917 and 1918 he temporarily commanded 5th Australian Division. Tivey was wounded at Westhoek Ridge, Belgium in October 1917 and was gassed in May 1918. During the war he was mentioned in dispatches six times, was appointed CB in 1917 and CMG in January 1919. From November 1918 to May 1919 Tivey was a temporary major general. He embarked for Australia in July 1919 and was promoted major general in the Reserve of Officers in June 1920. He commanded 2nd Cavalry Division of the Citizen Military Forces 1921–26 and was an honorary colonel in the Victorian Mounted Rifles 1928–32. He died at his Toorak home and is buried in Brighton General Cemetery, Melbourne. His son, Major Edwin Peter Tivey, died as an Italian prisoner of war in 1943.

the 6th Senior Officer's Course at Aldershot, Hampshire 7th January–16th March. He was granted leave 17th-30th March, although he is shown to have rejoined his unit with effect from 20th March and was appointed Second-in-Command. **Mentioned in Field Marshal Sir Douglas Haig's Despatch dated 7th April 1918, LG 28th May 1918.** Blair assumed temporary command of 32nd Battalion in June and July and was granted leave 24th August–11th September. On the eve of the great battle to breach the Hindenburg Line, GOC 5th Australian Division, Major General Hobbs, was away on leave and Commander 8th Australian Brigade, Brigadier General Edwin Tivey, was in command. Lieutenant Colonel CS Davies was in command of the Brigade and Blair was in temporary command of 32nd Battalion. At the last moment Major General Hobbs returned and Tivey resumed command of 8th Australian Brigade. As the troops were in position and Wark had issued his orders, Tivey decided to give the young major his chance in leading the Battalion. **Awarded the VC for his actions on 29th September–1st October 1918 between Bellicourt and Joncourt, France, LG 26 December 1918.**

Blair was granted leave in England from 5th January 1919. The VC was presented by the King in the ballroom at Buckingham Palace on 13th February. Blair rejoined his unit on 19th February. He was detached to 30th Battalion on 12th March and returned to England via Le Havre on 23rd April, disembarking at Southampton, Hampshire the following day. He joined 5 Group at Weymouth, Dorset. On 10th June, Blair embarked aboard SS *Port Lyttleton* for return to Australia and was appointed OC Troops. His appointment in the AIF was terminated in 2nd Military District, Sydney on 28th September 1919.

During his last period in England, Blair married Phyllis Marquiss Munro (24th December 1890–17th June 1967), born at Barton Regis, Gloucestershire, on 31st May 1919 at St George's Church, East Worthing, Sussex. Her address was Eardley House, Marine Parade, Worthing, Sussex. They were living at Darling Point Road, Sydney, when Phyllis travelled alone to the United States, embarking aboard SS *Tahiti* on 25th February 1921. She settled at San Francisco, California and was described on her immigration document as 5′ 2½″ tall, weighing 110 lbs, with light complexion, brown eyes and brown hair. Blair and Phyllis divorced in 1922. She was a writer, living at 274 North Raymond Avenue, Pasadena, California in 1934. She was living at 1661 North Orange Drive, Los Angeles when she applied for US citizenship on 9th December 1940. Citizenship was certified on 24th September 1943 (No.110073), by when she was living at 2424 Wilshire Boulevard, Los Angeles. She remarried as Woodard and was living at 90601 Whittier, Los Angeles at the time of her death.

Phyllis' father, William Marquiss Munro (1st July 1860–1922), born at Bristol, Gloucestershire, married Jemima Herbert née Lloyd (1860–1956), born at Gloucester, in 1885 at Barton Regis. He was a warehouseman in 1891, when they were living at 45 Kingsdown Parade, Bristol. By 1901 he was a manager of a wholesale clothier works and they were living at 79 Hampton Park, Bristol. By 1911 he was a commercial traveller and they were living at 48 Gloucester Street, London. They are also known to have lived at Eardley House, Marine Parade, Worthing, Sussex and at 16 Norfolk Mansions, Prince of Wales Road, London. William died at Steyning, Sussex and Jemima at Greenwich, London. In addition to Phyllis they had another daughter:

St George's Church in East Worthing was built in 1867–68 to serve new residential developments in the southeast of the town. It was extended in 1875 and 1884 and has three mission halls elsewhere in Worthing. It is listed as Grade C by English Heritage. Although a tower was planned, only a stump was ever built. St George's Church founded St George's National School in 1874 and it had been enlarged twice by 1897. However, it closed in 1940 and the site is now a supermarket.

- Margaret Marquiss Munro (4th June 1886–1955), born at Bristol, Gloucestershire, was an artist in 1911, living with her parents. She married Charles Cornwallis Wykeham-Martin (10th February 1893–1960), born at Kendal, Westmorland, in 1928 at St Martin in the Fields, London. He was educated at Winchester College and was boarding at 69 Kingsgate Street there in 1911. Charles was commissioned in the King's Royal Rifle Corps on 7th December 1914 and went to France on 22nd July 1915. Promoted lieutenant on 26th January 1916 and transferred to the Oxfordshire and Buckinghamshire Light Infantry on 4th May. He was a temporary captain while instructing at the Army Training School 17th June–26th July 1918. He was Mentioned in Despatches, LG 4th January 1919. Chares was dismissed from the Army by sentence of a general court martial on 23rd March 1923. He was a civilian clerk Grade 4 at the War Department in 1939, when they were living at World's End Cottage, Lexden and Winstree, Essex. Her death was registered at Braintree, Essex and his at Colchester, Essex. There were no children.

Blair was one of twenty-two VCs who attended a dinner at Hotel Australia, Castlereagh Street, Sydney, New South Wales on 11th November 1919, hosted by Hon Hugh Donald McIntosh MLC. Blair became a principal of Thompson & Wark, Quantity Surveyors, E&G Buildings, Elizabeth Street, Sydney. He was also:

Councillor of National Roads and Motorists' Association, NSW.
Director of Australian Motorists' Petrol Co Ltd.
Director of the National Roads and Motorists' Association Insurance Ltd.
Director of Car Credits (NSW) Ltd.
Director of Car Repairs Ltd.
Committee member of the Hawkesbury Race Club.
Director of the Royal North Shore Hospital.
Life Governor of the Benevolent Society of New South Wales.

During the visit of the Prince of Wales in June 1920, Blair introduced him to a group of eleven Australian VCs in the grounds of Government House. Blair remained on the Reserve of Officers and was promoted major on 30th March 1921. He became a Freemason, being Initiated into Lane Cove Lodge No.338, United Grand Lodge of New South Wales, meeting at Gore Hill, Sydney, on 8th November 1921. He resigned from Lane Cove Lodge after affiliating with The Millions Lodge No.476, in which he served as Steward. He resigned from this Lodge when he joined the Army and Navy Lodge No.517 on 9th November 1927.

Blair married Katherine 'Kit' Mary Davis (1901–10th May 1978), born at Paddington, NSW, on 10th December 1927 at St Stephen's Presbyterian Church, Sydney. They lived at 3 Spring Street, Sydney, New South Wales and later at Pentecost Highway, Pymble, New South Wales. Kit attended the VC Centenary Celebrations in London in 1956. They had three children:

- Pamela 'Pam' Mary Wark married John Armstrong Morris in 1954 at Sydney.
- Blair Geoffrey Wark (born 1933) married Beverley Fraser in 1967 at St Leonards, NSW. He was a surveyor and she was a secretary in 1968, living at 6/1 Cremorne Street, Cremorne, NSW. By 1977 she was a company director and they were living at 3 Walwera Street, North Sydney. Beverley had retired by 1980, when they were living at 33 Grandview Street, Bradfield, NSW.

Major Blair Wark meeting the Prince of Wales in June 1920.

- Katherine 'Kathie' Anderson Wark (1st November 1936–29th October 2003) married John Anthony Kemm (20th October 1932–14th March 2018), born at Epsom, Surrey, England, in 1966 at Sydney. John was commissioned as an acting sub lieutenant in the Royal Navy. He was promoted sub lieutenant on 1st May 1952 and lieutenant on 16th March 1955. He retired on 20th June 1956. He was a clerk and she was a secretary in 1968, when they were living at 9/48 Upper Pitt Street, North Sydney. By 1977 they were living at 6 Cooney Road, Artarmon, NSW. In 1980 Kathie was living at 1/81 Shirley Road, Wollstonecraft, North Sydney but John was still at 6 Cooney Road. They had a child.

Kit's father, Joseph John Davis (18th November 1870–20th November 1916), born at Araluen, NSW, married Mary Ann née O'Connor (21st May 1875–14th December 1954), born at Paddington, NSW, at Woollahra in 1901. He died at Lord Street, Roseville, NSW and she at Chatswood, NSW. In addition to Katherine they had three other children:

- Geoffrey Michael Davis (17th December 1904–5th December 1973) married Mary 'Mamie' Wemyss Leslie (8th September 1906–17th November 1997), born at Bellingen, NSW, in 1931 at Chatswood, NSW. He served in the Australian Army 14th November 1942–5th August 1946, enlisting at Strathfield, NSW (NX137628) and was discharged as a warrant officer class I. He died at Concord, NSW but was buried at St Luke's Anglican Church Cemetery, Tarragindi, Brisbane, Queensland. She died at Mount Gravatt, Queensland and was buried with her husband. They had a son, Michael Leslie Davis (1937–27th July 2003).
- Clare Davis (born 1905), born at Waverley, NSW.
- Terence 'Terry' O'Connor Davis (born 1911) married Alma May Dawes (born 13th August 1911), born at Waverley, NSW, in 1942 at Hamilton, NSW. He was an engineer in 1968, when they were living at 19 Dalmely Road, North Sydney. They are believed to have had two children.

Sydney Town Hall, where the first AIF Reunion Dinner was held on 8th August 1928. It was built in the 1870–80s and the architecture was inspired by the French Second Empire. In addition to the Sydney City Council Chamber, there are reception rooms, the Centennial Hall and offices for the Lord Mayor and councillors. The Centennial Hall contains the world's largest pipe organ, built between 1886 and 1889 and installed by the English firm of William Hill & Son. Before the opening of the Sydney Opera House, the Town Hall was Sydney's main concert venue.

Blair attended the 1st AIF Reunion Dinner at Sydney Town Hall on 8th August 1928, to celebrate the tenth anniversary of the commencement of The Big Push. Seven other VCs also attended – WE Brown, G Cartwright, W Currey, G Howell, B Kenny, P Storkey and J Whittle. He was entertained at a luncheon at Government House in November 1929 by the Governor General of Australia, Sir Dudley de Chair, together with thirteen other VCs – G Cartwright, W Currey, A Evans, J Hamilton, G Howell, W Jackson, B Kenny, J Maxwell J Newland, J Ryan, P Storkey, A Sullivan and J Whittle. Blair also attended the wedding of Walter Ernest Brown VC DCM at Christ Church, Bexley, NSW on 4th June 1932, together with seven other VCs – G Cartwright, W Currey, A Evans, J Hamilton, G Howell, TJB Kenny and A Sullivan.

Amongst his recreational activities, Blair listed fishing and golf. He won the War Services Cup at the Australian Imperial Forces Golf Tournament at Killara, NSW on 10th August 1937. He tied with three others for the Imperial Service Club trophy in the same event.

On 17th April 1940, Blair was appointed to command 1st Battalion (City of Sydney's Own Regiment) (Militia) (M35778) and was appointed temporary lieutenant colonel on 26th July. He was posted to Puckapunyal Camp, Victoria to attend the Senior Officers' Course at the Australian Armoured Fighting Vehicle School. During a field exercise he was sent back to camp after complaining of heartburn. He was diagnosed as suffering from dyspepsia and was treated with alkaline powder but died suddenly of coronary heart disease on 13th June 1941. At his funeral with full military honours, it was said that he 'liked the wind in his face and lived the life of three men'. He was cremated at Eastern Suburbs Crematorium, Botany, NSW and his ashes were interred in Woronora Crematorium Columbarium (Niche D-30). He is commemorated in a number of other places:

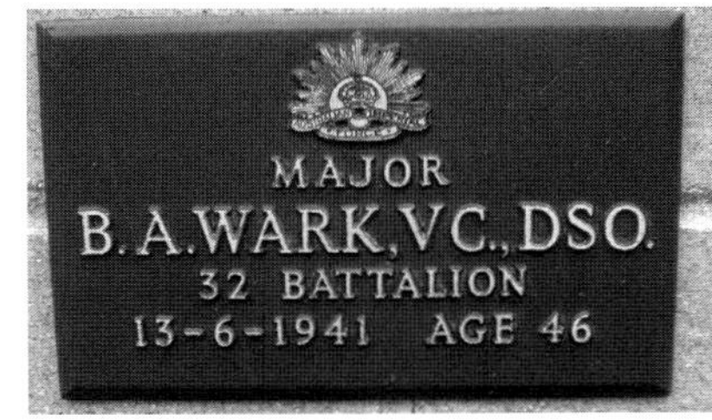

Commemorative plaque at Woronora Crematorium Columbarium.

Victoria Cross Memorial, Queen Victoria Building, George Street, Sydney (MaritimeQuest.com).

- New South Wales
    - Victoria Cross Memorial, Queen Victoria Building, George Street, Sydney dedicated on 23rd February 1992 to commemorate the visit of Queen Elizabeth II and Prince Phillip on the occasion of the Sesquicentenary of the City of Sydney. Sir Roden Cutler VC AK KCMG, Edward Kenna VC and Keith Payne VC were in attendance.
    - Victoria Cross Recipients Wall, North Bondi War Memorial donated to Waverley on 27th November 2011 by The Returned & Services League of Australia.
    - VC Memorial, Borella Road, Peards Complex, East Albury.
    - VC Memorial, Ingleburn RSL Club, Sydney.
    - Plaque in the Australian War Graves Garden of Remembrance, Rookwood.
    - Memorial Plaque, RSL, Bathurst.
- Australian Capital Territory
    - Australian Victoria Cross Recipients plaque on the Victoria Cross Memorial, Campbell, dedicated on 24th July 2000.
    - Named on one of eleven plaques honouring 175 men from overseas awarded the VC for the Great War. The plaques were unveiled by the Senior Minister of State at the Foreign & Commonwealth Office and Minister for Faith and Communities, Baroness Warsi, at a reception at Lancaster House, London on 26th June 2014 attended by The Duke of Kent and relatives of the VC recipients. The Australian plaque is at the Australian War Memorial, Canberra.
    - Commemorative display in the Hall of Valour, Australian War Memorial, Canberra.
    - One of the 77mm guns that he captured is displayed at the Australian War Memorial.
- Wark Street, Wodonga, Victoria on White Box Rise estate, built on land formerly part of Bandiana Army Camp.
- Communities and Local Government commemorative paving stones for the 145 VCs born in Australia, Belgium, Canada, China, Denmark, Egypt, France, Germany, India, Iraq, Japan, Nepal, Netherlands, New

The Australian VC plaque at the Australian War Memorial, unveiled at Lancaster House, London on 26th June 2014.

Zealand, Newfoundland, Pakistan, South Africa, Sri Lanka, Ukraine and United States of America were unveiled at the National Memorial Arboretum, Alrewas, Staffordshire by Prime Minister David Cameron MP and Sergeant Johnson Beharry VC on 5th March 2015.

One of the 77mm guns captured by Blair at the Australian War Memorial, showing some battle damage.

His widow travelled aboard P&O's SS *Arcadia* to attend the VC Centenary Celebrations at Hyde Park, London on 26th June 1956.

In addition to the VC and DSO he was awarded the 1914–15 Star, British War Medal 1914–20, Victory Medal 1914–19 with Mentioned-in-Despatches Oakleaf, War Medal 1939–45, Australia Service Medal 1939–45 and George VI Coronation Medal 1937. The VC group was purchased in 1999 by Mackay businessman and philanthropist Neil Jenman for A$134,000, using funds put up by a group of five anonymous Australian real-estate businessmen, known as SAVE (Some Australians Value Ethics). The group combined with the Victorian Returned Services League President, Bruce Ruxton OBE, to purchase the VC group. However, relations soured when it was alleged that Ruxton tried to bully Jenman into handing over the medals before he was ready to do so. The medals were returned to Jenman, who decided not to donate them to the RSL. Jenman went on to outbid the RSL for the Beatham VC in 1999, forcing the price up to a then record of A$185,000. Jenman then

The 1914–15 Star was instituted in December 1918 for personnel who served in any theatre between 5th August 1914 and 31st December 1915. Those awarded the 1914 Star, Africa General Service Medal or Khedive's Sudan Medal 1910, were ineligible to receive it. The 1914–15 Star was awarded with the British War and Victory Medals, the trio known as *Pip, Squeak and Wilfred* after comic strip characters. 2,366,000 medals were awarded to members of the British, Dominion and Empire forces.

The War Medal 1939–45 was instituted on 16th August 1945 and was awarded to all full-time personnel of the armed forces and Merchant Navy for serving for twenty-eight days, irrespective of where they were serving, between 3rd September 1939 and 2nd September 1945.

Australian War Memorial, Canberra.

The Australia Service Medal 1939–1945 was awarded to members of the Australian armed forces, Mercantile Marine and Volunteer Defence Corps during the Second World War. The qualifying period was eighteen months full-time service at home or overseas or three years part-time service between 3rd September 1939 and 2nd September 1945. There was no minimum qualifying period for those killed, wounded or disabled due to service. In August 1996 the qualifying period was reduced to thirty days for full-time service and ninety days for part-time service.

gifted the Wark VC to the United Service Club, 183 Wickham Terrace, Brisbane and also gave the club the Beatham VC for safe keeping. In 2004 the United Service Club decided to place both VCs in a bank vault for safe keeping and commissioned replicas for display in the club. Both VC groups were loaned to the Hall of Valour, Australian War Memorial, Australian Capital Territory February 2017–20th February 2019.

10/20408 COMPANY SERJEANT MAJOR JOHN HENRY WILLIAMS
10th Battalion, The South Wales Borderers

John 'Jack' Williams was born on 29th September 1885 at Greenfield Cottages, Nantyglo, Monmouthshire, Wales. His father, Henry Williams (1853–1932), born at Hagley, Herefordshire, started work in a boiler shop in Ebbw Vale, Monmouthshire in 1864 and is later believed to have gone to sea as a boiler maker. He was boarding at 27 Waterfall Row, Bedwellty, Monmouthshire in 1881. Henry married Elizabeth née Phillips (1856–1906), born at Ebbw Vale, Monmouthshire, on 4th March 1882 at the Parish Church, Bedwellty, Monmouthshire. She was a schoolteacher at Briery

Hill School, Ebbw Vale. After her marriage she was employed as a governess to the four sons of the De Winton family in the Brecon area. They were living at 14 Armoury Row, Bedwellty in 1891 and at 2 Reservoir Terrace, Ebbw Vale in 1901. Henry retired in 1926 and died at his home at 9 York Avenue, Garden City, Ebbw Vale. Jack had two siblings:

- George Philip Williams (1882–1903) was a boiler making smith's striker, living with his parents in 1901. He suffered from diabetes.

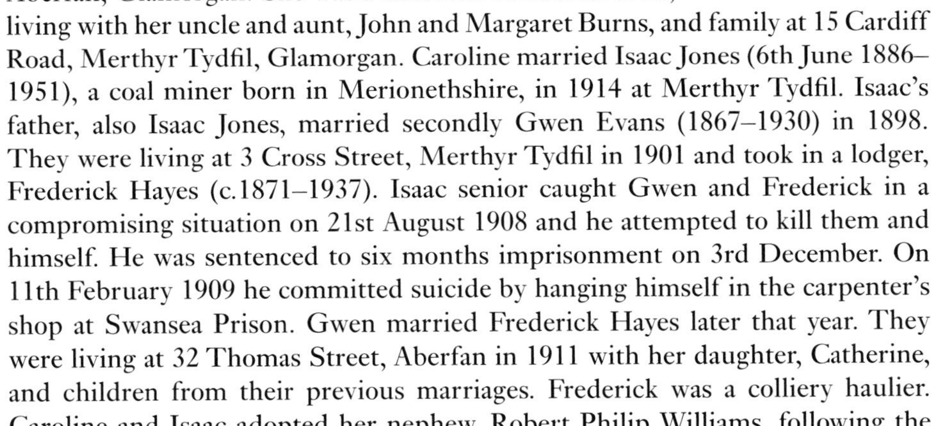

- Caroline Louisa Williams (15th July 1891–1975) moved to Aberfan, Glamorgan. She was a domestic servant in 1911, living with her uncle and aunt, John and Margaret Burns, and family at 15 Cardiff Road, Merthyr Tydfil, Glamorgan. Caroline married Isaac Jones (6th June 1886–1951), a coal miner born in Merionethshire, in 1914 at Merthyr Tydfil. Isaac's father, also Isaac Jones, married secondly Gwen Evans (1867–1930) in 1898. They were living at 3 Cross Street, Merthyr Tydfil in 1901 and took in a lodger, Frederick Hayes (c.1871–1937). Isaac senior caught Gwen and Frederick in a compromising situation on 21st August 1908 and he attempted to kill them and himself. He was sentenced to six months imprisonment on 3rd December. On 11th February 1909 he committed suicide by hanging himself in the carpenter's shop at Swansea Prison. Gwen married Frederick Hayes later that year. They were living at 32 Thomas Street, Aberfan in 1911 with her daughter, Catherine, and children from their previous marriages. Frederick was a colliery haulier. Caroline and Isaac adopted her nephew, Robert Philip Williams, following the

In 1811 Matthew Wayne and Joseph Bailey purchased the lease of the rundown ironworks at Nantyglo. In 1820 Matthew Wayne sold his share and Joseph's brother, Crawshaw, replaced him. By 1827 the two brothers had seven blast furnaces operating at Nantyglo, which became one of the great ironworks in the country. Nearby Beaufort Ironworks was added in 1833. By the mid-1840s the Baileys were employing 3,000 men and 500 women and children. They had disposed of their interests in Nantyglo by 1869–70. Although there was a slump in the demand for iron manufacturing after the Napoleonic Wars, Nantyglo increased its exports. Unrest throughout the country due to the high cost of wheat caused Matthew Wayne and Joseph Bailey to build the two fortified Nantyglo Round Towers in 1816. Zephaniah Williams, a master collier who also kept the Royal Oak Inn at Nantyglo, became a leader of the Chartist movement in southeast Wales. With others he led a large march from Nantyglo to the Westgate Hotel, Newport in 1839. For his part in the Newport Rising, he was convicted and deported to Australia, where he died a prosperous man in 1874.

Human activity in the Ebbw Vale area dates back to at least the Bronze Age. At the end of the 18th century the village had only 120 inhabitants but this changed rapidly during the Industrial Revolution. The Ebbw Vale Iron Works opened in 1778, followed by a number of coal mines around 1790. Growth continued and by the 1930s the steelworks were the largest in Europe. By the 1960s, 14,500 people were employed there but within a few decades the UK steel industry had collapsed. Closures and redundancies followed inevitably and in 2002 only 450 were employed in the old industries. That July the final works closed and there are now no steelworks or mines in the area. Ebbw Vale had one of the highest unemployment rates in the country but has gradually diversified and recovered. Amongst famous people born or associated with Ebbw Vale are:

- Aneurin 'Nye' Bevan (1897–1960), Labour MP for Ebbw Vale 1929–60, was appointed Minister of Health by Clement Attlee in the post-war Labour government. Bevan led the establishment of the National Health Service to provide free medical care for all, regardless of wealth. He became Minister of Labour in 1951, but resigned after two months, when the Attlee government proposed introducing prescription charges for dental and vision care and transferred funds from the National Insurance Fund to pay for rearmament.
- Michael Mackintosh Foot (1913–2010) succeeded Nye Bevan as MP for Ebbw Vale in 1960. He was a journalist and under a pseudonym co-wrote the 1940 polemic against appeasement of Hitler, *Guilty Men*. Before Ebbw Vale he was MP for Plymouth 1945–55. Foot was associated with the left wing of the Labour Party and was an ardent supporter of the Campaign for Nuclear Disarmament and for British withdrawal from the European Economic Community. He held a number of political appointments – Secretary of State for Employment 1974, Leader of the House of Commons (1976–79), Deputy Leader of the Labour Party 1976–80 and Leader of the Labour Party 1980–83.
- Vittorio 'Victor' Spinetti (1929–2012), actor, author, poet and raconteur was born in nearby Cwm. He was educated at Monmouth School and the Royal Welsh College of Music and Drama in Cardiff. He appeared in numerous films and stage plays including the three 1960s Beatles films. He received a Tony Award for the stage version of *Oh, What a Lovely War!* on Broadway. Amongst his many films were *The Taming of the Shrew*, *Under Milk Wood* and *The Return of the Pink Panther*.

death of his mother in 1927 and raised him as Robert 'Bob' Jones. Isaac was an unemployed surface worker in 1939, when they were living at 8 Pleasant View, Merthyr Tydfil. They had three children:

- Gertrude Elizabeth Jones (26th October 1914–6th June 2010) was a housemaid in 1939 at 24 Park Place, Cardiff, Glamorgan. She married James Clifford Evans (2nd April 1908–1978), born at Cardiff, later that year, when her name was recorded as Elizabeth G Jones. James was a gas fitter in 1939, living with his mother at 3 Bromfield Street, Cardiff. They had two children – James Bernard Evans 1943 and Angela Elizabeth Evans 1947.
- Eunice Jones (11th December 1918–17th January 1980) was a parlour maid in 1939 at Little Gate, Fairwater Road, Cardiff and served in the

St Sannan's Church, Bedwellty dates back to the 13th century. It was restored in 1858 and 1882 (Gerry Pritchard).

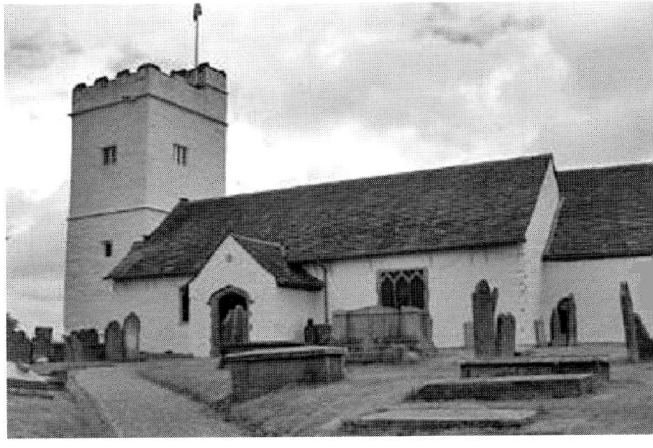

Auxiliary Territorial Service during the Second World War. She married Thomas Daniel Morgan (11th February 1908–30th January 1962), born at Ton Pentre, Rhondda Valley, in 1945 at Merthyr Tydfil. Thomas was a butcher's assistant in 1939, living with his father and siblings at 53 Parry Street, Rhondda Valley. He served in the Army during the Second World War. They were living at 53 Parry Street, Ton Pentre at the time of his death at Sully

Tredegar became an early centre of the Industrial Revolution in the Sirhowy Valley, which provided iron ore, coal to produce coke, power from the Sirhowy River and wood for buildings, pit props and fuel. By the early 1700s there were a few small iron works amongst the farms and woods. The Sirhowy Iron Works were built in 1750 and were developed into the first coal fired furnace. The furnace failed in 1794. In 1797 Samuel Homfray, with Richard Fothergill and Matthew Monkhouse, built a new furnace on land leased from the Tredegar Estate. Homfray was a hard taskmaster, running the town almost as a private fiefdom. He paid his workers in tokens that could only be used in shops that he leased to traders and took a percentage. Hours were long and the work was extremely dangerous, with almost no welfare provision. The Sirhowy Ironworks became the Tredegar Iron Co in 1800, which ceased iron production in 1891 but continued to produce coal. Whiteheads took over the southern section of the ironworks site in 1907 but this closed in 1931, when operations were moved to Newport. The Tredegar mines were nationalised in 1946 as part of the National Coal Board. There have been three major riots in the town. The first in 1868 resulted from the favourite candidate in an election not being elected. There was another in 1882 caused by tensions with the large Irish community in Tredegar. The Irish were run out of town and troops were called in to quell the violence. There were anti-Jewish riots in 1911 and the Army was brought in again. The Tredegar Medical Aid Society set up in the early 1920s became the model for the National Health Service. Amongst the town's famous people are:

- Neil Gordon Kinnock, Baron Kinnock PC, born in Tredegar in 1942, was Labour MP for Bedwellty and then Islwynis 1970–95. He was Leader of the Labour Party and Opposition 1983–92 and Vice-President of the European Commission 1999–2004. He was elevated to the House of Lords in 2005.
- Raymond Reardon MBE, born in Tredegar in 1932, won the World Snooker Championship in 1970, 1973, 1974, 1975, 1976 and 1978.

Hospital, Cardiff. She died at Pentre, Glamorgan. They had two children – Geoffrey Morgan 1947 and Janet Elizabeth Morgan 1949.
    - Cyril George Jones (1929–92) married Patricia Abbott in July 1957, registered at Merthyr Tydfil, and died at Harefield Hospital, London.

Little is known about Jack's paternal grandparents, other than his grandfather was Thomas Williams, who had died by 1882. His maternal grandfather, George Phillips (born c.1825 – died before 1881), born at Newport, Monmouthshire, married Elizabeth née Thomas (c.1816–93), also born at Newport, on 10th March 1845 at Tredegar, Monmouthshire. George was a puddler in 1851, when they were living at 150 Machine Row, Bedwellty, Monmouthshire. By 1861 he was a rougher and they were living at House 14, No.15 Forge Row, Bedwellty. By 1871 they had moved to 150 Forge Row. Elizabeth was living with her daughter, Elizabeth, at 14 Armoury Row, Bedwellty in 1881 and was still living there with Elizabeth and her family in 1891. In addition to Elizabeth they had two other children:

- Elizabeth Phillips (1846–51), born at Abergavenny.
- Margaret Phillips (c.1849–1919), born at Ebbw Vale, Monmouthshire, married John Philip Burns (1852–1926), born at Victoria, Bedwellty, in 1873 at Pontypool, Monmouthshire. He was an engineer in 1871, when they were living at 31 Powell Row, Bedwellty. By 1881 he was an engine fitter and they were living at No.5 Roderick Row, Ebbw Vale. By 1901 they had moved to 15 Cardiff Road, Merthyr Tydfil, Glamorgan and were still there in 1911. They had a daughter, Margaret Elizabeth Burns (born 1880).

Jack was educated at Briery Hill School, Ebbw Vale until c.1898. He started work as a boiler making smith's striker with Ebbw Vale Iron & Coal Co Ltd at Marine Colliery, Cwm. Jack enlisted in the South Wales Borderers in 1906 but purchased his discharge soon after and returned home. He was a coal inspector in 1912 and was a blacksmith at Cwm Colliery immediately before enlisting in 1914.

Jack married Gertrude Williams (1884–18th March 1927) on 6th June 1908 at English Baptist Chapel, Tredegar, Monmouthshire. They were living at 52 Canning Street, Cwm, Monmouthshire in 1911 before moving to Willowtown, Ebbw Vale and later to 9 York Avenue, Garden City, Ebbw Vale. They had eleven children:

Briery Hill School has since closed and has been demolished.

- Doris Elizabeth Williams (1909–10), born and died at Bedwellty.
- Ivor John Williams (28th May 1910–25th April 1990), a machine operator in a steelworks,

The Ebbw Vale Steel, Iron & Coal Co was founded in 1790 by a partnership led by Jeremiah Homfray. It was one of a chain of works along the northern rim of the south Wales coalfield, where the raw materials for making iron (iron ore, coal and limestone) occurred. In 1796 Homfray sold the works to the Harfords who built three more blast furnaces and puddling furnaces. The Harfords were bankrupted in 1842 but the works continued under trustees. In 1844, Abraham Derby IV, the Coalbrookdale ironmaster, formed the Ebbw Vale Company. The company expanded, taking over Victoria Ironworks in 1848, Abersychan Ironworks in 1852, Pentwyn Ironworks in 1858 and Pontypool Ironworks in 1872. When local iron ore was exhausted the Company bought iron mines in Somerset, Gloucestershire and Spain. A Bessemer converter plant was installed in 1868 and regular steel production began. The cost of expansion eventually crippled the Company. Pentwyn closed in 1868, Sirhowy and Abersychan in 1882–3, Pontypool in 1890 and by 1892 the Company was almost bankrupt. From the 1870s the Company was increasingly dependent on coal rather than iron and steel. In 1873 it was the largest coal producer in south Wales, but most was used to produce coke for its ironworks. It switched to take advantage of the demand for Welsh steam coal to drive the world's ships, trains and steam engines. As older collieries were exhausted two new collieries were sunk – Waunlwyd (1874–77) and Marine Colliery at Cwm (1889–91). Demand for Welsh steam coal increased in the early 20th century and the Company expanded and modernised its collieries. In twenty years output doubled to two million tons and the workforce rose to nearly 6,000. In 1892 control of the Company returned to iron and steel interests. In the pre-Great War period it employed 34,000 men. The last expansion before war broke out was the construction of sheet mills in 1912. After the Great War the Company expanded further. Two modern blast furnaces at Victoria replaced four old ones at Ebbw Vale and plants were installed to produce steel railway sleepers and weldless tubes and couplings. The international iron and steel trade slumped in the early 1920s at the same time as ships were switching to oil for fuel. During the 1920s and 1930s wages fell, collieries closed and unemployment soared. There were bitter industrial disputes in 1921 and 1926 and the financial crisis of 1929 affected the Company badly. Almost half of Ebbw Vale's population was unemployed. In 1935 the Company went into liquidation and its collieries were sold to Partridge Jones and John Paton Ltd. The British tinplate industry required an American-style steel stripmill, which was planned for Lincolnshire. However, the Government forced it to be built at Ebbw Vale. In 1936–38 the old works were cleared and an integrated iron, steel and tinplate plant was built. The three remaining collieries (Waunlwyd, Cwmcarn and Marine) were taken over by the National Coal Board under Nationalisation in 1947. They closed respectively in 1964, 1968 and 1988. The first electrolytic line outside the United States was built at Ebbw Vale in 1947–48. The Bessemer and open-hearth steel plants were expanded and in 1960 Britain's first Linz-Donawitz converter was installed. Two more electrolytic tinning lines were installed in 1961 and 1969 and galvanising lines in 1957 and 1969. However, rationalisation of the steel industry led to the steel plant at Ebbw Vale closing in 1978. The works then concentrated on tinplating and galvanising and became the largest tinplate producer in Britain until closure in 2002.

married Ruby Mary Oliver (19th February 1912–19th August 1971), born at 9 Pennant Street, Ebbw Vale, on 12th March 1932 at the General Register Office, Ebbw Vale. He was living at 76 Alexandra Street, Ebbw Vale at the time. He was a storekeeper engineer in 1939, when they were living at 12 Gardenia Avenue, Luton, Bedfordshire. He was also an Air Raid Precautions warden and stretcher bearer at the time of the 1939 Register. They later lived at 27 Moreton Road, Luton, Bedfordshire. Ruby died at Biggleswade, Bedfordshire and Ivor at Luton. They had three children:

The sinking of Marine Colliery was begun in 1889 by the Ebbw Vale Steel, Iron and Coal Co. There were two shafts, downcast and upcast, each about 380m deep. Coal was produced from 1893. By 1896, there were 833 men employed and this had risen to 2,407 by 1913. On 1st March 1927 an underground gas and coal dust explosion killed fifty-two men. The disaster would have been worse but the quick-thinking manager, Edward Gay, ordered the ventilation fan to be slowed so that it would not fan the flames. At the time 1,400 men were employed at the colliery but when the explosion occurred only the night shift was working underground. In 1935 ownership changed to Partridge, Jones & John Paton Ltd, who worked the colliery until Nationalisation in 1947. An incident at Marine Colliery led to an important legal case. A miner named Edwards was killed by a falling rock on 6th November 1947. The resultant case of Edwards v National Coal Board in 1949 established the concept of 'reasonable practicability' with avoiding workplace deaths. Marine was the last deep mine in the Ebbw valleys, closing in March 1989.

- Maureen Williams (born 1932), born at Bedwellty.
- Keith R Williams (born 1939), born at Luton.
- Susan M Williams (born 1950), born at Luton.

- Edgar G Williams (28th August 1911–1964) married Marion Jane Gibbon née James (30th June 1909–January 1993) in 1939 at Uxbridge, Middlesex. She was born at Bedwellty and was living with her parents at 33 Pochin Crescent, Tredegar, Monmouthshire in 1911. Edgar and Marion were living at 96 Raleigh Avenue, Hayes and Harlington, Middlesex in 1939, by when he was an electrician, specialising in electrical lift engineering and electrical wiring, and she was a bench hand, painting and assembling mechanical parts. They later lived

The sinking of Cwm Colliery commenced in 1909 by the Great Western Colliery Co and coal production commenced in 1914 for the Great Western Railway. There were two shafts each 685m deep. By 1918 there were 603 men working there and this had risen to 1,043 by 1923. Powell Duffryn Associated Collieries Ltd took over the colliery in 1928. In 1931 Cwm was linked underground to Marine Colliery. By 1938 the workforce had increased to 1,269 but had reduced to 1,154 by the time of Nationalisation in 1947. A reconstruction scheme between 1952 and 1960 included linking Cwm underground and working jointly with Coed Ely Colliery, which was over 5,000m to the west. By the 1970s the joint collieries were producing 515,000 tons of coal each year, with a workforce of 1,580. Due to high demand for coke the National Coal Board built an adjacent coking works to Cwm Colliery in 1958. Four collieries, including Cwm, fed the plant. Cwm Colliery closed in November 1986, with an estimated nine million tons of coal remaining. Cwm Coking Works continued as a private concern, supplying coke to the British Sugar Corporation and Britannia Zinc at Avonmouth, until it closed in 2003.

at Monkswood, near Usk, Monmouthshire. Marion had married Samuel Gibbon (9th January 1910–8th April 1935) in 1934 at Merthyr Tydfil, Glamorgan, where he was born. They were living at 27 Chelston Road, Ruislip, Middlesex at the time of his death at Nuneaton Road, Woodnesborough, Kent. They had a daughter, Rhona S Gibbon (born 1934), born at Uxbridge. Marion married Ivor John Pitt (born 1921) in 1969 at Pontypool, Monmouthshire. They lived at Monkswood, near Usk. Ivor had married Annie May Watkins (21st February 1921–1967) in 1944 at Abergavenny, Monmouthshire. She was living with her parents at Penarth Farm, Llanishen, Monmouthshire in 1939. Marion was living at Thistle Court Nursing Home, Ty Canol, Cwmbran, South Wales at the time of her death there.

English Baptist Chapel on Church Street, Tredegar has since been demolished and replaced with a pair of semi-detached dwellings.

- Mary Elizabeth Williams (2nd October 1913–1988) married Jack Herbert Clarke (21st April 1907–1961), born at Thames Ditton, Surrey, in 1932 at Kingston-upon-Thames, Surrey. He was living with his parents at Manor Cottage, Station Road, Thames Ditton, Surrey in 1907 and 1911. He was a plumber in 1939, when they were living at 5 Jubilee Villas, Esher, Surrey. They had five children:
    - Donald 'Don' J Clarke 1937.
    - Robert J Clarke 1938.
    - Linda M Clarke 1941.
    - Rosemary Clarke 1944.
    - Christopher JL Clarke (born 1946) married Fiona K Scott-Batey (born 1947) at Newcastle-upon-Tyne, where she was born, in 1971. They had three children – Lucy Ellen L Clarke 1973, Alistair Graham R Clarke 1975 and Isobel Mary F Clarke 1978.
- Henry 'Harry' Williams (10th August 1914–21st October 1990) enlisted in the South Wales Borderers on 22nd July 1933 (3908444) and served with the 1st Battalion at Rawalpindi, India and on the North West Frontier 1935–39. He was at Deolali Transit Camp, India in 1940 and was a member of the Deolali Reinforcements Camp football team that won the tankard against the Royal Navy on 27th October 1941. He suffered eleven attacks of malaria while in India. It is not known if Harry served with the Battalion in Iraq but, while playing football in India in 1941, he twisted his knee and was eventually treated at Hexham General Hospital, Northumberland. The cartilage slipped out again while he was playing netball with the nursing staff and a subsequent operation resulted in Harry being in hospital for three months. He is not believed to have served with the Battalion in North Africa. He was a prisoner of war escort aboard RMS *Aquitania* from

Cape Town, South Africa to New York, USA, arriving in Britain in May 1943. He joined C Company, 1st South Wales Borderers and served at Haybrake, Shetland Watering house, Orkney 16th December 1943–2nd September 1944. His tonsils were removed while in Orkney. Harry was based at Vinter's Park, Maidstone, Kent in 1944. He was discharged as a sergeant on 28th February 1946. Harry married Ada Rosalie Capeling (10th June 1927–7th December 2008) on 28th July 1945 at Maidstone, Kent, where she was born. She was living with her parents at 2 New Cottages, Farleigh Mill, Maidstone in 1939. Harry died at his brother Robert's home at Chipping Sodbury, Avon on the way to the re-dedication of his father's headstone. Ada died at Maidstone Hospital. They had three children:

  - John Henry Michael Williams (born 14th August 1945) married Freda D Waters (born 1946) in 1964 at Maidstone. They had two children – Gary John Williams 1965 and Michele Williams 1967. John married Kerin Margaret Edwards née Jones (born 1956), born at Bedwellty, on 10th August 2002 at Tintern, Monmouthshire. She had married Roffey C Edwards in 1980 at Pontypool.
  - Ann Rosalie Williams (born 23rd April 1948) married Alan Page (born 14th February 1946) on 3rd February 1973 at Maidstone. Alan enlisted in the Royal Navy on 8th January 1962 (D063623S) and qualified as a submariner in 1970. He was serving aboard the submarine HMS *Conqueror* as Charge Chief Marine Engineering Artificer (Electrical) (Submarines) during the 1982 Falklands War, when the Argentinian *General Belgrano* was sunk. He was discharged on 13th February 1986. Ann was the Admissions Officer at MidKent College. They had two daughters – Helen Louise Page 1974 and Karen Anne Page 1977.
  - Peter Williams (born 19th July 1959) married Daphne Joyce Simmonds (born 7th November 1958) on 1st March 1980 at Maidstone. They had two children – Nina Michele Williams 1980 and Michael David Williams 1982.

- Margaret 'Peggy' Victoria Williams (1920–2nd April 2007) is understood to have been adopted by a Colonel and Mrs Rees. He may have been Lieutenant Colonel Evan Thomas Rees OBE DSO MC (1883–1955) of the South Wales Borderers (1883–1955), who attended Jack Williams' funeral.
- John 'Jack' Windsor Williams (8th June 1921–2nd April 1977) served in the RAF. He married Helen 'Nell' Wilkinson (6th September 1922–23rd September 2016). He died in hospital at Columbus, Ohio, USA and she at Aylesbury, Buckinghamshire. They had three children – Bruce Williams 1946, Lynne Calder Williams 1949 and Rhys John Williams 1952.
- Gertrude Vera Williams (22nd November 1922–December 1986), known as Vera, served in the Women's Auxiliary Air Force during the Second World War. She married Augustus 'Gus' James Coates (13th April 1916–1st July 2002), born at Bath, Somerset, at Swanage, Dorset on 29th November 1943. Gus was a

commercial traveller (textiles) in 1939, when he was living with his parents at 91 Cheltenham Road, Gloucester. He was serving as a leading aircraftman (radio operator) in the Royal Air Force at the time of the marriage. They were living at 3 Rothsay Road, Bedford, Bedfordshire when Vera died there suddenly. Gus also died at Bedford. They had two sons:
    - David Coates (12th November 1945–April 1971) died in a car accident.
    - Paul J Coates (born 1949).
- Kathleen Williams (11th April 1924–26th June 1970) served in the Auxiliary Territorial Service as a driver for a brigadier. She married Ronald Bertram Fear (9th September 1915–27th June 1998), born at St John, New Brunswick, Canada, on 17th October 1947 at Edmonton, Middlesex. Ronald was a master builder and contractor in 1939, living with his parents at 45 Warwick Street, Cardiff. He enlisted in the Royal Armoured Corps and was promoted to lance corporal. He was commissioned in the Royal Engineers on 14th April 1942 (230381) and served as an acting captain in Burma (Mentioned in Despatches, LG 9th May 1946). They were living at 25 Victoria Square, Penarth, Glamorgan at the time of her death there. They had five children:
    - Richard Boyd Fear (born 26th July 1949) married Zyliha Gjolej in 1974.
    - Simon 'Sam' Fear (born 10th September 1950) married Katherine M Jones in 1978 and they had a daughter, Layla Fear, in 1979. They separated and Simon later lived with Linda Evens and they had three children – Callum Ross Evens 1989, Ellis Joel Evens 1990 and Briallen Savanna Evens 1992, the last two born in New Zealand.
    - Elizabeth Bennett Fear (born 31st January 1953) married Glyn George Gibson (born 1952) in 1974 and they had two children – Eliza Elenor Gibson 1986 and Jack William Gibson 1988.
    - Emma Jane Fear (7th March 1961–2018).
    - Dinah Kathryn Fear (born 12th July 1962) had two children – Louie Vincent Arcuri Fear 1992 and Lydia Elsbeth Arcuri Fear 1996.

Ronald married Gertrude Josefa Auner (10th March 1927–November 2004) on 24th April 1973. She qualified as a Registered Nurse on 12th August 1957 at the Royal Infirmary, Cardiff (251250).

- Robert 'Bob' Philip Williams (23rd August 1926–15th April 2013), a twin with Bertha, born at Ebbw Vale, was raised by his aunt and uncle, Caroline and Isaac Jones, from the age of six months following the death of his mother. He served in the Welch Regiment 1944–47, including in Egypt. He changed his name to Jones and married Jean Anderson (5th June 1930–23rd October 2003) on 17th September 1949 at Merthyr Tydfil, where she was born. She was living with her parents at 10 Alberta Street, Merthyr Tydfil in 1939. Her death was registered at South Gloucester and his at Chipping Sodbury, Gloucestershire. They had two sons – Roy Jones 1955 and Gary Jones 1962.

- Bertha Williams (23rd August 1926–May 1989), a twin with Robert, was raised by her uncle and aunt, Henry and Bertha Williams, from the age of six months. She married Ronald George Davies (10th April 1924–14th July 2009) in 1947 at Bedwellty. He was living with his parents at 61 Emlyn Avenue, Ebbw Vale in 1939. Her death was registered at Surrey South Eastern and his at Weston-super-Mare, Somerset. They had a daughter:
  - Shirley Anne Davies (born 24th January 1951), born at Ebbw Vale, married Christopher Robert Daly (born 1st January 1961), born at Bridgwater, Somerset, on 7th March 1987 at Weston-Super-Mare, Somerset. They had two children – Ashlee Curtis Daly 1987 and George Patrick Daly 1990.

Gertrude's father, Philip Williams (born c.1866) was born illegitimately and was adopted by Daniel and Ann Jones. He married Mary Williams (sic) (born c.1863), both born at Ebbw Vale, c.1884. He was a furnace labourer in 1891, when they were living at 17, 2nd Row, Newtown, Ebbw Vale, Monmouthshire and at 3, 2nd Row, Newtown in 1911. Philip is understood to have died in 1922. In addition to Gertrude, they had six other children:

- Daniel Williams (born 20th September 1887), a grocery haulier, married Alice Colbourne (c.1889–1924), born at Blaina, Monmouthshire, in 1911 at Bedwellty. She was living with her parents at 3 Parsons Row, Blaina at the time. They lived at 19 Mount Pleasant, Blain and had a son, Leslie Williams, later in 1911. Daniel married Adelaide Davey (14th July 1901–1972) on 6th August 1928 at Monmouth. She was living with her mother and siblings at 24 Clock Row, Blaina in 1911. He was a grocery warehouseman in 1939, when they were living at 13 Henwain Street, Blaina. Adelaide married Henry Brown in 1966 at Crickhowell, Monmouthshire.
- Henry 'Harry' Williams (16th August 1889–c.1959) was a coal miner hewer, living with his parents in 1911. He married Bertha Adams (born 1st February 1890) in 1917 at Bedwellty. He was a foreman colliery haulier in 1939, when they were living with their niece, Bertha Williams, at 45 Curre Street, Ebbw Vale.
- Philip John Williams (16th April 1891–1971), a coalminer, married Ellen Redden (1889–1964), born at Beaufort, Monmouthshire, in 1910 at Bedwellty. They were living at 26 South Street, Beaufort Hill, Beaufort in 1911. He was a Minister of Religion in 1939, when they were living at 4 Wellington Road, Helston, Cornwall. They had two children – Daniel Williams 1911 and Windsor Williams 1916.
- Annie Williams (born c.1895).
- Windsor Williams (1897–14th September 1918) was a coalminer in 1911, living with his parents. He was serving as a corporal in 13th Welsh (53878) when he died on active service (Ste Marie Cemetery, Le Havre, France – 62 V E 1).
- Mary Alice Williams (30th October 1904–May 1995) married William Benedict Sullivan (28th January 1901–1965), born at Dowlais, Glamorgan, in 1927 at

Jack's brother-in-law, Windsor Williams, is buried in Ste Marie Cemetery, Le Havre, France. During the Great War, Le Havre was an important port, base area and medical facility for the BEF. By May 1917 there were three general and two stationary hospitals, plus four convalescent depots. The first Commonwealth burials took place in August 1914. A memorial marks the graves of twenty-four fatalities from HMHS *Salta* and her patrol boat, sunk by a mine on 10th April 1917. The memorial also commemorates those lost whose bodies were not recovered from the *Salta*, or from HMHS *Galeka*, mined on 28th October 1916, and the transport SS *Normandy*, torpedoed on 25th January 1918. There are 1,690 Commonwealth burials of the Great War, including eight unidentified. Le Havre was an evacuation port for the BEF in June 1940. Towards the end of the war it was a supply and reinforcement base. There are 364 burials of the Second World War, of which fifty-nine are unidentified.

Bedwellty. He was an open-hearth furnace ladle man, in 1939, when they were living at 23 Second Row, Newtown, Monmouthshire. They had six children:

- Brenda M Sullivan (1928–2018).
- Peter Sullivan (19th January 1930–1st September 2020).
- Audrey E Sullivan (1934).
- Mary D Sullivan (1937).
- Gertrude Ann Sullivan (1946).
- Shan E Sullivan (1948) married Stuart Small in 1966 and they had three children – Carl Peter Small 1967, James Thomas Small 1977 and Rebecca Louise T Small 1979.

On 19th September 1914, David Lloyd George proposed the formation of a Welsh Army Corps at a meeting in London. The Welsh National Executive Committee formed in Cardiff on 29th September to organise recruitment. Sir Frederick Mills, Director of the Ebbw Vale Iron & Steel Co, sat on the Committee and set about raising a battalion from his businesses in Ebbw Vale. Recruitment commenced in October, including Jack Williams (20408), but the numbers fell short and the area was extended to Abertillery, Abercarn, Blackwood, Cwmcarn and Tredegar. Jack was formerly attested on 12th November, one of 631 men who formed the core of 10th South Wales Borderers, which moved to Colwyn Bay on 29th December. He was promoted sergeant on 1st January 1915 and went to France on 3rd December. **Awarded the DCM for his actions at Mametz Wood on the Somme 10th – 12th July 1916 during which he handled his men in the attack with great courage and skill and performed consistently good work throughout, LG 13th February 1917. Awarded the MM for his actions southwest of Langemarck on Pilkem Ridge, Belgium on 31st July 1917. The Battalion was in the support brigade to the main attack and one company went forward**

A group of wounded soldiers outside Whitecross Hospital, Warrington dressed in hospital blues. CSM Jack Williams is seated in the front row third from the left. On his left is Arnold Loosemore VC DCM, whose story appears in the fifth book in this series, *Victoria Crosses on the Western Front – Third Ypres 1917*.

Warrington Hospital began as an isolation hospital in 1893. The Warrington Union Workhouse Infirmary was built on the same site and opened in 1898. It was occupied by Whitecross Military Hospital during the Great War. In 1930 the infirmary became Warrington Borough General Hospital and it joined the National Health Service in 1948. The isolation hospital became known as Aiken Street Hospital and it was demolished in 1973. The site was redeveloped to create the Appleton Wing in 1980, Burtonwood Wing in 1988, Croft Wing in 1994 and Daresbury Wing in 1998. A new intensive care unit opened in 2009.

at 5.00 p.m. to reinforce 11th South Wales Borderers and 17th Royal Welsh Fusiliers and helped repel counterattacks, LG 28th September 1917.

Jack was appointed company sergeant major on 2nd October. **Awarded a Bar to the MM for his actions during a raid on the enemy lines in the Armentières area on 30th October 1917, in which he brought back a wounded comrade, LG 23rd February 1918. Awarded the VC for his actions at Villers-Outréaux, France on 7th – 8th October 1918, LG 14th December 1918.** He was severely wounded by shrapnel in the right arm and leg on 17th October and was evacuated to Britain for treatment at Whitecross Hospital, Warrington, Cheshire. He suffered constant pain in his arm and lost much of its functionality.

The VC, DCM, MM & Bar were presented by the King in the ballroom at Buckingham Palace on 22nd February 1919. This is believed to have been the first time that the King decorated the same man four times in one day. Jack had not recovered from his wounds and during the investiture the wound in his arm opened up and he had to be treated before he could leave the Palace. Jack is the most decorated Welsh NCO. He was discharged from the Army on 7th May 1919. **Awarded the French Médaille Militaire, LG 15th December 1919.** He was a member of the VC Honour Guard at the burial of the Unknown Warrior at Westminster Abbey on 11th November 1920. He was presented with a silver tea set by Briery Hill School. On 11th November 1921 he was presented with a silver tray by Ebbw Vale Steel, Iron & Coal Ltd. The tea set and tray were presented to Ebbw Vale Works Museum on long loan by 8th March 2014 by his grandchildren Ann Page, John Henry Michael Williams and Peter Williams.

Jack was employed as a commissionaire at the Steel, Iron & Coal Co, Ebbw Vale, until that company ceased trading in 1929. He then worked for Ebbw Vale Council Housing Department as a rent collector, moving from Garden City to Willowtown. In 1937 he was reinstated as a commissionaire at the general offices of Richard Thomas & Co, Ebbw Vale by the Chairman, Sir William Firth, when new works opened in 1937. Jack held this position until his death.

Jack met the Prince of Wales on a number of occasions, including at Cardiff Arms Park in 1921. He took part in a wreath laying ceremony at the Cenotaph, Newport on 8th March 1924, at which the Duke of York (later King George VI) was present. Jack met the Prince of Wales again at the unveiling of the National War Memorial in Cardiff on 12th June 1928. He was also introduced to the Prince, by then King Edward VIII, in November 1936, shortly before his abdication, when he inspected the British Legion at Pontypool, during a visit to South Wales to see the high unemployment and poor conditions there. As they shook hands, the King asked, *How many times is this, Jack?* To which he replied, *The first time since you had your new job, Sir*! The King bent forward in a hearty chuckle of appreciation.

The rebuilt steelworks after 1937.

Jack represented 10th South Wales Borderers at the unveiling of the South Wales Borderers memorial at Gheluvelt, near Ypres, Belgium on 19th May 1929 by General Sir Alexander Stanhope Cobbe VC GCB KCS DSO.

Jack married Morfydd Rees (20th March 1894–24th March 1980), born at Aberbeeg, Llanhilleth, Monmouthshire, on 19th December 1931 at Bedwellty Parish Church. She was living at 89 Penylan Road, Markham, Monmouthshire and she at Aberbeeg, Monmouthshire at the time. She was a domestic servant at 13 Glenview Terrace, Ynysddu, Monmouthshire in 1911. They met when Morfydd

Newport Cenotaph in Clarence Place was unveiled by Lord Tredegar on 7th June 1923. It also now commemorates people who died in subsequent wars. There are no names on the memorial (South Wales Argus).

The Welsh National War Memorial in Alexandra Gardens, Cathays Park, Cardiff was unveiled on 12th June 1928 by the Prince of Wales and the ceremony was broadcast by the BBC. It commemorates servicemen who died during the Great War and a plaque was added in 1949 for those who died during the Second World War (HT Beach).

was the Senior Telephonist at the General Offices, Messrs Richard Thomas & Baldwins, Ebbw Vale. They lived in a company house at 4 The Dingle, Queen's Square, Ebbw Vale from 1937 and received free coal and lighting through the company. He was also presented with a gold watch by the people of the town. Jack was an Air Raid Precautions Warden there at the time of the 1939 Register. She was living at 17 West End Avenue, Caldicot, Monmouthshire at the time of her death there.

The South Wales Borderers memorial at Gheluvelt, near Ypres, Belgium.

Morfydd's father, Henry Rees (6th August 1863–27th July 1939), born at Peterston-super-Ely, Glamorgan, was a goods guard when he married in 1892 and later a railway foreman and inspector with Great Western Railways. He married Jemima Pugh (1873–18th January 1937), on 30th January 1892 at the Parish Church, Bedwellty, where she was born. She was living at 12 Whitworth Terrace, Tredegar and he at Aberbeeg at the time. They were living at 17 Railway Terrace, Llanhilleth, Monmouthshire in 1901 and at Church Street, Rogerstone, Monmouthshire in 1911. Henry was a deacon and choir conductor at Commercial Road Baptist Church, Aberbeeg, Monmouthshire and Jemima was also a prominent member of the Church. They were living there at Brynamel Terrace, Aberbeeg when Jemima died at Aberbeeg Hospital. Henry lived with his daughter, Morfydd and her family, at 4 The Dingle, Queen's Square, Ebbw Vale and later died there. In addition to Morfydd they had six other children:

- Blodwen Rees (9th March 1893–26th March 1972), born at Aberbeeg, was a dressmaker living with her parents in 1911. She married Frederick Luke Ball (30th December 1892–21st April 1955), born at Cheltenham, Gloucestershire, in 1918 at Newport. He was a railway goods guard in 1939, when they were living at 17 The Avenue, Caldicot, Monmouthshire. They both later died there.
- Olwyn Rees (1897–1901). Her parents went to Pontypool for the day on 18th May 1901 leaving Olwyn and her siblings in the care of a neighbour, Rose James. Olwyn and another neighbour's son, Joseph Williams, aged four years and eleven months, of 18 Railway Terrace, Llanhilleth, went through a gap in a fence and played on the railway line. William Rose, a railway brakeman of 19 Railway Terrace, was returning home when he spotted Olwyn and Joseph. Olwyn was lying across the rails after a rail truck had passed across her chest, killing her instantly. Joseph was lying a few metres away in a pool of blood. He was unconscious but breathing and had a compound fracture of the right thigh and

his right hand was almost severed. Dr Timothy Daniel Sullivan arrived but was unable to save Joseph. A verdict of accidental death was reached by the inquest.

- Sanford Rees (26th July 1898–1970), a miner, sailed to Canada from Southampton, Hampshire aboard RMS *Ausonia* on 18th September 1926, arriving at Montréal, Québec on 26th September. He married Helen Addison Wishart (11th June 1898–1993), born at Dunfermline, Fife, Scotland, in 1931 at Edmonton, Alberta. She arrived in Canada with her parents in June 1930. Sanford and Helen returned to Britain from Montréal aboard RMS *Ausonia*, arriving on 4th August 1934. Their address was given as Homni, Aberbeeg, Monmouthshire, South Wales. They returned to Québec aboard SS *Athenia*, departing Glasgow, Lanarkshire on 5th October. They returned to Britain again aboard RMS *Aurania*, arriving at London on 13th September 1937, giving their address as 4 The Dingle, Queen's Square, Ebbw Vale. Sanford was a colliery ripper in 1939, when they were living at 38 North Lane, Astley, Lancashire. Their deaths were registered at Ewecross, Yorkshire. They had two children born in Canada – Kathleen Rees (born 1932) and Brenda Morfydd Rees (born 23rd November 1935).
- Gwyneth Rees (born 1902), born at Pontypool.
- Islwyn Rees (8th April 1905–26th July 1968), born at Aberbeeg, married Eva Blackmore (26th February 1902–1992) in 1925 at Pontypool, where she was born. She was living with her parents at 10 Springfield Terrace, Llanhilleth, Monmouthshire in 1911. Islwyn died at Ty Graig, Corris, Merionethshire. Eva's death was registered at Cardiganshire North. They had two children – Alan Rees 1925 and Enid M Rees 1926.
- Gurnos Rees (19th November 1910–15th March 1964), born at Rogerstone, married Doris May Barrett (12th May 1913–28th January 1978) in 1935 at Axbridge, Somerset. He was a physical training organiser for York Education Authority in 1939, when they were living at 45 Fellbrook Avenue, Acomb, York. He died at the Civilian Wing, Military Hospital, York. Doris was still living at 45 Fellbrook Avenue at the time of her death there. They had two children – David A Rees 1936 and Jennifer MB Rees 1944.

Jack was an Air Raid Precautions Warden in 1939 and served in the Local Defence Volunteers from 27th May 1940. He was a captain with 7th Monmouthshire (Ebbw) Battalion, Home Guard from 1st February 1941 but had to relinquish his commission due to ill health on 14th October 1942. As a consequence he did not qualify for the Defence Medal. He attended a number of VC Reunions – the VC Garden Party at Buckingham Palace on 26th June 1920, the VC Dinner at the Royal Gallery of the House of Lords, London on 9th November 1929 and the Victory Day Celebration Dinner & Reception at The Dorchester, London on 8th June 1946.

Jack Williams was admitted to St Woolos Hospital, Newport, Monmouthshire, where he died on 6th March 1953. His funeral with full military honours was held at Tabernacle Church, Ebbw Vale, with the South Wales Borderers providing a

The site for the hospital was donated by Sir Charles Morgan and it opened as the Newport Union Workhouse and Infirmary in 1837. A new infirmary building was completed in 1869 and the Workhouse was rebuilt in 1903. In 1915 it was converted into a military hospital under the control of 3rd Western General Military Hospital in Cardiff. The hospital joined the National Health Service as St Woolos in 1948.

Jack William's funeral and the new gravestone.

guard of honour, bearers and the firing party. He is buried in Ebbw Vale Cemetery, Gwent, Wales (Section K, Row 4, Grave 14). A newspaper at the time made the following tribute – *A loveable personality, esteemed and respected by every member of the community. With his unassuming character, his high ideals of service, he held a place in public admiration that no one else will fill.* His headstone was removed during cemetery renovations and was not replaced. However, a new headstone was dedicated on 21st October 1990 following a parade through Ebbw Vale. Jack is commemorated in a number of other places:

- John H Williams VC Hall, Army Reserve Centre, Abertillery, Gwent was dedicated by the Duke of Gloucester on 4th May 1988. Jack's children, Henry,

The Jack Williams Gateway Bridge is fifty metres tall and forms part of the A465 dualling project between Brynmawr and Gilwern. It dominates the westerly part of Clydach Gorge and is the largest of the structures on the project with a 118m span.

Bob and Bertha, and granddaughter Ann Page, were present at the ceremony together with other members of the family.

- The Jack Williams Gateway Bridge, Heads of the Valleys Road, Clydach Gorge, Blaenau, Gwent was dedicated in the presence of family members on 21st January 2019. Jack's great, great granddaughter, Adriana Smith, aged five, assisted the Economy and Transport Deputy Minister for Wales, Lee Waters, in unveiling the plaque.
- Ebbw Vale
  - Plaque at the general office building of the former Richard Thomas & Co steelworks, now Gwent Archives, dedicated on 8th March 2014.
  - Department for Communities and Local Government commemorative paving stones in English and Welsh were dedicated at the memorial outside Nantyglo Senior Citizens Hall on 22nd September 2018 in the presence of family members.
  - Memorial stone outside the Nantyglo Senior Citizens Hall on Chapel Road dedicated on 8th March 2014, in the presence of family members.
  - Framed photo and plaque in the main bar of Ebbw Vale Ex-Servicemen's Club and Institute.
- Brecon, Powys
  - Named on a panel in Harvard Chapel, Brecon Cathedral.
  - Named on the Victoria Cross Roll, The Royal Welsh Museum.
- Memorial at Villers-Outréaux, France dedicated on 7th October 2018 in the presence of family members, including his four-year old great granddaughter, Adriana Lee Smith, who laid a wreath.

The posthumous award of the Freedom of the Borough of Blaenau Gwent County Borough was presented to his granddaughter, Ann Page, on 27th October 2016. In addition to the VC, DCM and MM & Bar he was awarded the 1914–15 Star, British

Plaque in the Gwent Archives building.

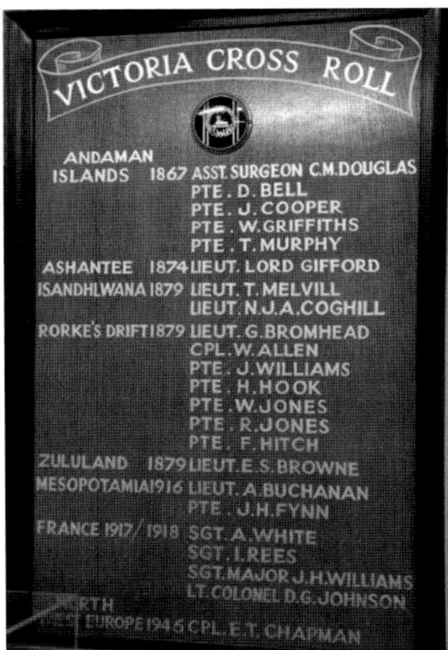

The Victoria Cross Roll at The Royal Welsh Museum.

Jack's memorial at Villers Outreaux. It is situated near the cemetery beside an old windmill north of the town on the D76.

The Regimental Museum of The Royal Welsh at Brecon.

War Medal 1914–20, Victory Medal 1914–19 with Mentioned-in-Despatches Oakleaf, George VI Coronation Medal 1937 and the French Médaille Militaire. Although the Victory Medal ribbon carries the MID Oakleaf, no trace of this award has been found. The VC is held at the Regimental Museum of The Royal Welsh, The Barracks, Brecon, Powys, Wales. Jack's miniature medal group was loaned to the Adult Education Centre, Ebbw Vale in October 1961 by his daughter, Mary Clarke. They were displayed in the old library until early 1976, when they were stolen. Jack's daughter, Bertha Davies, was not informed of this until July 1978. The miniatures have not been recovered.

16444 CORPORAL HARRY BLANSHARD WOOD
2nd Battalion, Scots Guards

Harry Wood was born on 21st June 1882 at Newton upon Derwent, near York, Yorkshire. His father, John Wood (c.1841–1928), an agricultural labourer also born at Newton upon Derwent, was baptised on 26th January 1841 at Wilberfoss, near York. He married Maria Nicol née Dey (24th December 1850–1946), born at Escrick, Yorkshire, on 29th October 1872 at Wilberfoss. She was related to James Melrose (1828–1929), Lord Mayor of York 1876–77 and was living with her grandparents at Newton upon Derwent in 1871. John and Maria were living there in 1881. By 1891 they had moved to Strensall, near York and later to 13 Grange Street, Fulford Road, York. John was visiting his daughter, Agnes Hughes and family, at No.4 Married Quarters, Fulford Road, York at the time of the 1911 Census. Maria was housekeeper to Alfred John Segar, dental surgeon, at 92 The Mount, York in 1911 and at 489 Gloster Road, Bristol, Gloucestershire in 1917. She was living with her daughter, Agnes, and family at 26 Kilburn Road, York in 1939. Harry had five sisters:

Newton upon Derwent is a small village eight kilometres west of Pocklington. There is little trace of occupation until after the Norman Conquest, although some evidence exists for Neolithic and Iron Age settlements. The first record of Newton appears in the mid 12th century. A chapel was known to exist in 1153, a sub-chapel of St Mary Priory, Wilberfoss. The earliest appearance on a map was in 1755.

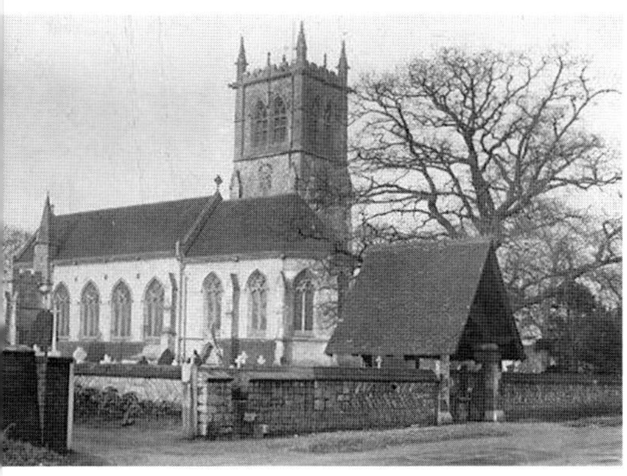

Escrick, between Selby and York, sits on a low ridge of terminal moraine left by the last ice age. A gold Anglo-Saxon ring was discovered in a field nearby in 2009. The village was named Ascri (Ash Ridge) in the Domesday Book, but by 1600 had been replaced by Escrick. Sir Thomas Knyvett became the first baron of Escrick after playing a key role in foiling the 1605 Gunpowder Plot. Sir Henry Thompson developed Escrick as an estate village, having acquired the village and hall in 1668. His great grandson, Beilby Thompson, extended the village towards York and the church of St Helen was relocated to its present position in 1783. The present church, seen here, was built in 1857. A manor existed in 1323 and by 1557 was named Escrick Hall. It was rebuilt c.1690 and was extended and improved in the 18th and 19th centuries. The Hall has been occupied by Queen Margaret's School since 1949. The grounds are now a holiday and pleasure park.

- Laura Preston Wood (24th December 1873–1965), born at Newton upon Derwent, married Sergeant Peter Cottrill (1869–1938), birth registered at Stafford, on 31st March 1897 at Strensall. He was a teacher when he enlisted in the North Staffordshire Regiment at Lichfield, Staffordshire on 13th February 1890 (2968). He gained 2nd Class Education on 24th April and was posted to the 2nd Battalion on 15th May. He was in hospital at Devonport with a sprain 14th–18th October. On 21st February 1891 he was appointed unpaid lance corporal and was in hospital at Portland with a chill and tonsilitis 5th–9th September. He was granted Good Conduct Pay from 13th February 1892 and was posted to the Depot on 18th February. He gained 1st Class Education on 29th March, was promoted lance corporal on 11th May and corporal and probationary staff clerk on 29th August. On 1st April 1893 Peter transferred to the Army Pay Corps and was promoted sergeant on 29th August 1895. He extended his service to complete twelve years at York on 29th October 1896 and re-engaged for twenty-one years at Lincoln on 22nd June 1899. Peter served in South Africa from 7th March 1900 and was promoted staff sergeant with Class I Service Pay on 1st April 1901. He

Strensall, seven kilometres north of York, was in the North Riding of Yorkshire until 1974, when it became part of the district of Ryedale in North Yorkshire and since 1996 has been part of the City of York unitary authority. Strensall is the possible site of the 664 Whitby Synod and is referred to in the Domesday Book. It belonged to the Archbishops of York from c.1214, except for a short period in 1547 when it was held by the Duke of Somerset and Lord Wharton. Strensall Camp was started by the War Office in 1884 to train troops and is now known as Queen Elizabeth Barracks.

was wounded accidentally in the left hand at Bloemfontein on 3rd September 1902 and was in hospital until 19th September. On 1st April 1904 he was appointed staff quartermaster sergeant and returned to Britain on 10th October 1908. He was permitted to continue service beyond twenty-one years on 21st March 1910. The family was living at Ashton Place, Cork, Ireland in 1911. He was in hospital there with gout 13th December 1912–3rd January 1913. His conduct was brought to the notice of the Secretary of State for War for valuable services in connection with the war on 24th February 1917. Peter elected to draw his pension while still serving at Blackheath on 21st January 1918 and re-engaged to continue service under the Military Service Act 1918 on 19th April. Promoted warrant officer class II on 22nd June. Peter was demobilised from Blackheath on 16th January 1920, entitled to one month's leave. He was discharged on 13th March 1920, having served a total of thirty years and thirty days. The family was living at 13 Mount Pleasant, Plumstead, London in 1920. Laura was living at 50 Littlefield Road, Edgware, Middlesex in 1939 and was still there at the time of her death at Mardale Nursing Home, Stratford Road, Watford, Hertfordshire. Laura and Peter had three children:

- Hilda May Cottrill (born 1898), born at Lincoln, married Alan Western Monger (8th May 1900–23rd March 1964), born at West Green, London, on 9th April 1928 at Woolwich. Alan was the son of Hilda's cousin, Blanche. His parents were living at 402 West Green Road at the time. Alan was a clerk, living at 28 Tylney Road, Forest Gate, when he was deemed to have enlisted in the Royal Air Force at Great Scotland Yard, London on 8th May 1918 (168923). He was called up on 16th May to the Central London Recruiting Depot and joined at No.1 Reception Depot RAF as a Clerk 3. He was described as 5′9″ tall, weighing 132 lbs with brown hair, brown eyes, fresh complexion and his religious denomination was Church of England. Alan changed trade to Clerk Stores on 1st January 1919 and re-mustered as an Equipment Assistant on 9th January. On 5th May he joined the seaplane carrier HMS *Empress* and served in Malta from 15th June. He returned to Britain on 1st October and was demobilised on 24th November 1919. On 30th April 1920 he transferred to the RAF Reserve but did not volunteer for reserve training. He enlisted in the Class B Reserve for four years on 9th January 1939. He was recalled during the Second World War and was serving as a corporal in December 1943. They were living at 35 St Andrews Drive, Stanmore, Middlesex at the time of his death there. They had a daughter, Audrey Margaret Monger, in 1930, who married Peter Smart in 1968.

- John Bernard Cottrill (21st February 1911–1974), born at Cork, Ireland, was an automatic telephone engineer in 1939, living with his mother. He married Eileen Mary Swinburne (13th February 1920–21st July 2008), born at Holborn, London, in 1942 at Hendon, Middlesex. She was a typist clerk in 1939, living with her parents at 134 Grays Inn Buildings, Holborn. John's death was registered at Harlow, Essex. Eileen died at Ripon, Yorkshire. They had a son, Alan B Cottrill, in 1947.
- George Phillip Cottrill (15th June 1914–4th January 1979), born at Woolwich, London, was a correspondence clerk in 1939, living with his mother. He married Joan Phyllis Gilkes (20th August 1921–April 1991), born at Pancras, London, in 1940 at Hendon, Middlesex. Joan was an assistant in a shoe shop in 1939, living with her mother and stepfather. The marriage ended in divorce. Joan married John R Batty on 16th September 1949 registered in Surrey South Western. She was living alone at 6 Bybrook Road, Gloucester in 1972 and her death was registered at Cheltenham, Gloucestershire. John and Joan had two children – Jane E Batty 1952 and Jeremy J Batty 1960. George married Agnes Doris Johnson née Thomas (30th October 1919–November 1991), born at Edmonton, Middlesex, in 1953 at Marylebone, London. They had a daughter, Jondene G Cottrill, in 1955. Agnes had married Clifford George Johnson (24th April 1916–15th May 2000), a metal finisher for a clock manufacturer living at 47 Ellanby Crescent, Edmonton, at Edmonton in 1939 and they had a son, Michael L Johnson, in 1941. Clifford enlisted on 6th May 1943 (14596878). He and Agnes divorced. Clifford married Mavis D Skells (born 1929), born at Islington, London, at Edmonton on 24th July 1954 at the Congregational Church, Lower Edmonton. They had two sons

– Kevin C Johnson 1961 and Graham G Johnson 1963. George was living at Hillside, 171 Swakeleys Road, Ickenham, near Uxbridge, Middlesex at the time of his death, registered at Chelsea, London. Agnes' death was registered at Hillingdon, Greater London.

- Margaret Elizabeth Wood (1875–77) died in an accidental shooting incident.
- Jessie Grace Wood (1878–1917) married John Davies in 1897 at York. John is believed to have died before 1901, by when Jessie was living with her parents. She married Frederick George Heale (28th April 1876–1957), an engine cleaner born at Torrington, Devon on 11th January 1906 at York. Frederick served in 3rd Somerset Light Infantry (Militia) before enlisting in 3rd (The King's Own) Hussars at Taunton, Somerset on 10th October 1892 (3286), joining at Dublin on 20th October. He was described as almost 5′ 6½″ tall, weighing 130 lbs, with fair complexion, dark eyes, black hair and his religious denomination was Church of England. He was kicked in the head by a horse on 9th November at Dublin, when a corporal struck the horse with a whip causing him to fall off. He was in hospital until 5th December. Frederick was posted to the Curragh, Ireland on 15th July 1893 and returned to Dublin on 2nd September. He was treated for ring worm 29th November–16th December and was posted to Newbridge, Co Kildare on 13th July 1894. He was treated for a tendon injury 2nd January–5th February 1895 and for a contusion 5th-11th May. He was posted to Aldershot on 22nd May. On 10th September 1897 he was posted to Chatham and to Shorncliffe on 8th June 1898. He was aboard SS *Rameses* when he was treated for phimosis 29th-30th June. He arrived in Egypt and was treated at a hospital in Cairo 12th-22nd July. Frederick landed in India on 8th November and was posted to Lucknow on 25th November. He was treated for ague 22nd-27th October 1900 but a medical on 3rd October 1901 found him fit for extension of service. He served in South Africa from November and returned to India aboard SS *Ionian* in October 1902 and was posted to Sialkot, Punjab on 3rd November. A medical on 5th September 1904 found him fit for extension of service and another at York on 6th January 1905 found him fit for service in India. He was posted to Sialkot on 1st April 1906 and to Aldershot on 3rd October 1907. He embarked aboard HMS *Hardinge* on 19th November and was posted to Pretoria, South Africa on 6th December. A medical on 22nd February 1909 found him fit for service abroad and he was aboard HT *Braemar Castle* 25th February–19th March. It is believed that he was serving with 7th Hussars at the time as that regiment sent a draft of eighty-six men to 3rd Hussars in South Africa on 24th February. Frederick had been promoted corporal by 1911 and embarked aboard HT *Soudan* on 18th November 1911, to be posted to Shorncliffe, Kent on 14th December. He was posted to Bristol on 18th March 1912 and was discharged on 9th October 1913. Jessie's death was registered at Bristol. Frederick married Harriet Edith Ada Reece (11th November 1888–October 1960), born at Bristol, on 17th December 1918 at Holy Trinity Church, Horfield, Bristol. She was living with her parents at 2 Willway Street,

St Philip & St Jacob, Bristol in 1891 and with her mother and stepfather at 20 Conduit Place, Bristol in 1901. Frederick was a clerk at the time of the marriage and they were both living at 489 Gloucester Road, Horfield. He was a postman in 1939, when they were living at 50 Belsize Lane, Hampstead, London. His death was registered at Paddington, London and hers at Westminster, London. Jessie and John had a son:

- ◦ John Douglas Stuart Davies (16th August 1898–16th September 1964), born at Newcastle upon Tyne, Northumberland, married Ann Morgan (9th June 1902–17th March 1980) in 1929 at Bristol, Gloucestershire. He was a wholesale salesman in sugar confectionary in 1939, when they were living at 22 Belvoir Road, St Andrews, Bristol. John subsequently died there. Ann was living at 68 Longmead Avenue, Horfield, Bristol at the time of her death there.

- Hilda Jane Wood (1880–92).
- Agnes Elizabeth Wood (19th January 1885–1963) married Sergeant James Hughes RAMC (23rd April 1877–1951), born at Lochwinnoch, Renfrewshire, in 1909 at York. They were living at No.4 Married Quarters, Fulford Road, York in 1911. Her father was visiting them at the time of the 1911 Census. James retired as a sergeant major and was living with his family at 26 Kilburn Road, York in 1939. They both subsequently died at York. They had seven children, all registered at York:
  - ◦ Donald James Hughes (13th May 1910–11th September 1985) married Edith Margaret Thornton née Allison (born 6th May 1907) in 1953 at York. She had married Austin Thornton (6th March 1907–25th April 1951) there in 1935. He was living with his uncle and aunt, John George and Ethel Britton at 22 Lewisham Street, York in 1911. Austin was a club steward and Edith was a club stewardess in 1939, living at 101 Fulford Road, York. They were still living there at the time of Austin's death at 418 Westgate Road, Newcastle upon Tyne, Northumberland. Donald was living at 23 Parkside Close, West Bank, Acomb, York at the time of his death there.
  - ◦ Audrey Mary Hughes (born 6th January 1912) married Edward Stanley Hills (4th September 1910–1976) in 1939 at York, where he was born. He was a local actuary with the Trustee Savings Bank in 1939, when they were living at 51 Wetherby Road, York. They had moved to 80 Hookstone Chase, Harrogate, Yorkshire by 1955. They had a son, Christopher David Hills (1941–2007).
  - ◦ Kenneth Gordon Hughes (19th December 1914–1984) was an electrician in 1939, living with his parents. He married Anne M Croker in 1952 at York. They had a son, Andrew J Hughes, in 1957.
  - ◦ Margaret Hughes (born 30th November 1916) was a photographer's assistant in 1939, living with her parents.
  - ◦ Dennis Hughes (29th September 1919–February 1986) was a joiner in 1939, living with his parents.

- Patricia Hughes (26th January 1921–7th February 2004) married Wilfrid Pinkney (24th September 1919–11th August 2001) in 1947 at York, where he was born. They had two daughters – Jennifer M Pinkney 1949 and Gillian E Pinkney 1952. Wilfred's father, Arthur Edward Pinkney, was a wagon repairer working for the Tramways & Electric Light Department, York Corporation when he enlisted in C Company, 2/5th West Yorkshire at York (2764 & 200923) on 17th October 1914. Promoted lance corporal 9th January–9th November 1915 and corporal 11th July–28th December 1916. He embarked with the Battalion at Southampton on 5th January 1917 and disembarked at Le Havre next day. Arthur received a shrapnel wound to the right big toe at Beaumont-Hamel on 4th March, which turned septic. He was treated at 3rd (Royal Naval) Field Ambulance, No.11 Casualty Clearing Station from 12th March and 13th Stationary Hospital, Boulogne from 20th March. He was evacuated to Southampton aboard HMHS *St Patrick* on 23rd March. He was treated at the Italian Hospital, Queen's Square, London 24th March–12th April and 4th London General Hospital on 14th April. He was on the strength of 5th Reserve Battalion, Rugeley, Cannock Chase from 24th April. Transferred to the Command Depot, Ripon 17th May and 5th Reserve Battalion 13th July. He was allocated to 2/7th Battalion on 27th July and joined 33rd Infantry Base Depot, Étaples, France next day. He was allocated to 2/5th Battalion on 12th August, joining on 17th August. Arthur was appointed unpaid lance corporal on 14th September and paid acting lance corporal on 4th October. On 20th November he received a gunshot wound to the right thigh at Cambrai. He was treated at 2/2nd West Riding Field Ambulance, No.3 Casualty Clearing Station and 1st South African General Hospital, Abbeville from 21st November. He was evacuated to Britain aboard HMHS *Essequibo* on 27th November and was treated at Lord Derby War Hospital, Warrington 28th November–19th January 1918, when he transferred to the TF Depot. On 28th January he joined 5th Reserve Battalion, transferred to 341st Protection Company, Royal Defence Corps, Oswestry on 20th April, to 18th Welsh (207100) on 5th July, to Tyne Electrical Engineers, Gosport on 15th July (477272) and to No.2 Group Depot Company, Royal Engineers, Gosport on 12th December. A final medical at Chatham, Kent on 4th March 1919 recorded that he was suffering from rheumatism and the two wounds. He was assessed to be 30% disabled. On 8th March he transferred to the RE Dispersal Camp, Ripon and transferred to the Class Z Reserve on 7th April 1919. His address was 42 Swan Street, Nunnery Lane, York. A medical board at York on 12th January 1920 found he had no disability.
- Thomas David Hughes (8th December 1923–May 1988) was an apprentice printer in 1939, living with his parents. He married Maureen Lily Hinchliffe (25th June 1930–January 1959) in 1954 at York, where she was born. She was living with her parents at 8 Alma Grove, York in 1939.

Elvington, a village eleven kilometres southeast of York, was in the East Riding of Yorkshire until local government boundary changes in 1974 moved it into the Selby District of North Yorkshire. In 1996 it became part of the City of York unitary authority. The village is mentioned in the Domesday Book. Elvington Hall was built during Elizabethan times and was re-modelled in the 18th century. RAF Elvington, a bomber airfield during the Second World War, was expanded during the Cold War with the main runway able to accept American B-52 bombers. The airfield is now the Yorkshire Air Museum and a venue for motorsports.

Fishergate, York.

Harry's paternal grandfather, George Wood (c.1797–4th July 1871), born at Kexby, Yorkshire, married Grace née Preston (c.1802–10th January 1876), born at Elvington, Yorkshire, on 10th July 1831 at Aldborough, near Hull, Yorkshire. He was a farmer of 106 acres, employing two labourers at Newton upon Derwent in 1851. They both subsequently died there. In addition to John they had seven other children:

- Mary Wood (14th February 1833–1880) was assisting her father on his farm in 1861. She died unmarried.
- Elizabeth Wood (born c.1835) was assisting her father on his farm in 1861.
- William Wood (born c.1837) is believed to have died between 1851 and 1861.
- Eliza Wood (born 1839).
- Anne Wood (born c.1843).
- George Wood (born 1846).
- Edward Preston Wood (1850–83).

His maternal grandfather, Edward Dey (c.1821–99), an agricultural labourer born at Acomb, near York, married Elizabeth née Blanshard (11th January 1814–1897), born at Aughton, Yorkshire, on 14th February 1843 at Escrick, Yorkshire. In 1851 they were living with his parents-in-law at Mount Pleasant, Escrick. By 1861 they had moved to Fishergate, St Lawrence, York with his parents-in-law and by 1871 he was farming at Newton upon Derwent. By 1881 he was running a farm of fifty acres there and by 1891 was living with his family at Pigeon Cote Farm, Newton upon Derwent. In addition to Maria they had five other children:

- William Francis Dey (c.1843–74), born at Fangfoss, near Pocklington, Yorkshire, was a commercial traveller in the bottle trade. He married Mary Castle (1840–8th January 1924), born at Greenwich, Kent, on 4th June 1864 at St Mary Magdalene's Church, Bermondsey, London. She was living with her parents at 12½ Weston Street, St Olave, London in 1851. William and Mary were living at 76 New Morton Street, Bermondsey in 1865 and at Northumberland Terrace, Bermondsey in 1871. His death was registered at Pocklington. They had two children:
    - Blanche Mary Dey (22nd January 1865–16th December 1943), a nurse born at Bermondsey, married Henry 'Harry' Western Monger (c.1862–1933), a bootmaker born at Athlone, Co Westmeath, Ireland, on 3rd August 1899 at Forest Gate, London. They were living at 28 Tylney Road, Forest Gate in 1911. His death was registered at West Ham, London. She was living at 35 St Andrews Drive, Stanmore, Middlesex at the time of her death at Redhill County Hospital, Edgware, Middlesex. They had a son, Alan Western Monger (8th May 1900–23rd March 1964), who married the VC's niece, Hilda.
    - Frank Edward Dey (1867–17th December 1937), born at Greenwich, was boarding at the Commercial Travellers' School in 1881 and later worked as a commercial traveller. He married Adeline Webster (1st March 1867–11th April 1946), born at Lincoln, Lincolnshire, in 1891 at West Ham. They were living at Liscard, Cheshire in 1911. They were living at 94 Penkett Road, Wallasey, Cheshire at the time of their deaths there. They had five children – Hilda Blanche Dey 1892, Herman Francis Dey 1893, Winifred Adeline Theresa Dey 1895, Marjorie Irene Dey 1899 and Adeline Mary Dey 1906.

Mary Dey was a nurse (domestic servant) in 1881 at Southwood, Eltham, Kent. She married Robert Herman Boughton (c.1837–23rd January 1922), the manager at a bottle manufacturing plant, in 1884 at Lewisham, London. They were living at 5 Ranelagh Villas, Hove, Sussex in 1911 and he later died there. Mary was living with her daughter, Blanche and family, at 28 Tylney Road, Forest Gate, Essex at the time of her death there.

- John Raimes Dey (c.1847–1910), born at Fangfoss, lived with his parents until at least 1891. He was a gardener's labourer in 1901, living with his sister, Williamina and family. He died unmarried.

- Blanchard George Dey (born and died 1849).
- Williamina Laura Dey (1855–1909), born at St Lawrence, Escrick, Yorkshire, was a domestic servant in 1881 with her niece, Blanche Mary Dey, working for the Reverend Thomas R Morton at Huntington, Yorkshire. She married Edwin Dixon (1858–1927), born at Huntington, on 17th September 1889 at Scarborough, Yorkshire. She was visiting her parents at the time of the 1891 Census. Edwin was a corn dealer (hay and straw) in 1901, when they were living at 9 Buckingham Street, York. They had a daughter, Elizabeth Blanshard Dixon (2nd December 1891–1979).
- Alfred Dey (born c.1857).

Harry was educated at Strensall village school, near York. He worked for the Midland Railway Company at York railway station as a cleaner. He enlisted in the Scots Guards on 4th February 1903 (4796) and joined at London on 7th February. He gained the 3rd Class Army School Certificate on 10th June and was promoted lance corporal on 14th August. He extended his service to complete eight years with the Colours on 19th August and qualified Class 1 on 1st April 1904. Harry was awarded the Good Conduct Badge on 4th February 1905 and gained the 2nd Class Army School Certificate on 15th April. He was promoted corporal on 22nd May and was appointed lance sergeant on 16th June. On 25th May 1907 he was promoted lance sergeant. However, he was reduced to private and forfeited Good Conduct Pay by Court Martial on 6th May 1908 for drunkenness. Harry served at Windsor, the Tower of London and Aldershot before being transferred to the Reserve on 4th February 1911.

Strensall village school dates back to 1718, when farmer, Robert Wilkinson, left some money in his will 'for the instruction and education of the young, to teach and instruct the children of Strensall forever.' Today, known as Robert Wilkinson Primary Academy, it has more than 600 pupils.

Harry was recalled from the Reserve on 5th August 1914 to join 2nd Battalion and was based at Lyndhurst, Hampshire. He sailed for Flanders aboard HMT *Lake Michigan*, arriving at Zeebrugge, Belgium on 7th October 1914. He became lost on 11th October whilst on outpost duty. There are conflicting accounts about the composition of the party and the events that followed. *The Bristol Observer* on 16th August 1924 reported that Harry was alone and met up with a Belgian soldier. The Battalion war diary states that Harry was lost with Sergeant Binks, whereas *The Scots Guards*

York railway station, a key junction halfway between London and Edinburgh, has historically been a major site for rolling stock manufacture, maintenance and repair. The first station, which opened in 1839, was a wooden building on Queen Street outside the city walls. It was replaced in 1841 by what is now known as York old railway station. The present station opened on 25th June 1877 with thirteen platforms. At the time it was the largest in the world. The Royal Station Hotel (now The Principal York) opened in 1878. The station was heavily bombed during the Second World War and extensive repairs were carried out in 1947. Since 1968 the station has been Grade II* listed. The collocated former motive power depot and goods station now houses the National Railway Museum.

in the Great War 1914–1918 states that he was accompanied by Sergeant JG Burke and Private O'Halloran. The same sources say that the Belgian soldier was either a Belgian boy or a railwayman. Harry lived off root crops, apples and whatever else he could forage until he made contact with friendly Belgian civilians who gave him food, shelter and clothing. He was able to cross the border into the Netherlands and returned to England aboard a boat carrying scrap iron that docked at Gravesend, Kent. He was congratulated by Lord Kitchener, the Secretary of State for War, and presented with a sovereign. Harry was on the held strength of 3rd Battalion from 17th October.

He returned to France on 23rd May 1915 and rejoined 2nd Battalion next day. He returned to England and 3rd Battalion on 27th January 1916. He was discharged on 3rd February, having completed thirteen years' service. He found work as a storekeeper and lived with his mother at 15 Worcester Street, Gloucester.

Harry was recalled on 17th January 1917 under the provisions of the Military Service Acts, 1916 and joined 3rd Battalion (16444). He was appointed unpaid lance corporal on 16th February. He was reprimanded for neglect of duty, when in charge of a hospital guard, for not reporting the escape of a man in close arrest at once on 26th May. Harry returned to France on 29th March 1918 and joined 2nd Battalion. He was promoted lance corporal on 12th May 1918. **Awarded the MM for leading a patrol of twenty men on 15th August near Boyelles railway station. He heard voices in a trench, went forward alone, killed three Germans and brought back a prisoner who was in possession of important papers and information. LG 11th December 1918.**

Awarded the VC for his actions at St Python, France on 13th October 1918, LG 14th December 1918. He was promoted corporal and unpaid lance

2nd Scots Guards at Lyndhurst September 1914.

SS *Lake Michigan* (8,200 tons), built by Swan & Hunter, Newcastle upon Tyne for Beaver Line (Elder Dempster & Co), Liverpool, was launched on 28th September 1901. She had berths for 122 first, 130 second and 500 third class passengers. In 1903 ownership transferred to Canadian Pacific Railway Co and in 1916 to Canadian Pacific Railway Ocean Lines. She was on the Liverpool to Québec and Montréal service until the Great War, when she was taken over as a troopship. At Gallipoli she was used to land 4th Australian Infantry Battalion and A Echelon, 1st Australian Brigade on 25th April 1915. On 16th April 1918 she was torpedoed by U-*100* en route from Liverpool to Saint John, New Brunswick and sank 155 kilometres west of Nova Scotia.

sergeant the same day and was appointed acting lance sergeant on 20th October. Harry returned to York on 17th February 1919 and was driven in a procession to the Mansion House. He was later a guest of honour at a West Yorkshire Regiment dinner and was presented with a wristwatch. The VC was presented by the King at Buckingham Palace on 22nd February. Harry went back to France and returned to England again on 9th March 1919. He was demobilised to the Class Z Reserve on 8th July 1919 with a small disability pension of six shillings a week.

The Mansion House, home of the Lord Mayors of York, is the earliest purpose-built house for a Lord Mayor existing, predating the Mansion House in London. The foundation stone was laid in 1725 and the building was completed in 1732.

In September 1919 Harry intervened when two military policemen were examining the documents of soldiers at the Buckingham Palace road hostel. Harry advised the soldiers that they should not produce their passes and continued to obstruct the military police in their duties. A passing Metropolitan police officer was summoned and Harry was arrested for being drunk and disorderly. He was bound over by a magistrate on good behaviour on the strength of his service record.

Harry was employed as a commissionaire with the Anglo-American Oil Company in Bristol, Gloucestershire, living at 14 Windsor Terrace, Totterdown, Bristol. He was presented with a gold watch and £100 by his employers. Harry also ran a stall at the Ideal Homes Exhibition in London in February 1920, where he met King George V. Harry attended the VC Garden Party at Buckingham Palace on 26th June and was one of the Honour Guard at the burial of the Unknown Warrior at Westminster Abbey on 11th November.

Harry Wood married Georgina Dorothy Naylor (c.1894–17th May 1950), born in Co Tipperary, Ireland, on 28th July 1920 at St James Church, Plumstead, London. He was living at 34 Sydenham Road, Knowle, Bristol and she at 13 Mount Pleasant at the time. They were living at 14 Windsor Terrace, Totterdown, Bristol, Gloucestershire in 1924. There were no children.

The back of the watch presented to Harry by the Anglo-American Oil Company.

Georgina's father, George James Naylor (born c.1843), born in Co Limerick, Ireland, married Charlotte née Belton (c.1856–25th January 1911), born in Co Wicklow, Ireland, on 22nd June 1876 at Limerick. He was a domestic gardener in 1901, when they were living at 16 Urra, Cloughprior, Co Tipperary and at Henry Street South, Limerick in 1911. By 1920 he was a head gardener. In addition to Georgina they had seven other children:

St James, Plumstead was built in 1855 as an independent church and transferred to the Church of England in 1878. It became a parish in 1880. It was disused from 1966 and has since been converted into flats.

- Samuel Belton Naylor (born 22nd May 1877), born at Limerick, married Sarah Lowe (born 10th April 1876), born at Newtown, Westmeath, on 1st August 1902 at Athlone, Co Westmeath. They had six children – Charlotte Naylor 1904, Emily Naylor 1905, George James Naylor 1906, Ellen Naylor 1908, Dora Naylor 1913 and Samuel Naylor 1916.
- John Naylor (born 8th April 1879).
- George James Naylor (23rd December 1881–18th March 1951) never married and died at Swords, Ireland.
- Elizabeth 'Lizzie' Naylor (born 18th October 1883), born at Boskill, Co Limerick, married Patrick O'Brien (17th April 1876–22nd November 1953), born at Nenagh, Co Tipperary, on 25th August 1905 at Dublin, Ireland. They were living at Sheriff Street, Dublin, Ireland in 1911. They had ten children – William George O'Brien 1907, Elizabeth O'Brien 1908, Patrick James O'Brien 1910, Thomas Christopher O'Brien 1916, Edward O'Brien 1918, Richard O'Brien 1919, Frederick O'Brien, Gabriel O'Brien, James O'Brien and June O'Brien.

By 1844 St Peter's Hospital for Pauper Lunatics was overcrowded and Bristol Corporation built a new hospital, the Bristol Lunatic Asylum, which opened in 1861. It was co-located with Stapleton Workhouse. Various extensions were added in 1875–77, 1882, 1887–91 and 1897–1902. In 1914 the Asylum was requisitioned by the War Office as Beaufort War Hospital and 931 patients were transferred to other asylums. Post war it resumed its former role as Bristol Mental Hospital. Before the Second World War it was renamed Glenside Mental Hospital and later Glenside Hospital. By 1961 the hospital had over one thousand patients. In January 1993, Glenside merged with neighbouring Manor Park Hospital to form Blackberry Hill Hospital. Wards were gradually closed as mental health issues were increasingly dealt with in the community. The site was converted into the Avon and Gloucestershire College of Health over three years and in 1996 became the University of the West of England Faculty of Health and Social Care, later the Faculty of Health and Applied Sciences.

- Charlotte Naylor (born 27th July 1886) born at Tipperary.
- Margaret Naylor (c.1891–4th February 1922), born in Co Tipperary, never married.
- Sarah 'Daisy' Jane Naylor (born 19th October 1897), born at Cloughprior, Nenagh, Co Tipperary, married James Greene (June 1889–1983), born at Banogues, Moate, Co Westmeath, on 18th January 1922 at St Mary's Church of Ireland, Moate. They emigrated to Hamilton, Ontario, Canada. They had four children – Richard Greene 1922, James Harold Greene 1926, William Marvin Greene and Gerald Roy Greene.

While holidaying with his wife at Teignmouth, Devon, a car mounted the kerb on a collision course with the couple. Georgina pushed her husband out of the way

Bristol Cathedral, originally the Cathedral Church of the Holy and Undivided Trinity, was founded in 1140 as St Augustine's Abbey and consecrated in 1148. The building was added to in the early 13th century and much of it was rebuilt during the 14th century. The transept and central tower are 15th century. The incomplete nave was demolished in 1539 and was replaced in the 19th century by a Gothic Revival version partly based on the original plans. With the Dissolution of the Monasteries it became the seat of the newly created Bishop of Bristol in 1542. The western twin towers were completed in 1888. Very little original stained glass remains as some was replaced in Victorian times and much was lost during the Bristol Blitz. In 1994 the first thirty-two women priests in the Church of England were ordained there. The building is Grade I listed.

but was pinned to the wall herself by the vehicle, fortunately only suffering minor cuts and bruises. However, Harry, who was severely affected by nerves from the war, became unconscious and fell into a coma from which he never recovered. He died on 15th August 1924 at Bristol Mental Hospital. His body lay in state in Bristol Cathedral and the funeral took place on 21st August. His coffin was drawn on a guncarriage, escorted by the Scots Guards with the Regiment's Band and Pipes & Drums. He is buried in Soldiers' Corner (Grave 1738) of Arnos Vale Cemetery, Brislington, Bristol. The turf stone was subsequently vandalised and a replacement was dedicated on 27th October 2001. Harry is commemorated in a number of other places:

Harry Wood's grave in Arnos Vale Cemetery.

- Plaque at his former school at Strensall, near York.
- Named on the War Memorial, Arnos Vale Cemetery, Bristol.
- Named on The Household Division (Foot Guards) Honour Roll for the Victoria Cross at the Sergeants' Mess, Guards Depot, Wellington Barracks, London.

Arnos Vale Cemetery was established in 1837 in the style of a Greek necropolis and the first burial was in 1839. Most of the area is now Grade II* listed. During the 20th century the cemetery fell into disrepair and in 1987 there were plans to exhume the remains and develop the site for housing. However, following a public campaign, the site was purchased compulsorily by Bristol City Council and much restoration work has been carried out. The cemetery has received a £4.8M Heritage Lottery Fund grant. In addition to Harry Wood there are two other VCs buried there – Daniel Burges and Gronow Davis. There are more than 500 CWGC burials, with most of the 356 servicemen from the Great War being interred in the Soldiers' Corner plot near the main entrance. Each grave in the Soldiers' Corner plot is covered with a square Portland Stone gravestone laid horizontally, which is unique to Arnos Vale Cemetery. The Second World War burials are mainly scattered except for one group in the upper part of the cemetery from the nearby Naval Hospital. Other notable burials include:

- Elsie Joy Davison (1910–40) of the Air Transport Auxiliary, the first female British aviator to die in the Second World War.
- Mary Carpenter (1807–77) a social and penal reformer who worked to improve the lives of destitute children in Bristol and across the country. She founded a 'ragged school' for the poor and for young offenders, campaigned against slavery, supported women's suffrage and education for girls in India.

- A Department for Communities and Local Government commemorative paving stone was dedicated at the corner of Jackson Lane and Main Street, Newton upon Derwent, East Riding of Yorkshire on 13th October 2018.

Georgina married George Tearle (1888–14th February 1940), born at Hendon, Middlesex, on 17th July 1926 at Holy Trinity Church, Kilburn, Middlesex. He was a foreman with London, Midland and Scottish Railway, living at 57 Charteris Road, Kilburn. George and Georgina lived at 145 Aboyne Road, Neasden, London. They moved temporarily to East Anglia before returning to their previous address in Neasden. George had married Helena Lucy Heath (10th May 1889–1920), born at Paddington, London, on 21st July 1912 at St Michael's Church, Stonebridge, Willesden. George was a railway fireman, living at 7 Melville Road, London and Helena was a domestic servant, living at 95 Carlyle Avenue, London at the time and were still living there in 1919. George and Helena had five children, all registered at Willesden:

- George John Tearle (born 2nd February 1913), a motor driver, married Margaret Bridges (born 21st April 1914) on 17th August 1935 at St Michael's, Stonebridge. They were living at 97 Exmouth Road, Ruislip, Essex in 1939. They had three children – Maureen J Tearle 1938, Sheila M Tearle 1941 and Philip J Tearle 1954.
- Ronald Edward Tearle (6th March 1914–26th December 1973) married Elizabeth O'Brien (17th March 1908–15th September 1991), born in Co Cork, Ireland, in 1936 at Willesden. He was a lorry driver in 1939, when they were living at 10 Lansdowne Grove, Willesden. They had three children – Patricia Elizabeth Tearle 1938, Philip G Tearle 1942 and Roderick Edward Tearle 1946.
- Ethel Ellen Tearle (3rd June 1915–2008) married Charles Victor/Victor Charles Wright (8th June 1907–1973), born at Chalvey Hough, Buckinghamshire, in 1935 at Willesden. He was living with his parents at 8 Wellington Place, Chalvey Hough in 1911. He was a porter in a wholesale clothing warehouse in 1939, living with his family at 101 Blenheim Crescent, Kensington, London. They both died in Norfolk. They had three children – Donald W Wright 1935, Brian GV Wright 1938 and Yvonne U Wright 1949. Charles' father, William Henry George Wright, was living at 8 Wellington Place, Chalvey when he enlisted in 13th

The Great War memorial at Arnos Vale Cemetery with Harry Wood's name at the top. The memorial, at Soldiers' Corner, consists of four bronze panels set within a loggia. The panels record the names of those buried in Arnos Vale Cemetery and the adjoining Holy Souls Catholic Cemetery. Most of those commemorated died in Bristol hospitals.

Works Battalion, Devonshire Regiment (28019) at Slough on 1st July 1916. He was described as 5′4″ tall, weighed 133 lbs and was flat footed. As a result he was graded medically B2. Next day he was attached to 4th East Surrey and was posted to 3rd Infantry Works Company, Devonshire Regiment on 14th July. He transferred to 312th (Home Service) Works Company, Labour Corps (172486) on 28th April 1917. He was demobilised on 3rd February 1919 and transferred to the Class Z Reserve on 3rd March.
- Cyril Charles Tearle (a twin with Donald) (29th July–October 1919).
- Donald Alfred Tearle (a twin with Cyril) (29th July 1919–July 1928).

Georgina married Arthur Frank Beney (19th May 1906–27th November 1968), a stoker born at Battle, Sussex, in 1945 at Willesden. Arthur was an Army train driver during the Second World War, billeted at Neasden, where the couple met. They lived at 145 Aboyne Road, Neasden. Arthur married Catherine Jean Hayden (5th April 1916–17th April 2001) on 10th March 1951 at Willesden, where she was born. She was living with her parents at 141 Aboyne Road, Neasden in 1939, when she was a wages and bonus clerk. They were living at 145 Aboyne Road at the time of his death. She died at Barnet, Hertfordshire. They had a daughter:

- Jean Catherine Beney MRCS MB BS LRCP (9th February 1952–4th May 2020), became a doctor. She married Derek RA Archer (3rd March 1936–8th October 1987), born as Madura, India, in June 1975 and they had two children – Felicity Edwina A Archer 1977 and Edward Andrew J Archer 1979. They were living at 16 Woodcroft Avenue, Mill Hill, London at the time of his death there. Jean married Leonard James Walters (12th November 1944–2021), a medical administrator born at Stoke-on-Trent, Staffordshire, in February 1989 at Hendon, London. They lived at 16 Woodcroft Avenue. Jean was Senior Partner at Oak Lodge Medical Centre, 234 Burnt Oak Broadway, Edgware, Middlesex and was a member of the Barnet Local Medical Committee until her retirement in March 2012. She died at the Royal Free Hospital, Pond Street, London.

Ethel Anne Priscilla 'Ettie' Fane (1867–1952), although born into an aristocratic family, had no title. She married William Grenfell (1855–1945) in 1887, an MP, firstly for the Liberal Party and later for the Conservatives. From 1911 Ettie was periodically Lady of the Bedchamber to Queen Mary, consort to King George V. Two of her sons died during the Great War – Julian Grenfell, the war poet, and Billy Grenfell. The third son, Ivo Grenfell, died in a car accident in 1926. Her nephew was Francis Octavius Grenfell VC. She was a well-known society hostess whose guests included Winston Churchill and five other PMs, HG Wells, Henry Irving, Vita Sackville-West, Edward Prince of Wales (later King Edward VII) and Oscar Wilde. She became Baroness Desborough when her husband was raised to the peerage as 1st Baron Desborough in 1905.

York Castle Museum is on the site of York Castle, originally built by William the Conqueror in 1068. The museum was founded in 1938, housed in prison buildings that were built on the site of the castle in the 18th century. The former debtors' prison was added in 1952, the Edwardian Half Moon Court in 1963 and Raindale Mill, an early 19th century flour mill moved from the North York Moors to the rear of the site in 1966. An £18M redevelopment was announced in 2017. The debtors' prison was originally the County Gaol. Its most notable inmate was the highwayman Dick Turpin who was incarcerated there in the 1730s before his trial at York Assizes.

In addition to the VC and MM, Harry was awarded the 1914 Star with 'Mons' clasp, British War Medal 1914–20 and Victory Medal 1914–19. The VC was purchased by Lady Desborough and on her death it was auctioned at Christie's on 11th December 1953. His family sought to buy it with additional funding from York Corporation and Mr William Lee, an antique dealer of Stonegate, York. The Scots Guards dropped out of the bidding at £200. The VC was purchased for £240 by Mr Lee, who presented it to Harry's sister, Mrs Agnes Hughes, of Kilburn Road, York, who was permitted to hold it for one year. On 31st December 1954 it passed to the military section of York Castle Museum and is held there at The Eye of York, York.

Sources

Regimental Museums

The following Museums and Regimental Headquarters kindly provided information:

Royal Engineers Museum, Chatham; RHQ Worcestershire and Sherwood Foresters, Beeston; HQ Scots Guards, London; Canadian War Museum, Ottawa; Lancashire HQ Royal Regiment of Fusiliers.

Individuals

The following individuals provided information and assistance:

Doug and Richard Arman, Norris Atthey, John Coltman, Maj John Cotterill, Russ Grimble, Alan Jordan, Robert Mansell, Graham McPhie, Col (Ret'd) Gerald Napier, Philip Paine, Ann Page, Vic Tambling, Ada Williams, Joan Yeatman.

Divisional Histories

Listed in numerical order, commencing with the Guards Division:

The Guards Division in the Great War. C Headlam. Murray 1929. Two volumes.
A History of the 38th (Welsh) Division. Editor Lt Col JR Munby CMG DSO. 1920.
Breaking the Hindenburg Line – The Story of the 46th (North Midland) Division. Maj R E Priestley. Fisher Unwin 1919.

Regimental/Unit Histories

Works appear by Regiment in precedence order:

Royal Engineers

History of the Corps of Royal Engineers, Volume V, The Home Front, France, Flanders and Italy in the First World War. Institute of the Royal Engineers 1952.

Grenadier Guards

The Grenadier Guards in the Great War of 1914–18. Compiler AS White. Society for Army Historical Research 1965.

Scots Guards
The Scots Guards in the Great War 1914–18. F Loraine Petre, W Ewart and Maj Gen Sir C Lowther. Murray 1925.

The Lancashire Fusiliers
The History of the Lancashire Fusiliers 1914–18, Volumes I and II. Maj Gen JC Latter. Gale & Polden 1949.
The Lancashire Fusiliers Annual. No.26–1916 and No.28–1918, Editor Maj B Smyth. Sackville Press 1917 and 1919.

The South Wales Borderers
The History of the South Wales Borderers 1914–18. CT Atkinson. Medici Society 1931.

Australian Imperial Force
Official History of Australia in the War of 1914–1918, Volume IV – The Australian Imperial Force in France, 1917. 11th Edition 1941.
They Dared Mightily. Lionel Wigmore, Jeff Williams & Anthony Staunton 1963 & 1986.
The Story of the Fifth Australian Division. Capt AD Ellis MC. Hodder & Stoughton 1920.
Snowy to the Somme. Timothy J Cook 2014. (55th Battalion AIF)

Canadian Expeditionary Force
Official History of the Canadian Army in the First World War – Canadian Expeditionary Force 1914–19. Col GWL Nicholson 1962.
The History of the Twentieth Canadian Battalion (Central Ontario Regiment) Canadian Expeditionary Force in the Great War 1914–1918. Maj DJ Corrigall DSO MC. Stone & Cox Ltd, Toronto 1935.

General Works
A Bibliography of Regimental Histories of the British Army. Compiler A S White. Society for Army Historical Research 1965.
A Military Atlas of the First World War. A Banks & A Palmer. Purnell 1975.
Topography of Armageddon, A British Trench Map Atlas of the Western Front 1914–18. P Chasseaud. Mapbooks 1991.
Before Endeavours Fade. R E B Coombs. Battle of Britain Prints 1976.
British Regiments 1914–18. Brig E A James. Samson 1978.

Biographical/Autobiographical
The Dictionary of National Biography 1901–85. Various volumes. Oxford University Press.
The Cross of Sacrifice, Officers Who Died in the Service of the British, Indian and East African Regiments and Corps 1914–19. S D and D B Jarvis. Roberts Medals 1993.

Australian Dictionary of Biography.
Dictionary of Canadian Biography.
Valiant Hearts. Atlantic Canada and the Victoria Cross. John Boileau. Nimbus Publishing, Halifax, Nova Scotia 2005.
The Christian Soldier: The Life of Lt Col the Rev Bernard William Vann, VC, MC & Bar, Croix de Guerre avec palme. Charles Beresford. Helion & Co 2017.

Specific Works on the Victoria Cross

The Register of the Victoria Cross. This England 1981 and 1988.
The Story of the Victoria Cross 1856–1963. Brig Sir J Smyth. Frederick Muller 1963.
The Evolution of the Victoria Cross, A Study in Administrative History. M J Crook. Midas 1975.
The Victoria Cross and the George Cross. IWM 1970.
The Victoria Cross, The Empire's Roll of Valour. Lt Col R Stewart. Hutchinson 1928.
The Victoria Cross 1856–1920. Sir O'Moore Creagh and E M Humphris. Standard Art Book Company, London 1920.
Heart of a Dragon, VCs of Wales and the Welsh Regiments 1914–82. W Alister Williams. Bridge Books 2006.
For Conspicuous Gallantry, A Brief History of the recipients of the VC from Nottinghamshire and Derbyshire. N McCrery. J H Hall 1990.
For Valour, The Victoria Cross, Courage in Action. J Percival. Thames Methuen 1985.
VC Locator. D Pillinger and A Staunton. Highland Press, Queanbeyan, New South Wales, Australia 1991.
The VC Roll of Honour. J W Bancroft. Aim High 1989.
A Bibliography of the Victoria Cross. W James McDonald. W J Mcdonald, Nova Scotia 1994.
Canon Lummis VC Files held in the National Army Museum, Chelsea.
Recipients of the Victoria Cross in the Care of the Commonwealth War Graves Commission. CWGC 1997.
Victoria Cross Heroes. Michael Ashcroft. Headline Review 2006
Monuments to Courage. David Harvey. 1999.
The Sapper VCs. Gerald Napier. The Stationery Office, London 1998.
Liverpool Heroes – Book 1. Ann Clayton. Noel Chavasse VC Memorial Association.
Our Bravest and Our Best. The Stories of Canada's Victoria Cross Winners. Arthur Bishop 1995.

Works on Other Honours and Awards

Recipients of Bars to the Military Cross 1916–20. J V Webb 1988.
Distinguished Conduct Medal 1914–18, Citations of Recipients. London Stamp Exchange 1983.
The Distinguished Service Order 1886–1923 (in 2 volumes). Sir O'Moore Creagh and E M Humphris. J B Hayward 1978 (originally published 1924).
Orders and Medals Society Journal (various articles).

Official Publications and Sources

History of the Great War, Order of Battle of Divisions. Compiler Maj A F Becke. HMSO.
History of the Great War, Military Operations, France and Belgium. Compiler Brig Gen Sir J E Edmonds. HMSO. Published in 14 volumes of text, with 7 map volumes and 2 separate Appendices between 1923 and 1948.
Unit War Diaries in the National Archives under WO 95
Military maps in the National Archives under WO 297.
Medal Cards and Medal Rolls in the National Archives under WO 329 and ADM 171.
Soldiers' Service Records in the National Archives under WO 97, 363 and 364.
Officers' Records in the National Archives under WO 25, 76, 339 and 374.
Army Lists
Location of Hospitals and Casualty Clearing Stations, BEF 1914–19. Ministry of Pensions 1923.
London Gazettes
Census returns, particularly for 1881, 1891 and 1901.
Births, Marriages and Deaths records
Service records and war diaries in the National Archives of Australia.
Service records from the Library and Archives of Canada.
Officers and Soldiers Died in the Great War.

Reference Publications

Who's Who and Who Was Who.
The Times 1914 onwards.
The Daily Telegraph 1914 onwards.
Kelly's Handbook to the Titled, Landed and Official Classes.
Burke's Peerage.

Internet Websites

History of the Victoria Cross – www.victoriacross.org.uk/vcross.htm – Iain Stewart.
Commonwealth War Graves Commission – www.cwgc.org
Free Births, Marriages and Deaths – www.freebmd.org.uk
Memorials to Valour – http://www.memorialstovalour.co.uk
Scotland's People – https://www.scotlandspeople.gov.uk

Periodicals

This England magazine – various editions.
Coin and Medal News – various editions.
Journal of The Victoria Cross Society – no longer published
Gun Fire – A Journal of First World War History. Edited by AJ Peacock – no longer published – including Reluctant Hero (Harry Blanshard Wood VC) Gun Fire No. 28.
Stand To – journal of the Western Front Association.

Useful Information

(Some details may be affected by Brexit)

Accommodation – there is a wide variety of accommodation available in France and Belgium. Search online for your requirements. There are also numerous campsites, but many close for the winter from late September.

Clothing and Kit – consider taking:

Waterproofs.
Headwear and gloves.
Walking shoes/boots.
Shades and sunscreen.
Binoculars and camera.
Snacks and drinks.

Customs/Behaviour – local people are generally tolerant of battlefield visitors but please respect their property and address them respectfully. The French are less inclined to switch to English than other Europeans. If you try some basic French, it will be appreciated.

Driving – rules of the road are similar to UK, apart from having to drive on the right. If in doubt about priorities at junctions, always be prepared to give way to the right, particularly in France. In many areas, particularly rural, you usually have to give way to vehicles coming in from the right, even from apparently minor roads onto major routes. Obey laws and road signs – police impose harsh on-the-spot fines. Penalties for drinking and driving are heavy and the legal limit is lower than UK (50mg rather than 80mg). Most Autoroutes in France are toll roads. In rural areas the speed limit is 80kph but in many places the old 90kph signs remain. The red-framed name board at the entrance to a village or town automatically imposes a 50kph speed limit.

Fuel – petrol stations are only open 24 hours on major routes and larger supermarkets. Payment by credit/debit card in automatic tellers is increasingly becoming the norm. The cheapest fuel is generally at hypermarkets.

Mandatory Requirements – if taking your own car you need:

Full driving licence.

Vehicle registration document.

Comprehensive motor insurance valid in Europe (Green Card).

European breakdown and recovery cover.

Letter of authorisation from the owner if the vehicle is not yours.

Spare set of bulbs, headlight beam adjusters, warning triangle, GB sticker, high visibility vest and breathalyzer. Requirements do vary, so check before departing.

An emission quality sticker (Crit'Air) is required if driving in Paris or certain other cities/areas.

Emergency – keep details required in an emergency separate from your wallet or handbag:

Photocopy passport, insurance documents and EHIC/GHIC (see Health below).

Mobile phone details.

Credit/debit card numbers and cancellation telephone contacts.

Travel insurance company contact number.

Who to contact in an emergency.

Ferries – the closest ports are Boulogne, Calais and Dunkirk. The Shuttle is quicker, but usually more expensive.

Health

European Health Insurance Card – entitles the holder to medical treatment at local rates. Apply online at www.ehic.org.uk/Internet/startApplication.do. It is issued free and is valid for five years. You are only covered if you have the EHIC with you when you go for treatment. Since Brexit, EHIC is being gradually replaced by a Global Health Insurance Card (GHIC).

Travel Insurance – you are also strongly advised to have travel insurance. If you receive treatment get a statement by the doctor (*feuille de soins*) and a receipt to make a claim on return.

Personal Medical Kit - treating minor ailments saves time and money. Pack sufficient prescription medicine for the trip.

Chemist (*Pharmacie*) – look for the green cross. They provide some treatment and if unable to help will direct you to a doctor. Most open 0900–1900 except Sundays. Out of hours services (*pharmacie de garde*) are advertised in Pharmacie windows.

Doctor and Dentist – hotel receptions have details of local practices. Beware private doctors/hospitals, as extra charges cannot be reclaimed – the French national health service is known as *conventionné*.

Rabies – contact with infected animals is very rare, but if bitten by any animal, get the wound examined professionally immediately.

Money

ATMs – at most banks and post offices with instructions in English. Check your card can be used in France and what charges apply. Some banks limit how much can be withdrawn. Let your bank know you will be away, as some block cards if transactions take place unexpectedly.

Credit/Debit Cards – major cards are usually accepted, but some have different names – Visa is Carte Bleue and Mastercard is Eurocard.

Exchange – beware 0% commission, as the rate may be poor. The Post Office takes back unused currency at the same rate, which may or may not be advantageous. Since the Euro, currency exchange facilities are scarce.

Local Taxes – if you buy high value items you can reclaim tax. Get the forms completed by the shop, have them stamped by Customs, post them to the shop and they will refund about 12%. Brexit may change this.

Passport – a valid passport is required.

Post – postcard stamps are often available from vendors, newsagents and tabacs.

Public Holidays – just about everything closes and banks can close early the day before. Transport may be affected, but tourist attractions in high season are unlikely to be. The following dates/days are public holidays:

1 January
Easter Monday
1 May
8 May
Ascension Day
Whit Monday
14 July
15 August
1 & 11 November
25 December

In France many businesses and restaurants close for the majority of August.

Radio – if you want to pick up the news from home, try BBC Radio 4 on 198 kHz long wave. BBC Five Live on 909 kHz medium wave can sometimes be received. There are numerous internet options for keeping up with the news.

Shops – in large towns and tourist areas they tend to open all day. In more remote places they may close for lunch. Some bakers open Sunday a.m. and during the week take later lunch breaks. In general shops do not open on Sundays and those that do have limited hours.

Telephone

To UK – 0044, then delete the initial 0 and dial the rest of the number.

Local Calls – dial the full number even if within the same zone.

Mobiles – check yours will work in France and the charges.

Emergencies – dial 112 for medical, fire and police anywhere in Europe from any landline, pay phone or mobile. Calls are free.

British Embassy (Paris) – 01 44 51 31 00.

Time Zone – one hour ahead of UK.

Tipping – a small tip is expected by cloakroom and lavatory attendants and porters. Not required in restaurants when a service charge is included.

Toilets – the best are in museums and the main tourist attractions. Towns usually have public toilets where markets are held; some are coin operated. Otherwise on the battlefields facilities are sparse. Finding a local café may be the best option, although they are closing as rapidly as British pubs.

Index

Notes

1. Not every person or location is included. Most family members named in the Biographies are not.
2. Armed forces units, establishments, etc are grouped under the respective country, except for Britain's, which appear under the three services – British Army, Royal Air Force and Royal Navy. Royal Naval Division units appear under British Army for convenience.
3. Newfoundland appears under Canada although not part of it at the time.
4. Cemeteries/Crematoria, Cathedrals, Churches, Hospitals, Museums, Schools, Ships, Trenches, Universities and Commonwealth War Graves Commission appear under those group headings.
5. All orders, medals and decorations appear under Orders.
6. Belgium, Britain, France and Germany are not indexed in the accounts of the VC actions, as there are too many mentions. Similarly, England, Britain and United Kingdom are not indexed in the biographies.